T0325570

PRAISE FOR

FINANCIAL PLANNING & ANALYSIS AND PERFORMANCE MANAGEMENT

"A comprehensive work on FP&A and Performance Management, covering fundamental topics through best practices and advanced topics. Terrific framework for assessing, improving and expanding the contribution of FP&A. The accompany website, with models and analysis introduced in the book, provides substantial additional value to finance teams."

Joseph Hartnett, COO and CFO, EventLink, LLC

"Financial Planning & Analysis and Performance Management *is a must-have reference manual for FP&A and Investor Relations teams. I found this text extremely helpful, with its useful tools for setting strategy and its practical guides to implementing process improvements and to innovating."*

Sally J. Curley, CEO, Curley Global IR, LLC and former Senior Vice President, Investor Relations, Cardinal Health, Inc.

"The concepts addressed in this book both challenged and inspired our team to reassess and identify the drivers of value in our enterprise, top to bottom. We are using the examples and suggestions contained throughout the book to develop a single page dashboard that will keep us focused on the key elements of our strategic plan, concentrate on the most relevant metrics, and react quickly to any unexpected deviations and opportunities. This book is a must read and will serve as a great resource for future reference."

Paul McGowan, Jr., CPA, CVA, Global Managing Partner, MDD International LTD.

"Using decades of experience as CFO and business consultant, Jack Alexander offers a practical guide to bridge the gap between planning and performance. The tools and models in this book will help leverage corporate assets and create shareholder value."

Jennifer Bethel, Professor, Babson College

FINANCIAL PLANNING & ANALYSIS AND PERFORMANCE MANAGEMENT

Founded in 1807, John Wiley & Sons is the oldest independent publishing company in the United States. With offices in North America, Europe, Australia, and Asia, Wiley is globally committed to developing and marketing print and electronic products and services for our customers' professional and personal knowledge and understanding.

The Wiley Finance series contains books written specifically for finance and investment professionals as well as sophisticated individual investors and their financial advisors. Book topics range from portfolio management to e-commerce, risk management, financial engineering, valuation, and financial instrument analysis, as well as much more.

For a list of available titles, visit our website at www.WileyFinance.com.

FINANCIAL PLANNING & ANALYSIS AND PERFORMANCE MANAGEMENT

Jack Alexander

WILEY

Published by John Wiley & Sons, Inc., Hoboken, New Jersey.

Published simultaneously in Canada.

For general information on our other products and services or for technical support, please contact our Customer Care Department within the United States at (800) 762-2974, outside the United States at (317) 572-3993, or fax (317) 572-4002.

Wiley publishes in a variety of print and electronic formats and by print-on-demand. Some material included with standard print versions of this book may not be included in e-books or in print-on-demand. If this book refers to media such as a CD or DVD that is not included in the version you purchased, you may download this material at http://booksupport.wiley.com. For more information about Wiley products, visit www.wiley.com.

Library of Congress Cataloging-in-Publication Data is Available

ISBN 9781119491484 (Hardback)
ISBN 9781119491439 (ePDF)
ISBN 9781119491453 (ePub)

Cover Design: Wiley
Cover Image: © Lava 4 images | Shutterstock

Printed in the United States of America.

SKY10079726_071724

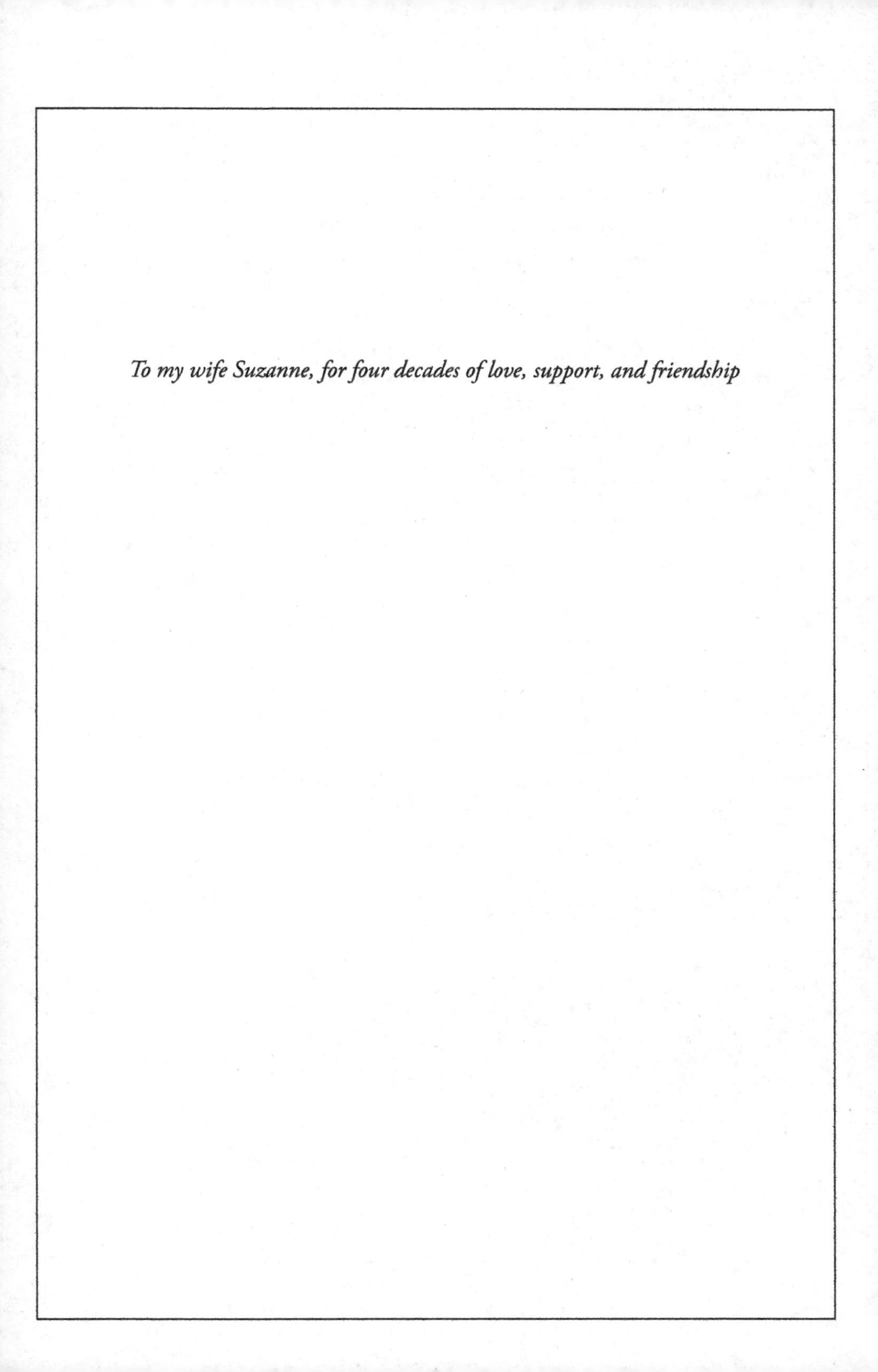

To my wife Suzanne, for four decades of love, support, and friendship

CONTENTS

Part Four Planning and Analysis for Critical Business and Value Drivers

PREFACE

WHY THIS BOOK?

In the late 1970s, as I was starting my career, I came across an article that identified the traits a chief executive officer was looking for in a chief financial officer. Since I had already set my sights on becoming a CFO, I jotted down the key takeaways from the article, something that I developed a habit of doing over my career and continue to this time. Unfortunately, I did not note the article, publication, or CEO to give them credit here or to recognize the soundness of the points articulated in the article. Here is a copy of my notes, that I have retained to this day:

TOP GUN CFO'S

WHAT CEO'S LOOK FOR IN CFO

- CREDIBILITY OF FORECASTS
- DISPASSIONATE, HARD HEADED ANALYSIS
- BALANCE: COST MODEL & GROWTH
- KINSHIP & TEAMWORK

Each of these recommendations has proven to be true in my experience. Of course, this assumes that financial controls and reporting are also well executed. CFOs and finance teams must be able to develop, evaluate, and assist in achieving planned and forecast results. The phrase "dispassionate, hard headed analysis" struck and stuck with me. Financial planning and analysis (FP&A) must be impartial and objective. Finance teams must be prepared to identify and expose both problems and opportunities, often in a hardheaded way. CFOs and their teams must strike a balance between focusing on the cost model and directly and indirectly contributing to growth. "Kinship" refers to a trusted adviser and partner relationship with the CEO. And of course, finance must be viewed as a member of the team, supporting and executing to achieve the organization's objectives.

It is interesting that three of the four characteristics speak directly to FP&A. Throughout my 40-year career, I have found that FP&A is one of the most important roles the finance team plays. I became a student of financial analysis early in my career and can directly attribute attaining my goal of becoming a CFO in large measure to a strong focus and emphasis on FP&A throughout my career.

I define FP&A very broadly, as evidenced by the scope of this book. FP&A draws on several academic areas, including managerial accounting, financial accounting, finance, and operations and process management, as well as new disciplines in analytics and data visualization. Today the FP&A organization is called upon to lead the development of plans and projections, evaluate trends and variances, evaluate complex investment decisions, and value and increase the value of the enterprise and acquisition candidates, among many others.

Even with the broad scope and increasing importance of FP&A, there are very few resources available to analysts and FP&A departments. The objective of this book is to address that void by providing a comprehensive and practical guide to FP&A.

USING THIS BOOK

The book can be utilized in three ways. First, it can be read from cover to cover by those deeply involved in all facets of FP&A. Second, many readers may peruse the entire book and then focus on a couple of specific areas of interest. Finally, my hope is that the book will be retained for use as a future reference.

This book is organized into five parts:

Part One: Fundamentals and Key FP&A Capabilities
Part Two: Performance Management
Part Three: Business Projections and Plans
Part Four: Planning and Analysis for Critical Business and Value Drivers
Part Five: Valuation and Capital Investment Decisions

Part One: Fundamentals and Key FP&A Capabilities

Part One provides a review of fundamentals of finance and key analytical tools. It also covers important FP&A capabilities, including developing models, building analytical capability, and presenting and communicating financial information.

Part Two: Performance Management

Part Two provides an introduction to performance management and best practices in developing key performance indicators and dashboards. It also provides guidance on institutionalizing performance management – that is, integrating it with other management processes. Additional topics include the measurement of innovation, agility, and human capital, as well as applying performance measurement to external forces, including benchmarking and competitive analysis.

Part Three: Business Projections and Plans

Part Three covers best practices in developing projections and plans. Topics include budgets, operating plans, rolling forecasts, business outlooks, and long-term projections. Special attention is given to techniques to deal with the uncertainty and rapid change that exist in the twenty-first century.

Part Four: Planning and Analysis for Critical Business and Value Drivers

Part Four covers techniques for planning, analyzing, and improving on key performance drivers: revenue growth and margins, operating effectiveness, capital management, and the cost of capital.

Part Five: Valuation and Capital Investment Decisions

Part Five addresses business valuation, value drivers, and analysis of mergers and acquisitions. In addition, the evaluation of capital investments is covered, from basic concepts through advanced topics such as dealing with risk and uncertainty.

ABOUT THE WEBSITE

WHAT'S ON THE WEBSITE

This book is accompanied by a companion website:

wiley.com/go/fpapm

The following sections provide a summary of the software and other materials you'll find on the website.

Content

A number of illustrative performance dashboards, analytical tools, and Excel models used in the book are included in the accompanying website. These items are identified in the book with a website logo. The dashboards and spreadsheets are intended as working examples and starting points for the reader's use. An important theme of this book is to underscore the importance of selecting the appropriate measures and dashboards. It is very important to carefully select the measures and analytical tools that are most appropriate for each circumstance. Accordingly, most of the dashboards and models will have to be tailored to fit the specific needs of each situation. Please note that in order to facilitate changes to the analyses, none of the formulas in the worksheets are protected. A copy of the original files should be retained in the event that formulas are inadvertently changed or deleted.

The spreadsheets contain the data used in the examples provided in the book. In order to fully understand the worksheets, including the objective, context, and logic of the analysis, the user should refer to the appropriate example in the text. For each worksheet, the data input fields are generally highlighted in color. All other fields contain formulas. The reader should save these files under a different name and use them to begin developing dashboards and analysis for the reader's specific needs. Using the models on the Website-ROM requires Microsoft Excel software and an intermediate skill level in the use of that software. Many of the worksheets are stand-alone analyses that are not linked to the other spreadsheets. However, some of the workbook files contain models that require data input on the first worksheet to drive the models on subsequent worksheets in that file.

The website also includes a Quick Reference Guide (Table 2.8) that can be printed, laminated, and retained as a reference for financial terms and ratios and key aspects of valuation and performance measurement.

All contents are Excel spreadsheets unless otherwise noted.

Chapter 2	**Fundamentals of Finance**
Table 2.5	Roberts Manufacturing Co. Historical and Estimated 2018 Financials
Table 2.7	Roberts Manufacturing Co. Performance Assessment Summary
Figure 2.2	Key Performance Trends for Roberts Manufacturing Co.
Table 2.8	Key Financial Terms and Measures: Quick Reference Guide
Chapter 3	**Key Analytical Tools and Concepts**
Table 3.1	Finished Goods Inventory – Vance Corp
Table 3.2	Finished Goods Inventory – Vance Corp: Descending Order
Table 3.3	Analysis of Finished Goods Inventory
Table 3.4	Stock Price Sensitivity Analysis
Table 3.5	Expected Value of Sales Plan
Figure 3.1	Decision Tree: Replace Existing Product
Table 3.6	Return on Equity Analysis
Figure 3.2	Revenue Process and Accounts Receivable Analysis
Table 3.7	Order Processing Costs Allocated by Sales Dollars

(*continues*)

Chapter 11	**The External View: Benchmarking Performance and Competitive Analysis**
Figure 11.1	Quarterly Performance Recap: Under Armour
Table 11.1	Comprehensive Benchmark Analysis
Figure 11.3	Apple Performance Trends
Figure 11.4	Amazon Performance Trends
Table 11.2	Benchmark Survey and Target Worksheet
Chapter 12	**Business Projections and Plans: Introduction and Best Practices**
Figure 12.2	Historical versus Plan Trends
Figure 12.3	Sales Run-Rate Analysis
Figure 12.4	Actual Revenue versus Forecast Range
Table 12.1	Upside and Downside Event Summary
Figure 12.5	Sensitivity Analysis: Key Assumptions
Figure 12.6	Scenario Recap
Table 12.2	Revenue Probability Analysis
Figure 12.7	Using Business Model to Develop Projections
Chapter 13	**Budgets, Operating Plans, and Forecasts**
Table 13.1	Traditional Departmental Budget
Figure 13.2	Budget Roll-Up Illustration
Figure 13.3	Dashboard: Evaluation of Operating Plan
Table 13.2	Rolling Forecast Method
Table 13.3	DBO Supporting Schedule: Product Margins
Table 13.4	DBO Supporting Schedule: Gross Margins
Table 13.5	DBO Supporting Schedule: Marketing
Table 13.6	DBO Income Statement
Table 13.7	DBO Supporting Schedule: Balance Sheet and Cash Flow
Figure 13.8	DBO Presentation Summary

(*continues*)

(*continues*)

Modifying the Charts and Graphs

The user may need to modify some of the charts and graphs on the website in order to substitute specific performance measures for those contained in the sample dashboard. In order to modify chart titles, alter axis labels, and make other changes to charts, click on the chart, then select Chart in the menu commands and then select Options. A menu of available chart options will be presented, including titles, labels, and scale selections.

The user may also want to change the scale of the charts to better present the data for each situation. This can be accomplished by double clicking on the "Value Axis" label on the graph and selecting Scale to change axis minimum and maximum values.

GLOSSARY

A glossary of commonly used financial, value, and performance management terms is included in the back of the book.

Jack Alexander

1

FINANCIAL PLANNING & ANALYSIS AND BUSINESS PERFORMANCE MANAGEMENT

CHAPTER INTRODUCTION

Financial Planning & Analysis (FP&A) and Performance Management (PM) are critical functions to the success of any enterprise. In this chapter, we will define what we believe productive FP&A and PM functions should include, and we will preview the contents of the remainder of the book. We will use the terms FP&A and PM interchangeably to encompass these two related and overlapping disciplines.

THE PROBLEM WITH TRADITIONAL MEASUREMENT SYSTEMS

Traditional financial reports have several limitations. First, they typically are prepared after the close of the accounting period, on a monthly, quarterly, or annual basis. Once these reports are prepared and distributed, managers attempting to use them for performance monitoring are looking in the rearview mirror. The report may tell them where they have been, but it will not be helpful in keeping the car on the road! A financial report for March, for example, may indicate that inventories increased above expected levels. While management can review causes of the increase and take corrective actions in April, they were unable to avoid the problem and are left with the unfavorable impact on working capital and cash flows.

A related limitation with traditional accounting reports is that their content is typically focused on "lagging" financial measures, such as gross margins, days sales outstanding (DSO), and so forth. Effective managers identify "leading" indicators of critical processes and activities that can be monitored on a current basis. This affords them the opportunity to identify exceptions and unfavorable trends and take immediate corrective action. In creating a system of effective performance improvement reports, managers need to identify the leading or predictive indicators of performance. For example, a key but lagging indicator of accounts receivable performance, DSO, requires knowing the ending receivables balance and sales for the period. However, a well-constructed performance report will track key leading indicators such as revenue patterns and collections on a weekly basis throughout the quarter. Management can estimate the ending receivables level based on the interim measures and take corrective action immediately *within* the quarter if exceptions or unfavorable trends emerge.

The third limitation with most accounting reports is that they are prepared by accountants in a way that is useful and intuitive to them, but is difficult for most nonfinancial managers and employees to understand and digest. These include traditional financial statements, supporting schedules, and spreadsheets that are easily understood by accountants, but can be confusing to the rest of the organization. Key trends or exceptions may be buried in the statements, but are extremely difficult for anyone to identify, let alone take action upon.

Another challenge is the endless bombardment of new financial measures and new management disciplines over recent decades, including economic profit, scorecards, key performance indicators (KPIs), dashboards, data visualization, analytics, and artificial intelligence (AI). In addition, performance measures have been developed for specific industries and special situations such as early-stage enterprises. Managers should look across these various initiatives and extract and combine the best features of each to develop an effective system of performance management for their enterprise.

OBJECTIVES OF FINANCIAL ANALYSIS AND PERFORMANCE MANAGEMENT

Figure 1.1 presents the instrument panel in the cockpit of the space shuttle. At a glance, the pilot can get a highly visual report on the shuttle's altitude, on its attitude, and on every major system in the aircraft. The radar in an airplane allows the pilot to spot and identify potential external threats long before visual contact. At first the panel appears very complex, but you can bet the pilots know where every needle and dial should be and the importance of any changes! They compare this information with the feel of the plane, visual observation, experience, and intuition to make adjustments in real time, as indicated, to operate the craft in safely executing the flight plan or mission.

In a nutshell, the objectives of FP&A and PM are to develop and provide information to run the business and achieve the organization's goals, just as the instrument panel assists the pilots of an aircraft to execute their mission.

Our definition and application of FP&A is very broad and inclusive. It includes all activities that assess, plan, improve, and monitor critical business activities and initiatives. PM is a critical aspect of the management processes of the enterprise. Performance management is closely aligned with and overlaps FP&A in many respects. Important characteristics of effective PM include:

- Achieving an organization's goals and objectives, including strategic and operational initiatives, forecasts, and planned results.
- Projecting and modeling future financial performance.

FIGURE 1.1 Space Shuttle Cockpit Instrument Panel

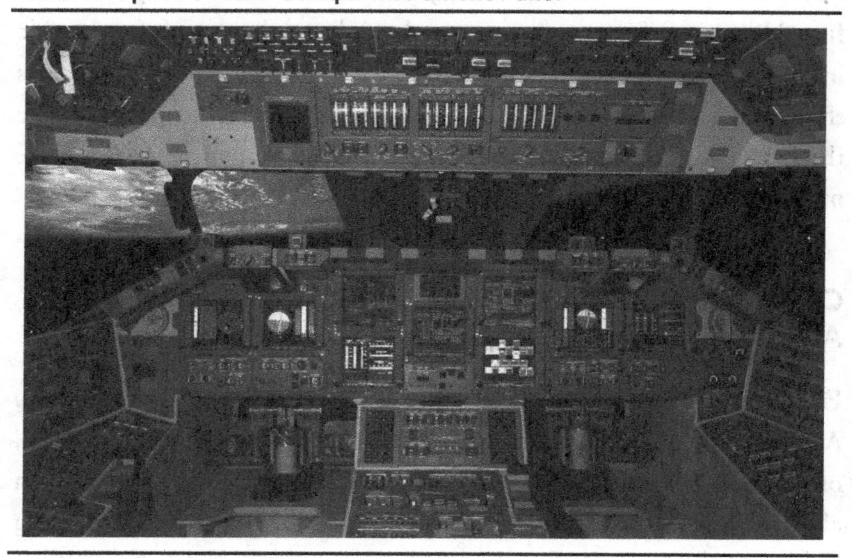

Photo courtesy of NASA.

- Monitoring performance on key value and business drivers.
- Increasing visibility into critical areas of business performance, allowing managers to assign and enforce accountability for performance.
- Providing an effective framework, allowing managers and employees to understand how their activities relate to operating and financial performance, and ultimately to the value of the company.
- Providing early detection of unfavorable events and trends, such as manufacturing problems, competitive threats, and product performance issues.
- Delivering critical information to managers and executives in effective displays or presentation formats that aid in identifying trends, problems, opportunities, and so on.
- Integrating into other management practices in the overall system of management processes that we will call the performance management framework (PMF).

- Identifying, monitoring, and mitigating risks.
- Providing information to managers to run the business.

FP&A and PM must be integrated into other management processes as shown in Figure 1.2. Analysts and others involved in PM must play an active role in the management of the organization. They are not reporters or historians; they should help shape the outcome of the enterprise's efforts.

Understanding How Decisions Are Made

Since a substantial part of FP&A involves developing and providing information and analysis to managers, the analyst should develop an understanding of how the human mind receives and processes information as part of evaluating options and making decisions. The analyst bears a responsibility to develop and present findings in an objective manner that reduces bias and the tendency to reach less than optimum decisions.

A primary theme throughout this book is the important need to present and communicate business information effectively. This subject is the focus of Chapter 6, Communicating and Presenting Financial Information.

FIGURE 1.2 FP&A and PM Must Be Integrated with Other Management Processes

	Project Management	Mergers and Acquisitions	Product Development	Sales	Performance Improvement	
Goal Setting						Management Reporting
Strategic Planning			Financial Planning & Analysis Performance Management			Performance Evaluation
Annual Planning						Value Creation
Forecasts						Investor Relations
	Risk Management	Human Capital Management	Performance Monitoring	Execution Accountability	Incentive Compensation	

PREVIEW OF THE BOOK

The book has been written to address key areas of Financial Planning & Analysis and Performance Management from a practical point of view. While theory and technical aspects are included throughout the book, I have tried to incorporate real business applications from my 40-year career in business accounting and finance. The book contains five parts:

Part One: Fundamentals and Key FP&A Capabilities
Part Two: Business Performance Management
Part Three: Business Projections and Plans
Part Four: Planning and Analysis for Critical Business and Value Drivers
Part Five: Valuation and Capital Investment Decisions

Part One: Fundamentals and Key FP&A Capabilities

Part One builds a foundation for effective planning, analysis, and performance management. It includes a comprehensive review of financial statement analysis and presents analytical tools that can enhance the effectiveness of FP&A. For most finance professionals, Chapter 2 is primarily a review, so a quick perusal of this material may suffice.

In order to complement technical subject areas in the book, we cover best practices in developing financial models and in developing analytical capability. Finally, we address a significant weakness in many finance organizations: presenting and communicating business information.

Part One contains these chapters:

2. Fundamentals of Finance
3. Key Analytical Tools and Concepts
4. Developing Predictive and Analytical Models
5. Building Analytical Capability
6. Communicating and Presenting Financial Information

Part Two: Business Performance Management

In Part Two, we focus on subject matters traditionally associated with PM. After introducing keys to effective business performance management (BPM), we present the best practices in selecting key performance indicators (KPIs) and creating dashboards. In order to fully achieve the benefits of PM, it needs to be integrated with other key management processes. We introduce a challenge to PM leaders to focus on *what's important*, not just what is easy to measure. Since PM should also look outside the enterprise, benchmarking and competitive analysis are also presented.

Part Two consists of these chapters:

7. Business Performance Management
8. Dashboards and Key Performance Indicators
9. Institutionalizing Performance Management
10. Measuring and Driving What's Important: Innovation, Agility, and Human Capital
11. External View: Benchmarking Performance and Competitive Analysis

Part Three: Business Projections and Plans

In Part Three, we will cover best practices and techniques for planning, projecting, and forecasting future performance. In addition to traditional budgeting and operational planning, the implementation of rolling forecasts or business outlooks is also presented. Finally, we cover the unique challenges in projecting performance over an extended time horizon.

Part Three includes these chapters:

12. Business Projections and Plans: Introduction and Best Practices
13. Budgets, Operating Plans, and Forecasts
14. Long-Term Projections

Part Four: Planning and Analysis for Critical Business and Value Drivers

Part Four presents best practices and illustrations for planning, measurement, analysis, and improvement of key business and value drivers, in the following chapters:

15. Revenue and Gross Margins
16. Operating Expenses and Effectiveness
17. Capital Management and Cash Flow: Working Capital
18. Capital Management and Cash Flow: Long-Term Assets
19. Risk, Uncertainty, and the Cost of Capital

Part Five: Valuation and Capital Investment Decisions

Part Five presents planning and analysis of critical business decisions, including capital investment decisions, techniques for valuing a business, and analyzing value drivers. The section concludes with techniques to value a business, and the planning, analysis, and evaluation of mergers and acquisitions (M&A).

Part Five includes these chapters:

20. Capital Investment Decisions: Introduction and Key Concepts
21. Capital Investment Decisions: Advanced Topics
22. Business Valuation and Value Drivers
23. Analysis of Mergers and Acquisitions

Supplemental Information

Supplemental information includes a glossary, an index, and information on the CD or website available to purchasers of this book.

SUMMARY

Most senior financial and operating executives single out FP&A as one of the most important and, unfortunately, underperforming functions of the finance organization. Combining elements of classic FP&A with PM can unleash significant analytical horsepower that can assist the organization in executing its mission and achieving its objectives.

Before embarking on an initiative to improve FP&A and performance management, practitioners should develop a context based on the company's strategy and objectives, performance, and critical initiatives. This will ensure that the focus of efforts is directed to critical areas in the organization. Material found in Chapter 5, Building Analytical Capability, and Chapter 7, Business Performance Management, will be helpful to this cause.

Part One

Fundamentals and Key FP&A Capabilities

2

FUNDAMENTALS OF FINANCE

CHAPTER INTRODUCTION

The traditional and most fundamental aspect of financial planning and analysis is the ability to understand and evaluate financial statements and financial performance. This chapter presents a brief introduction (or refresher) to financial statements and financial ratios. Many finance professionals will use these financial ratios as overall measures of a company's performance or as overall measures of performance on a particular driver of value.

BASICS OF ACCOUNTING AND FINANCIAL STATEMENTS

The three primary financial statements are the Income Statement, the Balance Sheet, and the Statement of Cash Flows. We need all three statements to properly understand and evaluate financial performance. However, the financial statements provide only limited insight into a company's performance and must be combined with key financial ratios and ultimately an understanding of the company's market, competitive position, and strategy, before evaluating a company's current performance and value. A significant limitation of financial statements is that they present historical results – that is, the past. Other measures and mechanisms must be utilized to see what is happening in the present and to predict and manage future outcomes.

Financial statements are based on generally accepted accounting principles (GAAP). A key objective of financial statements prepared under GAAP is to match revenues and expenses. Two significant conventions arise from this objective: the accrual method of accounting and depreciation. These two conventions are significant in our intended use of financial statements for economic evaluation and business valuation purposes, since they result in differences between accounting income and cash flow.

Accrual Accounting

Financial statements record income when earned and expenses when incurred. For example, the accrual basis of accounting will record sales when the terms of the contract are fulfilled, usually prior to collection of cash. Similarly, expenses are recorded when service is performed rather than when paid.

Depreciation

GAAP requires that expenditures for such things as property, plant, and equipment with long useful lives be recorded as assets and depreciated over the expected useful life of the asset. As a result, when a firm spends cash to purchase equipment, it records it as an asset on the balance sheet and depreciates the cost of that asset each year on the income statement.

Income Statement (aka Profit and Loss)

The income statement, or what is frequently referred to as the profit and loss (P&L) statement, is a summary of all income and expense transactions completed during the period (year, quarter, etc.). Typical captions and math logic for a basic income statement include these examples:

Sales	+ $1,000
Cost of Goods Sold	– 500
Gross Margin	= 500
Operating Expenses	– 200
Operating Income	= 300
Income Tax Expense	– 100
Net Income	= 200

Many different measures, terms, and acronyms are used in practice to describe various elements of the P&L. Table 2.1 illustrates how some of these common measures are determined as well as how they relate to one another.

Following are definitions of key terms used in Table 2.1:

Net Income: Residual of income over expense; sometimes referred to as profit after tax (PAT).

EBIT: Earnings before interest and taxes. This measure reflects the income generated by operating activities (generally equals or approximates operating income) before subtracting financing costs (interest) and income tax expense.

EBIAT: Earnings before interest and after taxes, aka net operating profit after taxes (NOPAT) or operating profit after tax (OPAT). This measure estimates the after-tax operating earnings. It excludes financing costs but does reflect income tax expense. It is useful in comparing and evaluating the operational performance of firms, excluding the impact of financing costs.

EBITDA: Earnings before interest, taxes, depreciation, and amortization. EBITDA adjusts EBIT (operating income) by adding back noncash charges for depreciation and amortization. This measure is used in valuation and financing decisions

TABLE 2.1 Comparison of Common P&L Measures

	Abbreviation		P& L	EBIT	EBIAT	EBITDA	EP
Sales			$100,000	$100,000	$100,000	$100,000	$100,000
Cost of Sales	COGS		50,000	50,000	50,000	50,000	50,000
Gross Margin	GM		50,000	50,000	50,000	50,000	50,000
% of Sales			50.0%	50.0%	50.0%	50.0%	50.0%
R&D			5,000	5,000	5,000	5,000	5,000
SG&A	SG&A		15,000	15,000	15,000	15,000	15,000
Depreciation & Amortization (D&A)			10,000	10,000	10,000	–	10,000
Operating Profit	OP		20,000	20,000	20,000	30,000	20,000
% of Sales			20.0%	20.0%	20.0%	30.0%	20.0%
Interest Expense			3,000				
Profit before Tax	PBT		17,000				
Income Tax		35.0%	5,950		7,000		7,000
Net Income	PAT		11,050				
%			11.1%				
Earnings before Interest and Taxes	EBIT			20,000			
Earnings before Interest after Taxes	EBIAT				13,000		13,000
Earnings before Interest, Taxes, D&A	EBITDA					30,000	
Capital Charge							10,000
Economic Profit	EP						3,000

since it approximates cash generated by the operation. It does not include capital requirements such as working capital and expenditures for property and equipment.

Economic Profit: Economic profit measures subtract a capital charge from the earnings to arrive at an economic profit. The capital charge is computed based on the level of capital employed in the business.

Balance Sheet

The balance sheet is a critical financial report and frequently does not get the attention it deserves in evaluating the performance of an entity. It is a summary of the company's assets, liabilities, and owners' equity, and, importantly, it represents a snapshot of all open transactions as of the reporting date. For example, the inventory balance represents all materials delivered to the company, work in process, and finished goods not yet shipped to customers. Accounts payable represents open invoices due to vendors that have not been paid as of the balance sheet date. As a result, the balance sheet can be a good indicator of the efficiency of an operation. A firm with a very efficient manufacturing process will have lower inventory levels than a similar firm with less effective practices.

The balance sheet is constructed as shown in Table 2.2.

Another way to look at the balance sheet is to reorder the traditional format (Table 2.2) to identify the net operating assets and the sources of capital provided to the organization. This presentation, as illustrated in Table 2.3, is more useful in understanding the dynamics of the balance sheet. The net operating assets are those assets that are required to operate and support the business. The net operating assets must be funded (or provided to the firm) by investors, either bondholders or shareholders.

Statement of Cash Flows (SCF)

The statement of cash flows (SCF) summarizes the cash generated and utilized by the enterprise during a specific period (year, quarter, etc.). Since

TABLE 2.2 Assets = Liabilities + Shareholders' Equity

Assets		Liabilities and Equity	
Cash	150	Accounts Payable	100
Receivables	200	Accrued Liabilities	100
Inventories	200	Debt	200
Fixed Assets, net	50	Total Liabilities	400
		Shareholders' Equity	200
Total Assets	600	Total Liabilities and Equity	600

TABLE 2.3 Net Operating Assets/Invested Capital Illustration

Net Assets		**Sources of Capital**	
Cash	150		
Receivables	200		
Inventories	200		
Fixed Assets, net	50		
		Debt	200
Total Assets	600		
Less Operating Liabilities		Shareholders' Equity	200
Accounts Payable	−100		
Accrued Liabilities	−100		
Net Assets	400	Total "Invested Capital"	400

cash flow will be a focus of our economic valuation and is an important business measure, we will pay particular interest to cash flow drivers and measures. The statement of cash flows starts with the net income generated by the company over the period, as reported on the income statement.

Since net income is based on various accounting conventions, such as the matching principle, the SCF identifies various adjustments to net income to arrive at cash flow. In addition, we also need to factor in various cash flow items that are not reflected in net income, such as working capital requirements, dividends, and purchases of equipment.

A simplified format for a statement of cash flow is shown in Table 2.4.

Since the cash flow statement starts with net income but then is adjusted by multiple different factors to arrive at the final cash flow amount, many

TABLE 2.4 Cash Flow Statement

Net Income	$ 200
Depreciation and Amortization	10
(Increase) Decrease in Working Capital	−25
Purchases of Property and Equipment	−25
Operating Cash Flow	160
Dividends	0
Debt Repayments	−60
Cash Flow	$ 100

nonfinancial folks (okay, some finance folks, too) find this cumbersome and not intuitive. Rest assured that the "cash flow" amount reported here will be the same result of all checks written and deposits recorded in the enterprise's checking account.

The three primary financial statements just discussed are interrelated. Understanding these relationships is critical to evaluating business performance and valuation and is presented in Figure 2.1. For example, net income (or PAT) flows from the income statement to increase shareholders' equity in the balance sheet. Net income for the period is also the starting point for the statement of cash flows. Other elements on the statement of cash flows are the result of year-to-year changes in various balance sheet accounts, including capital expenditures, changes in working capital, and reductions or increases in borrowings. Finally, financial ratios look at the relationship of various line items both within each financial statement and across all financial statements (e.g. return on assets).

FINANCIAL RATIOS AND INDICATORS

The basic financial statements are simply raw financial results and are of limited value. Financial ratios can be very useful tools in measuring and evaluating business performance as presented in the basic financial statements. Ratios can be used as tools in understanding profitability, asset utilization, liquidity, and key business trends and in evaluating overall management performance and effectiveness.

Usefulness

Using financial ratios can provide a great deal of insight into a company's performance, particularly when combined with an understanding of the company and its industry. In addition to providing measures of performance, ratios can be used to monitor key trends over time and compare a company's performance to that of peers or "best practice" companies.

FIGURE 2.1 Financial Statement Interrelationships

Income Statement	Year 2	Year 1	Change
Sales	1,000	900	100
Gross Margin	500	425	75
Operating Expenses	200	190	10
Operating Profit	300	235	65
Net Income	200	157	43

Cash Flow	Year 2
Net Income	200
+Depreciation	10
–Capital Expenditures	–25
(Inc) Decrease in Operating Capital	–25
Operating Cash Flow	160
Financing	–60
Cash Flow	100

Balance Sheet			
Cash	150	50	100
Receivables	200	150	50
Inventories	200	150	50
PP&E: Cost	100	75	25
PP&E: Accumulated Depreciation	–50	–40	–10
Total Assets	600	385	215
Accounts Payable	100	75	25
Accrued Liabilities	100	50	50
Debt	200	260	–60
Equity	200	–	200
Liabilities and Equity	600	385	215

Ratio Analysis		
Profitability		20%
Days Sales Outstanding		73.0
Asset Turnover		1.67
Return on Assets	Net Income / Assets	33%

Variations

There are a number of different financial terms and ratios, and variations of each of these in use. This leads to potential confusion when similar-sounding measures are computed differently or used interchangeably. It is important to clearly define the specific ratio or financial measure used.

Key Financial Ratios

To illustrate key financial ratios, we will use the information in Table 2.5 for Roberts Manufacturing Company (RMC). Unless otherwise indicated, the ratios will be computed using the estimated results for 2018.

Operating Measures

Operating measures will include ratios that provide insight into the operating performance of the company. These measures will typically utilize the information presented in the income statement.

Sales Growth

Sales growth is an important determiner of financial performance. Based only on information in the income statement, we are limited to measuring the sales growth rate over the periods reported. Two key sales growth measures are year-over-year growth and compound annual growth rate (CAGR):

Year-over-Year Growth: Roberts Manufacturing Company's sales are expected to grow from $92,593 in 2017 to $100,000 in 2018. This represents a growth of 8% in 2018:

$$= (\$100{,}000/\$92{,}593) - 1 = 8\%$$

TABLE 2.5 Roberts Manufacturing Company Historical and Estimated 2018 Financials

		2015	2016	2017	2018
P&L					
Net Sales		79,383	85,734	92,593	100,000
Cost of Goods Sold		35,722	38,580	41,667	45,000
Gross Margin		43,661	47,154	50,926	55,000
SG&A		25,403	27,435	29,630	32,000
R&D		6,351	6,859	7,407	8,000
Operating Income		11,907	12,860	13,889	15,000
Interest (Income) Expense		600	600	600	600
Other (Income) Expense		5	7	6	5
Income Before Income Taxes		11,302	12,253	13,283	14,395
Federal Income Taxes		3,843	4,166	4,516	4,894
Net Income		7,460	8,087	8,767	9,501
Balance Sheet					
Cash		25	2,404	4,400	7,944
Receivables		15,877	17,147	18,545	20,000
Inventories		14,289	15,432	16,667	18,000
Other		200	800	975	900
Current Assets		30,391	35,783	40,587	46,844
Net Fixed Assets		15,877	17,147	18,750	20,000
Net Goodwill and Intangibles		14,000	13,000	12,000	11,000
Other Long-Term Assets		200	210	428	205
Total Assets		60,467	66,140	71,765	78,049
Accounts Payable		3,572	3,858	4,167	4,500
Notes Payable, Bank		–	–	–	–
Accrued Expenses & Taxes		4,000	4,500	4,750	5,000
Current Liabilities		7,572	8,358	8,917	9,500
Long-Term Debt		10,000	10,000	10,000	10,000
Other		3,000	3,100	2,900	3,300
Stockholders Equity		39,895	44,682	49,949	55,249
Total Liabilities and Equity		60,467	66,140	71,765	78,049
Other Information:					
Stock Price		9.22	9.78	10.00	10.59
Shares Outstanding (in millions)		16.7	16.8	16.9	17.0
Market Value of Equity		153,974	164,304	169,000	180,030
Interest rate	6%				
Income Tax Rate	34%				
Dividends		3,000	3,300	3,500	4,200
Capital Expenditures		3,000	4,200	4,800	5,000
D&A		2,800	2,930	3,197	3,750
Employees		411	450	460	490

Other Information:

Comparable Companies are trading in the following ranges (trailing 12 months):

	LOW	HIGH
Sales	1.3	2.0
Earnings (P/E)	16.0	20.0
EBITDA	8.0	10.0
PEG	1.3	2.0

Cost of Capital (WACC) 12%

Compound Annual Growth Rate: This measure looks at the growth rate over time (*n* years). The CAGR from 2015 to 2018 is computed as follows:

$$= [(\text{Sales } 2018/\text{Sales } 2015)^{1/n}] - 1$$

$$= [(\$100{,}000/\$79{,}383)^{1/3}] - 1$$

$$= 8\%$$

Revenue growth contributed by acquisitions has significantly different economic characteristics than that contributed by the existing business. As a result, total revenue growth is frequently split between "acquired" and "organic" growth.

Chapter 15 provides an in-depth review of revenue drivers, measures, and analysis.

Gross Margin % of Sales

How Is It Computed? Gross margin % of sales is simply the gross margin as a percentage of total revenues.

$$\text{Gross Margin } \% = \text{Gross Margin}/\text{Sales}$$

$$= \$55{,}000/\$100{,}000$$

$$= 55\%$$

What Does It Measure and Reflect? Gross margin % is an important financial indicator. Gross margins will vary widely across industries, ranging from razor-thin margins of 10% to 15% (e.g. grocery retailers) to very high margins approaching 70% to 80% (technology and software companies).

The gross margin % will be impacted by a number of factors and therefore will require substantial analysis. The factors affecting gross margin include:

- Industry
- Competition and pricing

- Product mix
- Composition of fixed and variable costs
- Product costs
- Production variances
- Material and labor costs

Chapter 15 provides an in-depth review of gross margin drivers, measures, and analysis.

R&D % Sales

How Is It Computed?

$$= \text{R\&D/Sales}$$
$$= \$8{,}000/\$100{,}000$$
$$= 8\%$$

What Does It Measure and Reflect? This ratio reflects the level of investment in research and development (R&D) compared to the current-period total sales. This ratio will vary significantly from industry to industry and from high-growth to low-growth companies. Some industries, for example retail, may have little or no R&D, whereas other firms, such as pharmaceuticals or technology companies, will likely have large R&D spending. Firms in high-growth markets or those investing heavily for future growth will have very large levels of R&D % Sales, occasionally exceeding 20% of sales.

Chapter 16 provides an in-depth review of product development drivers, measures, and analysis.

Selling, General, and Administrative (SG&A) % Sales

How Is It Computed?

$$= \text{SG\&A/Sales}$$
$$= \$32{,}000/\$100{,}000$$
$$= 32\%$$

What Does It Measure and Reflect? Since this measure compares the level of SG&A spending to sales, it provides a view of spending levels for selling and distributing the firm's products and in supporting the administrative aspects of the business. The measure will reflect the method of distribution, process efficiency, and administrative overhead. In addition, SG&A will often include costs associated with initiating or introducing new products.

Chapter 16 provides an in-depth review of operating process and expense drivers, measures, and analysis.

Operating Income (EBIT) % Sales

How Is It Computed?

= Operating Income/Sales

= $15,000/$100,000

= 15%

What Does It Measure and Reflect? This is a broad measure of operating performance. It will reflect operating effectiveness, relative pricing strength, and level of investments for future growth.

Return on Sales (Profitability)

How Is It Computed?

= Net Income/Sales

= $9,501/$100,000

= 9.5%

What Does It Measure and Reflect? This is an overall measure of performance. In addition to the factors described under operating income % of sales, this measure reflects taxes and other income and expense items.

Asset Utilization Measures

Asset utilization is a very important element in total financial performance. It is a significant driver of cash flow and return to investors. Chapter 17 provides an in-depth review of working capital drivers, measures, and analysis.

Days Sales Outstanding (DSO)

How Is It Computed?

$$= (\text{Receivables} \times 365)/\text{Sales}$$

$$= (\$20{,}000 \times 365)/\$100{,}000$$

$$= 73 \text{ days}$$

What Does It Measure and Reflect? DSO is a measure of the length of time it takes to collect receivables from customers. It will be impacted by the industry in which the firm participates, the creditworthiness of customers, and even the countries in which the firm does business. In addition, DSO is affected by the efficiency and effectiveness of the revenue process (billing and collection), by product quality, and even by the pattern of shipments within the quarter or the year.

Inventory Turns

How Is It Computed?

$$= \text{Cost of Goods Sold (COGS)}/\text{Inventory}$$

$$= \$45{,}000/\$18{,}000$$

$$= 2.5 \text{ times (turns)}$$

What Does It Measure and Reflect? Inventory turns measure how much inventory a firm carries compared to sales levels. Factors that will affect this measure include effectiveness of supply chain management and production processes, product quality, degree of vertical integration, and predictability of sales.

Days Sales in Inventory (DSI)

How Is It Computed?

$$= 365/\text{Inventory Turns}$$

$$= 365/2.5$$

$$= 146 \text{ days}$$

What Does It Measure and Reflect? This measure is impacted by the same factors as inventory turns. The advantage to this measure is that it is easier for people to relate to the number of days of sales in inventory. It is easier to conceptualize the appropriateness (or potential improvement opportunity) of carrying 146 days' worth of sales in inventory than to conceptualize 2.5 inventory turns.

Operating Cash Cycle

How Is It Computed?

$$= \text{DSO} + \text{DSI}$$
$$= 73 + 146$$
$$= 219 \text{ days}$$

What Does It Measure and Reflect? Operating cash cycle measures the overall efficiency and the length of time it takes the business to convert inventory into cash. It is calculated by combining the number of days' worth of inventory on hand with the length of time it takes the firm to collect invoices from customers. The factors impacting this measure are the aggregate of those affecting DSO and inventory turns/DSI.

Operating Capital Turnover and Operating Capital % Sales

How Is It Computed?

$$= \frac{\text{Operating Capital}}{\text{Sales}}$$
$$= \frac{\$29{,}400}{\$100{,}000}$$
$$= 29.4\% \text{ or } 3.4 \text{ turns per year}$$

Operating capital computation:

Receivables	20,000
Inventory	18,000
Other Current Assets	900
Accounts Payable	−4,500
Accrued Expenses	−5,000
Operating Capital	29,400

What Does It Measure and Reflect? These measures reflect the net cash that is tied up in supporting the operating requirements of the business. The factors impacting these measures are the aggregate of those affecting DSO and inventory turns, as well as the timing of payments to vendors, employees, and suppliers.

Capital Asset Intensity (Fixed Asset Turnover)

How Is It Computed?

$$= \frac{\text{Sales}}{\text{Net Fixed Assets}}$$

$$= \frac{\$100{,}000}{\$20{,}000}$$

$$= 5 \text{ turns per year}$$

What Does It Measure and Reflect? This measure reflects the level of investment in property, plant, and equipment relative to sales. Some businesses are very capital intensive (i.e. they require a substantial investment in capital), whereas others have modest requirements. For example, electric utility and transportation industries typically require high capital investments. On the other end of the spectrum, software development companies would usually require minimal levels of capital.

Asset Turnover

How Is It Computed?

$$= \frac{\text{Sales}}{\text{Total Assets}}$$

$$= \frac{\$100{,}000}{\$78{,}049}$$

$$= 1.28 \text{ turns per year}$$

What Does It Measure and Reflect? This measure reflects the level of investment in all assets (including working capital; property, plant, and equipment; and intangible assets) relative to sales. It reflects each of the individual asset utilization factors discussed previously.

Capital Structure/Liquidity Measures

Capital structure measures are indicators of the firm's source of capital (debt vs. equity), creditworthiness, ability to service existing debt, and ability to raise additional financing if needed. Liquidity measures examine the ability of the firm to convert assets to cash to satisfy short-term obligations.

Our definition of debt includes all interest-bearing obligations. The following measures will include notes payable, long-term debt, and current maturities of long-term debt (long-term debt due within one year).

For Roberts Manufacturing Company:

Notes Payable	$ –
Current Maturities of Long-Term Debt	$ –
Long-Term Debt	$10,000
Total Debt	$10,000

Current Ratio

How Is It Computed?

$$\text{Current Ratio} = \frac{\text{Current Assets}}{\text{Current Liabilities}} = \frac{\$46{,}844}{\$9{,}500} = 4.93$$

What Does It Measure and Reflect? This measure of liquidity computes the ratio of current assets (that will convert to cash within one year) to current liabilities (that require cash payments within one year). As such, it compares the level of assets available to satisfy short-term obligations.

Quick Ratio

How Is It Computed?

$$\text{Current Ratio} = \frac{\text{Current Assets} - \text{Inventory}}{\text{Current Liabilities}} = \frac{\$46{,}844 - \$18{,}000}{\$9{,}500} = 3.04$$

What Does It Measure and Reflect? The quick ratio is a more conservative measure of liquidity than the current ratio, since it removes inventory from other assets that are more readily converted into cash.

Debt to Equity

How Is It Computed?

$$D/E = \frac{\text{Debt}}{\text{Equity}}$$

What Does It Measure and Reflect? Debt to equity measures the proportion of total book capital supplied by bondholders (debt) versus shareholders (equity).

Debt to Total Capital

How Is It Computed?

$$\begin{aligned} D/TC &= \frac{\text{Debt}}{\text{Total Capital (Debt + Equity)}} \\ &= \frac{\$10{,}000}{\$10{,}000 + \$55{,}249} \\ &= 15.3\% \end{aligned}$$

What Does It Measure and Reflect? This measure computes the percentage of total book value (as recorded on the books and financial statements) of capital supplied by bondholders. A low debt-to-total-capital percentage indicates that most of the capital to run the firm has been supplied by stockholders. A high percentage, say 70%, would indicate that most of the capital has been supplied by bondholders. The capital structure for the latter example would be considered highly leveraged. This measure is also computed using market value of debt and equity.

Times Interest Earned (Interest Coverage)

How Is It Computed?

$$\begin{aligned} TIE &= \frac{\text{EBIT (Operating Income)}}{\text{Interest Expense}} \\ &= \frac{\$15{,}000}{\$600} \\ &= 25X \end{aligned}$$

What Does It Measure and Reflect? This measure computes the number of times the firm earns the interest expense on current borrowings. A high number reflects slack, indicating an ability to cover interest expense even if income were to be reduced significantly. Alternatively, it indicates a capacity to borrow more funds if necessary. Conversely, a low number reflects an inability to easily service existing debt levels and borrow additional funds.

Overall Measures of Performance

Return on Assets (ROA)

How Is It Computed?

$$= \frac{\text{Net Income}}{\text{Assets}}$$

$$= \frac{\$9{,}501}{\$78{,}049}$$

$$= 12.2\%$$

What Does It Measure and Reflect? This measure computes the level of income generated on the assets employed by the firm. It is an important overall measure of effectiveness since it considers the level of income relative to the level of assets employed in the business.

Return on Equity (ROE)

How Is It Computed?

$$= \frac{\text{Net Income}}{\text{Equity}}$$

$$= \frac{\$9{,}501}{\$55{,}249}$$

$$= 17.2\%$$

What Does It Measure and Reflect? This measure computes the income earned on the book value of the company's equity.

Note that ROE is greater than ROA. This is because part of the capital of the firm is furnished by bondholders and this financial leverage enhances the return to stockholders (ROE).

ROE Tree

A very useful analytical tool that can be used to understand the drivers of ROE is to break the measure down into components. This methodology, often called the Dupont model or return tree, is illustrated here:

$$\text{ROE} = \text{Profitability} \times \text{Asset Turnover} \times \text{Financial Leverage}$$
$$= \frac{\text{Net Income}}{\text{Sales}} \times \frac{\text{Sales}}{\text{Assets}} \times \frac{\text{Assets}}{\text{Equity}}$$

For Roberts Manufacturing Company:

$$17.2\% = 9.5\% \times 1.28 \times 1.41$$

Using this formula, we can compare the performance of one company to another by examining the components of ROE. It is also useful to examine ROE performance over time and to determine how a change in each of the components would affect ROE. For example, if we improve profitability to 10.5%, ROE will improve to 19%. The individual components (profitability, asset turnover, and financial leverage) can be further broken down into a tree to highlight the contribution of individual measures (e.g. DSO or SG&A % of sales). An expanded ROE tree is illustrated in Chapter 4.

Return on Invested Capital (ROIC)

How Is It Computed?

$$= \frac{\text{EBIAT (Earnings before Interest and after Tax)}}{\text{Invested Capital}}$$
$$= \frac{\text{EBIT (1 - Tax Rate)}}{\text{Debt + Equity}}$$
$$= \frac{\$15{,}000 * (1 - 0.34)}{\$10{,}000 + 55{,}249}$$
$$= \frac{\$9{,}900}{\$65{,}249}$$
$$= 15.2\%$$

What Does It Measure and Reflect? ROIC measures the income available to all suppliers of capital (debt and equity) compared to the total capital provided from all sources (debt and equity). Another way of looking at ROIC is that this measure indicates the amount of income a company earns for each dollar invested in the company, including both debt and equity investment.

Return on Invested Capital – Market (ROICM)

A variation to ROIC is to use the market value of capital, rather than the historical book value.

How Is It Computed?

$$= \frac{\text{EBIAT (Earnings before Interest and after Tax)}}{\text{Invested Capital (Market)}}$$

$$= \frac{\text{EBIT (1 − Tax Rate)}}{\text{Debt + Equity}}$$

$$= \frac{\$15{,}000 * (1 - 0.34)}{\$10{,}000 + 180{,}030}$$

$$= \$9.900/\$190{,}030$$

$$= 5.2\%$$

What Does It Measure and Reflect? ROICM measures the income available to all suppliers of capital (debt and equity) compared to the total capital provided from all sources (debt and equity) at current market values. While ROIC is a good measure of management effectiveness, ROICM relates current income levels to the market value of a company. A very low ROICM may indicate that the company's market value is very high compared to current performance. This may be due to very high expectations for future growth or a potential overvaluation of the company's stock.

Cash Generation and Requirements

In addition to measures such as EBITDA, others have been developed to measure and evaluate cash flow.

Cash Effectiveness (CE%)

Some managers and analysts measure the operating cash flow relative to the income generated as a measure of cash effectiveness.

How Is It Computed?

The cash effectiveness for Roberts Manufacturing Company for 2018 is estimated to be 66% (Table 2.6).

What Does It Measure and Reflect? The cash effectiveness ratio can be a good indicator of the relationship between reported income and cash flow. A significant decrease may signal that receivables collections are slowing or inventories are growing faster than income. Conversely, an increase in the percentage may indicate that the company is doing a better job in managing receivables, inventories, and capital investments. However, this measure is highly dependent on the rate of growth and the maturity of a business. A fast-growing company may have very low or even negative cash effectiveness percentage, since asset levels must grow to support future sales growth. A company that is shrinking may find it easy to post CE% greater than 100% since capital investment levels will often decline faster than sales.

Self-Financing or Internal Growth Rate (IGR)

Managers must understand if the company is generating enough cash flow from operations to meet requirements to support future growth. A company that is self-financing will generate enough cash from operations to satisfy working capital and other requirements to support growth. Many companies test this requirement with future cash flow projections. Others use rules of thumb; for example, in order to support future growth levels

TABLE 2.6 Cash Effectiveness for Roberts Manufacturing Company

	$	%
Operating Profit after Tax	9900	100%
Depreciation & Amortization	3750	38%
Capital Expenditures	−5000	−51%
(Increase) Decrease in Operating Capital	−2130	−22%
Operating Cash Flow	6520	66%

of 15%, a company needs an ROIC of 20%. Ross et al. have developed a formula to estimate the self-financing growth rate given a firm's ROA and cash retention policy.[1]

How Is It Computed?

$$\text{IGR} = \frac{\text{ROA} \times r}{1 - (\text{ROA} \times r)}$$

where r is the percentage of net income retained in the business (i.e. not paid out as dividends to shareholders):

$$\begin{aligned} r &= 1 - \frac{\text{Dividends and Share Repurchases}}{\text{Net Income}} \\ &= 1 - \frac{\$4{,}200}{\$9{,}501} \\ &= 0.5579 \\ \text{IGR} &= \frac{12.2\% \times 0.5579}{1 - (12.2\% \times 0.5579)} \\ &= 7.3\% \end{aligned}$$

What Does It Measure and Reflect? The IGR measure provides a good estimate of the rate at which the firm can grow without requiring outside financing. If this company grows at a rate faster than 7%, it will need to raise additional funds. If growth is under 7%, then the firm is generating enough cash to fund the growth. If the firm desires to increase the internal growth rate, it can retain a greater percentage of earnings or increase ROA.

Limitations and Pitfalls of Financial Ratios

Since the measures are based on financial statements that are prepared after the close of the period, these ratios are referred to as "lagging" measures of performance. We will discuss leading/predictive indicators a bit later.

Some managers place too much emphasis in blindly comparing ratios from one company to another. In order to effectively compare ratios across companies, it is important to understand the strategy, market(s), and structure of each company. For example, a company that is vertically integrated will likely post significantly different financial results than one that is not. A company with a strong value-added product in a growing market will likely have very different characteristics than a company participating in a competitive, slower-growth market.

Financial ratios should be used as part of a broader diagnostic evaluation. These ratios will provide a great basis to identify trends, will complement other aspects of an overall assessment, and will be a great source of questions. Think of them in the same way a medical doctor uses key quantitative data about our health. Even in routine examinations, doctors will monitor key factors such as weight. But a patient's weight provides limited insight until combined with other insights, observations, and comparisons. How does the weight compare with others of the same age, height, and frame? Has the patient gained or lost weight since the last exam? If the patient has lost weight, why? This obviously could be good if intended as part of a fitness program or bad if a result of a health problem. Only through observation, discussion with the patient, and perhaps additional testing can the doctor reach conclusions. So it is with many elements of financial performance.

Another potential limitation is that there is a great variety of similar ratios employed in business. An example is return on capital, as there are a number of potential definitions for both the income measure and the capital measure in such a ratio. It is important to understand exactly what is being measured by a formula before reaching any conclusions.

Similarly, it is important to understand the period to which the measure relates. Many measures could apply to monthly, quarterly, or annual periods. Further, an annual measure could be based on a balance at the end of the period or an average of the quarterly balances.

Putting It All Together

These individual ratios and measures take on greater meaning when combined as part of an analytical summary as shown in Table 2.7.

Creating a set of graphs capturing selected performance measures will typically be helpful to analyze and communicate this information as shown in Figure 2.2.

A quick reference guide to key financial terms and measures is provided in Table 2.8.

TABLE 2.7 Roberts Manufacturing Company Performance Assessment Summary

	2015	2016	2017	2018	2015	2016	2017	2018	CAGR
P&L									
Net Sales	$79,383	$85,734	$92,593	$100,000	100%	100%	100%	100%	8.0%
Cost of Goods Sold	35,722	38,580	41,667	45,000	45%	45%	45%	45%	8.0%
Gross Margin	43,661	47,154	50,926	55,000	55%	55%	55%	55%	8.0%
SG&A	25,403	27,435	29,630	32,000	32%	32%	32%	32%	8.0%
R&D	6,351	6,859	7,407	8,000	8%	8%	8%	8%	8.0%
Operating Income	11,907	12,860	13,889	15,000	15%	15%	15%	15%	8.0%
Interest (Income) Expense	600	600	600	600	1%	1%	1%	1%	0.0%
Other (Income) Expense	5	7	6	5	0%	0%	0%	0%	0.0%
Income Before Income Taxes	11,302	12,253	13,283	14,395	14%	14%	14%	14%	8.4%
Federal Income Taxes	3,843	4,166	4,516	4,894	5%	5%	5%	5%	8.4%
Net Income	7,460	8,087	8,767	9,501	9%	9%	9%	10%	8.4%
EPS	0.45	0.48	0.52	0.56					
EBIAT	7,859	8,488	9,167	9,900					
Balance Sheet									
Cash	25	2,404	4,400	7,944	0%	3%	5%	8%	
Receivables	15,877	17,147	18,545	20,000	20%	20%	20%	20%	
Inventories	14,289	15,432	16,667	18,000	18%	18%	18%	18%	
Other	200	800	975	900	0%	1%	1%	1%	
Current Assets	30,391	35,783	40,587	46,844	38%	42%	44%	47%	
Net Fixed Assets	15,877	17,147	18,750	20,000	20%	20%	20%	20%	
Net Goodwill and Intangibles	14,000	13,000	12,000	11,000	18%	15%	13%	11%	
Other Long-Term Assets	200	210	428	205	0%	0%	0%	0%	
Total Assets	60,467	66,140	71,765	78,049	76%	77%	78%	78%	
Accounts Payable	3,572	3,858	4,167	4,500	5%	5%	5%	5%	
Notes Payable, Bank	–	–	–	–	0%	0%	0%	0%	
Accrued Expenses & Taxes	4,000	4,500	4,750	5,000	5%	5%	5%	5%	
Current Liabilities	7,572	8,358	8,917	9,500	10%	10%	10%	10%	

TABLE 2.7 ***(continued)***

		2015	2016	2017	2018	2015	2016	2017	2018	CAGR
Long-Term Debt		10,000	10,000	10,000	10,000	13%	12%	11%	10%	
Other		3,000	3,100	2,900	3,300	4%	4%	3%	3%	
Stockholders Equity		39,895	44,682	49,949	55,249	50%	52%	54%	55%	
Total Liabilities and Equity		60,467	66,140	71,765	78,049	76%	77%	78%	78%	
Operating Capital		22,793	25,021	27,270	29,400					
Invested Capital		49,895	54,682	59,949	65,249					
Market Value of Equity		153,974	164,304	169,000	180,030					
Cash Flow										
Net Income		7,460	8,087	8,767	9,501	9%	9%	9%	10%	
D&A		2,800	2,930	3,197	3,750	4%	3%	3%	4%	
Capital Expenditures		−3,000	−4,200	−4,800	−5,000	−4%	−5%	−5%	−5%	
(Inc) Decrease in OC			−2,228	−2,249	−2,130	0%	−3%	−2%	−2%	
FCF		7,260	4,589	4,914	6,121	9%	5%	5%	6%	
Employees		411	450	460	490					
Returns/Ratios:										
DSO		73.0	73.0	73.1	73.0					
Inv Turns		2.5	2.5	2.5	2.5					
DSI		146.0	146.0	146.0	146.0					
FA T/o		5.0	5.0	4.9	5.0					
Asset Turnover		1.3	1.3	1.3	1.3					
ROA		12.3%	12.2%	12.2%	12.2%					
ROIC		15.8%	15.5%	15.3%	15.2%					
ROE		18.7%	18.1%	17.6%	17.2%					
Economic Profit		7859	8488	9167	9900					
Interest Earned		19.8	21.4	23.1	25.0					
Debt to Total Capital (book)		20.0%	18.3%	16.7%	15.3%					
Debt to Total Capital (market)		8.1%	7.8%	7.7%	5.3%					
Leverage (Assets/Equity)		1.52	1.48	1.44	1.41					
Current Ratio		4.0	4.3	4.6	4.9					
ROE Analysis										
Profitability		9.4%	9.4%	9.5%	9.5%					
Asset Turnover	x	1.31	1.30	1.29	1.28					
Leverage	x	1.52	1.48	1.44	1.41					
ROE	=	18.7%	18.1%	17.6%	17.2%					
WACC					12%					

FIGURE 2.2 Key Performance Trends for Roberts Manufacturing Company

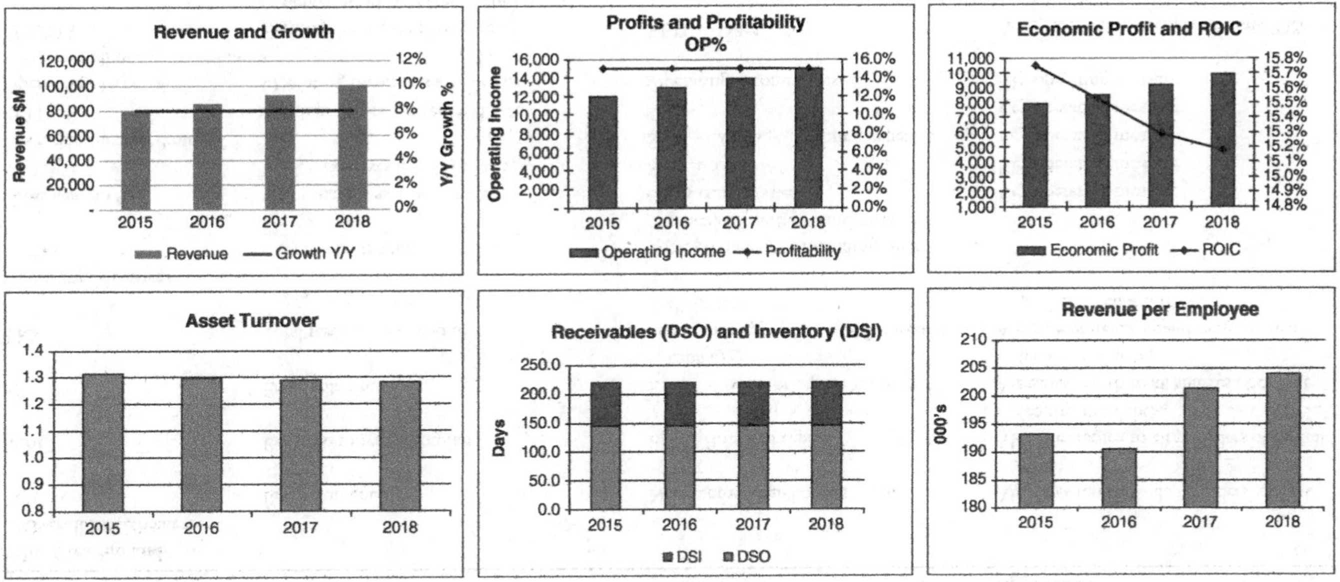

Revenue and Growth
Revenue $M
120,000
100,000
80,000
60,000
40,000
20,000
-
Y/Y Growth %
12%
10%
8%
6%
4%
2%
0%
2015 2016 2017 2018
Revenue — Growth Y/Y

Profits and Profitability
OP%
Operating Income
16,000
14,000
12,000
10,000
8,000
6,000
4,000
2,000
-
16.0%
14.0%
12.0%
10.0%
8.0%
6.0%
4.0%
2.0%
0.0%
2015 2016 2017 2018
Operating Income —♦— Profitability

Economic Profit and ROIC
11,000
10,000
9,000
8,000
7,000
6,000
5,000
4,000
3,000
2,000
1,000
15.8%
15.7%
15.6%
15.5%
15.4%
15.3%
15.2%
15.1%
15.0%
14.9%
14.8%
2015 2016 2017 2018
Economic Profit —♦— ROIC

Asset Turnover
1.4
1.3
1.2
1.1
1.0
0.9
0.8
2015 2016 2017 2018

Receivables (DSO) and Inventory (DSI)
Days
250.0
200.0
150.0
100.0
50.0
0.0
2015 2016 2017 2018
DSI DSO

Revenue per Employee
000's
210
205
200
195
190
185
180
2015 2016 2017 2018

TABLE 2.8 Key Financial Terms and Measures: Quick Reference Guide

Measure	Description	Computed as …	Application
Value Creation and Overall Effectiveness			
ROE	Return on equity	Net income/Shareholders' equity	Measures return to shareholders' capital (equity)
ROIC	Return on invested capital	EBIAT/Invested capital	Measures return to all providers of capital (equity and debt)
EP	Economic profit/	EBIAT – (Cost of capital × Invested capital)	Measures return to all sources of capital (equity and debt)
TRS	Total return to shareholders	Stock price appreciation + Reinvested dividends	Measure of management performance (and compensation)
Operating Measures			
COGS	Cost of goods sold	Total product cost, including labor, material, overhead, and variances	
Gross Margin %	Gross margin as a % of sales	Gross margin/sales	Key operating measure
SG&A %	SG&A expenses as a % of sales	SG&A/Sales	Key operating measure
Operating Income/Profit		Sales – COGS – Operating expenses	Key operating measure
EBIT	Earnings before interest and taxes		Key operating measure
Operating Margin % /"Profitability"	Operating Income as a % of sales	Operating Income/Sales	Key operating measure
EBITDA	Earnings before interest, taxes, depreciation, and amortization	EBIT + D&A	Adds back noncash expense items (D&A)
EBIAT/OPAT	Earnings before interest and after tax/Operating profit after tax	EBIT$(1 - t)$	Earnings available to all providers of capital
CAGR	Compound annual growth rate	CAGR = $[(LY/FY)^{1/n}] - 1$	Measures growth in a key variable over time (e.g. sales)

TABLE 2.8 ***(continued)***

Measure	Description	Computed as ...	Application
Asset Management			
DSO	Days Sales Outstanding	(Accounts receivable × 365)/Sales	Measures time to collect from customers
Inventory Turns	Inventory turnover	Cost of goods sold/Inventory	Supply chain effectiveness
DSI/DIOH	Days sales of inventory/Days inventory on hand	365/Inventory turns	A more intuitive measure of inventory levels/cycle time
Operating Capital Turnover	Operating capital levels relative to sales	Sales/Operating capital	Measures operating capital relative to sales
Operating Capital % Sales	Operating capital levels relative to sales	Operating capital/Sales	Measures operating capital relative to sales
Operating Capital Cycle		DSO + DSI	Measures key operating capital elements relative to sales
Asset Turnover	Asset levels relative to sales	Sales/Total assets	Asset requirements and effectiveness
Capital Structure			
TIE/C	Time interest earned/Covered	EBIT/Interest expense	Measures ability to service debt
Debt to total Capital	% of capital contributed by lenders	Debt/(Debt + Equity)	Measures financial risk and capital structure
Valuation			
WACC/Cost of Capital	Weighted average cost of capital	WACC = (ke * we) + (Kd * wd)	Expected returns of equity and debt investors
Invested Capital	Total capital contributed by investors	Book equity + Interest-bearing debt	Historical investment from all investors
Enterprise Value (EV)	Market value of debt and equity		Total value of the firm
Market Value/Market Cap	Market value of equity	Shares outstanding × Share price	Equity value of the firm

Note: Definitions and uses of ratios often vary.

SUMMARY

Understanding and interpreting financial statements is a required competency for effective management and investing. Combining this competency with an understanding of the business, industry, and strategic objectives of a firm can significantly improve management effectiveness and decision making. Historical and projected financial statements will serve as the basis for many decisions and are an important part of the foundation in building an effective performance management framework.

NOTE

1. S. A. Ross, R. W. Westerfield, and B. D. Jordan, *Fundamentals of Corporate Finance*, 5th ed. (New York: McGraw-Hill, 2000), 102.

3

KEY ANALYTICAL TOOLS AND CONCEPTS

CHAPTER INTRODUCTION

There are a number of great analytical tools that can be used to understand business performance, identify problems and opportunities, and help set a course toward improving performance. In this chapter, I will share a few of my favorites that I have relied on time and time again. Most of these tools are utilized throughout this text, but they are worth introducing here as general tools and techniques because they are both useful and underutilized by finance professionals.

BASIC STATISTICAL TOOLS

There are several useful tools buried in that textbook from your college statistics course. Many of the most useful assist in the analysis of a population or data set such as inventory, costs, transactions, or revenue by product, by project, or by customer. To illustrate, we'll review the finished goods inventory list for Vance Corp in Table 3.1. Management has asked

TABLE 3.1 Finished Goods Inventory – Vance Corp

Vance Corporation						
Finished Goods Inventory						
Product Number	Unit Sales	Quantity Y/E	Unit Cost	Extended Cost	% of Total	DSI
1001	500	100	800	80,000	0.1%	73
1002	2,000	800	3,224	2,579,200	3.5%	146
1003	200	60	250	15,000	0.0%	110
1004	6,000	1,000	400	400,000	0.5%	61
1005	1,000	500	650	325,000	0.4%	183
1006	750	270	800	216,000	0.3%	131
1007	2,500	600	800	480,000	0.6%	88
1008	4,200	1,800	4,800	8,640,000	11.6%	156
1009	1,800	300	1,800	540,000	0.7%	61
1010	1,400	400	900	360,000	0.5%	104
1011	9,000	2,088	2,800	5,846,400	7.8%	85
1012	22,000	3,200	1,475	4,720,000	6.3%	53
1013	10,000	2,600	1,190	3,094,000	4.1%	95
1014	7,400	1,200	264	316,800	0.4%	59
1015	10,000	3,100	4,700	14,570,000	19.5%	113
1016	800	200	104	20,800	0.0%	91
1017	600	159	250	39,750	0.1%	97
1018	6,200	1,700	2,500	4,250,000	5.7%	100
1019	820	100	500	50,000	0.1%	45
1020	7,425	825	600	495,000	0.7%	41
1021	1,600	200	300	60,000	0.1%	46
1022	1,200	300	400	120,000	0.2%	91
1023	3,200	600	700	420,000	0.6%	68
1024	7,400	2,243	3,015	6,762,645	9.1%	111
1025	3,200	1,125	484	544,219	0.7%	128
1026	5,500	950	400	380,000	0.5%	63
1027	2,300	700	280	196,000	0.3%	111
1028	1,875	680	374	254,320	0.3%	132
1029	3,000	1,034	3,100	3,205,400	4.3%	126
1030	1,312	1,100	693	762,300	1.0%	306
1031	750	88	900	79,200	0.1%	43
1032	180	35	250	8,750	0.0%	71
1033	235	60	350	21,000	0.0%	93
1034	2,000	680	988	671,840	0.9%	124
1035	7,000	2,880	4,100	11,808,000	15.8%	150
1036	4,800	1,800	522	939,600	1.3%	137
1037	3,200	500	360	180,000	0.2%	57
1038	1,600	895	439	392,502	0.5%	204
1039	2,150	900	504	453,600	0.6%	153
1040	3,100	750	503	376,875	0.5%	88
Total				74,674,201	100.0%	107

for an analysis of finished goods, believing that the inventory levels are high and need to be reduced. This is a relatively small population of only 40 products whereas many businesses have hundreds or even thousands of products. Yet, it will serve to demonstrate the power of these analytical tools. The raw table provides data but would require an analyst to spend considerable time to review and summarize it.

We start by sorting or reordering the product data by a key element, in this case the extended cost, in descending order. We then will divide the population into quartiles (in this case 10 products per quarter: 40/4) in Table 3.2.

Sorting the population based on revenue, cost, or inventory value begins to transform the raw data into meaningful information, facilitating analysis and insights. If you are going to "move the needle," you must focus on the larger items in any population. In this example, we have a product line that has excessive inventory as measured by inventory turns or days of inventory. Tackling the detail listing of part numbers is intimidating and inefficient. By sorting the inventory on extended cost in descending order, a mind-numbing list of products takes on meaning. The entire population can be easily characterized, and our attention can be focused on addressing the significant items first.

Even a focus on the top 10 or 20 items in a large population can be useful. As a CFO, I would routinely want to review our top 10 products, customers, and inventory items.

By adding some simple statistical measures to this analysis, we can characterize the revenue in much more meaningful ways, as summarized in Table 3.3.

Quartile Analysis. Dividing a population into fourths provides a useful start. In the case of inventory or sale values, the top quartile will general contain a disproportionate percentage of the total population. As a result, it presents an opportunity to identify the most significant line items in a large population. Management can focus on these large values, and addressing the top quartile will lead to improvements that will "move the needle."

TABLE 3.2 Finished Goods Inventory – Vance Corp: Descending Order 

3/15/2018 14:51		Vance Corporation				
		Finished Goods Inventory			2018	
Product Number	**2018 Unit Sales**	**Quantity Y/E**	**Unit Cost**	**Extended Cost**	**% of Total**	**DSI**
1015	10,000	3,100	4,700	14,570,000	19.5%	113
1035	7,000	2,880	4,100	11,808,000	15.8%	150
1008	4,200	1,800	4,800	8,640,000	11.6%	156
1024	7,400	2,243	3,015	6,762,645	9.1%	111
1011	9,000	2,088	2,800	5,846,400	7.8%	85
1012	22,000	3,200	1,475	4,720,000	6.3%	53
1018	6,200	1,700	2,500	4,250,000	5.7%	100
1029	3,000	1,034	3,100	3,205,400	4.3%	126
1013	10,000	2,600	1,190	3,094,000	4.1%	95
1002	2,000	800	3,224	2,579,200	3.5%	146
1st Quartile				65,475,645	87.7%	109
1036	4,800	1,800	522	939,600	1.3%	137
1030	1,312	1,100	693	762,300	1.0%	306
1034	2,000	680	988	671,840	0.9%	124
1025	3,200	1,125	484	544,219	0.7%	128
1009	1,800	300	1,800	540,000	0.7%	61
1020	7,425	825	600	495,000	0.7%	41
1007	2,500	600	800	480,000	0.6%	88
1039	2,150	900	504	453,600	0.6%	153
1023	3,200	600	700	420,000	0.6%	68
1004	6,000	1,000	400	400,000	0.5%	61
2nd Quartile				5,706,559	7.6%	93
1038	1,600	895	439	392,502	0.5%	204
1026	5,500	950	400	380,000	0.5%	63
1040	3,100	750	503	376,875	0.5%	88
1010	1,400	400	900	360,000	0.5%	104
1005	1,000	500	650	325,000	0.4%	183
1014	7,400	1,200	264	316,800	0.4%	59
1028	1,875	680	374	254,320	0.3%	132
1006	750	270	800	216,000	0.3%	131
1027	2,300	700	280	196,000	0.3%	111
1037	3,200	500	360	180,000	0.2%	57
3rd Quartile				2,997,497	4.0%	96
1022	1,200	300	400	120,000	0.2%	91
1001	500	100	800	80,000	0.1%	73
1031	750	88	900	79,200	0.1%	43
1021	1,600	200	300	60,000	0.1%	46
1019	820	100	500	50,000	0.1%	45
1017	600	159	250	39,750	0.1%	97
1033	235	60	350	21,000	0.0%	93
1016	800	200	104	20,800	0.0%	91
1003	200	60	250	15,000	0.0%	110
1032	180	35	250	8,750	0.0%	71
4th Quartile				494,500	0.7%	63
Total				74,674,201	100.0%	107

TABLE 3.3 Analysis of Finished Goods Inventory

Recap	Line Items	Value	% Total
Total Finished Goods	40	74,674,201	100%
Top Quartile	10	65,475,645	88%
Pareto (80/20)	8	59,802,445	80%
Mean (Average)		1,866,855	
Median		396,251	
Standard Deviation		3,352,101	

Pareto Analysis. Pareto analysis is similar to quartile analysis just described. For analysis purposes, the Pareto or 80/20 law essentially says that 80% of a population's value will be represented by 20% of the items. This has many applications in financial analysis: 80% of sales will generally result from sales to 20% of customers, and 80% of total inventory value will generally be made up of 20% of individual products or components.

Mean. As we know from our basic algebra class, the mean is the arithmetic average of all values in a set of numbers. In this case, the total value of finished goods ($74,674,201) is divided by the number of products (40), resulting in an average or mean value of inventory in finished goods of $1,866,855. While useful, the mean can be distorted by the presence of even a few outliers in the data set.

Median. The median is the middle value in a set of numbers. There will be an equal number of items above and below the median value. The median is particularly insightful when the mean is distorted due to outliers in the population.

Standard Deviation. Identifying the mean (average) or the median is helpful, but it is important to understand the dispersion of the population around the mean or average. One standard deviation indicates that 66% of the population is contained within that value. A normal distribution (bell curve) indicates that the data are equally dispersed above and below the mean. Most statistical software programs (and even Microsoft's Excel) have functions to compute the standard deviation. In this example, the standard deviation is very large, due to the number of very large values in the finished goods inventory. This indicates that there is a wide variation in finished goods inventory values.

The combination of these statistical tools can provide significant insight into any data set and help draw our attention to the most significant components in the set.

Sensitivity Analysis

This technique determines the sensitivity of an outcome (e.g. profit projection, value of a project, or valuation) to changes in key assumptions used in a base or primary case. Any projection or estimated value must be viewed as an estimate based on a number of inherent assumptions. Performing a sensitivity analysis is very useful to understand the dynamics of a particular projection or decision and to highlight the importance of testing assumptions. For example, in Table 3.4, we estimate the sensitivity of the stock price of Roberts Manufacturing Company to changes in key assumptions: the rate of sales growth and the level of profitability.

Sensitivity analysis will be used throughout this book. For the specific application of this sensitivity analysis, see Chapter 22, Business Valuation and Value Drivers.

Scenario Analysis

A projection or forecast version is based on a specific set of conditions and assumptions (e.g. economic recovery). Since projected performance will vary under different assumptions or scenarios, significant projections should be recast under different conditions, events, or scenarios. A scenario

TABLE 3.4 Stock Price Sensitivity Analysis

DCF Value Sensitivity Analysis						
					Stock Price	
Roberts Manufacturing Company			Sales Growth Rate			
Operating		4%	6%	8%	10%	12%
Income %	20.0%	$12.11	$13.49	$15.04	$16.80	$18.77
	17.5%	10.52	11.68	13.00	14.49	16.17
	15.0%	8.92	9.88	10.96	12.18	13.56
	12.5%	7.33	8.08	8.92	9.87	10.95
	10.0%	5.74	6.27	6.88	7.57	8.34

is an imagined sequence of future actions or events. Whereas sensitivity analysis provides insight into the impact of "flexing" or changing one or more assumptions, scenario analysis will examine the projection if a different course of action or chain of events occurs. For example, if the primary or base case of a projection assumes economic recovery, what would the results be if the recession continues? This requires the analyst to examine and revise all variables under a specific scenario. Scenario analysis requires substantial consideration to identify and change assumptions that are impacted under a different scenario. For example, a recession scenario could affect unit sales volumes, average selling prices, interest rates, inflation, labor costs, and commodity prices. One of the most important aspects of scenario planning is to identify the management actions that can be taken to mitigate unfavorable changes or to capitalize on potential upsides.

POTENTIAL APPLICATIONS OF SCENARIO ANALYSIS

Economic	New Product Development	Forecast
Recession	Terminated	Loss of contract
Recovery	Favorable market reaction	Competitive threat
Expansion	Moderate market reaction	

A simplistic form of scenario analysis is to develop best-case and worst-case scenarios. This will develop a range of potential outcomes that can be useful in evaluating a projection.

Probability and Expected Value

In developing financial projections and evaluating investment projects, probability analysis can be helpful. In the example in Table 3.5, executives had developed estimates of sales under five discrete scenarios. In addition to the base plan, two upside and two downside scenarios were identified. Managers had estimated the probability of each scenario. The simple

TABLE 3.5 Expected Value of Sales Plan

Sales Plan Expected Value			
Plan Scenario	**Sales Plan**	**Probability**	**Weighted Estimate**
Upside Scenario 1	140,000	5%	7,000
Upside Scenario 2	125,000	10%	12,500
Base	120,000	50%	60,000
Downside Scenario 1	110,000	20%	22,000
Downside Scenario 2	108,000	15%	16,200
Expected Value		100%	117,700

illustration provides an expected value (EV), or outcome, based on the probabilities assigned to each of the scenarios.

Of course, the most critical part of this analysis would be to identify the scenarios, estimate sales, and also estimate the probability of each scenario. In some cases, prior experience may provide a basis. Industry trends and data can be useful, for example the probability of product development success. Even where the probabilities can't be developed scientifically, use of reasonable estimates can prove helpful. In this case, the base projection of $120,000 appears aggressive when compared to the EV of $117,700. There is more downside exposure than upside to the base plan, and, pending additional information, the base forecast should be revised down to $117,700. Probability and expected value are utilized in Part Three (Business Projections and Plans), in Chapter 15 (Revenue and Gross Margins), and also in Part Five (Valuation and Capital Investment Decisions).

Decision and Event Trees

Decision and event trees are useful to visualize, evaluate, and communicate various scenarios, especially future projects or other decisions where the outcomes are uncertain. For example, a firm may face a decision to replace an existing product with a new one or continue to sell the existing product. This is unlikely to be a single decision or event. How successful will the new product be? What will happen to the sales of the existing product if not

FIGURE 3.1 **Decision Tree: Replace Existing Product**

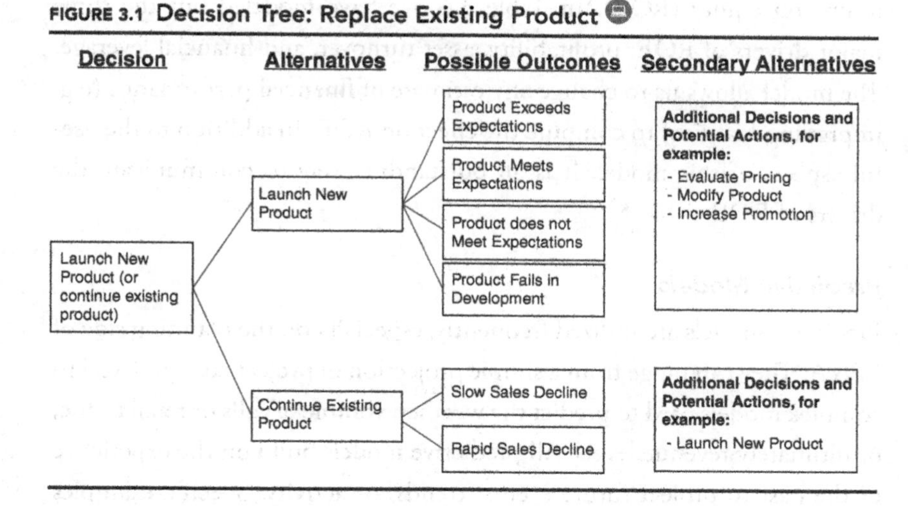

replaced? What subsequent options will management have in optimizing the result?

The simple illustration in Figure 3.1 is a very effective way to lay out various management decisions and to describe potential outcomes resulting from each alternative choice. Each of the six potential outcomes will have probability of occurrence and an estimated value (e.g. NPV, sales, earnings per share). Each of these six outcomes will also involve a second level of management options or decisions.

A more comprehensive review of decision trees and examples with values and probabilities is included in Chapter 21, Capital Investment Decisions: Advanced Topics.

Performance Trees

While we are on the subject of trees, another useful way to analyze and present financial data is through the use of tree analysis. Essentially, the analyst will create a visual model to drill down to almost any element of financial performance. These can be used to model/illustrate return on capital or equity, value drivers, or drivers of accounts receivable DSO. An early application is the so-called Dupont formula used to analyze or decompose return on equity (ROE). In Table 3.6, we have modeled out the three major drivers of ROE: profitability, asset turnover, and financial leverage. The model allows us to change any estimate of financial performance (e.g. improving margins) to compute the effect on ROE. In addition to the useful aspects of this model, it is an outstanding way to communicate the drivers of ROE.

Predictive Models

Predictive models are utilized frequently, especially on the planning side of FP&A. They can range from a simple projection of project costs in Excel to complex models used to predict the weather, volume of calls or retail traffic, or ultimately revenue levels. All predictive models build on the experience of the past to project future events, trends, or activity. Specific examples of predictive modeling are included in Chapters 13 (Budgets, Operating Plans, and Forecasts), 14 (Long-Term Projections), and 15 (Revenue and Gross Margins).

Performance Improvement and Diagnostic Tools

In Chapter 1, we suggested that the objectives of financial analysis are not simply to report on events, outcomes, and future projections. Analysts should be prepared to identify the root causes of variances, shortfalls, and overruns, and be prepared to recommend possible corrective actions. Even better, analysts should identify improvement opportunities and recommend actions to realize these opportunities. This type of analysis requires an understanding of business processes, process improvement, and diagnostic techniques. In many cases, these skills will not be resident within the traditional FP&A department. Many of these skills are developed in consulting firms or in quality or continuous improvement organizations within the enterprise. In Chapter 5, Building Analytical Capability, we review ideas for evaluating, developing, or acquiring talent with these skills (or teaming with resources outside FP&A).

TABLE 3.6 Return on Equity Analysis

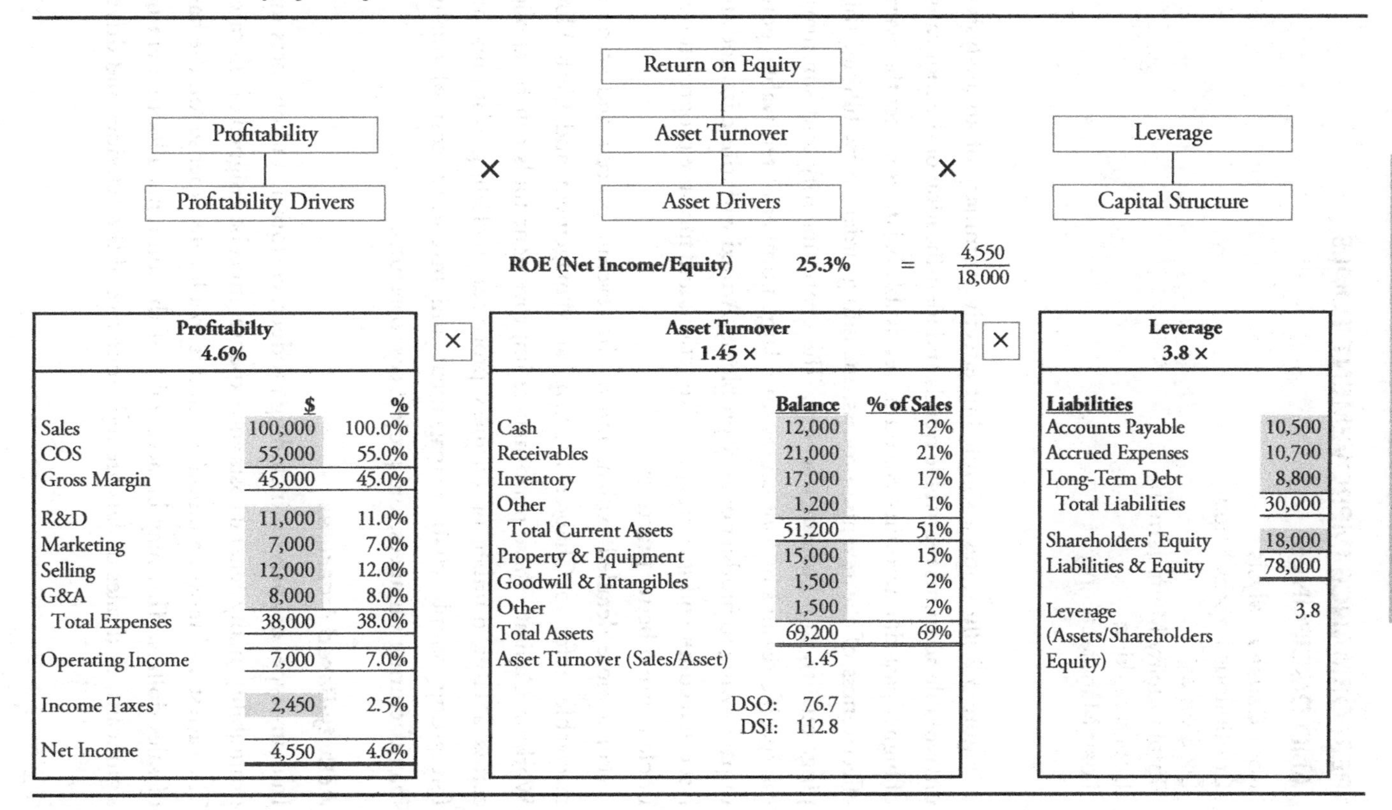

Return on Equity

Profitability (Profitability Drivers) × Asset Turnover (Asset Drivers) × Leverage (Capital Structure)

ROE (Net Income/Equity) **25.3%** = $\frac{4,550}{18,000}$

Profitabilty 4.6%

	$	%
Sales	100,000	100.0%
COS	55,000	55.0%
Gross Margin	45,000	45.0%
R&D	11,000	11.0%
Marketing	7,000	7.0%
Selling	12,000	12.0%
G&A	8,000	8.0%
Total Expenses	38,000	38.0%
Operating Income	7,000	7.0%
Income Taxes	2,450	2.5%
Net Income	4,550	4.6%

×

Asset Turnover 1.45 ×

	Balance	% of Sales
Cash	12,000	12%
Receivables	21,000	21%
Inventory	17,000	17%
Other	1,200	1%
Total Current Assets	51,200	51%
Property & Equipment	15,000	15%
Goodwill & Intangibles	1,500	2%
Other	1,500	2%
Total Assets	69,200	69%
Asset Turnover (Sales/Asset)	1.45	
DSO:	76.7	
DSI:	112.8	

×

Leverage 3.8 ×

Liabilities	
Accounts Payable	10,500
Accrued Expenses	10,700
Long-Term Debt	8,800
Total Liabilities	30,000
Shareholders' Equity	18,000
Liabilities & Equity	78,000
Leverage (Assets/Shareholders Equity)	3.8

PERFORMANCE IMPROVEMENT TOOLS AND DISCIPLINES

Root Cause Analysis
Continuous Improvement
Six Sigma
Total Quality Management
Benchmarking
Lean Manufacturing

Figure 3.2 illustrates a simple but effective summary of an analysis of unfavorable accounts receivable trends and identification of the root causes of higher past-due accounts. Accounts receivable balances reflect the overall effectiveness of the revenue process, including order entry, billing, shipping, quality, and customer service. The charts identify and summarize the specific reasons or root causes for a large number of receivables going unpaid owing to product quality problems. Armed with this data, the analyst can recommend specific corrective actions and measure progress toward implementing better practices.

For a more detailed explanation of the revenue process and accounts receivable, refer to Chapter 17, Capital Management and Cash Flow: Working Capital. These performance improvement tools can be applied across a large number of business processes, including planning and forecasting, supply chain management and inventory, cost of quality, manufacturing variances, and project cost overruns.

Activity-Based Measures

In many types of analysis, including product, customer, and business unit profitability, many general costs and expenses must be assigned or allocated. The easiest and most common method is to allocate expenses on the basis of sales dollars. This may be acceptable if the amounts allocated are not significant, or if sales dollars are representative of the activities and drivers

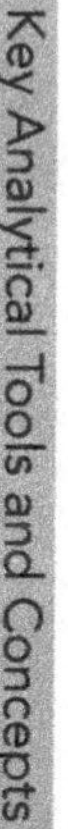

FIGURE 3.2 Revenue Process and Accounts Receivable Analysis

Receivables and DSO

Receivables: 0, 20, 40, 60, 80, 100, 120, 140, 160
DSO: 0, 20, 40, 60, 80, 100
Q317 Q417 Q118 Q218 Q318 Q418
Receivables — DSO

DSO Drivers

Days: 20, 30, 40, 50, 60, 70, 80, 90, 100
BPDSO | Customer CML | Revenue Linearity | Past Dues | Other | Current DSO

Past Due Receivables

$m: 0, 5, 10, 15, 20, 25, 30
Q317 Q417 Q118 Q218 Q318 Q418
— Goal

Past Due By Root Cause

$m
Other | Customer credit | Quality | Billing Errors
0 2 4 6 8 10 12 14 16

of that expense. For example, order processing, invoicing, and service activities may support all product lines within an enterprise. In preparing product line P&Ls, these costs are allocated on the basis of sales dollars. However, in most organizations, sales dollars are not reflective of the level of activity and time attributable to each product line. For example, the cost of processing and invoicing an order may be the same for a small-dollar repair order as it is for a $100,000 system. Service costs will be driven by the level of product failures and returns, not sales dollars. Inevitably, certain product lines will consume a disproportionate share or these activities.

Table 3.7 presents a comparison of these activities and measures and an allocation of total costs on the basis of sales dollars.

Note that the activity measures selected as representative of the drivers of time and cost for the department, namely number of invoices generated and returns, vary significantly from the percentage of sales dollars for each product line.

Table 3.8 assigns the cost for order processing and billing (OPB) on the basis of the number of transactions (invoices), and assigns the customer service costs on the basis of product returns. The table also compares the costs allocated by sales dollars to the costs assigned by activity measures, highlighting a significantly different assignment of costs. The analysis also identifies some other notable concerns that should be pursued, for example the large number of returns for parts. What are the root causes of returns and possible corrective actions? The company should also look at the profitability for parts, to ensure that pricing covers the relatively high transaction costs.

Benchmarking and External View

Most traditional efforts by FP&A professionals are directed at the internal aspects of the enterprise. However, these professionals can extend and expand the value they add by looking outside the enterprise. FP&A can

TABLE 3.7 Order Processing Costs Allocated by Sales Dollars

Activity-Based Cost Analysis

Order Processing and Customer Service	
Order Processing and Billing (OPB)	1,200,100
Customer Service	750,000
Total	1,950,100

	Sales	% Total	Allocation on Sales $	# Invoices	% Total	Average Transaction	Returns	% Total	Return Rate
Product Line 1	1,500,100	3%	56,519	862	11%	1,740	20	2%	2.3%
Product Line 2	2,105,000	4%	79,310	410	5%	5,134	61	6%	14.9%
Product Line 3	1,200,600	2%	45,235	600	8%	2,001	41	4%	6.8%
Product Line 4	8,001,000	15%	301,455	1600	20%	5,001	15	1%	0.9%
Product Line 5	4,200,500	8%	158,263	2300	29%	1,826	40	4%	1.7%
Product Line 6	12,400,500	24%	467,215	260	3%	47,694	12	1%	4.6%
Product Line 7	6,000,000	12%	226,063	525	7%	11,429	28	3%	5.3%
Product Line 8	14,750,000	28%	555,738	300	4%	49,167	1	0%	0.3%
Parts	1,600,486	3%	60,302	1000	13%	1,600	800	79%	80.0%
Total	51,758,186	100%	1,950,100	7,857	100%	6,588	1,018	100%	13.0%

TABLE 3.8 Costs Assigned Based on Activity

	Costs Assigned Based on Activity Measures						
					Comparison		
	% Invoices	OPB Cost Assignment	% Returns	Service Assignment	Total Assigned	Allocated Sales $	Change
Product Line 1	11.0%	131,664	2.0%	14,735	146,399	56,519	89,880
Product Line 2	5.2%	62,625	6.0%	44,941	107,566	79,310	28,255
Product Line 3	7.6%	91,646	4.0%	30,206	121,852	45,235	76,617
Product Line 4	20.4%	244,388	1.5%	11,051	255,440	301,455	(46,015)
Product Line 5	29.3%	351,308	3.9%	29,470	380,778	158,263	222,515
Product Line 6	3.3%	39,713	1.2%	8,841	48,554	467,215	(418,661)
Product Line 7	6.7%	80,190	2.8%	20,629	100,819	226,063	(125,244)
Product Line 8	3.8%	45,823	0.1%	737	46,560	555,738	(509,178)
Parts	12.7%	152,743	78.6%	589,391	742,134	60,302	681,832
Total	100.0%	1,200,100	100.0%	750,000	1,950,100	1,950,100	–

utilize benchmark and external information to add value in the following ways:

- Analysis of markets, customers, and competition.
- Using external information to benchmark and evaluate performance.
- Utilizing benchmark information to set enterprise goals for performance and value creation.

Benchmarking is more fully explored in Chapter 11, The External View: Benchmarking Performance and Competitive Analysis.

THE BUSINESS MODEL

Managers often describe the actual and targeted financial performance of their company as a "business model" or "financial model." The business model represents the quantification of a company's strategy and business practices. The business model concept provides a useful framework for a number of business decisions ranging from product/service pricing to setting investment and expense levels. However, managers may lock into a single business model concept, limiting their ability to effectively compete or grow into other markets.

The common view of a business model represents a target profit and loss (P&L) model. The manager thinks of the business in terms of the P&L captions and the relationship of each line item as a percentage of sales, as illustrated in Table 3.9.

Using this conceptual framework, managers will set prices, establish business plans, evaluate business proposals, set expense levels, and make other critical business decisions. For example, a company that is developing a product with a cost of $450 may set a target selling price of $1,000 to maintain the 55% margin. In establishing the R&D budget, the company may target spending at 8% of projected sales.

TABLE 3.9 Business Model Illustration: Traditional View

Roberts Manufacturing Co.	2006	% of Sales
Sales	$ 100,000	100.0%
Cost of Sales	45,000	45.0%
Gross Margin	55,000	55.0%
SG&A	32,000	32.0%
R&D	8,000	8.0%
Total Expenses	40,000	40.0%
Operating Income	15,000	15.0%
Other Income (Expense)	605	0.6%
Taxes	4,894	4.9%
Net Income	9,501	9.5%

Comprehensive Business Model Framework

The traditional P&L business model framework, while useful, provides an incomplete view of a company's economic performance since it does not reflect other critical aspects of business performance. Most important, it does not consider sales growth rates, capital requirements, cash flow, and returns. The two critical determiners in building long-term, sustainable value are growth and return on invested capital (ROIC). Therefore, any comprehensive business model framework must incorporate at least these elements to be a useful decision support tool.

A broader, more comprehensive view of the business model is illustrated in Table 3.10. By including the additional measures reflecting growth and invested capital, we present a more complete picture of the company's performance. For example, managers or investors should not reach a conclusion on the reasonableness of R&D spending levels without considering the potential sales growth rates.

In addition, the profitability measures alone are incomplete for evaluating the performance of the organization. Only when we include the capital levels employed in a business can we fully assess the financial performance

TABLE 3.10 Business Model Illustration: Comprehensive View

Roberts Manufacturing Co.		2017	% of Sales
Sales Growth Rate:	8.0%		
Profitability Model			
Sales		$ 100,000	100.0%
Cost of Sales		45,000	45.0%
Gross Margin		55,000	55.0%
SG&A		32,000	32.0%
R&D		8,000	8.0%
Total Expenses		40,000	40.0%
Operating Income		15,000	15.0%
Other Income (Expense)		605	0.6%
Taxes		4,894	4.9%
Net Income		9,501	9.5%
Asset Utilization			
Days Sales Outstanding			73.0
Days Sales Inventory			146.0
Operating Capital Turnover			3.4
Fixed Asset Turnover			5.0
Intangible Turnover			9.1
Total Asset Turnover			1.3
Leverage			1.4
Debt to Total Capital			15.3%
Returns			
ROE			17.2%
ROIC			15.2%

of that business. The inclusion of a balance sheet and key metrics will allow us to determine the ROIC. Many companies and entire industries generate significant returns despite relatively low profit margins as a result of low capital requirements or high asset turnover. The grocery industry is a prime example. This industry tends to operate with thin margins, but requires lower invested capital by turning assets, primarily inventory, faster than other industries. Many mass merchandisers have a similar low-margin, high-turnover model. Walmart's profitability (net income % sales) is relatively low, but the combination of asset turnover and leverage boosts the company's ROE to over 20%.

Conversely, other industries such as equipment manufacturers must post higher profitability to compensate for high capital requirements.

Review of Business Models

Table 3.11 provides a summary of various business models for some well-known companies. The table presents selected financial information for a number of companies that most of us are familiar with at some level. Take a moment to compare key performance measures across the companies, including growth, profitability, asset turnover, and financial leverage. The companies' performance on each of these variables can be related to the key ROE and valuation measures over a five-year period.

While this summary is used to illustrate the business model concept, the format is also a terrific way of benchmarking performance across value drivers. We will build on this concept of benchmarking business models in Chapter 11, The External View: Benchmarking Performance and Competitive Analysis.

Varying Business Models within a Company

Most companies have two or more distinct business units under one corporate roof. When this situation exists, it is important that managers understand the differences in the various businesses and don't attempt to force fit the model from one business to another without due consideration. This is especially important when a company has one dominant business, with smaller but different business units in the portfolio. Managers have a tendency to apply a single business model, expecting similar ratios and performance across the businesses, which can result in dysfunctional decisions and missed opportunities.

TABLE 3.11 Business Model Benchmark Summary Based on Company Reports and SEC Filings

	Business Models, Returns, and Valuation Metrics					
	Accenture	IBM	Amazon	Apple	Target	Southwest
Revenue and Growth						
Revenue	34,798	79,919	135,987	215,639	70,000	20,425
Rev. Growth (3 Year Hist CAGR)	4.6%	−7.2%	22.2%	8.1%	−0.8%	4.9%
Profitability						
Gross Margin %	30.0%	47.9%	35.0%	39.0%	30.0%	18.0%
R&D %		7.2%		5.0%	0.0%	0.0%
SG&A %	16.0%	24.3%	32.0%	7.0%	23.0%	0.0%
Operating Margin	4,811	13,105	4,186	60,024	5,000	3,760
Operating Margin %	13.8%	16.4%	3.1%	27.8%	7.1%	18.4%
EBITDA	5,540	17,486	12,302	70,529	7,000	4,981
%	15.9%	21.9%	9.0%	32.7%	10.0%	24.4%
Operating Profit after Tax	3,734	12,581	2,657	43,979	3,300	2,379
%	10.7%	15.7%	2.0%	20.4%	4.7%	11.6%
Asset Turnover and Returns						
DSO	65.3	134.0	22.4	26.7	0	9.8
DSI	0	13.6	47.4	5.9	61.9	7.4
Net Asset (IC) Turnover	4.23	1.32	5.04	1.00	2.92	1.73
ROIC	45.4%	20.8%	9.8%	20.4%	13.8%	20.1%
Valuation						
Enterprise Value	71,800	196,000	452,500	834,000	32,040	38,590
Enterprise Value/Revenue	2.1	2.5	3.3	3.9	0.5	1.9
Enterprise Value/EBITDA	13.0	11.2	36.8	11.8	4.6	7.7

This is a frequent problem when managers consider a related but different business opportunity. For example, there may be an opportunity to build a business based on the current product line, but requiring lower pricing and therefore lower costs. Managers may pass on this opportunity because of lower expected gross margins. However, it is possible that this product line may require lower levels of SG&A and inventory. This may result in returns approximating or even exceeding the levels achieved by the high-end business.

This phenomenon is striking at companies with diversified portfolios such as General Electric (GE), Textron, and United Technologies. These companies each contain business units with very different business characteristics. In GE's case, they range from jet engines to medical systems to power systems. Each of these businesses will be shaped by different market and competitive forces. The businesses will have different growth rates, gross margins, operating expense levels, and asset requirements. An illustration of a diversified portfolio is presented in Table 3.12. This portfolio has five businesses, each with very different characteristics. These businesses record gross margins that range from 65% to as low as single digits. Some have very large levels of invested capital; other businesses require essentially no capital. Some of these businesses are growing and require capital to fund the growth; others are mature and are generating substantial cash flow. This diverse set of businesses could not have a one-size-fits-all business model. If the managers of this firm insisted on a single business model, the results would likely be disastrous. For example, if managers evaluated each of these businesses on operating profitability alone, they could significantly misjudge the economic performance of each. To evaluate overall business performance, managers and investors need to consider expected growth rates and ROIC. Note in this example that the services business has the lowest operating margin, but, owing to low investment requirements, it posts one of the highest ROICs.

Even in companies with a more homogeneous set of businesses, there is likely to be significant variation in the performance characteristics of business segments. Businesses tend to have different product lines or end-use markets with different business models. Geographic markets, ancillary products, and services also contribute differently to financial performance. Managers must understand and evaluate the individual business models and the contribution that each makes to total corporate performance. Table 3.13 presents different business models that may exist in what appears to be a homogeneous business.

TABLE 3.12 Varying Business Models under the Same Roof

	Equipment		Components		
	Mature	High Growth	Mature	High Growth	Services
Estimated Sales Growth	5%	15–20%	5%	15–20%	3%
Gross Margin	65%	60%	45%	40%	15%
R&D	9%	12%	5%	3%	1%
SG&A	40%	35%	30%	18%	5%
Operating Margins	16%	13%	10%	19%	9%
Net Income	10%	8%	7%	12%	6%
DSO	60	60	50	45	75
DSI	120	90	70	50	0
Other Capital Requirements	L	M	M	H	L
Asset Turnover	3.0	4.0	5.0	4.0	8.0
ROIC	31%	34%	33%	49%	47%

TABLE 3.13 Business Models in a Homogeneous Company

	Base Business					New	
	End Use 1	End Use 2	End Use 3	Service	Parts	Market	Combined
Estimated Sales Growth	–2%	10–15%	20%	5%	6%	60%	12%
Gross Margin	60%	40%	54%	35%	30%	50%	53%
R&D	3%	8%	10%	0%	0%	15%	7%
SG&A	28%	20%	35%	7%	7%	20%	25%
Operating Margins	29%	12%	9%	28%	23%	15%	21%
Net Income	19%	8%	6%	18%	15%	10%	14%
DSO	60	60	100	45	45	90	70
DSI	90	115	200	100	160	150	118
Other Capital Requirements	L	M	H	L	L	H	M
Asset Turnover	5.0	4.0	2.5	5.0	5.0	2.7	3.5
ROIC	94%	31%	15%	91%	75%	26%	48%

Operating Leverage: The Business Model and Variability

Another important dimension to the business model is the dynamics of the model in terms of fixed and variable costs. This analysis for Roberts Manufacturing Company is presented in Table 3.14. The analysis starts with the basic P&L model. Then costs can be classified into one of two groups: fixed costs and those that vary with changes in sales levels. The schedule also estimates the variable contribution margin representing the additional margin realized on each additional sales dollar.

TABLE 3.14 Cost and Breakeven Analysis

Roberts Manufacturing Co	Fixed	Variable	2018 Variable % Sales	Total	% of Sales
Sales				100,000	100.0%
Cost of Sales					
Material		20,000	20.0%	20,000	20.0%
Direct Labor	12,000	1,000	1.0%	13,000	13.0%
Overhead	11,000	1,000	1.0%	12,000	12.0%
Total Cost of Sales	23,000	22,000	22.0%	45,000	45.0%
Operating Expenses					
R&D	8,000			8,000	8.0%
Selling Expense	20,000			20,000	20.0%
Commission Expense		3,000	3.0%	3,000	3.0%
Marketing Expense	4,000			4,000	4.0%
G&A	5,000			5,000	5.0%
Goodwill Amortization					0.0%
Total Operating Expenses	37,000	3,000	3.0%	40,000	40.0%
Total Costs	60,000	25,000	25.0%	85,000	85.0%
Operating Profit				15,000	15.0%
Variable Contribution Margin			75.0%	-	
Breakeven Point Sales per Year				$ 80,000	80.0%
Breakeven Point Sales per Week				1,538	

Note: Fixed costs are defined as costs fixed for the short term (i.e., 90–180 days).

With these estimates of fixed and variable components of the cost structure, managers can significantly improve their understanding of the business model and the relationship of costs and profitability to sales volume. Given this information, they can estimate the breakeven point in sales and project profit levels at various sales levels.

The breakeven level in sales can be estimated as follows:

$$\frac{\text{Total Fixed Costs}}{\text{Variable Contribution Margin}} \quad \frac{\$60{,}000}{75\%} = \$80{,}000$$

At $80,000, the operating income of Roberts Manufacturing Company (RMC) would be $0.00, or at breakeven. For every dollar of sales above this level, operating income will increase by 75 cents. Similarly, for every dollar below $80,000, RMC will lose 75 cents. A summary of this analysis is presented in Table 3.15.

Companies in cyclical industries often attempt to reduce the fixed component of the cost structures in favor of variable costs. If RMC is in a cyclical market with significant variation in sales levels, management may wish to lower the breakeven point or "variabilize" more of the costs. As illustrated in Table 3.16, managers could consider reducing the fixed component of the cost model from $60,000 to $40,000, converting these costs to variable. Management may accomplish this in a number of ways, for example by outsourcing manufacturing or by using outside distributors rather than internal sales employees. Note that the profits and profitability

TABLE 3.15 Operating Leverage Illustration: Current Situation

Current		−60%	−40%	−20%	Base	20%	+40%	+60%
Sales		40,000	60,000	80,000	100,000	120,000	140,000	160,000
Fixed Costs	60,000	(60,000)	(60,000)	(60,000)	(60,000)	(60,000)	(60,000)	(60,000)
Variable Costs	25.0%	(10,000)	(15,000)	(20,000)	(25,000)	(30,000)	(35,000)	(40,000)
Operating Profit		(30,000)	(15,000)	–	15,000	30,000	45,000	60,000
%		−75.0%	−25.0%	0.0%	15.0%	25.0%	32.1%	37.5%
Breakeven Sales Level	80,000							

TABLE 3.16 Operating Leverage Illustration: Revised Cost Structure

Reduce Breakeven		−60%	−40%	−20%	Base	+20%	+40%	+60%
Sales		40,000	60,000	80,000	100,000	120,000	140,000	160,000
Fixed Costs	40,000	−40,000	−40,000	−40,000	−40,000	−40,000	−40,000	−40,000
Variable Costs	45.0%	−18,000	−27,000	−36,000	−45,000	−54,000	−63,000	−72,000
Operating Profit		−18,000	−7,000	4,000	15,000	26,000	37,000	48,000
%		−45.0%	−11.7%	5.0%	15.0%	21.7%	26.4%	30.0%
Breakeven Sales Level	72,727							

are unchanged at the base sales plan from the levels projected under the current situation in Table 3.15.

The revision to the company's cost structure has several benefits. RMC will achieve profitability at a lower sales level ($72,727) compared to $80,000 in the current situation. Operating losses will be reduced from the current situation under any sales shortfall scenarios. This will also reduce risk, since the firm is more likely to avoid operating losses and resultant liquidity and cash flow problems. It is important to note that converting fixed costs to variable costs is not without downsides. One downside visible from this analysis is that profits will be reduced at the higher end of the sales range under the revised model. Other downsides may include reduced control over key business processes, such as outsourcing manufacturing, potentially resulting in reduced information flow or longer cycle times.

Limitations of the Business Model Concept

The use of the business model concept has limitations and can be misused. Blind adherence to the concept may discourage managers from considering sound business opportunities simply because they don't fit the prescribed model for the company. They may indeed be acceptable businesses, but with a variant business model.

Other companies fail to challenge their business models and may be vulnerable to potential competitors that approach the business from a dramatically different direction. Some very successful companies have done just that. For example, Dell redefined the business model for the personal computer market with a new distribution and supply chain strategy. This reduced costs and increased competitiveness as well as reducing inventory requirements and possible obsolescence risk. Similarly, Southwest Airlines attacked the traditional model for commercial airlines, and Walmart and subsequently Amazon, that of the retail industry.

SUMMARY

The analyst has a broad range of tools that can be utilized to add value in evaluating, planning, monitoring, and improving performance. Many of these tools are outside the traditional analytical toolbox. These tools will be incorporated in analysis throughout this book.

4

DEVELOPING PREDICTIVE AND ANALYTICAL MODELS

CHAPTER INTRODUCTION

One of the greatest tools in the business analyst's bag is the ability to create a model of future business results. Models are typically used to evaluate business decisions, analyze alternatives, or predict future business results. In this chapter, we will define models, highlight typical applications, review best practices, discuss best ways to present the results of a model, and explain how to establish a portfolio of models.

WHAT IS A FINANCIAL MODEL?

A model is essentially a mathematical representation of a transaction, event, or business, and typically involves the use of assumptions and relationships of various factors to predict an outcome.

A financial model allows us to project and test the dynamics of a business, project, or program. Developing an effective model of a business or significant project requires a sophisticated understanding of the business or opportunity at hand. The analyst will almost always need input from other business disciplines such as sales and marketing, operations, and research and development.

Several challenges arise in developing effective models. The first challenge is to create a model that will satisfy its objective. Second, almost all models include or develop projections of future performance, and therefore they incorporate assumptions about future performance, which introduces uncertainty and risk. Finally, the analyst must develop a method for creating output or presentation summaries to effectively communicate the results of the model to managers. We will discuss best practices to address these challenges in the remainder of this chapter. An illustration of a model to project revenues and product margins is included at the end of this chapter.

Applications for Financial Models

Under our broad definition, models are used in a wide range of applications. We will review a few of the most common applications of models, but the potential application of models is nearly unlimited.

Operating Plans and Budgets

Nearly all organizations develop operating plans and budgets. These plans include a set of projections about future performance based on a set of assumptions. While the emphasis will vary based on the nature of the organization, the operating plan should include projections of sales, margins, expenses, profits, balance sheet accounts, and cash flow. We will discuss operating plans and budgets in detail in Chapter 13.

Forecasts/Business Outlooks

Most organizations prepare forecasts or "business outlooks," which are essentially updates to the annual operating plans and budgets. These are an increasingly important part of business projections owing to the dynamic times in which we live and operate. Assumptions made in the annual operating plan will often have to be revised throughout the year. We will discuss forecasts and business outlooks in detail in Chapter 13.

Revenue Projections

Revenue projections are typically the most important and difficult-to-predict variables in developing a forecast or plan for an enterprise. Projections must reflect assumptions in the company's market and overall business environment as well as pricing, cost, and product introduction and life cycle. The illustrative model at the end of this chapter presents a simple case to project revenues over a multiyear horizon. Additional models and analysis addressing revenue are included in Chapter 15.

Cash Flow and Liquidity Projections

Most treasurers and CFOs must pay very close attention to cash flow, capital requirements, and liquidity. Often, the traditional financial statement approach is not the best method for short-term (even weekly or daily) projections. Cash flow models focus on specific drivers of short-term cash flow. We will explore these models in Chapter 17, Capital Management and Cash Flow: Working Capital.

Strategic Plans and Long-Range Forecasts

A strategic plan should include a set of financial projections. These projections are a financial representation of the estimated results of executing the strategic plan. The projections are typically done at a higher level than annual plans or forecasts. Owing to the difficulty in projecting financial results over an extended period of time (typically three to seven years), a number of scenarios are often included in the plan. We will explore these models in Chapter 14, Long-Term Projections.

Capital Investment Decisions

Capital investment decisions include any expenditure with a long-term horizon such as purchases of capital equipment, new product development, and acquisitions of businesses or companies. These decisions often require a series of projections of both investment outlays and future cash inflows. We will explore these models in Chapters 20 and 21, on capital investment decisions.

Compensation and Incentive Plans

As part of the process to design and test compensation systems, it is essential to model potential outcomes. These models illustrate incentives earned under different scenarios and help to prevent inclusion of unintended consequences. You can rest assured that executives and managers will spend a great deal of time modeling potential payouts and scenarios for their personal compensation plans!

Valuing a Business

Most sound methodologies for developing an estimated value for a business require projecting future performance and cash flows. The best valuation models will include key performance drivers, projected income statements, and balance sheet and cash flow projections. We will explore these models in Chapter 22, Business Valuation and Value Drivers.

Mergers and Acquisitions

The ability to project the results and evaluate the investment characteristics of a merger or an acquisition is simply a combination and refinement of the business valuation model and the capital investment model. Additional metrics are included to focus on critical success factors and other unique aspects of these investment decisions. We will explore these models in Chapter 23, Analysis of Mergers and Acquisitions.

Best Practices in Developing Models

The best practices reviewed next can be applied to almost any predictive or analytical model. Models will be illustrated and used throughout this book. We will use a simple model to develop long-term revenue projections to illustrate these best practices.

Define Objective

As a first step, analysts should step back and define the objective of a large modeling project. In many cases, the model is in response to a request from the CEO, CFO, or another operating executive. Taking a few minutes of time to define the objective and review with the internal client can save a great deal of time and rework later in the process. Defining the objective will also assist in designing the model and should address the following questions:

- Who is the client or user of the model?
- What answers (output) are we seeking?
- What are the key variables that will impact the analysis?
- What is the time horizon?
- How frequently will the model be used, and by whom?

Develop Architecture of Model

Many financial models are developed without a well-thought-out architecture. Pressed for time, the analyst sets up a spreadsheet or other tools without developing an overall framework for the model.

Preferably, the analyst, building on the stated objective, lays out the flow of the model, including required inputs, processing worksheets, and output summaries.

The architecture should include:

- Objective: What is the purpose of the model?
- Client: Who is the primary client/user of the report?
- Frequency: How often will the model be updated?
- Flow: In complex models, it is helpful to illustrate the flow of information in a model.
- Key assumptions: Identify, up front, the major assumptions and inputs required to use the model.
- Output and presentation: Based on the objective and identification of the client, develop the output summary.

Figure 4.1 is an example of the planning architecture for a long-term revenue projection model. This can be included as the first worksheet in an Excel model.

Documentation

One of the most common problems with financial models is that they tend to have little, if any, documentation. This presents a problem if another analyst attempts to use the model. In fact, for models that are used infrequently, even the developer of the model may waste a lot of time refreshing his or her memory (I am speaking from personal experience here!). Taking the additional time to properly document the model will save both the developer and other users substantial time in using and modifying the model in the future.

The documentation can include key inputs required and the steps required to update the model.

Identify Input Areas

For many models, it is very helpful to identify or even segregate input fields from processing or output fields. If input areas are not identified, the user must hunt and peck around the model looking for input fields. In large models, the input values may be several steps away from the final summary. A simple but effective technique is to simply shade all input areas in the model. This allows any user to quickly identify cells that can (and those that should not) be changed. Alternatively, some model developers prefer to have all key inputs and assumptions in one section of the model.

Identify Key Assumptions and Drivers

Models typically require making many estimates and assumptions. Not all inputs to a model have equal importance. Key assumptions and drivers in the model should be identified and highlighted. These critical inputs should be identified, documented, tested, reviewed, and varied in sensitivity and scenario analysis.

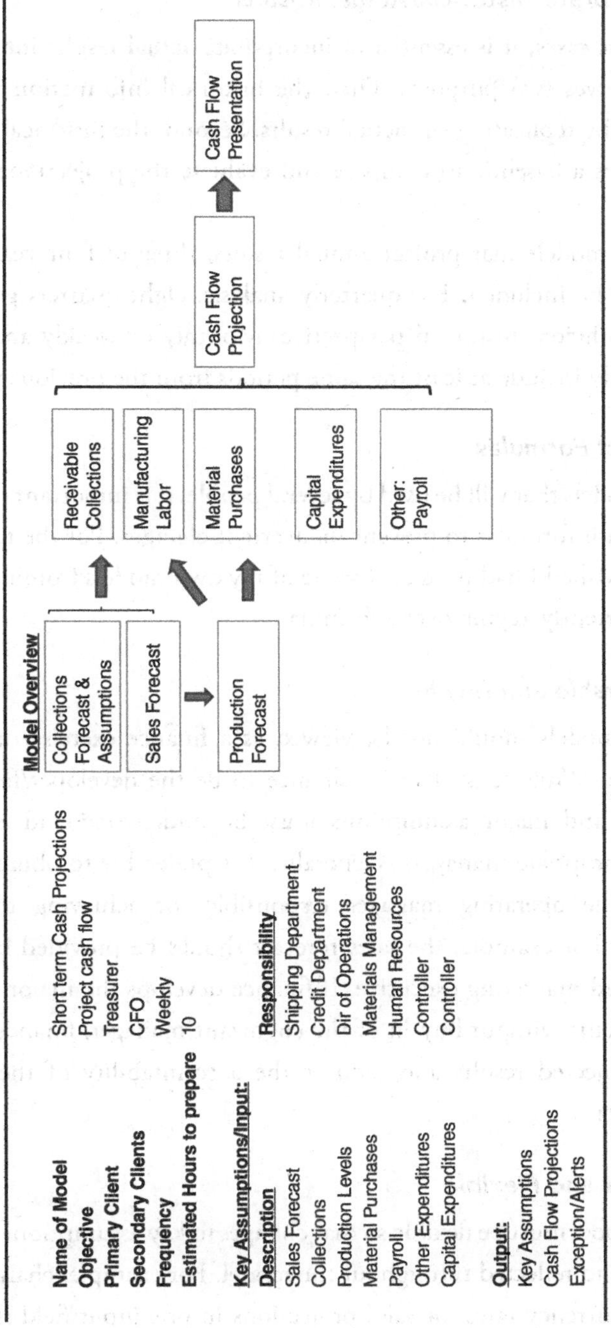

FIGURE 4.1 Financial Model Architecture

Incorporate Historical/Actual Results

In most cases, it is essential to incorporate actual results into the model. This serves two purposes. First, the historical information validates the model by replicating the actual results. Second, the historical information provides a baseline to compare and evaluate the projections used in the model.

For models that project annual results, three to four years of history should be included. For quarterly analysis, eight quarters generally provide sufficient historical perspective. Monthly or weekly analysis should generally include at least the same periods from the previous year.

Protect Formulas

For models that will be used by several people, it is important to protect the cells with formulas to prevent inadvertent changes. For the record, I have often wished I had protected some of my own models from myself – from inadvertently keying over a formula.

Ownership and Buy-In

Most models should not be viewed as a finance exercise or product of finance. While it is okay for finance to be the developer/facilitator, the inputs and major assumptions must be understood and agreed to by the appropriate managers. Generally, it is preferable to obtain key inputs from the operating manager responsible for achieving the projected results. For example, the sales forecast should be provided by the senior sales and marketing executive. If finance develops the major assumptions and inputs without buy-in of the cognizant manager, finance often owns the projected results and reduces the accountability of the responsible manager.

Robust and Flexible

The model must be flexible so that changes to key assumptions can easily be made and reflected throughout the model. For example, changing interest rates, currency rates, or sales projections in one input field should ripple throughout the model, resulting in revised outcomes. Too often, models are fragmented and require multiple manual entries to effect a single change.

In addition, contrary to the wildest dreams of the analyst, most models are not one and done. Typically, the client will want to change assumptions or run additional scenarios.

Review for Accuracy and Reasonableness

There is no quicker way to destroy personal credibility than to produce reports and analysis that contain errors. The analyst and FP&A team should implement measures to identify and correct any errors. The following review techniques can reduce errors and improve the overall quality of the analysis:

Independent Review. It can be very difficult to effectively review an analysis that we have personally prepared. Where possible, the analysis should be reviewed by an analyst or a manager who was not directly involved in the process.

Review of Key Inputs, Assumptions, and Flow of Analysis. The reviewer should perform a mini-audit of the model, to "tick and tie" key numbers to ensure they flow through the analysis, from detail worksheets to summaries.

Big Picture/Client Perspective. Review the analysis through the lens of the client. Does it address the objective and issue at hand? Is the presentation clear? Are the results of the analysis/model sensible? In too many cases, the answer (output) is nonsensical because of some minor error in the model; this could easily be detected (and most assuredly will be discovered by the client!). What additional questions does the analysis raise? What actions should be taken or recommended?

Sensitivity and Scenario Analysis

The model should also facilitate making changes to critical assumptions to create various scenarios and perform sensitivity analysis. The initial output of the model may be described as the "base" projection. Other versions of the model should be summarized and presented to the client since they add tremendous value in understanding the impact of assumptions and the overall dynamics of the situation or decision.

A sensitivity analysis will flex one or more sensitive assumptions. For example, what is the impact on total revenues if unit volumes are 10% under the base forecast? What is the result if unit volumes are 10% above?

A scenario analysis will attempt to address what-ifs. For example, what if a new competitor successfully introduces a product that competes directly with one of our key products? This scenario will likely result in reduced average sales prices *and* unit sales for this product. A model could easily accommodate estimating and presenting this and other scenarios. For additional examples of scenario analysis, refer to Chapter 21, Capital Investment Decisions: Advanced Topics.

Output and Presentation Summary

Nearly all analysis, spreadsheets, and models make poor presentation documents. Completing the analysis or model is just half of the job. Developing an effective way to summarize and present the results of the model is as important as the model itself.

For complex models, it is best to incorporate an output or presentation summary. By integrating the presentation summary into the model, it is updated any time the model is run or changed. I prefer a one-page summary highlighting key assumptions, a graphic presentation of results, and a sensitivity and scenario analysis. This summary should be the lead presentation summary, with most spreadsheets and tables as supporting schedules. The model, or even one output from the model, represents a small part of the potential value of a model. The real value is in increasing the understanding of the dynamics of a particular investment, projection, or decision and communicating this to the pertinent managers. We cover this topic in greater detail in Chapter 6, Communicating and Presenting Financial Information.

Establish a Portfolio of Models

In most organizations, the models are often stored by the individual who developed or uses the model. Many organizations have found it useful to develop an index of models and store them in a shared drive or cloud. This will serve to eliminate duplication of similar models. It will also encourage the sharing of best practices and techniques across the organization. A partial list of the models included in this book (Table 4.1) highlights the usefulness of this practice. More on building the analytical capability of the organization is presented in Chapter 5.

SUMMARY

Financial models are a critical part of the analyst's tool kit. Models are used to predict future results and to analyze actual performance. By employing best practices, the FP&A team can develop more effective models, save time, and present the results more effectively. Analysts should devote time at the beginning of a project to define the objective, identify their clients, determine key inputs and assumptions, design the architecture work flow of the model, and design how the results of the model will be presented. The model itself actually represents a small part of the potential value of a model. The real value is in increasing the understanding of the dynamics of a particular process or decision and communicating this to the pertinent managers.

APPENDIX: ILLUSTRATIVE MODEL

Our model to project revenues utilizes two separate spreadsheets, one for sales of existing products and another for sales of new products. The model was developed to reflect critical drivers and assumptions for this specific situation. Key variables and assumptions will vary for each specific company and situation. Other companies may need to modify the model to reflect other key drivers such as foreign currency rates, distribution channels, geographies, and other variables. It is also important to develop the

TABLE 4.1 Portfolio of Financial Models

Portfolio of Models and Analytical Tools				
Subject Area	**Title**	**Description**	**Developer**	**Last Used**
FS Analysis	Historical Performance Analysis	Ratio Analysis Financial Performance of Company Level	JFA	5/26/18
Revenue/Margins	Revenue and margin projections	Multi year, product through Company summary	SVA	1/02/17
Valuation	DCF Sensitivity Analysis	Displays the sensitvity of share price to changes in assumptions	MTV	6/26/18
Projections	Expected Value/Probability	Probability weighted forecast	RJA	3/06/18
FS Analysis	ROE Analysis (Dupont)	Drill down analysis -components of Return on Equity	GO	10/14/18
Working Capital	Revenue Process/Receivable Analysis	Dashboard of Receivable levels, Measures and Drivers	KRV	5/26/18
Assessment	Activity Based Analysis	Allocate/Assign Costs based on activity and drivers	BVD	1/02/17
FS Analysis	Business Model-Comprehensive View	Presents Comprehensive Performance Analysis	TJA	6/26/18
Assessment	Benchmarking Financial Performance	Compares company performance to peers and admired	JJC	3/06/18
FS Analysis	Operating Leverage Analysis	Fixed and variable costs, breakeven, variable cont. margin	JFA	10/14/18
Assessment	FP&A Assessment	Assess FP&A performance and Identify improvement steps	SVA	9/17/17
Assessment	Report/Analysis Assessment	Review and Survey Users on Report Effectiveness	MTV	5/06/18
Assessment	FP&A Survey	Surveys clients of FP&A	RJA	5/26/18
Presentation	Dual Access Graphs	Presents 2 variables in single graph, e.g. Receivables/DSO	GO	1/02/17
Presentation	Reconciliation Graph	(aka waterfall chart)	KRV	6/26/18
Valuation	Valuation Summary	Value a project or Business using Discounted Cash Flow	BVD	3/06/18
Assessment	Benchmarking Performance Graph	Compares company performance to peers and admired	TJA	10/14/18
Performance Measurement	KPI Development Worksheet	Develop KPI, objective, unintended consequences, etc.	JJC	5/26/18
Performance Measurement	Quarterly Corporate Dashboard	Displays key Corporate Trends	JFA	1/02/17

TABLE 4.1 *(Continued)*

Portfolio of Models and Analytical Tools				
Subject Area	**Title**	**Description**	**Developer**	**Last Used**
Performance Measurement	Weekly Dashboard	Tracks KPI weekly basis	JFA	6/26/18
Performance Measurement	Product Development Dashboard	Presents KPI for NPD function	SVA	3/06/18
Performance Measurement	Dashboard Specialty retailer	Overall Performance for specialty retailer	MTV	10/14/18
Performance Measurement	Dashboard Ski Resort	Overall Performance for Ski Resort	RJA	10/14/18
Performance Measurement	Dashboard Hospital	Overall Performance for Medical Center	GO	9/17/17
Performance Measurement	Assessing Environment for Innovation	Present KPI for Innovation	KRV	5/06/18
Performance Measurement	Agility Dashboard	Present KPI for Agility	BVD	5/26/18
Cost Driver Analysis	Cost of a New Hire	Computes the 5 year cost of a new hire	TJA	1/02/17
Performance Measurement	Human Capital Dashboard	Present KPI for Human Capital	JJC	6/26/18
Performance Measurement	Human Capital Portfolio Analysis	Visual Recap of Key Measures of Human Capital	JFA	3/06/18
Cost Driver Analysis	Headcount Trend	Visual Presentation of Headcount Levels and Trends	BVD	10/14/18
Projections	Rolling Forecast-Business Outlook	Projects future financial performance, with 12-month horizon	TJA	5/26/18

model so that it is consistent with the way the company runs the business. For example, in some organizations, product managers may be responsible for sales performance, whereas others may place primary responsibility with the sales organization.

REVENUE AND MARGIN MODEL DOCUMENTATION

Objective

This model will facilitate the development of long-term projections of revenues.

The working elements of the model are in two parts:

1. Existing Products
2. New Products

Key variables and assumptions are entered on these two working spreadsheets to project revenues and margins for each product or product group.

Major Assumptions

- Pricing
- List price and discounts
- Unit volumes
- Product costs
- Introduction of new products

Input fields are highlighted in green.

Summary Page

The summary page includes tables and a series of graphs (Tables 4.2 to 4.4 and Figure 4.2) to present the results of the projections. The tables and graphs are updated with any change to the underlying assumptions. Narrative comments must be manually updated to reflect changes in the model.

TABLE 4.2 Product Revenue and Margin Documentation 

Objective:

This model will facilitate the development of long-term projections of revenues.

The working elements of the model are in two parts:

1. Existing Products
2. New Products

Key variables and assumptions are entered on these two working spreadsheets to project revenues and margins for each product or product group.

Major assumptions:

- Pricing
- List price and discounts
- Unit volumes
- Product costs
- Introduction of new products

Input fileds are highlighted in green.

Summary Page

The summary page includes a table and a series of graphs to present the results of the projections. The tables and graphs are updated with any change to the underlying assumptions. Narrative comments must be manually updated to reflect changes in the model.

TABLE 4.3 **Revenue Plan Model – Existing Products**

Existing Products	2016	2017	2018	Future	2019	2020	2021	2022
Product 1200								
Unit Cost	400	416	433	4.0%	450	468	487	507
List Price	1000	1040	1080	4.0%	1123	1168	1215	1263
Average Discount	2.0%	2%	3%		4%	5%	5%	6%
Average Selling Price (ASP)	980	1019.2	1047.6		1078.272	1109.722	1154.11	1187.64
Unit Sales	245	270	300		320	275	260	240
Unit Sales Y/T Growth		10%	11%		7%	−14%	−5%	−8%
Revenue	240,100	275,184	314,280		345,047	305,173	300,069	285,034
Product Cost	98,000	112,320	129,900		144,102	128,792	126,637	121,572
Product Margin	142,100	162,864	184,380		200,945	176,382	173,432	163,462
%	59.2%	59.2%	58.7%		58.2%	57.8%	57.8%	57.3%
Product 1300								
Unit Cost		300	312	4.0%	324	337	351	365
List Price		799	820	4.0%	853	887	922	959
Average Discount		0%	1%		2%	2%	3%	5%
Average Selling Price (ASP)	0	799	811.8		840.008	873.6083	894.7168	911.3198
Unit Sales		86	199		320	275	260	240
Unit Sales Y/Y Growth			131%		61%	−14%	−5%	−8%
Revenue	-	68,714	161,548		268,803	240,242	232,626	218,717
Product Cost	-	25,800	62,088		103,834	92,801	91,249	87,599
Product Margin	-	42,914	99,460		164,969	147,441	141,377	131,118
%		62.5%	61.6%		61.4%	61.4%	60.8%	59.9%
Product 960								
Unit Cost	700	732	650	4.0%	676	703	731	760
List Price	1200	1200	1100	4.0%	1144	1190	1237	1287
Average Discount	10.0%	12%	5%		8%	15%	17%	20%
Average Selling Price (ASP)	1080	1056	1045		1052.48	1011.296	1027.001	1029.476
Unit Sales	600	570	500		475	400	300	200
Unit Sales Y/Y Growth		−5%	−12%		−5%	−16%	−25%	−33%
Revenue	648,000	601,920	522,500		499,928	404,518	308,100	205,895
Product Cost	420,000	417,240	325,000		321,100	281,216	219,348	152,082
Product Margin	228,000	184,680	197,500		178,828	123,302	88,752	53,813
%	35.2%	30.7%	37.8%		35.8%	30.5%	28.8%	26.1%
Total Existing Products								
Revenue	888,100	945,818	998,328		1,113,778	949,934	840,795	709,646
Product Cost	518,000	555,360	516,988		569,036	502,809	437,235	361,252
Product Margin	370,100	390,458	481,340		544,742	447,125	403,561	348,393
%	41.7%	41.3%	48.2%		48.9%	47.1%	48.0%	49.1%
Year/Year Growth Rate		6%	6%		12%	−15%	−11%	−16%

TABLE 4.4 Revenue Plan Model – New Products

New Products	2016	2017	2018	Future	2019	2020	2021	2022
Product 2000								
Unit Cost			275	4.0%	286	297	309	322
List Price			600	4.0%	624	649	675	702
Average Discount			0%		2%	2%	3%	4%
Average Selling Price (ASP)	0	0	600		612	636	655	674
Unit Sales			75		140	225	325	425
Unit Sales Y/Y Growth					87%	61%	44%	31%
Revenue	–	–	45,000		85,613	143,096	212,768	286,381
Product Cost	–	–	20,625		40,040	66,924	100,535	136,727
Product Margin	–	–	24,375		45,573	76,172	112,233	149,654
%			54.2%		53.2%	53.2%	52.7%	52.3%
Product 3000								
Unit Cost			125	4.0%	130	135	141	146
List Price			300	4.0%	312	324	337	351
Average Discount			0%		2%	2%	3%	5%
Average Selling Price (ASP)	0	0	300		307	320	327	333
Unit Sales					100	200	300	450
Unit Sales Y/Y Growth						100%	50%	50%
Revenue	–	–	–		30,732	63,923	98,201	150,034
Product Cost	–	–	–		13,000	27,040	42,182	65,805
Product Margin	–	–	–		17,732	36,883	56,018	84,230
%					57.7%	57.7%	57.0%	56.1%
Product 4000								
Unit Cost				4.0%	250	260	270	281
List Price				4.0%	600	624	649	675
Average Discount					8%	15%	17%	20%
Average Selling Price (ASP)	0	0	0		552	530	539	540
Unit Sales					40	125	250	300
Unit Sales Y/Y Growth						213%	100%	20%
Revenue	–	–	–		22,080	66,300	134,659	161,980
Product Cost	–	–	–		10,000	32,500	67,600	84,365
Product Margin	–	–	–		12,080	33,800	67,059	77,616
%					54.7%	51.0%	49.8%	47.9%
Total New Products								
Revenue	–	–	45,000		138,425	273,318	445,628	598,396
Product Cost	–	–	20,625		63,040	126,464	210,317	286,897
Product Margin	–	–	24,375		75,385	146,854	235,311	311,500
%			54.2%		54.5%	53.7%	52.8%	52.1%
Year/Year Revenue Growth					208%	97%	63%	34%

FIGURE 4.2 **Model Summary**

Revenue and Margin Projections

	Actual			Projections				
	2016	**2017**	**2018**	**2019**	**2020**	**2021**	**2022**	**CAGR**
Existing Products								
1200	240,100	275,184	314,280	345,047	305,173	300,069	285,034	
1300	–	68,714	161,548	268,803	240,242	232,626	218,717	
960	648,000	601,920	522,500	499,928	404,518	308,100	205,895	
Subtotal	888,100	945,818	998,328	1,113,778	949,934	840,795	709,646	
% of Total Sales	100%	100%	96%	89%	78%	65%	54%	
New Products								
2000	–	–	45,000	85,613	143,096	212,768	286,381	
3000	–	–	–	30,732	63,923	98,201	150,034	
4000	–	–	–	22,080	66,300	134,659	161,980	
Subtotal	–	–	45,000	138,425	273,318	445,628	598,396	
% of Total Sales	0%	0%	4%	11%	22%	35%	46%	
Total Revenue	888,100	945,818	1,043,328	1,252,202	1,223,252	1,286,423	1,308,042	7%
	8%	6%	10%	20%	–2%	5%	2%	
Gross Margin	370,100	390,458	505,715	620,126	593,980	638,871	659,893	
Gross Margin %	42%	41%	48%	50%	49%	50%	50%	

Revenue Recap:

- Revenue Plan is highly dependent on successful introduction of new products.

- Sales of new products will represent 46% of total sales in 2020.

- Sales of Model 1200 are projected to continue to decline due to competitive forces and product replacement introductions.

FIGURE 4.2 *(Continued)*

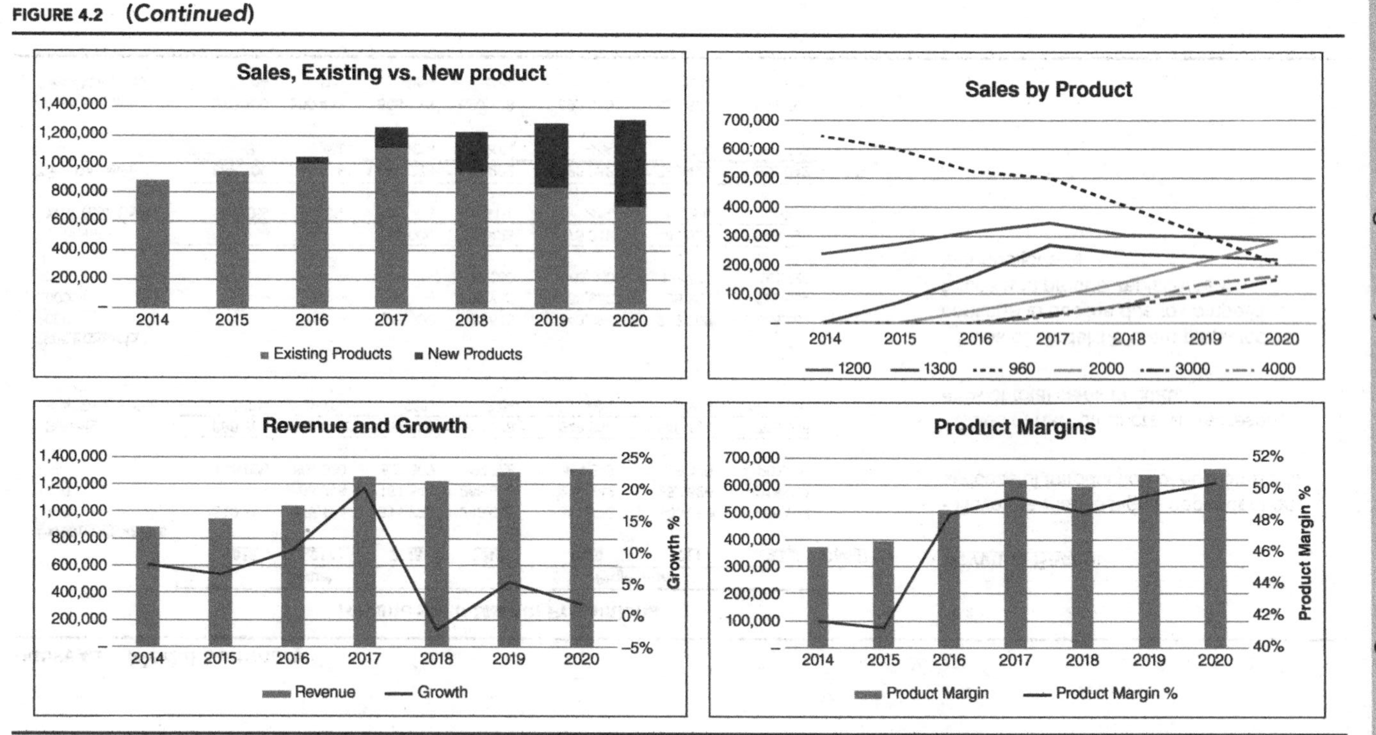

5

BUILDING ANALYTICAL CAPABILITY

CHAPTER INTRODUCTION

As evidenced by your opening the cover of this book, you have a desire to improve and develop your analytical capabilities. As a manager or executive responsible for FP&A, you may also want to strengthen the overall analytical capabilities within your organization. Many CEOs and CFOs rate their organization's FP&A as "satisfactory" or "needs improvement." FP&A is more important than ever, due to the pace of change and uncertainty in today's business environment. Many efforts to improve FP&A fail to achieve that objective because they focus on technology as the "silver bullet" and don't address opportunities to develop people and improve processes.

This chapter offers a number of ways the author has found helpful to improve financial planning and analysis (FP&A) and performance management (PM) for the individual as well as to improve the capabilities across the finance department of an organization.

Several factors typically arise as root causes of ineffective FP&A efforts:

- Insufficient time and resources: "Our team is too busy with closings, requests, and multiple iterations of plans, and has been reduced as a result of business conditions."
- Inadequate analytical skills: "Our team has fallen behind on the use of technology and best practices."
- Absence of business orientation: "Analysts are often accounting focused and do not understand the business."
- Poor communication and presentation skills: "Too often, I get a spreadsheet in response to a request. It is not easily understood, and there is no summary of findings."
- Technology: "Our software does not enable best practices."
- Leadership and organizational structure: "Finance leadership does not buy into or support FP&A" or "There is no alignment of FP&A resources to operating managers or business units."

This chapter will provide suggestions on how effective finance teams have overcome these barriers and challenges.

FOR THE INDIVIDUAL

Even if you are fortunate to be employed by an organization with a strong focus on organizational and people development, each of us has a responsibility to self-manage and contribute to our own career development. As one senior executive advised me early in my career: "You are in charge of your own career development." The following topics address specific actions that individuals can employ to broaden and enhance their skill sets and contributions to any organization.

Become a Student of Analysis

Formal Training

A large number of training programs exist that are geared to financial analysis. Unfortunately, many are very basic and do not extend very far beyond traditional financial statement and ratio analysis. These are fine for the junior analyst but fail to address important business drivers, current trends, and advanced topics.

For advanced levels of training, seek programs that cover a range of topics, offer practical tools, and cover new developments in the science.

- Planning and forecasting
- Business performance management
- Diagnostic tools, including the Pareto principle and root cause analysis
- Capital investment decisions
- Valuation and value drivers
- Presenting and communicating business information

Also choose a workshop or seminar leader who has practical experience in the application of these tools and experience that rounds out the technical aspects of FP&A.

Reference Materials (the Objective of This Book)

Few professional books or textbooks fully explore FP&A. Some works on corporate or managerial finance include a chapter or two on analysis, but the emphasis is on technical or academic finance subjects. Many books and publications focus on the theoretical aspects of a topic without exploring the real-world issues that the analyst encounters.

Recognizing the void in this area, I began creating my own reference materials and developing analytical tools. The objective of this book is to provide such a reference to others. Most of the analytical templates reviewed in this book are available to purchasers of the book. For more information, please refer to About the Website.

Read and Collect Examples of Outstanding Analysis

As a student of financial analysis and performance management, I set up a file (actually a paper file, back in the day!) in which I placed a copy of any superior analysis or presentation that caught my eye. Some were terrific spreadsheets; others had unique or very effective methods of summarizing and presenting complex information. In many cases, the analysis was not directly applicable to anything I was likely to need. However, there were often kernels that highlighted best practices in analyzing or presenting findings such as statistical summaries, dual axis graphs, and waterfall charts.

Many of these thought-provoking examples were plucked from magazine articles, conference materials, consultant reports, marketing and promotional materials, and research analyst reports.

Maintain a Portfolio of Your Analytical Works

Just as an artist maintains a portfolio of his or her works, so should the financial analyst. This portfolio can be electronic or paper, or both. It can serve as a source of ideas and will also limit "reinventing the wheel."

Today, my portfolio fills an entire file cabinet of paper, and a substantial part of my hard drive. I often find materials that I had long forgotten, but that are directly applicable to a current project. My ability to leverage this past work, of course, is very dependent on my ability to retrieve a paper or, better yet, the digital file. Good filing, indexing, and labeling are critical. These can also be useful in employment searches and for reference in performance reviews.

Improve Communication and Presentation Skills

One of the greatest improvement opportunities for most finance professionals is to develop their communication and presentation skills. Many finance professionals believe that the analysis is complete when the spreadsheet is complete. They simply pass on the spreadsheet without enough thought as to how best to communicate the findings. The analytical process is not complete until the results are presented and understood. Chapter 6 provides some specific and concrete ways for us to improve the way we present and communicate financial and business information.

Credibility and Objectivity

To be an effective analyst, it is important to be viewed as an objective party. Too often, we finance folks have a reputation of always having a negative perspective and being critical of all programs and performance. Operating managers will tune out input from analysts they believe are always pessimistic or negative. To counter this, we must strive to be balanced, and occasionally point out the positives! Our analysis and presentations should always be objective and fact based.

One effective technique for creating a balanced view is to present the "Highlights" and the "Improvement Opportunities." This balanced presentation will strengthen the weight of your findings and build credibility as an impartial reviewer of business performance and projects. Another technique is to present several scenarios, including both risks and upsides of projections, to point out concerns without always appearing negative about future prospects.

Business and Emotional Maturity

The FP&A team is engaged in analysis of highly sensitive business issues, problems, and opportunities. They will be interacting with senior executives and with a wide range of associates within the organization. Analysts need to build trust with associates to ensure access to information. In many cases, the analysis is a component of the evaluation of a project, business, team, or even an individual manager. In addition to the need for confidentiality of sensitive information, analysts must also be thoughtful and considerate in their interactions with other associates and managers.

Volunteer to Work on Important Analytical Projects and Presentations

Another way to develop and hone analytical and presentation skills is to volunteer or assist in important high-level presentations. Due to their importance, many projects and presentations get a lot of attention and therefore a lot of professional assistance. Volunteer to work on these projects, and you will be exposed to the big picture, solid thought leaders (consultants, investment bankers, senior managers, and executives), and good presentations of business information. A few examples of reports and projects:

- Reports and presentations to investors, analysts, and shareholders
- Reports to the board of directors
- Customer proposals
- Large capital decisions, including new products or acquisitions
- Strategic assessments and plans

Develop a Business Perspective

The best analysts develop an understanding of the business. To become an effective business partner, we must step back from our quantitative and technical orientation to develop a context and understanding of the overall business. Invest some time with operating managers to understand their challenges and objectives. Obtain and read marketing and strategic plans. Review investor presentations, analyst reports, and market reports. Inquire about areas where you may be able to assist by identifying opportunities or illuminating challenges. Our accounting jargon should be replaced by business terms; we should simplify the analysis rather than complicate it; we should act as players, not just reporters; and we should propose actions and solutions rather than offer criticism or just identify problems.

FOR THE ORGANIZATION

Leadership and Organization of the Finance Team

Financial executives must embrace the importance of FP&A and both support and drive improvements in organization and process. The structure and organization of the finance team can either limit or facilitate effective FP&A. Larger finance teams typically have a separate FP&A department reporting in to the controller, CFO, or other senior finance executive. In some cases, the FP&A team is distributed throughout the operating departments or business units.

Structure the Organization for Service

The structure and level of resources within the finance department directly impact the effectiveness of FP&A. Are there dedicated resources with a focus on FP&A? Are there adequate resources devoted to the needs of the organization? Does the staff have the requisite skills to serve the needs of the clients of FP&A?

The traditional organization is structured as shown in Figure 5.1.

Another way of accomplishing FP&A is to assign key FP&A functions to team members across the finance organization. For example, the accounting manager could be assigned to support marketing. This also helps to develop skills across the organization, since additional staff members will be involved in FP&A. An additional benefit is that the work is distributed across a larger group, which helps during peak reporting and planning cycles. Some organizations share the analysts with the department or function they are serving. These analysts may have a dual reporting structure and are viewed as members of both the operating organization (e.g. R&D or business unit) and finance (see Figure 5.2). Other companies are centralizing routine aspects of FP&A to gain economies of scale by creating a "center of excellence." While benefits of centralizing report generation and other products are self-evident, care must be exercised not to reduce personal contact or interaction with clients.

FIGURE 5.1 Traditional Finance Organization

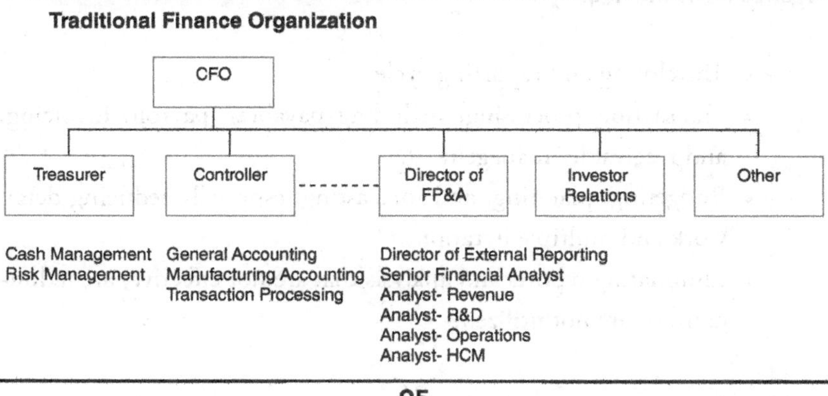

FIGURE 5.2 Integrated FP&A Structure

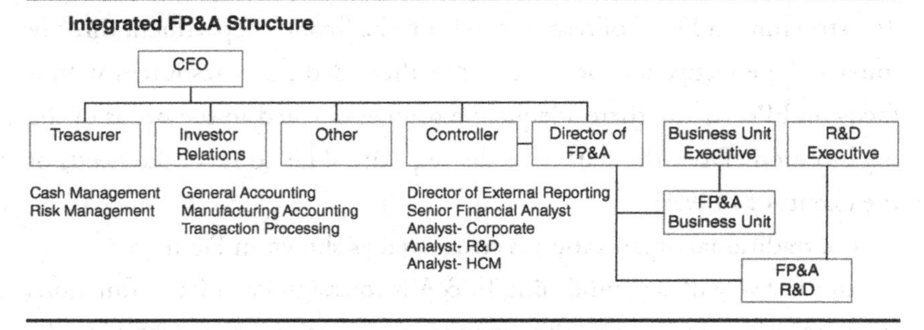

Whether structured as a separate department or as a process team from various finance departments, it is essential that a senior finance team manager coordinate and drive FP&A efforts, training, and development.

Creating the Slack for FP&A

One of the greatest impediments to improving FP&A in an organization is that "We are too busy processing transactions, closing the books, and working on annual and quarterly filings." Few, if any, organizations have excess resources; most have been purged of any excess years ago.

The key is for finance teams to continue pursuing process improvements across the nonvalue or lower value-add activities, so that more time is available for higher-value activities, including FP&A. In many organizations, there is still a huge opportunity to eliminate rework and redundant activities. Examples of areas where efficiency gains have been realized in many organizations include:

- The closing and reporting cycle.
- Transaction processing, including payables, payroll, invoicing, and receivables management.
- Budgeting, planning, and forecasting, especially reducing detail work and multiple iterations.
- Eliminating reports and analysis that are not effective, are redundant, or are not utilized.

Maintain a Repository/Portfolio of Analytical Tools

I often find that there is a lot of time spent across an organization duplicating spreadsheets, presentations, and financial models. This often occurs on nonroutine projects such as capital investment decisions and acquisition proposals. In addition, many analysis projects can utilize substantial parts of prior projects.

Models covering related subjects (e.g. gross margin analysis) should be standardized to achieve savings but also to make it easier for clients to review and process material presented with similar look and feel.

Organizations should set up a central repository of analytical projects and tools. I find that both paper and digital storage of these is helpful. There should be a keeper of these portfolios, often the director of FP&A or the director's designate in larger organizations. Of course, access to sensitive analysis must be considered and controlled. Best practices in developing and managing models are covered in Chapter 4.

Financial Literacy of Nonfinancial Managers

Throughout my career as an auditor, controller, CFO, lecturer, and consultant, it was apparent to me that most nonfinancial managers do not have a solid foundation in finance. Even worse, most finance folks do not attempt to compensate for or address this issue. It should not come as any surprise that many of our attempts to communicate fall on deaf ears. In addition, without a foundation of basic finance, it is difficult for nonfinance folks to understand the ways in which their functions impact financial results.

Several years ago, I conducted a survey across business managers, from first-line managers to middle managers to the executive suite. Although I had anticipated low scores, I was astonished at the results. (See Figure 5.3.) Even at the executive suite level, there is a limited understanding of financial terms and concepts.

We can help our associates at all levels to develop a better understanding of finance and accounting. The specific ways we can help will vary

FIGURE 5.3 Financial Acumen Scores

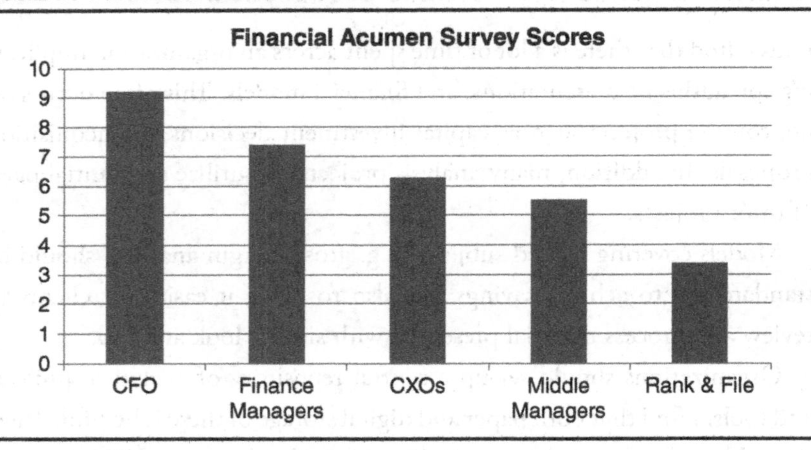

depending on the organization, level of manager or associate, and background of team members. Here are a few suggestions:

- Avoidance of accounting jargon: Work at explaining issues and opportunities in business, not financial, terms.
- Infomercials: Take the time during a presentation or meeting to provide an explanation or educate participants on the subject at hand. This can be a very effective way to reach senior managers, who are unlikely to sign up for a more formal training session. Another example of an opportunity for an infomercial is during a quarterly presentation to all associates.
- Lunch sessions: Best practices finance organizations have offered short sessions during lunch to cover important subjects.
- Formal programs: Business schools offer training in finance to managers.
- In-house workshops: Offering an in-house workshop has the advantage of tailoring the material to the organization.
- Comprehensive financial training programs: Very progressive organizations realize the importance of associates understanding the key elements of financial performance and for the associates

to understand how their individual functions impact key drivers of financial performance, value creation, and the organization's goals.

SUGGESTED TRAINING TOPICS

General

- Understanding Financial Statements and Business Performance
- Valuation and Value Drivers
- Linking Process and Activities to Value Drivers
- Capital Investment Decisions

Specific

- How to Develop a Forecast
- Budgeting and Operational Planning
- Basics of Cost Center Reporting
- Product Margins
- Chart of Accounts/Expense Coding
- Capital Investment Requests
- Working Capital Drivers

FP&A Assessment

I always find it useful to work through an assessment tool to evaluate the current effectiveness of FP&A, identify improvement opportunities, and develop an action plan to increase the effectiveness of FP&A. Text Box below is an outline of a high-level tool to assess current practices and identify improvement opportunities.

REPORTING AND ANALYSIS ASSESSMENT

- Organization and Resource Allocation
- Experience, Competency, and Skills Inventory
- Best Practices Review
- Client Surveys/Interviews
- Evaluation of Reports
- Plan to Address High-Impact Opportunities

TABLE 5.1 Experience, Skill, and Competency Inventory

	Skill and Competency Inventory												
Competency/Experience	**CFO**	**Controller**	**Treasurer**	**FP&A Dir Director**	**Senior Analyst**	**SEC Reporting**	**Analyst**	**Investor Relations Dir**	**Accounting Manager**	**Payroll**	**Payables**	**Credit Collection**	**Internal Audit**
General													
General Management	X												
Operations	X	X		X									
Business Sense				X	x								
Strategic Planning	X							X					
Treasury													
Cash Management	X		X										
Banking			X										
Investments			X										
Risk Management	X		X					X					
FP&A													
SEC (GAAP) Reporting		X				X			X				
Communication-Written		X				X		X					
Communication-Oral		X											
Presentation-Development		X					X	X					
Presentation-Delivery	X												
Graphics		X		X			X	X					
Statistics							X						
Business Application Software		X		X			X		X				
Process Mapping and Diagnostics				X	X				X				
Modeling				X	X		X		X				
Transaction Processing													
Accounts Payable									X		X		
Payroll									X	X	X		
Credit and Collection									X			X	
Audit	X	X											X

Organization and Resource Allocation

Review the organization chart, including senior management and the finance team. Are there staff members dedicated to FP&A? What are the reporting relationships within finance? How do they interact with senior managers and the rest of the organization?

Experience, Competency, and Skills Inventory

Finance managers should take an inventory of skills that exist within the organization. High-performing FP&A organizations recognize that the development of key competencies and experience is critical to their success. Business acumen, communication and presentation skills, exposure to other disciplines, statistics, and data visualization are just as important as technical skills, including report writing and modeling. Good analysts will typically be strong in several of the following skills and types of experience:

- Business Sense
- Operating Experience
- Reporting Applications
- Graphics
- Oral Communication and Presentation
- Written Communication
- Process Mapping and Improvement
- Statistics
- External Reporting

If these skills and competencies are underrepresented in the team, consideration should be given to developing or acquiring those skill sets. Formal training is available, but analysts should also become active learners by reviewing top-quality analysis and presentations from consultants, research analysts, and presentations to the board and investors. Very successful FP&A organizations also strive for diversity in thinking and skills. For example, individuals with experience in quality initiatives and process improvement can make a significant contribution to the overall FP&A effort. Table 5.1 is an example of a skills and experience inventory that highlights coverage and gaps. This inventory should be completed as part of an FP&A assessment and also as part of a comprehensive human capital management process (see Chapter 10).

Best Practices Review

Another assessment technique is to compare current FP&A practices to a list of best practices in FP&A. This is a very effective way to identify high-leverage improvement opportunities. Table 5.2 presents an excerpt from a best practices checklist.

Evaluate Your Current Reports and Analysis

One of the best ways to evaluate the effectiveness of your FP&A function is to collect all reports, dashboards, and on-demand reports that are distributed to managers, executives, directors, investors, and other important constituencies. These should include recurring reports (e.g. monthly or quarterly) as well as ad hoc requests for analysis. I recommend collecting paper copies of these reports and spreading them out on a conference table for full visual impact.

Evaluate these reports considering the following characteristics:

- Graphic or visual presentation versus spreadsheet tables.
- Relevancy: Do the reports cover key issues and progress toward goals, targets, and objectives?
- What themes are we emphasizing? Are they appropriate?
- Does our work support the attainment of strategic objectives and critical performance drivers of the organization?
- Are the reports professional and consistent with the image the finance organization strives to present?
- Time to produce.

The reports and analysis can be summarized as illustrated in Table 5.3. This process can be very illuminating! Typically, managers will be surprised

TABLE 5.2 Best Practices Checklist Excerpt

Best Practice Checklist				
	Yes	No		Comment
Clients of FP&A				
Have you identified users ("customers") of the FP&A?				
Have you interviewed or surveyed customers to determine satisfaction level and identify improvement opportunities?				
Have analysts been assigned to focus and support on specific functions or processes?				
Do you periodically review all reports prepared by finance and FP&A?				

Planning and Projections		Best practice		Top Quartile
How many iterations are prepared in the annual plan cycle?				
What is length of the plan process from start to Board approval?				
Does your organization utilize rolling forecasts or Continuous Business Outlooks?				

Organization and Development				
How many hours of training per analyst per year?				
Does your organization structure provide resources dedicated to FP&A?				
Is the FP&A function resourced for success?				

Models				
Do models reflect the following?				
o Documentation/Instructions				
o Identify Assumptions and Drivers				
o Robust design to facilitate sensitivity and scenario analysis				
o Include Output/Presentation Summary				
Do you maintain an inventory and portfolio of existing models?				

at the tremendous time invested in certain reports, including those with dubious utility. In some cases, reports can be eliminated. Others may be candidates for streamlining or developing a more efficient preparation process. This activity also identifies those reports that were introduced for a specific purpose at a point in time … that never get eliminated.

TABLE 5.3 Report and Analysis Inventory and Assessment

Tomasso Technology FP&A Reporting and Analysis Assessment										
Gather all Reports and Analysis Completed by the Finance Organization. List each report below:							Page 1 of 8			
Report Title	**Frequency**	**Estimated Time**	**Preparer**	**Clients**	**Client Assessment**	**Value H/M/L**	**Business Focus**	**Visual**	**Professional Appearance**	**Indicated Actions**
Monthly Package	Monthly	48 hours	Team	Sr Staff	Low Utilization, selected schedules valued-"Doesn't help me run the biz … I use one schedule"	L	Accounting Oriented	None-all financials	Needs Improve-ment	Reduce to high-value segments, add summary and narrative
Board Package	8x per year	30 hours	Sue B	Directors	Reference use, too historical	M	Accounting Oriented	Few	Tolerable	Add graphs, exec summary
Margin Analysis	Monthly	2 hours	John H	Product Managers	Important info-difficult to understand	M	Accounting Oriented		Needs Improve-ment	Revamp, add graphs and summary
Inventory Analysis	Monthly	4 hours	Jim B	Ops	No longer required	L	Accounting Oriented		Weak	Eliminate
Weekly Dashboard	Weekly	2 hours	John H	Sr Staff	"High Value"- single most useful thing coming out of finance	H	Biz Focus	Graphics	High	None Required
Forecast Summary	Monthly	3 hours	John H	CEO/CFO/ Staff	Great recap of ST goals-effective communication of targets	H	Biz Focus	Graphics	High	None Required

Next, interview key managers, executives, and other clients of your reports and analysis. In many cases, we have found that many managers do not utilize or even look at substantial parts of reports. In one instance, not one recipient (of 22 senior managers and executives) in the organization found the monthly finance report useful. Few reviewed the report. A couple referenced a single schedule for specific information. The report was old school, almost entirely focused on the past, and full of Excel spreadsheets. We decided to eliminate the report entirely, saving more than 12 days of preparation time! The report was replaced with more relevant weekly and monthly dashboards, and more emphasis was placed on current performance and progress toward future performance targets and goals.

Ask the managers what information they need on a recurring basis to execute their responsibilities. Inquire about any specific problems or issues that FP&A can assist in resolving.

Survey "Clients" of FP&A

In addition to informal discussions, some organizations also survey customers or clients of FP&A. While the ratings are informative, the greatest value tends to come in the comments and suggestions. Priority should be given to common themes. An example of a client survey is presented in the box.

CLIENT SURVEY

Financial Planning and Analysis

Your input is important to us!

FP&A is one of the most important functions of the finance organization: providing management and others with objective insight into the performance of the organization.

What best describes your level of responsibility?

Executive	Manager	Lead
Director	Supervisor	

	Low				High
Quality of presentation	1	2	3	4	5
Quality of content provided in reports and analysis	1	2	3	4	5
How would you rate your level of understanding of finance and accounting?	1	2	3	4	5
Timeliness of reports and responsiveness to requests	1	2	3	4	5
Overall, how do you rate the performance of FP&A?	1	2	3	4	5

What reports do you use on a regular basis?

In what business areas would you like more insight and analysis?

What improvements are needed?

Are the reports and analysis concise and well-presented business summaries of the topic covered?

What are your biggest challenges and key objectives? How can we help?

Do you view the FP&A team as a resource you can utilize?

Other comments and suggestions:

Improvement Plan

The results of the assessment can be overwhelming. Senior finance managers should review all assessment materials and identify the most important findings. Focus on high-leverage improvement opportunities that will have the greatest impact. Review with executives and senior managers (clients of FP&A) to validate your findings. The team should construct an implementation plan with specific objectives, responsibilities, and timeline. Progress on the plan should be reviewed each month. An example of an FP&A improvement plan is presented in Table 5.4.

TABLE 5.4 FP&A Improvement Plan

FP&A Assessment and Improvement
Timeline and Work Flow

					Week																														
	Resp	**Status**	**Date**	**Prior**	**1**	**2**	**3**	**4**	**5**	**6**	**7**	**8**	**9**	**10**	**11**	**12**	**13**	**14**	**15**	**16**	**17**	**18**	**19**	**20**	**21**	**22**	**23**	**24**	**25**	**26**	**27**	**28**	**29**	**30**	**Notes**
Assessment																																			
Skills and Competency Inventory	BR	Complete	6/15		X																														
Report Inventory	BR	Complete	6/22			X																													
Client Survey	BR	Complete	6/29				X																												
Summarize findings	BR	Complete	7/6																																
Develop Plan	Team	In Process	7/13					X	X																										
Low Hanging Fruit																																			
Eliminate Reports and Analysis	CD	In Process	7/22							X	--	X																							
Talent Acquisition and Management																																			
Additional Position Senior Analyst	JD	Open	7/31							X Define				X Hire																					
Group Training program	CD	Open	Var											X Contract					X Session 1				X Session 2				X Evaluate								
Communication Seminar	BR	Open	10/15																	XX															
Individual Development and Training Plan	BR	Open	11/5																							XX									
Develop Analysis																																			
List of new additions	JD	Complete	7/15					X																											
Develop Dashboard	CD	Open	Var						X Corporate					X Product Development							X Revenue Pipeline														
Revise Capital Investment Decision Package	BR	Open	8/1									X	X	X																					
Implement Rolling Business Outlook	BR	Open	9/15															X	x	x	x	x	x												
Evaluation and Next Steps																																			
Evaluate Progress																														X					
Additional Actions																															X				
Conflicts					Closing					CFO-Vaction					Closing										Closing			IR							

SUMMARY

Both individuals and organizations should make a conscious effort to improve their ability to generate and present analysis of business results, projections, and transactions. Financial analysis is one of the most important functions in the finance organization. Senior finance executives should develop or acquire talent that can meet the increasing demands of FP&A.

Finance teams must assess their overall performance in FP&A and other functions. This is best done from the client's perspective. Collect and assess all information pushed out or made available by the finance team. Interview clients of FP&A to understand whether the reports are relevant and helpful and to identify resources that can assist them in the future. A formal action plan to address issues and capitalize on opportunities should be developed.

6

COMMUNICATING AND PRESENTING FINANCIAL INFORMATION

CHAPTER INTRODUCTION

All analytical projects are made up of several phases. First, the objective must be understood, the client identified, and the work flow planned. Second, the analytical work is completed, including research and "crunching the numbers." The third and most important phase is to present and communicate the findings of the analytical work. The analysis should also call for some action and highlight alternative courses, and should recommend that a mechanism for monitoring progress be set in place. In this chapter, we will be focusing on the presentation and communication of the results of the analysis.

The greatest analysis will fail to achieve its objective if the results of the analysis are not presented or communicated effectively. In addition, financial managers should also recognize that, to a large extent, their careers may be limited if they cannot effectively communicate. What do you call a good accountant with excellent communication and presentation skills? The CFO!

LAYING THE FOUNDATION FOR SUCCESS

There are a number of behaviors and practices that can enhance the effectiveness of communicating finance and business information. These include outgrowing the behaviors of a stereotypical accountant, knowing your audience, developing a messaging strategy, educating nonfinance managers, and choosing the best delivery method.

Overcoming the Accounting Stereotype

Accountants and financial types are often stereotyped as cold, dry, and impersonal. We are often seen as impediments to getting things done. We also often seem to be too busy to help operating managers; we are either closing the books, doing forecasts, compiling tax returns, or whatever. Finance folks also typically do a poor job in communicating. It is not emphasized in our formal education, nor is it developed as a core competency in most companies. Accounting tends to attract quantitative types, not orators. We speak in "accounting-ese," citing FASBs, journal entries, accruals, and other items that are foreign to operating managers. Many operating managers perceive finance as only focused on the numbers. Too often we are perceived as not understanding the business.

Obviously, these stereotypes are not fair to all finance professionals or teams. One of the greatest ways to overcome these weaknesses, either real or just perceived, is to improve our delivery, communication, and presentation of business information to operating managers. Additional measures to improve capability were outlined in Chapter 5, Building Analytical Capability.

To become an effective business partner, we must step back from our quantitative and technical orientation to develop a context of the overall business. Invest some time with operating managers to understand their challenges and objectives. Obtain and read marketing and strategic plans. Review investor presentations, analyst reports, and market reports. Inquire about areas where you may be able to assist by identifying opportunities or illuminating challenges. Our accounting jargon should be replaced by business terms; we should simplify the analysis rather than complicate it; we should act as players, not just reporters; and we should propose actions and solutions rather than only offer criticism or just identify problems.

Understanding How Decisions Are Made

In order to effectively present business and analytical information, the analyst should develop an understanding of how the human mind receives and processes information as part of evaluating options and making decisions. The analyst bears a responsibility to present findings in an objective manner that reduces bias and the tendency to reach less than optimum decisions. Michael Lewis, in his book *The Undoing Project*, does a great job of chronicling the lives and research of two Israeli psychologists, Daniel Kahneman and Amos Tversky. Together, they documented and exposed how the human mind works and errs when making decisions in uncertain situations, which of course describes most business decisions.[1] Their observations strongly resonate with my personal experience. Analysts should consider the following in developing and presenting analysis:

Executive Intuition Can Be Wrong. Most executives overvalue their intuitive senses and judgment. In part, we seem not to obtain or effectively process the information available to us. In addition, we are heavily influenced by our experience and models of the past. We tend to oversimplify situations and look for standard, easy solutions based on our past experience. We also tend to be highly influenced by recent events or trends (e.g. the strong stock market will continue to grow) in spite of much empirical evidence to the contrary. The same holds for views on the economy, competitive threats, or the impact of demographic changes. All experienced analysts are already familiar with the bravado about executive intuition and should recognize the importance of providing context and background information to any decision.

Management Bias. We all recognize that bias plays a role in any decision. Managers and executives will almost certainly have preconceived views on any important subject (and so may the analyst). Humans tend to look for facts that support their positions and may ignore facts that are counter to their positions. Analysts must guard against their own biases and anticipate and address preconceived conclusions of their clients.

Assumptions. Managers are likely to make a number of implicit assumptions about a particular issue. Managers also will likely overestimate the probability of many important assumptions. The analyst can counter this by explicitly documenting and testing assumptions that underpin any projection or analysis. This subject is covered in detail in Chapters 12 to 14 on business planning and in Chapters 20 and 21 on capital investment decisions.

Presentation Matters. The way a particular issue is presented can have a significant effect on the interpretation and assessment by managers. In addition to the general subject covered in this chapter, analysts should be thoughtful about the way issues and decisions are framed and described. This is particularly true where downside risks are involved, since humans are risk averse by nature.

Base Case. Managers often view the base case or status quo as a high-probability scenario, even when the facts suggest otherwise. This may lead to deferring decisions or failing to act.

Tact, Diplomacy, and Emotional Intelligence

Analysts will find themselves working on analytical projects that are confidential or highly sensitive. They must accept this responsibility by safeguarding this information and by being discreet when communicating and presenting. In many cases the analysis is documenting or reporting negative performance that reflects on a team or executive, perhaps leading to the termination of a project, business, or even someone's career. Analysts should be sensitive to this aspect of their role.

Know Your Audience

Effective communicators tailor the message to their audience. Whenever I am engaged to make a formal presentation, I always strive to obtain a list of attendees or at least a profile of the group. What functions and industries do they represent? How many years of experience do they have? If possible, understand what key issues they face. What language and cultural differences will I encounter? How should each of these factors affect my presentation?

Another important factor to consider is the level of understanding of financial concepts. In addition to contemplating this in developing and communicating presentations, consider improving the level of financial literacy of colleagues as described in Chapter 5.

Here are a few audiences to consider. Obviously, the level of interest, understanding, and detail will vary significantly across these groups.

The CEO and Other Senior Executives

Senior executives are highly intelligent, are fast learners, and process information very quickly, or they wouldn't be senior executives. They are also very pressed for time. Most will not be interested in how you did the analysis or how long it took. Out of respect for their time and position (and your career advancement), you should bring your "A" game to any interaction with executives. Summarize the analysis, including a brief description of the objective, key findings presented in graphs and charts, and a summary with indicated actions. The detailed analysis should not be presented but can be included as an attachment, should there be a need or interest in "going into the weeds."

Watch the executive(s) for cues as to pace and reception. Make eye contact and look for signs of comprehension. If they start reading ahead, pick up the pace. Most conversations and presentations will be shorter than you expect. Be prepared to present the takeaways instead of working methodically through all of your materials.

The level of understanding of financial concepts across the executive suite varies significantly. For example, product development executives or technical scientists may have less exposure to finance and accounting than others, but no less cerebral capacity. Use commonsense, practical, business explanations.

The CEO and other executives must focus on the big picture and the next move. Always present the full implications of the analysis and be prepared to offer suggested actions. For example, if you explain a variance for the most recent quarter, executives will undoubtedly want to know the impact, if any, on the future projections and possible mitigating actions.

Many interactions with executives are impromptu (and brief!). The CEO steps onto the elevator with the analyst and inquires about some trend, issue, or projection. In these cases, you do not have an opportunity to prepare. Develop a way of formulating concise explanations... the so-called elevator pitch. Do your best to respond with the major points in a succinct manner.

Board of Directors

My first experience presenting to a full board of directors came when I was named acting CFO while serving as vice president and controller of a large publicly traded company. The board was very diverse: three CEOs of major corporations, two attorneys, two large company CFOs, and two university professors (one in business and the other in nuclear physics). The audience was brilliant and experienced, and most had deep business and finance experience. Information needed to be delivered in a concise manner and was absorbed at a rapid pace. Questions came fast and, due to the diversity of the group, they came from many different angles. It reinforced the need for deep preparation, including the need to anticipate likely questions.

Another learning experience occurred in that first board presentation: the flexible presentation. The financial presentation was the last item on the agenda and, as in most meetings, the board meeting was running behind schedule. I was often asked to condense a 30-minute slot into 10 or even 5 minutes. Rather than attempt to rush through the full presentation, I decided to turn to the summary page at the end of the report. I knew that we had summarized all the key points there, so I stepped through these and took questions from the directors. This experience repeated itself throughout my career. I always included an "Agenda/Discussion Topics" to preview and an "Executive Summary" to wrap up. Make sure that summaries are effective wrap-ups of the details of your presentation.

First-Line Supervisors and Middle Managers

I am usually pleasantly surprised by the relative level of financial knowledge by many supervisors and managers and even many associates within an organization. The wide adoption of 401(k) plans and the availability of Internet financial resources have substantially increased knowledge and interest in financial performance. However, most will not have a deep understanding of business accounting and finance. Always provide a link from financial outcomes to the processes and activities in which the employees are involved. Be especially careful to use general terms and commonsense explanations rather than accounting jargon. For example, say, "We need to reduce our customer payment cycle" versus "We need to reduce DSOs." Provide context for managers and supervisors if they are not generally exposed to this type of information. For publicly traded companies, the impact of a trend or variance can be linked to earnings per share (EPS) or even the share price.

Other Audiences

Senior finance managers may present to a wide set of audiences, even within a few days. Take the case of a CFO at the end of a quarter. He or she will likely present the results and business outlook to senior managers, the CEO, the board of directors, investment analysts, and associates. In some cases, the same core presentation material can be used, but the presenter's "voice-over" accompanying the visuals and supplemental information are tailored to each group.

Create a Messaging Strategy

If we were to talk to our marketing counterparts or a public relations firm about our communications and presentations, they would advise us to develop a "messaging strategy." This can be done for both our overall communications (e.g. focus on execution – hitting our goals) as well as each individual presentation (e.g. why have margins declined from last year?).

For individual analytical projects, be sure to state the objective. Examine the analytical worksheets and extract key observations. Step back and view the work as a senior business executive would review it. What is the best way to present these findings? What conclusions and recommendations should be made?

Develop talking points that focus on the key findings and observations, as well as conclusions and recommendations. Make these concise and limited to the top three to five points. Do not dilute the message with minor details or distractions.

As with any message, repetition may be required. I recall becoming frustrated early in my career because we had repeatedly communicated a finding that didn't seem to stick and for which no apparent action was taken. We must be prepared to repeat and reinforce key observations; it may take time for managers to internalize the observations and even more time to address them. And it is important to repeat key themes such as progress on critical initiatives and critical success factors (CSFs) for achieving plans or other objectives.

Educating Nonfinance Managers

One of the barriers to effectively communicating finance information is that many managers do not have a solid understanding of basic accounting and finance functions and terms. If the foundation is weak, then many of our analyses and recommendations will not be fully understood. Chapter 5 presented options to help managers gain a better understanding of finance and accounting, ranging from formal training to lunch sessions to including infomercials in our analysis.

Choosing the Best Delivery Method

Just a few short years ago, most reports and presentations were developed on paper and sent or presented in person to the recipient. While this still occurs in many situations, technology and other changes have added additional delivery channels, ranging from online access and query capabilities to dashboards to formal reports and presentations. Some reports are pushed by notification or alert; others are pulled (user initiated) as needed. Consideration must be given to client comfort with technology and whether clients will access information on their own initiative. We should never underestimate the potential importance of in-person communication to ensure that the information is understood.

DEVELOPING EFFECTIVE PRESENTATIONS AND REPORTS

The outline presented here is very effective in many situations, but should be tailored to fit the requirements of each specific situation. Context and structure are very helpful to the audience (and the presenter!). In addition, the inclusion of an "Agenda" and "Summary" can facilitate schedule and time change. Most business presentations are enhanced by visual aids such as handouts or PowerPoint slides.

Agenda/Discussion Topics

The Agenda/Discussion Topics is essentially a preview of your presentation: Here is what I'm going to tell you. This is a vital start to the pitch:

- It defines the objective of the presentation.
- It provides an overall context.
- It provides a flow of discussion topics, and it previews the topics to be covered. This may help prevent premature questions on topics that will be covered later in the presentation.

Do not assume that the audience, whether a single manager or a large group, understands the objective, scope, and context of the analysis. This overview can and should be brief, but developing a context and defining the objective of the exercise are very important.

Executive Summary-Preview

I often present the Executive Summary at the beginning of my presentations (as a preview) *and* at the end (to wrap up). I find it very effective to tell the group right up front the key findings and conclusions. The presentation then provides the basis of support for these findings. In other cases, especially where the findings are controversial or unexpected, I will hold the Executive Summary until the end of the presentation.

Presentation Content

Distill all the analytical material to high-impact visual summaries of your key findings. Do not include extraneous materials that are not relevant to the topic and key findings. Determine the best way to present your findings. Generally, this will involve graphs, tables, and other visual depictions to summarize the results of your detailed analysis. The order and flow of material are important. Avoid including detailed worksheets and tables in the presentation. These can be included in the appendix or as exhibits.

Briefly explain the methodology employed to complete the analysis. Did you review all transactions or just a sample? What was the scope? What period was covered? Be sure to credit others who assisted and provided input to the work. If the project involves projections, highlight the key assumptions utilized in the analysis. Do not describe the process in detail; no one cares!

The analytical tools used during the project are likely not the best tools to use in presenting the findings. Develop a few presentation slides that document and/or support key findings. Use highly visual tools to report findings. Graphs and charts with annotations are far superior to spreadsheets and tables. Eliminate any information that is not relevant or important to the objectives and findings of the analysis.

Identify Key Takeaways and Indicated Actions

In most cases, the objective of the analysis is not simply to *report* on a subject. The ultimate objective is to understand the implications of the findings and to develop and recommend one or more alternative courses of action. The value of the analysis is often exponentially increased if the analyst can recommend how to address the findings. Do not assume that the audience/reviewers would make the same observations or reach the same conclusions that you have reached. Since you have researched and studied the subject, your ability to understand the issue, implications, and possible actions is likely to exceed that of many managers.

In some situations, it may be desirable that conclusions and actions be determined by the audience, rather than presented as an outcome of the study. This can be especially important where you are trying to build consensus or have the team reach conclusions and develop indicated actions. In these situations, you should summarize findings and then facilitate a discussion and evaluation of solutions and alternatives.

Executive Summary and Recommended Actions

The Executive Summary, including recommended actions, is the most important part of your presentation. It is here that you will boil down and distill the results of your analytical work into key findings and recommended actions.

Often, there are alternative courses of action to address a problem. In this case, it is advised to list various alternatives and provide a financial evaluation of the various choices, in addition to your specific recommendation.

Exhibits

In our efforts to provide a very effective visual presentation of our findings, many supporting schedules and analyses are deemed not to be useful in the actual presentation. These can be included as an exhibit or in an appendix, should anyone wish to drill down.

OUTLINE FOR PRESENTATIONS AND REPORTS

Agenda/Discussion Topics
Executive Summary-Preview
Presentation Content
Takeaways
Executive Summary and Recommended Actions
Exhibits

DELIVERING THE PRESENTATION

After following the guidelines outlined, the analyst needs to prepare to *present* the material and should consider using these best practices to improve delivery of the presentation. Preparation leads to confidence and successful presentations.

Talking Points: Script out your talking points for each slide. Do not read content on the slides, since the audience will be viewing the material as you speak. Instead, use your "voice-over" to complement and guide the audience's visual process.

Rehearsing: Rehearse, but do not memorize your points. Time yourself as you rehearse to ensure that you can complete your presentation and address questions within the allotted time. If possible, visit the location of the meeting or presentation to familiarize yourself with the room.

Complex Slides: Introduce complex slides with a quick description of the tables, charts, and other material on the slide. Then walk through the observations and takeaways. Tables and graphs should be accompanied by bullets highlighting key points.

Flexibility: Be prepared for questions, changes in allotted time, and even appearances by "Mr. Murphy" of Murphy's Law: "Anything that can go wrong will go wrong." Time allotments may be reduced. Audiovisual devices may fail. Stay cool and develop a plan B. Always fall back on your primary objective and three to five primary talking points.

Brevity: Be as brief and concise as possible. Respect people's time, and remember that most people will stay more attentive if the pace is crisp. As Blaise Pascal, Mark Twain, Ben Franklin, Henry Thoreau, and others have said, in effect: "If I had more time, I would have made this shorter."

Eye Contact: Effective presenters make eye contact with the audience. This keeps the audience engaged. Also, effective eye contact allows you to determine the reception to your material, delivery, interest, and pace. Make adjustments as indicated.

Anticipating Questions: Consider the questions members of the audience may ask, and prepare responses. This is where knowing your audience is critical, since questions will generally be based on the participants' roles, responsibilities, and backgrounds.

Avoidance of Technical Terms and Explanations: Where possible use business terms, not accounting terms.

Stand-Alone Value: The report or handouts are often passed on to others who were not present and are without the benefit of your "voice-over." While it is not possible or desirable to include all your remarks, consider whether the printed material stands independent of verbal remarks. That is, could someone follow the main points of the presentation and follow observations and key takeaways? The use of bullet points to summarize key points and takeaways can be useful in achieving this objective.

Objectivity: It is important that analysts remain objective in fact and in appearance. Avoid tendencies to be negative or critical. Provide balance by highlighting *both* "What's going well?" *and* "What needs improvement?"

Confidentiality: If any of the information presented is confidential or is considered material nonpublic information, a cautionary statement may be warranted at the beginning of the material.

DATA VISUALIZATION AND PRESENTATION: A PICTURE IS WORTH A THOUSAND WORDS

A well-designed graphic, visual, or dashboard is worth a thousand words. "Data visualization" is the new label for this important concept. Our objective should be to determine the data or information that is important and then develop the best method to present the information to facilitate understanding by the viewer, including highlighting trends, variances, and other insights. If not properly presented, these key insights may not be evident or easily discernible by the client. Consider the revenue process dashboard shown in Figure 6.1.

This dashboard presents the trend in receivables level and days sales outstanding (DSO) and also includes graphs representing the key drivers and leading indicators. The graphs facilitate understanding trends and relative magnitude that would not be easily determined by looking at a table containing the raw data. Effective use of charts and graphs can significantly improve the presentation product:

- They create visual interest in the material.
- Scale and relative size are evident in a manner that is difficult, if not impossible, to describe in words or present in tables.
- Trends are easily identified.
- They allow the viewer to see the important aspects without having to work through the noise of a spreadsheet or table.
- Comprehension and retention rates skyrocket when you combine visual and hearing senses.

The graphs presented in this chapter are available on the book website. Refer to the "About the Website" for additional information.

Use the Best Visual for the Job

Utilizing charts, graphs, and other visuals is essential to developing effective presentations. However, the inclusion of graphs does not necessarily increase the effectiveness of the presentation. Providing graphs of flawed analysis or extraneous information is not the objective. Equally important is to select the best graphic form for presenting the information or analysis.

FIGURE 6.1 Revenue Process–Accounts Receivable Dashboard

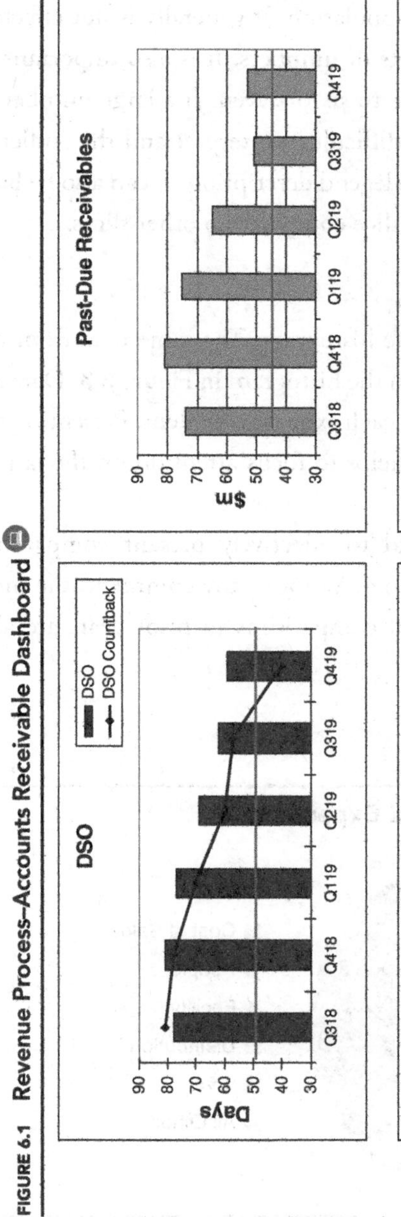

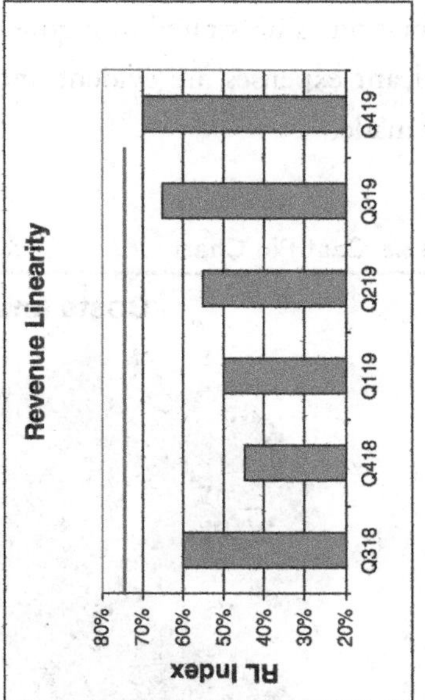

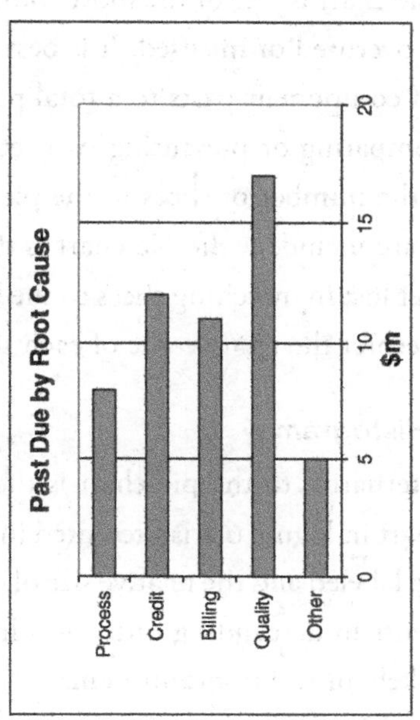

The Pie Chart

The pie chart is one of the most commonly used charts. In fact, it is sometimes overused or misused. It is best used to visually represent the relative size of component parts to a total population. It generally is not effective for comparing or presenting two sets of numbers. It is also important to limit the number of slices in the pie to six or seven. If a large number of slices are included, the pie chart is difficult to interpret and the audience will get lost in matching slices to the legend description. It can also be hard to interpret the relative size of each slice compared to other slices.

The Histogram

An alternative to the pie chart is the histogram. The same data from the pie chart in Figure 6.2 is presented in the histogram in Figure 6.3. Data are clearly labeled and the relative size of each expense is evident. Presenting the segments in descending order also helps to focus attention on the largest and likely most important items.

The histogram can also be used to effectively present comparative information as illustrated in Figure 6.4. Without any comment, the most significant expenses are evident and comparisons to prior years are also easily made.

FIGURE 6.2 Cost Pie Chart

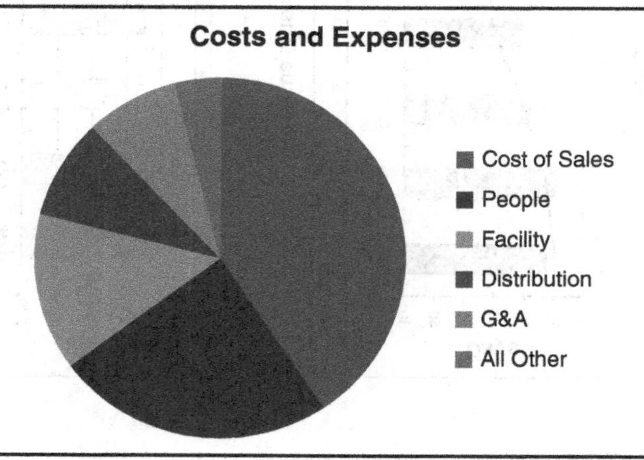

FIGURE 6.3 Histogram of Expenses

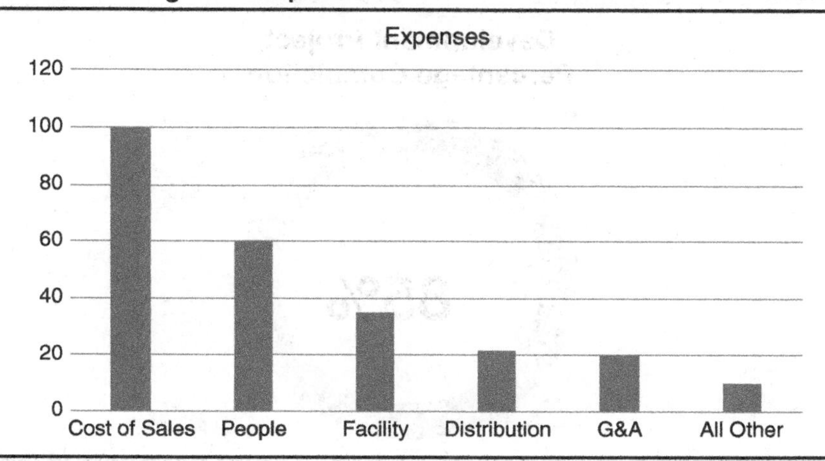

FIGURE 6.4 Comparative Histogram Chart

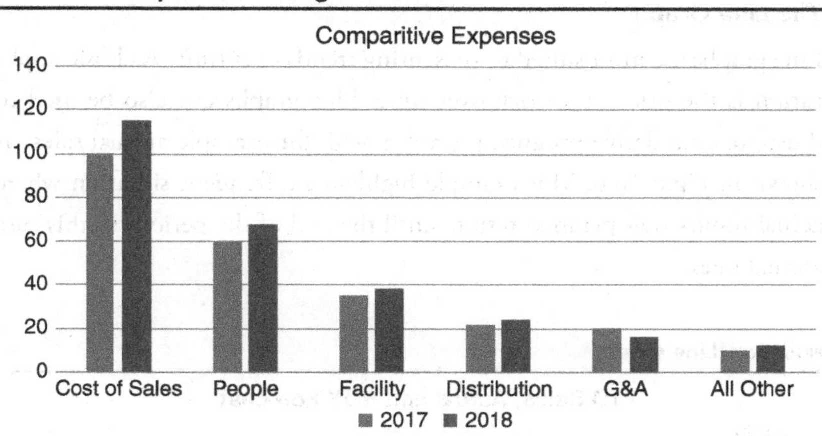

The Doughnut (or Ring) Chart

The doughnut or ring chart is a variant of the pie chart that has gained increasing popularity in recent years. This chart is illustrated in Figure 6.5. Some prefer this presentation, since the proportions are easier to determine than the slices of the pie. The same cautions that apply to pie charts also hold for doughnuts: too many segments complicate the visual effect and processing of the information.

FIGURE 6.5 Doughnut Graph – Percentage Completion 

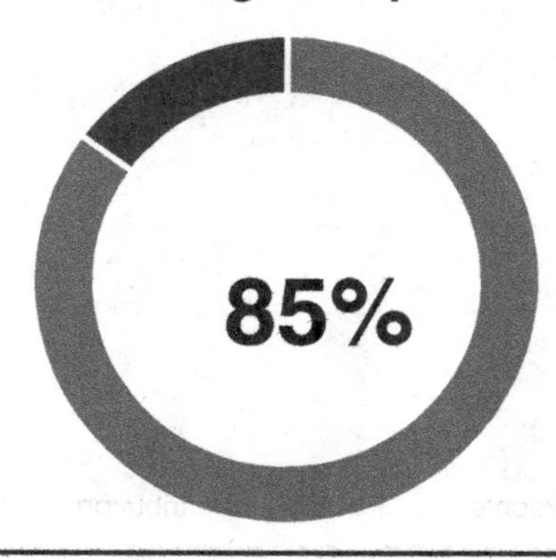

The Line Graph

Line graphs are most suited to presenting trends over time. A classic application is the price of a stock over time. Line graphs can also be used to illustrate cumulative progress toward a goal, for example annual sales, as shown in Figure 6.6. This example highlights a frequent situation where actual results trail planned results until the end of the period, in this case annual sales.

FIGURE 6.6 Line Graph

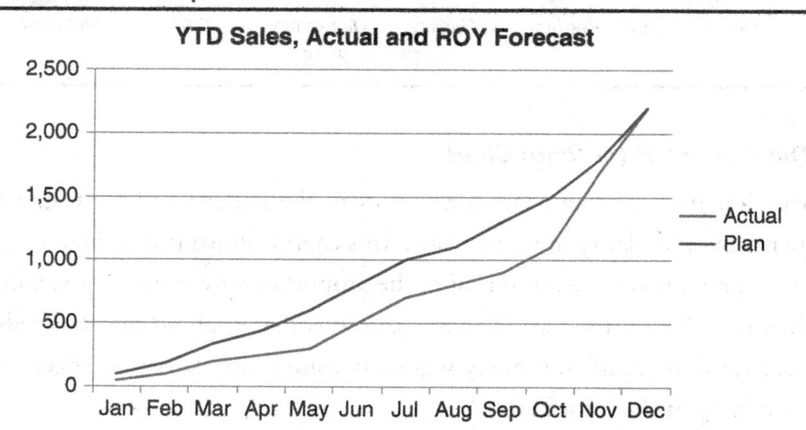

The Column Graph

The basic column chart is a great way to present comparative data sets, for example actuals to budget. It is also useful for presenting trends. Subsets of data can be presented by stacking the columns. The stacked column illustration in Figure 6.7 presents the value and mix of revenue over time.

The column graph can be further enhanced by presenting a variance column that appears to float. It is very effective in presenting variances in proportion to revenues and spending, for example sources and uses of cash and net cash flow as in Figure 6.8.

The Bar Chart

The bar chart is a variation of the column chart. In certain applications, the horizontal presentation fits better. In addition, by varying the mix of charts, we can create greater visual interest and attention. Figure 6.9 presents a summary of the performance evaluations for a company's associates.

The Dual Axis Graph

The dual axis graph is a great way to present two related data sets. It is a very effective method of overlaying a relative measure (e.g. days sales outstanding) over an absolute number (e.g. accounts receivable balance).

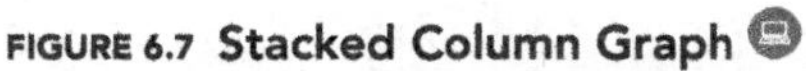

FIGURE 6.7 Stacked Column Graph

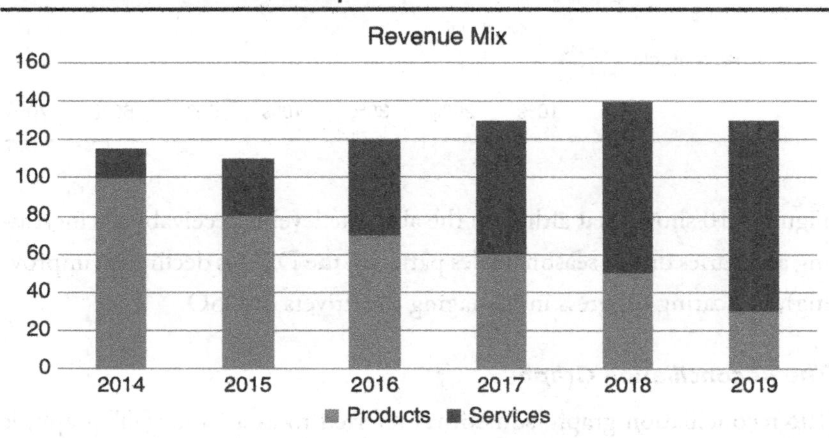

FIGURE 6.8 Stacked Columns with Float

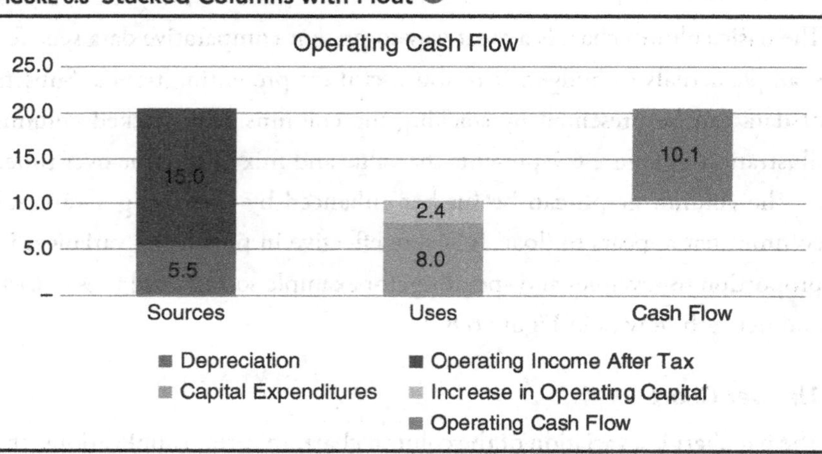

FIGURE 6.9 Bar Chart

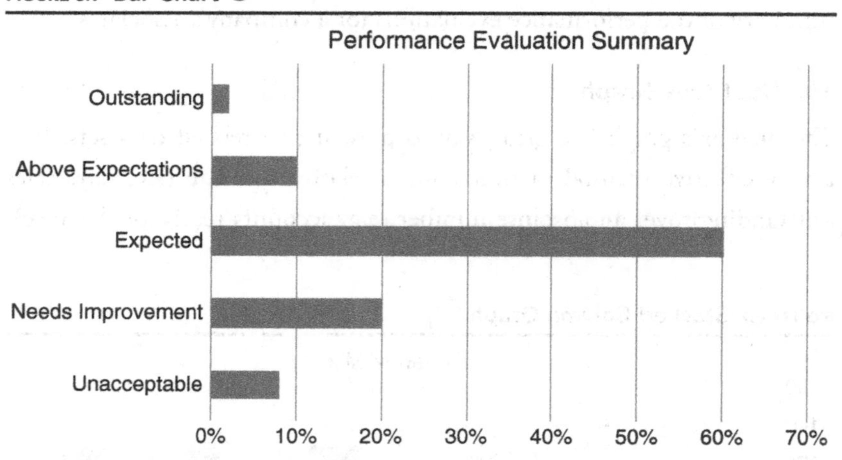

Figure 6.10 shows that although the absolute level of receivables is increasing and varies due to seasonal sales patterns, the DSO is declining (improving), indicating progress in managing the drivers of DSO.

The Reconciliation Graph

The reconciliation graph, sometimes referred to as a "waterfall" graph, is a terrific way to compare, reconcile, or roll forward a specific financial

FIGURE 6.10 Dual Access Graph

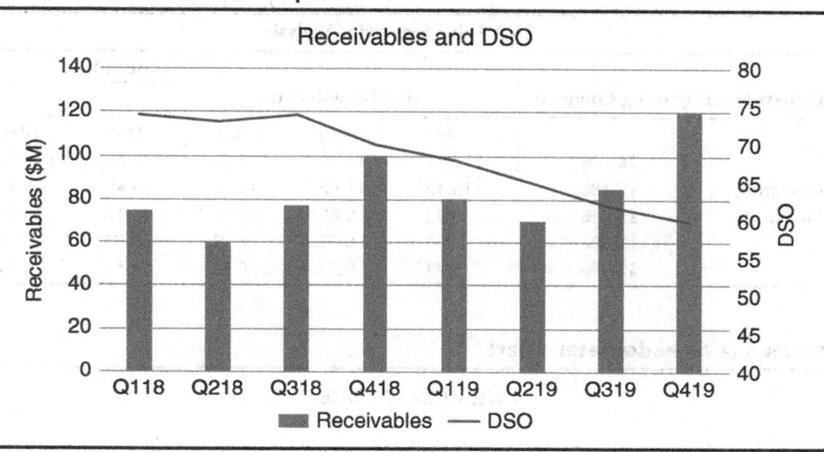

FIGURE 6.11 Reconciliation (Waterfall) Graph

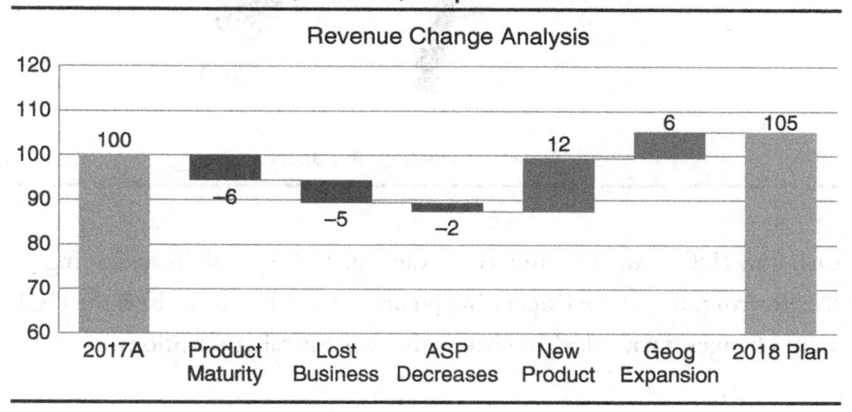

measure. In Figure 6.11 it is used to compare next year's planned revenue to last year's result. The visual is extremely effective to present key changes, drivers, or other variables. The visual is more effective if you first start with the negative changes followed by the increases.

The Sensitivity Chart

The sensitivity chart presents the sensitivity of an estimated result (base case) to changes in critical assumptions. In Table 6.1, the base case of a discounted

TABLE 6.1 Sensitivity Chart

DCF Value Sensitivity Analysis						
					Stock Price	
Roberts Manufacturing Company		Sales Growth Rate				
		4%	6%	8%	10%	12%
	20.0%	$12.11	$13.49	$15.04	$16.80	$18.77
Operating	17.5%	10.52	11.68	13.00	14.49	16.17
Income %	15.0%	8.92	9.88	10.96	12.18	13.56
	12.5%	7.33	8.08	8.92	9.87	10.95
	10.0%	5.74	6.27	6.88	7.57	8.34

FIGURE 6.12 Speedometer Chart

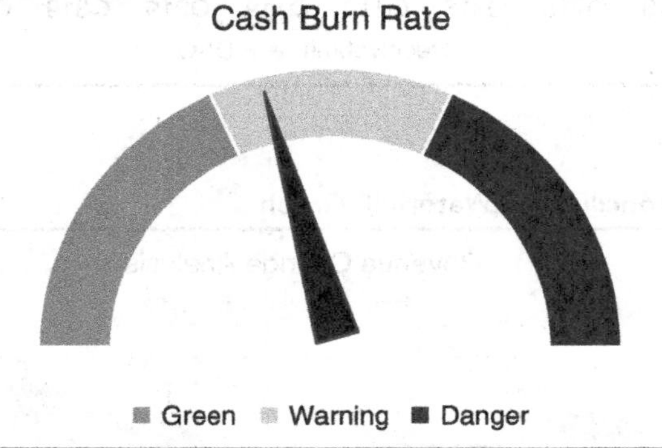

cash flow (DCF) analysis indicates a value of 10.96 per share, assuming an 8% growth rate and 15% operating income. The table shows how the DCF value changes if you "flex" or change the two critical assumptions.

The Speedometer Chart

A variation of the doughnut chart is the speedometer or gauge chart (Figure 6.12). It can add variety and visual interest to a dashboard to present progress or status of a project or to forecast performance.

To Scale or Not to Scale

The default setting on many graphic software tools, including Excel, generally sets the axis at zero. This may hide or mask trends or variances, particularly if there is a mix of large numbers and small variances or other data points. The scale can be set at a different level so that trends and variables are more visible.

However, caution must be exercised so that changes in the scale do not artificially magnify small changes or otherwise distort the presentation of the data.

Dashboards or Summary Charts

For certain purposes, it is useful to develop dashboards or summary charts that combine a number of graphs or charts into a single-page presentation. They allow for a quick review of several key variables or metrics. They facilitate a quick, comprehensive way to see all parameters of a process or an activity. A few examples are presented here. Note the effectiveness of combining graphs and highlight comments in Figures 6.13 (Human Capital Management Assessment) and 6.14 (Valuation Summary). Incorporating a variety of different chart types creates more visual interest and holds viewer attention for a longer period of time.

Dashboards are not ideal for every situation or client. For formal presentations, it may be preferable to present each graph separately. Some clients prefer individual views of the graphs versus a dashboard.

These dashboards are effective because they combine multiple views of performance. As mentioned, some executives prefer separate pages or slides to view performance. Formal presentations should generally break down the dashboards into separate slides.

Other Visuals

Images other than graphs and charts may also play an effective role in a presentation. They can be used to create visual interest and hold or extend the audience's attention. They can also add to or enhance the emotional attachment of the message. A photo of a team in a rowboat, a team in a meeting, a patriotic flag, or children living in poverty will evoke a response well beyond any spoken or written words.

FIGURE 6.13 Human Capital Management Assessment

HCM Assessment

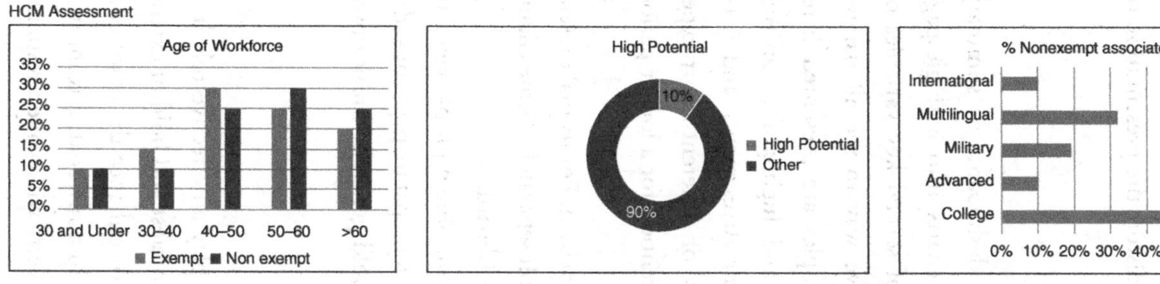

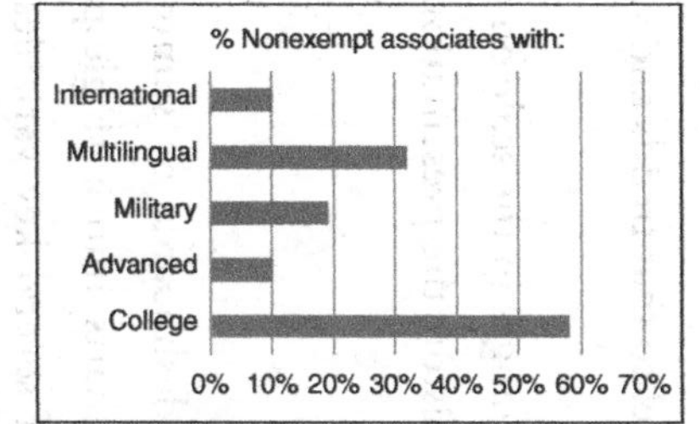

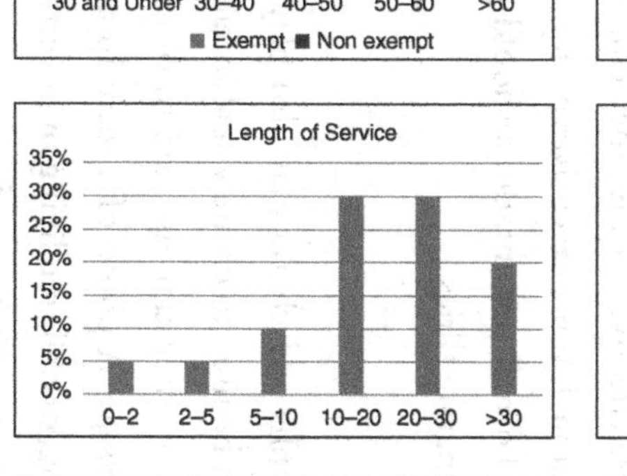

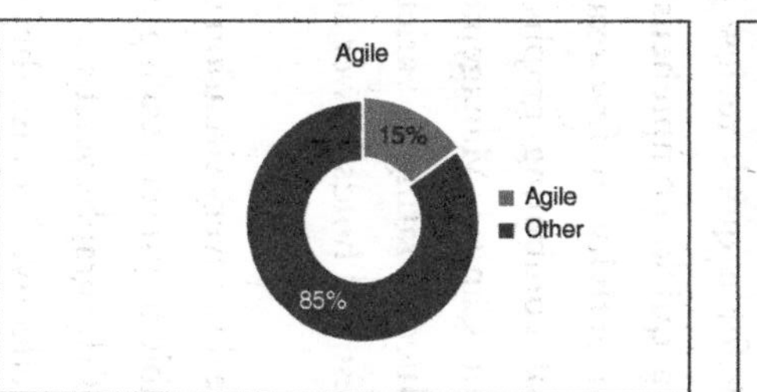

Takeaways:

Age of Workforce
We have an aging workforce. We will need to address significant turnover as the base reaches retirement age.

LOS:
Most employees have long tenure with company. While a positive, it can also stifle innovation and change.

Time in Position:
Most employees have held their position for extended periods. This may indicate lack of upward mobility

High Potential and Agile Associates
We have a very small number of high potential/ agile associates

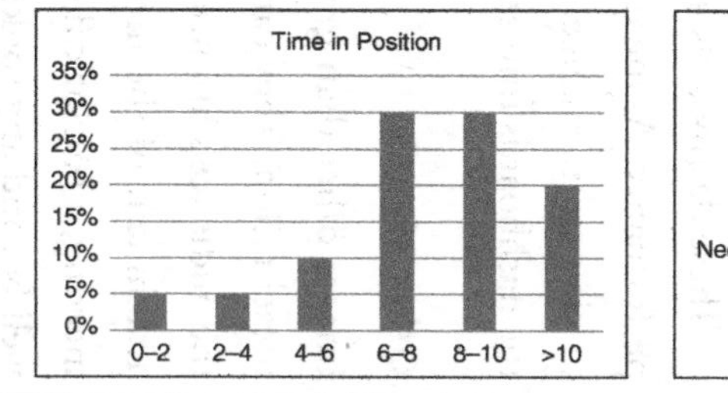

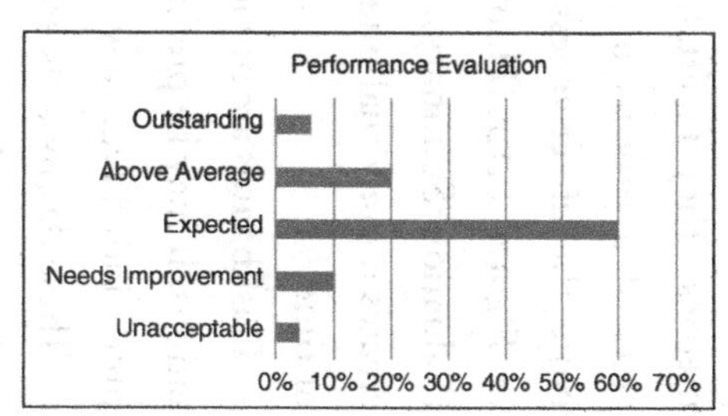

FIGURE 6.14 Valuation Summary

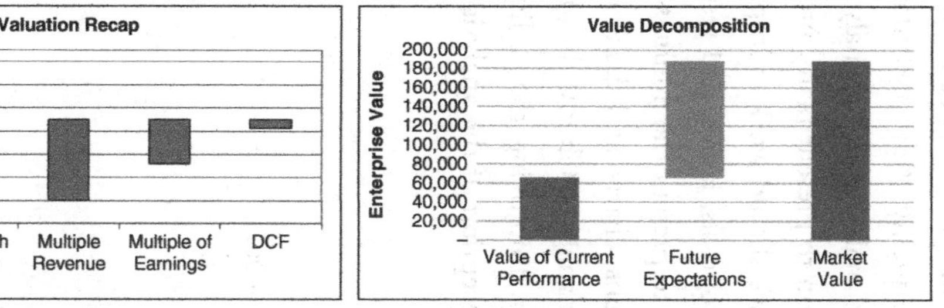

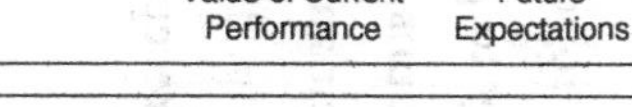

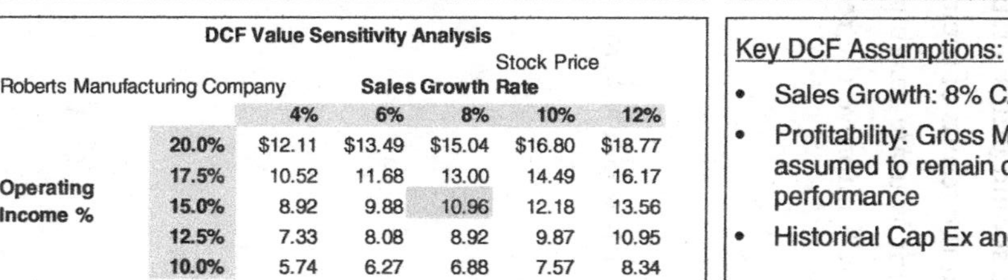

DCF Value Sensitivity Analysis

Roberts Manufacturing Company — Stock Price

		Sales Growth Rate				
		4%	**6%**	**8%**	**10%**	**12%**
Operating Income %	**20.0%**	$12.11	$13.49	$15.04	$16.80	$18.77
	17.5%	10.52	11.68	13.00	14.49	16.17
	15.0%	8.92	9.88	10.96	12.18	13.56
	12.5%	7.33	8.08	8.92	9.87	10.95
	10.0%	5.74	6.27	6.88	7.57	8.34

Key DCF Assumptions:

- Sales Growth: 8% CAGR
- Profitability: Gross Margins and Expenses are assumed to remain constant from 2018 performance
- Historical Cap Ex and Operating Capital %'s

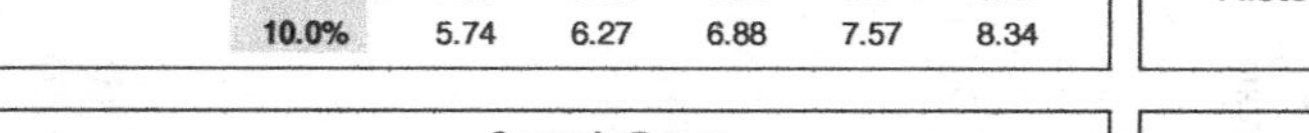

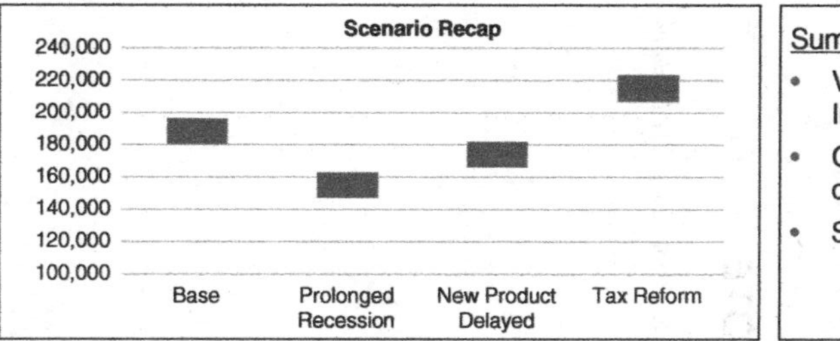

Summary

- Valuation is highly sensitive to Operating Income and Revenue Growth
- Current Performance accounts for only 35% of total value
- Sales Growth is Critical to valuation!

SUMMARY

Communicating and presenting the findings of our work is the most important aspect of the analysis. If not communicated effectively, the analysis is unlikely to achieve its objective. The quality of the presentation significantly impacts the credibility of both the analysis and the analyst.

Financial staff members are often called upon to present plans, project analysis, financial results, and other analysis. We should work to improve our ability to develop and present business proposals, issues, and results. The actual analysis is typically not a good way to present the findings and recommendations. Analysts should utilize graphs, charts, and dashboards to communicate and present the results of their analysis. Choose the graph that best illustrates the point you are making. Improving the ability to crisply deliver the message will improve the reception of the analysis and the standing of the analyst.

NOTE

1. Michael Lewis, *The Undoing Project* (New York: W.W. Norton, 2016).

Part Two

Performance Management

7

BUSINESS PERFORMANCE MANAGEMENT

CHAPTER INTRODUCTION

Business Performance Management (BPM) is an essential aspect of leading and managing an enterprise. Contrary to the views of many authors and consultants, this is not a twenty-first-century epiphany, but an evolution and enhancement of practices that have roots in the earliest management principles. BPM is far broader than developing glitzy dashboards!

In this chapter, we will introduce key concepts of business performance management (BPM), including developing a context for establishing performance measures.

In Chapter 8, we will cover the selection and development of key performance indicators (KPIs) and the development of dashboards.

In Chapter 9, we will outline key steps in implementing BPM and how to institutionalize and integrate performance management into other key management processes.

In Chapter 10, we will cover measuring and driving what's important, including innovation, agility, human capital, and other intangibles.

In Chapter 11, we will discuss using performance management to develop an external view of performance, including competitive analysis and benchmarking.

WHAT IS BUSINESS PERFORMANCE MANAGEMENT?

Our definition and application of BPM is very broad and includes all activities that plan, assess, improve, and monitor critical business activities and initiatives. So how does financial planning and analysis (FP&A) relate to performance management? Under this broad definition of performance management, FP&A is actually an important dimension of BPM. The "F" in FP&A often limits the scope or perception of the function, since we want to examine all aspects of performance. Many traditional FP&A activities are integral parts of performance management, including planning and forecasting, variance analysis, and financial reporting. FP&A may be an ideal function to expand into performance management, since that function is already involved in many important aspects and has an overall context of important performance drivers.

Performance management analysis (PMA) represents a key part of the management process, as pictured in Figure 7.1.

Performance management plays a role in each of these activities.

Assessment

Before setting goals and performance targets, there should be an assessment of the external environment and the current performance of the organization. Market and competitive forces must be assessed and factored into the overall view of performance. Current levels of performance, including performance drivers and improvement opportunities, must be documented and understood.

The organization must also continually assess performance against established goals.

FIGURE 7.1 Overview of Performance Management Process

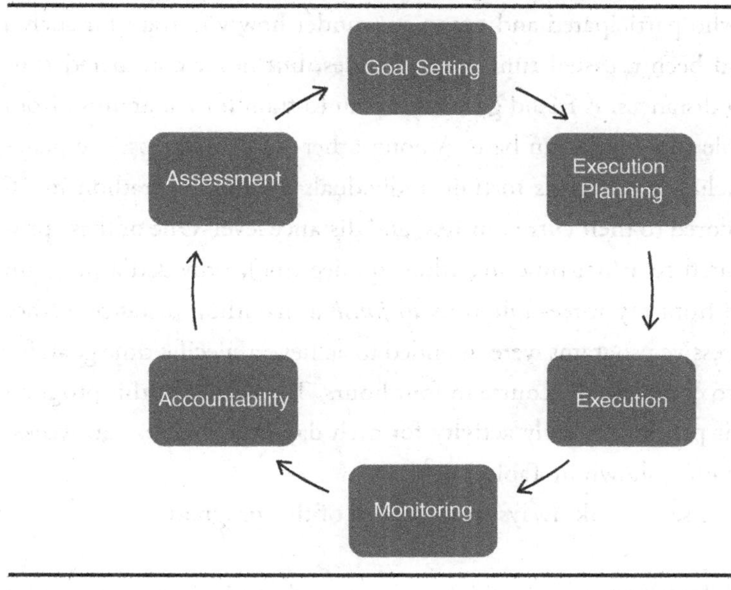

Goal Setting

Based on the assessment of the current environment and performance levels, goals can be established for the organization. The goals will eventually cascade down into objectives and targets for strategic and operating plans.

Benchmarking is a useful method of grounding performance expectations with the performance of competitors, customers, or best practices companies. Benchmarking is explored in detail in Chapter 11.

Execution Planning

Execution planning is the process of determining how, in specific terms, the goals and performance targets will be achieved. We have all heard some variation of this statement: "Organizations don't plan to fail, they fail to plan."[1] In other words, an important aspect of achieving goals is developing a plan to accomplish them.

Frequently, nonbusiness experiences provide great insight into business issues. One example from my personal experience relates to the Boston

Marathon. Living and working near the marathon route, I marveled at the runners who participated and began to wonder how you train for such a feat. I had been a casual runner for decades, but never considered running long distances. A friend gave me a plan to train for a marathon from my humble three-mile-run base. Among other invaluable tips, the plan's author included programs to train individuals to run a marathon in 26 weeks, tailored to their current fitness and distance level. One of these programs, suited to a first-time marathon trainee (me), provided a program to get me from my three-mile runs to *finish* a marathon distance. Other more aggressive programs were intended to achieve a specific time goal, for example to complete the course in four hours. The beauty of this program was that it provided a daily activity for each day over the next 26 weeks. The program is shown in Table 7.1.[2]

There are several takeaways from my use of this program:

- I knew what I should be doing, each and every day, until I achieved the goal.
- Each time I referred to this program (daily), I could connect my current activity (run) to the ultimate goal, completing the marathon.
- It reinforced accountability since I could see that missing a training session would jeopardize the attainment of the goal.
- I didn't reinvent the wheel; I used a program followed by thousands of aspiring marathoners.
- It worked!

In the business world, I often observe the success of teams that had well-developed execution plans. Conversely, the root cause of teams that failed to achieve objectives was often the absence of, or a poorly developed, execution plan.

Even a simple plan, as illustrated in Table 7.2, can be effective.

The existence of such a plan demonstrates that a considered, thoughtful approach to the project has been developed. The plan clearly identifies

TABLE 7.1 Marathon Training Program

Marathon Plan: To Finish							
Week	**Monday**	**Tuesday**	**Wednesday**	**Thursday**	**Friday**	**Saturday**	**Sunday**
	Run		**Run**		**Run**	**Run**	
1	3	Strength	3	Strength	3	3	Rest
2	3	Strength	3	Strength	3	4	Rest
3	3	Strength	3	Strength	3	3	Rest
4	3	Strength	3	Strength	3	6	Rest
5	3	Strength	3	Strength	3	3	Rest
6	3	Strength	3	Strength	3	8	Rest
7	3	Strength	3	Strength	3	4	Rest
8	3	Strength	3	Strength	3	10	Rest
9	3	Strength	3	Strength	3	5	Rest
10	3	Strength	3	Strength	3	12	Rest
11	3	Strength	3	Strength	3	6	Rest
12	3	Strength	3	Strength	3	14	Rest
13	3	Strength	3	Strength	3	7	Rest
14	3	Strength	3	Strength	3	16	Rest
15	3	Strength	3	Strength	3	8	Rest
16	3	Strength	3	Strength	3	18	Rest
17	3	Strength	3	Strength	3	9	Rest
18	3	Strength	3	Strength	3	20	Rest
19	3	Strength	3	Strength	3	10	Rest
20	3	Strength	3	Strength	3	22	Rest
21	3	Strength	3	Strength	3	11	Rest
22	3	Strength	3	Strength	3	24	Rest
23	3	Strength	3	Strength	3	12	Rest
24	3	Strength	3	Strength	3	26	Rest
25	3	Strength	3	Strength	3	10	Rest
26	3	Strength	3	Strength	3	Marathon	3

responsibilities, ensuring that each team member is aware of tasks and expected completion dates. Assigning responsibility and completion dates also facilitates accountability. The simple visual lays out the project flow, including sequencing and prerequisite tasks. The plan is a very effective way to communicate with the team, and serves to provide assurance to senior executives that the program is supported by a solid plan.

Execution

The entire organization should be engaged in executing the goals, plans, and critical functions of the organization. This includes everything from

TABLE 7.2 Project Timeline

FP&A Assessment and Improvement
Timeline and Work Flow

	Resp	Status	Date	Week 1	2	3	4	5	6	7	8	9	10	11	12	13	14	15	16	17	18	19	20	21	22	23	24	25	26	27	Notes
Assessment																															
Skills and Competency Inventor	BR	Complete	6/15	X																											
Report Inventor	BR	Complete	6/22		X																										
Client Survey	BR	Complete	6/29			X																									
Summarize findings	BR	Complete	7/6																												
Develop Plan	Team	In Process	7/13				X	X																							
Low Hanging Fruit																															
Eliminate Reports and Analysis	CD	In Process	7/22						X	–	X																				
Talent Acquisition and Management																															
Additional Position Senior Analyst	JD	Open	7/31						X Define				X Hire																		
Group Training Program	CD	Open	Var										X Contract					X Session 1				X Session 2				X Evaluate					
Communication Seminar	BR	Open	10/15																XX												
Individual Development and Training Plan	BR	Open	11/5																						XX						
Develop Analysis																															
List of New Additions	JD	Complete	7/15				X																								
Develop Dashboard	CD	Open	Var					X Corporate					X Product Development							X Revenue Pipeline											
Revise Capital Investment Decision Package	BR	Open	8/1								X	X	X																		
Implement Rolling Business Outlook	BR	Open	9/15														X	x	x	x	x	x									
Evaluation and Next Steps																															
Evaluate Progress																													X		
Additional Actions																														X	
Conflicts				Closing					CFO-Vacation					Closing										Closing			IR				

developing new products and talent to delivering products and services. Getting things done and done on time is, in large part, a cultural aspect of the organization. The tone must be set from the top. Make your plan. Get it done.

One caveat to this emphasis on execution is that it must be clear that legal and ethical boundaries are not to be breached as part of achieving goals and plans. Many examples of fraud are a direct result of high performance targets and an unqualified mandate to "make your numbers."

The chances of successfully executing any task or activity increase substantially as the effectiveness of execution planning increases. Another critical element to successful execution is the expectation of monitoring and enforcing accountability.

Monitoring

Monitoring progress on key initiatives and projects, as well as monitoring the overall performance of the organization on key business processes, is an essential activity. Identifying problems, delays, exceptions, and changing assumptions on a timely basis will increase the probability of successful execution. PMA must also focus on events and trends external to the organization. The greatest threats and opportunities typically arise outside the organization.

In order to be effective, the monitoring process must provide visibility into these key programs, processes, and performance drivers. Historically, progress and results in business were measured after the fact and reported on in financial reports. A far more effective method is to develop a series of reports or displays that present the key factors in a presentation format that has high visual impact, including graphs, charts, and tables. These user-friendly reports can be summarized in one or more dashboards that will allow managers and employees to quickly scan the series of charts, as a pilot would scan the instrument panel on an airplane. Running a business, or any organization, is similar to flying an airplane. Managers also need timely visual reports on key aspects of their business. How well is the company performing on major systems? Where is the company headed? Are there threats on the horizon? In Chapter 8, we will explore performance monitoring by using KPIs and dashboards.

Accountability

Many organizations fail to achieve goals, or fail outright, because of lack of accountability. To hold people accountable, you first must state clear expectations in terms of responsibility, timing, scope of project or activity, and results. It is also necessary to be able to measure performance against expectations. Performance targets must be well defined and *measurable*. There must be rewards for achieving objectives and consequences for failing to achieve them. Accountability should be a primary objective of monthly or quarterly meetings on product development or business unit performance.

Organizations that are successful in holding associates accountable for performance integrate the goals, plans, and targets of the company into setting performance objectives and reviews for associates. Promotions, compensation increases, and incentive compensation must be consistent with the organization's overall performance management framework (PMF).

DEVELOPING OR ENHANCING BPM IN AN ORGANIZATION

Nearly all companies use performance measures. Many attempts to use or implement performance measures and to develop an overall framework for BPM fail to achieve the full potential value of such efforts. Many organizations jump to creating dashboards and selecting performance measures without creating a context that considers the company's strategy, financial performance, key initiatives, and other important considerations. Figure 7.2 highlights a four-step, systematic process for building an effective performance management framework leading to the maximization of shareholder value.

FIGURE 7.2 **Implementing Performance Management Framework**

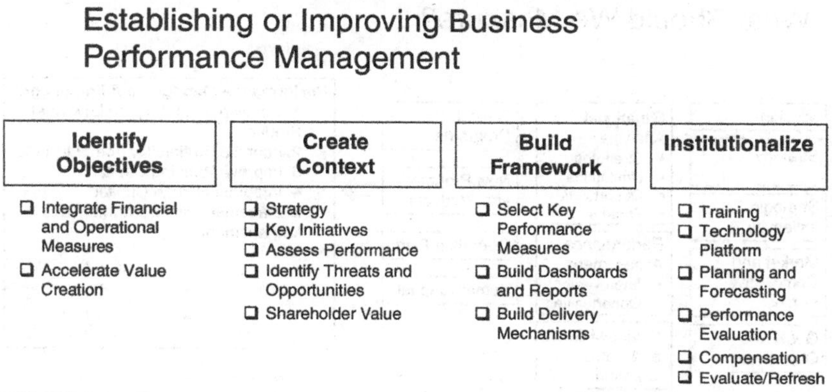

Establishing or Improving Business Performance Management

Identify Objectives	Create Context	Build Framework	Institutionalize
❑ Integrate Financial and Operational Measures ❑ Accelerate Value Creation	❑ Strategy ❑ Key Initiatives ❑ Assess Performance ❑ Identify Threats and Opportunities ❑ Shareholder Value	❑ Select Key Performance Measures ❑ Build Dashboards and Reports ❑ Build Delivery Mechanisms	❑ Training ❑ Technology Platform ❑ Planning and Forecasting ❑ Performance Evaluation ❑ Compensation ❑ Evaluate/Refresh

Creating the proper context and integration with other elements of the management system will also ensure that managers and employees will not view this project as just another "flavor of the month" initiative. This is not a short-term initiative; instead it will be integrated into the core of the company's management systems.

By utilizing a thoughtful and systematic way of developing an overall framework for performance management, the effort will ensure that it will be directed toward areas of significance and importance. In addition, this approach will build credibility with executives and associates.

Define Specific Objectives

The organization should consider and agree on the specific objectives of BPM. While many of the objectives will be common across most organizations (e.g. value creation, improve visibility), others will vary from organization to organization based on specific circumstances.

What Should We Measure? Creating Context

Developing a context for performance management will ensure that the efforts will focus on areas that are important to the organization. Figure 7.3

FIGURE 7.3 **Creating Context for Performance Management**

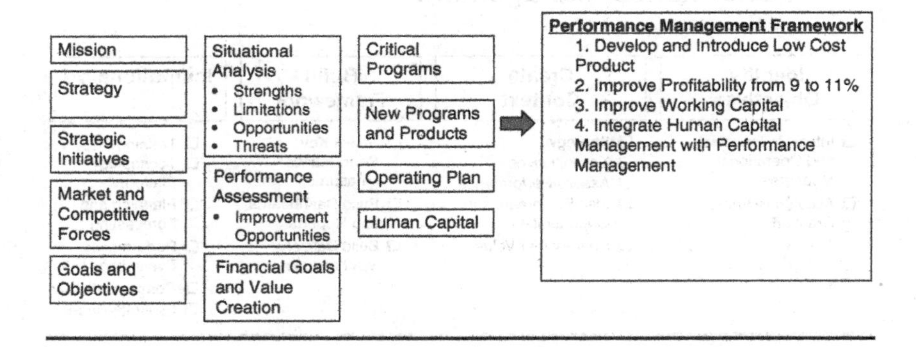

illustrates the areas that should be considered as part of developing the context. This is a critical step toward building an effective PMF.

Mission. What is the mission of the organization?

Strategy. What is the organization's strategy? What are the most important strategic objectives? What are the critical assumptions that should be monitored?

Market and Competitive Forces. Is the market growing or contracting? Are there specific forces that are shaping the market? Are new competitors entering the market? Is the market subject to disruptive technologies or business models? How can we identify emerging threats?

Strategic Initiatives. Effective managers have a short list of essential projects and programs that are critical to executing the strategic plan and achieving the long-term goals of the company. Examples of key strategic initiatives may be the introduction of a series of new products, the establishment of a distribution channel, or significant reduction to manufacturing costs for improving profitability and price competitiveness. These strategic initiatives should be documented and fully integrated into the development of a performance management system.

Situational Analysis. The SLOT (or SWOT) analysis, as defined next, can be helpful, particularly in developing a clear view of weaknesses, opportunities, and threats.

- Strengths: How can we leverage our existing advantages?
- Limitations/Weaknesses: Do we have a plan to address our major weaknesses and limitations?
- Opportunities: What are the largest opportunities? What are our plans to capitalize on these?
- Threats: What are the potential vulnerabilities? How can we develop plans to correct them?

Assessing Performance. Before proceeding with the selection of performance measures, it is important to complement the strategic focus with an objective assessment of the company's performance. The assessment can begin with the performance evaluation introduced in Chapter 2. It should include a review of financial performance and recent trends as illustrated for Roberts Manufacturing Company in Table 2.7. While this analysis contains a great deal of useful information on the financial performance of the company, it will be more useful if key elements are summarized in graphical form as shown in Figure 2.3. The evaluation should also include benchmarking key elements of operating, financial, and value measures against a peer group and to best practices companies.

Benchmarking Performance. Benchmarking the performance of your organization against a peer group and best practices companies can identify significant improvement opportunities. The selection of companies to be included in the benchmark group is very important. Many managers limit benchmarking to a peer group of similar companies or competitors. The potential for learning can be greatly expanded if the universe of companies in the benchmark is expanded to include best practices companies and most admired organizations.

Performance Framework

Where possible, it is best to establish a framework for BPM that flows down from overarching goals of the organization. Examples include value creation for most businesses or a specific goal for mission-oriented organizations (e.g. eradicating polio or world hunger).

Value Creation

The fundamental objective for most companies is to create value for shareholders. For these enterprises, we have successfully utilized a framework that links value creation and value drivers to key business processes and activities.

The value performance framework (VPF) (Figure 7.4) identifies six drivers of shareholder value:

1. Revenue/sales growth
2. Relative pricing strength
3. Operating effectiveness
4. Capital effectiveness
5. Cost of capital
6. The intangibles

Factors such as interest rates, market conditions, and irrational investor behavior will, of course, affect the price of a company's stock. However, the six value drivers identified are those that management teams and directors can drive in order to build long-term sustainable shareholder value.

It is important to recognize that the significance of each driver will vary from firm to firm and will also vary over time for a particular firm. For example, a firm with increased competition in a low-growth market will likely place significant emphasis on operating and capital effectiveness. By contrast, a firm with a significant opportunity for sales growth is likely to focus on that driver and place less emphasis on capital management or operating effectiveness. At some time in the future, however, this

FIGURE 7.4 The Value Performance Framework

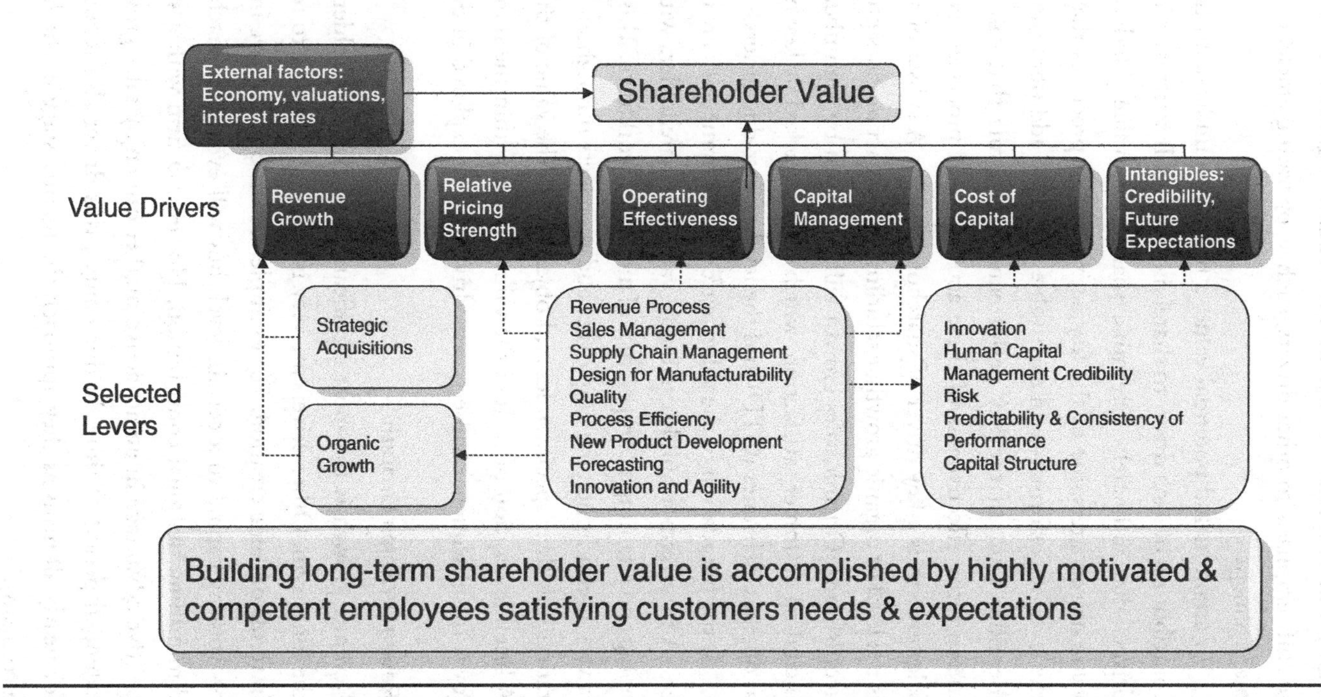

Source: Adapted from Jack Alexander, *Performance Dashboards and Analysis for Value Creation* (John Wiley & Sons, 2006).

high-growth firm may have to deal with a slower growth rate and may have to shift emphasis to other drivers, such as operating efficiency and capital management.

To attain its full potential value, a firm must understand the potential contribution of each driver to shareholder value. It starts with the six value drivers that ultimately determine shareholder value. Underneath these value drivers are some of the key activities and processes that determine the level of performance in each value driver. In addition, the framework identifies some of the key performance indicators that can be used to measure the effectiveness of these activities and processes. For example, sales growth is a key driver of shareholder value. A subset of sales growth is the level of organic growth, excluding the impact on sales growth of any acquisitions. Organic sales growth will be driven by a number of factors, including customer satisfaction, which can be tracked by key metrics such as on-time deliveries (OTD) and the level of past-due orders.

At the foundation of the value performance framework are the employees. A firm cannot build sustainable value for shareholders without developing and retaining a competent and motivated workforce. This framework is very useful in helping employees and managers throughout the organization link their specific roles and objectives to the value of the company. A brief description of each of the value drivers within the framework follows. In subsequent chapters, each driver will be explored in detail.

Revenue/Sales Growth

Revenue growth is the most significant driver of shareholder value over the long term. Other drivers are very important, but tend to reach a limit in terms of value creation. For example, a firm can improve management of working capital to a certain level, but will eventually reach a point of diminishing marginal contribution. However, a firm with a strong competitive advantage in an attractive market can enjoy sales growth over an extended period of time. In due course, this driver also tends to slacken for nearly all firms as they approach the mature stage in the life cycle of a company.

Despite its importance, managers must not focus exclusively on sales growth. To reach full potential value, some level of attention must be paid to each value driver. Additionally, it is important to note that not all sales growth leads to value creation. Sales growth must be profitable and capable of generating positive cash flow and economic returns in a reasonable period of time in order to create value.

It is fairly straightforward and relatively easy to measure and track sales growth over time. Two common measures are the growth in sales over the prior year, and the growth over an extended period of time, usually measured as compound annual growth rate (CAGR). Predicting future revenue levels, however, is much more difficult and requires considerable thought and analysis. In fact, estimating future sales and sales growth is typically the most difficult element of any planning or forecasting process.

Under the VPF, we understand that value will be driven to a significant extent by the expectation of *future* revenue growth. Therefore, considerable emphasis will be placed on understanding the factors impacting future revenue levels. Key factors in evaluating potential revenue growth include the market size and growth rate, the firm's competitive position in the market, pricing pressures, costs, product mix, new product introductions, product obsolescence, customer satisfaction, and impact of foreign currency exchange rates, to name a few. The sales growth driver is reviewed in greater detail in Chapter 15.

Growing the firm through acquisitions is a very different proposition than organic growth. This subject is reviewed in detail in Chapter 23, Analysis of Mergers and Acquisitions.

Relative Pricing Strength

The firm's ability to command a strong price for its products and services will have a significant impact on financial performance and building shareholder value. Clearly, if a firm has a strong competitive position, it should have greater pricing flexibility. This will allow the firm to set its pricing at a level that covers its costs and investments, and earns an acceptable return for shareholders. However, if the firm is in a relatively weak position in a highly competitive market, it could be subject to significant pricing pressure that will limit financial returns and drive cost containment and reduction. The subject of relative pricing strength is explored more fully in Chapter 15.

Operating Effectiveness

Operating effectiveness is a broad term that covers how effectively and efficiently the firm operates. It is an extremely important value driver and is often measured in terms of costs, expenses, and related ratios. Consider a firm that has operating margins of 15% of sales. This firm consumes 85% of its revenues in operational costs and expenses. If this firm can improve its productivity and reduce costs, a significant improvement in its financial performance, and ultimately its valuation, will occur.

A couple of obvious topside measures of operational effectiveness are gross margin and selling, general, and administrative (SG&A) expenses expressed as a percentage of sales. These measures can be supported by a number of indicators of process efficiency. A less obvious, but no less important, element of operational efficiency relates to the level of investments a company is making in future growth and the manner in which the firm manages these investments. Many firms have high levels of investment directed toward future growth. The disciplines around evaluating growth programs and eliminating dubious investments are important contributors to future financial performance and value creation. Eliminating investments in dubious projects at the earliest possible time allows managers to redirect the investment dollars to other projects or to improve margins.

An analogous issue for many companies is the frequency and diligence management applies to evaluating business units and/or products that routinely lose money. Thoughtful and disciplined managers can add significant shareholder value by addressing underperforming businesses or product lines. In addition to the ability to make the tough calls on these businesses, managers must have visibility into the true economic performance of the units and/or products.

Chapter 16 explores in further detail these and other business processes and key measures for operating effectiveness.

Capital Effectiveness

An underutilized lever for improving cash flows and shareholder value is effective capital management. Capital effectiveness has two broad categories: operating capital requirements and investments in property and equipment. Failing to manage investments in operating capital and in property and equipment has a significant impact on cash flows and return on assets, and ultimately on valuations.

Our definition of operating capital in the VPF includes accounts receivable and inventory, offset by accounts payable and accrued expenses. We will focus primarily on the business processes and conditions that drive the levels of receivables and inventories for a firm.

For property, plant, and equipment (PP&E), we will look at the processes for reviewing and approving large expenditures, measuring utilization, and conducting postimplementation reviews. In addition, we will address the hidden potential value of assets that are quite frequently carried at low accounting values.

Capital effectiveness is explored in detail in Chapters 17 and 18.

Cost of Capital

The firm's cost of capital is a significant value driver because it is the rate used to discount future cash flows. Cost of capital is influenced by a number of factors, including the firm's capital structure, perceived risk of future performance, operating leverage, and stock price volatility. General economic factors such as interest rates also play a role in determining the cost of capital for a firm. Cost of capital, capital structure, and related topics are discussed in Chapter 19.

The Intangibles

In addition to the more quantitative, hard factors discussed previously, there are any number of intangible, soft factors that play a significant role in driving share value. These include expectations of future performance, the reliability and consistency of financial performance, and the credibility of management. The intangibles are discussed in Chapters 11 and 19.

The key is to develop an effective performance management framework that supports the overall objective of the corporation, to create value for shareholders. In Chapter 22, the VPF is integrated with valuation techniques to maximize shareholder value. Projecting improved performance on spreadsheets is very easy. Achieving these improvements in actual results requires substantial planning, effort, and follow-through. Central to achieving these performance goals is the selection and development of effective performance measures.

Setting Targets

Realistic performance targets should be set for each measure that will lead to the achievement of strategic objectives and goals for value creation. This should be done by cascading the broad goals for value creation and performance down to the value drivers and individual process and activity measures. Setting targets must also consider the improvement opportunities identified in the process assessments.

Mission-Oriented Frameworks

While financial performance is critical to all organizations, mission-focused (aka not-for-profit) organizations are not created to build wealth. Instead, these organizations are founded to achieve (mostly) noble objectives such as curing cancer, eradicating polio, ending starvation, or educating youth. Accordingly, the focus of performance management in these organizations should be the attainment of specific objectives. However, financial management will still play a significant part in the overall success of the organization.

With a clear identification of the mission/goal, key activities required to support and achieve that goal can be identified as shown in Figure 7.5. Then specific objectives and measures can be established for each of these activities.

FIGURE 7.5 Performance Framework for Mission-Oriented Organization

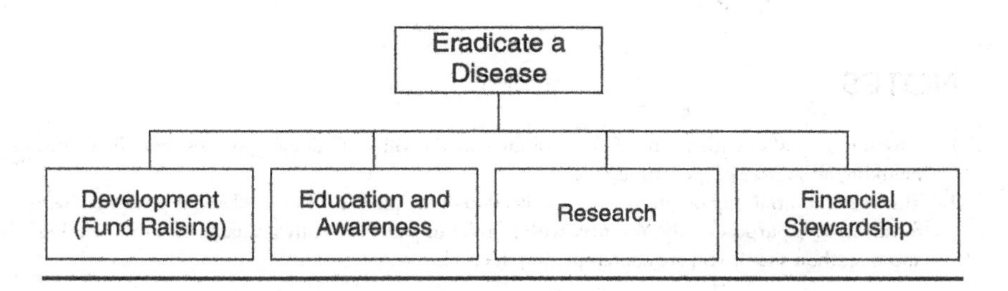

SUMMARY

Many companies use performance measures. Few have achieved the full potential benefits that a well-designed and well-implemented performance management framework can offer. The objective of a PMF is to provide a systematic way of measuring progress on strategic initiatives and performance on key value drivers. A successful framework will increase visibility into critical areas of business performance and allow managers to assign and enforce accountability for performance. Managers and employees will understand how their activities relate to operating and financial performance and, ultimately, the value of the company.

The single most important factor for achieving success with a PMF is to create context for the measurement system. This is achieved by creating linkage among strategy, performance management, process and quality initiatives, financial performance, and shareholder value. It is also critical to integrate and link operating measures to financial measures and then to shareholder value measures. The time spent in establishing this linkage will improve understanding and ultimately the effectiveness of the framework.

We will explore the concepts introduced in this chapter throughout the rest of the book. In Chapters 15 through 19, we drill down into each of the key value drivers, linking to critical business processes and identifying key performance measures. Chapter 8 covers the selection of performance measures and the development of dashboards. Chapter 10 discusses the application of performance management to important areas, including innovation, agility, and human capital. Chapter 11 presents the use of BPM in developing an external view and benchmarking.

NOTES

1. Variants of this statement are often attributed to the Bible, Chinese proverbs, and Benjamin Franklin, all sources of great thoughts!
2. This marathon training program is my recollection of the plan that I utilized and is presented here for illustrative purposes only. You may wish to refer to plans currently available on most running and marathon sites if you are contemplating the challenge.

8

DASHBOARDS AND KEY PERFORMANCE INDICATORS

CHAPTER INTRODUCTION

The use of performance measures and dashboards has exploded over the past 20 years. The effective use of key performance indicators (KPIs) and dashboards is illustrated throughout this book. This chapter will deal with some specific techniques in selecting and developing measures and dashboards.

OBJECTIVES OF DASHBOARDS AND KEY PERFORMANCE INDICATORS

Organizations that effectively use performance measures and dashboards spend a great deal of time thoughtfully selecting appropriate measures and developing dashboards that are relevant to the organization's objectives and challenges.

Too often, organizations adopt measures or start using so-called canned dashboards without properly vetting what should be measured. Before

FIGURE 8.1 Space Shuttle Cockpit Instrument Panel

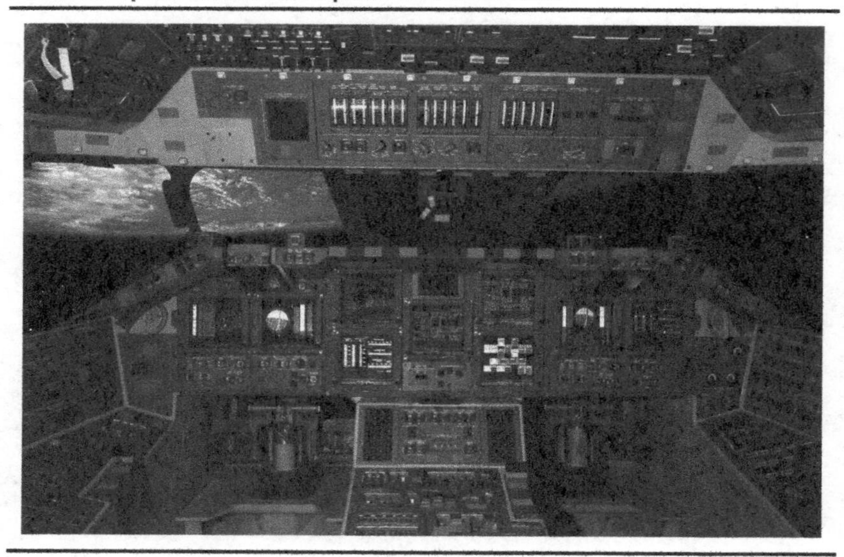

Photo used with permission of NASA.

jumping into key performance indicators (KPIs) and dashboards, it is very important to develop a context and framework, as explained in the preceding chapter, an introduction to business performance management (BPM).

As a potentially very useful part of BPM, we must start by focusing on the objective of BPM. We want to provide executives and managers with the information they need to run the business. The cockpit of an aircraft provides us with a very useful visual to guide us in the selection of measures and the development of dashboards. I reflect on this image frequently during any BPM project (Figure 8.1).

The instrument panel is essential in aviation. There are a number of important performance management principles that are illustrated by the cockpit.

Real-Time and Predictive Insights

The pilot and crew of this aircraft are not asked to blindly fly the mission and then be handed a series of narratives and reports after the flight to tell them how it went. The crew is able to monitor the performance of the aircraft in real time.

The instrument panel provides *real-time insight* into the performance of every major system on the aircraft, from engine performance to fuel levels and consumption, hydraulics, and landing systems. The cockpit has a number of alerts (flashing lights or sound alarms) to call the pilot's attention to potential problems or threats.

High Visual Impact

This pilot does not have to interpret long-winded narratives or Excel spreadsheets to see how things are going. With a quick scan of the instrument panel the pilot can see how every major system is performing and what's happening in the external environment. The pilot is not flying blind, only to then be presented with a 50-page report of Excel spreadsheets after the plane has landed.

Initially this instrument panel is complex, but you can be assured that the commander knows where every dial and reading should be. This illustrates an important concept in BPM, now generally described as "data visualization." Transforming important data into visual presentations that allow the user to quickly identify trends, scale, direction, and variances has great utility. The use of graphics and dashboards has greatly increased the effectiveness of reviewing business results.

Focus on the Important Measures

The instruments are measuring what's *important and relevant* to the mission. The pilot has confidence that a lot of thought, 100 years of aviation experience, and substantial tax dollars went into selecting the measures that are vital to a successful mission.

Providing Insight into External Factors and Environment

The instrument panel also provides insight about the aircraft's position and relationship with the *external environment*. There is external radar for potential threats, a navigation system, wind speed, altitude, and attitude. The pilot can identify storms and alter course. In many planes the pilot will be alerted that an adversary has the aircraft in its sights or on missile lock!

Combining with Observation, Experience, and Intuition

Finally, the pilot doesn't rely on the panel exclusively, but rather *combines* it with observation, intuition, and experience to complete the mission.

One of the biggest mistakes we make is to presume that performance measures, dashboards, and other aspects of BPM eliminate or replace the need for executive judgment, decisions, and even intuition. Instead, these measures should be utilized to better inform decisions and, where appropriate, to challenge intuition to ensure that the best possible decision is made by the executive.

SELECTING APPROPRIATE PERFORMANCE MEASURES AND KEY PERFORMANCE INDICATORS

A Nonbusiness Illustration

Let's assume that we have a goal to improve our health and fitness. We then decide that we want to measure our current state and future improvements by tracking our weight, cholesterol levels, and resting heart rate. We can measure our weight by jumping on the scale every hour, but we will not make progress until we identify and manage the key drivers, primarily food intake and our level of activity. The measures we have identified are really "results" or "outcomes" of our lifestyle (diet and exercise). To achieve different results or outcomes, we must identify, manage, and measure food intake and activity.

Fitness and nutrition journals have been used successfully by athletic trainers, weight-loss programs, and nutritionists. They also underscore an important principle of BPM: that is, what gets measured gets attention.

Activity Measures	Result/Outcome Measures
Food Intake (Calories, Fat, Carbs)	Weight
Activity Levels	Cholesterol
Number of Steps	Resting Heart Rate
Minutes of Cardio Exercise	Blood Sugar Levels
Strength Sessions/Week	
Alcoholic Drinks/Day	

By recognizing the likely cause-and-effect relationships among these measures, we can begin to track the results that our lifestyle changes have on the health indicators (weight, etc.). By capturing the activity levels and displaying the measures on a dashboard with outcomes, we create a visual that typically tells a compelling story. Figure 8.2 is an illustrated dashboard for health and fitness. By tracking the measures, we create a discipline that makes us more likely to achieve our targets for increased activity and reduced food intake. By building a dashboard, we provide the linkage required to connect the dots and reinforce the cause-and-effect relationship.

Developing Appropriate Measures

After documenting the key strategic issues and initiatives, assessing performance, and setting improvement goals in the context of valuation creation described in Chapter 7, we can begin to select the measures that will be important for monitoring performance and progress across the company. What measures will track our progress in achieving strategic objectives and goals for value creation? What are the critical elements of our business that I want to see on a daily, weekly, monthly, or quarterly basis? What measures will serve as leading indicators to alert us to potential problems in time

FIGURE 8.2 Personal Health and Fitness Dashboard

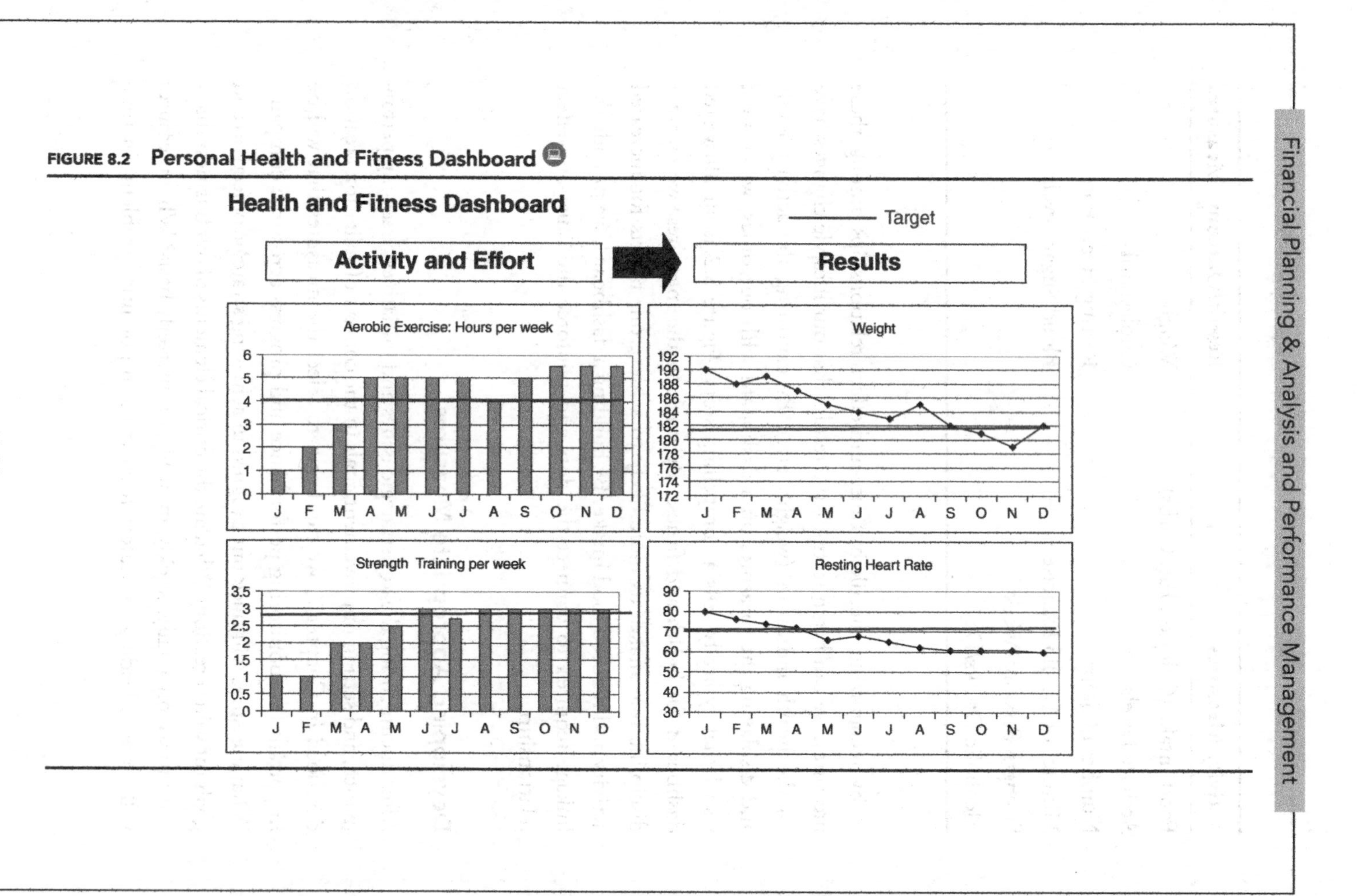

FIGURE 8.2 ***(Continued)***

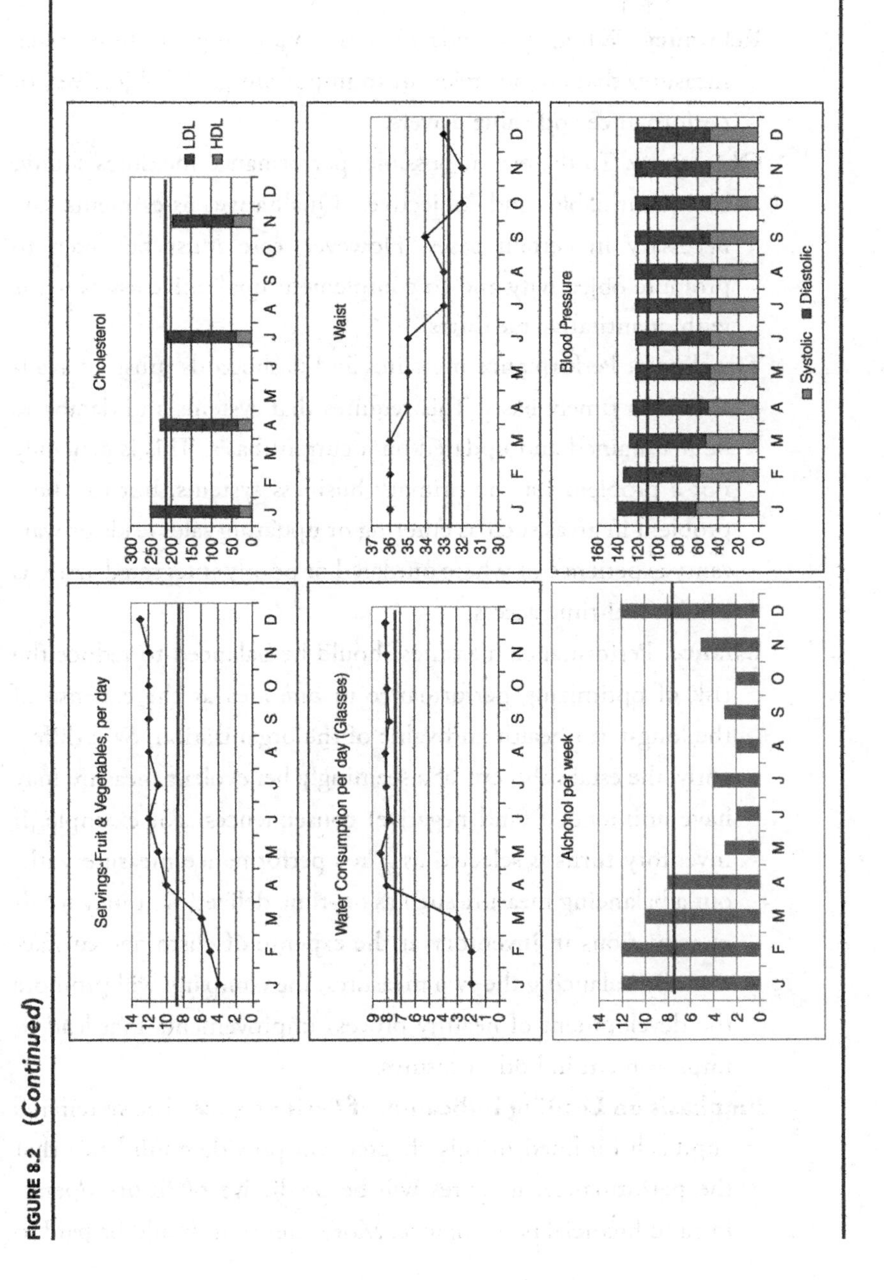

to make meaningful adjustments? Guidelines for selecting and developing performance measures include the following:

Relevancy. While it sounds obvious, many organizations track measures that are not relevant to important goals, objectives, or performance and value drivers.

Objectivity. To the extent possible, performance measures should be quantifiable and objective. Qualitative assessments are necessary in certain cases. However, care must be taken to promote objectivity and to complement qualitative assessments with quantitative measures.

Timeliness. Performance measures and dashboards must be available on a timely basis. This requires that systems and databases be maintained and updated on a current basis. This is generally not a problem for the primary business systems, but can be a problem in areas such as entering or updating sales leads or warranty experience or where outdated or poorly integrated systems inhibit real-time access.

Balance. Performance measures should be balanced to reduce the risk of optimizing performance in one area at the expense of the long-term health and value of the organization. Said differently, the establishment of a seemingly benevolent measure may have unintended (and negative) consequences. For example, if inventory turns is selected as a key performance measure without a balancing measure such as on-time deliveries, it may result in reductions in inventory at the expense of customer satisfaction. By balancing the two measures, the company will promote the development of healthy process improvements that lead to improvement in both measures.

Emphasis on Leading Indicators of Performance. The systematic approach outlined in this chapter will provide confidence that the performance measures will be predictive of future operating and financial performance. More attention should be paid to measuring and improving the leading indicators of performance. For example, if a company sets a target of improving DSO from 75 to 55 days, it must develop targets and measure performance on leading indicators such as revenue linearity, quality, and collections.

Measurement Definitions. Specific definitions must be developed and documented for each measure. For example, what is the definition of on-time delivery to customers? Is it the date that the company committed to delivery or the date the customer originally requested? In one extreme case, we discovered that the date used to measure on-time delivery was changed to the most recent internal schedule update. Since this measure is an important part of customer satisfaction, we want to view this measure through the eyes of the customer, generally the availability when the customer placed the ordered or received order confirmation. Definition of performance measures is important and must be consistent with the objective of the measure. These definitions should be documented and approved by management.

Data Integrity. Implementing BPM without having the ability to generate performance measures and dashboards that present accurate data may be worse than not having a BPM at all. It is fairly typical for a company to encounter problems with data accuracy as it begins to use performance measures. In fact, this is a side benefit of the process: improving the accuracy of reported data. Each measure should be defined and approved by the appropriate managers. Data gathering and processing can be improved over time. It is a good idea to have performance measures reviewed by internal audit teams or the controller's staff to ensure the integrity of the measurement system.

Unintended Consequences. As we focus on certain measures of performance with the best of intentions, we must be alert to the potential of unintended consequences. This potential should be considered before adopting any specific measure and the broad set of collective measures selected to be used.

Less Is More. Since the team will focus on the performance measures we select, it is important to limit the number of measures utilized. We should emphasize key priorities, drivers, programs, improvement opportunities, and other important stuff. If we measure too much, the message is diluted and the team is overwhelmed. Generally, six to eight measures represent a reasonable number on which to focus attention for a team, department, or individual. Additional metrics may be used that are subordinate to these primary measures.

Several years ago, I met with an enthusiastic finance team that had begun the performance management journey. They had adopted a great practice of posting KPIs in the work area of the responsible team. The trouble was that I counted more than 40 measures for a team with a relatively straightforward mission and simple operating model. Most of the measures were not understood and were not associated with any specific projects or key business drivers. This organization lost an opportunity to select and emphasize a few very important measures, and likely confused the members of the team.

The selection of measures and building performance dashboards can be improved by using a performance measurement worksheet, illustrated in Figure 8.3. This worksheet forces us to define, identify the objective, address the critical success factors (CSFs), anticipate unintended consequences, and place the measure in context.

CREATING PERFORMANCE DASHBOARDS

Having developed the objectives and a context for performance management as described in Chapter 7, we then set off to build a reporting mechanism to provide insight into these critical activities. It is essential to provide managers and all employees with critical information about the health of the business and the effectiveness of the activities in which they participate.

FIGURE 8.3 Performance Measure Worksheet

Be Careful (Thoughtful) What You Measure and Report!

Performance Measure Worksheet	
Measure: Asset Turnover	**Next Higher Measure:** ROA, ROE, ROIC
Objective: Measure the effectiveness of asset management, a key driver of ROE and a good overall measure of operating effectiveness	**Key Subordinate Measures:** Inventory Turnover Days Sales Outstanding Fixed Asset Turnover
Definition/Computation: Sales/Assets	**Processes Covered:** Supply Chain Management Revenue Process Management
❑ **Leading** ✓ **Lagging**	**Owner:** Controller
Unintended Consequences: May place too much emphasis on reducing assets at potential expense of revenues or efficiency	**Compensating Measures:** Customer Service Levels, Profitability Revenue Growth

And if performance improvement is to be successful, information must be provided consistently and in a timely manner relative to the activity.

Managers have two key decisions to address in implementing dashboards across the organization. The first decision is to determine what dashboards should be developed. Beyond the corporate-level dashboard, it will also be appropriate to have dashboards for various processes, divisions, functions, and departments. Many managers and employees also develop their own personal dashboards.

The second important consideration for developing any dashboard is to consider the optimum frequency for measuring performance and refreshing the dashboard contents. Some process and activity measures need to be monitored daily or continuously. Examples may include product yields from production processing in refinery or fabricating operations, order levels, or weather conditions. Other measures such as return on invested capital (ROIC) are typically measured at quarterly and annual intervals. Selecting the appropriate frequency for each measure is nearly as important as selecting the right measures.

Some organizations prefer the term *scorecards* over dashboards. While to some extent this is just a matter of semantics, words do matter. I prefer the concept of a dashboard or instrument panel because the inference is that we are visually monitoring a system in real time and have the ability to control at least some functionality within that system. A scorecard is often a document that records the results or outcome, as in recording the strokes on a hole of golf or runs scored in an inning of baseball.

GUIDING PRINCIPLES IN BUILDING DASHBOARDS

Focus on what's important:

- Value creation, strategic objectives, key drivers
- Mix of leading/predictive and lagging measures
- Balance across financial, strategic, customer, operational, and human capital
- Limit of 8 to 12 measures
- High visual impact
- Integration with key management processes
- Being careful (thoughtful) about what you measure

Corporate or Division Summary. The corporate dashboard is the most critical dashboard (see Figure 8.4). Selecting the most important 8 to 12 measures that capture the key performance variables for the company is both important and difficult. Managers must ensure that all key value drivers are represented. All other dashboards should be developed to support the corporate-level summary.

Note that at first the dashboards can be visually overwhelming. However, after a few cycles, managers become familiar with where each dial and needle should be on the dashboard. Having a complete and highly visual dashboard covering the business provides great insight across all key value drivers and affords managers the opportunity to assess performance and progress on key strategic objectives.

FIGURE 8.4 Quarterly Corporate Dashboard

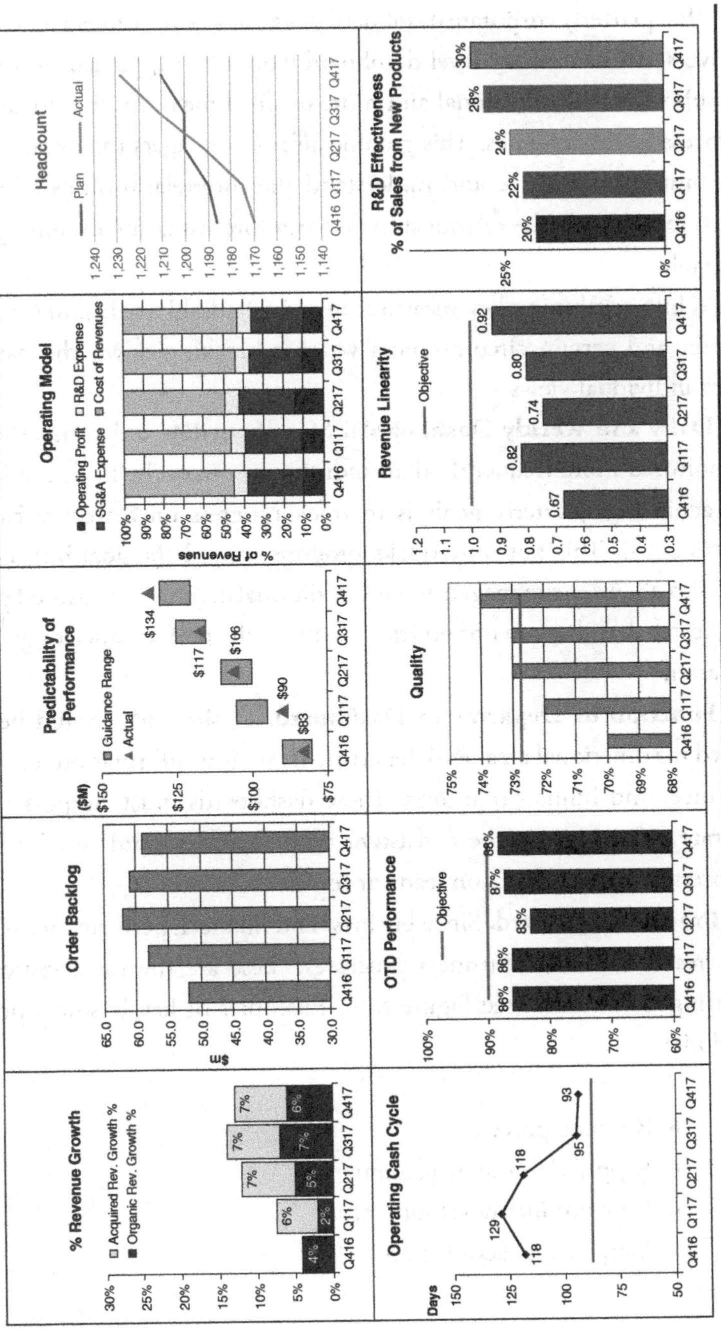

The quarterly corporate dashboard contains key measures across all value drivers. This summary-level dashboard would be supported by a series of dashboards with additional and more detailed measures that focus on key processes and activities. This graphic affords managers the opportunity to examine performance and understand the interrelationships of key factors, for example the relationship between forecast accuracy and operating capital.

While combining key measures in a single dashboard, some executives prefer and certain circumstances warrant breaking down the dashboard into individual views.

Daily and Weekly Dashboards. Many activities and events should be monitored more frequently than monthly or quarterly. In fact, a key part of achieving quarterly goals is to track progress on a weekly basis (see Figure 8.5). This not only tracks progress toward the goal but, in doing so, also allows the managers to take additional actions if measured progress indicates that they are not on track to attain the performance target for the quarter.

Function or Department Dashboard. Dashboards should be developed for functional areas and departments such as information technology, finance, and human resources. These dashboards must support the corporate objectives and be consistent with the dashboards established for processes that the function leads or serves.

Process Dashboard. Since business and financial performance is largely the result of critical business processes, these are the most critical supporting dashboards (see Figure 8.6). Examples of key business processes include:

- Revenue process
- Supply chain management
- New product development
- Mergers and acquisitions

FIGURE 8.5 Example of Weekly Dashboard

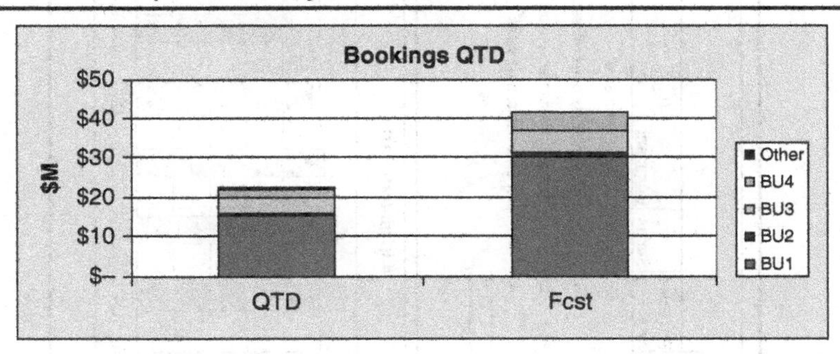

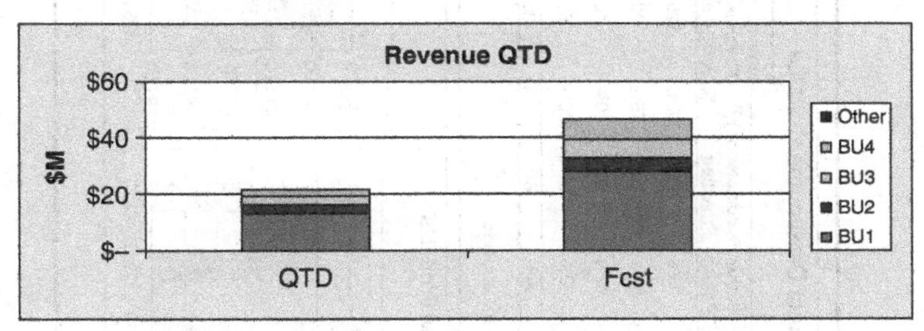

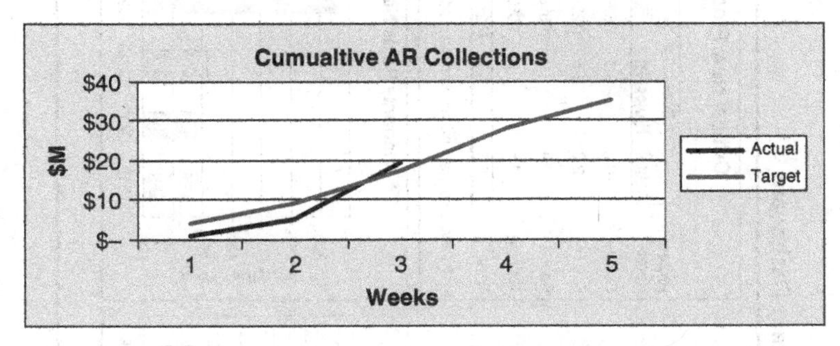

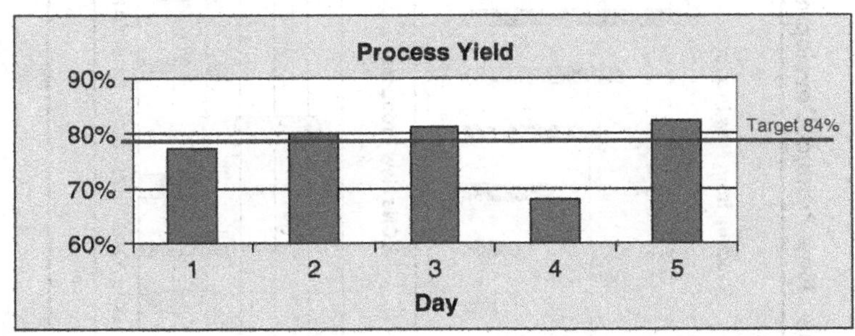

FIGURE 8.6 New Product Development Dashboard

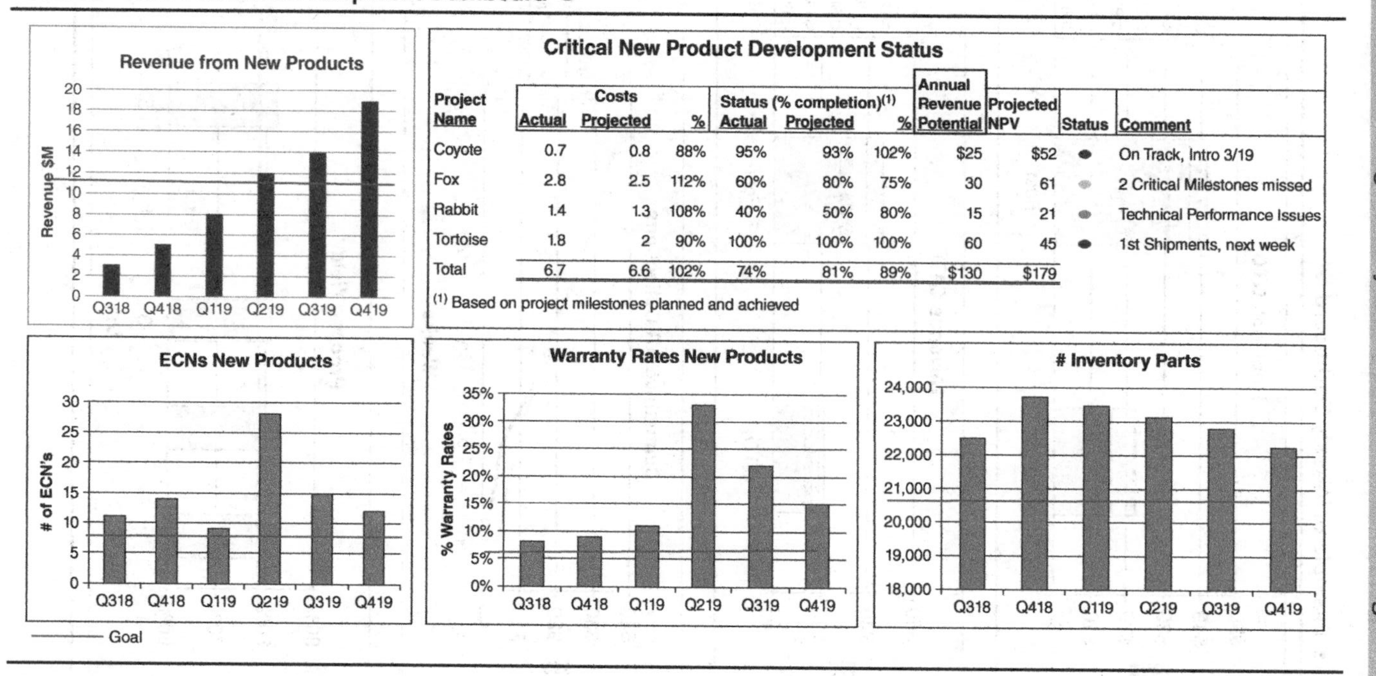

Critical New Product Development Status

Project Name	Costs Actual	Costs Projected	%	Status (% completion)[1] Actual	Status (% completion)[1] Projected	%	Annual Revenue Potential	Projected NPV	Status	Comment
Coyote	0.7	0.8	88%	95%	93%	102%	$25	$52	●	On Track, Intro 3/19
Fox	2.8	2.5	112%	60%	80%	75%	30	61	●	2 Critical Milestones missed
Rabbit	1.4	1.3	108%	40%	50%	80%	15	21	●	Technical Performance Issues
Tortoise	1.8	2	90%	100%	100%	100%	60	45	●	1st Shipments, next week
Total	6.7	6.6	102%	74%	81%	89%	$130	$179		

[1] Based on project milestones planned and achieved

Dashboards for other processes are presented in Part Four, Planning and Analysis for Critical Business and Value Drivers.

Project Dashboards. A very useful application for dashboards is to set goals and track performance on key projects.

Performance Improvement Dashboards. Dashboards are terrific ways to evaluate and diagnose performance issues and to track progress on performance improvement initiatives, for example improving the management of receivables in Figure 8.7.

Individual Manager Dashboards. In some cases, an individual's dashboard may correspond to a process, functional, or corporate dashboard. For example, the CEO can look at the corporate dashboard as his or her personal dashboard. Similarly, a vice president of R&D may choose the new product development dashboard. Other individuals may develop dashboards that include performance measures that cover critical activities and objectives within their respective responsibilities. Care must be exercised to ensure that these individual dashboards are consistent with the objectives and measures of the company and to the function or process to which the individual contributes.

Exception-Based Reporting (EBR) and Alerts. A very effective tool that is gaining wide acceptance is a notification or alert to an analyst or manager when a transaction, trend change, or event occurs. As the result, the manager does not have to constantly monitor a process or activity, but will be alerted to some activity warranting attention. EBR leverages analysts' and managers' time by eliminating the need to review every transaction or event and allowing them to focus only on those that have certain characteristics or are outside of predetermined boundaries.

Examples include:

- Accounts past due
- Sales transactions with excessive discount or low margin
- Retail transactions that may be fraudulent

FIGURE 8.7 Revenue Process/Receivables Improvement Dashboard

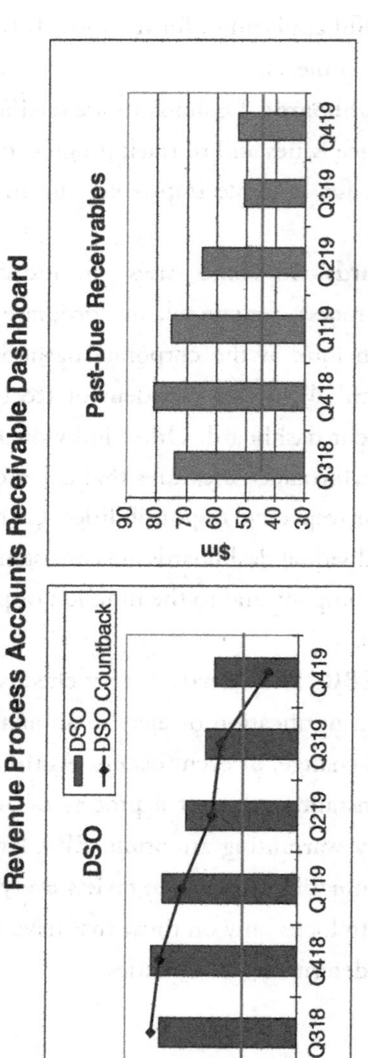

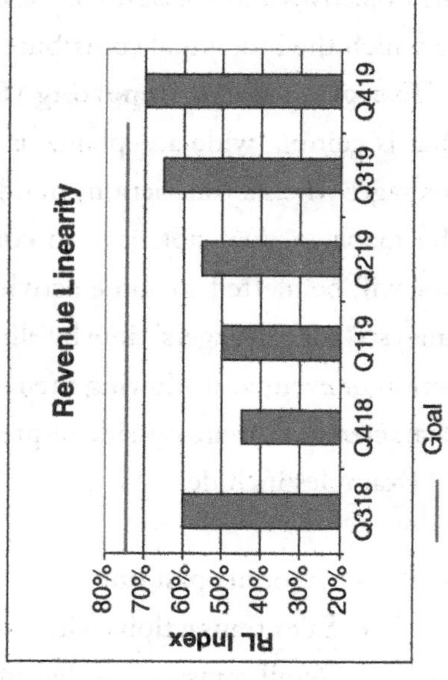

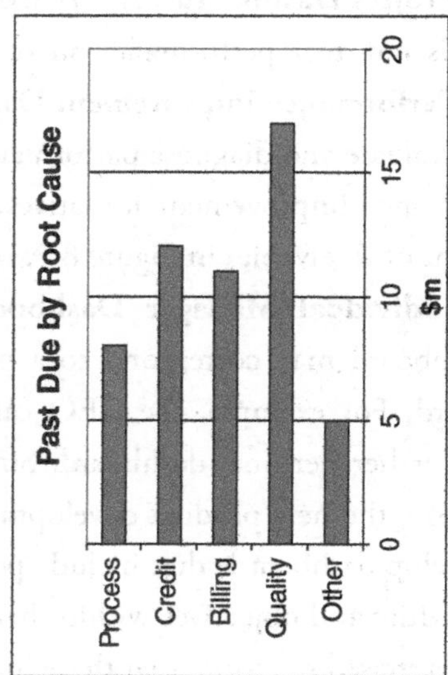

SAMPLE DASHBOARDS FOR SELECTED INDUSTRIES

It can be insightful to think about key performance indicators and dashboards for businesses other than our own. What are the key value drivers and performance measures? The sample dashboards in Figures 8.8 to 8.10 included at the end of this chapter are focused on revenue, which is critical to any business. Note how these dashboards focus on leading indicators of performance, including critical assumptions and variables affecting revenue levels. These variables will always include external factors. For example, weather impacts each of these businesses and would be reflected on the revenue dashboard. Lower temperatures and greater snowfall would have a negative impact on many businesses, but not for a ski resort or a retailer selling snow throwers or winter apparel.

SUMMARY

Key performance measures and dashboards are two very useful tools in developing effective BPM. However, the selection of measures and the development of dashboards are extremely important since they implicitly state priorities and key areas of emphasis for the organization. People and organizations respond to the use of measures. The mere fact that performance is being tracked often leads to improvements in productivity. This is even more dramatic if compensation plans are tied to the measures. As a result, care must be exercised to select appropriate measures. Establishing measures that are not well vetted may lead to behavior changes that have unintended consequences. In addition, it is critically important to achieve a balance in the measures. For example, measuring inventory turns could lead to the unintended consequence of impacting customer deliveries if not balanced with appropriate measures of on-time deliveries and customer satisfaction. The selection of performance measures should be done in the context of building a comprehensive BPM.

FIGURE 8.8 Dashboard for Specialty Retail: Lawn and Garden

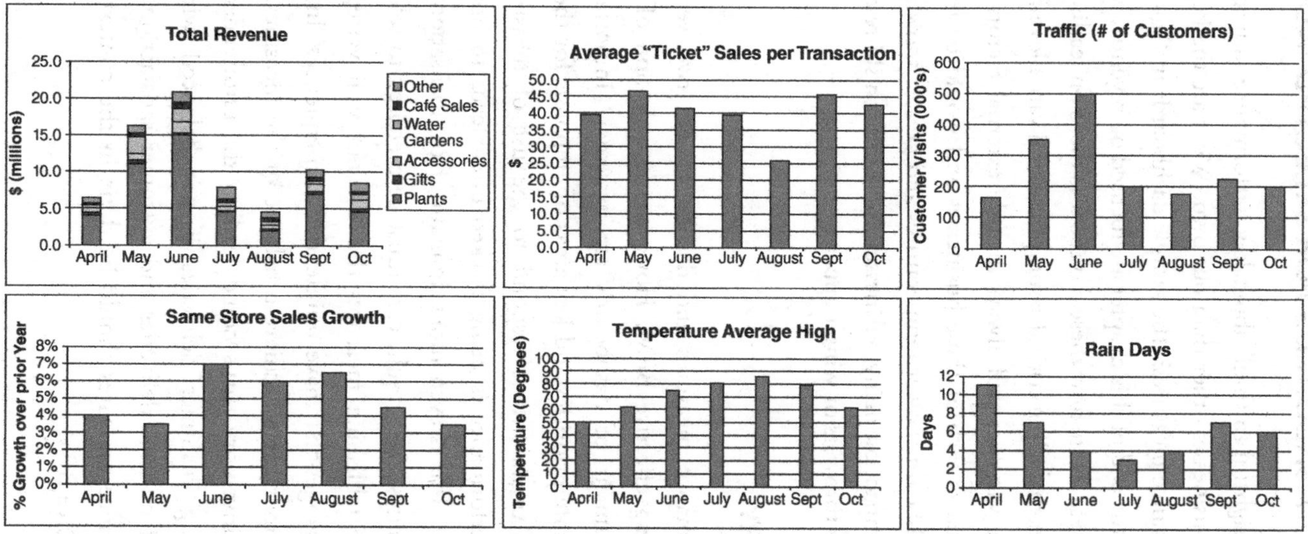

FIGURE 8.9 Dashboard for Ski Resort

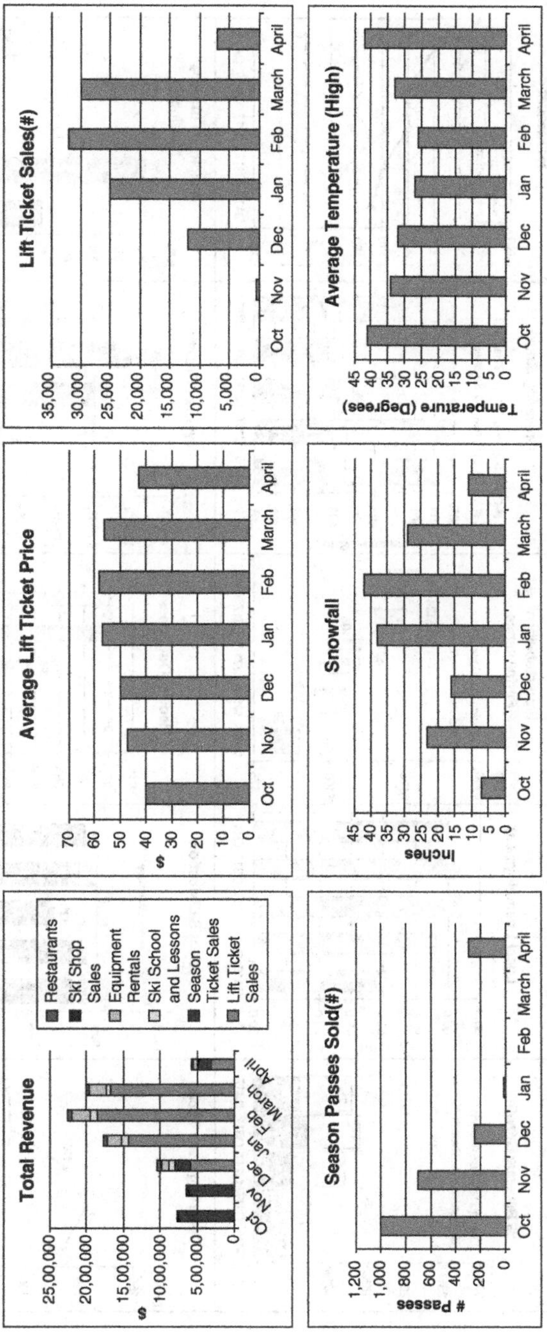

Total Revenue

$

25,00,000
20,00,000
15,00,000
10,00,000
5,00,000
0

Oct Nov Dec Jan Feb March April

Restaurants
Ski Shop Sales
Equipment Rentals
Ski School and Lessons
Season Ticket Sales
Lift Ticket Sales

Average Lift Ticket Price

$

70
60
50
40
30
20
10
0

Oct Nov Dec Jan Feb March April

Lift Ticket Sales(#)

35,000
30,000
25,000
20,000
15,000
10,000
5,000
0

Oct Nov Dec Jan Feb March April

Season Passes Sold(#)

Passes

1,200
1,000
800
600
400
200
0

Oct Nov Dec Jan Feb March April

Snowfall

Inches

45
40
35
30
25
20
15
10
5
0

Oct Nov Dec Jan Feb March April

Average Temperature (High)

Temperature (Degrees)

45
40
35
30
25
20
15
10
5
0

Oct Nov Dec Jan Feb March April

FIGURE 8.10 Dashboard for Medical Center

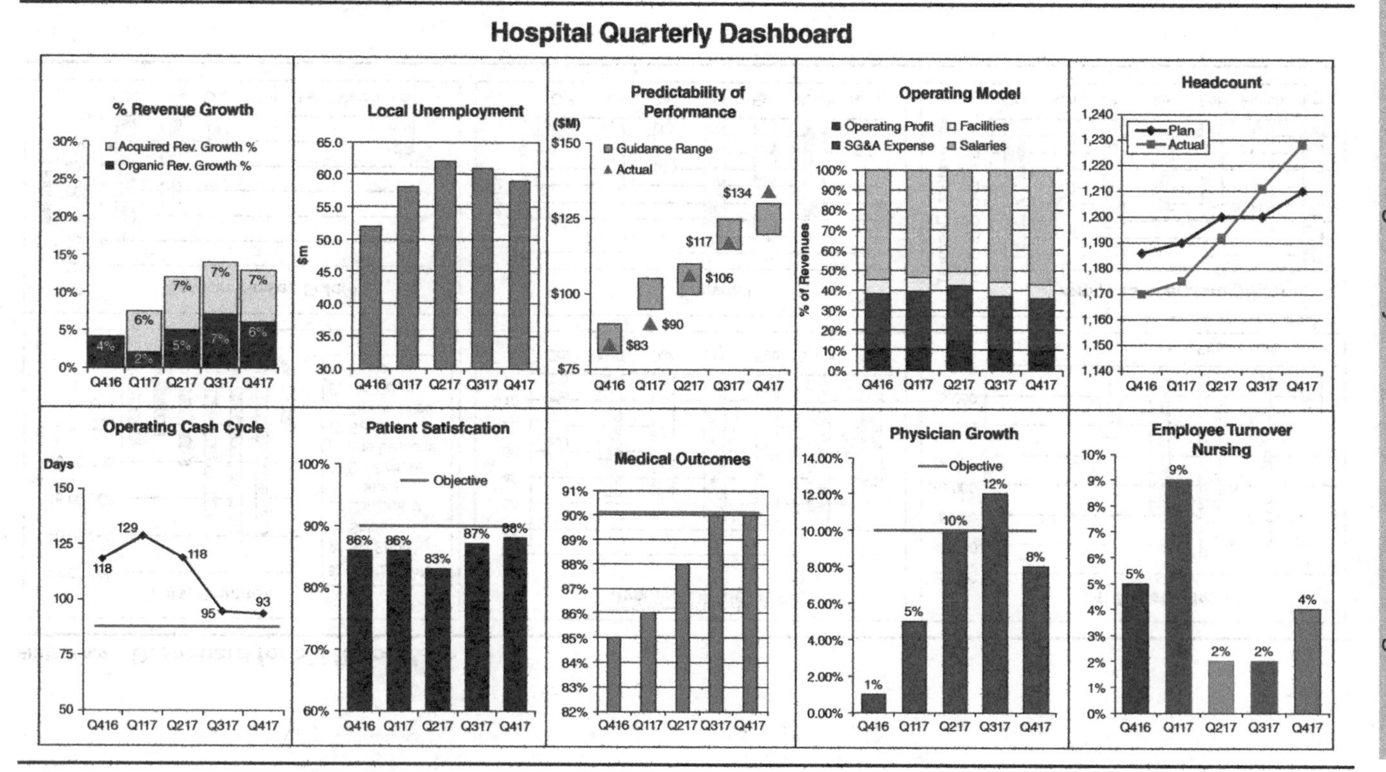

9

INSTITUTIONALIZING PERFORMANCE MANAGEMENT

CHAPTER INTRODUCTION

In earlier chapters in this section on performance management we covered the importance of stating objectives and developing a context. We then outlined best practices in selecting key performance indicators and building dashboards. We now turn to the process of institutionalizing performance management – that is, successful implementation and integration into all critical management processes. This step is the final and arguably most important aspect of successful performance management. If performance management is not integrated with other management processes, it will not be successful.

GAINING TRACTION

There are several critical steps that are necessary to effectively adopt performance management (PM) (see Figure 9.1). These include obtaining executive support, communication and training, using performance improvement tools, and developing a delivery mechanism.

FIGURE 9.1 Establishing a Performance Management Framework

Establishing or Improving Business Performance Management

Identify Objectives	Create Context	Build Framework	Institutionalize
❑ Integrate Financial and Operational Measures ❑ Accelerate Value Creation	❑ Strategy ❑ Key Initiatives ❑ Assess Performance ❑ Identify Threats and Opportunities ❑ Shareholder Value	❑ Select Key Performance Measures ❑ Build Dashboards and Reports ❑ Build Delivery Mechanisms	❑ Training ❑ Technology Platform ❑ Planning and Forecasting ❑ Performance Evaluation ❑ Compensation ❑ Evaluate/Refresh

Executive Support

Few initiatives are successful in a company without the passion and support of the CEO, CFO, and other members of the senior management team. Managers and employees are very adept at reading the level of commitment of leadership to any new project. Senior managers must support performance management in both word and action. The CEO will determine the ultimate success of performance management. Is she insisting on a review of dashboards at management meetings? Is he using the performance measures as a critical element of evaluating managers' performance? Is performance management going to be integrated across all management processes? If the answer is no, then PM will be an interesting activity but will fail to achieve its full potential impact on the organization. It is extremely important to win the support and buy-in across the executive suite before proceeding with PM.

Communication and Training

After selecting and developing the performance measures, it is important to provide managers and employees with appropriate training and other tools to use the measures and make performance improvements.

The effectiveness of a performance management system and related initiatives will be greatly enhanced if accompanied by manager and employee training. A substantial part of the value in performance management is in connecting the dots between operating performance, financial performance, and value creation. A comprehensive training program for managers and executives should include the following topics:

- Fundamentals of Finance
- Valuation and Value Drivers
- Linking Performance to Value
- Developing and Using Key Performance Indicators
- Use of Dashboards to Monitor and Improve Performance

The training should be tailored to various levels within the organization. The core concepts can be modified to be appropriate to the executive team, midlevel managers, and other employees.

Managers should also be educated on the development and use of key performance indicators (KPIs), the use of dashboards to monitor and improve performance, and the use of any software employed to deliver this vital information. For example, if actual results are falling short of targets, the manager must be able to identify the root causes of the variance and even possible actions to improve performance.

Additional assessment tools and training topics are discussed in Chapter 5.

Process Improvement Tools

In order to achieve improvements in performance in critical areas and measures, managers and employees must be provided with tools to evaluate and improve key business processes. In Chapter 17, we review examples of process evaluation tools for the revenue and supply chain management processes. In addition, there are several very useful process evaluation and quality management tools that work across all business processes, including:

- Six Sigma
- Total Quality Management (TQM)
- Process assessment and improvement
- Lean management
- Benchmarking

Delivery Mechanism

Many software vendors have developed and are refining products that will deliver key performance indicators and financial results in real time to designated managers throughout the organization. Critical information is available on demand and using best practices to present business information, including data visualization. These are effective long-term solutions in many cases. However, many companies become bogged down in attempting to use or even evaluate and procure these technology tools. Often, the introduction of the software solution is done without defining the objectives and context described in Chapter 7. Many of the "canned" KPIs and dashboards miss the mark in terms of measuring what is most important and relevant to this specific organization. The performance measures and dashboards that are developed in this way often fail to fully achieve the objectives of implementing PM. In addition, the implementation is often delayed until the technology is procured and installed. In some cases, valuable time is lost in critical performance areas.

While generally not a good long-term, *total* solution, many companies begin producing dashboards on spreadsheet tools such as Microsoft Excel. The advantage in this approach is that a few key dashboards can be produced in hours or days rather than in weeks or months. This can be a good way to get started, especially in situations where improving business performance is a matter of urgency, for example in a business turnaround situation. Long-term technology solutions can then be put in place as time permits and objectives and definition of needs are understood. Due to the power and flexibility of Excel, it or other similar products will always play a role in FP&A and PM.

Oversight of Performance Management

Who should be responsible for designing, implementing, and overseeing performance management? The answer to this question varies from one organization to another depending on several factors, including the skill set and experience of key managers and functions within the organization.

Many organizations that have successful performance management initiatives develop a steering committee or PM council to oversee the implementation and ongoing execution of PM. The council should include representation from all critical functions, including strategy, operations, finance, information technology (IT), and sales and marketing. This broad representation will ensure that PM will consider diverse perspectives and will encourage buy-in and acceptance across the organization.

The responsibility for the implementation and direction of PM on a day-to-day basis is usually assigned to a working group or related function. Two obvious functions to lead the working group are the IT and FP&A departments. I have generally found that the director of FP&A or equivalent is usually best suited to lead the working group. PM and FP&A must be fully integrated to be successful. An effective FP&A group is already aware of and analyzing critical areas of performance and understands drivers of financial performance and shareholder value. In addition, their role typically exposes them to all critical functions, strategic issues, and initiatives across the organization.

INTEGRATING BUSINESS PERFORMANCE MANAGEMENT WITH OTHER MANAGEMENT PROCESSES

To be effective, the performance measurement framework must be integrated with other key management processes and activities, including

FIGURE 9.2 Integrating PM with Other Management Processes

	Project Management	Mergers and Acquisitions	Product Development	Sales	Performance Improvement	
Goal Setting						Management Reporting
Strategic Planning		**Financial Planning & Analysis**				Performance Evaluation
Annual Planning		**Performance Management**				Value Creation
Forecasts						Investor Relations
	Risk Management	Human Capital Management	Performance Monitoring	Execution Accountability	Incentive Compensation	

planning, management meetings, performance reviews, project management, and evaluating and compensating human resources (see Figure 9.2).

Strategic and Operational Planning. Most companies develop strategic and annual operating plans each year. Planning activities will be greatly improved by incorporating the key elements of performance management. What level of shareholder value is likely if the planned results are achieved? The financials included in the plan should not be a spreadsheet exercise; rather, they must be grounded by execution plans and projected levels of performance on key operating measures. For example, if a company plans to achieve improved inventory turnover in the future, this goal should be supported by a detailed plan and targets for key performance indicators that impact inventory levels, such as revenue linearity, production cycle times, past-due deliveries, and forecasting accuracy. Each plan or alternative should be valued; that is, the team should estimate what the likely market value of the company will be if the plan is achieved. Is this an acceptable return to shareholders? Can we identify other actions that will enhance value? Finally, the planning process should identify the measures that will be monitored to track and evaluate assumptions and performance in executing the plan.

Forecasting and Business Outlook. Most companies spend a great deal of time forecasting business performance. In a successful performance management framework, companies will place more emphasis on forecasting and tracking key performance drivers and measures that will result in achieving the financial projections. These managers recognize that it is easier to track progress and drive improvement to performance measures that will impact financial results rather than attempt to drive improvement directly to financial results.

Project Management. At any one point in time, most organizations will have hundreds of projects under way. These will include projects in information technology, product development, process improvement, developing plans, and many others that have a direct and significant effect on performance. Project management can be improved by incorporating PM, including execution planning, monitoring, and visibility.

Product Development. As the pipeline for new product and revenue growth, product development is a very important process for value creation. Product development activity includes the evaluation of potential new programs and products and the management of several development projects. Both project evaluation and management lend themselves to PM, and their importance mandates the attention.

Monthly and Quarterly Business, Project, and Operational Reviews. Executive teams typically review the performance of operations of business units on a monthly or quarterly basis. These sessions often represent the most important exchange of information and also the best opportunity to focus on execution and hold managers accountable for performance. Discussions at monthly and quarterly management meetings should center on key objectives, important issues, progress toward goals and targets, KPI, and the performance dashboards. All too often, these meetings drift away from critical performance objectives aided by long discussions around lengthy slide show presentations. If the team has implemented the performance framework by developing context and linking to strategic initiatives and value drivers, then the dashboards will provide visibility into performance in critical areas and programs. Meetings will stay focused on key issues, and managers can be easily held accountable to the performance tracked by these objective measures.

It's hard to hide from the information on the slide shown in Figure 9.3. When required to be presented, it prevents long-winded, diversionary

FIGURE 9.3 **Business Unit Accountability Dashboard**

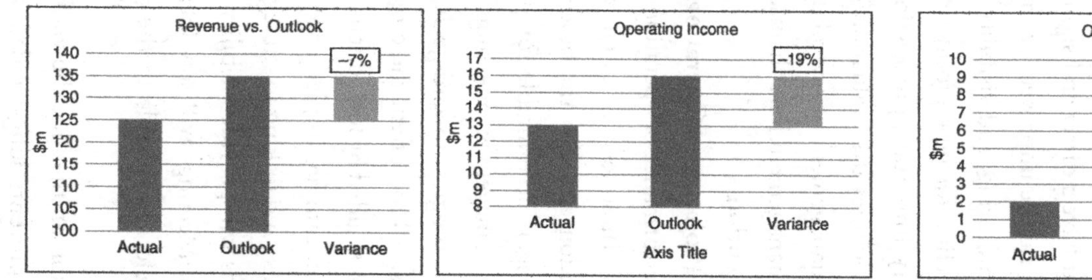

Critical New Product Development Status

Project Name	Costs Actual	Costs Projected	Costs %	Status (% completion)(1) Actual	Status (% completion)(1) Projected	Status (% completion)(1) %	Annual Revenue Potential	Status	Comment
Coyote	0.7	0.8	88%	95%	93%	102%	$25	Green	On Track, Intro 3/17
Fox	2.8	2.5	112%	60%	80%	75%	30	Yellow	2 Critical Milestones missed
Rabbit	1.4	1.3	108%	40%	50%	80%	15	Red	Technical Performance Issues
Tortoise	1.8	2	90%	100%	100%	100%	60	Green	1st Shipments, next week
Total	6.7	6.6	102%	74%	81%	89%	$130		

(1) Based on project milestones planned and achieved

Summary:

- **Significant shortfall in revenue and profit**
- **Delay in new product introductions**
- **Cash Flow levels also impacted by rising inventories due to revenue shortfall and new product delays**
- **Corrective action plan developed**

presentations that mask or fail to address the important elements of performance.

Talent Acquisition, Evaluation, Development, and Compensation (Human Capital Management). It is very unlikely that any performance management system will be completely successful unless it is integrated into the talent acquisition, evaluation, development, and compensation processes. Performance objectives should be established for each manager that are consistent with achieving the company's goals for value creation and strategic and operational objectives. Too often, individual and functional objectives are set independently, without adequate linkage to overall corporate objectives. Incorporating the principles from the PM into the evaluation of managers' performance will increase the effectiveness of the performance reviews and underscore the organization's commitment to performance management. Of course, aligning compensation and incentive practices with PM ensures ultimate connectivity.

Performance management can also be directed to human capital management (HCM). Since an organization's team of associates may be considered its greatest asset, performance management can be used to analyze the workforce and critical HCM processes. The use of KPI and analytics in HCM is explored in Chapter 10.

Management Reporting. Monthly financial and management reports should be modified to include the key performance indicators and drivers selected in developing the PM. Typical monthly reports include traditional financial statements, supporting schedules, and spreadsheets that are easily understood by accountants but are difficult for most nonfinancial managers and employees to understand and digest. Key trends or exceptions may be buried in the statements and are extremely difficult to identify or act on. More visual content (graphs) should replace pages of financial tables and reports. Focus should shift away from lagging financial results toward providing crisp, predictive (leading) indicators of future performance. The reports should also focus more attention on revenue drivers and analysis of external factors rather than the traditional measures of internal financial performance.

Board and Investor Communication. For both publicly traded and privately owned firms, communication with investors is a very important activity. Many investors are intensely focused on company performance and the future potential to create shareholder value. Investors will appreciate managers who recognize that a broad set of performance drivers factors into long-term value creation. They fully understand that successful execution on key strategic initiatives and improvement on value drivers will lead to long-term shareholder returns. Shareholders applaud managers who are focused on execution, accountability, and performance management, since they know that these are precursors to value creation.

Executives running publicly traded companies should communicate the performance on key business and value drivers and related performance measures, and not just focus on sales or earnings per share (EPS). Investors that use economic valuation methods such as discounted cash flow (DCF) need inputs for sales and earnings growth as well as capital requirements and cost of capital. Even those investors using multiples of revenue or earnings must consider these factors in selecting an appropriate price-earnings (P/E) or revenue multiple to value the company. Presenting and emphasizing the long-term value drivers also encourages investors to focus less attention on short-term quarterly financial results.

Corporate Development. The corporate development function is typically responsible for mergers and acquisitions (M&A) activity within most companies. The M&A process and resultant deals are important contributors or detractors to performance and value in many companies. For companies that are active in mergers and acquisitions, it is important that M&A activity be viewed as a process and that the key elements of the PM be incorporated into the identification, evaluation, valuation, and integration of acquisitions. The analysis of M&A is fully explored in Chapter 23.

Periodic Review and Revision

The selection of KPIs and the creation of dashboards will be based on numerous factors, including many that relate to specific issues and opportunities, events, and projects. The KPI and dashboards should be reviewed periodically to evaluate the ongoing utility of each measure and dashboard. For example, some measures can be eliminated because the underlying issue or project has been addressed or completed. New priorities and challenges arise that may warrant inclusion in the measurement system going forward. An excellent time to review measures and dashboards is in the later stages of the annual and/or strategic process, when new objectives, initiatives, and targets are established. Of course, measures that are no longer useful can be replaced at any point.

AVOIDING COMMON MISTAKES

Don't Drive the Car by Staring at the Dashboard

You won't keep the car on the road if you stare at the dashboard. Look out the front window, and check the rearview mirror. Pay attention to road conditions, traffic patterns, and aggressive drivers, as well as the dashboard. Similarly, pilots seldom fly by staring at the instrument panel. They utilize this visual input, but also rely on their intuition, feel, conditions, and other input. Get out of the office. Talk to employees, customers, and suppliers. Combine this input with your intuition and the objective information from the dashboards.

Don't Make It a Finance or Information Technology Project

Many projects fail because they are driven exclusively by the finance or information technology function. In order to be successful, PM must be driven from the top and integrated into the fabric of the management systems. Functions such as finance and IT are critical in the development, implementation, and support of PM, but all disciplines must buy into and support this activity to be successful.

Don't Measure Everything

Organizations that follow the process outlined in Chapter 7 to define objectives and develop context for PM will develop a framework that focuses the organization's attention on important value and performance drivers. Failure to do so will result in selecting too many measures and some measures that are not consistent with priorities and important performance drivers.

Don't Measure Only What Is Easy and Available

There is a tendency to select KPIs and build dashboards based on the information that is readily available. Examples include financial ratios and trends or operational metrics. In many cases, the most important information on key businesses processes, threats and opportunities, intangibles, and other important drivers is not readily available. While it may be challenging to measure things like innovation or human capital, their importance to success justifies attempts at measuring and evaluation. Even if the measures are imperfect, they will focus attention and provide insight into these critical areas. We explore measuring and driving what's important in Chapter 10.

Don't Attempt to Replace Judgment or Intuition

Some executives resist performance management initiatives because they argue that PM is an attempt to replace or limit their management judgment and intuition. While analysis and performance management can significantly improve decision making and management, many important decisions must incorporate the experience and judgment of the executive. PM can facilitate and bring full information, leading to better decisions.

Don't Measure Too Frequently

New information availability may encourage managers to "take the pulse" of the business and key activities too often. This will lead to frustration for managers and team members alike and may also result in decisions or actions based on small sample size, cycles, or minor perturbations.

Software Is Not a Silver Bullet

Many organizations look to a software product as the silver bullet in measuring and improving performance. While software can be an important element of performance management, it is at least as important, if not more so, to develop context, select measures, train, and integrate with other management processes.

SUMMARY

Performance management cannot succeed as a separate and distinct management process. To be successful, it must be integrated into key management processes, including strategic and operational planning, monthly or quarterly business and operational reviews, and talent evaluation and compensation. PM must also be driven from the top to be successful. The CEO and CFO must demand utilization of performance management throughout critical management processes. In order to remain relevant and vital, PM must be evaluated and adjusted periodically to ensure that it remains focused on the critical drivers of performance and value.

10

MEASURING AND DRIVING WHAT'S IMPORTANT

Innovation, Agility, and Human Capital

There is a strong tendency in FP&A and performance management (PM) to focus on areas and activities that are easy to measure. In addition, we also tend focus on those areas that are traditionally measured, principally financial and operational measures.

In this chapter, we provide an introduction to critical areas that are difficult to measure but of vital importance to today's challenging environment:

- Innovation
- Agility
- Human capital management (HCM)

While difficult to measure and to directly link to overall performance and value creation, there is little doubt of the role they play in an organization's success.

INNOVATION

Innovation has been hailed as a magic source of value. In fact, it has been the basis for value creation in a number of enterprises over the past 25 years. As an intangible, innovation is difficult to measure.

While difficult to quantify, key conditions and enablers of innovation can indeed be measured. Innovation can be aimed at product development, business processes, or business models – or at a combination of these. In particular, measurement of innovation requires identifying key performance indicators of critical business processes and activities that are targets for innovative practices, for example radical improvements in time to market. It is also possible to identify and assess certain conditions that tend to support and encourage innovations.

Types of Innovation Programs

Innovation initiatives can be grouped into three broad categories: product, business model, and process. Product innovation is generally described as developing revolutionary new products or increasing the speed at which creative new products are introduced to the market – think of Apple's stream of new iPods, iPhones, and smart watches. Business model innovation involves developing a new approach to delivering products and services that create significant competitive advantages in cost, customer service, or other important drivers. Examples include Southwest Airlines' "low-cost no-frills" model in air travel and Netflix's mail-delivery, then digital, model of movie rentals and content development.

Process innovation includes efforts to improve the quality and effectiveness of key business processes such as customer fulfillment or supply chain management. Walmart, for example, is notable as an innovator in supply chain, inventory, and vendor management. Other organizations, such as General Electric, create innovative *management* processes around organization and management development; still others, like Amazon, innovate processes such as business intelligence and analytics.

Some initiatives cut across two of these categories, and there is often a fine line between process and business model innovation. In addition, efforts to improve the new product development process reflect both process and product innovation. These distinctions can indeed be subtle, but the key point is that innovation is much broader than simply rolling out new products and can be directed to any business activity.

Will Innovation Efforts Move the Needle?

Before developing innovation programs and measures that can help move the needle, we first need to determine which dial we have in mind. What exactly are we trying to accomplish *through* innovation? Common objectives include growth in sales, boosts in profitability, and improvements in processes or product development effectiveness. Ultimately, most executives hope to accelerate progress on key strategic objectives, financial measures, and shareholder value.

Most consultants and academics and most independent rankings of innovation focus on two or three measures of overall performance to evaluate effectiveness. These measures, such as total return to shareholders (TRS), revenue, or profit growth, are good starting points, but they are by no means perfect or exclusive measures of innovation. Their principal deficiencies are that they are lagging indicators; historical measures don't help companies see where they are going. In addition, each of these measures is impacted by multiple factors besides innovation; TRS, for instance, is also subject to stock market variations, errors in valuation, cost reductions, and other factors.

Developing an effective set of measures necessitates the identification of leading indicators that emphasize the direct contribution from innovation. This process, the development of a "dashboard for innovation," can be facilitated by identifying key measures and activities that cascade from the objective of creating shareholder value.

Performance and Value Creation in Innovative Organizations

How have innovative companies performed on overall financial and value creation measures? Consider the dashboard of key financial and value indicators for Apple, which includes the following measures (see Figure 10.1):

- Revenue growth
- Operating margins
- Return on invested capital
- Asset turnover
- Growth in market value

It is noteworthy that the growth rate has slowed in recent years. This is inevitable for two reasons. First, as the organization grows, it becomes more difficult to maintain a high-percentage growth rate on larger numbers. Increasing sales by $50 million on a $100 million base is 50% growth; growing by $50 million on a $500 million base is only 10% growth. Second, maintaining the innovation edge often seems to wane over time, and it is often more difficult to identify new products and new markets for extended periods of time. Some organizations, including Amazon, have continued to refresh growth by extending offerings to new markets and even leveraging technology competencies into new business opportunities (e.g. Amazon Web Services).

The power of innovation to drive differentiation within an industry is noteworthy as well. Look at the contrast between the performance of the business model innovator Netflix (NFLX) and its traditional competitor Blockbuster (BBI) (see Figure 10.2) in the early 2000s.

FIGURE 10.1 **Historical Performance Recap: Apple**

Apple

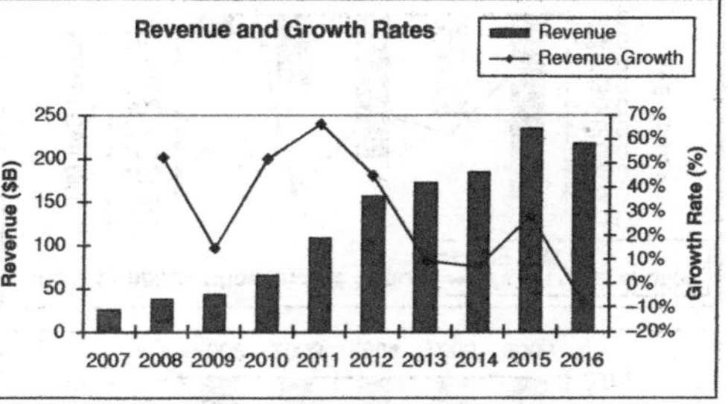

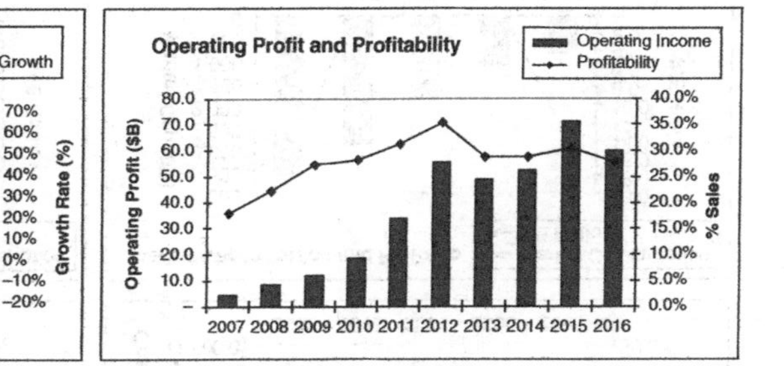

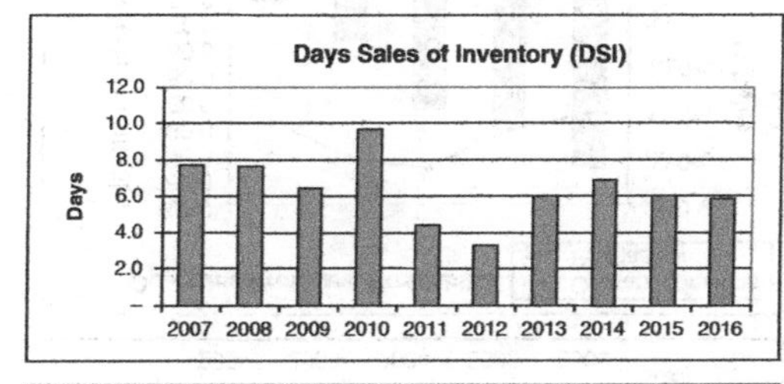

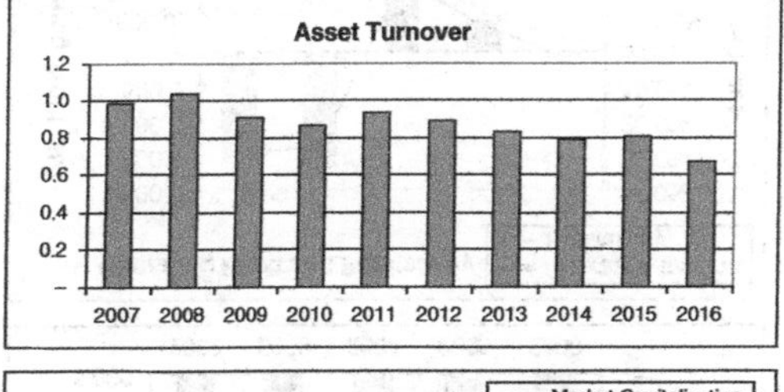

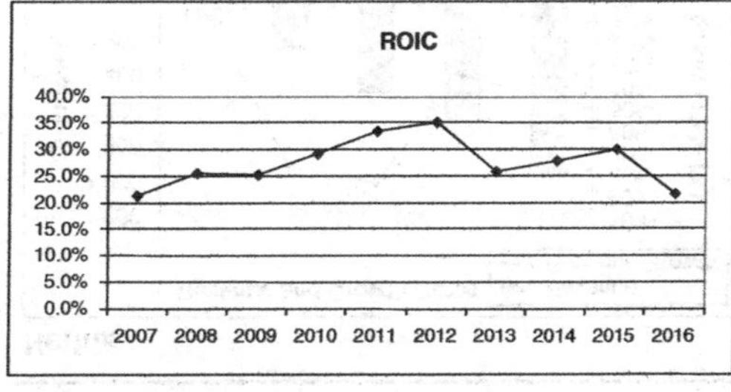

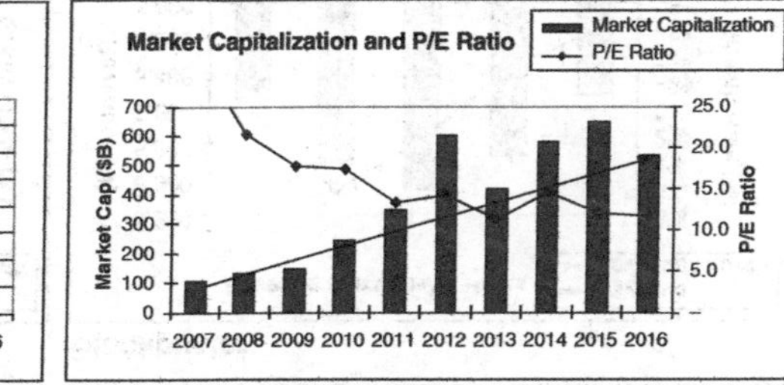

Source: Analysis based on company reports.

FIGURE 10.2 Comparative Performance: Netflix and Blockbuster

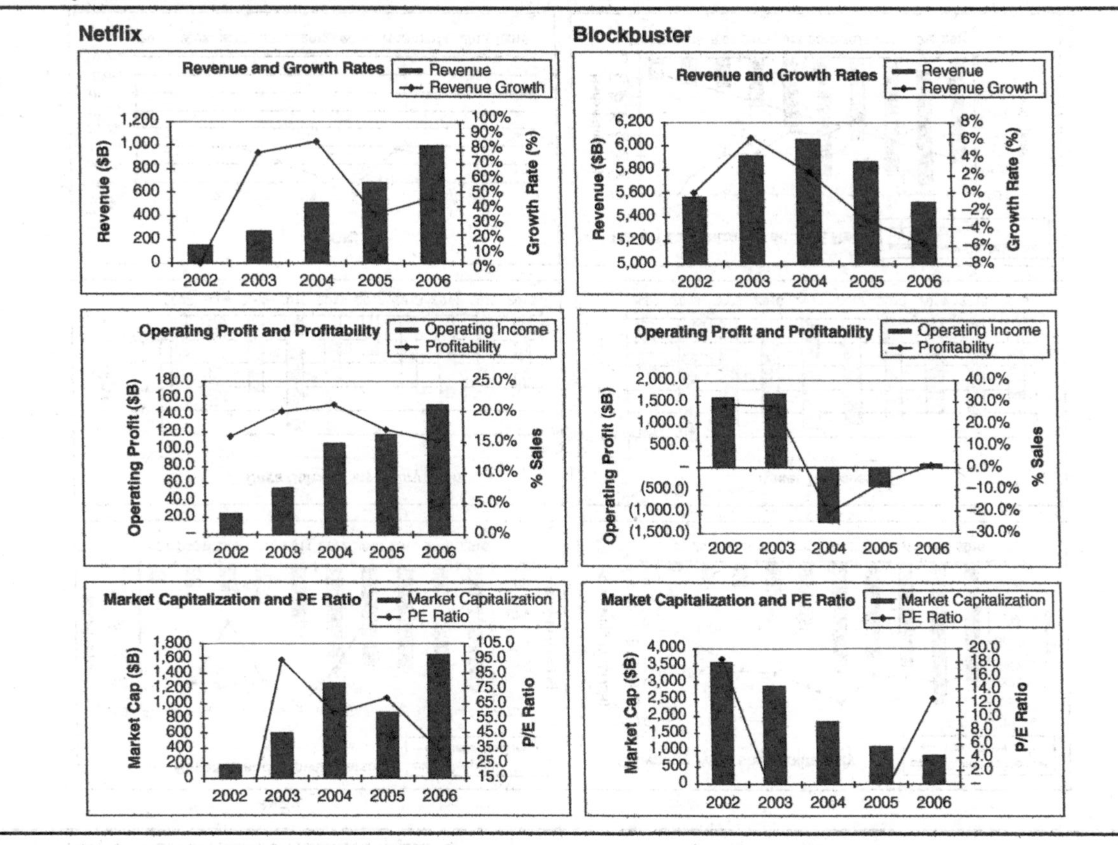

Netflix's innovative business model for DVD rental resulted in very rapid sales growth – at Blockbuster's expense. The Netflix business model also produced strong operating margins, even during high growth periods, while Blockbuster's profits plummeted. Blockbuster's market capitalization and price-earnings (P/E) multiple cratered as a result, whereas Netflix created substantial value. Netflix then pivoted away from the mail order DVD business to a digital platform and ultimately began developing its own programming content. A similar transformation has been underway in retail. Amazon and other Internet retailers have transformed the retail market, taking market share from traditional retailers at levels that threaten the traditionalists' very survival.

Innovator	**Victims**
Netflix	Blockbuster
Amazon	Walmart, Target, many others

Connecting the Dots: Innovation, Financial Performance, and Value

Innovation is most often discussed in the context of revenue growth. For this purpose, we will focus on the four key drivers of organic growth: market size and growth, new product introduction, new customer acquisition, and customer satisfaction/retention (see Figure 10.3).

The importance of each of these drivers at this level will vary over time and from company to company. Organizations should select measures that address an improvement opportunity or a specific strategic objective. For example, if new product development is a priority, measures such as revenue from new products, project status, and other key metrics can be incorporated into a new product development dashboard.

FIGURE 10.3 Drilling Down into Sources of Revenue Growth

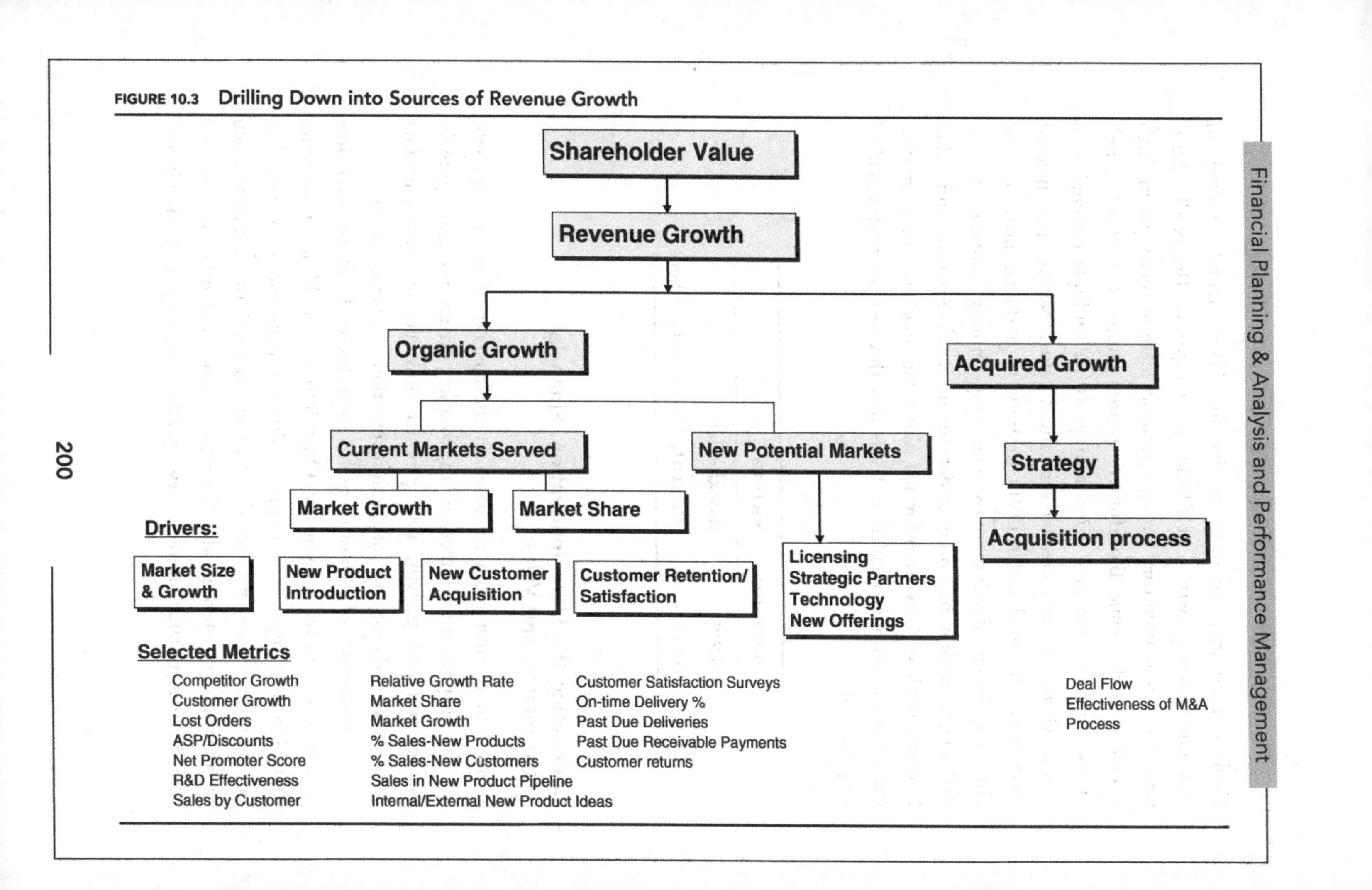
Shareholder Value
Revenue Growth
Organic Growth
Acquired Growth
Current Markets Served
New Potential Markets
Strategy
Market Growth
Market Share
Acquisition process
Drivers:
Market Size & Growth
New Product Introduction
New Customer Acquisition
Customer Retention/ Satisfaction
Licensing
Strategic Partners
Technology
New Offerings
Selected Metrics
Competitor Growth
Customer Growth
Lost Orders
ASP/Discounts
Net Promoter Score
R&D Effectiveness
Sales by Customer
Relative Growth Rate
Market Share
Market Growth
% Sales-New Products
% Sales-New Customers
Sales in New Product Pipeline
Internal/External New Product Ideas
Customer Satisfaction Surveys
On-time Delivery %
Past Due Deliveries
Past Due Receivable Payments
Customer returns
Deal Flow
Effectiveness of M&A Process

(See Figure 10.4.) Such a dashboard would be appropriate for Apple but not relevant for Walmart's process focus or Netflix's focus on business model innovation. If we were to create the revenue growth drill-down chart for Netflix, it would most likely focus on customer acquisition, retention (churn), activity, content development, and related measures.

Note that this new product development dashboard is balanced: in addition to containing vital information on new product status and development performance, it also presents information on the quality of the design process (engineering change notices [ECNs] from new products) and design for manufacturability (number of inventory parts).

Additional measures that provide insight into innovation effectiveness by specific value drivers are included in Table 10.1 and Figure 10.5. Managers should select measures from the list that best represent key business priorities and issues.

In addition to developing key measures and dashboards, we can assess the conditions for innovation, and can utilize benchmarking and process evaluation tools and project planning execution and tracking techniques. Do the culture, management systems, and practices of the company encourage or inhibit innovation? (See text box.)

TABLE 10.1 Key Innovation Measures

Overall	New Product	Business Model	Process
Revenue Growth-Organic	Relative Growth Index	Value Added per Employee	Asset Turnover
Total Return to Shareholders	Annual Revenue in Development Pipeline	Operating Leverage %	Customer Satisfaction (Warranty, OTD)
Profitability	Project Completion vs. Plan (Milestones and Cost)	ROIC (Asset Turnover × Profitability)	Cycle Time
Return on Invested Capital	% Sales from New Products	Customer Life Cycle Cost	Production Yields

FIGURE 10.4 New Product Development Dashboard

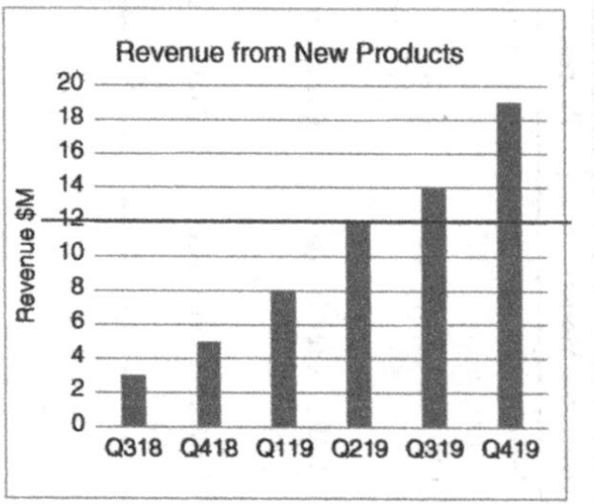

Critical New Product Development Status

Project Name	Costs Actual	Costs Projected	Costs %	Status (% completion)[1] Actual	Status (% completion)[1] Projected	Status (% completion)[1] %	Annual Revenue Potential	Projected NPV	Status	Comment
Coyote	0.7	0.8	88%	95%	93%	102%	$25	$52	●	On Track, Intro 3/19
Fox	2.8	2.5	112%	60%	80%	75%	30	61	●	2 Critical Milestones missed
Rabbit	1.4	1.3	108%	40%	50%	80%	15	21	●	Technical Performance Issues
Tortoise	1.8	2	90%	100%	100%	100%	60	45	●	1st Shipments, next week
Total	6.7	6.6	102%	74%	81%	89%	$130	$179		

[1] Based on project milestones planned and achieved

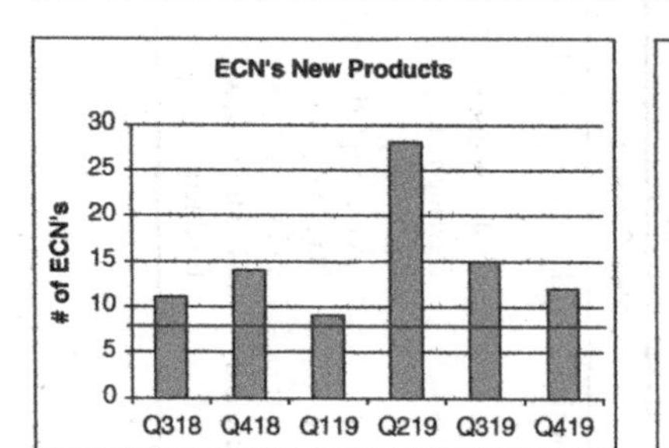

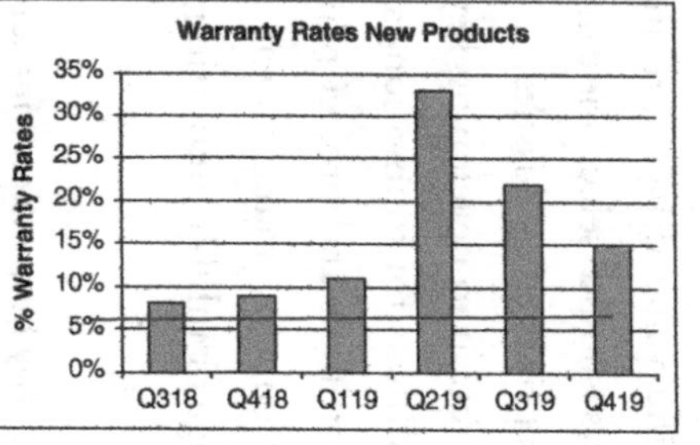

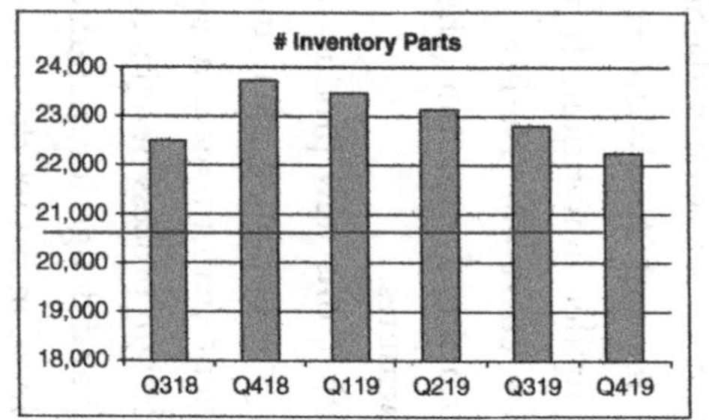

FIGURE 10.5 **Innovation Dashboard**

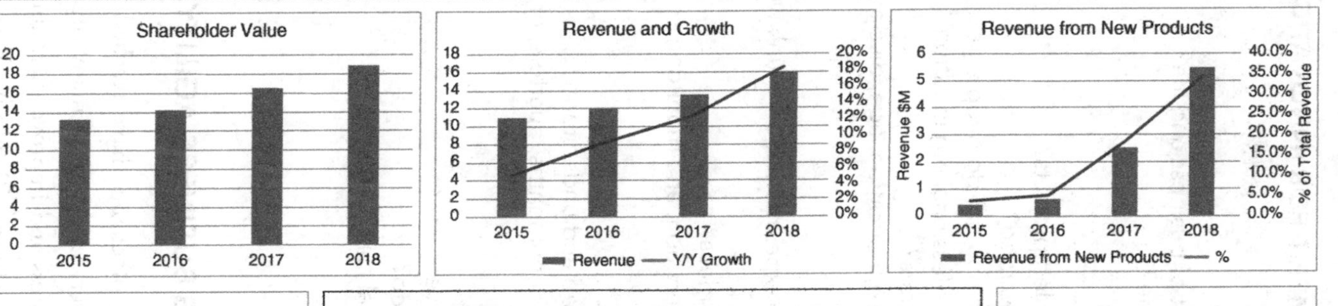

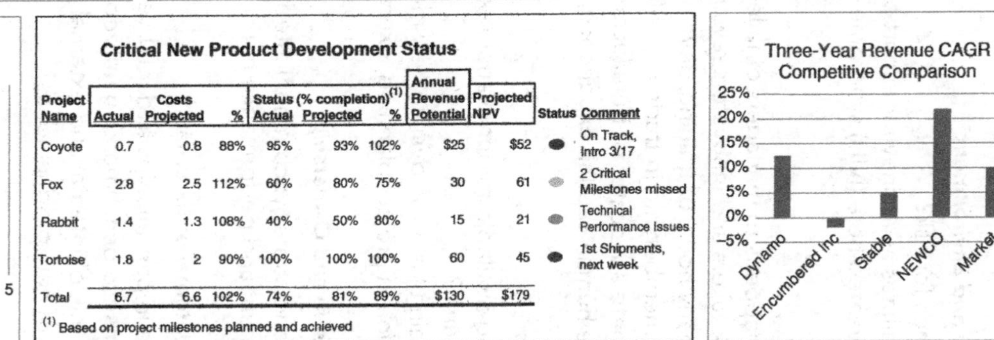

Critical New Product Development Status

Project Name	Costs Actual	Costs Projected	Costs %	Status (% completion)[1] Actual	Status (% completion)[1] Projected	Status (% completion)[1] %	Annual Revenue Potential	Projected NPV	Status	Comment
Coyote	0.7	0.8	88%	95%	93%	102%	$25	$52	●	On Track, Intro 3/17
Fox	2.8	2.5	112%	60%	80%	75%	30	61	●	2 Critical Milestones missed
Rabbit	1.4	1.3	108%	40%	50%	80%	15	21	●	Technical Performance Issues
Tortoise	1.8	2	90%	100%	100%	100%	60	45	●	1st Shipments, next week
Total	6.7	6.6	102%	74%	81%	89%	$130	$179		

[1] Based on project milestones planned and achieved

ASSESSING THE ENVIRONMENT FOR INNOVATION

Culture and Environment

Tolerance for risk?
View failures as an inevitable part of business and life?
Not invented here (NIH) syndrome?

People

What happens to managers of failed projects?
Are risk takers and innovators rewarded?
How many hours of training/development do people get?
Active membership in trade or professional organizations?
Passionate advocates or bureaucrats?
Diverse human capital: experience, education, age, discipline?

Process

Funding available for innovation/experimentation/skunk works/true research?
How painful is it to advance new ideas?
Discipline in project planning, execution, and monitoring?

Leadership and Ownership

Vision and strategy: communicated and understood?
Investment and performance horizon: months, quarters, or years?

Focus: Internal or External

Engage in partnerships and joint ventures?
Performance benchmarking utilized?
Hiring: mix of internal and external candidates?
Source of new product ideas?

MEASURING AND DRIVING BUSINESS AGILITY

Both the pace and the magnitude of change have reached levels that threaten the success and even the very existence of many organizations. Leaders of all organizations must assess and improve their ability to see, recognize, respond to, and adapt to change. They must have the ability to move quickly to address threats and to capitalize on opportunities. Finally, in addition to measuring and assessing agility, it is essential for executives to provide tools for improving the organization's agility.

What Is Business Agility?

We define business agility as the ability to anticipate, recognize, and effectively respond to do the following:

- Capitalize on opportunities.
- Mitigate risks and downside events.
- Prepare for and weather storms, including economic cycles.

It is helpful to view agility as a three-part process as shown in Figure 10.6. First, do we have the *vision* to see a potential threat or opportunity? This is the most important component, since if a threat or an opportunity goes undetected, the organization cannot effectively respond. In addition, seeing the threat or opportunity at the earliest possible time extends the total time the enterprise can respond to the event. Second, the organization must be able to *recognize* that an event or circumstance represents a threat or an opportunity. Finally, the organization must have the ability to *respond*.

Can Your Organization Call an Audible?

One of the best examples of agility is found on the (American) football field. Prior to each play, the team huddles to call the next play. The plays were selected as part of a game plan (operating plan) that was tailored to address the specific competitor, accounting for strengths and weaknesses of

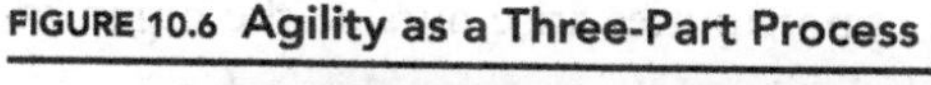
FIGURE 10.6 **Agility as a Three-Part Process**

both teams. After calling a play in the huddle, the team lines up to execute the play. As the quarterback comes to the line of scrimmage, he quickly surveys the opposing defensive personnel and formation to determine if the play he just called can be executed. If he decides that the play will not work, he can call an audible, changing the play called in the huddle to a different play that is more favorable to the defensive situation he observes. The ability to communicate this change to the team results in a different role or assignment for each player. This entire process takes only seconds.

Businesses and other organizations can learn a lot from this analogy (see Figure 10.7). Many of us look across the "field" and see very different circumstances from what we had expected when we "called the play." Unfortunately, we do not have the ability to call an audible!

Let's examine the skills and preparation that enable the "audible" on the football field using the vision-recognition-response framework, and extend these to the business environment.

Vision. When the quarterback comes to the line of scrimmage, he does so with tremendous vision. While his eyes likely possess greater-than-average capabilities such as clarity and peripheral vision, he has been trained to survey the whole field. He scans key matchups and assignments and accounts for so-called high-impact opponents. At first opportunity, he will review photographs taken to see the entire defensive alignment.

Businesses must also develop and improve their vision. FP&A and BPM play a large role in developing and improving the organization's vision. Play callers (executives) must have a view of how their internal processes, players, and projects are performing to ensure they are ready to execute. Do they have the right players on the team? Does everyone understand the plan and their respective roles?

Organizations also need to focus substantial attention on external forces. The vast majority of threats and opportunities arise outside the organization. Therefore, executives must have the ability to see what is happening in the economy, in their market, and to their competitors, as well as regulatory and geopolitical events. Extending the techniques and horsepower

FIGURE 10.7 Improving Agility

	Vision	Recognition	Response
Football	- Improve Vision - See the whole field - Review Film (real time views) - Account for impact opponents	- Experience - Study Game films - Scenario Planning - Operate at Game Speed	- Versatile athletes - Agility drills - Real time decisions - Half-time adjustments

Business	- External Focus:
	  - Customers and Competitors
	- Improve Vision:
	  - Business Intelligence
	  - Rolling Business Outlooks
	- Robust operating plans
		- Build experienced team with diversified experience
		- Training
		- Change Planning activity
		  - SWOT Analysis
		  - Competitor Intelligence
		  - Scenario Planning
		- Real time insights
		  - Dashboards
			- Acquire and develop agile associates
			- Develop Bench strength
			- Keep some powder dry (cash, borrowing capacity)
			- Anticipate and prepare for surprises
			- Radically change planning and monitoring processes
			- Scenario Planning
			- Flexible biz model

of financial analysis and performance management to external factors can significantly improve the vision of the enterprise. Chapter 11 explores the focus on the external environment and competitor analysis.

Capturing and presenting critical information are essential to improving the organization's vision. The use of rolling forecasts and outlooks facilitates the processing of new information and events and understanding the impact on the company's performance.

Recognition. The best vision in the world would not help the quarterback if he did not have the ability to recognize and evaluate what he was seeing on the field of play. This ability comes from both preparation and experience. The preparation includes long hours spent studying films of opponents in prior games. Coaches and players review the tendencies of the other team in certain situations. The team develops different actions under various what-if scenarios.

Similarly, in business we must be able to interpret what we see and hear and to understand the implications for our ability to execute our plans and achieve our objectives. A diversified and experienced executive team and board can increase the likelihood that events and patterns will be recognized and addressed. For example, an executive from another industry may recognize patterns from his or her experience that are new to this industry. Identifying potential surprises and considering various scenarios will improve the ability of the organization to recognize and respond.

Response. After seeing and recognizing changing circumstances, the team must have the ability to respond. One of the most important factors is having the right personnel. Since the team is not sure what it will encounter, a premium is placed on having highly versatile players who can play a variety of different roles as required. For example, a linebacker who can drop back in pass coverage or attack the line of scrimmage on a run play provides more flexibility than a specialist. The players are coached and trained and study the game plan. The hours of preparation allow the players to react at game speed. Teams practice both physical and mental agility. They practice and drill to ensure their ability to react quickly under many diverse situations.

Companies improve their ability to respond by acquiring and developing versatile (agile) associates who can be quickly redeployed to address issues and opportunities the company faces. How deep is the bench? Do we prepare for changing circumstances by anticipating potential future events and developing responsive actions? By developing planning processes that identify and evaluate critical assumptions and possible scenarios, the organization will be better able to respond to any change in circumstances. Maintaining a flexible business model and keeping some financial powder dry (cash and borrowing capacity) will facilitate developing and executing responses.

The Agile (Versatile) Associate

Since our associates are vital contributors to our overall success, it also holds that they play a huge role in enabling the organization's agility and flexibility. Agile associates are learners and are highly adaptable; they can be reassigned based on changing conditions and priorities. Characteristics of agile-versatile associates include:

- Continual learner
- Communicator
- Analytical individual
- Project manager
- Team player
- General business perspective
- Able to jump across silos to contribute
- A go-to person

Organizations can acquire or develop agile associates by employing the following practices:

- Identifying and evaluating key competencies when hiring
- Rotational assignments
- Training and development
- Promoting external activities and interests to broaden experience

Agility and Business and Economic Cycles

Nearly all businesses are subject to business and economic cycles (Figure 10.8). Business leaders must recognize that business downturns (and subsequent recoveries) are inevitable and must build an enterprise that can both thrive on upturns and survive on downturns:

- Develop business models that are successful across economic cycles.
- Utilize tools that provide a view forward, increasing the time to react.

In addition, all products, businesses, and markets are also impacted by a finite life cycle. New products or businesses are developed, grow, reach a peak at maturity, and then tend to decline. Successful companies are fully aware of this cycle and monitor product life cycle stages. The impact can be offset by developing and introducing new products as the older products reach maturity.

Many businesses fail to recognize that they are approaching the peak and heading toward slower or even negative growth. Signs that an organization is approaching the peak are:

- Growth rate slows.
- Revenue projections are missed.
- Product and gross margins decline.

FIGURE 10.8 Economic and Life Cycles

Economic Cycles Are Cyclical!
Products and Businesses Have a Life Cycle

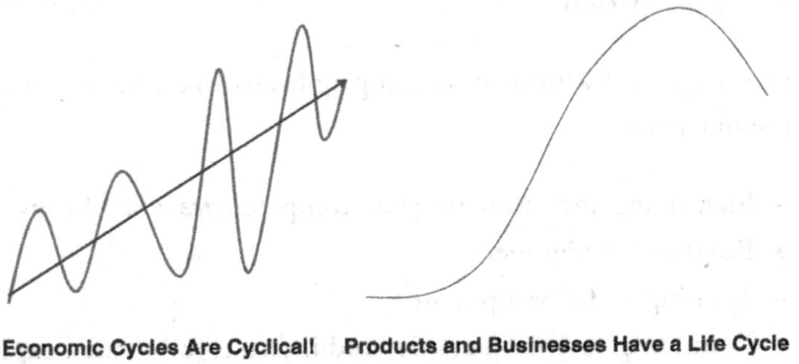

Ignoring these signposts and reality prevents the organization from revamping the business model to adjust for the road ahead or to accelerate the development of new businesses to refresh the growth curve. As a result, these organizations suffer from significant profit hits as sales decline. In addition, pressure mounts to develop an acquisition program to replace the lost organic revenue growth.

What can FP&A do to better prepare the organization for the impact of business and life cycle changes?

Provide Context. Many executives and especially founders have great difficulty in accepting that growth may be slowing. Preparing analyses that show growth curves for products and the entire business can help. Overlaying other well-known life cycle curves can provide further support for the alert.

Establish Signposts or Trigger Events. Predetermining KPI levels or events that clearly indicate that a kink in the curve is imminent can help to prevent denial and facilitate earlier responses.

Develop Cyclical Scenarios. As part of developing strategic plans, long-term forecasts, and even business outlooks, a business cycle or life cycle scenario should be prepared. This will introduce the possibility of a downturn into the thinking and allow the team to contemplate signposts and contingency efforts.

Develop Business Models and Practices Accordingly. Companies that are in cyclical industries should develop a flexible business model. Shifting selected expenses from fixed to variable will afford more flexibility and reduce the impact of the shortfall on profits. For companies approaching maturity, investment levels, costs, and expense levels can be adjusted for the road that lies ahead.

Dampen Irrational Exuberance during Peaks. Human beings tend to extrapolate the present conditions into the future. Include a historical perspective in planning and analytical products to remind executives that it is not if, but when, there may be a bump in the road.

Prepare for Recovery during Downturns. Companies that participate in cyclical industries should identify signal events and prepare plans to ramp up to capitalize on the recovery.

Agility Assessment and Metrics

Key performance indicators that provide a perspective on the level of agility within an organization include:

Percentage of Agile Employees. It is not necessary that all associates are versatile. However, it is important to establish a target level that will provide flexibility and to develop practices to move toward that level. The organization should set a clear definition of an "agile associate" incorporating characteristics from the previous list that are most relevant.

Associate Length of Service or Time in Position. Measuring the length of service and/or time in position can provide a view of versatility and agility. If a substantial number of associates have been locked in their present positions for long periods, it may indicate a lack of mobility or a need to increase rotational development assignments.

Breakeven Sales Level. This old-school measure is still very useful. It estimates the level of sales required to break even based on contribution margins and fixed versus variable costs. It is an indication of preparedness, by highlighting the extent that revenue can decrease before incurring losses. Measuring the level over time will track progress in bracing for downturns; a decrease in breakeven sales is a positive result of converting fixed costs to variable costs.

Planning Cycle. Companies should measure the length of time to generate the strategic and operating plan as well as business outlooks. A shorter cycle usually indicates a more efficient process that can lead to a timely response to any changing circumstance.

Manufacturing/Procurement Cycles. Shorter manufacturing and procurement cycles allow for greater flexibility in responding to change in demand.

FIGURE 10.9 Agility Dashboard

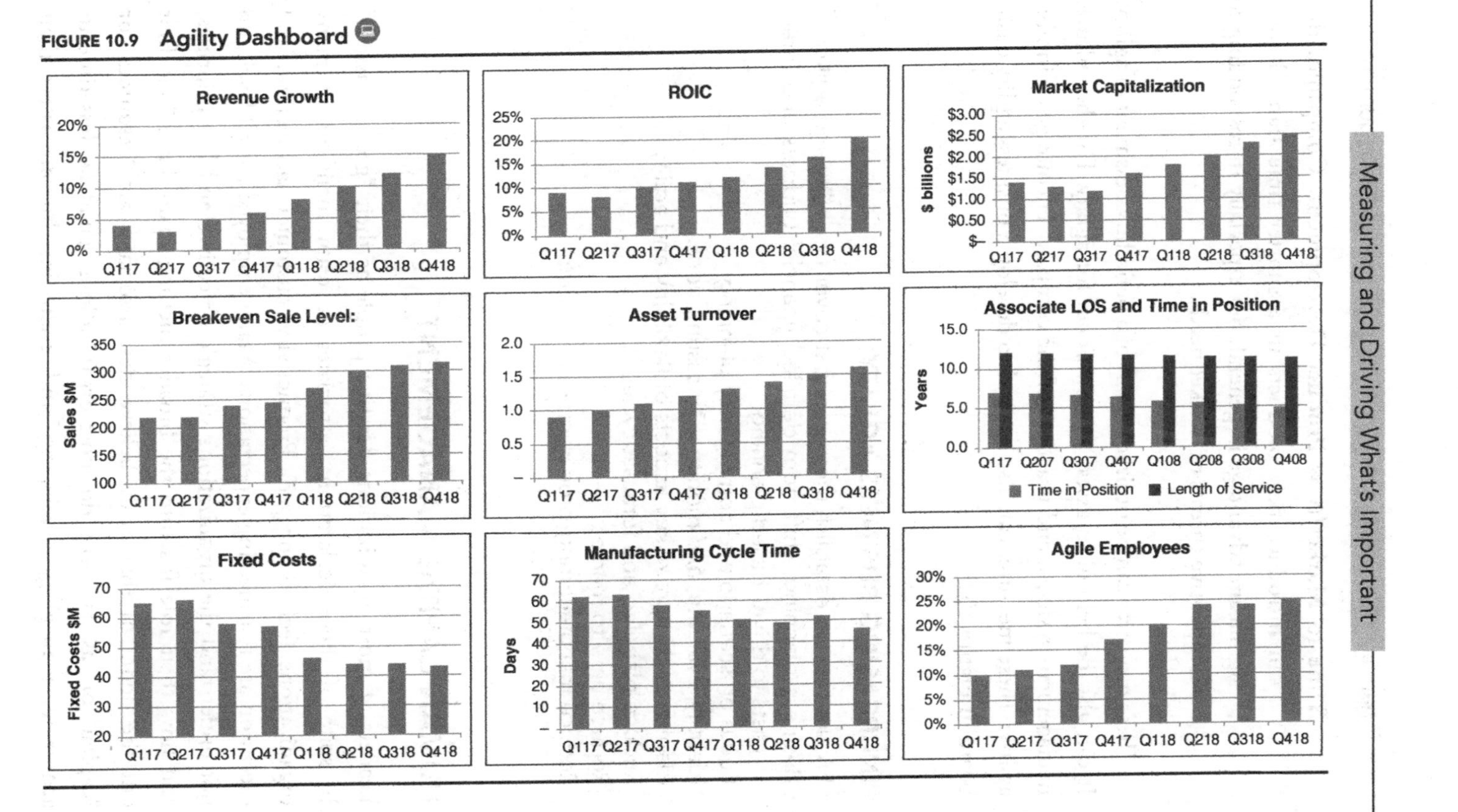

Time to Market/New Product Development. Companies that can introduce new products in a shorter time frame have a significant advantage in general, but especially in responding to competitive threats or market needs.

These measures can be utilized as part of a periodic assessment of agility. It can also be helpful to assess the *conditions* for agility. Do the culture, management systems, and practices of the company encourage or inhibit agility? These measures can also be used to develop a business agility dashboard in Figure 10.9.

INCREASING BUSINESS AGILITY

Ensure that we establish measures that cover flexibility and agility.
Business planning: shift from detailed financial budgets and forecasts to driver-based planning.
Focus on scenario and contingency planning.
Identify, evaluate, and monitor key assumptions.
Identify and improve key aspects of flexibility and agility.
Reduce planning and forecast cycles.
Reduce time to market.
Reduce manufacturing/procurement cycle time.

HUMAN CAPITAL MANAGEMENT

Leaders of most organizations describe people as their "greatest assets." In spite of these declarations, associates or team members of many organizations feel disengaged. Productivity, customer satisfaction, and execution are not meeting expectations. Many employees, at all levels, do not understand the organization's strategic objectives and key priorities, and how their role fits into the broader picture; many have "one foot out the door." If they truly believe that associates are "resources" or "capital" or "assets," why do most organizations spend far less time in acquiring, managing, developing, and evaluating human assets than they do other capital investments such as new products or programs, businesses, and equipment? How can they assess whether their human capital is appreciating (growing and developing) or depreciating? While it is often difficult to establish direct math relationships between human capital management (HCM) and financial results, it is worth the effort to develop useful, even if imperfect, measures of our most important asset.

There are two ways employees impact performance and value creation. First, *people costs*, defined broadly, are typically a major, if not the largest, cost in any organization. This fact is often not evident from examining most financial reports, budgets, and analysis. These tend to be prepared on a functional basis, rather than looking at cost drivers or natural expense codes such as total people costs (see natural expense analysis in Chapter 16). Second, with very few exceptions, it is our people who execute the strategy, develop products, deal with customers and suppliers, and deliver or manufacture the company's services or products. Finance and business analysts can partner with HCM to assess and identify improvement opportunities.

Total workforce costs are always a significant percentage of total costs. If an organization wants to be more productive, profitable, and successful, HCM must be more effective. Consider the investment made in a new hire in Table 10.2. In this case, the company is making an investment of more than $937,500, when considering recruiting fees, internal staff time spent recruiting and evaluating candidates, annual salary, fringe benefits,

TABLE 10.2 Investment in New Hire

Investment Description		Notes	Investment
Annual Salary	125,000	5 Year	625,000
Recruitment Fees	25%		31,250
Internal Recruiting Effort	20%	Interviews, Selection	25,000
Training and Learning Curve	33%	Assume 4 Month	41,250
Estimated Annual Bonus	10%		62,500
Benefits	24%		152,500
Total Investment 5 Year			937,500

annual bonus, and training and learning curve. This should get our attention on the importance of the recruitment and immersion process as well as engagement and satisfaction.

This analysis is a cost-based analysis. Assuming the position is of importance, there is a huge opportunity cost if the hire is not successful or does not add full value to the company. For example, if he or she was a hire critical to the development and introduction of a new product, the potential value could be substantially greater than the cost view.

Human capital impacts all value drivers (Figure 10.10). Satisfaction and engagement play a critical role in key performance drivers such as customer satisfaction, execution, productivity, and quality, just to name a few! We can all recall experiences as customers of an organization with a disaffected workforce. We can also contrast that with a highly engaged workforce. Is there any question that the customer experience is impacted by the level of engagement and satisfaction of associates?

FIGURE 10.10 Human Capital Impacts All Value Drivers

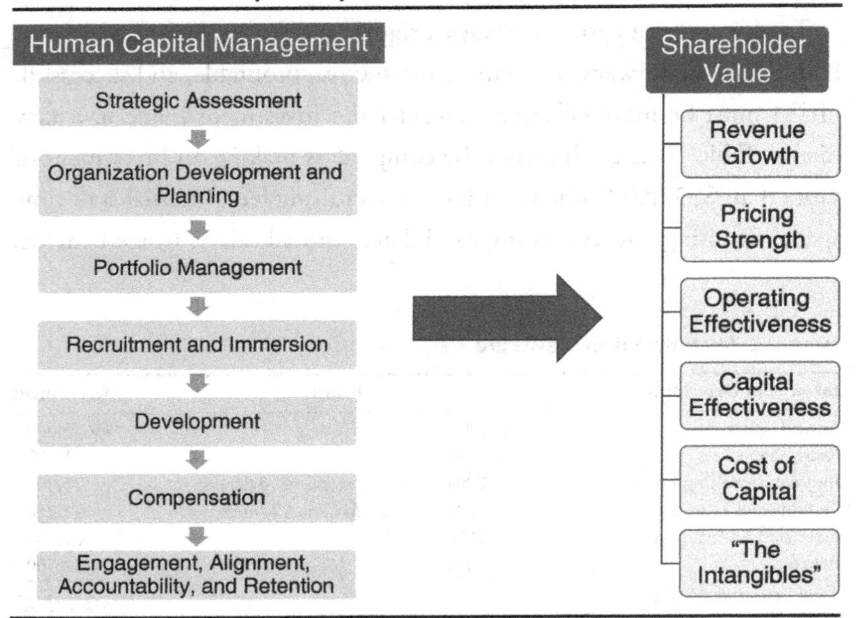

Critical HCM Processes and Activities

Strategic Planning

HCM must be an integral part of the strategic planning process.

- Can our existing team execute the plan?
- What additional resources and new competencies will be required to execute the plan?

Identify and address demographic changes and impact on costs, experience, and turnover.

Organization Development

If you buy into the "people are our greatest assets" view, then you must support efforts to build a solid organization and develop talent. Many successful organizations have formal processes to review and evaluate the organization structure, demographics, workforce characteristics, and talent acquisition and development.

Portfolio Management

If we do view associates as assets, can we borrow techniques from financial portfolio management to evaluate and improve our talent portfolio? We can develop various views of the workforce across key elements, including demographics, performance, aptitude for growth, agility, experience, and diversity. This analysis almost always identifies issues and opportunities in our portfolio of human resources.

Periodically, as part of the HCM portfolio assessment process (Figure 10.11) or the annual organization/development review, we should look at the workforce across several variables, including:

- Turnover: general, high potential, top quartile
- Age
- Length of service
- Time in position

FIGURE 10.11 HCM Portfolio Analysis

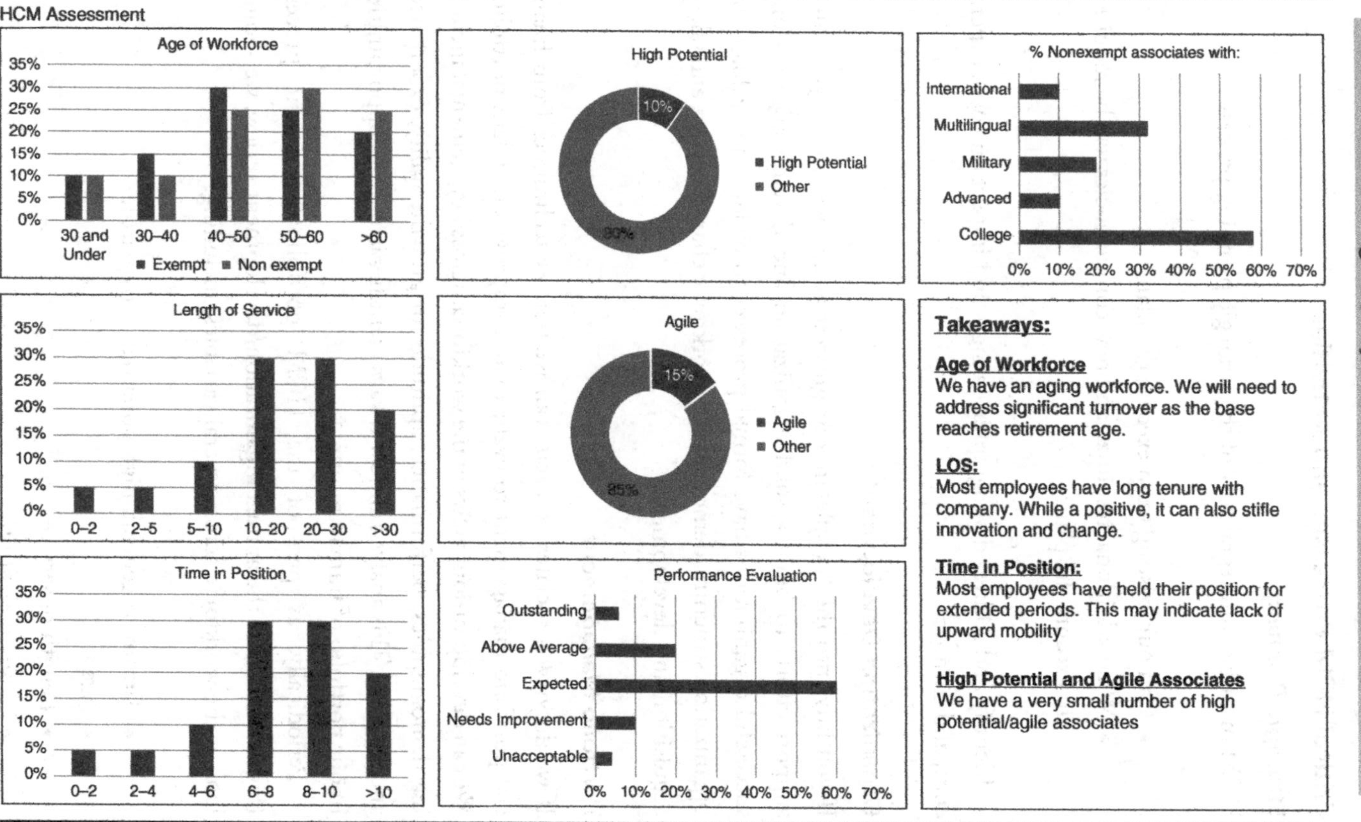

- Education
- Languages
- International experience
- Performance
- Aptitude for growth (high potential associates)
- Agility
- Experience
- Diversity

Recruitment and Immersion

Recruiting new talent is critical to the success of the organization. An effective process will define the position requirements and characteristics of an ideal candidate, effectively screen candidates, have a basis for predicting success, and effectively immerse or "onboard" the new associate to increase probability of a successful hire.

Engagement, Alignment, Evaluation, Accountability, and Retention

After effectively recruiting and onboarding associates, the organization must keep them engaged and ensure that their work is aligned with corporate objectives. It also must have effective methods for evaluating performance and holding associates accountable for responsibilities and achieving objectives. Finally, it needs to work to ensure that employees are satisfied and see future opportunities for growth in the organization.

Development and Training

Among the most important functions within HCM are the identification of development needs and providing effective programs to meet those needs. Development is much broader than training, and should include effective feedback, rotational assignments, mentoring, and other steps.

Compensation and Incentives

The development of compensation and incentive plans is extremely important in attracting, retaining, and motivating associates. These plans must be fully integrated with BPM in order to optimize effectiveness and ensure accountability for performance.

HCM Measures

A number of measures, analyses, and other tools can be utilized to evaluate and improve human capital. Some of these may be part of a continuous reporting process, whereas others may be utilized periodically, for example as part of an annual or quarterly review. Still others may be used on an ad hoc or when needed basis.

Human Resources (HR) Costs per Employee. How efficient is the HR department? What are the costs incurred in recruiting, providing benefits, employee development, and evaluating performance? How do these costs compare to those at other companies in the industry? To best practices companies?

Benefits per Employee. Employee benefits are a significant cost. Some of these costs, including health care premiums, have risen significantly in recent years. This measure is better than benefits as a percentage of payroll, since payroll can be skewed by the inclusion of highly compensated managers and executives. Note that reducing the cost of employee benefits by reducing *benefits* may have implications on retaining and attracting talent.

Headcount Analysis. People-related costs are typically a significant percentage of total costs. Tracking headcount levels is essential to cost management. Significant changes to the cost model will result from additions or deletions to headcount. Tracking headcount by department over time can provide significant insight into changes in costs. Some companies include the full-time equivalent (FTE) of part-time, temporary, or contract employees in the analysis to provide a comprehensive view and to prevent gaming the measure by using resources that might fall outside the employee definition. In addition, tracking open employment requisitions, new hires, and terminations provides a leading indicator of future cost levels. An example of a headcount analysis is presented in Table 10.3.

TABLE 10.3 Headcount Analysis

Department	Q416	Q117	Q217	Q317	Q417	Q118	Q218	Q318	Q418	Increase (Decrease) Q417-Q418
Operations										
Manufacturing	125	123	126	135	126	127	125	140	132	6
Quality Control	7	7	7	7	7	7	7	7	7	0
Inspection	3	3	3	3	3	3	3	3	3	0
Procurment	8	8	8	8	8	8	8	8	8	0
Other	9	9	9	9	9	9	9	9	9	0
Total	152	150	153	162	153	154	152	167	159	6
R&D										
Hardware Engineering	15	15	15	15	15	15	15	15	15	0
Software Engineering	17	17	17	17	17	19	23	25	30	13
Other	2	2	2	2	2	2	2	2	2	0
Total	34	34	34	34	34	36	40	42	47	13
SG&A										
Management	7	7	7	7	7	7	7	7	7	0
Sales	15	15	15	15	15	15	15	15	15	0
Finance	11	11	12	12	14	14	14	14	14	0
Human Resources	4	4	4	4	4	4	4	4	4	0
Total	37	37	38	38	40	40	40	40	40	0
Company Total	223	221	225	234	227	230	232	249	246	19
Increase (Decrease)		−2	4	9	−7	3	2	17	−3	

Open Requisitions	Number	Annual Cost (000's)
Operations	3	$ 150
R&D	6	750
Finance	1	95
Human Resources	1	75
Total	11	$1,070

Employee Engagement and Satisfaction Surveys. Employee surveys are typically done on a quarterly or annual basis. Occasionally, management may also want to take the pulse of the workforce after specific events, such as a change in leadership or a workforce reduction. Quantitative results can be very useful, especially when combined with commentary. Survey questions, frequency, and methods should be designed by professionals. Management must be committed to providing feedback and action, where appropriate, to associates, or the surveys can do more harm than good.

Effectiveness of Training and Development Programs. Development programs, including training, can lead to growth and improved performance. The programs must be thoughtfully chosen, and quality programs must be offered. It can be difficult to measure the effectiveness of training. Where possible, develop specific objectives for the training. For example, to improve customer service on help lines, this objective could be supported by measuring call wait times, customer survey results, and other specific measures. By putting a stake in the ground, the company can then measure improvements against that performance.

It is also useful to survey program participants and their superiors and clients. Did the participants learn from the session, and did it meet the stated objectives? Did clients and superiors see improved performance after the session? For example, after the FP&A team attended a session on presenting and communicating business information, did the clients of FP&A notice the difference?

Average Training Hours per Employee. This measure provides a good indicator of the level of training and learning within the organization. Since training needs may vary across the organization depending on the level and function of employees, this measure is often tracked separately for engineers, managers, technicians, and other groups.

Retention, Engagement, and Satisfaction

Employee Satisfaction. Many companies survey employee satisfaction annually or on a rotating basis. These surveys test overall satisfaction as well as specific areas such as compensation, perceived growth opportunities, communication, level of engagement, and management effectiveness. Another good way to take the pulse of employee satisfaction and underlying causes is for senior managers to meet with small groups of employees without other managers and supervisors present. Some companies refer to these as "skip-level" meetings, since several levels of managers may be skipped in the sessions. Employees are incredibly candid, especially when the process gains credibility by providing anonymity of comments and action on issues they raise. The effectiveness of surveys and skip-level meetings is highly dependent on how employees perceive management's commitment to address the findings. If the findings are not communicated to employees or acted upon, the process will lose employee participation and engagement.

Employee Turnover. Employee turnover can be very costly. There is significant time and cost incurred in recruiting, hiring, training, and terminating employees. Some level of turnover may be good. If employees are leaving for great opportunities, the turnover can be a reflection of a strong company that is developing talent. A variation of this measure is to split it between involuntary and voluntary turnover. What are the root causes of each? Is the turnover due to employee dissatisfaction, compensation levels, poor hiring practices, culture, or lack of growth? It is also important to look at the characteristics of those departing. Is the company losing high-potential and high-performing associates? What are the root causes?

Recruitment and Immersion

Time to Fill Open Positions. Since it is important to fill open positions in the shortest possible time, measuring the length of time to fill open positions is important. In keeping with balancing measures, it will be important to view this measure in the context of the overall effectiveness of recruitment. We wouldn't want to encourage hiring the wrong individuals faster!

Percentage of Openings Filled Internally. Some companies have a philosophy of promoting internally. Others prefer a mix of internal promotions and hiring from the outside. This measure captures the

FIGURE 10.12 Human Capital Management and Financial Performance

Human Capital
Engagement and Satisfaction
% of Employees "Highly Engaged"
Turnover
High Potential Turnover
Average Cost of Turnover
Training and Development
Training Hours per Employee
Training Effectiveness Score
% Training Courses w/Drivers Focus
Workforce Demographics
% High-Potential Associates
% Agile Associates
% Highly Employable Associates
Median LOS
Median Time in Position
Hiring Mix: Internal/External
Competency Analysis
Demographic Matrix

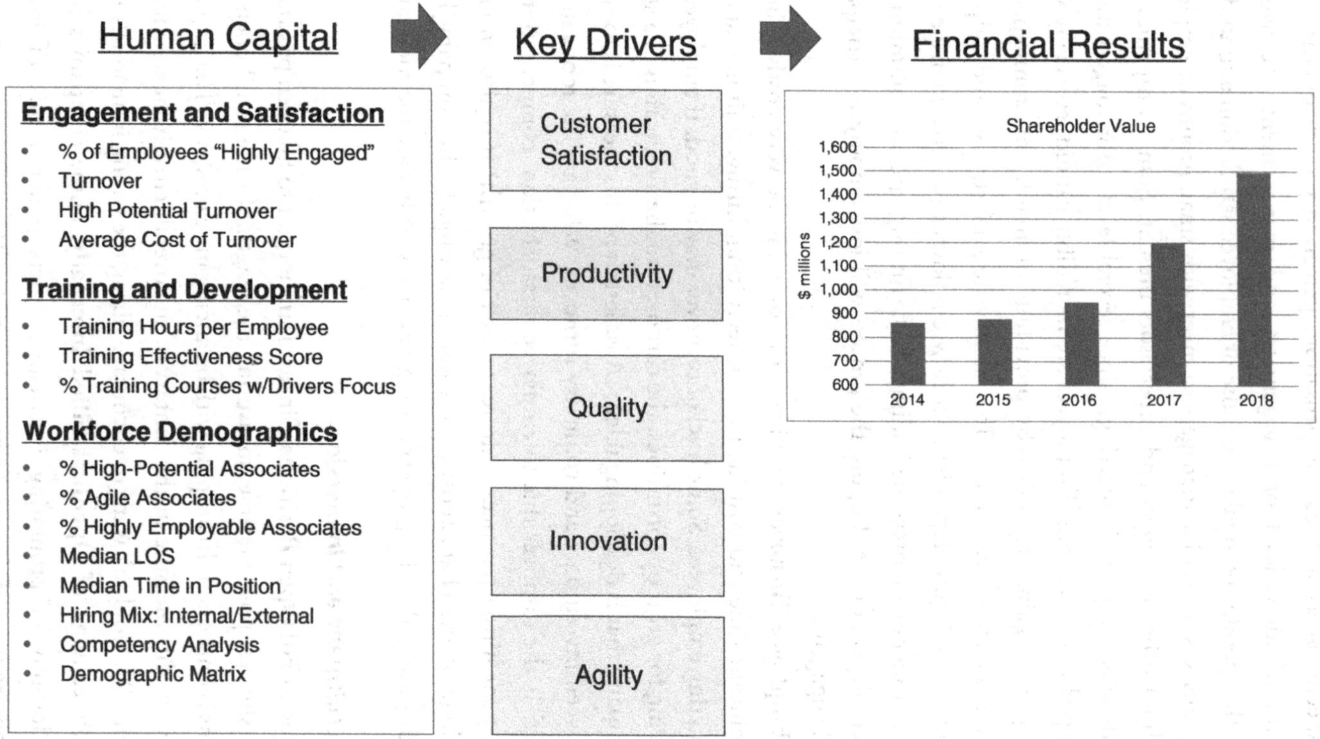

Key Drivers
Customer Satisfaction
Productivity
Quality
Innovation
Agility

Financial Results
Shareholder Value
$ millions
1,600
1,500
1,400
1,300
1,200
1,100
1,000
900
800
700
600
2014
2015
2016
2017
2018

FIGURE 10.13 HCM Dashboard

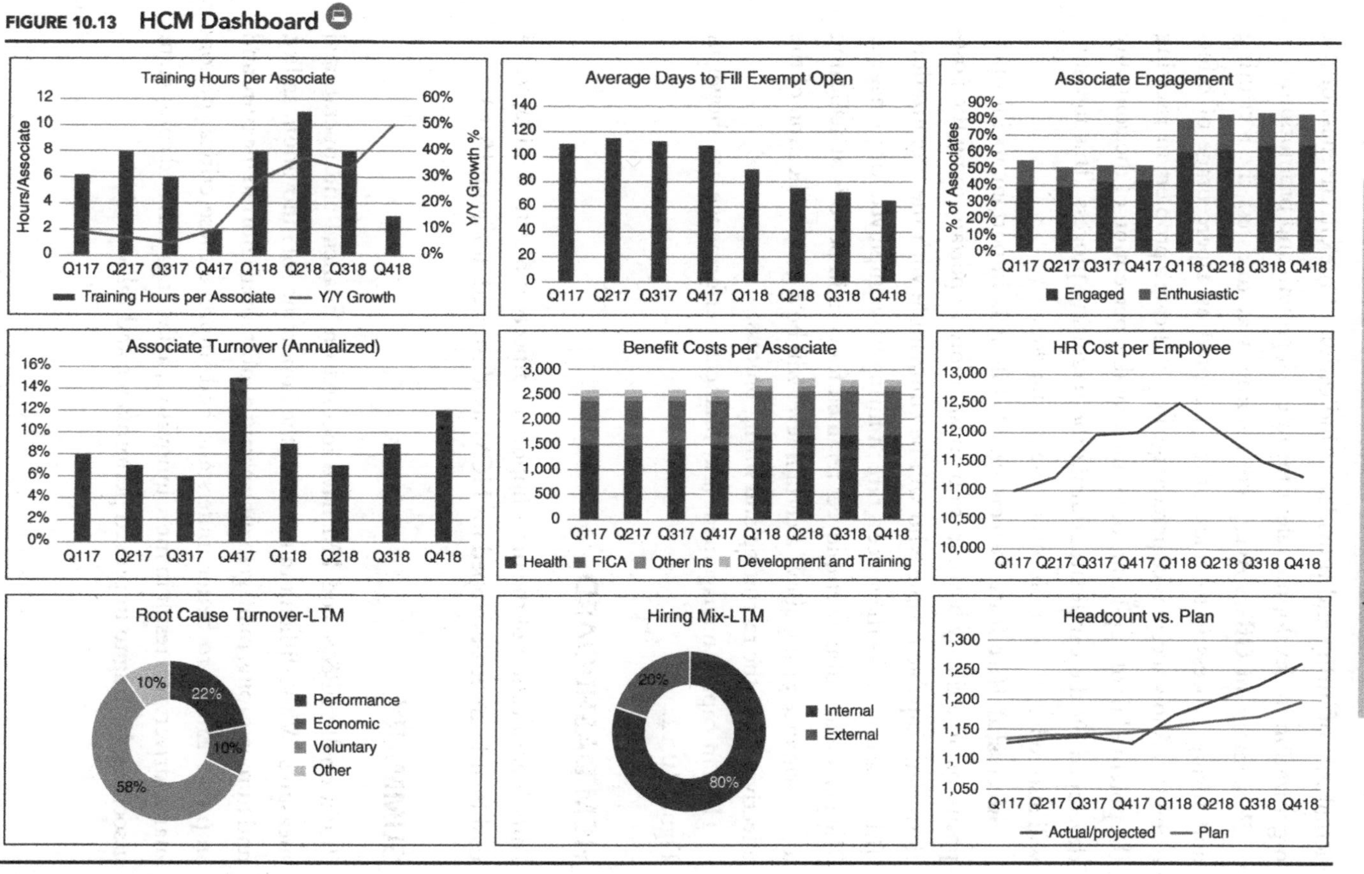

actual mix of hiring and provides an indication of the effectiveness of the organization in developing talent for internal growth and promotion.

Percentage of Offers Accepted. Another way to assess the recruiting and hiring process is to track offers accepted as a percentage of offers extended. A low acceptance percentage may indicate a problem in assessing the potential fit of applicants or an unfavorable perception of the company developed by the candidates during the recruiting process. This measure will also reflect the conditions in the job market.

Successful Hire Rate Percentage. While it is important to fill open positions on a timely basis, it is obviously more important to fill the positions with capable people who will be compatible with the organization. This measure tracks the success rate in hiring new employees or managers. The percentage of new employees retained for certain periods or achieving a performance rating above a certain level will be a good indication of the effectiveness of the recruiting and hiring process.

Human capital management and financial performance are shown in Figure 10.12.

HCM DASHBOARD

After identification of the most important aspects and critical initiatives, a dashboard can be developed for HCM as illustrated in Figure 10.13.

SUMMARY

Traditionally FP&A and PM have focused on financial and operational measures. While difficult to measure, the importance of innovation, agility, and human capital management warrant a substantial effort to measure and improve. Efforts to better understand and improve these critical performance drivers will result in more innovative, agile, engaged, and competent associates, leading to improved performance and value creation.

11

THE EXTERNAL VIEW

Benchmarking Performance and Competitive Analysis

CHAPTER INTRODUCTION

Most traditional efforts by FP&A professionals are directed at the internal aspects of the enterprise, including financial and operational performance. FP&A professionals can extend and expand the value they add by looking outside the enterprise. This chapter will focus on three broad subjects:

1. Analysis of markets, customers, and competition.
2. Using external information to benchmark and evaluate performance.
3. Utilizing benchmark information to set enterprise goals for performance and value creation.

ANALYSIS OF MARKETS, CUSTOMERS, AND COMPETITORS

Since most of the greatest threats and the greatest opportunities an organization faces arise externally, it stands to reason that FP&A resources should not focus all of their attention on the internal aspects of the organization.

Sources of Information

The digital age has resulted in a plethora of data that is readily available from multiple sources on the Internet. In fact, the challenge has shifted from the availability of data to evaluating and selecting the most credible and relevant information to utilize.

Industry Reports

Most markets are covered by industry analysts or trade groups that follow market trends and key events. These reports also often provide rankings by revenue growth or other financial performance measures and include news on product introductions and other important events.

Research Analyst Reports

Companies whose securities are traded on public exchanges (e.g. New York Stock Exchange or NASDAQ) are typically covered by analysts from large investment and brokerage firms. These reports range from puff pieces to very thorough reports that go well beyond basic financial analysis to include performance drivers, problems and opportunities, and a perspective on valuation. These reports can (and should) be an independent assessment of performance, and often include a comparison to competitors or overall market trends.

Company Website

Publicly traded companies (and certain private companies) disclose considerable information on their websites, including press releases, financial statements, executive profiles, product information, corporate governance, and other information. Most of the relevant financial information can be found in the investors section of the website.

Required Disclosures by Publicly Traded Companies

Securities laws mandate that publicly traded companies disclose substantial information to investors (and as a result, many others!). Much of this report is written by lawyers and accountants for other lawyers and accountants. As such, much of the meaning is lost on folks outside the legal and accounting professions. An FP&A professional who has experience in Securities and Exchange Commission (SEC) reporting can decode and interpret these reports.

Annual Report and Form 10-K. Areas of these reports that can be the most fertile sources for relevant information are the following:

- Business Description: This section can provide a useful perspective, including how the company defines its business and markets. It includes descriptions of the company's business strategy and of its products, intellectual property, marketing and promotion, and competitors.
- Management's Discussion and Analysis (MD&A): The MD&A is one of the most important disclosures in the Form 10-K. It is intended to be a review of the company's performance and financial condition through the eyes of management. Topics that must be addressed in the MD&A include:
  - Business overview
  - Results of operations
  - Review of current performance compared to prior years, addressing revenues, margins, expenses, and cash flow
  - Business combinations, acquisitions, and divestitures
  - Liquidity
- Footnotes: While most footnotes will bore people to tears, there are very important disclosures here, especially descriptions of business, financial overview, accounting policies, acquisitions, and contingencies.

- Risk Factors: Companies are required to disclose factors that may adversely impact financial results and the value of the company's shares.

Proxy Statement. The proxy statement includes information on management, directors, and compensation and incentive levels and programs.

Press Release/Form 8-K. Publicly traded companies must disclose material events and provide updates on previous guidance on earnings.

Supplemental Disclosures. Additional filings and disclosures are often required for special events or transactions, for example acquisitions requiring shareholder approval or financing. These would include detailed information on the strategic case supporting the transaction as well as the basis for valuing the acquisition.

Company Presentations to Investors. Companies that meet or present to shareholders are required to share that same information with all investors under the SEC's Regulation FD (Full Disclosure). These presentations are generally posted to the company's website.

Earnings Conference Calls. Most companies hold quarterly conference calls where senior executives review the last quarter's performance and discuss the business outlook for the future.

Analysis and Presentation

Much of the information from the sources just described would be too time-consuming to gather and too technical to be effectively utilized by executives and business unit managers. The analyst can consolidate and distill this information into useful analyses and reports. This information is useful in:

- Competitive intelligence for executives.
- A component of situational analysis for strategic and operational planning.

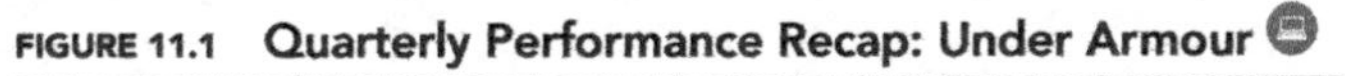

FIGURE 11.1 Quarterly Performance Recap: Under Armour

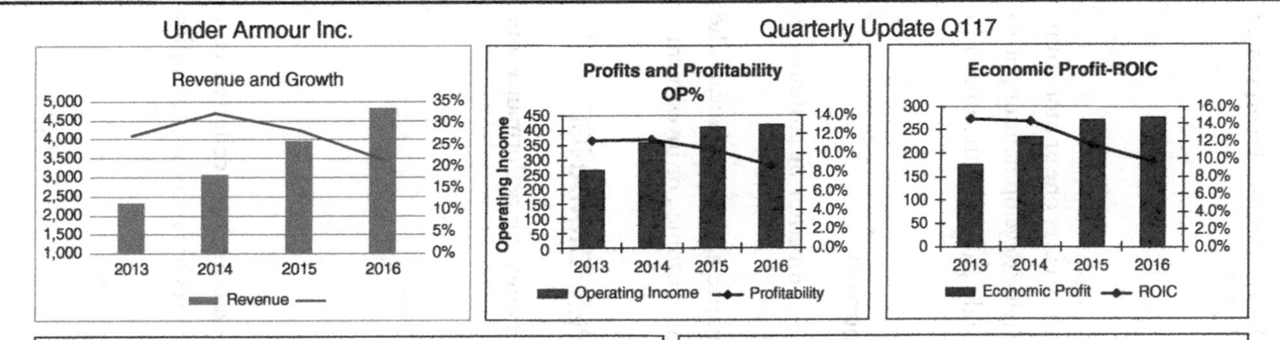

Company Description

Under Armour is a leading developer, marketer and distributor of branded apparel footwear and accessories. Products are sold worldwide and target athletes of all ages.

Business Segments

Apparel
Footwear
Accessories
Connected Fitness
Licensing

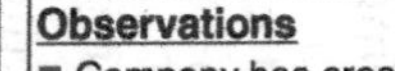

Observations

- Company has created a terrific brand
- Excellent marketing, including celebrity athletes
- North America represents approximately 83% of revenues
- Growth in apparel business has slowed
- UA has extended brand to Footwear and Connected Fitness, representing higher growth opportunities

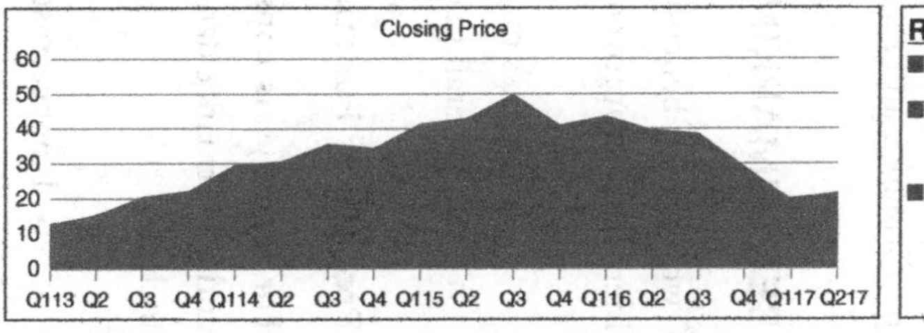

Recent Events

- After extended period of high growth, revenue miss Q4 2016
- Growth challenged due to disruption in North America retail environment
- CFO resigned January 2017, acting CFO appointed

Source: Compiled from company reports and SEC filings.

- A basis for evaluating strategic and operating plans by comparing competitor and customer trends to the assumptions incorporated into plans and forecasts.
- Quarterly updates for executives.
- Alerts for special events.

Some best practices companies assign analysts to cover one or more competitors or customers. This also represents a terrific development opportunity for analysts due to the perspective and insight gained by the analyst in this process.

Quarterly Update on Customer Competitor

A one-page quarterly performance recap for a competitor or customer is presented in Figure 11.1.

This recap is a very effective way to summarize and communicate the performance and recent events of a competitor, customer, or investment.

BENCHMARKING TO EVALUATE PERFORMANCE

Two types of benchmarking can be useful in evaluating performance and identifying improvement opportunities:

1. Process or functional benchmarks
2. Overall performance

Process or Functional Benchmarks

For many years consultants and trade organizations have collected cost and performance data on various business processes or functions. Examples include:

- Finance costs as a pertentage of sales
- Cost of processing an invoice
- Length of time to close books

- Duration of budget or plan cycle
- Product development – time to market
- Revenue process management
- Supply chain management
- Information technology

For example, these studies allow you to compare the cost of finance and key processes in your organization to the costs of companies included in the study. Most surveys emphasize the importance of using consistent definitions, since the scope of finance functions may vary from organization to organization. These surveys are very useful in identifying performance gaps and improvement opportunities, especially in transaction processing (e.g. payroll, accounts payable, and accounts receivable). They also should allow you to understand the mix of functions (e.g. transaction processing vs. FP&A) relative to average and best practices companies. The better benchmark surveys enable you to compare organizations of similar size and allow you to ascertain the reasons for gaps between your company's performance and the benchmark averages. In my experience, the most useful aspect of benchmark studies is the identification of best practices and trends. When utilizing benchmark surveys, select one that considers the overall effectiveness, not simply efficiency and cost.

Evaluating Overall Performance

In Chapter 3, we introduced the expanded view of the business model. The expanded view of the business model is a useful tool to benchmark performance across value drivers. We can compare performance on key elements such as revenue growth, margins, expense levels, and return on investment.

Many managers limit benchmarking to a peer group of similar companies or competitors. Their logic is that it is meaningful to compare performance only across companies in the same industry, so-called comparables. Companies in the same industry tend to adopt similar business practices.

In addition, their financial performance is shaped by the same market forces, since they typically would share common customers and suppliers. While benchmarking comparable companies is useful, it does not capture many of the potential benefits of a broader benchmarking process.

The potential for learning can be greatly expanded if the universe of companies in the benchmark is expanded, as shown in Figure 11.2. If you want to identify the best and the most innovative practices in supply chain management, do you want to study a competitor that has achieved a mediocre level of performance, or a best practices or wild card company like Apple or Amazon? While these companies may be in a very different business from yours, understanding the business practices that they have employed and the resultant impact on the business model is very enlightening and may lead to potential improvements for your business.

It is also helpful to look at the performance of key customers and companies in related or adjacent industries. A primary factor in a company's success will be the performance of key customers. How fast are

FIGURE 11.2 Expanded Benchmarking View

Assessing Performance: Expanded Benchmarking View

The value (learning) of benchmarking is far greater if the field is broader than "comparable companies."

they growing? Are they profitable? Are they cash strapped or cash flush? Comparing your company's performance to these companies on key metrics such as sales growth, operating costs, and capital requirements can be useful in evaluating your company's performance on a relative basis and in setting future performance targets. In addition, you may find it meaningful to contrast your business to other models. Understanding the different financial results in light of varying business practices may identify potential improvement opportunities as well as potential vulnerabilities. A comprehensive benchmark approach is illustrated in Table 11.1.

This one-page summary will allow managers to easily compare critical elements of their company's financial performance and valuation to those of competitors and customers as well as most admired and best practices companies. The summary was prepared using the sources identified in the beginning of the chapter and analyzed using the assessment model introduced in Chapter 2.

In the example in Table 11.1, let's assume we want to evaluate the performance and opportunities of RA Outdoor. The company is considering an aggressive growth strategy in the sports apparel market. We compared performance to two notable direct competitors, Nike and Under Armour. In addition, we included retailers that carry sports apparel, Dick's Sporting Goods and Cabela's. It is also worth including mass merchandisers such as Target and Walmart, since they also have a significant market share in sports apparel. These large retailers are worth studying since they employ best practices in merchandising and are impacted by the current turbulence in the traditional retail market. Also included are two wild card or most admired companies, Amazon and Apple. These companies have practices and track records that warrant our attention.

Even in this simple example, several takeaways are evident:

The traditional retail market is under siege, primarily from online companies such as Amazon. Brick-and-mortar participants have seen declining sales (or declining growth) and are forced to change the in-store experience as well as add online capability to complement the physical stores.

TABLE 11.1 Comprehensive Benchmark Analysis

	RA Outdoor	Nike	UA	Dick's	Cabela's	Sports Authority	Target	Amazon	Apple
Revenue	115.0	34,350.0	4,825.0	7,922.0	4,129.0	Closed	69,495.0	135,987.0	215,639.0
Revenue CAGR (3 Year Historical)	10.0%	7.3%	27.4%	8.4%	4.7%		−0.8%	22.2%	8.1%
Gross/Contribution Margin %	41.0%	44.6%	46.0%	30.0%	41.2%		30.0%	35.0%	39.0%
SG&A % Revenue	38.0%	31.0%	38.0%	24.0%	35.0%		23.0%	32.0%	7.0%
R&D % Revenue									5.0%
Operating Profit	3.5	4,749.0	418.0	450.0	274.0		4,969.0	4,186.0	60,024.0
Operating Profit % Revenue	3.0%	13.8%	8.7%	5.7%	6.6%		7.2%	3.1%	27.8%
EBITDA $	4.5	5,455.0	563.0	683.8	424.0		7,267.0	12,302.0	70,529.0
EBITDA %	3.9%	15.9%	11.7%	8.6%	10.3%		10.5%	9.0%	32.7%
Net Income	2.1	4,240	257	288	147		2,737	2,477	42,991
Net Income % Revenue	1.8%	12.3%	5.3%	3.6%	3.6%		3.9%	1.8%	19.9%

TABLE 11.1 *(Continued)*

	RA Outdoor	Nike	UA	Dick's	Cabela's	Sports Authority	Target	Amazon	Apple
Asset Utilization and Returns									
Days Sales Outstanding (DSO)	48.0	39.1	47.1	3.5	6.7		0.0	22.4	26.7
Days Sales Inventory (DSI)	167	96.9	129.5	107.6	129.4		62.1	47.4	5.9
Intangibles % Revenue	0.0%	1.2%	13.0%	4.9%	0.0%		0.0%	2.8%	4.0%
Asset Turnover	0.6	1.5	1.3	5.2	0.5		1.9	1.6	0.7
ROIC	1.5%	25.4%	9.7%	14.6%	7.3%		14.2%	9.8%	20.4%
Enterprise Value	98.0	70,000.0	7,230.0	3,030.0	8,330.0		32,000.0	455,490.0	834,490.0
Value Metrics:									
EV/Revenue	0.9	2.0	1.5	0.4	2.0		0.5	3.3	3.9
EV/EBITDA	21.8	12.8	12.8	4.4	19.6		4.4	37.0	11.8

One retail player, Sports Authority, didn't survive the current market challenges. Its successful stores and website were taken over by the remaining retailers, including Dick's.

The business models are similar across apparel companies and traditional retailers, including gross margins, SG&A levels, and working capital requirements (DSO and DSI). Similarly, there are patterns across most of the retailers. There are also differences in the performance of these companies that are worth exploring. For example, Nike maintains substantially lower inventories than Under Armour (96.9 DSI vs. 129.5).

The lines between apparel suppliers and retailers is blurring. Under Armour, Nike, and other suppliers sell directly to consumers in physical stores and online. Many retailers are developing private labels (store brands) to offset some of this trend.

Many of the successful subjects have extended their brands to related areas. For example, many apparel companies have added footwear and digital products, and are expanding to additional geographic markets. The Apple brand started in computers and extended to music, phones, watches, and other devices. Amazon started in books and now offers just about everything!

Brand is an important driver of growth and value. Even those who do not follow sports could recognize logos and products offered by Nike and Under Armour.

While this top-level benchmarking provides a view into the performance of all companies selected, it does not always provide detailed insight into the practices and drivers of the financial results. Without an understanding of the businesses practices and other factors, it provides limited benefit. For example, in the early 2000s, it was useful to observe that Dell turned computer inventory nearly 100 times per year. But just how did it do that? Are there best practices here that can be considered for use in your company?

The second and more meaningful method of benchmarking requires us to climb under the numbers to understand the practices and drivers of one firm's performance versus others'. This requires detailed knowledge of the market, business model, processes, and practices of the firm. For example, Dell's performance in inventory management is a result of creating a breakthrough business model with significant attention to managing the supply chain, assembly, order fulfillment, and distribution processes. Much has been written and published about best practices at Dell and other innovative companies. It is also possible to enhance insight by reviewing the disclosures in the company's reports and presentations. Many of these companies have also been open about sharing the methods they employed in achieving breakthrough performance in a particular area. In addition, many consulting firms have developed practices in this area or offer training courses in implementing best practices in various business processes. By comparing your performance to competitors' as well as best practices companies, it is possible to identify gaps in your performance that represent significant opportunities to increase shareholder value. Understanding the best practices that lead to extraordinary performance provides a road map to closing these performance gaps.

There are many different business models and combinations of value drivers that will lead to building long-term shareholder value. For example, some companies operate with very low operating margins, but earn respectable levels of return on invested capital (ROIC) based on effective utilization of assets. Others earn high margins but are very capital intensive. Companies that have built and sustained shareholder value over an extended time period have blended a mix of the two critical ingredients for value creation: revenue growth and ROIC.

Most Admired or Wild Card Benchmarks

Understanding the performance and shareholder value created by most admired or wild card companies can be inspiring and identify opportunities that a company can evaluate for their own use.

Apple has developed one of the most recognized brands and enjoys customer loyalty approaching cult-like obsession (Figure 11.3). It has developed a steady pipeline of revolutionary and evolutionary products. Apple has worked at developing a culture that fosters innovation.

FIGURE 11.3 Apple Performance Trends

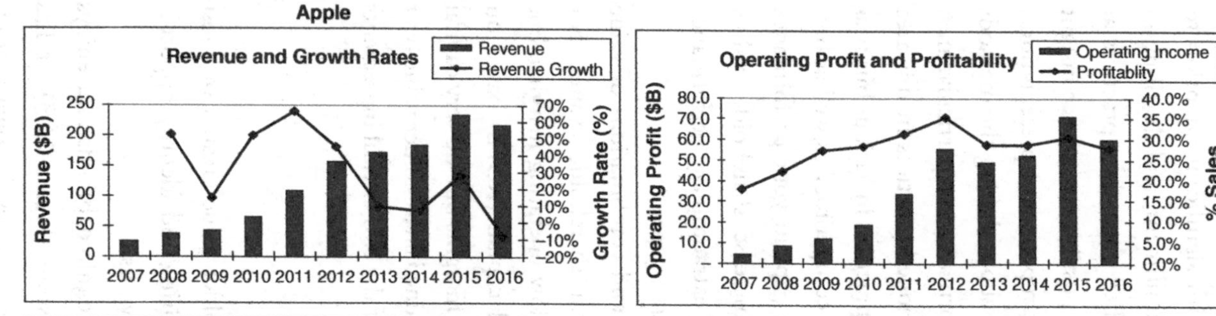

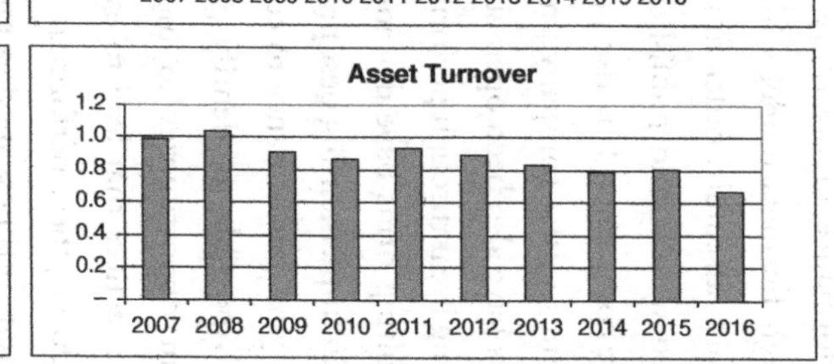

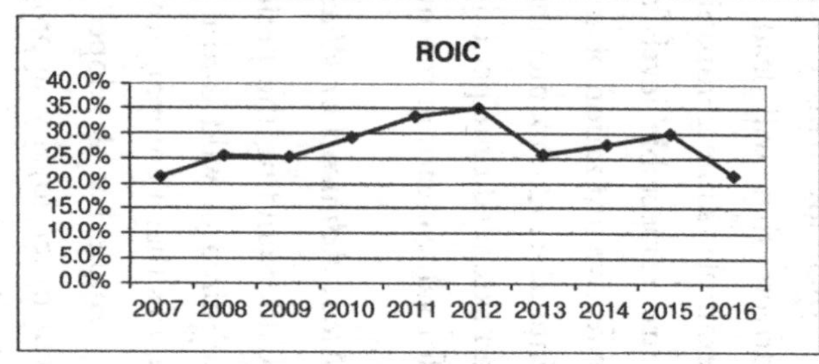

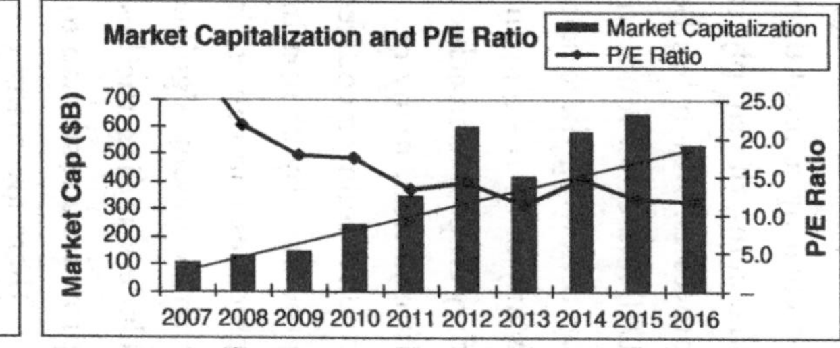

Source: Compiled from Annual and other company reports.

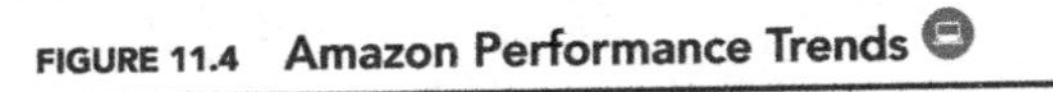

FIGURE 11.4 Amazon Performance Trends

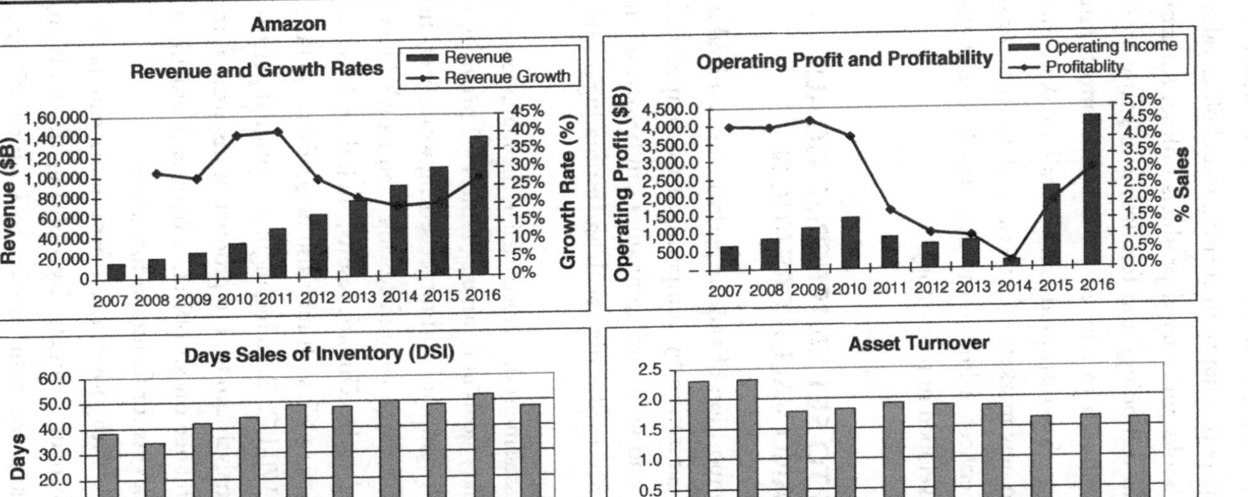

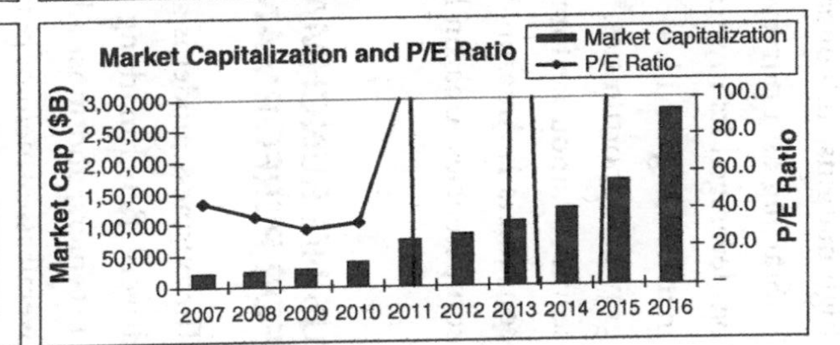

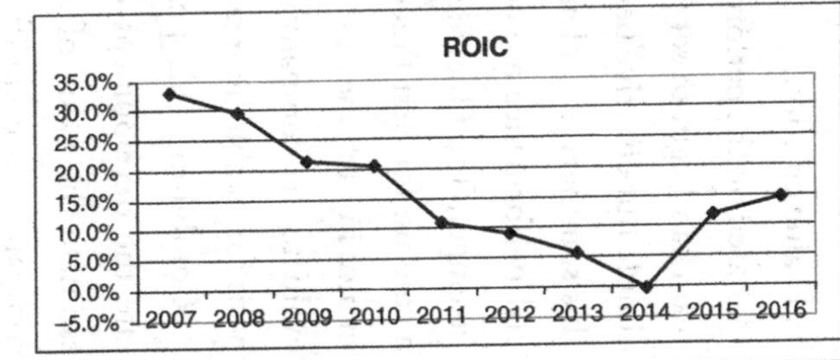

Source: Annual and other company reports.

The results are reflected in high sales growth over an extended period, very high margins, and outstanding performance in creating shareholder value.

Starting as a purveyor of books and related products online, Amazon has leveraged its investment in technology and fulfillment to many other markets (Figure 11.4). It has chosen to reinvest most profits into future growth opportunities. Amazon has disrupted many retail markets and seems to announce forays into new markets each week. Unknown to most consumers is Amazon Web Services, a line of business that leverages the competencies Amazon has developed in technology.

USING BENCHMARKS TO SET ENTERPRISE GOALS FOR PERFORMANCE AND VALUE CREATION

The business model is a decomposition of various performance and value drivers. Benchmarking the organization by comparing it to competitors, customers, and most admired and wild card companies can be part of an overall assessment of performance, establishing goals and estimating potential value creation.

Based on the performance assessment described earlier, the management team can begin to set preliminary goals and targets. Table 11.2 provides a simple but effective benchmark summary and target setting worksheet. In this summary, key elements of Roberts Manufacturing Company's financial performance are compared to benchmark results, including Median (average), Top Quartile, and Best in Class. It may also be useful to include a column for Best Practices or Wild Card, to highlight exceptional performance in each measure. This analysis can lead to productive discussions to evaluate the company's performance on an objective basis and provide a basis for establishing credible targets for future performance.

Combining this perspective with other assessment tools can facilitate the development of performance targets. By utilizing the tools to estimate the value of a company and value drivers in Chapter 22, the company can quantify the potential effect of achieving these targets on shareholder value.

TABLE 11.2 Benchmarking Summary and Target Worksheet

	Roberts Co.	Median	Top Quartile	Best in Class	Best Practice	Performance Target
Revenue Growth	8.0%	8.0%	12.0%	15.0%	25.0%	12.0%
Gross Margin %	55.0%	52.0%	56.0%	60.0%		56.0%
Operating Expenses	40.0%	40.0%	38.0%	35.0%		38.0%
Operating Margins	15.0%	12.0%	18.0%	20.0%	25.0%	18.0%
Tax rate	34.0%	30.0%	25.0%	15.0%	10.0%	25.0%
Operating Capital % Sales	30.0%	25.0%	15.0%	10.0%	15.0%	15.0%
WACC	11.99%	10.59%	10.13%	9.77%	9.07%	10%
Cost of Equity	12.4%	11.3%	11.0%	10.7%	9.8%	
Beta	1.24	1.05	1.00	0.95	0.80	
Debt to Total Capital						
Book	15.3%	30.0%	40.0%	50.0%	50.0%	
Market	5.3%	10.0%	13.3%	16.7%	16.7%	

SUMMARY

FP&A teams should extend their focus and attention to the enterprise's markets, customers, and competitors. Monitoring external events and trends is important because the greatest threats and opportunities arise outside the organization.

By monitoring and analyzing the performance of competitors and customers, analysts can provide insight into critical performance trends, events, and relative performance of those companies.

An external view is also a terrific way to evaluate the company's performance. Benchmarking is a very useful way to evaluate performance and to identify potential improvement opportunities.

Part Three

Business Projections and Plans

12

BUSINESS PROJECTIONS AND PLANS

Introduction and Best Practices

CHAPTER INTRODUCTION

The most challenging aspect of financial planning and analysis (FP&A) centers on the need to develop and evaluate projections of future financial performance. Almost every important managerial decision requires some estimation of future financial results. Owing to the dynamic nature of the world in which we now operate, the task of predicting future performance has become very challenging. Many finance teams have stepped up to this challenge and made significant changes to planning, budgeting, and forecasting processes over the past 25 years. In this chapter, we will provide an overview of financial projections. Succeeding chapters will cover planning and budgeting, forecasts and outlooks, and long-term financial projections. Planning and estimating specific areas, such as revenues and gross margins, operating expenses, and working capital are covered in Part Four, Planning and Analysis for Critical Business and Value Drivers.

OVERVIEW OF BUSINESS PLANNING AND PROJECTIONS

Historical Perspective

Budgets, in some form, were originally used by the British Empire and other governments hundreds of years ago. They were in common use by commercial enterprises in the late nineteenth century. Budgeting became very popular in the twentieth century and was adopted as a key part of managing the business by most companies and organizations. Incremental improvements were made to the process, and significant gains in information technology facilitated preparation.

Typically, the organization would prepare a budget once each year, several months before the new fiscal year began. For example, the budget for 1954 would likely have been prepared in the fall of 1953. This process served most businesses well during this time. Revenues were relatively stable and predictable. Costs and expenses were, for the most part, easily controlled and estimated on a detail basis. The pace of change and innovation was far slower than recent experience. The process typically included four steps, as illustrated in Figure 12.1.

Evolution of Financial Projections

Over time, deficiencies in the annual budget process were recognized. As a result of economic, political, technological, and global developments, the pace of change increased, often resulting in the budget being obsolete or at

FIGURE 12.1 Historical Budget and Control Process

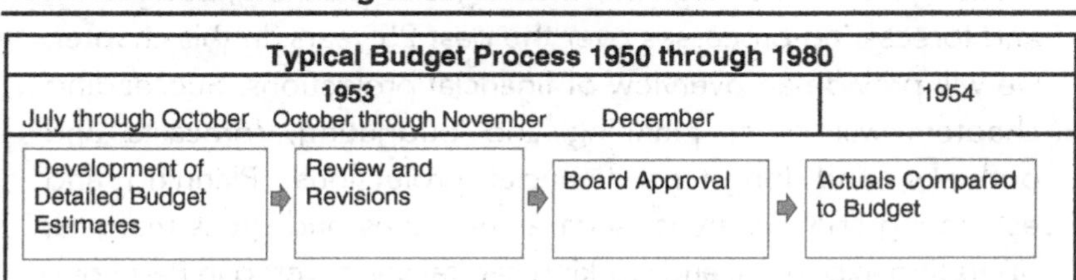

least dated soon after it was prepared. Many organizations began updating the budget or reforecasting the expected performance several times each year. In addition, pressure from the capital markets for updated forecasts of earnings (and severe and disproportionate reactions to missed forecasts) drove many finance teams to update and monitor projections frequently. Organizations began preparing strategic plans, which required the ability to produce estimates of financial performance over an extended time period.

Actual Results Often Fall Short

Actual results often vary significantly from plans and forecasts. Most variances represent *shortfalls* from projected results. There are several causes of this bias. First, most humans, and particularly managers, are inherently optimistic. Second, many plans or projections are incorrectly prepared as goals rather than probable outcomes. Third, less attention is paid to identifying and managing potential risks and downsides to the plan. This phenomenon is particularly evident in long-term projections, due to the long period between developing the projections and the day of reckoning. This makes it difficult to hold managers accountable for long-term projections, even if they are still in the chair several years later.

Improved practices in planning and developing projections as well as improvements in performance management can significantly improve the effectiveness of planning. Specifically, identifying and testing critical assumptions, identifying risks and upside events, and developing scenarios will greatly improve the effectiveness of developing projections. In addition to the general practices and techniques advocated in these chapters, the optimistic bias of plans can be countered with stated guidelines, development of multiple scenarios, focus on execution and accountability, and measuring forecast variances.

Types of Financial Projections

Financial projections are utilized in a multitude of applications in managing and optimizing performance. Because of this wide usage, it is important to hone projection skills within an enterprise. This can be facilitated by adopting best practices detailed later in this and succeeding chapters. A few of the most common FP&A and management uses of projections are identified next.

Budgeting

Budgeting continues to be employed by many organizations. In some cases, detailed budgets are required by customers or for statutory purposes. Some organizations continue to significantly reduce or even eliminate the detailed budget process by developing rolling forecasts or on-demand business outlooks (DBOs). Some continue to prepare budgets, but have implemented changes to the process to address deficiencies. Budgeting will be more fully explored in Chapter 13.

Annual Operating Plan

I define the annual operating plan as a broader and evolved form of the budget. The term *budget* typically has negative connotations and is viewed as a financial drill without substantive value to many other functions in the enterprise. Labels are important, and shifting the focus from financial projections to the development of a game plan for the organization can be significant.

As a game plan, the organization must develop a framework to operate the business in the coming year. The financial projections for the coming year are an important element of the operating plan and are a primary way to measure actual results of the operating plan. Operating plans will also be addressed in Chapter 13.

Forecast or Business Outlook

Due to the rate of change experienced in the late twentieth and early twenty-first centuries, the need for frequent updates to the budget or operating plan became necessary. Early efforts involved replicating much of the annual process more frequently or, alternatively, preparing high-level estimates of financial performance. Neither is a very good solution.

In recent years the rolling forecast (or on-demand business outlook, as I like to call it) has become an important part of the overall management process. It represents a more effective and efficient means to develop and update projections by focusing on *important* drivers and assumptions. Forecasts and business outlooks will be covered in Chapter 13.

Long-Range Projections

Long-range projections are required to evaluate investment and business decisions, acquisitions of businesses, and the evaluation of strategic plans and alternatives. Depending on the objective, these projections will have a horizon of two to seven or more years. Occasionally, for projects with long investment and life cycles, the horizon may be extended to 20 years or longer. We will explore long-range projections in Chapter 14.

Capital Investment Decisions (CIDs)

Projections are required to evaluate the economic case of investing in equipment, product development, new business, and business acquisitions. The projections are of vital importance in these capital investment decisions (CIDs) because they are the basis for determining if the project will create value for shareholders. Additional techniques for evaluating projections as part of CIDs and integrating them with decision criteria are covered in Chapters 20 and 21.

Special Purpose Projections

Projections are implicit in nearly all business decisions. Decisions such as lease versus buy, produce in-house versus outsource, and many others are based on expectations of future revenues, costs, and capital requirements.

Tools, techniques, and best practices for projecting revenue, working capital, other assets, and cash flow are covered in detail in Part Four.

BEST PRACTICES IN PROJECTING FUTURE FINANCIAL RESULTS

Whether predicting financial performance for the next quarter or the next 20 years, there are several considerations and best practices that should be employed in most projections.

The projections used in estimating value, evaluating a capital project, and evaluating financing alternatives will be a significant input to the decision-making process. There are a few concepts and elements that apply across all financial projections.

Projections Are Not a Finance Exercise!

While the finance team is typically the facilitator and process owner, it is important that all projections reflect the best estimate of the manager, executive, or team responsible for achieving them. Unfortunately, in many organizations, the ownership of the projections is often transferred to finance. Operating managers must be fully engaged in developing projections, including assumptions, estimates, decisions, risks, and upsides, and the execution plan to achieve the results. The executives with overall responsibility for achieving the results should also formally approve the final plan. Labels are also important! Changing "Forecast" to "Business Outlook" or "Budget" to "Operating Plan" can help to shift the perception of these exercises from financial to operational.

Trend Analysis and Extrapolation

Most financial projections for established businesses contain some element of extrapolation – that is, basing the projections on recent financial performance trends. We could start with recent financial statements and extrapolate financial trends into the future. Recent sales growth rates can be extended into the future. We could assume gross margins, expenses, and asset levels maintain a constant percentage of sales. This method is reasonable in very stable environments, which are increasingly becoming the exception rather than the rule.

This is generally not the best way to project financial performance. Most businesses are dynamic, and key variables will change over time. However, it may provide a useful view in serving as one potential scenario – that is, assuming that recent trends will continue into the future. This can be very useful in cases where other scenarios appear optimistic relative to historical performance. Extrapolation can also be used for certain areas that are stable or unlikely to vary over time.

Strike Balance between Bottom-Up and Top-Down

The traditional budget process started at the lowest level of revenue, costs and expenses. My first exposure to a budget process in the early 1980s highlights many of the pitfalls with this approach. The entire organization, which was very profitable but slow growing, embarked on the process with little direction. The result was a huge effort, spanning six weeks and involving hundreds of work hours across the organization. When the results were processed and tabulated, we presented a projection that included a 40% increase in staffing, 30% increase in other expenses and a tripling of capital expenditures, turning a profitable business unit into a substantial loss. Since the management team had not developed a game plan or macro view of expected performance, department managers submitted wish lists of investments, staffing, and expenses. There were five iterations of this bottom-up detail process spanning a total of four months before it approached a reasonable plan.

Other organizations operate at the other end of this spectrum, essentially dictating performance expectations for the coming year from the top. They may or may not consider fundamental drivers, changes, risks, and upsides in this process.

The best solution in my experience is a combination of realistic guidelines, boundaries, and targets in the form of planning guidelines.

Of course, managers should always be encouraged to present additional opportunities and risks. If the organization is effectively using rolling forecasts or DBOs, the process is more efficient and effective, since a view into next year's performance is already on the table.

Go Beyond the Numbers

For most significant decisions, managers should prepare well-thought-out financial projections. A well-developed planning process will have less detail than the bottom-up approach and will focus attention on the most critical drivers of performance. In addition to historical performance and trends, the projections should consider the impact of several factors, including:

- Strategic objectives
- Actions and potential actions of customers and competitors
- Anticipated changes in prices, costs, and expense levels
- Investments required to achieve the strategic objectives
- Economic variables

Managers must carefully address several questions in order to estimate future performance on key value drivers. We will discuss key financial inputs to each value driver in Part Four. A few examples are provided here.

Revenue

- How fast is the market growing?
- Is our market share expected to increase or decrease? Why?
- Will we be able to increase prices?
- What new products will be introduced (by our company and competitors)?
- What products will post declining sales due to product life cycles or competitive product introductions?
- What general economic assumptions are contemplated in the plan?

Costs and Expenses

- What is the general rate of inflation?
- What will happen to significant costs such as key raw materials, labor, and related expenses such as employee health care?
- What increases to headcount will be required to execute the plan?
- What operating efficiencies and cost reductions can be achieved?

Asset and Investment Levels

- What level of receivables and inventories will be required in the future?
- Will we need to increase capacity to achieve the planned sales levels?

Financing and Cost of Capital

- Will we need additional financial resources to execute the plan?
- Do we plan to change the mix of debt and equity in the capital structure?
- Is our business profile becoming more risky or less risky?
- What is likely to happen to interest rates over the plan horizon?

Identify and Test Assumptions

Developing projections of any type requires the use of assumptions. Critical assumptions should be identified, evaluated, and "flexed" to determine a range of potential outcomes and sensitivity. Managers should test the sensitivity of the projections and the decision criteria to each critical assumption. Once identified, these critical assumptions can be closely monitored as leading indicators of the firm's ability to achieve the plan.

Link to Performance Management

Most projections are presented and evaluated through a financial lens with a focus on outcomes. Cost center reports, profit and loss statements, and working capital and cash flow projections are all financial tools and reports that are based on expected performance of people, processes, projects, and other activities. With the possible exception of a few acceptable areas, you cannot directly manage financial outcomes; you can only manage people processes and activities that result in those outcomes. Many organizations utilize key performance indicators (KPIs) and dashboards as part of an overall performance management framework. By integrating these KPIs into the planning process, we directly link the financial results to business processes and activities.

A simple example is the projection of accounts receivable. Many organizations plan the receivables level based on past days sales outstanding (DSO) levels. However, receivables balances and DSO are the financial result of several important drivers, including:

- Credit terms and creditworthiness
- Timing and pattern of revenues
- Product and revenue process quality
- Customer service, problem resolution, and collection activities

It is far more effective to model future receivables levels based on these drivers and assumptions. Any projected improvements in DSO will be based on achieving improved performance on these drivers. These activities are leading indicators of future receivables levels and DSOs. They can be monitored against plan assumptions to ascertain that the projected outcome is likely or that some management intervention is required.

Evaluating Financial Projections (Note: Nearly All Projections Are Wrong!)

It is important to recognize that it is difficult to predict the future and that all projections incorporate a large number of assumptions. Therefore, nearly all projections of performance will be incorrect. However, there are several things that managers can do to improve the financial projections, their understanding of the dynamics affecting future performance, and the probability of achieving planned results. Multiple scenario and sensitivity analyses of financial projections will provide an understanding of how the key decision variables will be impacted under various scenarios and assumptions.

Another useful way to evaluate projections is to simply compare them to recent performance trends. For long-term projections, it is always useful to compare projected results to an extrapolation of recent history. This is not to say that future performance cannot depart from historical trends, but it clearly presents the issue and would lead to identifying and reviewing the factors that would lead to the projected reversal. In the example provided in Figure 12.2, a slow decline in revenues is projected to reverse in the future. Notice how effectively the graph presents this comparison compared to the table. Evaluation of this forecast should focus on the factors that will lead to this sudden and dramatic change in performance. If we don't soon change our direction, we will wind up where we are headed!

Short-term projections can be compared to recent trends and against last year's results. In Figure 12.3, we compare the weekly run rate of revenues year to date (YTD) to last year (YTD-LY) and to the plan (YTD-Plan), and compare the rest of year forecast (ROY) to last year (ROY-LY) and to the plan (ROY-Plan). This year's run rate of sales is slightly below last year's, but the forecast projects a significant increase

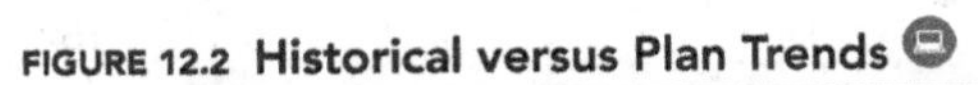

FIGURE 12.2 Historical versus Plan Trends

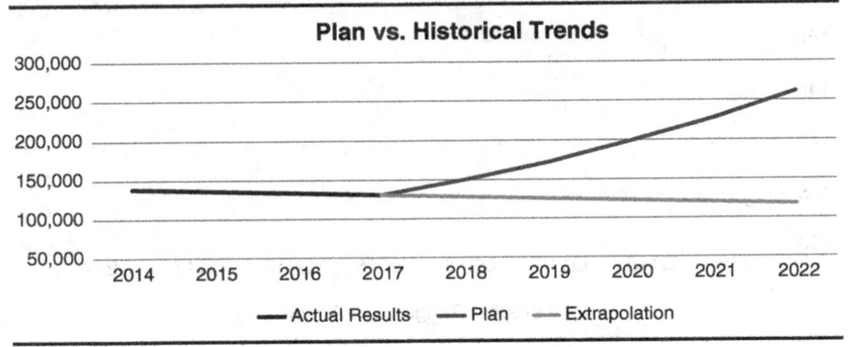

FIGURE 12.3 **Sales Run-Rate Analysis**

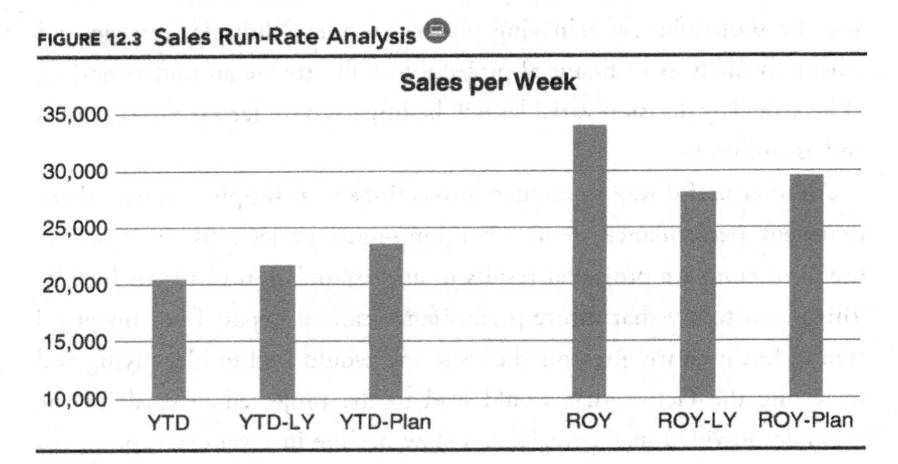

over the same period last year and the plan. Again, what are the specific drivers that support the dramatic change from the past?

Another useful tool to evaluate forecast performance is to track actual performance against forecast amounts. Figure 12.4 shows the actual revenue level achieved compared to the forecast range for recent quarters.

FIGURE 12.4 **Actual Revenue versus Forecast Range**

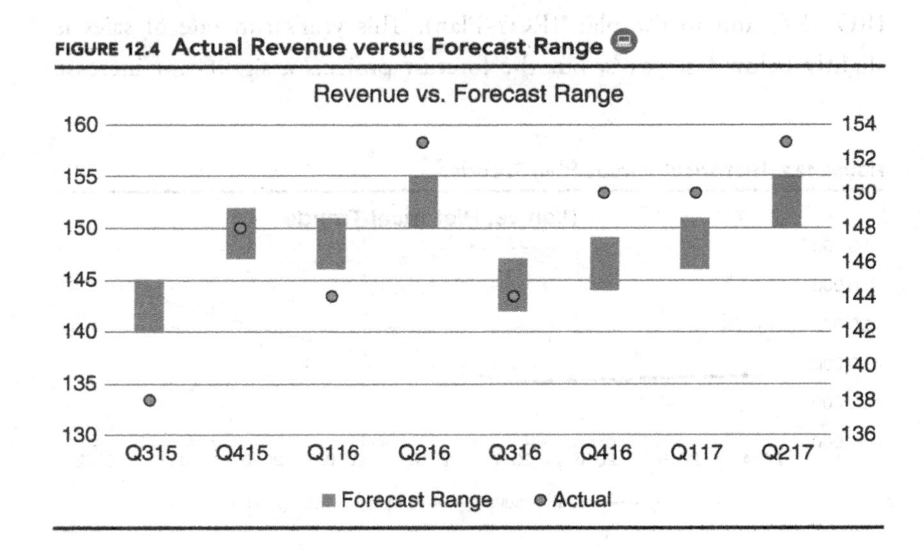

Identify Assumptions, Risks, and Upsides to the Projection

Unless otherwise intended, managers should set the expectation that a projection should be the best estimate of the outcome under the present strategy and expected market and economic conditions. Some organizations clarify this expectation by using language such as "most probable" or establishing desired confidence levels. This base plan includes numerous assumptions, including the probability and estimated impact of potential events. It is useful to identify and present how these potential events have been reflected in the plan. For example, if the plan assumes a continued favorable economic expansion, then a potential downside would be an economic recession. Other downside events may include competitive threats or loss of a major customer or contract. A summary of upside and downside events is presented in Table 12.1.

In addition, to assess the potential impact on the financial projections, this analysis allows management to monitor these potential factors and to develop preliminary contingency and response plans.

The summary presented in Table 12.1 raises several concerns. First, the absolute value of downside risks is two times greater than potential upsides. Second, the probability of two downside events is quite high, 50% and 60%. This suggests the plan is unbalanced, with greater downside exposure than upside. Since two of the downside risks have at least 50% probability, these risks should be further evaluated and perhaps incorporated into the base plan.

Scenario and Sensitivity Analysis

Multiple scenario and sensitivity analyses provide context and insight into the dynamics of expected performance.

Sensitivity Analysis. This technique determines the sensitivity of an outcome (e.g. profit projection) to changes in key assumptions used in a base or primary case. Any projection or estimated value must be viewed as an estimate based on many inherent assumptions. Sensitivity analysis is very useful to understand the dynamics of a projection or decision and to

TABLE 12.1 Upside and Downside Event Summary

$M						
Event Desciption	**Leading Indicators**	**Event Criteria**	**Potential Impact on Projections(PAT)**	**Probability This Plan Horizon**	**Probability Weighting**	**Management Action**
Upsides (U)						
Project XYZ Extension	Customer intiates extension	Extension signed	1.2	20%	0.24	(1) Monitor (2) Revise/extend termination plan'
Contract Win Tonk Corp	Selected as Finalist	Award	5	10%	0.5	
Total Upsides			6.2		0.74	
Downsides (D)						
Loss of Donaldson Contract	Feedback on Proposal	Award Notification	−5.2	60%	−3.12	(1) Monitor (2) Develop Contingency Plan
Recession	CPI	Backlog down 10%	−3.2	50%	−1.6	(1) Monitor and develop contingency plan
	Backlog					
Product Licensing Lawsuit			−4.2	20%	−0.84	(1) Monitor, consider appeal (2) Develop plan for technology alternative
Total Downside Events			−12.6		−5.56	
Total all U and D Events			−6.4		−4.82	

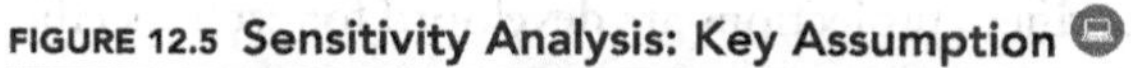

FIGURE 12.5 Sensitivity Analysis: Key Assumption

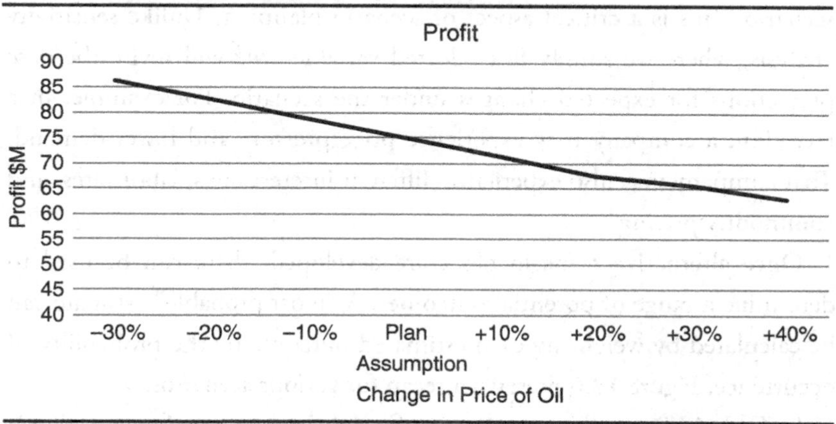

highlight the importance of testing assumptions. For example, Figure 12.5 presents the estimated sensitivity of a company's profit projection to changes in a key assumption, the price of fuel.

Scenario Analysis. While a sensitivity analysis provides insight into the importance of one variable, a scenario analysis contemplates the effect of an event or change in circumstances. The scenario will typically require reevaluation of several different variables in the plan. For critical projections including plans, it is essential to run several different versions of financial projections; for example:

- Base Case: This is the most likely outcome.
- Extrapolation of Recent Performance: Provides a reference point to evaluate other scenarios.
- Conservative Scenario: A scenario reflecting lower expectations or downsides.
- Upside or Stretch Scenario: A scenario reflecting the potential of certain upside events.
- Recession Scenario: What will happen to the projections if a recession occurs?
- Competitive Attack.

Once scenarios are identified, projections are developed for each specific scenario. This is a critical aspect of scenario planning. Unlike sensitivity analysis, where we simply flex selected variables, we will revise the base projections for expected changes under the scenario. For example, in a recession, a company may experience price pressure and lower demand. That company may also experience different interest rates, labor rates, and commodity pricing.

Once alternative scenario plans are developed, these can be used to determine a range of potential outcomes. A "most probable" estimate can be calculated by weighting each estimated outcome by the probability of occurrence. Figure 12.6 presents a recap for various scenarios.

In Table 12.2, we illustrate the use of weighting a range of revenue levels by the estimated probability of each occurring. In this case, the analysis shows that there appears to be more downside than upside to the base forecast of $115,000.

Building on the Business Model

In Chapter 3 we introduced the business model as an analytical tool. Using this conceptual framework, managers will set prices, establish business plans, evaluate business proposals, set expense levels, and make other

FIGURE 12.6 Scenario Recap

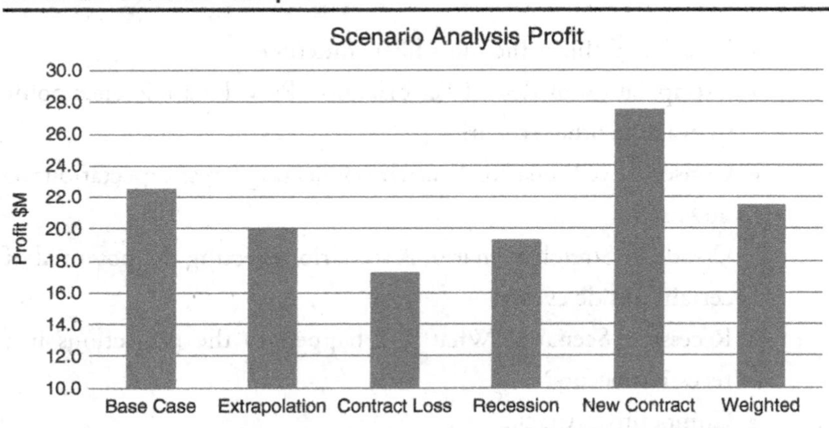

TABLE 12.2 Revenue Probability Analysis

	Revenue Level	Revenue Projection Probability Analysis Probability	Weighting
Upside 1	125,000	5%	6,250
Upside 2	120,000	10%	12,000
Base Plan	115,000	60%	69,000
Downside 1	110,000	25%	27,500
Downside 2	105,000	5%	5,250
Probable Outcome		100%	113,750

critical business decisions. For example, a company that is developing a product with a cost of $450 would likely set a target selling price of $1,000 to maintain a 55% margin. In establishing the research and development (R&D) budget, the company may target spending at 8% of projected sales.

The business model can be a useful way to initiate or to set high-level targets for the operating plan, as illustrated in Figure 12.7. Starting with the actual or forecast results for the current year (2017), a preliminary model for 2018 can be estimated by maintaining key ratios and measures. Executives can then adjust this preliminary result for known or anticipated changes for 2018, for example increased revenue growth and expenses related to new product introductions.

The considered estimate can be used as a starting point or basis for setting targets and boundaries for the development of the 2018 operating plan.

Comprehensive Financial Picture

There is a tendency to evaluate business decisions solely based on the effect on profit and loss (P&L) or earnings per share (EPS). In order to provide a complete summary of expected financial performance, financial projections should include the P&L, balance sheet, and statement of cash flows. Exceptions would include limited-scope exercises such as a forecast of quarterly EPS or expense savings.

FIGURE 12.7 Using Business Model to Develop Projections

Business Model Illustration
Comprehensive View

Roberts Manufacturing Co.

		2017	% of Sales	Prelim 2018	% of Sales	Considered 2018	% of Sales	Notes
Historical Sales Growth Rate:		8.0%		8%		10%		New Product Introduction
Profitability Model								
Sales		$ 100,000	100.0%	$ 108,000	100.0%	$ 110,000	100.0%	
Cost of Sales		45,000	45.0%	48,600	45.0%	50,600	46.0%	Lower margin on new product
Gross Margin		55,000	55.0%	59,400	55.0%	59,400	54.0%	
SG&A		32,000	32.0%	34,560	32.0%	35,200	32.0%	
R&D		8,000	8.0%	8,640	8.0%	9,500	8.6%	Increased R&D, large development project
Total Expenses		40,000	40.0%	43,200	40.0%	44,700	40.6%	
Operating Income		15,000	15.0%	16,200	15.0%	14,700	13.4%	
Other (Income) Expense		605	0.6%	653	0.6%	666	0.6%	
Taxes	32%	4,894	4.9%	5,327	4.9%	0	0.0%	
Net Income		9,501	9.5%	10,219	9.5%	14,035	12.8%	
Asset Utilization								
Days Sales Outstanding			73.0		73.0		65.0	Revenue Process Project
Days Sales Inventory			146.0		146.0		140.0	Supply Chain Initiative
Operating Capital Turnover			3.4		3.4		3.4	
Fixed Asset Turnover			5.0		5.0		5.0	
Intangible Turnover			9.1		9.1		9.1	
Total Asset Turnover			1.3		1.3		1.4	
Leverage			1.4		1.4		1.4	
Debt to Total Capital			15.3%		15.3%		15.3%	
Returns								
ROE			17.2%		17.2%		22.0%	
ROIC			15.2%		15.2%		19.0%	

Many decisions should be based on the economic analysis of projected results, including measures such as net present value and return on investment, and capital requirements and cash flow should be incorporated into the analysis. In addition, many projections will result in additional financing requirements or may test and even exceed existing debt covenants. Where important, these should be incorporated into the projections model and presentations.

The Value Is in the Planning, Not the Plan

While developing a plan is important, the far greater value is likely in the assessment of factors impacting the organization, critical thinking, and the ability to monitor performance against the plan. While financial projections are an important element of all decisions and plans, it can be argued that there is even more value created by the thinking necessitated in developing the financial projections. For example:

- Identifying critical assumptions that can be tested and monitored (an important management activity).
- Identifying and thinking through different scenarios and developing contingency plans.
- Understanding how critical management decisions impact the financial model and shareholder value.

Presenting and Communicating Projections

Too often, the presentation and review of projections, including operating plans and capital investment decisions, center on the financial outcomes as represented in the P&L. To effectively present and review significant plans and projections, a comprehensive package should be developed, including the following:

- Strategic Issues
- Market Forces, Including Customers and Competitors
- Critical Business Assumptions

- Critical Success Factors
- Execution Plan
- Execution Risks
- Sensitivity Analysis
- Recap of Possible Scenarios

Examples of plans and recaps are included in the chapters on plans and budgets, long-term projections, capital investment decisions, and mergers and acquisitions.

SUMMARY

Projections and plans are an essential aspect of managing any enterprise. Projections are utilized in most business decisions. Owing to the rapid level of change, increased uncertainty, and variability in business and economic activity, additional measures must be taken to develop financial projections. Firms should employ best practices that fit their specific circumstances to develop high-quality and robust projections.

In Chapter 13 we will cover budgets, operating plans, and forecasts/business outlooks. In Chapter 14, we turn our attention to unique aspects of developing long-term projections.

13

BUDGETS, OPERATING PLANS, AND FORECASTS

CHAPTER INTRODUCTION

This chapter will focus on projections that estimate performance over a 3- to 18-month period, including budgets, operating plans, and forecasts. Many of the techniques and practices utilized in this chapter were introduced in Chapter 12.

THE BUDGETING PROCESS

In spite of its shortcomings, the budgeting process lives on in many organizations. In some cases, it is required by charter or statute. In other cases, it either suffices or has not been evaluated against new tools, and against best practices and techniques in financial management. We will review the typical budget process and tools in this section to serve as a foundation for improved planning tools for the twenty-first century.

Traditional Budgeting Process

In chapter 12 we described the traditional budget process that became a cornerstone of management systems in the twenty-first century. While many organizations have adopted more evolved methods of developing business projections explored later in this chapter, others continue to use the traditional budget process.

The traditional budget process follows an annual cycle. The budget for next year would be developed several months before the new year begins. It is characterized by a very detailed and financially oriented process illustrated in Figure 13.1.

Departmental managers complete budget forms for their respective areas of responsibility as illustrated in Table 13.1.

These are then rolled up into cost summaries and ultimately profit and loss (P&L) projections as shown in Figure 13.2. After a series of reviews and revisions, the budget would be presented to senior executives and the board of directors for approval. The budget then served as the basis for operating and evaluating actual performance against these budget expectations.

Problems with Traditional Budgeting

Annual plans and budgets have been the subject of criticism for years. While many organizations have made substantial improvements, most organizations do not extract the potential utility out of this very time-consuming activity.

FIGURE 13.1 Traditional Budget and Control Process

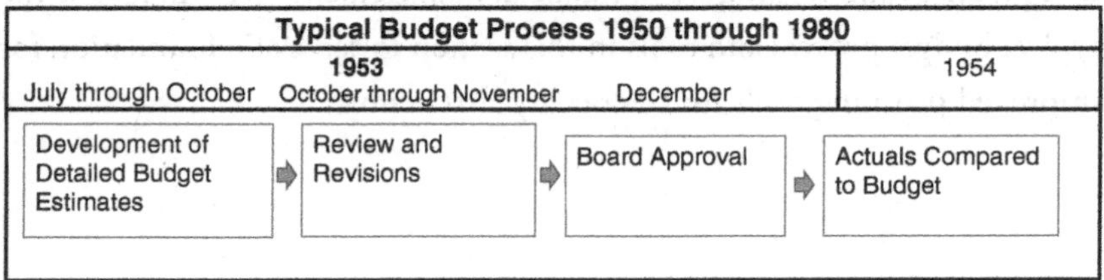

TABLE 13.1 Traditional Departmental Budget

Company:	Maugham Distributors $000's	Inside Sales				
		Q1	Q2	Q3	Q4	Year
Labor and Related Costs						
	Salary	145.0	145.0	145.0	160.0	595.0
	Bonus				40.0	40.0
	Commissions					0.0
	Total	145.0	145.0	145.0	200.0	635.0
	Fringe Benefits	36.3	36.3	36.3	40.0	148.8
	% to Total Labor	25%	25%	25%	20%	23%
	Total Labor and Related Costs	181.3	181.3	181.3	240.0	783.8
Other	Travel	4.0	4.0	4.0	4.0	16.0
	Meetings	2.0	2.0	2.0	2.0	8.0
	Consultants	2.0	2.0	2.0	2.0	8.0
	Professional Services	2.0	2.0	2.0	2.0	8.0
	Telecommunications					0.0
	Materials	8.0	8.0	8.0	8.0	32.0
	Contract Services					0.0
						0.0
						0.0
	Depreciation					0.0
	Allocations In	5.0	5.0	5.0	5.0	20.0
	Other	2.0	8.0	30.0	35.0	75.0
	Total Other Expenses	25.0	31.0	53.0	58.0	167.0
	Total Expense	206.3	212.3	234.3	298.0	950.8
	Year to Year Growth		2.9%	10.4%	27.2%	219.0%
	Sales	1100.0	1125.0	1135.0	1200.0	1300.0
	Selling % of Sales	18.8%	18.9%	20.6%	24.8%	73.1%
Labor Detail (000's)						
	Manager	38.0	38.0	38.0	38.0	152.0
	Admin	10.0	10.0	10.0	10.0	40.0
	New Hire				15.0	15.0
	Lead Internal Sales	25.0	25.0	25.0	25.0	100.0
	Sales Assistant	35.0	35.0	35.0	35.0	140.0
	Internal Sales (3)	37.0	37.0	37.0	37.0	148.0
						0.0
	Total ($000's)	145.0	145.0	145.0	160.0	595.0
	Year to Year Growth %		0.0%	0.0%	10.3%	271.9%
	Year to Year Growth $		0.0	0.0	15.0	435.0

FIGURE 13.2 Budget Roll-Up Illustration

Company: Mangham Distributors
$000's

Inside Sales

		Q1	Q2	Q3	Q4	Year
Labor and Related Costs						
	Salary	145.0	145.0	145.0	160.0	595.0
	Bonus				40.0	40.0
	Commissions					0.0
	Total	145.0	145.0	145.0	200.0	635.0
	Fringe Benefits	36.3	36.3	36.3	40.0	148.8
	% to Total Labor	25%	25%	25%	20%	23%
	Total Labor and Related Costs	181.3	181.3	181.3	240.0	783.8
Other	Travel	4.0	4.0	4.0	4.0	16.0
	Meetings	2.0	2.0	2.0	2.0	8.0
	Consultants	2.0	2.0	2.0	2.0	8.0
	Professional Services	2.0	2.0	2.0	2.0	8.0
	Telecommunications					0.0
	Materials	8.0	8.0	8.0	8.0	32.0
	Contract services					0.0
						0.0
						0.0
	Depreciation					0.0
	Allocations In	5.0	5.0	5.0	5.0	20.0
	Other	2.0	8.0	30.0	35.0	75.0
	Total Other Expenses	25.0	31.0	53.0	58.0	167.0
	Total Expense	206.3	212.3	234.3	298.0	950.8
	Year to Year Growth		2.9%	10.4%	27.2%	219.0%

Company: Mangham Distributors

Selling Expense

		Q1	Q2	Q3	Q4	Year
Field Sales						
	Sales Region 1	50.0	50.0	54.0	56.0	210.0
	Sales Region 2	49.0	50.0	54.0	55.0	208.0
	Sales Region 3	50.0	50.0	54.0	53.0	207.0
	Sales Region 4	51.0	50.0	54.0	55.0	210.0
	Sales Region 5	0.0	0.0	54.0	55.0	109.0
	Total	200	200	270	274	944.0
Office	Inside Sales	206.3	212.3	234.3	298.0	950.8
	Sales Management	60.0	50.0	54.0	62.0	226.0
	Order Processing	32	35	36	37	140.0
	Total Selling Expense	498	497	594	671	2,261

Profit & Loss	2017 Budget
Sales	15,000
Cost of Goods Sold	7,600
Gross Margin	7,400
%	49%
Operating Expenses:	
R&D	800
Marketing	1,600
Selling	2,261
G&A	1,100
Total Operating Expenses	5,761
Income from Operations	1,639
%	10.9%

One of the major problems with budgeting is the focus on finance, including general ledger accounts and financial statement captions, rather than processes, activities, customers, projects, and critical assumptions. Department managers often had to create "shadow" planning tools to develop budget estimates from an operating perspective and link to their processes and activities.

The output of a traditional budget process would often lock into a single-scenario document; the emphasis was on the document rather than the potential value of the process. As President Dwight Eisenhower said, "Plans are useless, but planning is essential."[1] In other words, the value is not in the plan document itself or in a single course of action set forth in the plan. Once the battle begins, the conditions and circumstances will depart from those used in developing the plan. The value in planning lies in the thought process, including assessing strengths and weaknesses, evaluating critical assumptions, and developing potential scenarios and contingency plans. Budgets tend to be numbers driven and tend not to focus attention on issues and opportunities, on risks and upsides, or on execution planning.

Traditional budgets do not adequately identify and test critical assumptions and performance drivers. The financial focus often means that assumptions are buried in the details and not adequately identified and tested.

Budgets were useful for a time, when business was more static. Their utility has declined significantly, resulting from the development of the global economy, the accelerated rate of change, and significant geopolitical events that reshape markets dramatically and frequently. Traditional budget processes are very labor intensive. Due to the level of detail and the typical need for multiple revisions, the budget process can often lead to a substantial investment (or waste) of time by finance and operating managers alike. Many companies issue planning guidelines and boundaries (discussed in Chapter 12) to establish goals and targets in order to create a starting point and to minimize the number of revisions.

In most cases, the organization would be better served by developing an operating plan as described in the next section.

THE OPERATING PLAN

A key distinction between a budget and an operating plan is that the latter is a complete execution plan for the coming year whereas the former has a focus on the *financial* projections. The financial projections are an essential aspect of the plan, but not the only objective or focus of the process. An effective operating plan will:

- Assess the current situation.
- Review strategic objectives and initiatives.
- Establish performance goals and targets.
- Identify business drivers and critical assumptions.
- Develop the game plan for next 12 months.
- Develop multiple scenarios.

Assess Current Situation

Before a plan can be effectively developed for the coming year, management must assess the current situation. Has the external environment changed? Has the competitive landscape changed? Are we meeting or exceeding strategic goals? Are we meeting current performance targets? This assessment should include a review and an evaluation of recent financial results as well as key performance indicators (KPIs). Many organizations find it useful to benchmark competitors and customers (refer to Chapter 11, The External View: Benchmarking Performance and Competitive Analysis) as part of this situational analysis.

Review Strategic Objectives

The annual operating plan should be an installment of the company's strategic plan. The operating plan process should include a review of the strategy. Are the critical assumptions supporting the strategic plan still valid? Where do we stand on the implementation or attainment of strategic objectives?

The operating plan is an opportunity to develop an execution plan for the strategic objectives for the next year. It should ensure that the objectives are still valid, and plan for human and financial resources to execute and achieve those objectives.

Establish Performance Goals and Targets

Prior to turning the troops loose on developing the operating plan, the leadership team and board should develop performance goals and targets. In establishing goals and targets, the organization should consider the following:

- Strategic plan
- Business model
- Recent performance trends
- Benchmarking and competitor analysis
- Objectives for value creation

Develop a Game Plan

Next, managers should develop a preliminary execution or game plan for the coming year. This should be based on the situational analysis and preliminary goals. In order to prevent the chaos of a bottom-up wish list, it is useful to establish parameters or high-level targets of revenue growth and expense and investment levels, and communicate to all involved in developing the plan.

Develop Preliminary Financial Projections

The organization should develop a preliminary model of projections for the plan year. Not all revenues, costs, and expenses are created equal. The team should focus on the most significant and most variable, using the Pareto rule introduced in Chapter 3.

This phase will be very easy if the organization uses rolling forecasts or an on-demand business outlook (DBO), discussed later in this chapter, since the team has already developed and evaluated projections for the plan year. In fact, most organizations utilize the DBO model to develop the preliminary projections for the operating plan. These preliminary projections must identify and present key assumptions.

Identify Critical Assumptions and Key Actions

The operating plan for next year has hundreds of assumptions. These assumptions likely include everything from general economic conditions to weather, from inflation to pricing, and from the availability of critical materials to their cost. In many plans, these assumptions are buried in the details and are not explicitly identified. Key assumptions should be identified and reviewed. Managers should understand how sensitive the planned results are to changes in critical assumptions. These assumptions should be tracked over the plan horizon, and any signals indicating that the assumptions may not be valid should trigger a review and a response. Identifying and reacting to changes in significant assumptions early will allow you to minimize the impact of downside events and trends and to fully capitalize on the upsides.

Successful plans place significant attention on the activities required to achieve the planned results. For example, sales growth arising from the introduction of a new product in the next year requires a series of activities related to the development, production, marketing, and selling of the product. Each of these activities must be thoroughly planned out and adequately resourced to ensure that the planned sales are achieved. In addition, each of the responsible managers must be committed to the completion dates to support the product introduction and revenue plan.

Identify Upside and Downside Events and Develop Multiple Scenarios

Owing to the rate of change and uncertainty that exists in the current environment, the use of a single-point plan generally is not valid or meaningful. A single plan estimate, by definition, must reflect a position on the probability and estimated impact of numerous events, transactions, and conditions. Managers should set the expectation that a base projection should be the best estimate of the outcome under the present strategy and expected market and economic conditions. Some organizations clarify this expectation by using language such as "most probable" or establishing desired confidence levels. This base plan includes a multitude of assumptions, including the probability and estimated impact of potential events. It is useful to identify and present how these potential events have been reflected in the plan. For example, if the plan assumes a continued favorable economic expansion, then a potential downside would be an economic recession. Other downside events may include competitive threats or loss of a major customer or contract.

In addition to assessing the potential impact on the financial projections, this analysis allows management to monitor these potential factors and to develop preliminary contingency and response plans. The development of multiple scenarios and upside/downside events was discussed in detail in Chapter 12.

Communicate Plan Objectives and Targets

The objectives and targets set during the plan process must be communicated throughout the organization. Failure to communicate is the equivalent of a coach not sharing the game plan with the team prior to the start of the game. Of course, the specific content shared will depend on several factors such as the need for confidentiality and the level and role within organization.

A good test of the organization's understanding of the plan is to ask: Can our managers and employees list the five critical priorities for the coming year? Significant leverage is possible by communicating key objectives and activities included in the plan. For example, imagine the potential benefits to a critical project if all finance, human resources, and procurement teams recognized and supported the project as the number one priority for the company. Even more effective results can be achieved if the objective setting and performance management process for individual managers and employees is a part of the annual planning process, instead of an independent, subsequent drill.

Develop Process to Monitor Key Assumptions and Track Progress

In many companies, performance tracking and monitoring are focused on financial results. This is problematic since financial results are lagging measures of business activities and processes. If you wait until trends or problems are visible in the financials, it is already too late to correct for that period. Many problems are easily addressed at an early stage, but grow and compound as time passes. Dashboards should be developed to track performance on leading indicators that will alert managers to unfavorable trends in near real time so that corrective action can be taken.

You can't manage financials; you can manage people, processes, transactions, and projects. The financials are a result of these business activities and inputs. For example, if you want to improve accounts receivable days sales outstanding from 75 to 60 days, it won't happen unless you focus on the critical business processes that impact receivables. Create a plan that identifies improvement opportunities on critical drivers of receivables: revenue hockey sticks, improving quality and on-time delivery, and resolving customer problems faster. Establish targets and then monitor KPIs covering revenue linearity, quality, past-due orders and collections, and problem resolution. KPIs were discussed in greater detail in Chapter 8, Dashboards and Key Performance Indicators.

Evaluate the Annual Plan Process

Each year, the annual plan process should be evaluated to identify potential improvement opportunities. Start by reviewing the current planning and forecasting processes and products. Measure the duration of the entire planning process. Document the process flow, including required inputs, processing, review and revision, and presentation. Identify the most critical assumptions and most significant revenue and cost drivers. Identify time spent in major stages of the process. Review the critical output/presentations of the plan. Do a postreview of the planning process, identifying impediments, issues, and improvement opportunities. Also review actual performance against the original plan, identifying the root causes of any variances. This will highlight bottlenecks, identify redundant and inefficient aspects, and provide a recap of critical assumptions and performance drivers.

Figure 13.3 is a dashboard summarizing KPIs for the planning process. This team started with some significant issues including a long plan duration, multiple revisions and ineffective results in the form of large variances to plan. By identifying and addressing root causes, the team implemented changes to make the process both more efficient and effective. The two most important changes were the use of planning guidelines and boundaries at the start of the process and the implementation of a rolling forecast.

BUSINESS FORECASTS AND OUTLOOKS

Due to the rapidly changing business conditions, it has become increasingly important to be able to recast expected performance periodically during the year, and even on demand. In many organizations, the rolling forecast or business outlook has become the cornerstone of the planning, projecting, and management control activities. The forecast or outlook model must be robust enough to easily reflect changes in key assumptions, performance trends, events, or management decisions.

Historical Evolution of Forecasts

Forecasts emerged because of the need to update or recast the budgets. As business became more complex and the pace of change increased, the original budgets often were outdated early in the year. These updates were often done at a higher level than the original budget projections.

FIGURE 13.3 **Dashboard: Evaluation of Operating Plan**

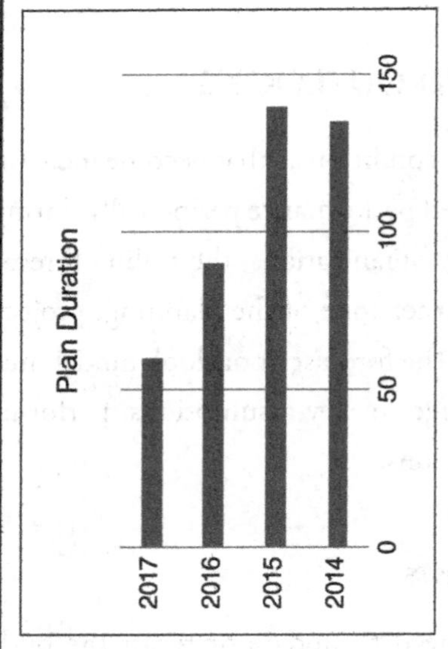

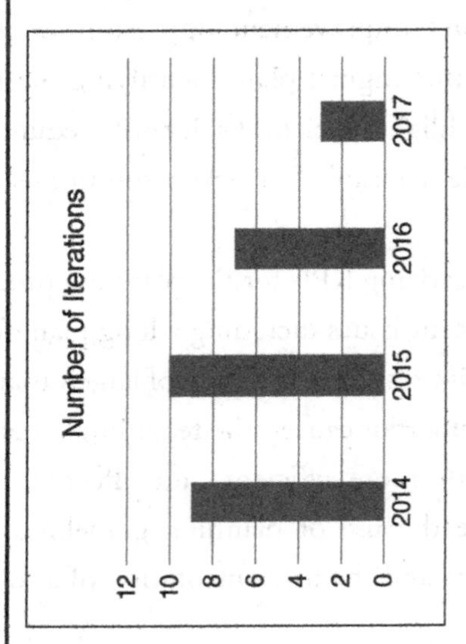

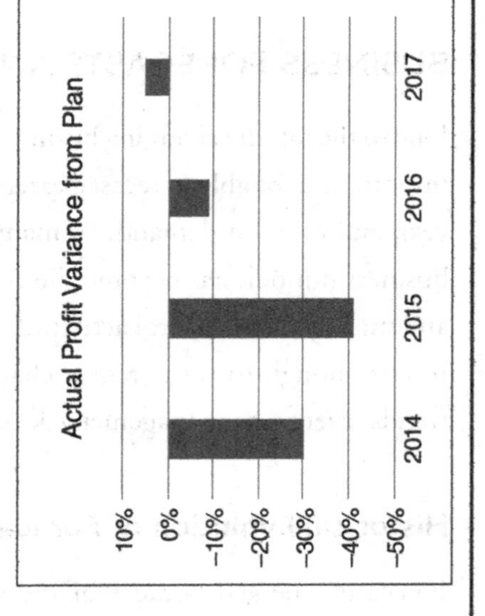

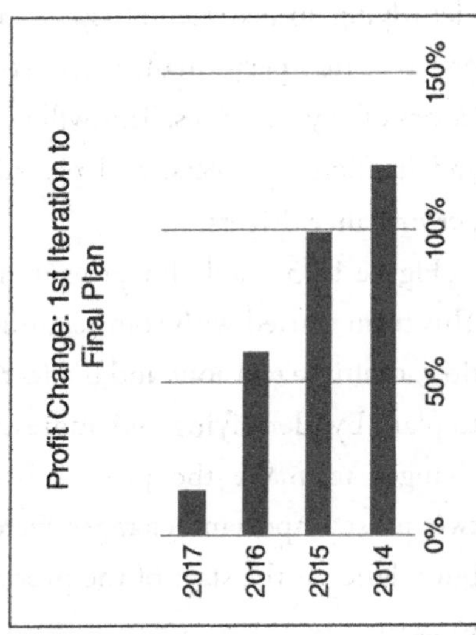

Many organizations began preparing an update to the budget on a monthly or quarterly basis. As the actual results were available, the remaining forecast period was evaluated to reflect known trends and any additional information that had surfaced since the original plan or budget had been prepared. Companies with stock owned by the public were pressured to confirm or adjust annual estimates. The forecast horizon ended abruptly at the end of the company's fiscal year (see Figure 13.4).

In the 1980s a number of companies began extending the forecast horizon as they progressed through the year. For example, as the first quarter actual results were known, the forecast was extended to include the first quarter of the following year. Described as a "rolling forecast," this methodology provided a full-year future outlook on the financial results, as illustrated in Figure 13.5. This became extremely helpful in the final several months of a fiscal year, providing a view into the next year before the budget process had been complete.

My first encounter with rolling forecasts occurred in 1985. At that time, I was a division CFO of a technology unit of a large publicly traded company, and the corporation began requiring us to provide rolling forecasts. At first this was simply a mechanical exercise by the folks in finance to extrapolate or extend the current forecast one additional quarter. The projections were based on the prior-year actuals and adjusted for any significant expected changes. Of course, we were not excited by the additional work and the perceived difficulty in developing an extended estimate of performance.

The true value of the rolling forecast became apparent after several months. A few major changes to our business had become apparent. We had several major nonrecurring sales that needed to be reflected as "one-timers" and not built into our run rate or trend for setting expectations for the following year. We also recognized a serious competitive threat that would have a significant impact on our performance in the next fiscal year, now seven to eight months away. We included our initial estimated impact of these factors into our extended projections. More important, the management team developed a plan to address the threats,

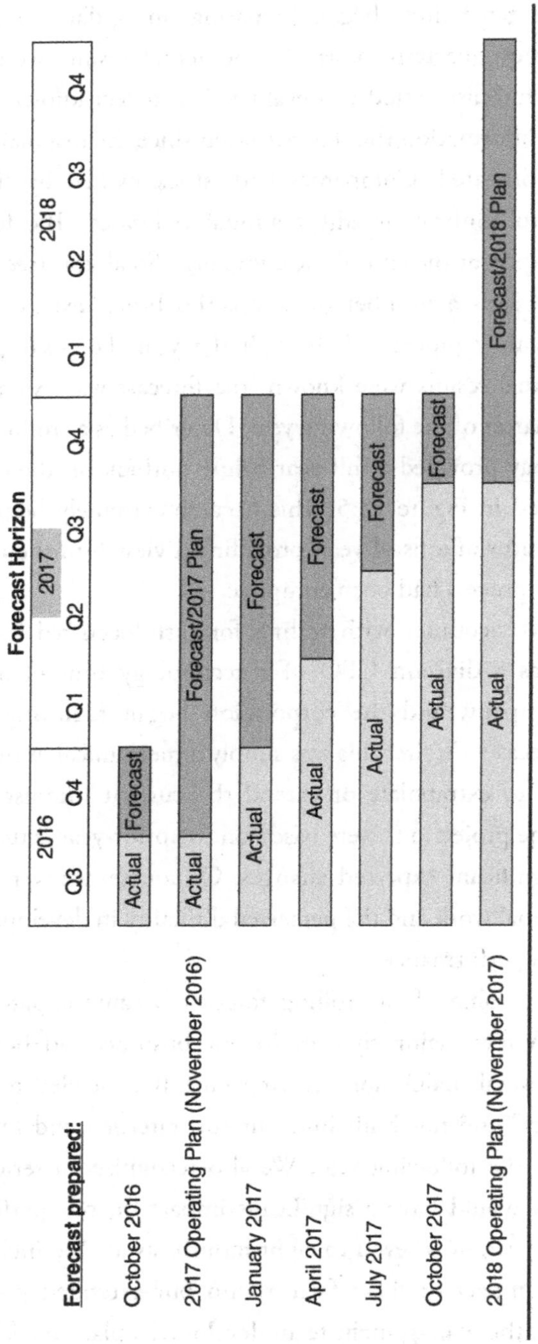

FIGURE 13.4 Traditional Forecast Horizon

Forecast Horizon

Forecast prepared:	2016 Q3	2016 Q4	2017 Q1	2017 Q2	2017 Q3	2017 Q4	2018 Q1	2018 Q2	2018 Q3	2018 Q4
October 2016	Actual	Forecast								
2017 Operating Plan (November 2016)	Actual	Forecast/2017 Plan	Forecast/2017 Plan	Forecast/2017 Plan	Forecast/2017 Plan	Forecast/2017 Plan				
January 2017	Actual	Actual	Forecast	Forecast	Forecast	Forecast				
April 2017	Actual	Actual	Actual	Forecast	Forecast	Forecast				
July 2017	Actual	Actual	Actual	Actual	Forecast	Forecast				
October 2017	Actual	Actual	Actual	Actual	Actual	Forecast				
2018 Operating Plan (November 2017)	Actual	Actual	Actual	Actual	Actual	Forecast/2018 Plan	Forecast/2018 Plan	Forecast/2018 Plan	Forecast/2018 Plan	Forecast/2018 Plan

FIGURE 13.5 Rolling Forecast: Business Outlook Horizon

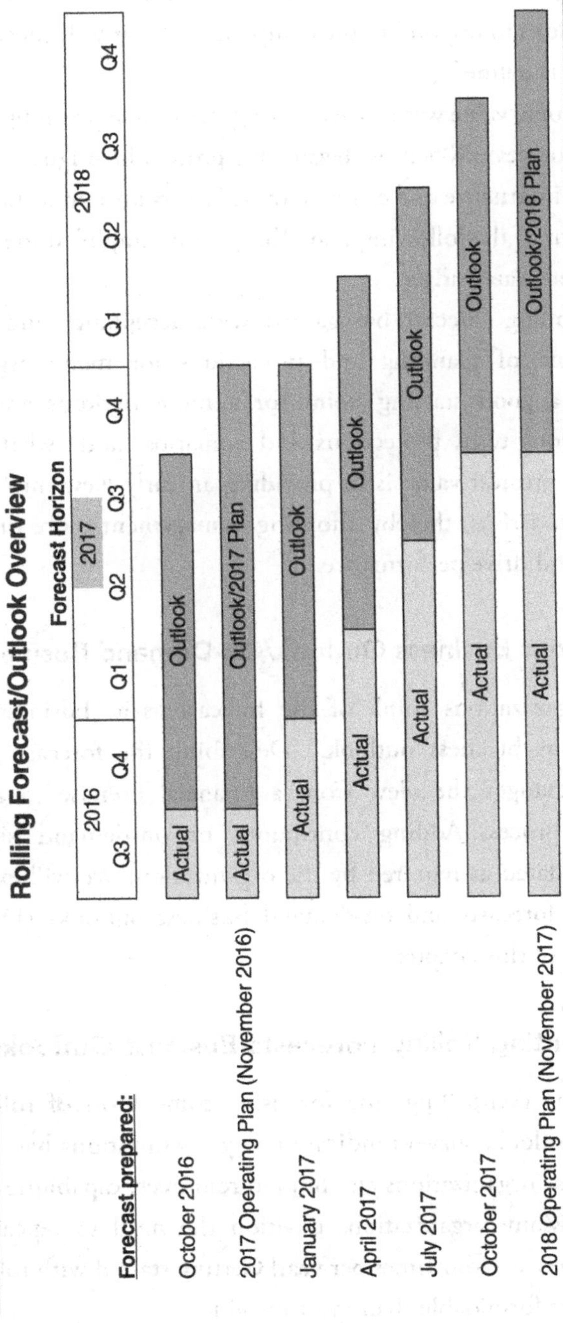

including the introduction of new products, revisions to pricing, and other actions to respond to the competitive threat well ahead of the annual planning timeline.

Additional value was realized during the annual planning process for the subsequent year. When we began this process in August, we had already begun to internalize and estimate these factors into projections for the first six months of the following year. This greatly simplified the preparation of our annual plan/budget.

The rolling forecast has gained wide acceptance and serves as the cornerstone of planning and projections for many organizations. It provides a good starting point for a more rigorous annual planning process, long-term projections and scenarios, and "what if?" analysis. By far its greatest value is in providing an early view into future trends, upsides, and risks, thereby affording management more time to react to changes and drive performance.

Continuous Business Outlook/On-Demand Business Outlook

Many organizations think of the forecast as a "business outlook" or "continuous business outlook." Describing the forecast as a business outlook changes the view from a financial exercise to a business or operating process. Adding "continuous" or "on-demand" signifies that it can be updated as required by the organization. We will explore the use of rolling forecasts and on-demand business outlooks (DBOs) for the remainder of this chapter.

Implementing Rolling Forecasts/Business Outlooks

Despite the compelling case for using some form of rolling forecast/business outlook, surveys indicate many organizations have not adopted them. These organizations cite limited resources, capabilities, or enabling software. Many organizations envision the need to repeat the annual planning process four times per year! Getting started with rolling forecasts is much less formidable than most imagine.

Getting Started: A Practical Approach

To overcome the inertia inherent in starting a DBO initiative, I have found that a practical, phased approach is the best way to get started. Utilizing Microsoft Excel is recommended, especially since it is hard to define needs and evaluate and procure other software products without prior experience in using DBO models.

Articulate the Objectives of Developing the On-Demand Business Outlook

A clear statement of objectives will focus attention on developing a process that meets important needs and requirements. Most organizations point to one or more of the following objectives:

- Provide a view into expected performance for the next 12 months. This will engage the organization more frequently and reduce surprises that arise in one-year planning cycles.
- Provide a timely basis for setting future expectations with executives, boards of directors, and investors.
- Identify performance trends and estimate future impact.
- Identify issues and opportunities that will impact future performance.
- Afford the greatest lead time possible to address problems and opportunities.
- Reduce inefficiencies and effort in the annual planning process.

Document and Review Current Operating Plans, Budgets, and Forecasts

Start by reviewing the current planning and forecasting activities and products as described earlier in the chapter. What are the major problems and improvement opportunities? What are the most significant performance drivers? What issues give rise to variances from the plan?

IMPLEMENTING A ROLLING FORECAST/BUSINESS OUTLOOK

1. Articulate objectives of rolling forecast/business outlook model.
2. Review current operating plans and management reports.
3. Identify critical business drivers:
   - Most significant (Pareto's 80/20 rule)
   - Most variable
   - Critical assumptions
4. Design architecture:
   - Focus on critical business drivers.
   - Optimize trade-off: detail versus summary.
   - Explicitly incorporate assumptions.
   - Integrate model.
   - Lay out flow.
   - Analysis and presentation.
5. Practical implementation path:
   - Step 1: Start with 12-quarter trend schedule.
   - Step 2: Develop high-level, one-page summary for each financial statement caption.
   - Step 3: Revise based on experience; intensify focus on drivers.

Identify Critical Business Drivers

Identification of critical business drivers is a critical step in developing a more effective and efficient forecast process, with the intent to extend the horizon of the projections. The key is to move away from a process that affords equal attention to all costs, expenses, and revenues. Identify the most significant drivers of performance. Here we can apply the 80/20 rule: 20% of the line items will represent 80% of the value. For example, the top 20% of products or programs will typically account for 80% of total revenues. The top 20% of line items of expenses (labor, facilities, materials, etc.) will typically account for 80% of all expenses.

Another important analysis is to identify those significant drivers that are most likely to fluctuate – that is, are most variable. Examples include revenues from new products or contracts, contract services, commodity prices, foreign currency fluctuations, and new home starts. These can be contrasted with drivers that are relatively stable and are more easily predicted by aggregation and extrapolation using trend analysis, such as salaries, facilities, and other costs. Critical assumptions should also be identified, including macroeconomic factors such as gross domestic product (GDP), political policy, and interest rates.

As we construct a DBO process and model, we will ensure that these critical drivers and assumptions are fully considered and emphasized, and that less important factors are deemphasized. Figure 13.6 highlights typical drivers that are emphasized in the development of business outlooks.

Design Process and Model Architecture

After stating the objectives and identifying critical performance drivers, we can begin to visualize an overview of the model. Most organizations should define the product (output) of the model to include the three basic financial statements (income statement, balance sheet, and statement of cash flows), analysis, and a presentation summary. Beginning with this end in mind, we

FIGURE 13.6 Reflect Critical Drivers in Business Outlook

Business Outlooks/Rolling Forecasts

Typical Areas of Emphasis

Revenue and Margins:	Significant Cost Drivers	Macro Economic Factors
❑ Pricing ❑ Product Life Cycles ❑ New Product Intros ❑ Contract/Programs ❑ Macroeconomic Factors ❑ Market and Competitive Forces ❑ Currency	❑ Human Resources ❑ Commodities ❑ Significant Inputs	❑ GDP ❑ Interest Rates ❑ Geopolitical ❑ Public Policy ❑ Demographics
Major Investments	**Human Capital Plan**	**Risks and Upsides**
❑ New Products, Programs ❑ Information Technologies ❑ Major Expansion ❑ Acquisitions	❑ Headcount ❑ New Hires, Recruiting ❑ Incentives, COLA ❑ Health Care and Other Benefits	❑ New Product/Program Delays ❑ Loss of Contract ❑ Major Expansion ❑ Acquisitions

- ❑ For most organizations, 80% of attention should be focused on Revenue and Margins
- ❑ Do not try to replicate annual budget/plan
- ❑ Every business has unique drivers and the DBO should be tailored to specific circumstances

FIGURE 13.7 Business Outlook Architecture Map

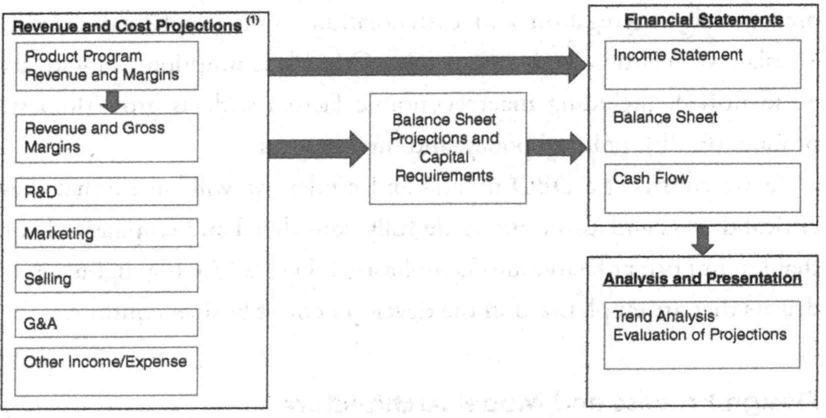

can lay out the supporting schedules to forecast key elements of financial performance. For example, the revenue and product (or service) margin projections are of critical importance in all organizations. These supporting schedules should be constructed to incorporate the most significant and most variable business drivers and assumptions identified above.

This is a critical step in the process. We must be careful not to replicate the annual planning process here. Instead we need to be disciplined and thoughtful to construct a working model that incorporates the key drivers and assumptions, without resorting to the lowest level of detail. (See Figure 13.7.)

Practical Implementation Path

At the center of any outlook is a performance trend schedule (typically quarterly). This trend schedule should include prior year history, the current year plan/outlook, and provision for the next year's outlook. Table 13.2 illustrates a trend schedule for Thomas Technologies, Inc. The company has just closed out the second quarter of 2017. Under a

TABLE 13.2 Rolling Forecast Method

Thomas Technologies, Inc.
Income Statement

		2016				2017				2018	
		Q1	Q2	Q3	Q4	Q1	Q2	Q3	Q4	Q1	Q2
Revenue		28,642,500	28,571,250	28,575,000	35,858,750	30,071,250	31,910,000	32,867,500	39,786,250		
Cost of Revenue		14,848,000	14,805,600	14,804,400	18,568,000	15,347,000	16,303,700	16,817,100	20,377,400		
Gross Margin		13,794,500	13,765,650	13,770,600	17,290,750	14,724,250	15,606,300	16,050,400	19,408,850		
Gross Margin %		48.2%	48.2%	48.2%	48.2%	49.0%	48.9%	48.8%	48.8%		
R&D		3,750,400	3,756,400	3,757,900	4,240,400	3,956,850	4,352,934	4,538,347	4,928,330		
Selling		4,255,500	4,255,500	4,256,500	4,357,500	4,427,200	4,428,200	4,428,200	4,518,200		
Marketing		1,665,050	1,682,050	1,681,550	2,060,050	1,773,383	1,773,649	1,757,649	2,312,699		
G&A		2,185,300	2,185,300	2,185,300	2,625,300	2,292,715	2,292,715	2,292,715	2,762,715		
Operating Expenses		11,856,250	11,879,250	11,881,250	13,283,250	12,450,148	12,847,498	13,016,911	14,521,945		
Operating Income		1,938,250	1,886,400	1,889,350	4,007,500	2,274,103	2,758,802	3,033,489	4,886,905		
Operating Income %		6.8%	6.6%	6.6%	11.2%	7.6%	8.6%	9.2%	12.3%		
Interest Income (Expense)		(3,500)	(3,500)	(3,500)	(3,500)	(3,500)	(3,500)	(3,500)	(3,500)		
Other Income (Expense)		2,000	1,800	1,800	1,500	2,000	1,800	1,800	1,500		
Profit Before Tax		1,936,750	1,884,700	1,887,650	4,005,500	2,272,603	2,757,102	3,031,789	4,884,905		
Tax	30.0%	(581,025)	(565,410)	(566,295)	(1,201,650)	(681,781)	(827,131)	(909,537)	(1,465,472)		
Net Income		1,355,725	1,319,290	1,321,355	2,803,850	1,590,822	1,929,971	2,122,252	3,419,434		

(continues)

TABLE 13.2 *(Continued)*

	2016				2017				2018	
	Q1	Q2	Q3	Q4	Q1	Q2	Q3	Q4	Q1	Q2
Y/Y										
Revenue	10.0%	12.0%	14.0%	15.0%	5.0%	11.7%	15.0%	11.0%		
Operating Expenses	5.0%	6.0%	7.0%	8.0%	5.0%	8.2%	9.6%	9.3%		
Operating Income	12.0%	14.0%	13.0%	12.0%	17.3%	46.2%	60.6%	21.9%		
% of Sales										
Revenue	100.0%	100.0%	100.0%	100.0%	100.0%	100.0%	100.0%	100.0%		
Cost of Revenue	51.8%	51.8%	51.8%	51.8%	51.0%	51.1%	51.2%	51.2%		
Gross Margin	48.2%	48.2%	48.2%	48.2%	49.0%	48.9%	48.8%	48.8%		
R&D	13.1%	13.1%	13.2%	11.8%	13.2%	13.6%	13.8%	12.4%		
Selling	14.9%	14.9%	14.9%	12.2%	14.7%	13.9%	13.5%	11.4%		
Marketing	5.8%	5.9%	5.9%	5.7%	5.9%	5.6%	5.3%	5.8%		
G&A	7.6%	7.6%	7.6%	7.3%	7.6%	7.2%	7.0%	6.9%		
Operating Expenses	41.4%	41.6%	41.6%	37.0%	41.4%	40.3%	39.6%	36.5%		
Operating Income	6.8%	6.6%	6.6%	11.2%	7.6%	8.6%	9.2%	12.3%		

traditional approach, the forecast horizon is compressed to the rest of 2017 (i.e. Q3 and Q4). To implement a rolling outlook, we simply need to extend the projections to include Q1 and Q2 for the subsequent year (2018). What is the minimal information we need to make reasonable estimates? We can start by reviewing the actual results of Q1 and Q2 of 2017. What items can be extrapolated from the previous periods or trends? What significant factors will shape the performance for these future periods? For example, for revenue, the projection must consider major product introductions and contract wins and losses.

For each income statement caption, I like to construct a one-page supporting schedule that provides a capsule of information, including actual and projected financial results (presented in a way that is meaningful to the responsible operating manager) and includes all major assumptions and key drivers. By focusing on a one-page summary at this level, we are forced to identify the most significant factors and drivers. It is important to tailor these schedules to each specific situation. Supporting schedules for product margins, gross margins, and marketing are illustrated in Tables 13.3 to 13.5. A complete, fully integrated forecast model is illustrated in the book's companion website.

The supporting schedules roll up to an income statement presenting the forecast for the extended forecast horizon in Table 13.6.

Comprehensive Financial Picture

To provide a complete view of expected financial performance, financial projections in the rolling forecast should include the P&L statement, balance sheet, and statement of cash flows. Many forecasts focus only on the P&L, which does not provide a complete picture of the financial performance of the organization.

There are two reasons for this. First, the focus for many companies is on earnings per share (EPS) and therefore all attention is directed to the P&L. Even where the CEO is primarily focused on the P&L and EPS, finance should continue to prepare and present the key balance sheet

TABLE 13.3 DBO Supporting Schedule: Product Margins

Thomas Technologies, Inc.
Product Margins — Trend Schedule

Product/Product Line	2016 Q1	2016 Q2	2016 Q3	2016 Q4	2017 Q1	2017 Q2	2017 Q3	2017 Q4	2018 Q1	2018 Q2	2018 Q3	2018 Q4
Product 1												
Average Selling Price	4,850	4,850	4,850	4,850	4,900	4,900	4,900	4,900	4,900	4,900	4,900	4,999
Product Cost	2,500	2,500	2,500	2,500	2,517	2,517	2,517	2,517	2,532	2,532	2,532	2,532
Unit Volume	800	1,000	1,100	2,000	1,000	1,100	1,300	2,200	1,300	1,500	1,600	2,300
Revenue	3,880,000	4,850,000	5,335,000	9,700,000	4,900,000	5,390,000	6,370,000	10,780,000	6,370,000	7,350,000	7,840,000	11,497,700
Product Costs	2,000,000	2,500,000	2,750,000	5,000,000	2,517,000	2,768,700	3,272,100	5,537,400	3,291,600	3,798,000	4,051,200	5,823,600
Product Margin	1,880,000	2,350,000	2,585,000	4,700,000	2,383,000	2,621,300	3,097,900	5,242,600	3,078,400	3,552,000	3,788,800	5,674,100
%	48.5%	48.5%	48.5%	48.5%	48.6%	48.6%	48.6%	48.6%	48.3%	48.3%	48.3%	49.3%
Product 2												
Average Selling Price	5,600	5,600	5,600	5,600	5,800	5,800	5,800	5,800	6,000	6,000	6,000	6,000
Product Cost	2,912	2,912	2,912	2,912	2,950	2,950	2,950	2,950	3,200	3,200	3,200	3,200
Unit Volume	4,000	3,800	3,700	4,000	3,600	3,700	3,500	3,800	3,050	3,000	3,100	3,050
Revenue	22,400,000	21,280,000	20,720,000	22,400,000	20,880,000	21,460,000	20,300,000	22,040,000	18,300,000	18,000,000	18,600,000	18,300,000
Product Costs	11,648,000	11,065,600	10,774,400	11,648,000	10,620,000	10,915,000	10,325,000	11,210,000	9,760,000	9,600,000	9,920,000	9,760,000
Product Margin	10,752,000	10,214,400	9,945,600	10,752,000	10,260,000	10,545,000	9,975,000	10,830,000	8,540,000	8,400,000	8,680,000	8,540,000
%	48.0%	48.0%	48.0%	48.0%	49.1%	49.1%	49.1%	49.1%	46.7%	46.7%	46.7%	46.7%
Product 3												
Average Selling Price	1,575	1,575	1,575	1,575	1,575	1,575	1,575	1,575	1,575	1,575	1,575	1,575
Product Cost	800	800	800	800	800	800	800	800	800	800	800	800
Unit Volume	1,500	1,550	1,600	1,650	1,550	1,600	1,700	1,750	1,950	1,950	2,100	2,050
Revenue	2,362,500	2,441,250	2,520,000	2,598,750	2,441,250	2,520,000	2,677,500	2,756,250	3,071,250	3,071,250	3,307,500	3,228,750
Product Costs	1,200,000	1,240,000	1,280,000	1,320,000	1,240,000	1,280,000	1,360,000	1,400,000	1,560,000	1,560,000	1,680,000	1,640,000
Product Margin	1,162,500	1,201,250	1,240,000	1,278,750	1,201,250	1,240,000	1,317,500	1,356,250	1,511,250	1,511,250	1,627,500	1,588,750
%	49.2%	49.2%	49.2%	49.2%	49.2%	49.2%	49.2%	49.2%	49.2%	49.2%	49.2%	49.2%

TABLE 13.3 ***(Continued)***

Thomas Technologies, Inc.
Product Margins **Trend Schedule**

	2016				2017				2018			
Product/Product Line	**Q1**	**Q2**	**Q3**	**Q4**	**Q1**	**Q2**	**Q3**	**Q4**	**Q1**	**Q2**	**Q3**	**Q4**
Product 4												
Average Selling Price				2,900	2,900	2,900	2,900	2,900	3,000	3,000	3,000	3,000
Product Cost				1,500	1,500	1,500	1,500	1,500	1,500	1,600	1,600	1,600
Unit Volume				400	500	600	800	900	900	1000	1300	1500
Revenue	–	–	–	1,160,000	1,450,000	1,740,000	2,320,000	2,610,000	2,700,000	3,000,000	3,900,000	4,500,000
Product Costs	–	–	–	600,000	750,000	900,000	1,200,000	1,350,000	1,350,000	1,600,000	2,080,000	2,400,000
Product Margin	–	–	–	560,000	700,000	840,000	1,120,000	1,260,000	1,350,000	1,400,000	1,820,000	2,100,000
%				48.3%	48.3%	48.3%	48.3%	48.3%	50.0%	46.7%	46.7%	46.7%
Product 5												
Average Selling Price					4,000	4,000	4,000	4,000	4,200	4,200	4,200	4,200
Product Cost					2,200	2,200	2,200	2,200	2,200	2,200	2,200	2,250
Unit Volume					100	200	300	400	800	1,000	1,100	1,500
Revenue	–	–	–	–	400,000	800,000	1,200,000	1,600,000	3,360,000	4,200,000	4,620,000	6,300,000
Product Costs	–	–	–	–	220,000	440,000	660,000	880,000	1,760,000	2,200,000	2,420,000	3,375,000
Product Margin	–	–	–	–	180,000	360,000	540,000	720,000	1,600,000	2,000,000	2,200,000	2,925,000
%					45.0%	45.0%	45.0%	45.0%	47.6%	47.6%	47.6%	46.4%
Total												
Revenue	28,642,500	28,571,250	28,575,000	35,858,750	30,071,250	31,910,000	32,867,500	39,786,250	33,801,250	35,621,250	38,267,500	43,826,450
Product Cost	14,848,000	14,805,600	14,804,400	18,568,000	15,347,000	16,303,700	16,817,100	20,377,400	17,721,600	18,758,000	20,151,200	22,998,600
Product Margin	13,794,500	13,765,650	13,770,600	17,290,750	14,724,250	15,606,300	16,050,400	19,408,850	16,079,650	16,863,250	18,116,300	20,827,850
%	48.2%	48.2%	48.2%	48.2%	49.0%	48.9%	48.8%	48.8%	47.6%	47.3%	47.3%	47.5%
Y/Y Growth Rate					5.0%	11.7%	15.0%	11.0%	12.4%	11.6%	16.4%	10.2%

TABLE 13.4 DBO Supporting Schedule: Gross Margins

Thomas Technologies, Inc.
Gross Margin

		2016				2017				2018			
		Q1	Q2	Q3	Q4	Q1	Q2	Q3	Q4	Q1	Q2	Q3	Q4
Sales		28,642,500	28,571,250	28,575,000	35,858,750	30,071,250	31,910,000	32,867,500	39,786,250	33,801,250	35,621,250	38,267,500	43,826,450
Product COGS		14,848,000	14,805,600	14,804,400	18,568,000	15,347,000	16,303,700	16,817,100	20,377,400	17,721,600	18,758,000	20,151,200	22,998,600
Product Margin		13,794,500	13,765,650	13,770,600	17,290,750	14,724,250	15,606,300	16,050,400	19,408,850	16,079,650	16,863,250	18,116,300	20,827,850
% to Sales		48.2%	48.2%	48.2%	48.2%	49.0%	48.9%	48.8%	48.8%	47.6%	47.3%	47.3%	47.5%
Other Costs													
Production Variances		25,000	25,000	25,000	25,000	25,000	25,000	25,000	25,000	25,000	25,000	25,000	25,000
Warranty	1.0%	286,425	285,713	285,750	358,588	300,713	319,100	328,675	397,863	338,013	356,213	382,675	438,265
Inventory Provisions		5,000	5,000	5,000	5,000	5,000	5,000	5,000	5,000	5,000	5,000	5,000	5,000
Royalty		750	750	750	750	750	750	750	750	750	750	750	750
Scrap		1,200	1,200	1,200	1,200	1,200	1,200	1,200	1,200	1,200	1,200	1,200	1,200
Sustaining Engineering		800	800	800	800	800	800	800	800	800	800	800	800
Other		24,535	24,392	24,400	38,967	27,392	31,070	32,985	46,822	34,852	38,492	44,285	54,902
Total Other COGS		343,710	342,855	342,900	430,305	360,855	382,920	394,410	477,435	405,615	427,455	459,710	525,917
% to Sales													
Total COGS		15,191,710	15,148,455	15,147,300	18,998,305	15,707,855	16,686,620	17,211,510	20,854,835	18,127,215	19,185,455	20,610,910	23,524,517
Gross Margin		13,450,790	13,422,796	13,427,700	16,860,446	14,363,396	15,223,380	15,655,990	18,931,416	15,674,036	16,435,796	17,656,590	20,301,934
% to Sales		47.0%	47.0%	47.0%	47.0%	47.8%	47.7%	47.6%	47.6%	46.4%	46.1%	46.1%	46.3%
Headcount		2,864	2,857	2,858	3,586	3,007	3,191	3,287	3,979	3,380	3,562	3,827	4,383

TABLE 13.5 DBO Supporting Schedule: Marketing

Thomas Technologies, Inc.
Marketing — Trend Schedule

		2016				2017				2018			
		Q1	Q2	Q3	Q4	Q1	Q2	Q3	Q4	Q1	Q2	Q3	Q4
People Costs													
Salary		745,000	745,000	745,000	745,000	782,250	785,138	785,138	900,138	939,395	939,397	939,397	939,397
Bonus					195,000				150,000				221,000
Other													
Total		745,000	745,000	745,000	940,000	782,250	785,138	785,138	1,050,138	939,395	939,397	939,397	1,160,397
Fringe Benefits	17%	126,650	126,650	126,650	126,650	132,983	133,473	133,473	153,023	159,697	159,697	159,697	159,697
Total Labor and Related Costs		1,616,650	1,616,650	1,616,650	2,006,650	1,697,483	1,703,749	1,703,749	2,253,299	2,038,487	2,038,491	2,038,491	2,480,491
Travel		6,000	6,000	6,000	6,000	8,500	8,500	10,000	12,000	12,000	12,000	12,000	12,000
Meetings		1,500	1,500	1,500	1,500	1,500	1,500	1,500	1,500	1,500	1,500	1,500	1,500
Consultants		–	2,000	1,500	5,000	–	2,000	1,500	5,000	–	2,000	1,500	5,000
Professional Services		2,000	2,000	2,000	2,000	2,000	2,000	2,000	2,000	2,000	2,000	2,000	2,000
Materials		4,200	4,200	4,200	4,200	4,200	4,200	4,200	4,200	4,200	4,200	4,200	4,200
Contract Services		1,200	1,200	1,200	1,200	1,200	1,200	1,200	1,200	1,200	1,200	1,200	1,200
Advertising		5,000	5,000	5,000	5,000	5,000	5,000	5,000	5,000	5,000	5,000	5,000	5,000
Trade Show			15,000				17,000			22,000			
Product Launch				15,000		25,000							
Depreciation		6,000	6,000	6,000	6,000	6,000	6,000	6,000	6,000	6,000	6,000	6,000	6,000
Allocations In		15,000	15,000	15,000	15,000	15,000	15,000	15,000	15,000	15,000	15,000	15,000	15,000
Other		7,500	7,500	7,500	7,500	7,500	7,500	7,500	7,500	7,500	7,500	7,500	7,500
Total Other Expenses		48,400	65,400	64,900	53,400	75,900	69,900	53,900	59,400	76,400	56,400	55,900	59,400
Total Marketing		1,665,050	1,682,050	1,681,550	2,060,050	1,773,383	1,773,649	1,757,649	2,312,699	2,114,887	2,094,891	2,094,391	2,539,891

(continues)

TABLE 13.5 ***(Continued)***

Thomas Technologies, Inc. Marketing Trend Schedule													
		2016				2017				2018			
		Q1	Q2	Q3	Q4	Q1	Q2	Q3	Q4	Q1	Q2	Q3	Q4
Year to Year Growth						6.5%	5.4%	4.5%	12.3%	19.3%	18.1%	19.2%	9.8%
Sales		28,642,500	28,571,250	28,575,000	35,858,750	30,071,250	31,910,000	32,867,500	39,786,250	33,801,250	35,621,250	38,267,500	43,826,450
Marketing % of Sales		5.8%	5.9%	5.9%	5.7%	5.9%	5.6%	5.3%	5.8%	6.3%	5.9%	5.5%	5.8%
Salaries													
CMO	1	145,000	145,000	145,000	145,000	152,250	152,250	152,250	152,250	159,863	159,863	159,863	159,863
Advertising Manager	1	125,000	125,000	125,000	125,000	131,250	131,250	131,250	131,250	137,813	137,813	137,813	137,813
Web Techs	2	180,000	180,000	180,000	180,000	189,000	189,000	189,000	189,000	198,450	198,450	198,450	198,450
Advertising Manager	1	125,000	125,000	125,000	125,000	131,250	131,250	131,250	131,250	137,813	137,813	137,813	137,813
Marketing Manager	1	115,000	115,000	115,000	115,000	120,750	120,750	120,750	120,750	126,788	126,788	126,788	126,788
Admin	1	55,000	55,000	55,000	55,000	57,750	60,638	60,638	60,638	63,670	63,670	63,670	63,670
New Hire Web Manager	1								115,000	115,000	115,000	115,000	115,000
Total Salaries		745,000	745,000	745,000	745,000	782,250	785,138	785,138	900,138	939,395	939,397	939,397	939,397
Headcount	8	7	7	7	7	7	7	7	8	8	8	8	8

TABLE 13.6 DBO Income Statement

Thomas Technologies, Inc.
Income Statement

	2016				2017				2018			
	Q1	Q2	Q3	Q4	Q1	Q2	Q3	Q4	Q1	Q2	Q3	Q4
Revenue	28,642,500	28,571,250	28,575,000	35,858,750	30,071,250	31,910,000	32,867,500	39,786,250	33,801,250	35,621,250	38,267,500	43,826,450
Cost of Revenue	14,848,000	14,805,600	14,804,400	18,568,000	15,347,000	16,303,700	16,817,100	20,377,400	17,721,600	18,758,000	20,151,200	22,998,600
Gross Margin	13,794,500	13,765,650	13,770,600	17,290,750	14,724,250	15,606,300	16,050,400	19,408,850	16,079,650	16,863,250	18,116,300	20,827,850
Gross Margin %	48.2%	48.2%	48.2%	48.2%	49.0%	48.9%	48.8%	48.8%	47.6%	47.3%	47.3%	47.5%
R&D	3,750,400	3,756,400	3,757,900	4,240,400	3,956,850	4,352,934	4,538,347	4,928,330	5,149,837	5,364,475	5,589,846	5,826,485
Selling	4,255,500	4,255,500	4,256,500	4,357,500	4,427,200	4,428,200	4,428,200	4,518,200	4,603,648	4,603,648	4,603,648	4,707,648
Marketing	1,665,050	1,682,050	1,681,550	2,060,050	1,773,383	1,773,649	1,757,649	2,312,699	2,114,887	2,094,891	2,094,391	2,539,891
G&A	2,185,300	2,185,300	2,185,300	2,625,300	2,292,715	2,292,715	2,292,715	2,762,715	2,405,501	2,405,505	2,405,505	2,929,505
Operating Expenses	11,856,250	11,879,250	11,881,250	13,283,250	12,450,148	12,847,498	13,016,911	14,521,945	14,273,872	14,468,520	14,693,391	16,003,530
Operating Income	1,938,250	1,886,400	1,889,350	4,007,500	2,274,103	2,758,802	3,033,489	4,886,905	1,805,778	2,394,730	3,422,909	4,824,320
Operating Income %	6.8%	6.6%	6.6%	11.2%	7.6%	8.6%	9.2%	12.3%	5.3%	6.7%	8.9%	11.0%
Interest Income (Expense)	(3,500)	(3,500)	(3,500)	(3,500)	(3,500)	(3,500)	(3,500)	(3,500)	(3,500)	(3,500)	(3,500)	(3,500)
Other Income (Expense)	2,000	1,800	1,800	1,500	2,000	1,800	1,800	1,500	2,000	1,800	1,800	1,500
Profit Before Tax	1,936,750	1,884,700	1,887,650	4,005,500	2,272,603	2,757,102	3,031,789	4,884,905	1,804,278	2,393,030	3,421,209	4,822,320
Tax 30.0%	(581,025)	(565,410)	(566,295)	(1,201,650)	(681,781)	(827,131)	(909,537)	(1,465,472)	(541,283)	(717,909)	(1,026,363)	(1,446,696)
Net Income	1,355,725	1,319,290	1,321,355	2,803,850	1,590,822	1,929,971	2,122,252	3,419,434	1,262,994	1,675,121	2,394,847	3,375,624

(continues)

TABLE 13.6 *(Continued)*

Thomas Technologies, Inc.
Income Statement

	2016				2017				2018			
	Q1	Q2	Q3	Q4	Q1	Q2	Q3	Q4	Q1	Q2	Q3	Q4
Y/Y												
Revenue	10.0%	12.0%	14.0%	15.0%	5.0%	11.7%	15.0%	11.0%	12.4%	11.6%	16.4%	10.2%
Operating Expenses	5.0%	6.0%	7.0%	8.0%	5.0%	8.2%	9.6%	9.3%	14.6%	12.6%	12.9%	10.2%
Operating Income	12.0%	14.0%	13.0%	12.0%	17.3%	46.2%	60.6%	21.9%	−20.6%	−13.2%	12.8%	−1.3%
% of Sales												
Revenue	100.0%	100.0%	100.0%	100.0%	100.0%	100.0%	100.0%	100.0%	100.0%	100.0%	100.0%	100.0%
Cost of Revenue	51.8%	51.8%	51.8%	51.8%	51.0%	51.1%	51.2%	51.2%	52.4%	52.7%	52.7%	52.5%
Gross Margin	48.2%	48.2%	48.2%	48.2%	49.0%	48.9%	48.8%	48.8%	47.6%	47.3%	47.3%	47.5%
R&D	13.1%	13.1%	13.2%	11.8%	13.2%	13.6%	13.8%	12.4%	15.2%	15.1%	14.6%	13.3%
Selling	14.9%	14.9%	14.9%	12.2%	14.7%	13.9%	13.5%	11.4%	13.6%	12.9%	12.0%	10.7%
Marketing	5.8%	5.9%	5.9%	5.7%	5.9%	5.6%	5.3%	5.8%	6.3%	5.9%	5.5%	5.8%
G&A	7.6%	7.6%	7.6%	7.3%	7.6%	7.2%	7.0%	6.9%	7.1%	6.8%	6.3%	6.7%
Operating Expenses	41.4%	41.6%	41.6%	37.0%	41.4%	40.3%	39.6%	36.5%	42.2%	40.6%	38.4%	36.5%
Operating Income	6.8%	6.6%	6.6%	11.2%	7.6%	8.6%	9.2%	12.3%	5.3%	6.7%	8.9%	11.0%

and cash flow projections. Most competent finance and general managers understand that profit must be evaluated in the context of the investment levels required. Therefore, measures such as asset turnover and return on investment should be presented. Attention to cash balances, liquidity, intermediate financing, and loan covenants are all important responsibilities of financial management and should be incorporated into all projections.

The second reason is that finance teams are much more comfortable in the mechanics of revenue and expense projections. However, once key models are established, it is relatively easy to project key balance sheet and cash flow information. An illustration of a balance sheet and cash flow model is provided in Table 13.7. Techniques to project the balance sheet and cash flow are found in Chapters 17 and 18.

Summarizing and Presenting Business Forecasts and Outlooks

The most effective way to review and present the results of a revised forecast or outlook is to incorporate a presentation summary directly into the forecast model. This will facilitate review, discussions with managers, and revisions. It enables a high-level quality control review of the projections, since the presentation summary will include key variables. Key items that are typically included are major assumptions, changes from prior outlook, key performance metrics, and major risks and upsides. An example of a presentation summary is provided in Figure 13.8.

Frequency and Timing of Forecasts

The frequency and timing of forecasts will depend on several factors. A very dynamic environment will require more frequent updates than a stable environment. Companies that report earnings and provide earnings or other guidance to public capital markets typically use a quarterly cycle. Private companies typically update the outlook around management or board

TABLE 13.7 DBO Supporting Schedule: Balance Sheet and Cash Flow

Thomas Technologies, Inc.
Balance Sheet Cash Flow

		2016				2017				2018			
		Q1	Q2	Q3	Q4	Q1	Q2	Q3	Q4	Q1	Q2	Q3	Q4
Cash		3,200,000	5,357,998	7,766,628	1,424,420	11,386,158	11,388,505	12,720,574	7,591,316	16,594,076	16,246,931	15,631,502	12,252,044
Receivables	90.0	28,642,500	28,571,250	28,575,000	35,858,750	30,071,250	31,910,000	32,867,500	39,786,250	33,801,250	35,621,250	38,267,500	43,826,450
Inventories	3.0	19,797,333	19,740,800	19,739,200	24,757,333	20,462,667	21,738,267	22,422,800	27,169,867	23,628,800	25,010,667	26,868,267	30,664,800
Other													
Current Assets		51,639,833	53,670,048	56,080,828	62,040,503	61,920,075	65,036,771	68,010,874	74,547,432	74,024,126	76,878,847	80,767,269	86,743,294
PP&E		25,000,000	25,750,000	26,150,000	27,250,000	28,250,000	29,250,000	30,250,000	31,250,000	32,250,000	33,250,000	34,250,000	35,250,000
Accumulated Depreciation		12,000,000	13,000,000	14,000,000	15,000,000	16,000,000	17,000,000	18,000,000	19,000,000	20,000,000	21,000,000	22,000,000	23,000,000
Net Fixed Assets		13,000,000	12,750,000	12,150,000	12,250,000	12,250,000	12,250,000	12,250,000	12,250,000	12,250,000	12,250,000	12,250,000	12,250,000
Net Goodwill and Intangibles		24,000,000	23,500,000	23,000,000	22,500,000	22,000,000	21,500,000	21,000,000	20,500,000	20,000,000	19,500,000	19,000,000	18,500,000
Other Noncurrent Assets													
Total Assets		88,639,833	89,920,048	91,230,828	96,790,503	96,170,075	98,786,771	101,260,874	107,297,432	106,274,126	108,628,847	112,017,269	117,493,294
Accounts Payable	20.0%	5,728,500	5,714,250	5,715,000	7,171,750	6,014,250	6,382,000	6,573,500	7,957,250	6,760,250	7,124,250	7,653,500	8,765,290
Notes Payable, Bank		1,000,000	1,000,000	1,000,000	1,000,000	1,000,000	1,000,000	1,000,000	1,000,000	1,000,000	1,000,000	1,000,000	1,000,000
Accrued Expenses & Taxes	18.0%	5,155,650	5,142,825	5,143,500	6,454,575	5,412,825	5,743,800	5,916,150	7,161,525	6,084,225	6,411,825	6,888,150	7,888,761
Current Liabilities		11,884,150	11,857,075	11,858,500	14,626,325	12,427,075	13,125,800	13,489,650	16,118,775	13,844,475	14,536,075	15,541,650	17,654,051
Long-Term Debt		12,000,000	12,000,000	12,000,000	12,000,000	12,000,000	12,000,000	12,000,000	12,000,000	12,000,000	12,000,000	12,000,000	12,000,000
Other		-											
Stockholders' Equity		64,498,658	65,805,948	67,115,303	69,907,153	71,485,975	73,403,946	75,514,198	78,921,632	80,172,626	81,835,747	84,218,594	87,582,218
Total Liabilities and Equity		88,382,808	89,663,023	90,973,803	96,533,478	95,913,050	98,529,746	101,003,848	107,040,407	106,017,101	108,371,822	111,760,244	117,236,269
Proof		257,025	257,025	257,025	257,025	257,025	257,025	257,025	257,025	257,025	257,025	257,025	257,025
Operating Capital		37,555,683	37,454,975	37,455,700	46,989,758	39,106,842	41,522,467	42,800,650	51,837,342	44,585,575	47,095,842	50,594,117	57,837,199
Total Debt		13,000,000	13,000,000	13,000,000	13,000,000	13,000,000	13,000,000	13,000,000	13,000,000	13,000,000	13,000,000	13,000,000	13,000,000
Invested Capital													

TABLE 13.7 *(Continued)*

Thomas Technologies, Inc.
Balance Sheet Cash Flow

	2016				2017				2018			
	Q1	Q2	Q3	Q4	Q1	Q2	Q3	Q4	Q1	Q2	Q3	Q4
Cash Flow												
Net Income	1,355,725	1,319,290	1,321,355	2,803,850	1,590,822	1,929,971	2,122,252	3,419,434	1,262,994	1,675,121	2,394,847	3,375,624
D&A	1,400,000	1,500,000	1,500,000	1,500,000	1,500,000	1,500,000	1,500,000	1,500,000	1,500,000	1,500,000	1,500,000	1,500,000
Capital Expenditures	600,000	(750,000)	(400,000)	(1,100,000)	(1,000,000)	(1,000,000)	(1,000,000)	(1,000,000)	(1,000,000)	(1,000,000)	(1,000,000)	(1,000,000)
(Inc) Decrease in OC	500,000	100,708	(725)	(9,534,058)	7,882,917	(2,415,625)	(1,278,183)	(9,036,692)	7,251,767	(2,510,267)	(3,498,275)	(7,243,082)
OCF	3,855,725	2,169,998	2,420,630	(6,330,208)	9,973,738	14,346	1,344,069	(5,117,258)	9,014,761	(335,146)	(603,428)	(3,367,458)
Dividends	(2,000)	(2,000)	(2,000)	(2,000)	(2,000)	(2,000)	(2,000)	(2,000)	(2,000)	(2,000)	(2,000)	(2,000)
Share Proceeds (Repurchases)	(10,000)	(10,000)	(10,000)	(10,000)	(10,000)	(10,000)	(10,000)	(10,000)	(10,000)	(10,000)	(10,000)	(10,000)
Other												
Debt (Payments) Borrowing												
Cash Flow	3,843,725	2,157,998	2,408,630	(6,342,208)	9,961,738	2,346	1,332,069	(5,129,258)	9,002,761	(347,146)	(615,428)	(3,379,458)
Sales	28,642,500	28,571,250	28,575,000	35,858,750	30,071,250	31,910,000	32,867,500	39,786,250	33,801,250	35,621,250	38,267,500	43,826,450
DSO	90.0	90.0	90.0	90.0	90.0	90.0	90.0	90.0	90.0	90.0	90.0	90.0
Inventory Turns	3.0	3.0	3.0	3.0	3.0	3.0	3.0	3.0	3.0	3.0	3.0	3.0
DSI	121.7	121.7	121.7	121.7	121.7	121.7	121.7	121.7	121.7	121.7	121.7	121.7
Asset Turnover	1.3	1.3	1.3	1.5	1.3	1.3	1.3	1.5	1.3	1.3	1.4	1.5
Debt to Total Capital (Book)	16.8%	16.5%	16.2%	15.7%	15.4%	15.0%	14.7%	14.1%	14.0%	13.7%	13.4%	12.9%

FIGURE 13.8 DBO Presentation Summary

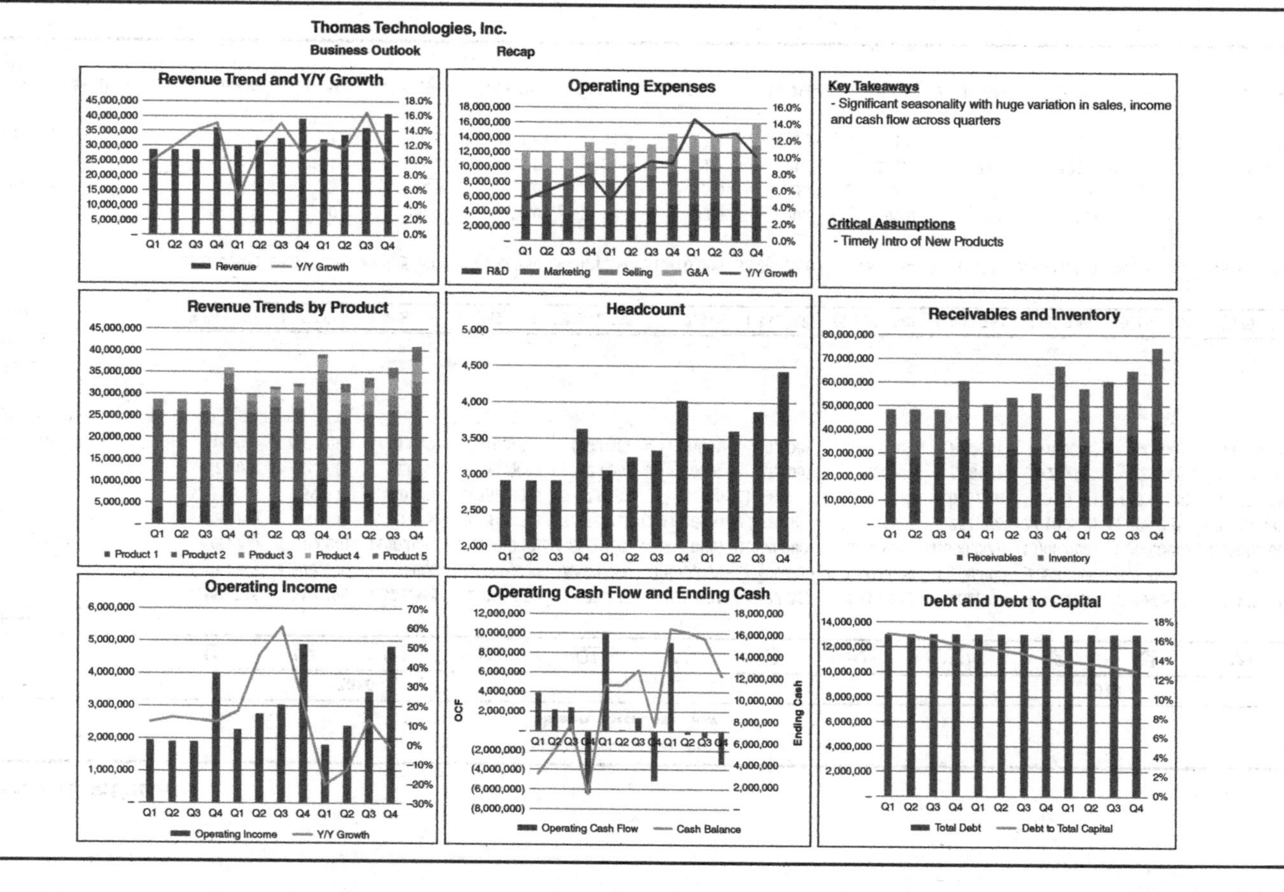

of directors meetings. Significant events, such as contract awards or losses, may dictate a special revision to the business outlook.

Analysis and Evaluation of Financial Projections

In Chapter 12, we introduced tools for analyzing and evaluating projections. These tools should be incorporated into the DBO model. For short-term projections, revenue and expense levels can be compared to current run rates and results from the prior period. It is vital to identify and evaluate critical assumptions included in the projections.

SUMMARY

The pace of change in the world today requires most organizations to create more effective planning and forecasting processes. Most organizations have developed an operating plan to replace the financially focused budget process of old. Due to the pace of change, organizations must frequently update business projections. Organizations need a process to project financial performance periodically, as well as on demand, to perform what-if analysis to evaluate the impact of potential changes and strategic alternatives.

The on-demand business outlook is yet another evolution in planning and forecasting. *On-demand* refers to the ability to update the business projections at any time. The term *business outlook* shifts the perception from a financial drill to an outlook of business trends and factors.

NOTE

1. Several variations of this quote are widely attributed to General (and subsequently President) Dwight Eisenhower. He attributes it to a long-held view in the army about planning for battle and the recognition of unexpected aspects; that is, battles (and businesses) will not play out the way people have planned. The only official documentation of these remarks is in a speech to the National Defense Executive Reserve Conference in Washington, DC (November 14, 1957); in *Public Papers of the Presidents of the United States, Dwight D. Eisenhower, 1957*, National Archives and Records Service (Washington, DC: Government Printing Office), 818.

14

LONG-TERM PROJECTIONS

CHAPTER INTRODUCTION

In this chapter, we will focus on developing projections over the long term. We will build on the practices and techniques introduced in Chapter 12, Business Projections and Plans. Long-term projections (LTPs) are required to evaluate new products, acquisitions, capital investments, and strategic plans.

In simpler times, LTPs could be easily developed by extrapolating historical performance trends or extending static business models. Over the past 30 years, factors such as globalization, technology developments, geopolitical events, demographics, and economic factors have significantly impacted markets and businesses.

Developing projections of performance over an extended period introduces some unique challenges that require a robust process to overcome. Uncertainty about the future should imply that most LTPs should be accompanied by multiple scenarios and thorough identification, testing, and evaluation of underlying assumptions.

UNIQUE CHALLENGES IN ESTIMATING LONG-TERM PERFORMANCE

Longer Forecast Horizon

Long-term projections (LTPs) will have an extended time horizon, ranging from two to five or more years. The methods and considerations used for short- to midterm projections are usually not well suited to LTPs. There should be less emphasis on performance details and more understanding of strategic issues, market forces, and long-term performance drivers.

Greater Uncertainty

The longer the horizon of our plan or projections, the greater the uncertainty. Few of us standing here now could have reasonably expected many of the events and changes experienced in just the past several years. Many of the strategic plans developed five years ago may appear absurd in hindsight, given the changes that could not have been anticipated. So why plan? Again, the value is in the planning, not the plan itself. If these organizations identified risks and opportunities and developed alternative scenarios, then they likely were better prepared to react to unforeseen changes that have unfolded.

Capability Required to Model Strategic Alternatives and Scenarios

The value in any plan is not the document or a single projection. The value is the critical thinking, anticipation, and identification of critical assumptions, critical success factors (CSFs), and performance drivers.

The model must be robust to consider radical changes to an organization's market, distribution channel, business model, and cost structure over a three- to five-year period. One scenario should be a simple extrapolation of recent performance trends. Other scenarios should flex key assumptions about the economy, market drivers, key cost drivers, and other factors. An important aspect of strategic planning is the identification of alternative courses of action. The long-term model must be able to portray the financial implications and results of various alternatives.

The key lies in the critical thinking the management team steps through in thinking about a range of potential scenarios.

Comprehensive View of Performance

Many organizations limit the content of long-term projections to the income statement. Long-term projections must include a complete view of the expected performance, including the balance sheet, cash flow and investment evaluation, and valuation. Any evaluation of future decisions or alternatives must include expected capital requirements, liquidity, a determination of the economic value created, and an evaluation of the investments contemplated in the plan. Why would any responsible executives embark on a plan that, if achieved, does not create value or cannot be financed by the firm?

APPLICATIONS OF LONG-TERM PROJECTIONS

Long-term projections are developed and utilized for a number of applications. The format and content of the projections must be tailored to the specific application.

Strategic Planning

LTPs must be developed as part of any strategic planning process. These projections will estimate the results of a certain strategy and allow for the evaluation of strategic alternatives. The LTPs must be developed using a robust model that can project financial results over several years (the planning horizon).

New Product Development

The evaluation of potential new products should include a complete plan containing strategic plan, execution plan, and financial projections. New product development activities are investments and should be analyzed as such. The financial projections must include all investments in development and capital as well as projected sales and expenses. New product development projections are covered in Chapters 20 and 21.

New Business Creation

The evaluation of potential new businesses should also include a complete plan containing strategic plan, execution plan, and financial projections. New business creation activities are investments and should be analyzed as such. The financial projections must include all investments in development and capital as well as projected sales and expenses. Projections for new business plans are covered in Chapters 20 and 21, and the valuation of businesses is covered in Chapter 22.

Mergers and Acquisitions

Mergers and acquisitions (M&A) represent substantial investments that must yield a return in the form of future financial results. The evaluation of potential acquisitions should also include a complete plan containing strategy, execution, and financial projections. The investment in an acquisition includes the purchase price, associated costs, and costs to implement synergies. Future projections must consider the stand-alone results of the acquirer and the target and the projected synergies resulting from the combination. M&A is covered in detail in Chapter 23.

Other Capital Investment Decisions

In addition to new products, new business, and M&A decisions, many other capital investment decisions will require long-term projections.

Examples include geographic expansion, purchases of manufacturing equipment, and plant expansions, which will all require the development of long-term projections.

DEVELOPING LONG-TERM PROJECTIONS

The process of developing an LTP is not simply a number-crunching exercise. The analyst must work closely with key managers and become extremely familiar with the strategic issues and opportunities of the organization. Significant consideration of strategic issues, opportunities, markets, and competitors must be reflected in the LTP. Best practices such as market analysis, benchmarking, competitor analysis, and SLOT analysis should be employed.

Assess Current Situation

As with any projection, LTPs must start with an assessment of the current situation and environment. This is particularly true with long-term projections. This process must include an assessment of the organization's strengths, limitations (or weaknesses), opportunities, and threats (SLOT) (Figure 14.1). The external environment must be monitored and reflected in the plan. The analyst must also be familiar with the strategic plan. A determination of the status of previous strategic objectives must be made. Recent performance trends must be identified and their impact on future performance considered.

Incorporate and Review Historical Results

In developing the model for use in developing LTPs, it is important to incorporate history. This has two advantages. First, the inclusion of history helps to identify key drivers and assumptions that are critical to projecting future projections. Second, it provides confidence in the relationship between these drivers and the actual financial results posted in prior years represented in the LTP model.

FIGURE 14.1 **SLOT Analysis**

SLOT Analysis

Strengths	**Limitations (Weaknesses)**
☐ Significant market share ☐ Products with strong competitive advantages	☐ High debt levels ☐ Reduced cash flow ☐ Aging workforce
Threats	**Opportunities**
☐ Emerging competitor ☐ Key customer evaluating in-sourcing ☐ Potential (disruptive) technology possible	☐ Several acquisition opportunities ☐ Potential to extend current products to new market

Identify Strategic Issues

Strategic issues must be considered in the development of LTPs. These may include changes in the overall market, competitive threats, weaknesses that must be overcome, and many other issues that will impact future financial performance.

Identify and Model Critical Assumptions and Business Drivers

Critical assumptions and business drivers that will affect future performance must be explicitly identified. Too often, these are buried in formulas in a model that prevent review and testing. These items will vary for each individual business. In some cases, market forces will be the most important. In others, product life cycles and introduction plans are critical. Key costs drivers must be identified and incorporated into LTP models.

Critical assumptions must be documented, reviewed, and tested. Sensitivity and scenario analysis should be integral elements of the plan.

Evaluate Strategic Alternatives and Scenarios

One of the objectives of strategic planning is to consider alternatives to the company's existing or primary strategic direction. This may be the most important contribution of the strategic planning and LTP process. Examples of strategic alternatives include alternative distribution channels, entering new product or geographic markets, and acquisitions. Other scenarios that are often explored are competitive threats, disruptive technologies, or flexing broad economic assumptions. The LTP model must be flexible enough to develop these alternative scenarios efficiently.

Projecting Key Performance Drivers

This section briefly covers techniques for projecting key areas of financial performance. These will be illustrated with two models in this chapter. Of course, any model must be tailored to the specific situation of each organization. Additional models and best practices are included in Part Four, Planning and Analysis for Critical Business and Value Drivers.

Revenue

Revenue is typically the most important driver and generally the most difficult to predict, both in the long term and in the short term. Accordingly, it warrants the most thought and attention. The drivers that are most important will vary greatly from company to company and may vary over time. In some cases, key revenue drivers will be product related and must consider new product introductions and product life cycles. This would certainly be important for Apple and other technology device providers. Other drivers may include market forces, foreign currency rates, macroeconomic trends, and competitors. Table 14.1 focuses on product drivers and market and competitive share.

Gross Margins

Gross margins are impacted by several factors, including product mix, margins on new products, production and commodity costs, transportation costs, and currency. In our example in Table 14.1, the gross margin projection is incorporated into the revenue plan.

TABLE 14.1 LTP: Revenue and Margin Projections

02-04-2018 14:23	Revenue and Margins				LRP							
	History			CY	Projections					CAGR		
	2014	2015	2016	2017	2018	2019	2020	2021	2022	History	Future	Assumptions/Notes
Sales Product 1200	500	495	485	475	469	450	430	420	400	−1.5%	−3.4%	Successful model slowly showing lower volume
Gross Margin	250	245	237.65	232.75	225.12	211.5	197.8	189	180			
%	50%	50%	49%	49%	48%	47%	46%	45%	45%			
Sales Product 1250	0	15	50	100	125	130	132	130	125		4.6%	Introduced 2015
Gross Margin	0	8.25	27.5	55	68.75	70.2	71.28	68.9	65			
%	#DIV/0!	55%	55%	55%	55%	54%	54%	53%	52%			
Sales Product 1300	300	250	200	150	100	20	0	0	0	−18.4%	−100.0%	Older model at tail end of product life cycle
Gross Margin	150	125	100	75	50	10	0	0	0			
%	50%	50%	50%	50%	50%	50%	#DIV/0!	#DIV/0!	#DIV/0!			
Sales Product 1400	50	52	48	47	53	58	62	66	70	−2.0%	8.3%	
Gross Margin	24	26	24	23.5	26.5	29	31	33	35			
%	48%	50%	50%	50%	50%	50%	50%	50%	50%			
Sales Product 2000	0	0	0	25	75	200	300	500	600	–	88.8%	Introduced 4th quarter of 2019
Gross Margin	0	0	0	12.5	37.5	80	120	200	240			
%	#DIV/0!	#DIV/0!	#DIV/0!	50%	50%	40%	40%	40%	40%			

TABLE 14.1 *(Continued)*

02-04-2018 14:23	Revenue and Margins				LRP							
	History			CY	Projections					CAGR		
	2014	**2015**	**2016**	**2017**	**2018**	**2019**	**2020**	**2021**	**2022**	**History**	**Future**	**Assumptions/Notes**
Sales Total	850.0	812.0	783.0	797.0	822.0	858.0	924.0	1,116.0	1,195.0	−4.0%	8.4%	
Gross Margin	424.0	404.3	389.2	398.8	407.9	400.7	420.1	490.9	520.0			
%	50%	50%	50%	50%	50%	47%	45%	44%	44%			
Revenue Growth Y/Y ($M)	−10	−38.0	−29.0	14.0	25.0	36.0	66.0	192.0	79.0			
Revenue Growth Y/Y %	2%	−4.5%	−3.6%	1.8%	3.1%	4.4%	7.7%	20.8%	7.1%			
Market Size and Share												
This Company	850.0	812.0	783.0	797.0	822.0	858.0	924.0	1,116.0	1,195.0	−4.0%	8.4%	
Competitor 1	50.0	50.0	50.0	50.0	50.0	50.0	50.0	50.0	50.0	0.0%	0.0%	
Competitor 2	500.0	600.0	700.0	800.0	900.0	950.0	1,050.0	1,125.0	1,250.0	18.3%	9.3%	
Competitor 3	145.0	159.5	175.5	193.0	200.0	220.0	242.0	266.2	292.8	10.0%	8.7%	
Competitor 4	200.0	175.0	150.0	100.0	75.0	50.0				−13.4%	−100.0%	
Total Market	1,745.0	1,796.5	1,858.5	1,940.0	2,047.0	2,128.0	2,266.0	2,557.2	2,787.8	3.2%	7.5%	
Market Share	48.7%	45.2%	42.1%	41.1%	40.2%	40.3%	40.8%	43.6%	42.9%			
Market Growth		51.5	62.0	81.5	107.0	81.0	138.0	291.2	230.6			
Market Growth Rate		3%	3%	4%	6%	4%	6%	13%	9%			
Our Share of Market Growth		−74%	−47%	17%	23%	44%	48%	66%	34%			

Costs and Expenses

Projecting costs and expenses over several years presents some unique challenges (Table 14.2). Many organizations start with a simple extrapolation of historical costs. For some types of expenses this is a practical approach. However, for significant expenses or those subject to high volatility, this approach is too simplistic, especially over a term of three to five years. Some expenses will vary with revenue levels. Others are driven by projects or investments that are incurred long before the associated revenue. Many others are highly volatile, including health care, commodity prices, and staffing. For these volatile and unpredictable costs, different scenarios or sensitivity analysis should be incorporated into the plan. They also should be reviewed for potential mitigating actions over the course of the plan.

Capital Requirements

In developing LTPs we must consider two capital requirements: (1) working capital and (2) property and equipment.

Working Capital. Working capital requirements can be a significant cash requirement, especially in growth situations. These can easily be estimated in the future by using key metrics such as days sales outstanding (DSO) and inventory turns to project receivables and inventory balances in the future. However, these metrics may change in the future owing to changes in distribution channels, markets, manufacturing, and integration decisions.

The Capsule Financial Summary table at the end of this main section includes projected working capital based on historical measures for DSO, days sales of inventory (DSI), and accounts payable and accrued as a percentage of sales.

Property, Plant, and Equipment (PP&E). If significant, future estimates of PP&E should be based on the existing bases of assets and future capital requirements. Depreciation and accumulated depreciation should be based on the anticipated additions.

Most organizations have a base level of expenditures to support general business and replacement requirements. To this base level of capital

TABLE 14.2 LTP: Operating Expense Projections

	Operating Expenses				LRP							
	History			CY	Projections					CAGR		
	2014	2015	2016	2017	2018	2019	2020	2021	2022	History	Future	Assumptions/Notes
Research and Development												
Base	75.0	79.5	84.3	89.3	94.7	100.4	106.4	112.8	119.5	6.0%	6.0%	
Incremental Project Expenses												
Product 1250	12.0	7.0	4.0									Competed 2016
Product 2000				10.0	40.0	20.0						Product Development started 2017
All Other		5.0	7.0					12.0	17.0			
Total R&D	87.0	91.5	95.3	99.3	134.7	120.4	106.4	124.8	136.5	4.6%	6.6%	
Y/Y Growth ($M)	0.05	5%	4%	4%	36%	−11%	−12%	17%	9%			
% of Sales	10%	11%	12%	12%	16%	14%	12%	11%	11%			
Marketing												
Base	50.0	53.0	56.2	59.6	63.1	66.9	70.9	75.2	79.7	6.0%	6.0%	
Product Launch 1250		12.0										Launch Costs based on Product Development
Product Launch 2000					5.0	22.0						
Product Launch Other			1.5						1.0			
Total Marketing	50.0	65.0	57.7	59.6	68.1	88.9	70.9	75.2	80.7	7.4%	6.3%	
Y/Y Growth ($M)	0.05	30%	−11%	3%	14%	31%	−20%	6%	7%			
% of Sales	6%	8%	7%	7%	8%	10%	8%	7%	7%			

TABLE 14.2 (Continued)

	Operating Expenses				LRP							
	History			CY	Projections					CAGR		
	2014	2015	2016	2017	2018	2019	2020	2021	2022	History	Future	Assumptions/Notes
Selling, General and Administrative												
Base	115.0	121.9	129.2	137.0	145.2	153.9	163.1	172.9	183.3	6.0%	6.0%	
Initiatives-Cyber Security Program				2.0	12.0	5.0	3.0	3.0	3.0			
Legal Settlement	2.0		12.0									
Consultant Strategic Plan				4.0								
IT New System	1.0	4.0										
Total SG&A	117.0	121.9	141.2	143.0	157.2	158.9	166.1	175.9	186.3	9.9%	5.4%	
Y/Y Growth ($M)	5%	4%	16%	1%	10%	1%	5%	6%	6%			
% of Sales	14%	15%	18%	18%	19%	19%	18%	16%	16%			
Total Operating Expenses	254.0	278.4	294.2	301.8	360.0	368.2	343.4	375.9	403.5	7.6%	6.0%	
% of Sales	29.9%	34.3%	37.6%	37.9%	43.8%	42.9%	37.2%	33.7%	33.8%			
Y/Y Growth ($M)		24.4	15.8	7.7	58.2	8.2	−24.7	32.4	27.7			
Y/Y Growth %		10%	6%	3%	19%	2%	−7%	9%	7%			

expenditures, we must estimate any large expenditures to support strategic initiatives, for example manufacturing facilities to support new product introductions and also to expand manufacturing facilities.

Once the capital plan is developed, depreciation expense can be estimated using a model similar to Table 14.3.

Balance Sheet and Cash Flow

The LTP model generally should include balance sheet and cash flow projections. In addition to working capital and PP&E, other important balance sheet captions can be incorporated into the model. For many captions such as prepaids, other assets, or accruals, these can be estimated using the historical percentage to sales. Each should be examined for any unique driver that would warrant further analysis and thought.

After estimating future these future asset and liability levels (and profit and loss), we can model the financing and capital requirements and cash balances or shortages. Some strategic plans will result in self-financing scenarios, whereas others will require significant additional capital to fund future growth and investments. By developing an integrated model, we can estimate the cash generation or requirements derived by the plan. We can also project and evaluate any potential conflicts with existing financing restrictions or loan covenants.

Our simple model effectively projects cash flow, cash balances, and financing requirements in Table 14.4.

Returns and Value Creation

For most organizations, the overall objective is to create value for shareholders. It would be inappropriate to prepare a strategy and an LTP that do not estimate and evaluate the levels of returns (e.g. ROIC) and value creation (estimated share price or value of business). The results for ROIC and shareholder value in Table 14.3 would certainly provide cause for reevaluating this plan!

TABLE 14.3 LTP: Capital Assets and Depreciation

Property, Plant & Equipment
Capital Requirements

		History			CY	Projections				
		2014	2015	2016	2017	2018	2019	2020	2021	2022
Capital Expenditures										
Prior	Prior	45.0								
General	2014	7.0								
General	2015		12.0							
General	2016			13.0						
General	2017				15.0					
Fabrication Plant New Product	2018					30.0				
General	2018					15.0				
General	2019						17.0			
Plant Expansion-Growth	2020							45.0		
General	2020							18.0		
General	2021								19.0	
General	2022									21.0
Total Capital Expenditures		7.0	12.0	13.0	15.0	45.0	17.0	63.0	19.0	21.0

		History			CY	Projections				
		2014	2015	2016	2017	2018	2019	2020	2021	2022
Depreciation Expense*										
Prior	Prior	7	5	3	2					
General	2014	1.4	1.4	1.4	1.4	1.4				
General	2015		2.4	2.4	2.4	2.4	2.4			
General	2016			2.6	2.6	2.6	2.6	2.6		
General	2017				3.0	3.0	3.0	3.0	3.0	
Fabrication Plant New Product	2018					1.5	1.5	1.5	1.5	1.5
General	2018					3.0	3.0	3.0	3.0	3.0
General	2019						3.4	3.4	3.4	3.4
Plant Expansion-Growth	2020							2.3	2.3	2.3
General	2020							3.6	3.6	3.6
General	2021								3.8	3.8
General	2022									4.2
Total		8.4	8.8	9.4	11.4	13.9	15.9	19.4	20.6	21.8

* Assumes 5 year straight-Line depreciation, except for Fab Plant and Plant Expansion (20 years)

Property, Plant & Equipment Recap	History			CY	Projections				
	2014	2015	2016	2017	2018	2019	2020	2021	2022
Property Plant and Equipment									
Beginning Balance	45.0	52.0	64.0	77.0	92.0	137.0	154.0	217.0	236.0
Capital Expenditures	7.0	12.0	13.0	15.0	45.0	17.0	63.0	19.0	21.0
Retirements									
Ending Balance	52.0	64.0	77.0	92.0	137.0	154.0	217.0	236.0	257.0
Accumulated Depreciation									
Beginning Balance	30.0	38.4	47.2	56.6	68.0	81.9	97.8	117.2	137.7
Depreciation	8.4	8.8	9.4	11.4	13.9	15.9	19.4	20.6	21.8
Retirements									
Ending Balance	38.4	47.2	56.6	68.0	81.9	97.8	117.2	137.7	159.5
PP&E, net of depreciation	13.6	16.8	20.4	24.0	55.1	56.2	99.9	98.3	97.6

TABLE 14.4 LTP: Capsule Financial Summary

	History			CY	Projections					Historical	Future
	2014	2015	2016	2017	2018	2019	2020	2021	2022	CAGR	CAGR
Income Statement											
Sales	850.0	812.0	783.0	797.0	822.0	858.0	924.0	1,116.0	1,195.0	−2%	8%
Gross Margin	424.0	404.3	389.2	398.8	407.9	400.7	420.1	490.9	520.0		
%	50%	50%	50%	50%	50%	47%	45%	44%	44%		
Operating Expenses	254.0	278.4	294.2	301.8	360.0	368.2	343.4	375.9	403.5	6%	6%
Income from Operations	170.0	125.9	95.0	96.9	47.9	32.5	76.6	115.0	116.5		
%	20.0%	15.5%	12.1%	12.2%	5.8%	3.8%	8.3%	10.3%	9.7%		
Other Income (Loss)	1.0	−1.0	1.5	0.7	0.5	0.7	0.8	0.6	0.5		
Profit Before Taxes	171.0	124.9	96.5	97.6	48.4	33.2	77.4	115.6	117.0		
Net Income	111.2	81.2	62.7	63 .4	31.4	21.6	50.3	75.2	76.0		
%	13.1%	10.0%	8.0%	8.0%	3.8%	2.5%	5.4%	6.7%	6.4%		
Balance Sheet											
Cash	47.8	83.9	134.0	161.6	139.0	130.9	107.2	125.9	169.8		
Receivables	158.0	175.0	170.0	174.7	168.9	176.3	189.9	229.3	245.5		
Inventory	120.0	145.0	140.0	147.3	153.2	169.1	186.4	231.2	249.7		
Property & Equipment	52.0	64.0	77.0	92.0	137.0	154.0	217.0	236.0	257.0		
Accumulated Depreciation	−38.4	−47.2	−56.6	−68.0	−81.9	−97.8	−117.2	−137.7	−159.5		
Other											
Total Assets	339.4	420.7	464.4	507.5	516.1	532.5	583.3	684.7	762.6		
Accounts Payable	125.0	132.0	141.0	119.6	98.6	103.0	110.9	133.9	143.4		
Accrued Liabilities	60.0	68.0	51.0	63.8	74.0	77.2	83.2	100.4	107.6		
Other	4.4										
Long-Term Debt	0.0	0.0	0.0	0.0	0.0	0.0	0.0	0.0	0.0		
Other											
Capital	40.0	40.0	40.0	40.0	40.0	40.0	40.0	40.0	40.0		
Retained Earnings	110.0	180.7	232.4	284.2	303.5	312.4	349.3	410.4	471.6		

TABLE 14.4 (continued)

	History			CY	Projections					Historical	Future
	2014	2015	2016	2017	2018	2019	2020	2021	2022	CAGR	CAGR
Total Liabilities and Equity	339.4	420.7	464.4	507.5	516.1	532.5	583.3	684.7	762.6		
Proof	0.0	0.0	0.0	0.0	0.0	0.0	0.0	0.0	0.0		
Operating Capital	88.6	120.0	118.0	138.7	149.5	165.3	182.2	226.2	244.3		
Cash Flow											
Net Income	111.2	81.2	62.7	63.4	31.4	21.6	50.3	75.2	76.0		
Add: D&A	8.4	8.8	9.4	11.4	13.9	15.9	19.4	20.6	21.8		
Capital Expenditures	−7.0	−12.0	−13.0	−15.0	−45.0	−17.0	−63.0	−19.0	−21.0		
(Increase) Decrease in Operating Capital	−5.0	−31.4	2.0	−20.7	−10.8	−15.8	−16.9	−44.0	−18.1		
Operating Cash Flow	107.6	46.6	61.1	39.2	−10.4	4.7	−10.3	32.8	58.7		
Debt Borrowings (Payments)											
Dividends	−10.0	−10.5	−11.0	−11.6	−12.2	−12.8	−13.4	−14.1	−14.8		
Cash Flow	97.6	36.1	50.1	27.6	−22.6	−8.1	−23.7	18.7	43.9		
Key Metrics											
Y/Y Revenue Growth		−4%	−4%	2%	3%	4%	8%	21%	7%		
Operating Expense % of Sales	29.9%	34.3%	37.6%	37.9%	43.8%	42.9%	37.2%	33.7%	33.8%		
Tax Rate	35%	35%	35%	35%	35%	35%	35%	35%	35%		
Days Sales Outstanding	68	79	79	80	75	75	75	75	75		
Days Sales Inventory	103	130	130	135	135	135	135	135	135		
Accounts Payable % Sales	14.7%	16.3%	18.0%	15.0%	12.0%	12.0%	12.0%	12.0%	12.0%		
Accrued Expenses % Sales	7.1%	8.4%	11.0%	8.0%	9.0%	9.0%	9.0%	9.0%	9.0%		
Debt to Total Capital	0	0	0	0	0	0	0	0	0		
Return on Assets	32.7%	19.3%	13.5%	12.5%	6.1%	4.1%	8.6%	11.0%	10.0%		
Return on Equity	74.1%	36.8%	23.0%	19.6%	9.2%	6.1%	12.9%	16.7%	14.9%		
Return on Invested Capital	73.7%	37.1%	22.7%	19.4%	9.1%	6.0%	12.8%	16.6%	14.8%		
Estimated Enterprise Value	1,020.0	755.3	569.9	581.4	287.3	195.2	459.8	690.2	698.9		
Estimated Value of Equity	1,020.0	755.3	569.9	581.4	287.3	195.2	459.8	690.2	698.9		

PRESENTATION OF LONG-TERM PROJECTIONS

The models used to develop projections of performance well into the future are likely to be complex. The results of the LTP model must be summarized and presented for effective communication and presentation. The best way to accomplish this is to prepare a well-designed presentation summary (see Figure 14.2) and integrate it directly into the LTP model. This will facilitate presenting the outcome of revisions and scenario analysis.

FIGURE 14.2 LTP: Presentation Summary 

Critical Assumptions

Significant growth over horizon of plan, primarily due to introduction of Model 2000.

Gross margins decline from 50% to 44% due to lower margins on Model 2000.

Strong balance sheet and cash flow maintained over plan horizon.

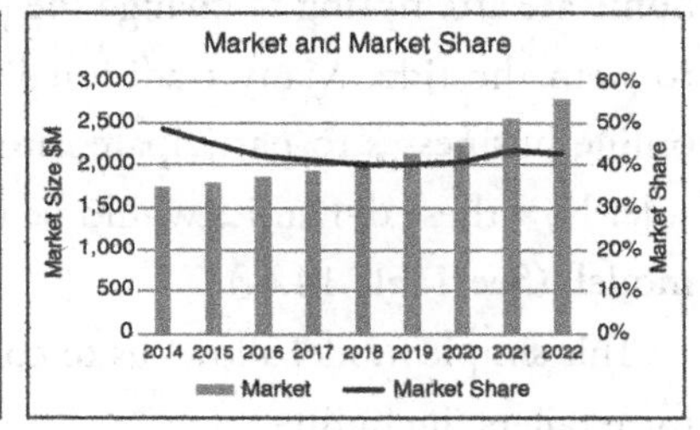

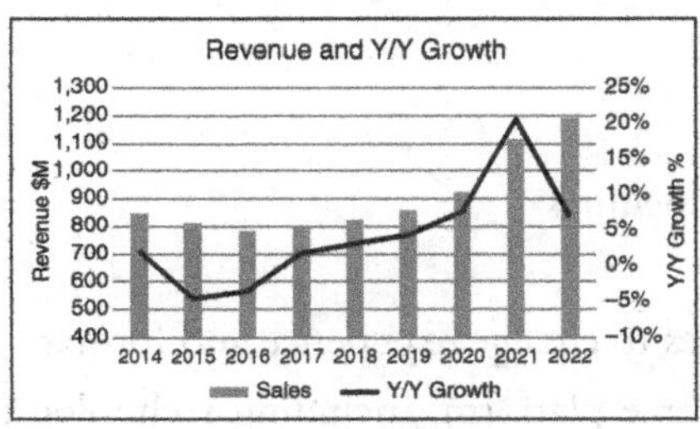

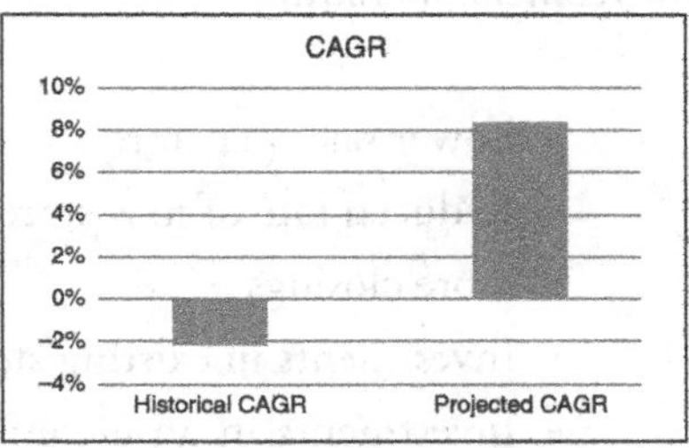

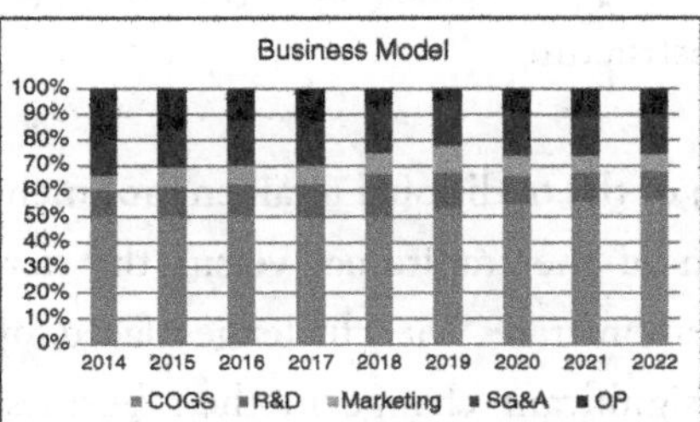

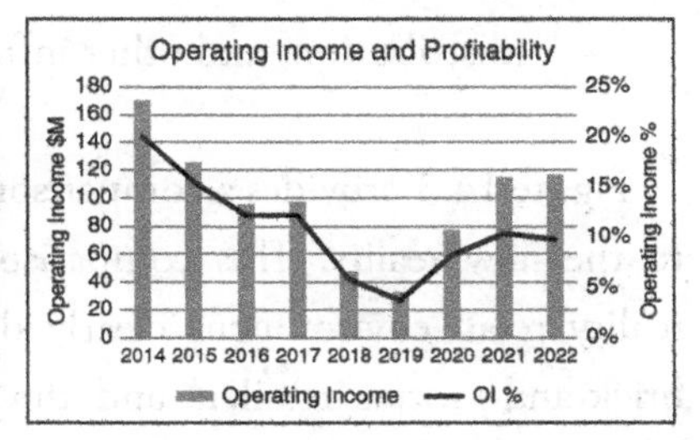

Strategic Model for Tumultuous Industries

Many organizations are facing significant changes in their market or disruptive forces such as technology or nontraditional competitors. Such is the fate of traditional brick-and-mortar retailers as e-commerce retailers continue to drastically cut into their market share.

In the past, a projections model for a retailer would focus on maintaining sales for existing stores and opening new stores. Table 14.5 is a high-level summary of the key drivers. Revenue growth would be driven by opening new stores and increasing sales per store.

Now these retailers are faced with declining sales in their stores and are forced to offer more promotions and discounts to retain customers. Some are attempting to change the product offerings and store experience to stem the tide. Many traditional retailers are also attempting to build online businesses to participate directly in this new retail segment. Consider how these dynamics would be represented in a long-term projections model. (See Table 14.6.)

This simple model allows us to consider the dynamics of the new reality for retailers, including:

- Lower sales per store
- Reduced rate of new store openings
- Store closings
- Investments in existing stores to change experience and format
- Investments in an e-commerce platform, including technology, distribution, and other infrastructure

Figure 14.3 provides a comparison of the traditional retail environment to the new reality. This comparison of the traditional versus the new reality retail environment clearly demonstrates the challenges faced by brick-and-mortar retailers and the significant change in their business models going forward.

TABLE 14.5 **Traditional Retail Model**

		Retailer Traditional Model							
Existing Stores		**2012**	**2013**	**2014**	**2015**	**2016**	**2018**	**2019**	**2020**
# of Stores		865	911	957	1008	1064	1120	1181	1242
Average Revenue per Store ($M)		12.5	12.6	12.7	12.8	12.9	12.9	12.9	12.9
Revenue Existing Stores		10,813	11,479	12,154	12,902	13,726	14,448	15,235	16,022
Total Store Margin		2,163	2,296	2,431	2,580	2,745	2,890	3,047	3,204
%		20.0%	20.0%	20.0%	20.0%	20.0%	20.0%	20.0%	20.0%
Store Closings		4	4	4	4	4	4	4	4
New Store Openings									
# of Stores		50	50	55	60	60	65	65	70
1st Year Revenue per Store ($M)		4.0	4.0	4.0	4.0	4.0	4.0	4.0	4.0
Revenue from New Stores		200.0	200.0	220.0	240.0	240.0	260.0	260.0	280.0
Capital Investments									
Capital Investment New Store	1.2	60.0	60.0	66.0	72.0	72.0	78.0	78.0	84.0
Capital Investment Store Refurb*	0.5	43.3	45.6	47.9	50.4	53.2	56.0	59.1	62.1
Total Capital Investment Stores		103.3	105.6	113.9	122.4	125.2	134.0	137.1	146.1
* Remodel/Update 10% of stores per year									
Total Store Operations									
# of Stores, end of year		915	961	1,012	1,068	1,124	1,185	1,246	1,312
Total Revenue		11,013	11,679	12,374	13,142	13,966	14,708	15,495	16,302
Store Margins		2,163	2,296	2,431	2,580	2,745	2,890	3,047	3,204
%		20%	20%	20%	20%	20%	20%	20%	20%
Capital Investments		103.3	105.6	113.9	122.4	125.2	134.0	137.1	146.1
Y/Y Growth			6.0%	6.0%	6.2%	6.3%	5.3%	5.4%	5.2%

TABLE 14.6 New Reality for Established Retailers

		Retailer The New Reality							
Existing Stores		**2012**	**2013**	**2014**	**2015**	**2016**	**2018**	**2019**	**2020**
# of Stores		865	911	957	987	967	932	904	900
Average Revenue per Store ($M)		12.5	12.6	12	11	10.5	10.5	10	9
Revenue Existing Stores		10,813	11,479	11,484	10,857	10,154	9,786	9,040	8,100
Total Store Margin		2,163	2,296	2,297	2,171	2,031	1,957	1,808	1,620
%		20.0%	20.0%	20.0%	20.0%	20.0%	20.0%	20.0%	20.0%
Store Closings		4	4	10	25	40	40	16	16
New Store Openings									
# of Stores		50	50	40	5	5	12	12	12
1st Year Revenue per Store ($M)		4.0	4.0	4.0	4.0	4.0	4.0	4.0	4.0
Revenue from New Stores		200.00	200.00	160.00	20.00	20.00	48.00	48.00	48.00
Capital Investments									
Capital Investment New Store	1.2	60.0	60.0	48.0	6.0	6.0	14.4	14.4	14.4
Capital Investment Store Refurb*	0.5	43.3	45.6	95.7	98.7	96.7	93.2	90.4	90.0
Total Capital Investment Stores		103.3	105.6	143.7	104.7	102.7	107.6	104.8	104.4

* Remodel/Update 20% of Stores per Year

TABLE 14.6 ***(Continued)***

		Retailer The New Reality							
Existing Stores		**2012**	**2013**	**2014**	**2015**	**2016**	**2018**	**2019**	**2020**
Total Store Operations									
# of Stores, end of year		915	961	997	992	972	944	916	912
Total Revenue		11,013	11,679	11,644	10,877	10,174	9,834	9,088	8,148
Store Margins		2,163	2,296	2,297	2,171	2,031	1,957	1,808	1,620
%		20%	20%	20%	20%	20%	20%	20%	20%
Capital Investments		103.3	105.6	143.7	104.7	102.7	107.6	104.8	104.4
Y/Y Growth			6.0%	–0.3%	–6.6%	–6.5%	–3.3%	–7.6%	–10.3%
Same store sales growth									
E-Commerce									
Invest in E-commerce Platform				100					
Sales				50.0	250.0	500.0	1,000.0	1,700.0	2,500.0
Margin	15%			7.5	37.5	75.0	150.0	255.0	375.0
%				15%	15%	15%	15%	15%	15%
Total Retail Operations									
Revenue		11,013	11,679	11,694	11,127	10,674	10,834	10,788	10,648
Margins		2,163	2,296	2,304	2,209	2,106	2,107	2,063	1,995
%		20%	20%	20%	20%	20%	19%	19%	19%
Y/Y Growth			6.0%	0.1%	–4.8%	–4.1%	1.5%	–0.4%	–1.3%
Capital Investment		103.25	105.55	243.70	104.70	102.70	107.60	104.80	104.40

FIGURE 14.3 Comparison of Traditional versus New Reality Retail

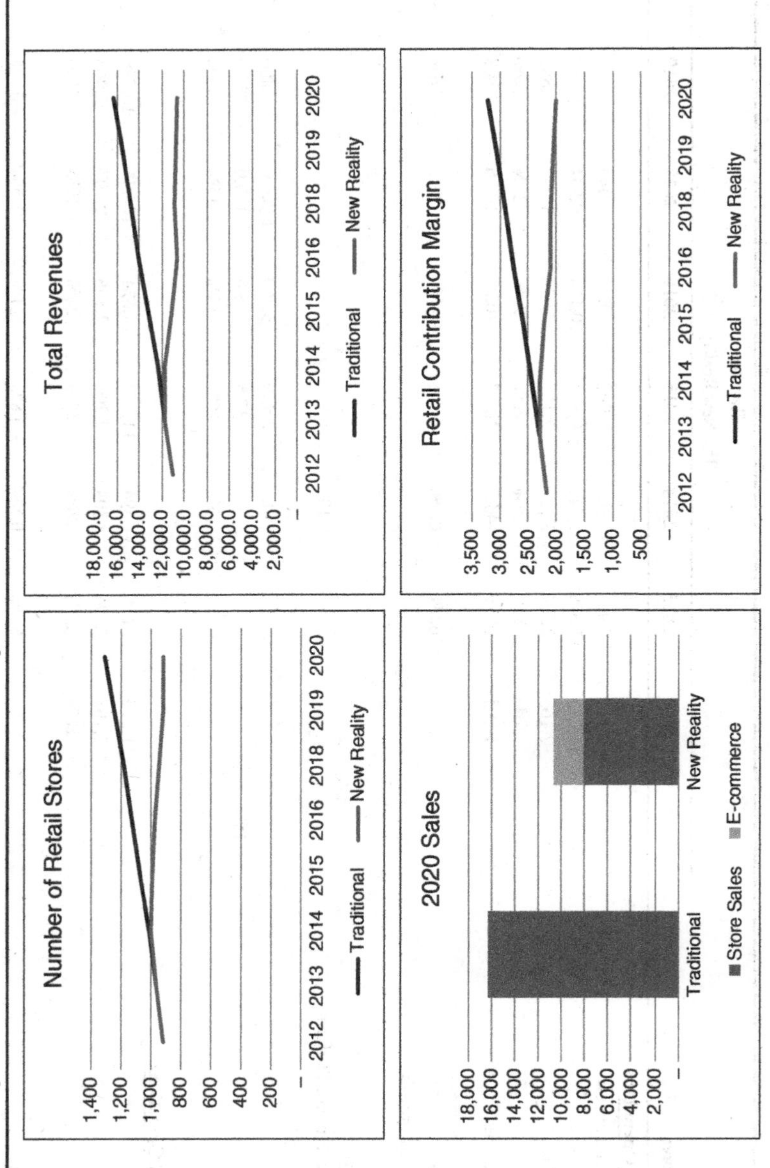

SUMMARY

Long-term projections are utilized to evaluate a wide range of business decisions. The longer horizon introduces more risk and greater uncertainty in the projections. The models need to focus on critical assumptions and performance drivers and allow the user to flex these assumptions and easily estimate performance under various scenarios.

LTPs should present a comprehensive view of performance, extending beyond the income statement to investment requirements, cash flow, returns, and valuation.

Part Four

Planning and Analysis for Critical Business and Value Drivers

15

REVENUE AND GROSS MARGINS

CHAPTER INTRODUCTION

Revenue growth is one of the most important drivers in building and sustaining shareholder value. Understanding the drivers of revenue growth, estimating future revenue levels, and achieving sustainable growth rates are some of the most difficult challenges that managers face. This chapter is not intended to be a work on strategy or creative marketing. The objective in this chapter is to enable more discipline and analysis in predicting, driving, and evaluating future revenue projections.

Gross margins are an important indicator of efficiency and competitive position. Product and service pricing, discounting, new product introductions, and competitor challenges all impact gross margins. Design effectiveness and material, manufacturing, and supply chain effectiveness impact the costs of products or services and gross margins.

REVENUE GROWTH: KEY DRIVERS

Figure 15.1 presents a summary of key drivers of revenue growth. Revenue growth arises from two sources: growth resulting from internal activities and growth resulting from acquisitions. Growth resulting from internal activities is often referred to as organic growth. Growth resulting from acquisitions will have very different drivers and economic characteristics from organic growth. The economics of acquired growth are covered in detail in Chapter 23, Analysis of Mergers and Acquisitions. We will focus on organic growth for the remainder of this chapter. Organic growth may result from growth in the overall size of the market, by gaining share from competitors within the market, or by entering new markets.

Market

Whether chosen by luck or as a result of great strategic thinking, the market that a company serves will be a key driver in determining potential sales growth. Some markets are mature and will grow at slow rates. Others are driven by external forces that will result in high growth rates for a number of years. In markets with high growth rates, even marginal competitors may thrive as all market participants are raised by the rising tide.

Competitive Position

Within a market, the competitive environment and the competitive position of a particular company will determine its ability to grow by increasing market share. A number of factors will determine a company's competitive position, including innovation, customer satisfaction and service, cost and pricing, and the number and size of competitors. Analysis of competitive position should be performed from a customer's perspective. What are the key decision criteria that drive a customer's purchase evaluation and decision? Analysis of competitive position is a relative concept; it is the performance of a company on key factors relative to another firm's offering similar products or services.

FIGURE 15.1 Drill-Down Illustration: Revenue Growth Drivers

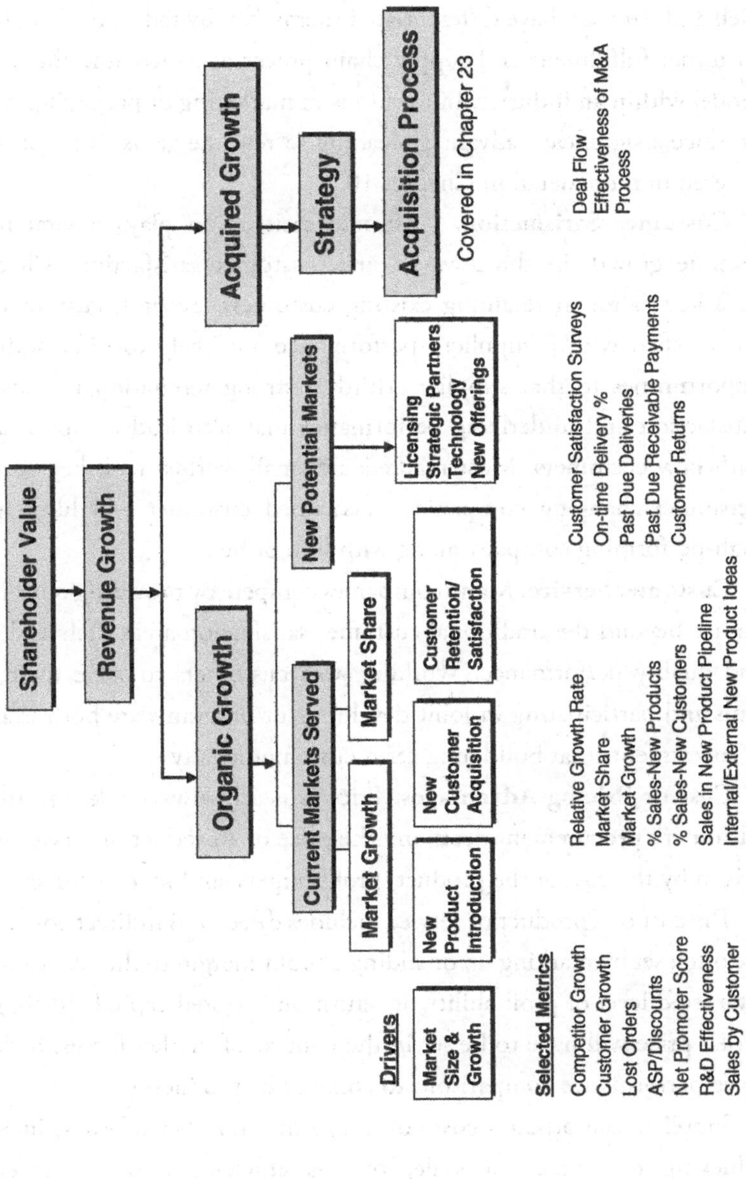

Innovation. Innovation can be a leading source of competitive position and should be considered in broad terms and not simply limited to product innovation. In addition to product innovation, firms such as Dell and Amazon have differentiated themselves by radically changing the customer fulfillment and supply chain processes to redefine the business model within an industry. Innovations in marketing or packaging can also produce a significant advantage leading to revenue gains. Innovation was covered in more detail in Chapter 10.

Customer Satisfaction. Customer satisfaction plays a vital role in revenue growth in three ways. First, customer satisfaction will always be a key factor in retaining existing customers. Second, customers that are satisfied with a supplier's performance are likely to offer additional opportunities to that supplier. Third, a strong reputation for customer satisfaction and underlying performance may also lead to opportunities with new customers. Most markets are small worlds, with key customer personnel changing companies. A satisfied customer will likely pull a high-performing company along with him or her.

Customer Service. Many companies compete by providing outstanding service beyond the traditional customer satisfaction areas such as delivery and quality performance. Working with customers to solve their problems and participating in joint development programs are both examples of investments that build long-term customer loyalty.

Cost or Pricing Advantages. Price is nearly always a key factor in a customer's procurement decision. The price of a product or service will be driven by the cost of the product, profit targets, and market forces.

The cost of a product or service includes direct and indirect costs. Prices are often set by marking up or adding a profit margin to the cost to achieve a targeted level of profitability or return on invested capital (ROIC). The actual price will have to be set in the context of market forces, including price-performance comparisons to competitor products.

Suppliers can attain a cost advantage in a number of ways, including achieving economies of scale, process efficiencies, or improvements in quality. Most sophisticated customers look at the total life cycle cost of a procurement decision, of which the product selling price is one component. Other elements of life cycle cost may include installation and training, service, maintenance, and operating and disposal costs. Suppliers that can demonstrate a lower life cycle cost can achieve an advantage over competitors, even if the product price component is more expensive.

Competitor Attributes and Actions. The performance of competitors in the areas that are important to customers will have big impact on a company's ability to grow or even maintain sales. It is not meaningful to project or evaluate revenue projections without a view of competitor intentions, tendencies, and actions. What is the competitor's strategy? How will its financial performance impact its performance in the market? If the competitor has other related businesses, how does that impact its ability to serve this market? What new product or service will the competitor introduce? How will the competitor respond to the introduction of a new product? Do competitors define the market differently? What new competitors may enter the market?

Many revenue projections are prepared without fully considering the answer to these questions. Revenue from new products is assumed to gain market share without reflecting the competitor response. Again, the value in planning is not in the precise quantitative values on the spreadsheet, but rather in the evolution in thinking as a result of the planning process.

Entering New Markets: Opportunities to Broaden or Migrate to Other Segments

Many companies have been successful at growing over extended periods of time. In addition to growing with their primary market and gaining share within that market, companies have found ways to expand the size of the market they serve by moving into adjacent markets. Amazon, for example, leveraged its competencies in distribution and supply chain management to expand its market from books to just about everything!

Projecting and Testing Future Revenue Levels

Since revenue growth is an important driver of economic value, it is critical for managers and investors to fully identify, understand, and evaluate the factors impacting future revenues. Despite the relative importance of revenue compared to other drivers, it often suffers from less disciplined analytical approaches than other drivers such as cost management and operating efficiency. This is due in part to the complexity of the driver and to the significant impact of external forces such as customers, competitors, and economic factors. Managers should develop and improve tools and practices for projecting future revenues and monitor leading indicators of revenue levels. Best practices include:

- Improve revenue forecasting process.
- Prepare multiple views of revenue detail.
- Measure forecast effectiveness.
- Deal effectively with special issues.

Improve Revenue Forecasting Process

Forecasting. In addition to providing a projection of future performance for planning, budgeting, and investor communication, the revenue forecast typically drives procurement and manufacturing schedules and activities. Forecasting revenue is an extremely important activity within all enterprises. Forecasting future business levels is also generally a significant challenge!

Predicting the future is inherently difficult. Having said that, there are a number of things managers can do to improve the forecasting process. First, it is of vital importance that all managers understand the importance of forecasting as a business activity. It impacts customer satisfaction and service levels, costs and expenses, pricing, inventories, and investor confidence, to name a few. Businesses that are predictable and have consistent levels of operating performance will have lower perceived risk, leading to a lower cost of capital. Second, huge gains can be made by measuring forecast effectiveness and assigning responsibility and accountability to appropriate managers. Third, there are a number of techniques that can be applied to improve the effectiveness of forecasts, such as using ranges of expected performance, identifying significant risks and upsides, and developing contingency plans. However, because forecasting involves an attempt to predict the future, it will always be an imperfect activity.

Forecast Philosophy and Human Behavior. The starting point in improving forecasting is to recognize tendencies in human behavior. Most managers are optimistic. They are positive thinkers. They are under pressure to achieve higher levels of sales and profits. They are reluctant to throw in the towel by lowering performance targets. They recognize that decreasing the revenue outlook may result in a decrease in value, necessitate cost and staff reductions or even the loss of their job. Managers who are ultimately responsible for the projections, in most cases the CEO and CFO, must recognize these soft factors and their impact on projections. They must communicate and reinforce the need for realistic and achievable forecasts.

Base Forecast. Many companies have improved their ability to project revenues by using multiple scenarios. A base forecast is developed, which is often defined as the most probable outcome. Managers find it helpful to define an intended confidence level for the base forecast. Is it a 50/50 plan or 80/20? The former would indicate that there is as much chance of exceeding the forecast as falling short. The latter confidence level implies a greater level of confidence in achieving the forecast: there is an 80% chance of meeting or exceeding the forecast. A practical way of defining this would be that 8 out of 10 forecasts would be met or exceeded.

Upside and Downsides. After planning the base case, upside and downside events can be identified. These can be economic factors, competitor actions, or acceleration or delays in new product introductions. For each possible event, managers should identify how they will monitor the possible event and the probability of the event occurring during the plan horizon. In most cases, upside and downside events with high probabilities should be built into the base forecast.

Development of Aggressive and Conservative Forecast Scenarios. Using the base case scenario and potential upside and downside events, managers can prepare an aggressive scenario and a conservative scenario. The aggressive scenario can be achieved if some or all of the upside events materialize, for example if product adoption rates exceed the estimates incorporated into the base case. The conservative scenario contemplates selected downside events. What actions will we take if it becomes apparent that we are trending toward either the aggressive or the conservative scenario? If trending to the aggressive scenario, do we need to accelerate production, hiring, and other investments? If trending to the downside scenario, do we need to reduce or delay investments or hiring? Pedal harder to close the gap?

Identify, Document, and Monitor Key Assumptions. As with any projection, it is important to identify and document key assumptions that support the revenue forecast. Projecting revenues is typically the most difficult element of business planning and involves many assumptions, including factors external to the organization. Key assumptions for revenue projections typically include:

- Market size and growth rate
- Pricing
- Product mix
- Geographic mix
- Competitor actions/reactions
- New product introductions
- Product life cycle of existing products
- Macroeconomic factors, including interest rates, GDP growth, and others

After identifying and documenting these key assumptions supporting revenue projections, these factors must be monitored. Any changes in assumptions must be identified and the potential impact on sales must be quantified and addressed. Critical assumptions should be included on the performance dashboard for revenue growth as illustrated later in this chapter.

Prepare Multiple Views of Revenue Detail

Key dynamics of revenue projections can be identified by reviewing trend schedules of revenue from various perspectives. Table 15.1 is a sample summary of revenue by product. This level of detail identifies contributions from key products and provides visibility into dynamics such as product introduction and life cycles. Other views may be sales by region or geography, customers, and end use market.

Another insightful analysis is to evaluate the projections in light of recent performance and comparisons to the plan and to prior year results. Table 15.2 compares year to date (YTD) actual and rest of year (ROY) projected performance to last year and the plan. Since it is comparing the

TABLE 15.1 Revenue Planning Worksheet: Product Detail

	Revenue Planning Illustration				
	Actual		Projected		
Existing Products	**2017**	**2018**	**2019**	**2020**	**2021**
1	100	90	80	60	50
2	100	100	100	100	100
3	50	40	20	10	0
4	30	60	70	90	110
Subtotal	280	290	270	260	260
New Product Pipeline					
5			20	35	60
6			5	20	35
7				20	45
8					
Subtotal	0	0	25	75	140
Total Sales Projection	280	290	295	335	400
Year-over-Year Growth		3.6%	1.7%	13.6%	19.4%
CAGR: 2017: 2021P					9.3%

TABLE 15.2 Forecast Evaluation Worksheet

	YTD			ROY			Year		
Revenue ($m)	**Actual**	**Last Year**	**Plan**	**Fcst**	**Last Year**	**Plan**	**Fcst**	**Last Year**	**Plan**
Product 1	1,175	1,208	1,300	1,525	1,325	1,400	2,700	2,533	2,700
Product 2	950	985	1,100	1,350	1,102	1,200	2,300	2,087	2,300
Product 3	1,250	1,310	1,400	1,650	1,433	1,500	2,900	2,743	2,900
Product 4	850	825	900	1,000	879	950	1,850	1,704	1,850
Product 5	733	715	750	800	775	800	1,533	1,490	1,550
Product 6	1,650	1,612	1,700	1,860	1,725	1,800	3,510	3,337	3,500
Total	6,608	6,655	7,150	8,185	7,239	7,650	14,793	13,894	14,800

	YTD		ROY		Year	
Revenue %	**Last Year**	**Plan**	**Last Year**	**Plan**	**Last Year**	**Plan**
Product 1	97%	90%	115%	109%	107%	100%
Product 2	96%	86%	123%	113%	110%	100%
Product 3	95%	89%	115%	110%	106%	100%
Product 4	103%	94%	114%	105%	109%	100%
Product 5	103%	98%	103%	100%	103%	99%
Product 6	102%	97%	108%	103%	105%	100%
Total	99%	92%	113%	107%	106%	100%

same periods, seasonality is accounted for in the analysis. This forecast needs some explaining! On a year to date basis, revenues are 99% of last year and 92% of plan. However, the forecast revenue for the remainder of the year is 113% of last year and 107% of plan. Coincidentally, the forecast projects that the total year plan will be achieved. There may be some very good reasons for this inconsistency. I sure would like to hear and evaluate them!

The graphic presentation in Figure 15.2 vividly portrays the inconsistency between actual year to date performance relative to plan and last year, compared to projections for the remainder of the year.

Revenue Change Analysis. A useful way to evaluate revenue projections is to compare them to the prior year and identify significant changes. Each source of significant change can be evaluated and tested. There is a tendency to project future revenues by identifying future sources of revenue growth and adding these increments to existing revenue levels.

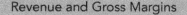

FIGURE 15.2 Revenue Variance

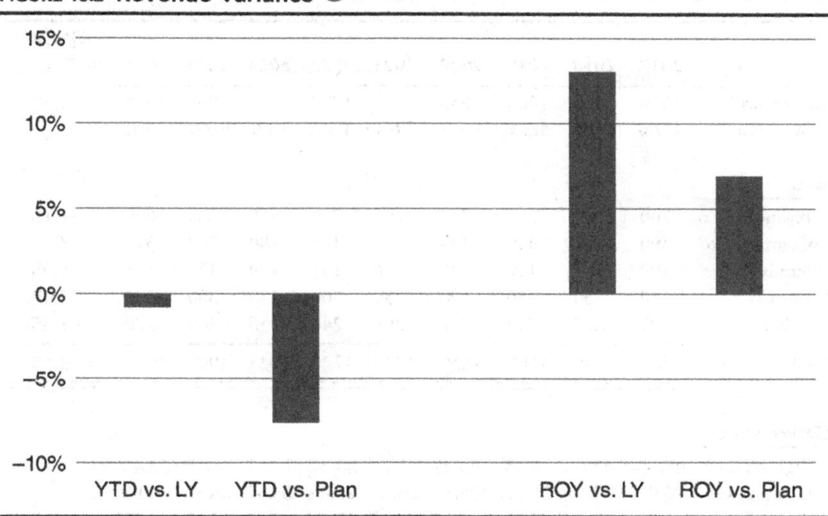

FIGURE 15.3 Revenue Change Analysis

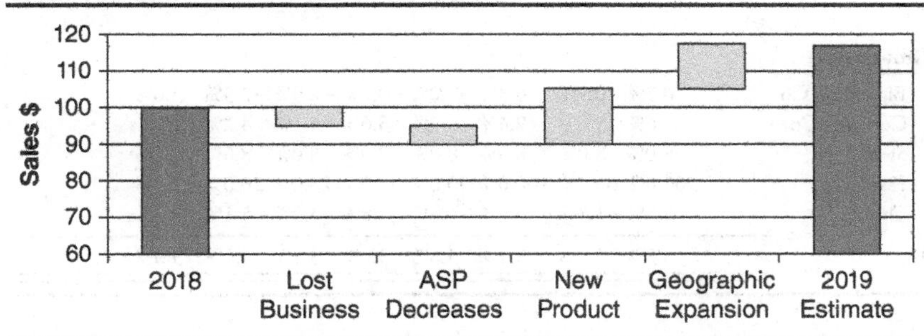

For example, additional revenues may result from new product introductions or geographic expansion. It is also important to identify factors that will decrease revenues. For example, many industries will experience decreases in average selling prices (ASPs) over time. In addition, all products are subject to life cycles with the eventuality of declining sales levels at some point. Figure 15.3 provides a good visual summary of significant changes in sales from 2018 to 2019.

TABLE 15.3 Market Size and Share Analysis

	2017	2018	2019	2020	2021	2022	2023	2024	2025	CAGR 2017–2025
Market Size	1500	1550	1600	1650	1710	1770	1825	1900	1975	3.5%
Growth Rate	4.0%	3.3%	3.2%	3.1%	3.6%	3.5%	3.1%	4.1%	3.9%	
Sales										
BigandSlo Co	700	705	710	712	705	700	680	660	640	−1.1%
Complex Co	390	400	420	430	450	475	480	500	510	3.4%
Steady Co	100	108	117	126	136	147	159	171	185	8.0%
Fast Co	10	30	50	100	150	200	250	300	370	57.0%
Other	300	307	303	282	269	248	256	269	270	−1.3%
Total	1500	1550	1600	1650	1710	1770	1825	1900	1975	3.5%
Market Share										
BigandSlo Co	46.7%	45.5%	44.4%	43.2%	41.2%	39.5%	37.3%	34.7%	32.4%	
Complex Co	26.0%	25.8%	26.3%	26.1%	26.3%	26.8%	26.3%	26.3%	25.8%	
Steady Co	6.7%	7.0%	7.3%	7.6%	8.0%	8.3%	8.7%	9.0%	9.4%	
Fast Co	0.7%	1.9%	3.1%	6.1%	8.8%	11.3%	13.7%	15.8%	18.7%	
Other	20.0%	19.8%	18.9%	17.1%	15.7%	14.0%	14.0%	14.2%	13.7%	
Total	100%	100%	100%	100%	100%	100%	100%	100%	100%	
Growth Rate										
BigandSlo Co		0.7%	0.7%	0.3%	−1.0%	−0.7%	−2.9%	−2.9%	−3.0%	
Complex Co		2.6%	5.0%	2.4%	4.7%	5.6%	1.1%	4.2%	2.0%	
Steady Co		8.0%	8.0%	8.0%	8.0%	8.0%	8.0%	8.0%	8.0%	
Fast Co		200.0%	66.7%	100.0%	50.0%	33.3%	25.0%	20.0%	23.3%	
Other		2.3%	−1.3%	−6.9%	−4.6%	−7.8%	3.2%	5.1%	0.4%	
Total		3.3%	3.2%	3.1%	3.6%	3.5%	3.1%	4.1%	3.9%	

Market Size and Share Summary. Another view that is useful for evaluating revenue projections is to consider them in the context of the overall market size and growth and market share. Table 15.3 presents the market for Steady Co. For each year, the size of the market is estimated and the growth rate is provided. Sales for each competitor are also estimated, forcing a consideration of competitive dynamics and identification of share gains. In this case, we see that Steady Co.'s 8% growth projected for each year is higher than the market growth. Who will the company take market share from? Why? Is 8% growth each year possible? Is it consistent with the real-life market dynamics such as product introductions and life cycles, economic factors, and competitive factors?

Measuring Forecast Effectiveness

A very effective way to improve the forecast accuracy is to monitor and track actual performance against the forecasts. Table 15.4 presents the changes made to each quarterly projection over the course of 12 months. It is very effective in identifying biases and forecast gamesmanship. In this example, the analysis surfaces a number of concerns and questions. Note that the actual revenue achieved for each quarter is consistently under the forecast developed at the beginning of that quarter. In addition, shortfalls in one quarter are pushed out into subsequent quarters. However, the team does seem to be able to forecast revenues within one month of the quarter end.

Figure 15.4 tracks the evolution of the total year forecast over a 12-month period. Note that the forecast for the year was not decreased until two quarterly shortfalls were posted.

TABLE 15.4 Revenue Forecast Accuracy

Month Forecast Submitted:	Q1	Q2	Q3	Q4	Year
January	7,500	8,000	8,700	9,200	33,400
February	7,200	8,300	8,700	9,200	33,400
March	7,000	8,500	8,700	9,200	33,400
April	7,045	8,400	8,800	9,200	33,445
May		8,400	8,800	9,200	33,445
June		8,000	9,200	9,200	33,445
July		7,076	9,200	9,200	32,521
August			9,100	9,200	32,421
September			8,700	9,600	32,421
October			8,725	9,600	32,446
November				9,600	32,446
December				9,200	32,046
January (Final)				9,250	32,096
Variance, from beginning of quarter ($)	(455)	(1,324)	(475)	(350)	(1,304)
Variance, from beginning of quarter (%)	−6.1%	−15.8%	−5.2%	−3.6%	−4.1%

FIGURE 15.4 Forecast Progression Analysis

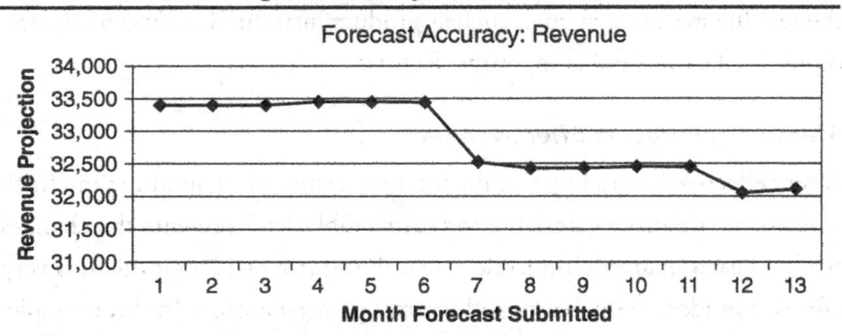

Additional Tools for Projecting Revenue

There are additional tools that can be effectively utilized in developing and evaluating revenue projections. These topics are covered in several other chapters, principally in Part Three, Projecting Financial Performance and in Chapter 21, Capital Investment Decisions: Advanced Topics.

Special Issues

There are a number of special circumstances that present challenges in developing and evaluating revenue projections. These include sales projections for new products, chunky or lumpy businesses with uneven sales patterns, and large programs.

Sales Projections for New Products. The development and introduction of new products are always a factor in growing or maintaining sales. Revenue plans for new products must be directly linked to new product development schedules. These schedules must be monitored closely and any changes in the development timeline must be considered in the related revenue projections. A delay in the product schedule will almost certainly delay introduction and the revenue ramp. Product introduction plans must be broad, expanding beyond product development to incorporate key marketing and customer activities. Critical assumptions should be reviewed as well. Any changes in these underlying assumptions should be tested to support revenue plans and even project viability. Examples include changes in key customer performance, economic conditions, and competitor actions.

Chunky and Lumpy Businesses. Some businesses are characterized by large orders resulting in lumpy business patterns from the presence or absence of these orders. These chunks wreak havoc in trend analysis and short-term projections. Depending on the cost structure and degree of operating leverage, these swings in revenue can result in extremely large fluctuations in profits. Care must be taken in setting expense levels in these situations. It may be appropriate to set expectations and expense levels for a base level of revenue and consider these lumps as upsides. Communicating with investors and other stakeholders about the business variability and disclosing the inclusion of lumpy business are essential to avoid significant fluctuations in the company's valuation and loss of management credibility.

Large Programs and Procurements. In many industries, large procurements, programs, or long-term contracts are awarded periodically, for example every three years. Revenue changes in these situations are often binary and significant: if the contract is awarded to your firm, significant sales growth will be achieved for the contract period. If unsuccessful, your firm loses the opportunity to obtain that business for that contract period. If a firm loses that business at the end of the contract period, there is a significant decrease to sales. This presents a number of management, financial planning, and stakeholder communication issues.

When pursuing a large procurement opportunity, it is useful to prepare a base forecast without the inclusion of the large procurement and prepare an upside forecast reflecting the award. If a company's existing contracts are up for grabs, consideration should be given to a downside scenario, reflecting conditions if the contract is lost. Investors should have visibility into the presence and expiration dates of significant contracts.

KEY PERFORMANCE MEASURES: REVENUE GROWTH

A number of key performance measures can provide insight into historical trends and future revenue potential.

Sales Growth: Sequential and Year over Year

A critical measure of business performance is simply to measure the rate of growth in sales from one period to another. Table 15.5 illustrates a typical presentation of sales growth rates. Two different measures are frequently used. The first is simply to compute the growth from the previous year. The second measure computes sequential growth rates – that is, from one quarter to another.

While these growth rate measures are important top-level performance measures, they are of limited usefulness without additional insight and analysis. Some managers and investors will extrapolate past sales growth rates into the future. This works in certain circumstances for a period of time; however, it does not take into consideration the underlying dynamics that will drive future revenues. These factors include market forces, competitive position, innovation, and customer satisfaction discussed earlier in this chapter.

Customer/Competitor Growth Index

The evaluation of a company's performance is best done in the context of competitors, customers, and overall market performance. This is very important in assessing a company's performance in growing sales. For example, if Steady Co. grew 8% last year, the market grew by 3%, and one of the competitors grew 25%, would we consider this acceptable performance?

TABLE 15.5 Quarterly Sales Trend

	2018					2019				
$m	**Q1**	**Q2**	**Q3**	**Q4**	**Year**	**Q1**	**Q2**	**Q3**	**Q4**	**Year**
Sales	62	64	60	75	261	65	70	58	82	275
Year-over-Year Growth	5.1%	6.7%	11.1%	8.7%	7.9%	4.8%	9.4%	−3.3%	9.3%	5.4%
Sequential Growth	−10.1%	3.2%	−6.3%	25.0%		−13.3%	7.7%	−17.1%	41.4%	

FIGURE 15.5 Year-over-Year Growth

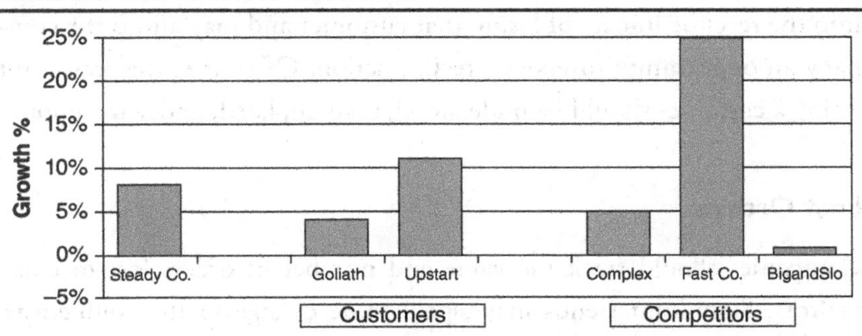

Comparing growth to rates experienced by key competitors and customers places the company's performance in an appropriate context. It can also be important input to strategic analysis. For example, what are the causes and implications of customer growth exceeding our own? Are we missing potential opportunities to grow with our customers? A summary of comparative growth rates is provided in Figure 15.5. In this case, Steady Co. is growing faster than the market, and at a rate between the company's two largest customers. Steady Co.'s growth rate is ahead of two competitors' rates, but is significantly under Fast Co.'s rate.

Percentage of Revenue from New Products

Most companies seek to maintain and grow sales by developing and introducing new products. An important indicator of the success of the new product development and introduction activities is the percentage of revenue from products recently introduced. Some companies would define *recently* as within two years. Others may shorten the period to reflect shorter product life cycles. This measure is highly susceptible to gaming, so it is critical to have considered definitions, including "What is a new product?"

Customer Retention, Churn Rate, and Lost Customers

Given the cost and difficulty in obtaining new customers, companies must go to great lengths to retain existing customers. Identifying the loss or potential loss of a customer on a timely basis provides immediate visibility into the revenue impact of losing that customer and may afford the company an opportunity to take corrective action. Of course, the reason for losing a customer should be understood, contemplated, and acted upon.

Lost Orders

Companies should track the value and number of orders lost to competitors. Significant trends may signal some change in the competitive environment. Drilling down into lost orders to identify the root cause can also be enlightening. Most companies expect to lose some orders. For example, a high-end equipment supplier expects to lose some orders to a low-end supplier where price is a driving factor in the customer's buy decision. However, if the company began to lose orders based on performance or service, the alarm should sound.

Revenue from New Customers

Companies may expect future growth by acquiring new customers. In these cases it would be useful to track revenue derived from sales to new customers. *New* is defined by individual circumstance, but is frequently defined as revenue derived from customers acquired over the prior 12 months.

Customer Satisfaction

An important factor in maintaining current sales levels and in growing sales is customer satisfaction. An increasing number of companies periodically solicit overall performance ratings from their customers. Many customers have sophisticated supply chain processes that include the evaluation of overall vendor performance. These performance ratings are used as a basis for selecting and retaining vendors.

Key elements of the customer's total experience will include price, quality, delivery performance, and service. Therefore, management should measure these factors frequently. It is important to measure these factors from the customer's viewpoint. For example, the customer may measure quality or service levels differently than the supplier. What matters, of course, is only the customer's perspective.

Past-Due Orders

Monitoring the number and value of past-due orders can provide important insight into customer satisfaction. An increase in the level of past-due orders may indicate a manufacturing or supply problem that resulted in delayed shipments to customers. In addition to tracking (and attacking) the level of past-due orders, much can be learned by identifying and addressing recurring causes of past-due orders. Many companies actively "work" past-due orders. Reducing the level of past-due sales orders will increase sales and customer satisfaction and reduce inventories and costs.

On-Time Delivery

On-time delivery (OTD) is a very important determiner of customer satisfaction. Some companies measure delivery to quoted delivery dates. Progressive companies measure delivery performance against the date the customer originally requested, since that is the date the customer originally wanted the product. This is another measure that can be gamed. Extending the original delivery date or updating the delivery date is counterproductive, but results in a higher OTD performance if the measure is not properly established.

Quality

Measuring the quality of product and other customer-facing activities is an important indicator of customer satisfaction. Examples include product returns, warranty experience, and the volume of sales credits issued.

FIGURE 15.6 Revenue in Product Development Pipeline

$m Project Name	2018	2019	2020	2021	Annual Revenue Potential	Status	Comment
Coyote	0	7	18	24	$25	Green	On Track, Intro 3/19
Fox	0	12	26	30	30	Yellow	2 Critical Milestones Missed
Rabbit	15	15	15	12	15	Red	Technical Performance Issues
Tortoise	0	20	30	50	60	Green	1st Shipments, next week
Total	$15	$54	$89	$116	$130		

Projected Revenue in Product Pipeline

If future growth is highly dependent on new product development and introduction, then management should have a clear view of the revenue potential and project status in each product in the development pipeline. Figure 15.6 is an example of a summary of revenue in the product development pipeline.

A key benefit to this summary is that development, marketing, sales, and other personnel involved in the introduction of new products have clear visibility of the connection of their activities to future revenue targets. This helps to create linkage in many enterprises where product development teams may not be acutely aware of the timing and potential magnitude of the projects they are supporting. The impact of any delay or acceleration in the development timeline on revenue expectations is easily understood.

Revenue per Transaction

Tracking revenue per transaction can provide important insight into sales trends. Is average transaction or order value increasing or decreasing? Can we capture more revenue per order by selling supplies, related products, service agreements, or consumables? In retail industries, revenue per customer visit is a key revenue metric, and retailers put substantial effort into increasing customer spend per visit by offering related products, cross merchandising, and impulse buy displays.

Revenue per Customer

Reviewing the revenue per customer in total and for key customers can identify important trends. Identifying and tracking sales to top customers is useful in understanding revenue trends, developing future projections, and maintaining an appropriate focus on satisfying and retaining the partners. Analysts must be thoughtful in defining the customer. Many order-processing systems fragment customers by plant and ship to addresses or divisions, resulting in a less than complete view of the customer's total revenue and activity.

Quote Levels

For certain businesses with long purchasing cycles, tracking the level of open quotes over time can be a leading indicator of future revenue levels. However, not all quotes are created equal. Some may be for budgetary purposes, indicating a long-term purchase horizon. Others may indicate order potential in the short term. For this reason, quote levels are often summarized by key characteristics to enhance the insight into potential order flow.

Order Backlog Levels

Some businesses have long lead times or order cycles. Customers must place orders well in advance of requested delivery dates. Examples include aircraft, shipbuilding, and large equipment industries. In these industries, the order backlog levels are an important leading indicator of revenue and general business health.

FIGURE 15.7 **Backlog Analysis**

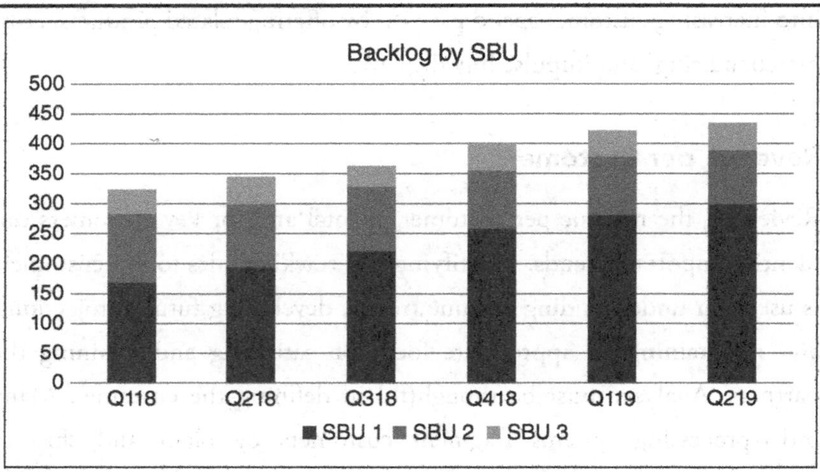

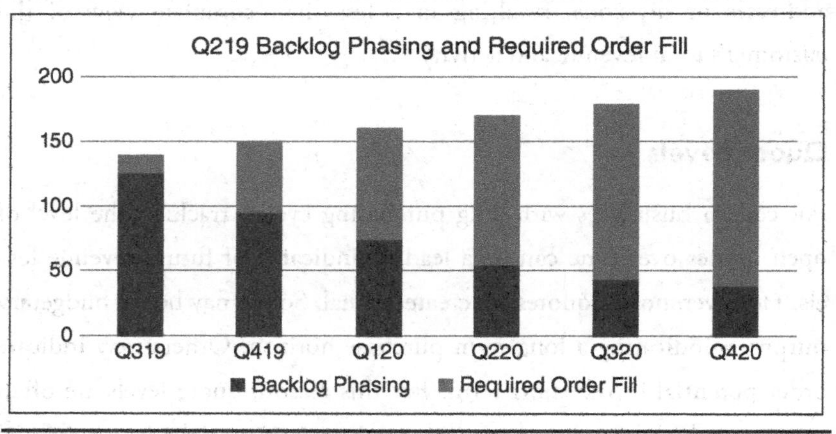

Figure 15.7 provides two views of backlog. In the chart on the top, the backlog by SBU at the end of each quarter is presented. The graph on the bottom presents a phasing of the backlog at Q219 into the future quarter when the revenue is projected to be recorded.

Anecdotal Input

Nothing beats customer letters or survey responses containing specific feedback. Post them with the quantitative measures and watch the reaction of employees. Many include points actionable by employees at various levels in the company. A few examples:

> "Customer Service never answers the phone. Voice mail messages are not returned for several days."
> "Service levels have declined. We are contemplating an alternative supplier."
> "The delay in scheduling installation and training is unacceptable."

Comprehensive Analysis of Revenue Measures

Collecting and analyzing a broad set of measures supporting revenue growth, lost customers, new product introductions, and other revenue drivers can provide a comprehensive picture into underlying trends and identify issues and opportunities. Table 15.6 illustrates a tool used to collect data that may be useful in the analysis of revenues.

REVENUE DASHBOARD

Based on the most important drivers and issues impacting current and future revenue growth, a performance dashboard as shown in Figure 15.8 can be created to track and present these measures to managers. The selection of the individual measures to include in the dashboard is an extremely important process. There should be an emphasis on leading and predictive indicators of revenue growth. The measures should focus on the most important drivers and should be changed out over time as appropriate. Properly constructed, this one-page summary of critical factors is sure to focus the team's attention to appropriate issues and opportunities.

GROSS MARGINS AND RELATIVE PRICING STRENGTH

It is easy to look at a company with high gross margins and profitability and assume that it is highly efficient from an operating perspective. However, a company may be inefficient but still achieve high margins on the basis of a strong competitive advantage that affords it a premium price. This relative

TABLE 15.6 Comprehensive Revenue Measures

	Performance Measure Collection Worksheets									
	Revenue						Illustrative			
	2017		2018				2019			
	Q3	Q4	Q1	Q2	Q3	Q4	Q1	Q2	Q3	Q4
Revenue	21	26	18	18.7	21	28	20	20	22	30.6
Seq Growth		24%	−31%	4%	12%	33%	−29%	0%	10%	39%
Y/Y Growth					0%	8%	11%	7%	5%	9%
Year		79.4				85.7				92.6
Y/Y Growth										8%
Lost Orders										
#	15	16	14	12	11	15	11	7	6	5
$	1.2	1.5	2	1.5	1.7	1.8	0.5	0.9	1.5	1.2
% of Sales	5.7%	5.8%	11.1%	8.0%	8.1%	6.4%	2.5%	4.5%	6.8%	3.9%
Lost Customers										
#	15	16	14	12	11	15	11	7	6	5
$	1.3	1.7	2	1	4	2	3	1.5	0.8	1.8
% of Sales	6.2%	6.5%	11.1%	5.3%	19.0%	7.1%	15.0%	7.5%	3.6%	5.9%
New Product Sales	3	2	2	2	2	3.5	3.8	3.9	4.5	4.7
% of Total	14%	8%	11%	11%	10%	13%	19%	20%	20%	15%
New Customer Sales	2	2.5	3	3.2	3	3.5	3.6	3.8	2.2	0.5
% of Total	10%	10%	17%	17%	14%	13%	18%	19%	10%	2%
On-Time Delivery %	88%	75%	89%	91%	84%	87%	91%	92%	91%	89%
Past-Due Orders $	1.7	2.2	3.2	2.8	2.7	2.5	2.6	2.3	2.1	1.9

	2017		2018		2019	
Customer Concentration Trend	**Customer**	**$**	**Customer**	**$**	**Customer**	**$**
1	Goliath	11.0	Goliath	12.0	Goliath	12.6
2	DEG	10.5	DEG	11.0	DEG	12.0
3	XYZ	5.6	XYZ	7.0	XYZ	9.0
4	PQR	4.8	PQR	5.0	PQR	8.0
5	MNO	2.2	MNO	3.0	MNO	7.0
6	Upstart	1.1	Upstart	1.2	Upstart	1.3
7	HIJ	0.8	HIJ	0.9	HIJ	4.0
8	TUV	0.7	TUV	0.8	TUV	3.0
9	RST	0.6	RST	0.8	RST	2.0
10	ZAB	0.5	ZAB	0.7	ZAB	1.0
Total	0	37.8	0	42.3	0	59.9
% Total Revenue		47.6%		49.4%		64.7%

TABLE 15.6 (*continued*)

Historical Revenue

1995	1996	1997	1998	1999	2000	2001	2002	2003	2004	2005
57	58	60	62	63	64	68	73.5	79.4	85.7	92.6

CAGR		
	2 Year	8.0%
	3 Year	8.0%
	5 Year	7.7%
	10 Year	5.0%

Shading indicates input area

pricing advantage can mask operating inefficiencies and high costs, which can be a source of competitive vulnerability. Over time, relative pricing advantages tend to dissipate, leading to margin erosion unless cost and operating efficiencies are achieved.

Gross margins are primarily a function of two variables, cost of goods sold and pricing. (See Figure 15.9.) Pricing will be driven by a combination of cost and market forces. What typically drives relative pricing strength for a company is a unique product or service offering or an offering with significantly higher performance attributes than competitors' offerings. The leading market indicators for pricing will center on the competitive position and landscape. Factors such as excess industry capacity, aggressive competitor strategies to gain share, and industry health also will play a role.

Cost of Goods Sold or Cost of Revenues

Costs and operating effectiveness are covered in greater depth in Chapter 16. Costs comprise direct or product cost of goods sold (COGS) and indirect COGS. Product or service COGS generally includes those costs that are directly associated with the product or service. For example, product costs will include the cost of materials, labor, and overhead to assemble or manufacture that product. Other or indirect COGS includes items such as warranty, manufacturing variances, and cost overruns. Service costs include time, materials, and overhead.

FIGURE 15.8 Revenue Growth and Innovation Dashboard

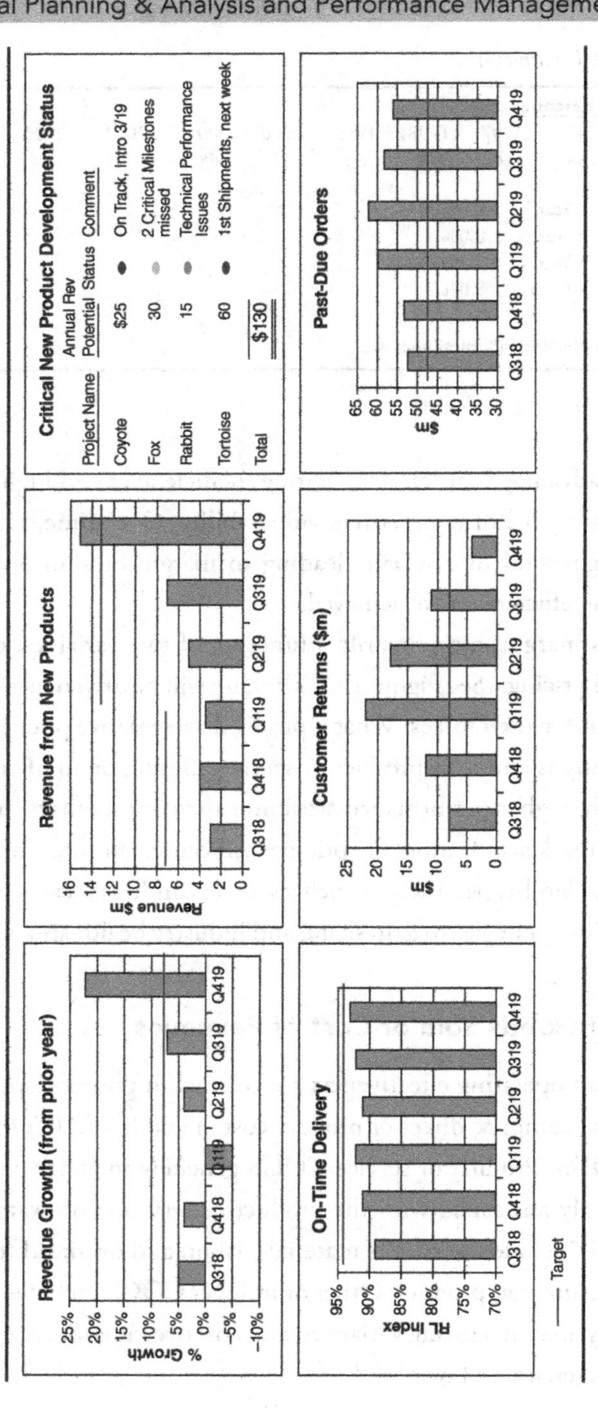

Project Name	Annual Rev Potential	Status	Comment
Coyote	$25	●	On Track, Intro 3/19
Fox	30	●	2 Critical Milestones missed
Rabbit	15	●	Technical Performance Issues
Tortoise	60	●	1st Shipments, next week
Total	$130		

FIGURE 15.9 Gross Margins and Relative Pricing Strength

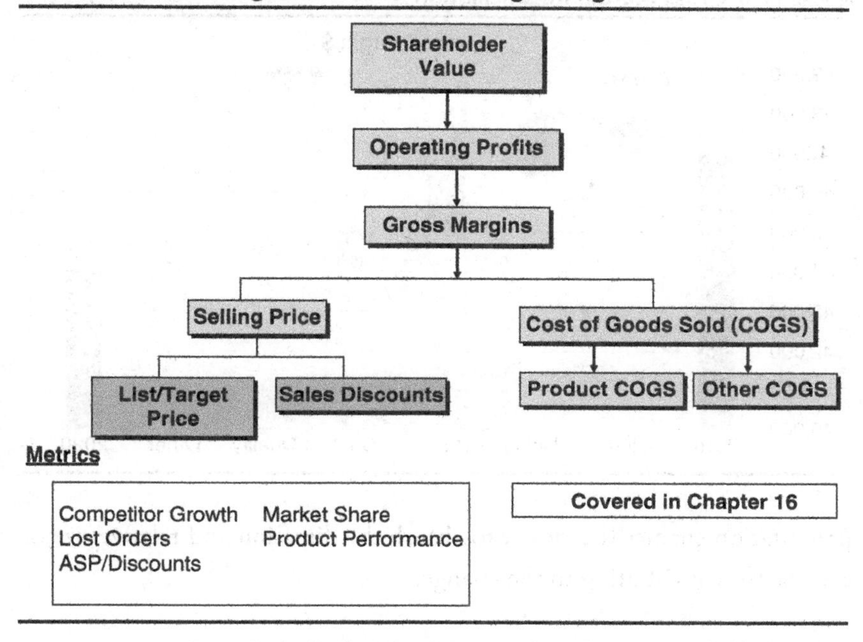

TABLE 15.7 Gross Margin Analysis

	Gross Margin Analysis			Variance Analysis						
	2019	2020	Variance	Volume Increase	Pricing Changes	Mix	Cost Increases	Quality Savings	Other	Total
Sales	125,000	126,000	1,000	2,500	−1,500					1,000
Cost of Sales	78,000	82,000	−4,000	−1,560		−1,500	−820	280	−400	−4,000
Gross Margin	47,000	44,000	−3,000	940	−1,500	−1,500	−820	280	−400	−3,000
Gross Margin %	37.6%	34.9%	−2.7%	0.0%	−0.8%	−1.2%	−0.7%	0.2%	−0.3%	−2.7%

Gross margin analysis is also impacted by other factors, including changes in product mix and foreign currency fluctuations. Most well-run companies examine gross margin trends carefully and identify the factors accounting for changes between periods, as illustrated in Table 15.7.

Figure 15.10 presents the analysis in graphical form, highlighting the major changes in gross margin between the two years. This visual

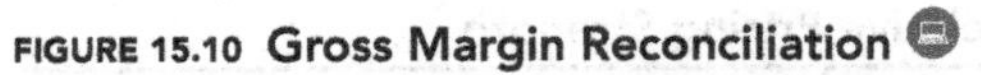

FIGURE 15.10 Gross Margin Reconciliation

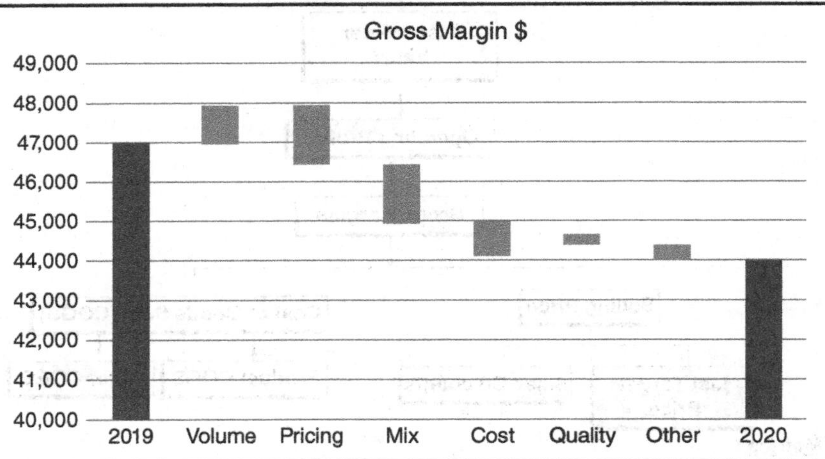

presentation enables the viewer to absorb the direction and relative size of each factor contributing to the change.

MEASURES OF RELATIVE PRICING STRENGTH

A number of measures can provide visibility into a company's pricing strength.

Average Selling Price

Tracking and monitoring the average selling price (ASP) of products over time is a good indicator of the relative pricing strength of a product in the market. ASP will decline, often rapidly, in highly competitive situations. In many markets, customers expect lower pricing over time as a result of expected efficiencies and savings.

Discounts as a Percentage of List Price

Tracking the level of pricing discounts is a useful indicator of pricing strength that also quantifies the magnitude of any pricing erosion.

Lost Orders

The lost orders measure provides insight into future revenue and pricing trends. Orders lost on the basis of pricing are of particular concern, since they foreshadow a decrease in both revenue and margins.

Product Competitive Analysis

Capturing and monitoring price and performance characteristics of competitive products is a good way to anticipate changes in relative pricing strength. If a competitor introduces a product with better performance attributes, the pricing dynamics in the market are likely to change in very short order.

Market Share

The pricing and performance measures previously described can be combined with the market share analysis and other measures discussed under revenue growth to help form a complete view of the competitive landscape in the context of pricing and gross margins. For example, it is possible that a company is holding firm on pricing but losing market share to lower-priced competitors.

Gross Margin and Pricing Strength Dashboard

Based on the most important drivers and issues impacting current and future pricing and gross margins, a performance dashboard as shown in Figure 15.11 could be created to provide visibility for managers. Again, the selection of the individual measures to include in the dashboard is extremely important. There should be an emphasis on leading and predictive indicators of competitive forces and pricing. The measures should focus on the most important drivers and should be modified over time as appropriate.

FIGURE 15.11 Dashboard: Gross Margin and Pricing Strength

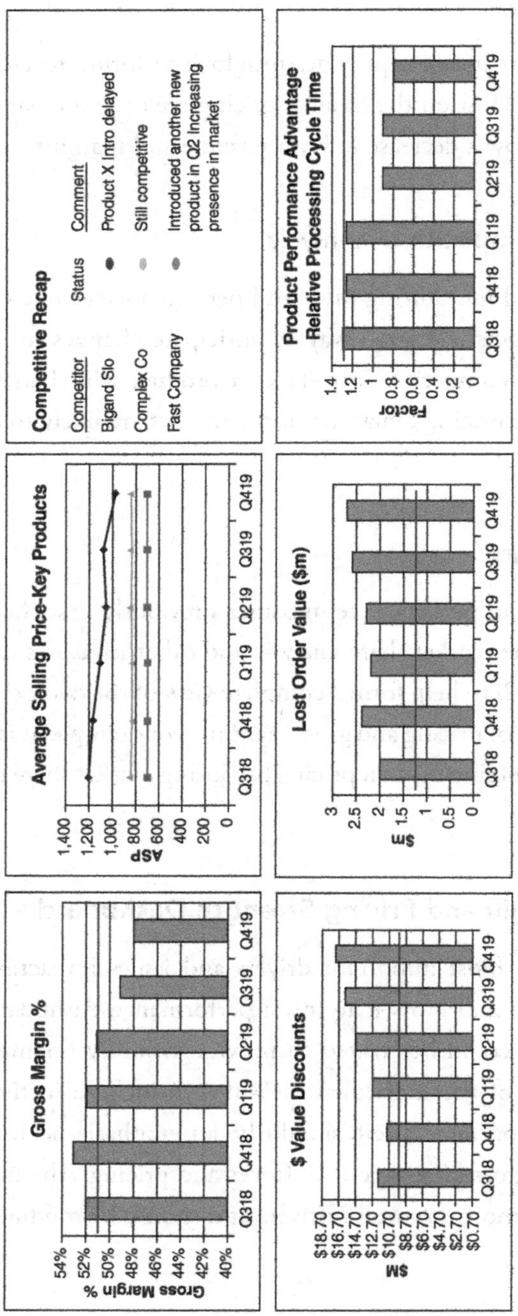

Competitive Recap

Competitor	Status	Comment
Bigand Slo		Product X Intro delayed
Complex Co		Still competitive
Fast Company		Introduced another new product in Q2 Increasing presence in market

SUMMARY

Revenue growth and relative pricing strength are among the most important value drivers. Yet in spite of this importance, managers often do a better job in measuring and managing other value drivers. Revenue planning is inherently difficult owing to the complexity of drivers and the impact of external factors. However, managers can greatly increase their ability to build and sustain shareholder value by improving their discipline over projecting, measuring, and growing revenue.

Relative pricing strength is a key driver of value and is realized by holding a strong competitive advantage. Companies that enjoy a strong competitive advantage or have a unique product offering will enjoy strong product margins. It is important to distinguish between strong operating margins resulting from pricing strength and those due to operational efficiency. Over time, competitive advantage and pricing strength often dissipate. This unfavorable impact to margins can be offset by improving operational effectiveness, our topic for Chapter 16.

16

OPERATING EXPENSES AND EFFECTIVENESS

CHAPTER INTRODUCTION

In this chapter, we will focus on another critical value driver: operating effectiveness. Managers and consultants often debate about their preference for either the word *effectiveness* or *efficiency* in this context. While effectiveness is often interpreted as doing things well or selecting the right things to address, efficiency connotes doing things faster and more cheaply. We will use the term *effectiveness* to encompass both interpretations. Obviously, managers do not want to become highly efficient in an unimportant process or activity. On the other hand, improving efficiency by reducing cycle time, costs, and errors can be a tremendous source of value.

Many observers look to profitability as a key indicator of operating effectiveness. It is a good start, but we recognize that it is possible for a highly inefficient organization to post high profit margins if it possesses a strong competitive advantage leading to pricing strength. In this case, it can pass along high costs arising from its inefficiencies to its customers. This is rarely a sustainable position over the long term, however, since potential competitors are attracted to these opportunities. Additionally, profitability does not directly account for the asset levels required to support a business. Return on invested capital (ROIC) and return on equity (ROE) are considered better overall measures of management effectiveness, since they reflect both profitability and asset effectiveness measures.

There is significant crossover between operating effectiveness and capital effectiveness. While working capital has some independent critical drivers, accounts receivable and inventories are directly related to the effectiveness of the revenue and supply chain processes, respectively. We will discuss these two processes in this chapter and again in more detail in Chapter 17, Capital Management and Cash Flow: Working Capital.

DRIVERS OF OPERATING EFFECTIVENESS

Operating effectiveness has a significant impact on cost and therefore value. Even a highly profitable company recording 15% operating margins is "high cost" since the company incurs costs and expenses equal to 85% of the company's revenue. This represents a tremendous pool of opportunity for value creation. (See Figure 16.1.)

A primary driver of operating effectiveness and profit margins is the effectiveness of business processes. Figure 16.2 identifies critical business processes, including supply chain management, revenue process management, and new product development (NPD), that will impact key financial factors such as costs, revenue levels, working capital requirements, and cash flow.

Typically, a given process will cross several functional areas. For example, new product development may start in marketing with product managers for conceptual definition, then move to research and development for product design. During product development, procurement and manufacturing will begin purchasing materials and developing the manufacturing process for the product. Marketing and sales will become engaged in the promotion and distribution of the product. The effectiveness of this new

FIGURE 16.1 Operating Effectiveness Diagram

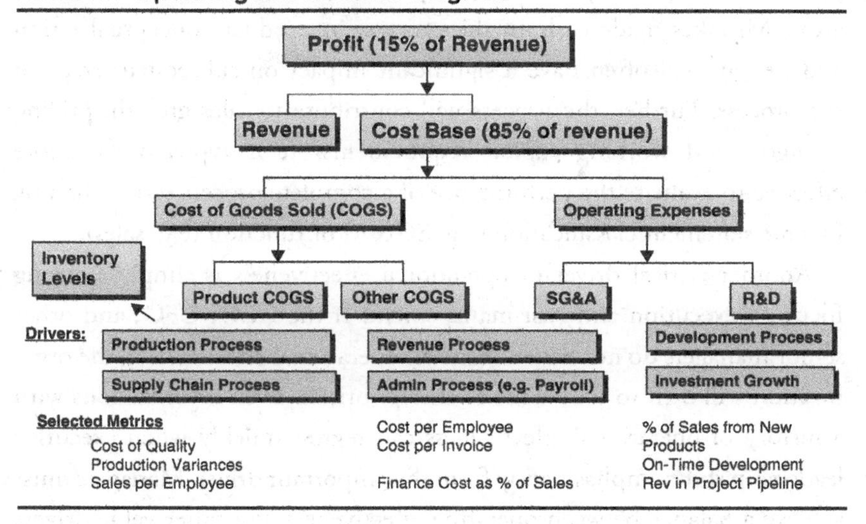

FIGURE 16.2 Process View

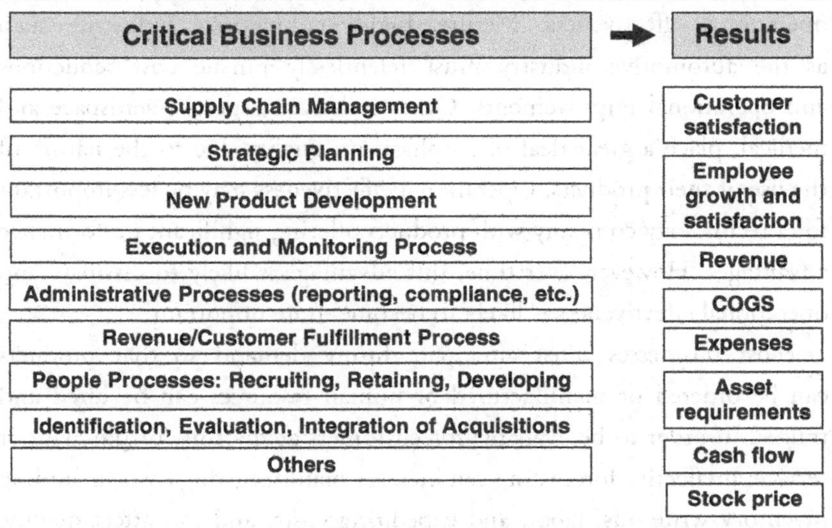

The process view appropriately recognizes cross-functional interaction versus functional silos. In order to improve performance in most critical processes, cross-functional cooperation and teaming are required.

product development process will impact costs in each of these functional areas. Mistakes made early in the process, in product conceptualization and design, will often have a significant impact on subsequent steps in the process. Further, the process will contribute to sales growth, pricing strength, and working capital requirements. It is typically far more effective to evaluate the performance of a complete process rather than by income statement classification (e.g. SG&A) or function (e.g. sales).

Another critical driver of operational effectiveness is simply a strong focus on execution and cost management. If the CEO, CFO, and other senior managers do not have a focus on operational effectiveness, the organization will drift to follow their other priorities. Even organizations with a history of operational effectiveness can regress quickly when executive leadership shifts emphasis away from this important driver. Managers must achieve a balance between operating effectiveness and other value drivers in order to be successful over the long run.

The specific industry or market served by a company will also impact operational effectiveness. Mature, highly competitive industries such as the automotive industry must relentlessly pursue cost reductions and operational improvements. Other industries, such as aerospace and medical, place a great deal of emphasis on quality due to the nature of the use of their products. Operational effectiveness may be less important for a technology company with products offering significant performance advantages. However, over time, this advantage is likely to dissipate and operational effectiveness is likely to become more important.

Most businesses must anticipate future demand so that products can be ordered or manufactured or human resources can be hired and trained in order to be available for customers at the time of purchase or service. Ineffective forecasting can increase manufacturing costs, including inventory write-offs, labor, and expediting costs, and can affect quality, customer satisfaction, and working capital levels. However, because forecasting involves an attempt to predict the future, it will always be an imperfect activity. Therefore, in addition to improving the forecasting process, managers should also strive to increase flexibility and response times, for example by reducing lead times. Forecasting future revenue levels was covered in detail in Chapter 15.

KEY PERFORMANCE INDICATORS: OPERATING EFFECTIVENESS

We will review selected measures covering several areas, including overall effectiveness, the business model, asset utilization, revenue patterns, key business processes, quality, and functional and people management. For additional background and explanation on the financial statement ratios that follow, please refer to Chapter 2, Fundamentals of Finance.

Overall Measures of Operating Effectiveness

The following measures represent top-level indicators of overall operating effectiveness.

Return on Invested Capital (ROIC). ROIC is one of the best overall measures of operating effectiveness since it reflects both profitability and investment levels. ROIC is computed as:

$$= \frac{\text{EBIAT (Earnings before Interest after Tax)}}{\text{Invested Capital}}$$

Asset Turnover. This measure reflects the level of investment in all assets, including working capital; property, plant, and equipment; and intangible assets, relative to sales. It reflects each of the individual asset utilization factors discussed in Chapter 2. This measure and underlying drivers are covered in detail in Chapters 17 and 18.

$$= \frac{\text{Sales}}{\text{Total Assets}}$$

Profitability: Operating Income as a Percentage of Sales. This is a broad measure of operating performance. In addition to operating effectiveness, it will reflect other factors including pricing strength and the level of investments for future growth. Profitability is computed as follows:

$$= \frac{\text{Operating Income}}{\text{Sales}}$$

Gross Margin Percentage. Gross margin percentage is simply the gross margin as a percentage of total revenues, computed as:

$$= \frac{\text{Gross Margin}}{\text{Sales}}$$

The gross margin percentage will be impacted by several factors and therefore will require comprehensive analysis. The factors affecting gross margin include operating effectiveness and other factors:

Operational effectiveness:
- Composition of fixed and variable costs
- Product costs
- Production variances
- Material and labor costs

Other:
- Industry
- Competition and pricing
- Product mix

R&D Percentage of Sales. Research and development (R&D) as a percentage of sales is computed as follows:

$$= \frac{\text{R\&D}}{\text{Sales}}$$

This ratio determines the level of investment in research and development compared to the current period sales. R&D as a percentage of sales ratio will vary significantly from industry to industry and from high-growth to low-growth companies. Objective analysis is required to determine if a high R&D percentage of sales is due to ineffective processes or large investments to drive future revenues.

Selling, General, and Administrative (SG&A) Percentage of Sales. Since this measure compares the level of SG&A spending to sales, it provides a view of spending levels in selling and distributing the firms' products and in supporting the administrative aspects of the business. The measure will reflect the method of distribution, process efficiency, and administrative overhead. SG&A will also often include costs associated with initiating or introducing new products. Recall that SG&A percentage of sales is computed as follows:

$$= \frac{\text{SG\&A}}{\text{Sales}}$$

Sales per Employee. This measure is often used as a high-level ratio to measure employee productivity. It is computed as:

$$= \frac{\text{Sales}}{\text{\# Employees}}$$

The problem with sales per employee is that the measure is very dependent on the business model of a company. If a company outsources a substantial part of manufacturing, for example, the revenue per employee may be much higher than it is for a company that is vertically integrated. This makes it difficult to compare performance to other companies or industries. For example, most retail companies have a high ratio of sales per employee since the retailers typically have purchased, not manufactued, all products that are then sold in their stores by employees. Certain manufacturing companies, in contrast, purchase a relatively small level of raw materials and manufacture or transform these materials with substantial labor into finished products, resulting in a lower ratio of sales per employee. Nevertheless, it is useful to look at trends over time and to benchmark performance and business models.

Value Added per Employee. This measure attempts to address the major criticism of the sales per employee measure. Instead of computing the sales per employee, we estimate the value added per employee. Value added would be computed by subtracting purchased labor and materials from sales. The example in Table 16.1 illustrates the difference between the two employee productivity methods.

Test the Business Model

In Chapter 3, we discussed the importance of a company's business model, including the composition of costs between fixed and variable and the level

TABLE 16.1 Sales and Value Added per Employee

Employee Productivity Measures	
$ 000's	
Sales	$ 100,000
External (Purchased or Contract) Costs	
Purchased Product	15,000
Purchased Labor	12,000
Outside Processing	5,000
Other	7,000
Total	39,000
Internal Costs	
Salaries	30,000
Labor	10,000
Rent	5,000
Other	2,000
Total	47,000
Operating Profit	14,000
Employees	900
Sales per Employee	111
Total Value Added (Sales-External Costs)	61,000
Value Added per Employee	68

of sales required to achieve a breakeven level of profits. A few measures provide insight into the dynamics of the cost structure and breakeven sales levels.

Fixed Costs per Week. In Table 3.14 we estimated the annual level of fixed costs. It can be helpful to compute the weekly (divide by 52) fixed cost level and track it over time. In doing so, the organization will become sensitive to the level of fixed costs and to any changes in the fixed costs levels on a timely basis. The impact of increasing staffing levels or committing to additional space will be reflected in real time in this measure.

Breakeven Sales Levels per Week or Month. Breakeven sales levels can also be easily estimated and tracked on a weekly or monthly basis. This measure translates any changes to the cost model immediately into required increases in sales to break even. It also tends to subliminally influence the organization to level shipments within a given quarter.

Factory or Asset Utilization

In many businesses, there is a substantial fixed cost in factories, stores, or other assets, including people. The extent to which these assets are utilized in a period is a significant driver of breakeven levels and profitability. Until the facility reaches a breakeven level of utilization, these fixed costs will not be covered. Once production exceeds these levels, there is usually a significant increase in profitability, since a substantial part of the costs are fixed and do not increase with production.

Factory Utilization. Depending on the nature of the business, factory utilization may be measured on the basis of labor hours, material or process throughput, or production output. If a factory has resources in place with a capacity to work a certain number of hours, then you can measure the utilization of these resources based on the amount of time spent working on product as a percentage of total available hours. Similarly, it would be critical to understand the capacity, breakeven level, and utilization of a refinery operation on a continuous basis. Actual production levels would be closely monitored since they would be very significant drivers of the operating performance.

Professional Services – People Utilization. A significant driver of revenue and profitability for a professional services firm would be the level of professional staff hours that can be billed to clients. Typically, the total billable hours for a professional would be estimated by taking total available hours for a year (40 hours per week × 52 weeks = 2,080 hours per year), and then subtracting time for holidays, vacations, company meetings, and the like. Partners and managers in these firms may also be expected to spend a significant time in business development and administrative activities. The utilization rate would be computed as follows:

$$= \frac{\text{Hours Billed to Clients}}{\text{Billable Hours}}$$

Space Utilization. For businesses that incur significant occupancy costs, measures are often put in place to monitor the utilization of space. These can range from sales per square foot in a retail setting to headcount per square foot for manufacturing and office space. Headcount per square foot can vary significantly between manufacturing, research, office, and other uses. Standards have been developed that allow companies to compare their density levels to other companies.

Headcount Analysis. People-related costs are typically a significant percentage of total costs. Tracking headcount levels is essential to cost management. Significant changes to the cost model will result from additions or deletions to headcount. Tracking headcount by department over time can provide significant insight into changes in costs. Some companies include the full-time equivalent (FTE) of part-time, temporary, or contract employees in the analysis to provide a comprehensive view and to prevent gaming the measure by using resources that may fall outside the employee definition. In addition, tracking open employment requisitions, new hires, and terminations provides a leading indicator of future cost levels. An example of a headcount analysis is presented in Table 16.2.

Revenue Patterns

Many companies have revenue patterns that are significantly skewed to the end of the quarter or the end of the fiscal year. Revenue patterns impact such areas as receivables, inventories, costs, and risk. Some firms are successful in leveling production and revenue evenly throughout a quarter; others ship as much as 60% or more in the final two weeks of a 13-week quarter. This latter pattern is often described as a "hockey stick" based on the shape of the curve of weekly shipments shown in Figure 16.3.

This graph is a presentation of revenue patterns within a quarter. The revenue linearity index can be used to track revenue patterns over time, computed as follows:

$$\frac{\text{Shipments Last 45 days}}{\text{Shipments First 45 days}}$$

$$\text{Hockey stick} = \$140.5\text{m}/\$28.0\text{m} = 5.02$$

$$\text{Level} = \$84.25\text{m}/\$84.25\text{m} = 1.00$$

TABLE 16.2 Headcount Analysis

Department	Q416	Q117	Q217	Q317	Q417	Q118	Q218	Q318	Q418	Increase (Decrease) Q417-Q418
Operations										
Manufacturing	125	123	126	135	126	127	125	140	132	6
Quality Control	7	7	7	7	7	7	7	7	7	0
Inspection	3	3	3	3	3	3	3	3	3	0
Procurement	8	8	8	8	8	8	8	8	8	0
Other	9	9	9	9	9	9	9	9	9	0
Total	152	150	153	162	153	154	152	167	159	6
R&D										
Hardware Engineering	15	15	15	15	15	15	15	15	15	0
Software Engineering	17	17	17	17	17	19	23	25	30	13
Other	2	2	2	2	2	2	2	2	2	0
Total	34	34	34	34	34	36	40	42	47	13
SG&A										
Management	7	7	7	7	7	7	7	7	7	0
Sales	15	15	15	15	15	15	15	15	15	0
Finance	11	11	12	12	14	14	14	14	14	0
Human Resources	4	4	4	4	4	4	4	4	4	0
Total	37	37	38	38	40	40	40	40	40	0
Company Total	223	221	225	234	227	230	232	249	246	19
Increase (Decrease)		−2	4	9	−7	3	2	17	−3	

Open Requisitions	Number	Annual Cost (000's)
Operations	3	$ 150
R&D	6	750
Finance	1	95
Human Resources	1	75
Total	11	$1,070

FIGURE 16.3 Revenue Patterns

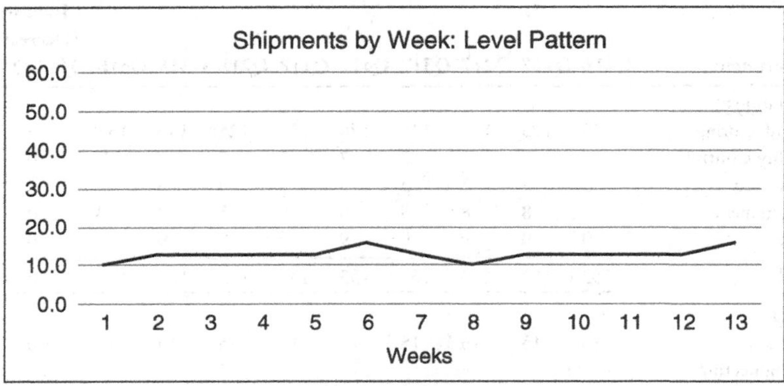

Revenue Linearity Index 1.00

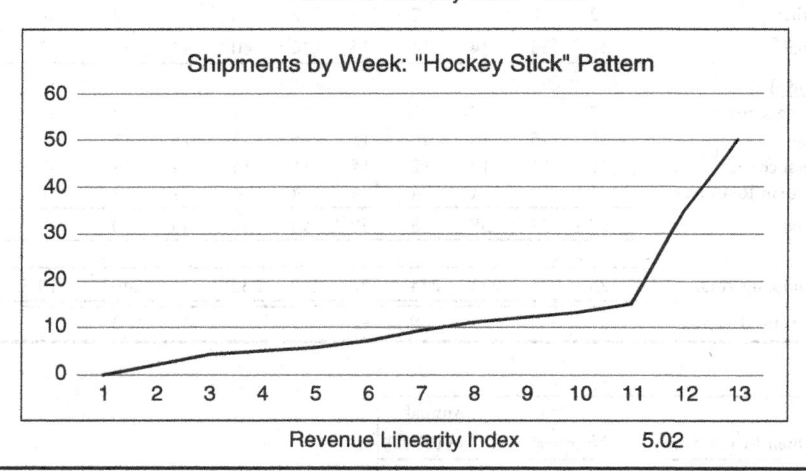

Revenue Linearity Index 5.02

Revenue patterns can have a significant impact on cost, quality, and risk. Revenue patterns that are skewed to the end of a quarter result in higher costs, since overtime and other costs to match product with demand are likely to be incurred. Quality may suffer as the flurry at the end of a quarter can lead to errors in building, testing, documenting, and shipping product. "Hockey sticks" increase the risk that a problem or event leads to a significant shortfall in revenue for a given period. Revenue patterns also have a significant impact on working capital levels, specifically accounts receivable and inventory. This aspect is addressed in detail in Chapter 17.

Forecast Accuracy

Measuring and improving the accuracy of sales forecasts compared to actual demand levels will provide visibility into a key performance driver and serve to establish accountability for sales projections. Inaccurate forecasts lead to operating inefficiencies and higher levels of working capital. The measurements presented in Chapter 15 for measuring revenue forecast accuracy can be easily adapted to other variables including costs, expenses, and profits.

Revenue Process

The revenue process covers all activities around a customer order, from the presales activities to order entry, shipping, invoicing, and collections. This process is covered in detail in Chapter 17. A few additional measures that focus on efficiency of the revenue process are covered next.

Cost per Revenue Transaction. What is the total cost to process a revenue transaction, including order processing, shipping and handling, billing, and collections? This measure can be computed by estimating the cost incurred in each department and dividing by the number of transactions. The cost is typically higher than expected and may lead to further analysis to identify process or technology issues. This measure may also lead to the consideration of minimum order levels necessary to cover the cost of transaction processing.

Invoice Error Rate. Invoicing errors can result in a number of problems. They are costly to correct, requiring the issuance of credit memos or additional invoices. They impact customer satisfaction, since customers must also address invoicing errors in their systems. Invoicing errors will delay collection, resulting in higher levels of accounts receivable. They may also go undetected, likely affecting margins and profitability.

New Product Development Process

Key elements of R&D performance include innovation, cost and time to develop, and impact of design on downstream process activities, for example manufacturing. Measuring R&D effectiveness presents a number of challenges. New product development (NPD) often involves planning for new projects that contain tasks that haven't been performed before. Another challenge is that some engineering professionals resist performance measures in a creative environment. However, there are many aspects of the process that are repeatable and for which feedback on past projects can be extremely useful in planning and managing future projects. In addition, some aspects may be compared to the performance at other companies, for example the time and cost to develop a printed circuit board with certain characteristics.

Key performance indicators (KPIs) for new product development are also discussed in Chapter 15, Revenue and Gross Margins, and include percentage of revenue from new products and projected revenue in the R&D project pipeline. Additional measures that should be considered to evaluate the effectiveness of the new product development process are actual performance versus target development schedule and cost, and target product cost. To measure the broad effectiveness of new product development, other measures should also be considered, including production yields, engineering change notices/orders (ECNs), and warranty costs for new products.

Actual versus Target Development Costs. This measure compares actual costs incurred to the costs estimated for each project. This can be done at the conclusion of the project, but is more useful if it is also examined periodically during the project. Underspending is not necessarily a good thing if it is the result or cause of delays in the development process. This issue can be addressed by combining the cost evaluation with a measure of project progress. This requires disciplined project planning that details key project phases and checkpoints in addition to cost. This type of discipline could result in the analysis shown in Table 16.3.

Actual Product Costs versus Target Costs. Even if the product is developed on time and within the development cost estimate, it is unlikely to be a successful project unless the product can be manufactured at a

TABLE 16.3 Critical New Product Development Status

Project Name	Costs Actual	Projected	%	Status (% completion)[1] Actual	Projected	%	Annual Revenue Potential	Status	Comment
Coyote	0.7	0.8	88%	95%	93%	102%	$25	● Green	On Track, Intro 3/17
Fox	2.8	2.5	112%	60%	80%	75%	30	● Yellow	2 Critical Milestones Missed
Rabbit	1.4	1.3	108%	40%	50%	80%	15	● Red	Technical Performance Issues
Tortoise	1.8	2	90%	100%	100%	100%	60	● Green	1st Shipments, next week
Total	6.7	6.6	102%	74%	81%	89%	$130		

[1] Based on project milestones planned and achieved

cost approximating the cost target developed in the project proposal. Adopting this measure will help to ensure that the product managers and development team will be attentive to estimating and achieving target costs.

Production Yields on New Products. It is understandable that a new product may incur some problems in the first few production runs. The learning curve and process efficiencies will typically kick in over time. However, if manufacturing incurs large cost overruns, rework, or excessive production variances on new products, it may be an indication of design problems or a failure to design the product for manufacturability.

Engineering Change Notices/Orders (ECNs) on New Products. After a product is designed and released to manufacturing for production, any subsequent changes to the design or manufacture process are initiated by ECNs. ECNs are very expensive in terms of time, rework, and inventory costs. An excessive level of ECNs on new products may indicate process issues or premature release to manufacturing.

Warranty and Return Levels. The new product development (NPD) process has a significant impact on downstream activities in manufacturing and in quality and customer service levels. These measures are typically tracked for other reasons, but should be included in the NPD dashboard, since these measures will be affected by the development process.

Supply Chain Management and Production

Supply chain management is covered in detail in Chapter 17, since it is a critical driver of inventory. Additional measures related directly to operating effectiveness are discussed here.

Cycle Time. A very effective measure of supply chain and inventory management is the amount of time required to produce a unit of inventory. The shorter the cycle time for a product, the less time the product spends in the factory. Reducing cycle times typically leads to lower manufacturing costs, lower inventory balances, and increased flexibility. Cycle time can be estimated by using the days in inventory for the company in total or by looking at days in inventory for specific products or processes. Specific cycle times can be measured by tracking the flow of material through the factory until completion. This detailed method is likely to identify opportunities to reduce the cycle time by exposing bottlenecks and dead time in the process.

First-Time Production Yield. During most manufacturing or process activities, there are critical steps where the product must be tested for conformity to specifications, including performance, appearance, and other characteristics. Significant costs will be incurred if there is a large percentage of product that must be scrapped or reworked. Measuring the yield rate of products that pass inspection and reviewing the root causes of failures will provide good visibility into critical production processes.

Number of Vendors. There is a significant cost in dealing with vendors. Each buyer can deal with only a certain number of vendors. Contracts must be negotiated. Vendor performance must be assessed. Many companies have reduced procurement and overhead costs and inventory levels by reducing the number of vendors, subject to good business sense on maintaining alternative suppliers.

Number of Unique Parts. The number of unique parts a company carries in inventory is a significant driver of both costs and inventories.

Each part number must be ordered, received, stored, and counted. Each part is susceptible to obsolescence and forecasting errors. Companies with a focus on supply chain management attempt to reduce the number of parts. They often start by identifying low-volume or redundant parts. This may lead to decisions to prune the product line of old or low-volume products and drive the development team to use common components where possible.

Vendor Performance Assessment. Companies with an effective supply chain management process will monitor vendor performance and typically evaluate performance formally at least once per year. Underperforming vendors may be counseled or terminated in favor of suppliers that consistently meet or exceed pricing, delivery, and quality expectations.

Quality

Quality is an important factor in business performance. It will affect costs and expenses, revenues, receivables, inventories, and customer satisfaction. Corporations have focused significant attention on quality over the past 20 years. A few additional measures not covered in other areas are described next.

Cost of Quality (or Cost of Quality Failures). This measure can be a very effective way to estimate the cost of quality issues across the organization. Typical costs that should be considered for inclusion in this measure include:

Manufacturing. Include any costs arising from quality problems or that are incurred because of the need to test for frequent quality lapses. Examples are:

- Warranty costs
- Rework
- Scrap
- Inventory write-offs
- Customer returns

- Inspection
- Quality control

Back office. The quality of back-office activities should also be considered. Examples include:

- Accounts receivable problem resolution
- Cost of issuing credit memos
- Cost of journal entries to correct mistakes

Revenue. Quality issues can have a significant impact on customer satisfaction and may result in lost customers and revenue.

These costs can be aggregated and used to track the dollar level of quality failures and the cost of quality failures as a percentage of sales:

$$= \frac{\text{Total Cost of Quality Failures}}{\text{Sales}}$$

Defined broadly, the cost of quality failures can easily exceed 10% for many companies. It will typically identify a significant opportunity to address the root cause of these failures and can lead to improved profitability, inventory, receivables, and customer satisfaction.

Error or Defect Rates. We have covered error rates in a number of areas, including invoicing errors and production failures. Many companies have achieved great success with initiatives to measure error rates, including Six Sigma. This program has an objective of decreasing error or failure rates to an extremely low level. Care must be exercised to select and focus on critical activities and processes so that the level of effort in driving to Six Sigma performance will impact important performance drivers.

People and People Management

Many CEOs are often quoted as saying that people are their company's greatest assets and resources. Progressive companies treat these assets well and measure the effectiveness of people-related processes. Human capital management (HCM) and related measures are more fully explored in Chapter 10, Measuring and Driving What's Important.

In addition to KPIs for human capital management, that chapter introduces a "portfolio analysis" of these important assets. Examples of important HCM measures include:

- Associate turnover
- Associates' satisfaction/engagement
- Days to fill open positions
- Training days per associate

Functional Perspective

While it is better to look at process measures in general, some measures of functional performance are useful, particularly where an entire process falls within that function. For example, closing the books of the company is primarily an accounting activity. Functional managers should strive to ensure that their organizations are competitive and incorporate best practices in key activities. Consulting firms developed comprehensive benchmarks and best practices for certain functions for this purpose beginning in the 1990s. Many consulting firms and professional and trade associations also conduct and publish benchmark surveys. Examples of measures that can be used to evaluate performance of functional areas are discussed next.

Finance: Budget Cycle. Preparing the annual operating plan or budget can be a time-consuming and inefficient process in many organizations. The cost and time involved in preparing the budget go well beyond the finance organization, since nearly every function in the organization is involved in the process. The budget cycle can be measured in terms of days, from initial planning through management or board approval.

Financial Closing Cycle. The "closing cycle" can be a time when accounting folks work excessive hours and are unavailable to support the business. The closing cycle begins some time before the end of the accounting period (e.g. quarter end) and ends with the review of financials with the CEO or audit committee. Many organizations have reduced this cycle significantly while maintaining or improving quality by implementing process and technology improvements. This reduces time spent in this activity and provides the management team with critical business information sooner.

Finance: Percentage of Time Spent on Transaction Processing and Compliance Activities. During the 1990s many finance organizations began to measure the percentage of time spent on transaction and compliance versus value-adding activities such as decision support and financial analysis. The objective was to become more efficient (but not less effective) in the areas of compliance and processing in order to devote more time to business support.

Human Resources (HR): Costs per Employee. How efficient is the human resources (HR) department? What are the costs incurred in recruiting, providing benefits, employee development, and evaluating performance? How do these costs compare to those of other companies in our industry? To best practices companies?

HR: Average Days to Fill Open Positions. This measure captures the speed in filling vacant positions. This is a good productivity measure as long as it is balanced by a measure of hiring effectiveness.

HR: Successful Hire Rate Percentage. While it is important to fill open positions on a timely basis, it is obviously more important to fill the positions with capable people who will be compatible with the organization. This measure tracks the success rate in hiring new employees, including managers. The percentage of new employees retained for certain periods or achieving a performance rating above a certain level will be a good indication of the effectiveness of the recruiting and hiring process.

Information Technology (IT) Costs as a Percentage of Sales. Information technology (IT) has become both a significant asset and a major cost to most businesses. Measures should be used to monitor both effectiveness and efficiency of this critical function. IT costs as a percentage of sales have risen sharply over the past 10 years. Capturing this spending rate and evaluating benefits is a necessity.

IT: Network Uptime. Nearly all business functions are dependent on the reliability of the IT network. Measuring the percentage of time that the network is up and running is an important indicator of service levels and performance.

IT Help Desk: Request Levels and Response Times. How many requests are received by the help desk for application or desktop support? What are the root causes of these requests? They may be due to inadequate training, software problems, user errors, or equipment problems that indicate needed action. How fast and effective are we in responding to help desk requests?

Other Measures

Over time there may be certain specific issues or challenges that warrant special consideration and visibility. These may be due to a dramatic shift in the market or increased regulatory pressure, for example the costs associated with being a public company.

Costs Associated with Being a Public Company. There has always been a focus on the cost of public versus private ownership of a firm. With the enactment of the Sarbanes-Oxley Act and subsequent attempts to comply with the new requirements implied in the legislation, the cost of compliance has risen significantly. These costs should be captured and be part of an overall evaluation of whether a company should be taken (or remain) public. The costs of being a public company fall into two categories: obvious and subtle.

Obvious:

- Investor relations program
- Professional fees (legal and audit) associated with public company filings and compliance
- Cost of annual reports and meetings
- Increased directors' and officers' insurance premiums
- Potential costs associated with shareholder suits and actions
- Cost of evaluating and certifying internal controls

Subtle:

- Cost of maintaining a public company board
- Executive time spent in communicating with investors
- Compensation consultants for proxy documentation
- The cost and impact of the focus on short-term and quarterly performance

TOOLS FOR ASSESSING AND IMPROVING OPERATING EFFECTIVENSS

In addition to the performance measures covering operating effectiveness, two other tools may used to understand costs and business processes: the natural expense code analysis and business process assessment.

Natural Expense Code Analysis

While it is generally better to focus on costs and efficiency from a process perspective, another helpful view is what accountants call the "natural" expense accounts. Instead of looking at expenses based on the typical income statement classifications such as R&D or SG&A, we look at the type of spending, for example salaries, wages, and fringe benefits, across the entire company. A top-level summary of natural expense codes is presented in Table 16.4. Note that it is essentially a roll-up of information typically presented in a department or cost center report.

This view provides a great way to examine costs. If we are attempting to control or reduce costs, it is important to understand the largest cost categories. The 80/20 rule typically applies here. A small number of expense categories are likely to account for 80% of the total cost. For example, if people and related costs approximate 40% of the total cost base, then these expenses would likely have to be addressed in order to have an impact on total costs. If purchased materials are significant, then we must look at our procurement practices, vendor pricing, and perhaps alternative sources. Can we attack the cost of health care premiums? Can we negotiate better terms with travel vendors to reduce costs? These opportunities do not come

TABLE 16.4 Natural Expense Code Analysis

	Cost of Sales					$M	Illustrative		
	Product	Other	R&D	Selling	Marketing	General	Other	Total	%
Salaries and Wages	175.0	10.0	15.0	10.0	6.0	15.0	2.0	233.0	32%
Fringe Benefits	35.0	2.0	3.0	2.0	1.2	3.0	0.4	46.6	6%
Travel	4.0	0.5	0.8	2.0	1.5	2.0		10.8	1%
Telecommunications	4.0	0.5	1.0	2.0	1.5	3.0		12.0	2%
Rent	15.0	1.0	1.0	1.4	0.5	0.7		19.6	3%
Depreciation	15.0	1.0	3.0	2.0	3.0	4.0		28.0	4%
Purchased Materials	275.0	4.0	2.0		1.0			282.0	39%
Purchased Labor	55.0	3.0	4.0	1.0				63.0	9%
Consultants	3.0		2.0		1.0	6.0		12.0	2%
Other	4.0	1.0	3.0	2.0	4.0	3.0	1.0	18.0	2%
Total	585.0	23.0	34.8	22.4	19.7	36.7	3.4	725.0	100%

into sharp focus if expense analysis is limited to either income statement classification or process view. The results of the natural expense code analysis can then be graphically presented as in Figure 16.4, sorted in descending order to highlight the most significant costs. This analysis is at a summary level. Each of the categories can be broken down into more detail. For example, fringe benefits can be further broken down into medical costs, retirement contributions, and payroll taxes, including Social Security.

Process Evaluation

Each significant business process can be reviewed to assess the effectiveness and the efficiency of the process. The following critical business processes are likely to have a significant impact on overall business performance, and therefore should be assessed periodically:

- New product development
- Supply chain management
- Revenue/customer fulfillment
- Strategic and operational planning
- Mergers and acquisitions

FIGURE 16.4 Natural Expense Code Analysis Histogram

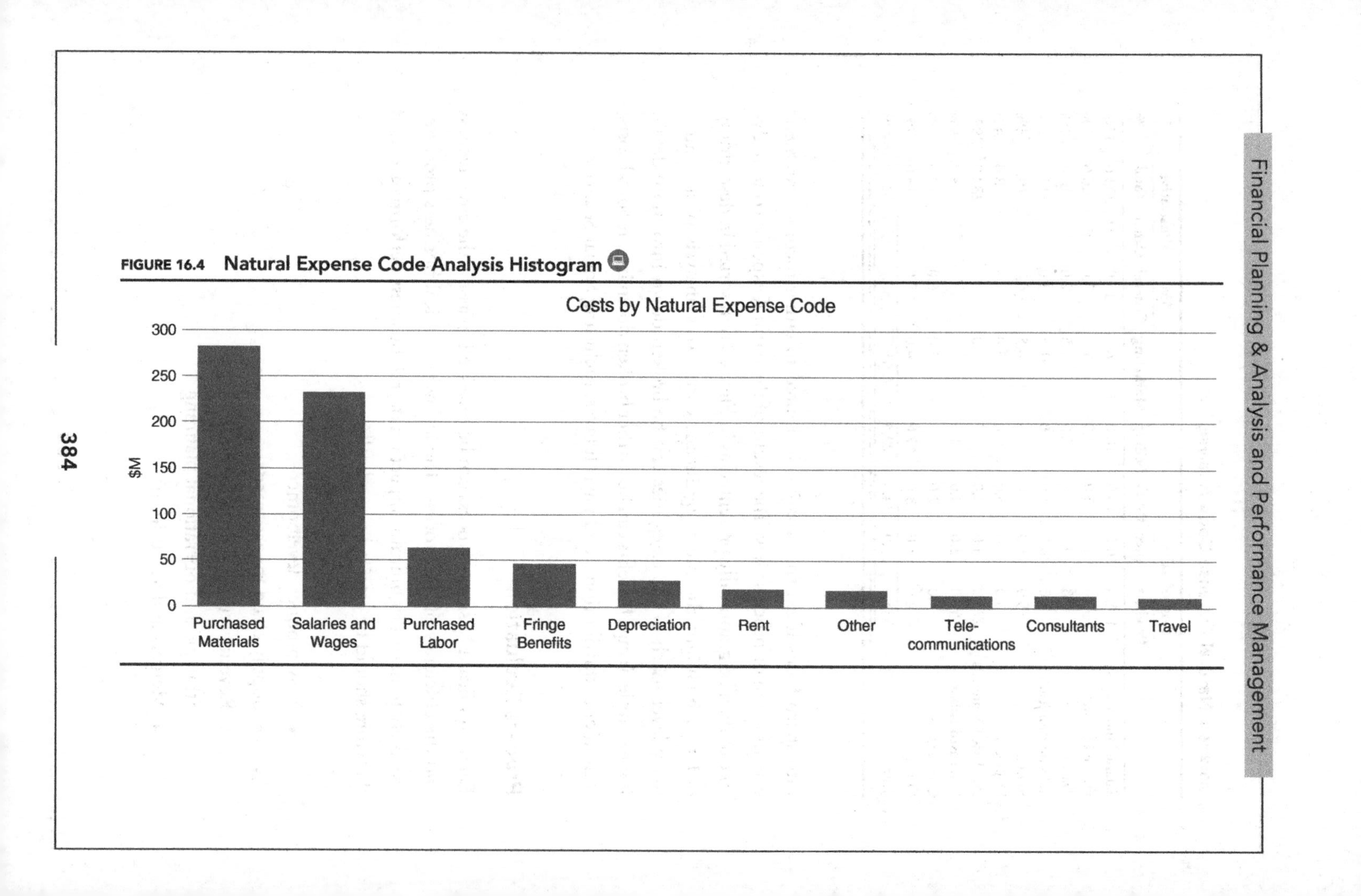

FIGURE 16.5 Operating Effectiveness Dashboard

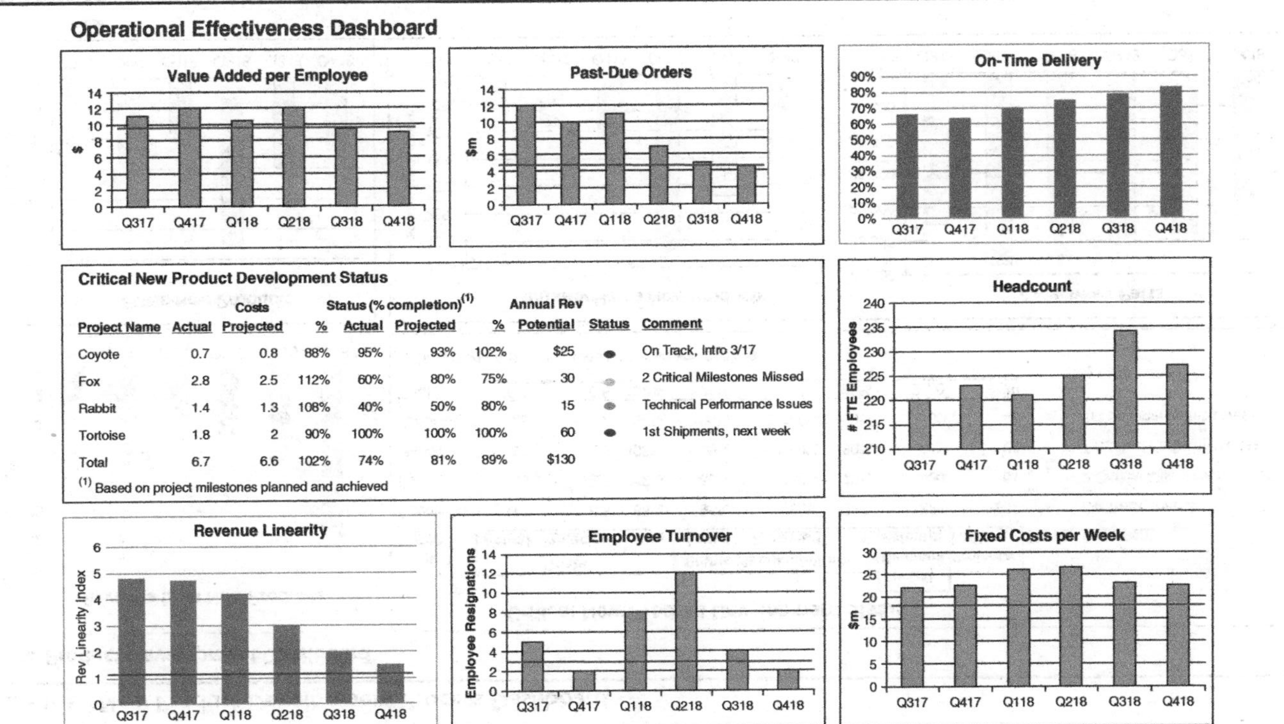

Critical New Product Development Status

Project Name	Costs Actual	Costs Projected	%	Status (% completion)(1) Actual	Status (% completion)(1) Projected	%	Annual Rev Potential	Status	Comment
Coyote	0.7	0.8	88%	95%	93%	102%	$25	●	On Track, Intro 3/17
Fox	2.8	2.5	112%	60%	80%	75%	30	●	2 Critical Milestones Missed
Rabbit	1.4	1.3	108%	40%	50%	80%	15	●	Technical Performance Issues
Tortoise	1.8	2	90%	100%	100%	100%	60	●	1st Shipments, next week
Total	6.7	6.6	102%	74%	81%	89%	$130		

(1) Based on project milestones planned and achieved

FIGURE 16.6 New Product Development Process Dashboard

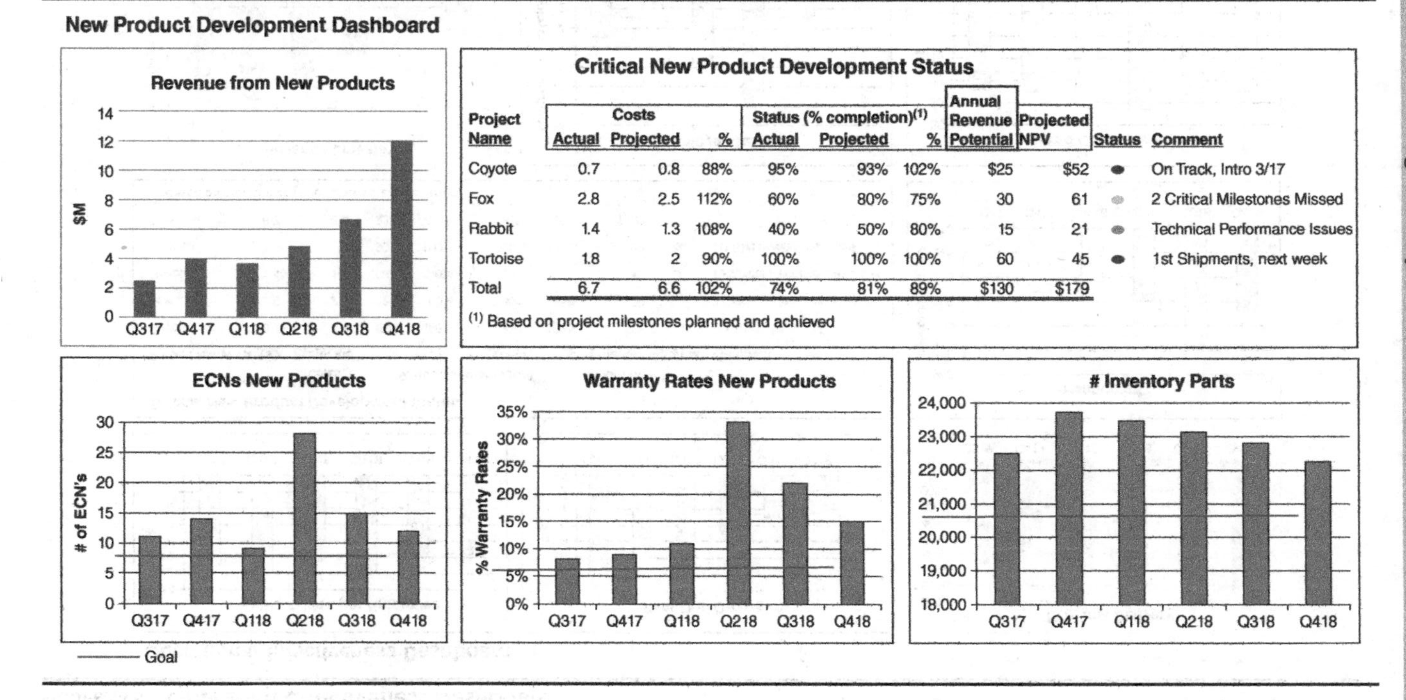

Critical New Product Development Status

Project Name	Costs Actual	Costs Projected	Costs %	Status (% completion)[1] Actual	Status (% completion)[1] Projected	Status (% completion)[1] %	Annual Revenue Potential	Projected NPV	Status	Comment
Coyote	0.7	0.8	88%	95%	93%	102%	$25	$52	●	On Track, Intro 3/17
Fox	2.8	2.5	112%	60%	80%	75%	30	61	●	2 Critical Milestones Missed
Rabbit	1.4	1.3	108%	40%	50%	80%	15	21	●	Technical Performance Issues
Tortoise	1.8	2	90%	100%	100%	100%	60	45	●	1st Shipments, next week
Total	6.7	6.6	102%	74%	81%	89%	$130	$179		

[1] Based on project milestones planned and achieved

Examples of process assessment tools for the revenue process and supply chain management are reviewed in Chapter 17.

Operating Effectiveness Dashboards

Sample dashboards are shown for overall operating effectiveness (Figure 16.5) and new product development (Figure 16.6). The measures selected by an individual company should be based on their specific circumstances and priorities.

SUMMARY

Operating effectiveness is a tremendous source of potential shareholder value. Operating effectiveness has an impact on profitability, sales growth, and asset requirements. There are hundreds of potential measures to choose from to measure different aspects of operating effectiveness. Great care must be exercised in selecting the measures that are most appropriate to a firm at a specific point in time. The performance dashboards must reflect key business priorities. The measures should be evaluated periodically and revised to reflect ever-changing priorities and conditions. It is also critical to provide balance to ensure that a focus on efficiency is not achieved at the expense of quality, customer satisfaction, or growth.

17

CAPITAL MANAGEMENT AND CASH FLOW

Working Capital

CHAPTER INTRODUCTION

Capital efficiency is a critical driver of shareholder value. Improving the management and turnover of assets can significantly improve cash flow and returns. Unfortunately, due to the emphasis on sales and earnings per share growth at many companies, capital management often doesn't get the attention it deserves. Managers and investors who understand the importance of working capital in cash flow appreciate the role that effective capital management plays in value creation. Figure 17.1 drills down into the key drivers of capital efficiency and asset management and highlights the major components of capital employed in a typical business:

- Operating capital
- Capital assets, including property, plant, and equipment
- Intangible assets, including goodwill

FIGURE 17.1 Drill-Down Illustration: Capital Efficiency and Asset Management

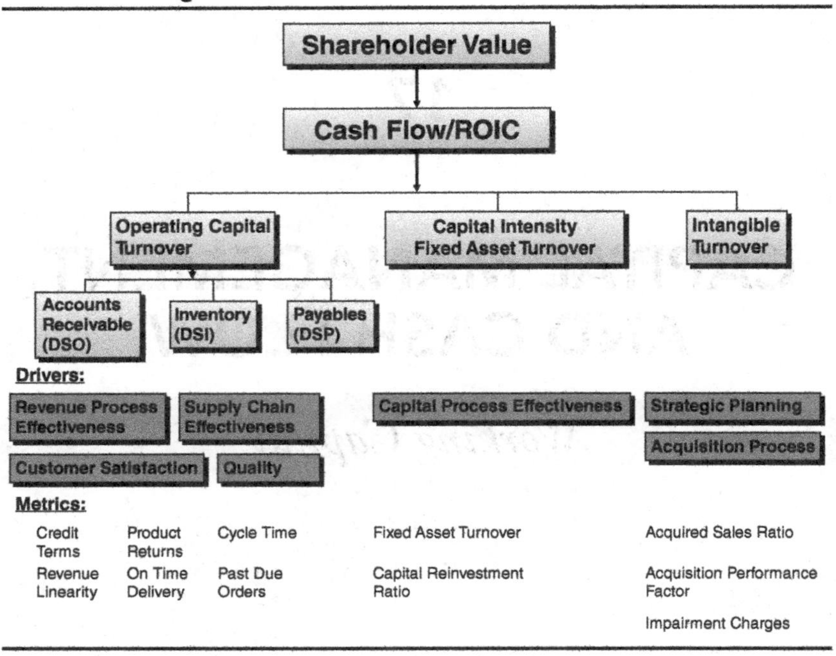

The balance sheet is a snapshot of transactions in process. Therefore, it stands to reason that a company with greater process efficiency will have a leaner balance sheet than a company that is less efficient. This leaner balance sheet is evident by better performance on measures of asset utilization and turnover such as accounts receivable days sales outstanding (DSO), inventory turns, and asset turnover. In addition to eroding returns and decreasing cash flow, companies that have bloated balance sheets (i.e. excessive inventories or receivables) are also inherently more risky than their leaner counterparts. A company with excess inventory or slow-paying customers is more likely to have future write-offs. A wise CFO once told me, "There are only two things that happen to inventory: you either sell it to a customer or write it off." A rising DSO may indicate a number of problems, including potential collection problems, aggressive revenue recognition policies, or a delay of shipments to the end of the quarter. Key asset utilization and turnover measures described later in the chapter can also be used to identify potential risks due to excessive asset levels.

In Chapter 3, we noted that different businesses will have distinct operating or business models. Among other differences, capital requirements and asset turnover will vary significantly across businesses. Some will require large capital outlays for manufacturing plants; others will require little capital for this purpose. For example, a consulting firm typically requires little in the way of capital assets, since people and intellectual property are the firm's primary assets. These firms do not require large expenditures for plants, warehouses, and the like that other firms may need. Some businesses will sell products or services on credit and will carry large accounts receivables. Others will collect the money up front in cash or credit card sales. Each of these extremes must be considered in developing the overall business model in order to earn an acceptable to superior return for shareholders. Within specific industries, there is also a wide range of asset and turnover levels. Effective operating capital management is driven by several factors, including management attention and process efficiency.

CRITICAL SUCCESS FACTORS

The critical success factors for achieving improved capital management include management attention, performance visibility, process efficiency, context creation, and accountability.

Management Attention

The extent to which managers emphasize and attend to any specific process, project, or measure will have a large impact on the effort and result of that endeavor. This is very true in capital management. If a manager is only sales or earnings driven, it will follow that operating capital levels will be higher. Conversely, if a manager recognizes the importance of working capital and actively drives and monitors performance, operating capital levels will be lower. In addition, a well-designed management compensation plan that includes capital utilization (or uses a broad measure such as ROIC that reflects capital) will ensure focus in this important area.

Performance Visibility

Capital management will be improved if managers have appropriate visibility into key performance indicators (KPIs) on a timely basis. Well-designed performance dashboards provide managers with key process measures and leading indicators of capital performance.

Process Efficiency

Capital requirements are very closely associated with process efficiency. Companies that have well-established process and quality programs will typically require less capital to support the business. Conversely, a manufacturing process that is not efficient and has a high level of rejected products will result in high inventories (and costs).

Creating Context: Understanding the Importance of Capital Management

When managers and employees fully understand the dynamic impact of capital in creating value, more attention is paid to this driver and related processes. However, organizations with an exclusive focus on sales or earnings growth will often view capital as "free," with the result of higher than required asset levels.

Accountability

Assigning appropriate accountability for assets such as inventory and receivables is difficult. Out of convenience, many companies look at the functional area responsible for the last step in the related process.

For example, manufacturing is often held responsible for inventory, and finance is held responsible for receivables levels since finance people are typically involved in collections. However, most financial measures and other outcomes are the result of a business process that crosses a number of functional areas. For example, inventory levels are certainly a result of manufacturing activities. But they are also a result of the design of products and the product demand forecasts typically furnished by sales or marketing management. Each driver must be disaggregated and assigned to the appropriate process team and leader.

The remainder of this chapter will focus on measuring and improving the management of operating capital. We will explore the other components of capital investment, fixed assets, and intangibles in Chapter 18.

OPERATING CAPITAL MANAGEMENT

We will focus on measuring and improving the operating components of working capital, primarily accounts receivable, inventories, and accounts payable. We are treating the remaining components of working capital, cash and short-term debt, as "nonoperating" or financing accounts. Table 17.1 presents the major components of operating capital and includes key activity measures for these accounts. Operating capital assets such as receivables and inventories represent a past investment in cash or a future claim to cash. Reducing either of these balances will increase cash and improve returns.

Accounts payable and accrued liabilities offset these "investments" and reduce the total cash required to support the business. Although increasing accounts payable by delaying payments to vendors will reduce the total investment and improve returns, caution must be exercised with this tactic. It runs counter to developing a partnership with vendors and is inconsistent with motivating vendors to higher performance and service levels. Vendors may seek compensation for delayed payment in the form of higher prices or in other subtle ways.

TABLE 17.1 Operating Capital (Working Capital Less Cash and Debt) 

Roberts Manufacturing Co.

Component	2018	Measure Description	Measure Result	% of Sales	Sales Turnover
Receivables	20,000	DSO	73	20%	5.0
Inventory	18,000	Inventory Turns	2.5	18%	5.6
Other	900			1%	111.1
Payables	−4,500	DSP	−16.4	−5%	−22.2
Accrued Liabilities	−5,000			−5%	−20.0
Operating Capital (OC)	29,400	OC Turnover	3.4	29%	3.4
Sales	100,000				
COGS	45,000				

UNDERSTANDING THE DYNAMICS OF OPERATING CAPITAL

In order to understand the dynamics of working capital and to be able to predict future levels of operating capital and cash flows, managers should employ the operating capital forecast, illustrated in Table 17.2. This tool is very helpful in understanding the inputs and outputs to receivables and inventories. The basic idea is to start with a projected profit and loss by month. Then, based on past experience and management practices, receivables, inventories, and payables can be projected. Let's take a look at the projected levels and activity for accounts payable. We will discuss receivables and inventories in each respective section later in the chapter.

Payables represent amounts due to vendors. When inventory is delivered to a company, an addition to the company's inventory and payables is recorded. When the invoice is paid, the payment is subtracted from the balance. In Table 17.2, payables will increase by the amount of inventory purchases each month. In January, the company received $84 million worth of inventory and typically pays vendors in 30 days. This transaction will increase both inventory and payables by $84 million. Payables will

TABLE 17.2 Operating Capital Forecast – Thomas Industries

		History			Projections			
		Oct	Nov	Dec	Jan	Feb	March	April
Income Statement								
Sales		600.0	660.0	1,000.0	400.0	500.0	550.0	600.0
COGS		420.0	462.0	700.0	280.0	350.0	385.0	420.0
Gross Margin		180.0	198.0	300.0	120.0	150.0	165.0	180.0
GM % Sales		30.0%	30.0%	30.0%	30.0%	30.0%	30.0%	30.0%
Operating Expenses		165.0	174.0	225.0	135.0	150.0	157.5	165.0
Operating Profit		15.0	24.0	75.0	−15.0	0.0	7.5	15.0
Tax Expense		6.0	9.6	30.0	−6.0	0.0	3.0	6.0
Net Income		9.0	14.4	45.0	−9.0	0.0	4.5	9.0
Accounts Receivable								
Beginning Balance		950	1,150	1,310	1,810	1,452	1,310	1,285
Sales		600	660	1,000	400	500	550	600
Collections		−400	−500	−500	−758	−642	−575	−510
Other								
Ending Balance		1,150	1,310	1,810	1,452	1,310	1,285	1,375
DSO		57.5	59.5	54.3	108.9	78.6	70.1	68.8
% sales (annualized)		16.0%	16.5%	15.1%	30.3%	21.8%	19.5%	19.1%
Collections	CM	M+1	M+2	M+3				
Assumptions	10.0%	40.0%	30.0%	20.0%				
Inventories								
Beginning Balance		1,300	1,220	1,112	832	762	902	1,077
Purchases		140	154	168	84	196	224	280
Labor		100	100	168	84	196	224	280
OH		100	100	84	42	98	112	140
COGS		−420	−462	−700	−280	−350	−385	−420
Ending balance		1,220	1,112	832	762	902	1,077	1,357
Inventory turns		4.1	5.0	10.1	4.4	4.7	4.3	3.7
DSI		87.1	72.2	35.7	81.6	77.3	83.9	96.9
% sales		16.9%	14.0%	6.9%	15.9%	15.0%	16.3%	18.8%
Accounts Payable								
Beginning Balance		160	170	184	198	114	226	254
Purchases		140	154	168	84	196	224	280
Payments		−130	−140	−154	−168	−84	−196	−224
Other								
Ending Balance		170	184	198	114	226	254	310
% of annualized sales		2.4%	2.3%	1.7%	2.4%	3.8%	3.8%	4.3%

be reduced in February when the company pays vendors $84 million for deliveries received in the prior month.

It is also necessary to develop estimates of working capital levels for long-term projections. Projecting operating capital requirements for long-term projections for strategic plans, valuations, and capital investments is covered in Chapter 14, Long-Term Projections.

UNLEASHING THE VALUE TRAPPED IN OPERATING CAPITAL

It is not uncommon to find companies that have operating capital levels between 20% and 30% of annual sales levels. Many companies have been able to improve on these levels and achieve ratios of 5% to 10%, and in some cases even negative operating capital levels. In other words, companies such as Dell have created business models that provide for payables and accrued liabilities that exceed receivables and inventory levels. The potential value associated with dramatic improvements is significant. Table 17.3 presents a summary of the benefits of a company reducing operating capital levels by 10%, 20%, and 30%. An income statement, a balance sheet, and key activity ratios are presented. To fully understand the benefits, key measures of operating and financial performance are also shown on the analysis, including earnings per share, asset turnover, return on equity (ROE), and economic profit.

Most attention should be focused on reducing receivables and inventories rather than increasing accounts payable or other liabilities. A focus on receivables and inventories will reduce investment levels and can lead to improvements in the revenue and supply chain management processes, customer service, and profitability.

The base case presents a company with $1,200 million in sales and net income of $135.6 million. The company has accounts receivable of $250 million (76 DSO) and inventories of $200 million (3.0 turns). Let's look at the 20% improvement scenario. What would be the benefit

TABLE 17.3 Working Capital Improvement Illustration

				Improvement Scenario					
		Base		10%		20%		30%	
P&L	**$m**	**$**	**% Sales**	**$**	**% Sales**	**$**	**% Sales**	**$**	**% Sales**
Sales		1,200.0	100.0%	1,200.0	100.0%	1,200.0	100.0%	1,200.0	100%
COGS		600.0	50.0%	600.0	50.0%	600.0	50.0%	600.0	50%
Operating Profit		240.0	20.0%	240.0	20.0%	240.0	20.0%	240.0	20%
Interest Expense		14.0	1.2%	10.9	0.9%	7.7	0.6%	4.6	0%
Profit before Taxes		226.0	18.8%	229.2	19.1%	232.3	19.4%	235.5	20%
Taxes	40%	90.4	7.5%	91.7	7.6%	92.9	7.7%	94.2	8%
Net Income		135.6	11.3%	137.5	11.5%	139.4	11.6%	141.3	12%
Balance Sheet									
Cash		100.0	8.3%	100.0	8.3%	100.0	8%	100.0	8%
Accounts Receivable		250.0	20.8%	225.0	18.8%	200.0	17%	175.0	15%
Inventory		200.0	16.7%	180.0	15.0%	160.0	13%	140.0	12%
Net Fixed Assets		100.0	8.3%	100.0	8.3%	100.0	8%	100.0	8%
Total Assets		650.0	54.2%	605.0	50.4%	560.0	47%	515.0	43%
Accounts Payable		75.0	6.3%	75.0	6.3%	75.0	6.3%	75.0	6.3%
Accrued		50.0	4.2%	50.0	4.2%	50.0	4.2%	50.0	4.2%
Debt		200.0	16.7%	155.0	12.9%	110.0	9.2%	65.0	5.4%
Equity		325.0	27.1%	325.0	27.1%	325.0	27.1%	325.0	27.1%
Total Liabilities & Equity		650.0	54.2%	605.0	50.4%	560.0	46.7%	515.0	42.9%
Cost of Capital	12%								
Interest Rate	7.0%								
Key Measures									
DSO		76.0		68.4		60.8		53.2	
Inventory Turns		3.0		3.3		3.8		4.3	
Asset Turnover		1.8		2.0		2.1		2.3	
Working Capital		425.0	35.4%	380.0	31.7%	335.0	27.9%	290.0	24.2%
Net Operating Assets		525.0	43.8%	480.0	40.0%	435.0	36.3%	390.0	32.5%
Invested Capital		525.0	43.8%	480.0	40.0%	435.0	36.3%	390.0	32.5%
ROE Analysis		41.7%		42.3%		42.9%		43.5%	
Profitability		11.3%		11.5%		11.6%		11.8%	
Asset Turnover		1.85		1.98		2.14		2.33	
Leverage		2.00		1.86		1.72		1.58	
ROIC		27.4%		30.0%		33.1%		36.9%	
Additional Cash Generated				45		90		135	
Earnings				1.9	1%	3.8	3%	5.7	4%

of reducing receivables to $200 million (60.8 DSO) and inventories to $160 million (3.8)? The following changes would result:

The sum of $90 million additional cash is generated.

The additional cash could be used to repurchase shares, pay down debt, or make strategic investments, including acquisitions. In this case, the company pays down debt from $200 million to $110 million.

Reducing debt also reduces annual interest expense from $14.0 million to $7.7 million. Net income increases from $135.6 million to $139.4 million.

Asset turnover increases from 1.85 to 2.14.

ROIC increases from 27.4% to 33.1% (a 21% improvement).

ACCOUNTS RECEIVABLE

Figure 17.2 presents a drill down into the drivers and critical measures for accounts receivable. Key among these drivers are credit terms, quality of products and paperwork, the effectiveness of the revenue process, and revenue patterns.

Best Potential DSOs

A significant determiner of a company's actual DSOs is the credit terms extended to customers. There tends to be wide variation in credit terms by industry, country, and competitive situation. Even within a company, it is fairly typical to see a wide range of terms extended to customers for different products, channels, and regions. A useful way to evaluate receivable management is to compare actual DSO to the "best possible DSO" (BPDSO). This computation estimates the DSO level if all customers paid invoices on the contractually agreed date. It is computed by weighting the credit terms for each type of customer, region, or business line by annual sales and is illustrated later in this chapter in the "Best Possible DSO Estimate" table. Companies should also consider the possibility and merits of reducing credit terms to customers, resulting in a reduction to the BPDSO.

FIGURE 17.2 **Drill-Down Illustration: Accounts Receivable**

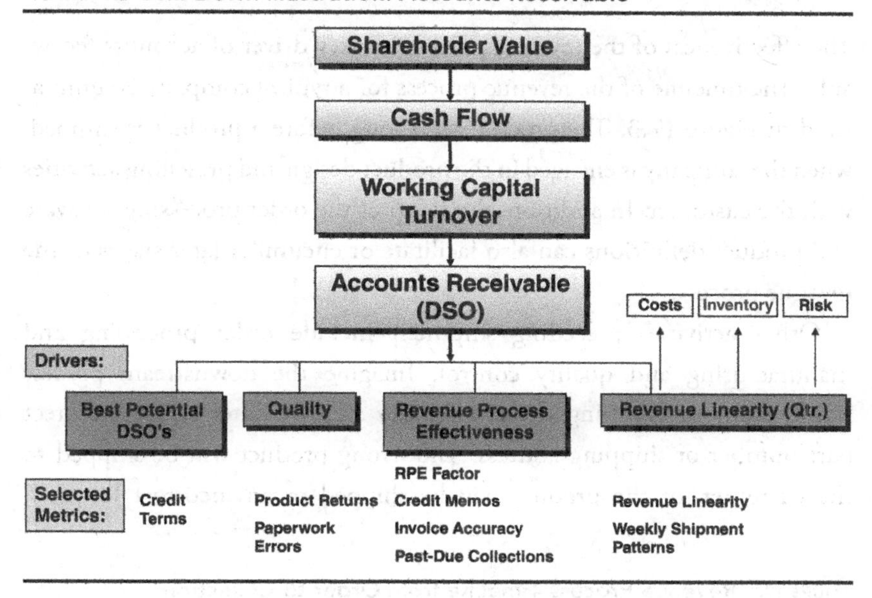

Quality

It stands to reason that receivables collections will be affected by the quality of products and services and customer-facing processes such as billing. The typical customer is not anxious to part with cash in the first place. Obviously, if the product is not performing, the customer will not pay. The same is true for nonconforming or incomplete paperwork. If the invoice does not match the customer purchase order or does not provide required supplemental information, the payment cannot be processed without additional action.

We all recognize that the impact of quality problems goes far beyond slow collections. It reduces customer satisfaction and loyalty, increases costs for both you and your customer and may jeopardize future sales. By examining slow-paying accounts and identifying underlying reasons, managers can learn a great deal about any customer dissatisfaction and take steps to deal with underlying product or process problems.

Effectiveness of the Revenue Process

The effectiveness of the revenue process is a key driver of accounts receivable. The timeline of the revenue process for a typical company is summarized in Figure 17.3. The process starts long before a product is shipped, when the company is engaged in the product design and preselling activities with the customer. In addition, the setup of the order processing software and product definitions can also facilitate or encumber later stages of the revenue process.

Other activities preceding shipment include order processing and manufacturing and quality control. Imagine the downstream process implications of botching the order entry step by entering an incorrect part number or shipping address. The wrong product will be shipped to the customer, or the product will be shipped to an incorrect location.

FIGURE 17.3 Revenue Process Timeline from Order to Collection

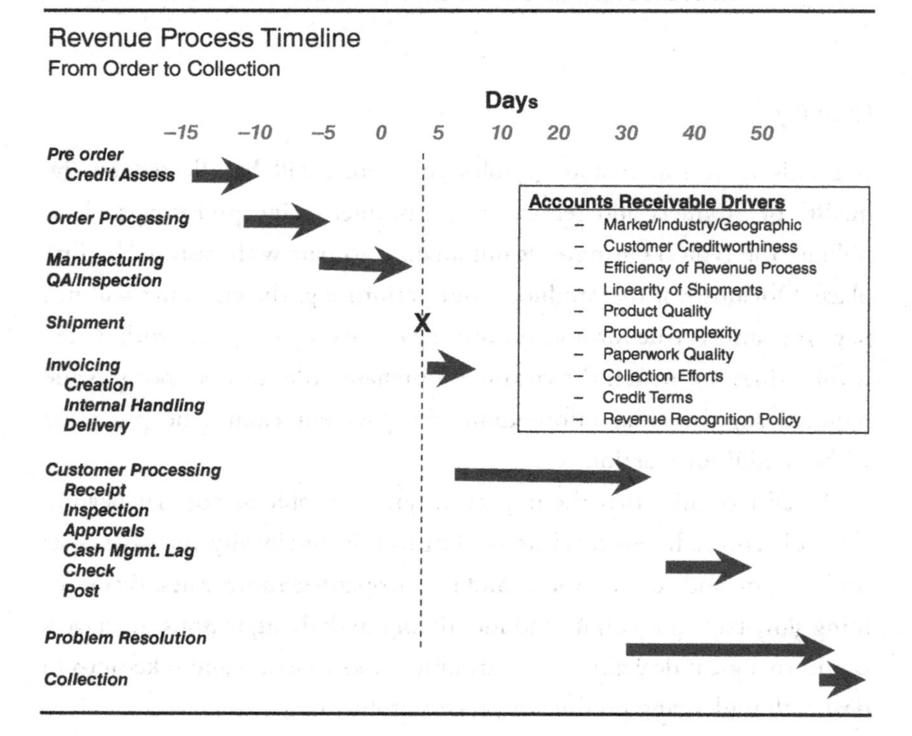

The ability to reduce defects at this stage in the process can save a great deal of time, money, and customer goodwill.

When available, the product is shipped and an invoice is generated and delivered to the customer by post or electronic means. Understanding what happens at the customer's facility to process purchases and payments is essential to speed collections. What process and system does the customer employ to receive the product, test that it works properly, review the transaction, and initiate payment? Does the customer require special paperwork to facilitate processing? How does the customer identify and resolve problems and discrepancies? Does the customer pay on negotiated terms or routinely delay payment to help its own cash flow, often called the cash management lag (CML)?

A best practice is for customer service to contact the customer shortly after delivery to ensure that the customer has received and is satisfied with the product and has everything necessary to pay the invoice. If any issues exist, they are identified early and can be addressed at this time. Unfortunately, many companies wait until the receivable is past due to contact the customer. They may be unaware that there is a problem with the product or paperwork preventing payment. Under even the best of circumstances, this situation results in an unsatisfied customer and delayed payment for 40 days or more.

KEY PERFORMANCE INDICATORS FOR THE REVENUE PROCESS AND ACCOUNTS RECEIVABLE

The specific measures utilized will vary based on the individual circumstances. However, there are some common measures that are useful in evaluating and measuring improvements in this area.

Days Sales Outstanding (DSO). DSO is a measure of the length of time it takes to collect from customers. It will be affected by the industry in which the firm participates, the creditworthiness of customers, and even the countries in which the firm does business. In addition, DSO is affected by the efficiency and effectiveness of the revenue process (billing and collection), by product quality, and even by the pattern of shipments within the quarter or the year.

The basic DSO formula is:

$$= \frac{\text{Receivables} \times 365}{\text{Sales}}$$

In Chapter 2, we computed the DSO for Roberts Manufacturing Company (RMC) as follows:

$$= \frac{\$20{,}000 \times 365}{\$100{,}000}$$

$$= 73 \text{ days}$$

The basic formula can be adjusted for use as a quarterly or monthly measure by annualizing sales for the period. For example, DSO for a quarter would be computed as follows:

$$= \frac{\text{Receivables} \times 365}{\text{Quarterly Sales} \times 4}$$

Assuming that Q4 sales for Roberts Manufacturing Company were $35,000, the quarterly DSO would be computed as follows:

$$= \frac{\$20{,}000 \times 365}{\$35{,}000 \times 4}$$

$$= 52.1 \text{ days}$$

Many financial and operating managers prefer to examine DSOs based on average levels of receivables throughout the year, since year-end receivables levels may be large due to the year-end push (hockey stick):

$$= \frac{\text{Average Monthly Receivables} \times 365}{\text{Annual Sales}}$$

DSO Count-Back Method. This measure is a terrific variation of the basic DSO concept that considers variations in shipment patterns. The traditional DSO measure described earlier can be significantly impacted by shipment or billing patterns during a period. For example, if a disproportionate levels of shipments are made at the end of the quarter, DSO will rise since it is very unlikely that these invoices will be collected within 10 to 15 days after shipment.

The DSO count-back method accumulates sales starting with the last day of the quarter and continuing backward until the total equals the receivables balance as illustrated in Table 17.4. The number of days counted results in the DSO count-back.

The count-back method results in a DSO of 35 days, approximately 17 days lower than the traditional DSO computation. The difference is a good estimate of the impact of a nonlinear revenue pattern during the quarter.

Best Potential DSOs. A useful way to evaluate the actual DSO performance is to compute the best possible DSO (BPDSO) (Table 17.5). This computation estimates the DSO level if all customers paid invoices

TABLE 17.4 DSO Count-Back Illustration

	Sales	Cumulative Countback	Days
October			
Week 1	700.0	35,000.0	
Week 2	900.0	34,300.0	
Week 3	1,200.0	33,400.0	
Week 4	2,000.0	32,200.0	
November			
Week 1	2,200.0	30,200.0	
Week 2	2,300.0	28,000.0	
Week 3	2,700.0	25,700.0	
Week 4	3,000.0	23,000.0	
December			
Week 1	3,800.0	20,000.0	7.0
Week 2	3,200.0	16,200.0	7.0
Week 3	3,700.0	13,000.0	7.0
Week 4	3,800.0	9,300.0	7.0
Week 5	5,500.0	5,500.0	7.0
Total Sales	35,000.0		
Ending Receivables	20,000.0		
DSO, Quarterly Basis	52.1		
DSO, Countback			35.0

TABLE 17.5 Best Possible DSO Estimate

Geography/Channel	Credit Terms	Estimated Revenue ($m)	% of Total	Weighted
Product Line 1 Direct	30	30.5	31%	9.2
Product Line 1 Distributor	45	7.5	8%	3.4
Product Line 1 Export	60	15.0	15%	9.0
Product Line 2 Direct	30	30.0	30%	9.0
Product Line 2 Distributor	50	5.0	5%	2.5
Product Line 2 Export	60	12.0	12%	7.2
Total		100.0	100%	40.2
				Best Possible DSOs

Weighting is computed as: Credit Terms x % of total

on the contractually agreed date. It is computed by weighting the credit terms for each type of customer, region, or business line by annual sales. This is a key step in understanding an important variable in receivables management and in setting realistic targets for DSO levels.

Past-Due Collections. Receivables that are not collected in a reasonable period (a cushion beyond agreed-upon terms) will obviously have a significant impact on DSOs. Tracking this level of past-due receivables on a monthly, weekly, and even daily basis allows for timely identification and faster resolution of emerging problems and is a leading indicator of accounts receivable performance.

Returns. Product that is returned by customers represents a costly transaction on a number of fronts. Performance problems culminating in product returns are likely to have a significant negative impact on customer satisfaction. By identifying the root cause of these returns, process failures and problems can be identified and addressed. There is also a significant transaction cost of shipping, receiving, and carrying the returned product. Depending on the specific circumstance, some companies choose to track the dollar value of returns; others prefer to measure the number of transactions.

Revenue Patterns. In Chapter 16, the impact of revenue patterns on operating efficiency was discussed. Revenue patterns, especially those with revenue skewed toward the end of the quarter, also impact working capital requirements. As evident in the count-back method, accounts receivable will be higher if the revenue pattern is a hockey stick since a greater percentage of revenue will be uncollected at the end of the period. Inventories will likely be higher since more inventory must be carried to meet last-minute orders.

Revenue patterns within a quarter can be plotted as shown in Figure 16.3 in Chapter 16. The revenue linearity index is a useful measure to track revenue patterns over time.

Revenue Process–Accounts Receivable Dashboard

Depending on the specific facts and circumstances, several of these measures should be selected and combined to create a dashboard for the revenue process and accounts receivable, illustrated in Figure 17.4.

Tools for Assessing and Improving Revenue Process and Accounts Receivable

A number of tools can be employed to help in assessing and improving the revenue process and accounts receivable management.

Accounts Receivable–DSO Drivers Chart. The chart in Figure 17.5 presents a high-impact visual summary of DSOs. We begin with the best possible DSOs (BPDSOs) of 40 days and then identify the number of days associated with significant factors resulting in an actual DSO of 64 days. In this illustration, three factors account for most of the 24 days: customer cash management lag (CML), revenue linearity, and past-due collections. Each of these items represents high-leverage improvement opportunities for managers to address.

Accounts Receivable Aging Schedule. A useful tool for managing accounts receivable, customer satisfaction, and the revenue process is the standard accounts receivable aging report. An example of an accounts

FIGURE 17.4 Revenue Process–Accounts Receivable Dashboard

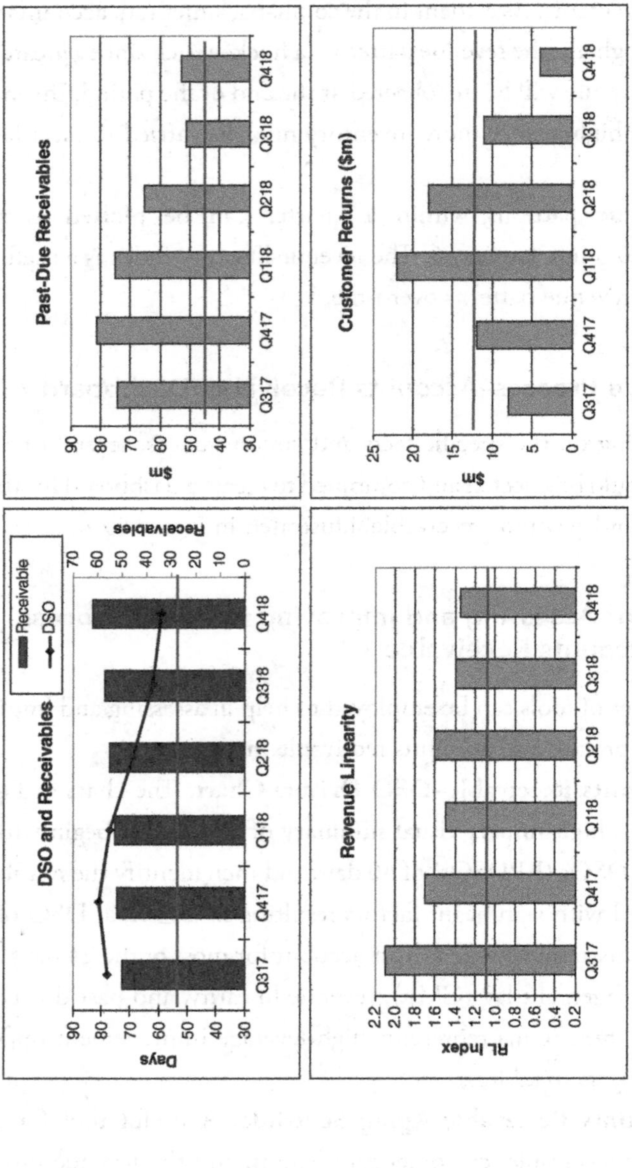

DSO and Receivables

Days: 90, 80, 70, 60, 50, 40, 30

Receivables: 70, 60, 50, 40, 30, 20, 10, 0

Receivable

DSO

Q317 Q417 Q118 Q218 Q318 Q418

Past-Due Receivables

$m: 90, 80, 70, 60, 50, 40, 30

Q317 Q417 Q118 Q218 Q318 Q418

Revenue Linearity

RL Index: 2.2, 2.0, 1.8, 1.6, 1.4, 1.2, 1.0, 0.8, 0.6, 0.4, 0.2

Q317 Q417 Q118 Q218 Q318 Q418

Goal

Customer Returns ($m)

$m: 25, 20, 15, 10, 5, 0

Q317 Q417 Q118 Q218 Q318 Q418

FIGURE 17.5 DSO Drivers

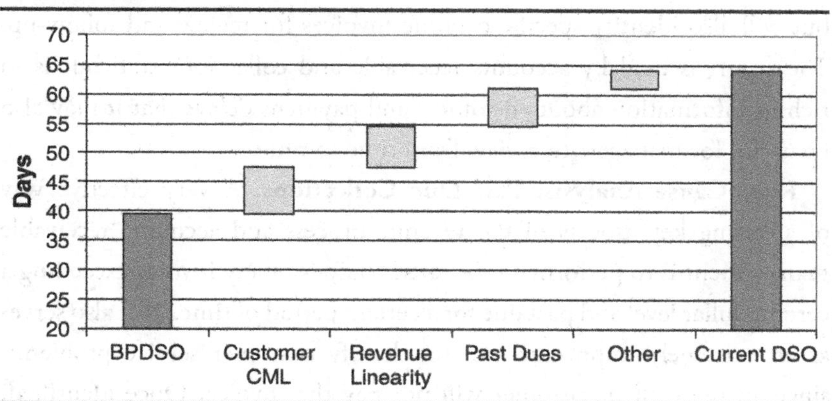

receivable aging report is presented in Table 17.6. This report simply details the current accounts receivable balance for each customer by age of invoice. Invoices issued in the past 30 days would be included in the 0–30 days column. Invoices issued in the previous month would be reported in the 31–60 days column, and so on. This report allows the

TABLE 17.6 Accounts Receivable Aging Schedule for Morehouse Company

Customer	Total	Current	30–60	60–90	90–120	>120
A	83,000	50,000	20,000	10,000	–	3,000
B	54,000	20,000	20,000	10,000	2,000	2,000
C	40,000	10,000	20,000	10,000	–	–
Others	50,000	30,000	20,000			
Totals	227,000	110,000	80,000	30,000	2,000	5,000
Sales	1,500,000					
DSO Impact	55.2	26.8	19.5	7.3	0.5	1.2
Aging % of Total Balance:						
%	100.0%	48.5%	35.2%	13.2%	0.9%	2.2%
Last Month %	100.0%	60.0%	30.0%	5.0%	5.0%	0.0%

identification of macro payment patterns such as slow-to-pay customers, but will also identify specific overdue invoices for review and follow-up. The report is used by accounts receivable and collections staff but is so rich in information about customers and payment delays that it may also be useful for managers to review from time to time.

Root Cause Analysis: Past Due Collections. A very effective way of assessing key aspects of the revenue process and accounts receivable management is to perform a root cause analysis of any invoice exceeding a certain dollar level and past due for a certain period of time. This also serves as an extremely important tool to identify customer service problems, since an unsatisfied customer will not pay the invoice. Once identified, overdue invoices can be reviewed to determine the root cause for the delay. Overdue receivables generally will fall into one of several root cause categories. For example, key process problems such as invoicing errors or poor quality associated with a particular product may be contributing to overdue receivables. An example of a simple root cause analysis is shown in Table 17.7.

The analysis can then be summarized to provide useful insight into the root cause of problems that can lead to the development of a corrective action plan as shown in Figure 17.6.

Accounts Receivable Roll-Forward Summary. This tool is a subset of the operating capital budget tool discussed earlier in the chapter. It is a great way to understand and communicate the dynamics of accounts receivable. Accounts receivable represent amounts due from customers for products delivered or services rendered. Receivables are increased by sales and reduced by amounts collected from customers. Sales for each month

TABLE 17.7 Accounts Receivable Past Due Analysis

Invoice	Date	Division	Customer	Product	Amount	Root Cause
220921	11/3/2005	A	Mangham	M-1	22,000	Dead on arrival
230073	10/4/2005	B	Rhodes	B-1	15,000	Installation problem
223578	9/30/2005	B	Webster	C-1	140,000	Paperwork discrepancy

FIGURE 17.6 Past Due by Root Cause 

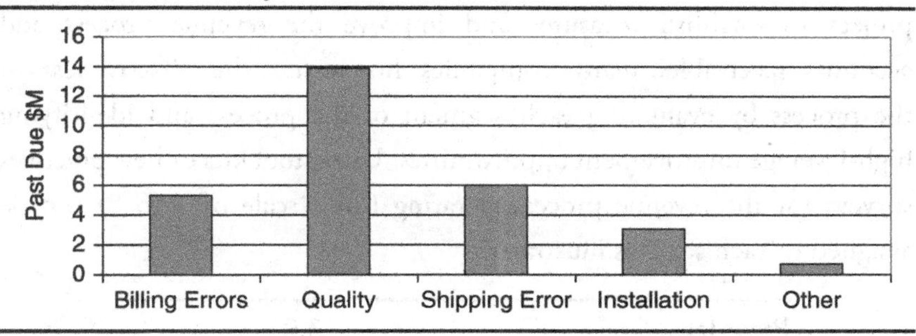

TABLE 17.8 Accounts Receivable Roll-Forward Summary

Accounts Receivable		Oct	Nov	Dec	Jan	Feb	March	April
Beginning Balance		950	1,150	1,310	1,810	1,452	1,310	1,285
Sales		600	660	1000	400	500	550	600
Collections		−400	−500	−500	−758	−642	−575	−510
Other								
Ending Balance		1,150	1,310	1,810	1,452	1,310	1,285	1,375
DSO		57.5	59.5	54.3	108.9	78.6	70.1	68.8
% Sales (annualized)		16.0%	16.5%	15.1%	30.3%	21.8%	19.5%	19.1%
Collections	CM	M+1	M+2	M+3				
Assumptions	10.0%	40.0%	30.0%	20.0%				

are taken from the profit and loss (P&L) forecast. Collections will be estimated based on past and projected payment patterns. In the example in Table 17.8, it is estimated that 10% of sales will be collected in the current month, 40% in the next month, and then 30% and 20% in months 2 and 3, respectively.

For example, collections in January of $758 million are estimated as follows:

January shipments: 10% of $400m	$40m
December shipments: 40% of $1,000m	400m
November shipments: 30% of $660m	198m
October shipments: 20% of $600m	120m
Total estimated January collections	$758m

Assess Effectiveness of Revenue Process. Before embarking on a project to establish measures and improve the revenue process and accounts receivable, many companies first assess the effectiveness of the process by evaluating each segment of the process and identifying high-leverage improvement opportunities. Using tool kits or best practices surveys for the revenue process, a rating (on a scale of 1 to 5) can be assigned to each stage as illustrated:

Preorder	3.0
Credit assessment	4.0
Manufacturing	4.0
Quality	4.5
Invoicing	2.5
Follow-up	2.0
Problem resolution	4.0
Visibility: metrics and reporting	1.5
Overall	25.5 (out of 40)

This evaluation will set the focus on weak segments of the process, in this case invoicing, follow-up, and visibility.

INVENTORIES

Many businesses must build, manufacture, or hold products for resale to customers. Inventory levels are the result of several key drivers and the effectiveness of the procurement and conversion process as shown in Figure 17.7.

Drivers of Inventory Levels

Market and Industry. The very nature of certain businesses and industries often determines the level of inventory required. For example, retailers must purchase and hold inventories for resale to consumers. Manufacturing companies must acquire materials, assemble products,

FIGURE 17.7 Procurement and Conversion Processes

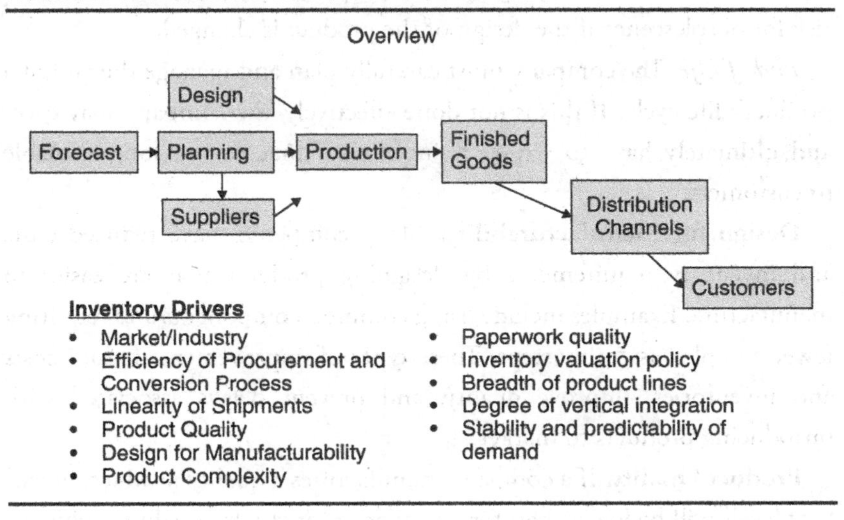

and distribute finished goods to their customers. However, service companies, including consulting firms, do not have to hold significant levels of inventory.

Effectiveness of Procurement and Conversion Processes. Inventories as well as manufacturing costs can be reduced by improving procurement and manufacturing or conversion processes. For example, by evaluating and then improving vendor quality and delivery performance, the company can reduce lead times and inventory levels. Over the past 25 years, tremendous improvements have been made by many companies in improving the flow and efficiency of the manufacturing process.

Product Life Cycle Issues. The evolution of a product from conception to full-scale production and to end of life has significant impact on inventory levels. Two critical phases in the product life cycle are new product introduction and the end of the product's life.

New Product Introduction. Many companies carry high inventory levels associated with problems in the design and introduction of new products. If a new product is transferred to manufacturing before all design issues are resolved, there are likely to be high inventory levels associated with the product. In addition to tying up excess capital, this inventory may be at risk for obsolescence if the design of the product is changed.

End of Life. The company must carefully plan and manage the end of a product's life cycle. If this is not done effectively, the company may carry and ultimately have to write off inventories that are no longer salable to customers.

Design for Manufacturability. Many companies have reduced costs and inventory requirements by designing products that are easier to manufacture. Examples include using common components and requiring fewer complex assembly steps. These types of improvements reduce costs and inventories, improve quality, and prevent delays associated with introducing products to market.

Product Quality. If a company manufactures a quality product, inventory levels will be lower than for a similar product with quality problems. A firm with high-quality manufacturing processes will require lower levels of material input; less time and inventory in test, repair, and rework; and lower levels of inventory returned from customers.

Breadth of Product Line. The company that offers a broad selection of products will typically require higher inventory levels. Conversely, a firm with limited product alternatives will typically have less inventory. Many firms have reduced inventory levels by limiting product variety to fewer options and choices (e.g. color, size, configurations, and power).

Vertical Integration/Outsourcing. Companies that are highly vertically integrated will carry higher inventory balances than a firm that outsources a substantial part of the manufacturing process to other firms.

Forecasting. In Chapter 15 we discussed that most businesses must anticipate future demand for their products so that products can be ordered or manufactured and be available for customers at the time of purchase. The revenue forecast typically drives procurement and manufacturing schedules and activities. The accuracy of forecasts will have a significant impact on inventory levels. If demand is overestimated, excess inventory will result. Even if the total revenue forecast is accurate, if the mix of products is different than projected, the company may miss sales and build products that were not ordered, leading to an increase in inventory. In Chapter 16, we outlined several measures that can be taken to improve the forecasting process. In addition to improving the forecasting process, managers should also strive to increase flexibility and response times, for example by reducing lead times.

Key Performance Indicators for Supply Chain Management and Inventory

There are a number of performance measures that can be developed and tracked to provide visibility into key drivers of supply chain and inventory management.

Inventory Turns. In Chapter 2, we computed inventory turns and days sales of inventory (DSI) for Roberts Manufacturing Company (RMC), as follows:

$$= \frac{\text{Cost of Goods Sold (COGS)}}{\text{Inventory}}$$

$$= \frac{\$45{,}000}{\$18{,}000}$$

$$= 2.5 \text{ times (turns)}$$

Inventory turns measure how much inventory a firm carries compared to sales levels. Factors that will affect this measure include effectiveness of supply chain management and production processes, product quality, breadth of product line, degree of vertical integration, and predictability of sales.

Days Sales of Inventory (DSI). This measure is a derivative of inventory turns and is computed as follows:

$$= \frac{365}{\text{Inventory Turns}}$$

$$= \frac{365}{2.5}$$

$$= 146 \text{ days}$$

This measure is affected by the same factors as inventory turns. The advantage to this measure is that it can be easier for people to relate to the number of days of sales in inventory. As a result, it may be easier to conceptualize the appropriateness (or potential improvement opportunity) of carrying 146 days' worth of sales in inventory than to conceptualize 2.5 inventory turns.

Slow-Moving and Obsolete Inventory Levels. It is important to identify and manage excess and obsolete inventory. Excess inventory is the inventory on hand in excess of foreseeable demand over a defined period such as 12 months. Excess inventory results from overestimating demand or from radical changes in demand patterns. Obsolete inventory results from holding inventory that is no longer salable or usable in the ordinary course of business. A useful summary of excess and obsolete inventory is illustrated in Figure 17.8. A good first step in managing excess and

FIGURE 17.8 Excess and Obsolete Inventory Summary

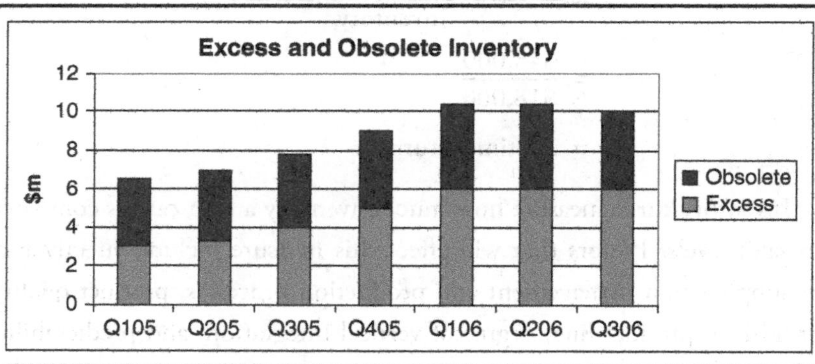

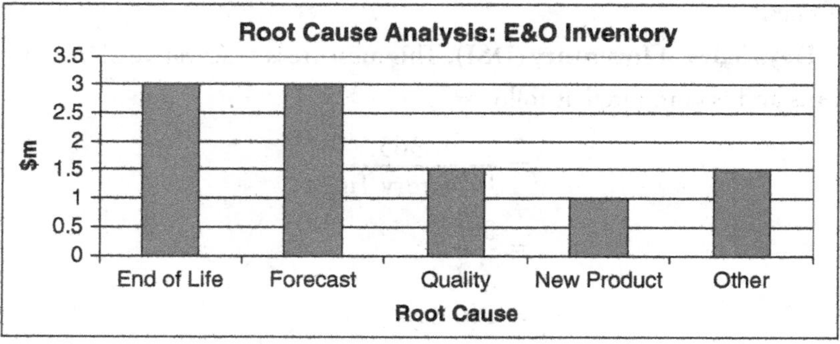

obsolete (E&O) inventory is to trend the levels over time. Measuring levels of E&O inventory will provide visibility and identify trends. This measure is complemented by a root cause analysis that provides insight into the underlying causes of E&O inventory. Typical causes include product life cycle issues (end-of-life issues, new product introductions) and forecasting errors.

Number of Unique Inventoried Parts. Tracking the number of unique inventoried parts may provide insight into a key driver of inventory management. The company may be able to reduce inventory levels by reducing the number of unique inventoried parts. This objective may take time to achieve and must consider supplier, customer, and manufacturing issues.

Past-Due Customer Orders. If customer orders are delayed past the requested delivery date, the inventory must be carried until the order can be completed. Perhaps the inventory for an order is completed except for a single integral part that is out of stock. Obviously, past-due orders are likely to negatively affect customer satisfaction as well.

Supplier Performance. Companies should measure the quality of parts supplied by vendors. Poor quality of incoming parts will delay internal processes and result in higher inventories. Late deliveries from suppliers will also wreak havoc with production schedules, resulting in higher inventories and potential delays in shipments to customers.

Forecast Accuracy. Measuring the accuracy of sales forecasts compared to actual demand levels will help to explain inventory shortages and excesses. It will also provide visibility into a key performance driver and serve to establish accountability for sales projections. Measures of forecast accuracy were presented in Chapter 15.

Cycle Time. A very effective measure of supply chain management and inventories is the amount of time required to produce a unit of inventory. The shorter the cycle time for a product, the less time the product spends in the factory. Reducing cycle times typically leads to lower manufacturing costs, lower inventory balances, and increased flexibility. It can also lead to higher levels of customer satisfaction.

Additional measures for supply chain management are discussed in Chapter 16.

Supply Chain Management and Inventory Dashboard

Several of the measures just discussed can be selected and combined to create a dashboard for supply chain management and inventory. (See Figure 17.9.)

Tools for Understanding and Assessing Inventory and Related Processes

Assess Related Business Process. Similar to the approach suggested for accounts receivable earlier in the chapter, it may be helpful to assess the supply chain and related processes before selecting performance measures. Using tool kits or best practices surveys for the supply chain management process, a rating (on a scale of 1 to 5) will be assigned to each stage as illustrated:

Product design and new product introduction	2.0
Forecasting and production planning	3.0
Manufacturing	3.5
Quality	4.5
Management of end-of-life, excess and obsolete inventory	2.5
Visibility: metrics and reporting	3.5
Overall assessment	19 (of 30)

This assessment will focus on attention on weak segments of the process, in this case, product design and new product introduction, forecasting, and management of excess and obsolete inventory.

Improving Visibility: Useful Analytical Reports

In addition to the dashboard and assessment, there are a number of reports and tools that are very useful in identifying trends and providing visibility into key drivers of inventory.

FIGURE 17.9 Supply Chain and Inventory Dashboard

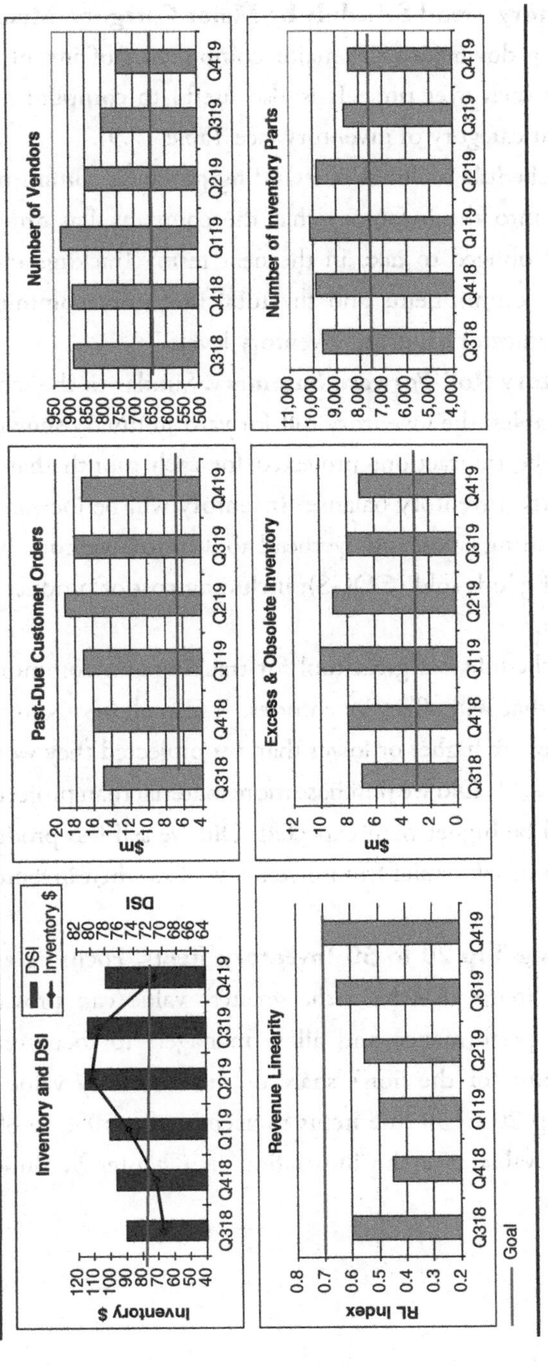
Inventory and DSI
DSI
Inventory $
Past-Due Customer Orders
Number of Vendors
Revenue Linearity
Excess & Obsolete Inventory
Number of Inventory Parts
RL Index
$m
DSI
Q318 Q418 Q119 Q219 Q319 Q419
Goal

Inventory Trend Schedule by Major Category. Much can be learned by drilling down into the major components of inventory and tracking trends in each over time. It is also useful to compute turnover for each significant category of inventory (see Table 17.9).

This schedule includes outstanding purchase commitments to provide visibility into the inventory that the company has ordered and is contractually obliged to take in the near term. Tracking and managing the purchase commitments and the total inventory commitment provide a leading indicator of future inventory levels.

Inventory Roll-Forward Summary. Similar to the schedule presented for receivables, the inventory roll-forward summary shown in Table 17.10 displays the transactions projected for each month that will increase or decrease the inventory balance. Inventory will be increased by purchases, manufacturing labor, and overhead applied to inventory. It will be reduced by cost of goods sold (COGS); including cost of product sold, write-offs, and so on.

This schedule is a great tool for tracking and communicating the key variables that will affect inventories. It also allows us to understand why inventories are higher or lower than we projected they would be as shown in Table 17.11. Did we purchase more material than projected? If so, inventories will be higher than expected. Did we sell less product, resulting in lower cost of sales relief from inventory? If so, then inventories would also be higher.

Tracking Top 20 to 50 Inventory Items. Focusing attention on the inventory items that have the greatest value can provide insight into inventory performance and allow managers to focus on specific items that account for the lion's share of the inventory value. It is common for the top 20 to 50 line items to account for 50% to 80% of the total inventory value. See the illustration in Chapter 5, Building Analytical Capability.

TABLE 17.9 Inventory Trend Schedule by Category

	Jan	Feb	$m March	April	May
Raw Material					
Incoming Inspection	2	2	5	7	7
Supplies	6	6	6	6	6
Electronic Components	22	25	27	22	22
Total	30	33	38	35	35
Work In Process					
Fabrication	4	4	4	4	4
Assembly	12	13	14	18	18
Burn In	1	1	1	1	1
Rework	3	3	3	3	3
Test	1	1	1	1	1
Final Inspection	4	4	4	4	4
Total	25	26	27	31	31
Finished Goods					
Manufacturing Plants	5	4	6	4	5
Warehouse	7	7	7	7	7
International Locations	12	12	13	12	10
Sales Offices	6	6	6	6	6
Total	30	29	32	29	28
Total Gross Inventory	85	88	97	95	94
Less: Inventory Reserves	−15	−15	−16	−16	−17
Net Inventory	70	73	81	79	77
Purchase Commitments	15	17	22	25	30
Total Inventory Commitments	85	90	103	104	107
Key Performance Indicators					
Inventory Turns	2.9	2.7	2.5	2.5	2.6
Days Inventory	127.8	133.2	147.8	144.2	140.5
% of Total					
Raw Materials	35.3%	37.5%	39.2%	36.8%	37.2%
WIP	29.4%	29.5%	27.8%	32.6%	33.0%
Finished Goods	35.3%	33.0%	33.0%	30.5%	29.8%
Inventory Reserves % of Total	17.6%	17.0%	16.5%	16.8%	18.1%
Committed Inventory % Cost of Sales	43%	45%	52%	52%	54%
Cost of Sales (annual)	$ 200				

TABLE 17.10 Inventory Roll-Forward Summary

Inventories	Oct	Nov	Dec	Jan	Feb	March	April
Beginning Balance	1,300	1,220	1,112	832	762	902	1,077
Purchases	140	154	168	84	196	224	280
Labor	100	100	168	84	196	224	280
Overhead	100	100	84	42	98	112	140
COGS	−420	−462	−700	−280	−350	−385	−420
Ending Balance	1,220	1,112	832	762	902	1,077	1,357
Inventory Turns	4.1	5.0	10.1	4.4	4.7	4.3	3.7
DSI	87.1	72.2	35.7	81.6	77.3	83.9	96.9
% of Sales	16.9%	14.0%	6.9%	15.9%	15.0%	16.3%	18.8%

TABLE 17.11 Inventory Forecast Analysis

	December		
Inventories	Actual	Forecast	Variance
Beginning Balance	1,112	1,112	0
Purchases	235	168	−67
Labor	185	168	−17
Overhead	93	84	−9
COGS	−710	−700	10
Ending Balance	915	832	−83
Inventory Turns	9.3	10.1	
DSI	38.7	35.7	
% sales	7.5%	6.9%	
Sales	1,021	1,000	
COGS	710	700	

SUMMARY

The capital required to support a business and the effectiveness of management in managing capital assets are significant drivers of performance and value. Major components of capital include operating capital; property, plant, and equipment; and intangible assets. The level of assets required to support a business is driven by a number of factors, including the nature of the industry, the business model, and the level of efficiency in key business processes such as supply chain management and revenue processes. Significant improvement in asset utilization is possible by improving the effectiveness of the related business processes.

18

CAPITAL MANAGEMENT AND CASH FLOW

Long-Term Assets

CHAPTER INTRODUCTION

In Chapter 17, we described capital efficiency as a key value driver and explored operating capital in detail. This chapter examines the remaining components of capital effectiveness, including property, plant, and equipment and intangible assets. Figure 18.1 drills down into the components of capital investment and asset management.

CAPITAL INTENSITY

The term *capital intensity* is used to describe the level of property, plant, and equipment (PP&E; also known as fixed assets) that is required to support a business. Capital intensity will vary significantly from firm to firm, from industry to industry, and from one business model to another. Key among

FIGURE 18.1 Drill-Down Illustration: Capital Effectiveness and Asset Management

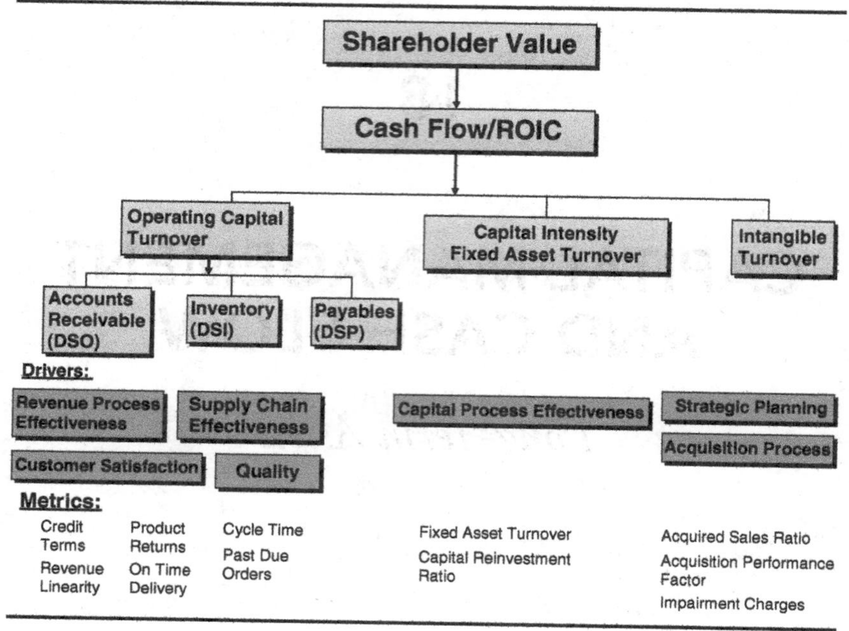

the drivers of capital intensity are the nature of the industry, the effectiveness of capital processes, and the degree of vertical integration.

Nature of Industry

Certain industries, such as automotive manufacturing, refining, and transportation require high levels of capital assets. Others, such as consulting, require very little in the way of capital assets. Other industries fall somewhere in the middle of these two extremes.

Effectiveness of Capital Process

Companies that require substantial investments in capital assets must develop effective decision and control processes over capital spending and asset management. Key process controls will include review of proposed expenditures to ensure business and economic justification, reviews to monitor project implementation, postaudits, physical control over existing assets, and identification and disposal of underutilized assets. The process of making capital investment decisions is discussed in detail in Chapters 20 and 21.

Vertical Integration

Vertical integration refers to the extent to which a company directly owns supply chain activities and resources. A company that is considered vertically integrated will produce a substantial part of the final product. An example of a vertically integrated organization would be a company engaged in growing, harvesting, processing, and distribution of food products. Other companies, by contrast, will purchase or acquire a substantial part of the product from third parties, commonly referred to as contract manufacturing or outsourcing. In recent years, there has been a strong movement toward outsourcing activities such as manufacturing, so that the enterprise can focus attention and resources on core activities such as product design and marketing. A company that outsources a substantial part of its manufacturing will require substantially less plant and equipment (and of course inventory) than a company that is more vertically integrated.

Depreciation Policy

Capital assets are defined as assets with a utility greater than one year. Accounting practices require that these investments be "capitalized" (recorded as assets) and depreciated over an estimated useful life. While there are general guidelines for depreciation methods and periods for each type of asset, companies can adopt either a conservative or an aggressive practice within the acceptable range. Companies that use shorter lives and faster depreciation methods will depreciate assets faster, resulting in higher depreciation expense and lower book values for these assets on the balance sheet.

TOOLS FOR IMPROVING THE MANAGEMENT OF LONG-TERM CAPITAL

Tools and best practices can be employed to improve the utilization and effectiveness of long-term assets. These include developing an effective capital investment process, monitoring projects, and conducting postimplementation reviews.

Effective Capital Review and Approval Process

A fundamental driver of effective utilization of capital is the strength of the capital investment process. Figure 18.2 recaps key steps in an effective capital investment process.

Companies should identify potential capital projects as part of their strategic and annual operating planning activities. The capital budget will be an important element of each plan. For strategic plans, the managers should look out three to five years and anticipate significant capital expenditures to support growth, strategic initiatives, and other requirements. Integrating the capital plan into the financial projections will afford the opportunity to review cash flow projections and determine the adequacy of returns over the strategic planning horizon.

For significant expenditures, a capital investment proposal (CIP) should be prepared to document key aspects of the project, including business justification, economic case, alternatives, and implementation plan. The scope of the CIP and the management approval level should scale with the size and importance of the project. The CIP would typically include:

- Business case
- Economic case
- Alternatives
- Implementation plan

If a capital project has been supported by a well-documented proposal, including a detailed implementation plan, managers can review the

FIGURE 18.2 Capital Investment Process Overview

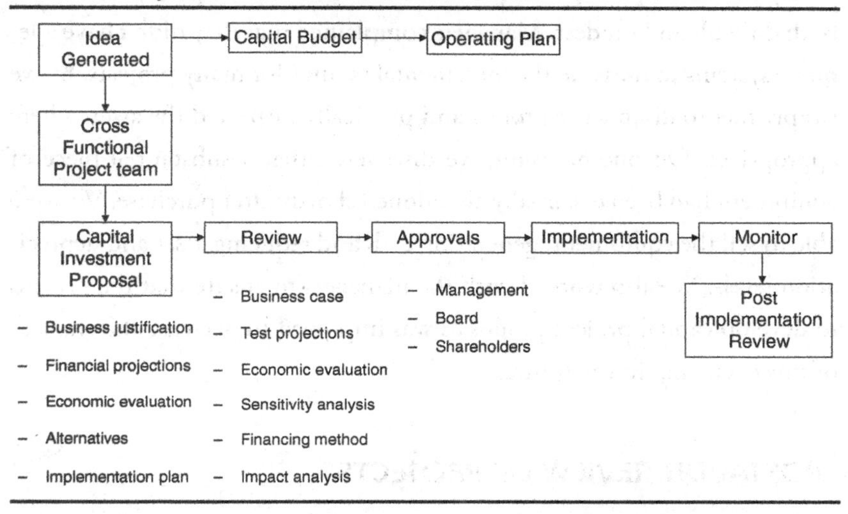

progress of the project at various points. Is the project on schedule? If not, why? Have the underlying assumptions changed? If so, is the project still worth doing? The capital investment decision process is covered in detail in Chapter 20.

Postimplementation Review

A terrific way to improve the utilization of capital and the capital investment process is to review the actual performance of capital investments compared to the original CIP (see sidebar: "Postaudit Review of Projects"). While this can be a difficult exercise for many projects, there is great value in the effort. First, managers will know, in advance, that the project results will be formally evaluated. This will encourage well-thought-out and realistic proposals. Second, even where the results may be difficult to measure, much can be learned about the project results as well as lessons for future projects. Third, the review can identify improvement opportunities in the capital investment process or management issues such as unrealistic projections or inadequate project oversight.

My first attempt at postimplementation reviews of capital projects was both difficult and modest. Managers complained that they didn't have adequate systems to measure the incremental savings for many projects. So we simply met to discuss the project and physically inspected the asset, where appropriate. On one occasion, we discovered that a substantial piece of equipment had been essentially abandoned shortly after purchase. We were able to sell the equipment, generating cash and reducing asset and depreciation levels. We also worked with the managers to ensure that the process to develop capital project proposals was improved to decrease the chances of this occurring in the future.

POSTAUDIT REVIEW OF PROJECTS

- Objectives:
  - Hold managers accountable.
  - Identify indicated actions (project specific):
    - Example: Dispose/shut down/stay course.
  - Global feedback on process and execution.
- Feedback:
  - How many projects have met or exceeded planned results?
  - Identify and address estimation bias.
  - What are the root causes of underperforming projects?
  - What are the key ingredients in successful projects?
  - What should we do differently on future projects?
- Post audit reviews are sometimes difficult to perform.
- Results are not always easily identifiable.
- The process is worth the effort.

Asset Inventory and Utilization Review

Periodically, companies should perform a physical inventory of fixed assets and compare to accounting records. This process should be part of a company's internal control framework. The inventory can easily be expanded to review the estimated utilization of significant assets. If certain assets are not utilized, these assets may be sold (or otherwise disposed of), which will generate cash, reducing associated expenses (e.g. taxes, depreciation, maintenance, and insurance), and increase asset turnover.

In some cases, an asset's fair value may appreciate significantly over the value carried in the accounting records. This occurs frequently with real estate assets. Management should consider if the potential value realized by liquidating that asset exceeds the value of continuing to hold and operate that asset. Table 18.1 illustrates an asset utilization recap for the top 20 line items in property, plant, and equipment.

TABLE 18.1 Asset Utilization Review

Asset Description	Service/ Acq Date	Original Cost	Net Book Value	Estimated Utilization	Market Value	Indicated Action
Machining Station	1992	800,000	0	10%	200,000	Sell and outsource machining
Warehouse 1	1990	2,400,000	160,000	90%	3,700,000	No action
Warehouse 2	1994	1,600,000	177,778	10%	1,800,000	Consolidate into Whse. 1, sell
Corporate Headquarters	1997	1,350,000	300,000	80%	1,250,000	Lease excess space
R&D Facility-wet lab	2005	900,000	360,000	0	750,000	Project terminated; lease or sell
Manufacturing Line 1	1995	600,000	22,000	0.8	20,000	No action
Manufacturing Line 2	2004	850,000	340,000	88%	800,000	No action
Land						
Lots-Sheridan Business Park	2004	1,600,000	1,600,000	0%	2,200,000	New complex indefinitely postponed; consider selling

Ensure Key Business Decisions Include Capital Requirements

Frequently, capital requirements are not fully considered in business decisions. This is may occur in companies with a narrow focus on sales and earnings per share (EPS) growth and in companies with cash surpluses. Capital is sometimes viewed as "free" in these situations because of the muted effect of capital on EPS (depreciation expense is spread out over several years) and limited alternatives for utilizing excess cash.

PROJECTING CAPITAL INVESTMENTS AND DEPRECIATION

Estimating future capital expenditures, depreciation, and related balance sheet accounts is an important part of developing projected profits, asset requirements, and cash flow.

Estimated capital expenditures should be integrated with the strategic and operational planning process as well as the short-term forecast or business outlook. Drivers of capital expenditures include growth and expansion; new product development, introduction, and production; replacement and refurbishment; and statutory requirements (e.g. environmental regulations). Developing and reviewing capital investment decisions is covered in Chapter 20.

There is a tendency to shortcut the process of estimating depreciation expense and accumulated depreciation in the balance sheet. Unlike many other financial elements, depreciation generally cannot be trended or extrapolated. It is driven by the timing of acquisitions, depreciation methods, and lives. Significant changes in depreciation occur:

- When an asset is acquired or placed in service.
- When an asset has been fully depreciated.

Table 18.2 illustrates the methodology for forecasting depreciation expense. The worksheet captures the estimated depreciation for assets

TABLE 18.2 Projecting Property and Equipment and Accumulated Depreciation

Property and Equipment	2017				2018				Total Year	
	Q1	Q2	Q3	Q4	Q1	Q2	Q3	Q4	2017	2018
Beginning Balance	139.0	149.0	161.0	166.0	178.0	203.0	265.0	307.0	139.0	178.0
Additions	10.0	12.0	5.0	12.0	25.0	62.0	42.0	12.0	39.0	141.0
Retirements		–					–		–	–
Other									–	–
Ending Balance	149.0	161.0	166.0	178.0	203.0	265.0	307.0	319.0	178.0	319.0

Accumulated Depreciation	2,017.0				2,017.0				Total Year	
	Q1	Q2	Q3	Q4	Q1	Q2	Q3	Q4	2,017.0	2,018.0
Beginning Balance	70.0	74.7	79.7	84.8	89.6	95.3	103.2	112.3	70.0	89.6
Depreciation Expense	4.7	5.0	5.0	4.8	5.7	7.9	9.1	9.6	19.6	32.3
Retirements										–
Other									–	–
Ending Balance	74.7	79.7	84.8	89.6	95.3	103.2	112.3	121.9	89.6	121.9

TABLE 18.2 *(continued)*

Depreciation Estimate	Acquisition	2017				2018				Total Year		Avg
Acquisition Period	Cost	Q1	Q2	Q3	Q4	Q1	Q2	Q3	Q4	2017	2018	Depr Life
Prior	40.0	0.8	0.8	0.7	0.7	0.7	0.6	0.6	0.7	3.1	2.6	12
2012	50.0	1.8	1.7	1.6	1.0	1.0	1.0	0.9	0.9	6.0	3.8	7
2013	15.0	0.5	0.5	0.5	0.5	0.5	0.5	0.4	0.4	2.1	1.9	7
2014	10.0	0.4	0.4	0.4	0.4	0.4	0.4	0.4	0.3	1.4	1.4	7
2015	12.0	0.4	0.4	0.4	0.4	0.4	0.4	0.4	0.4	1.7	1.7	7
2016	12.0	0.4	0.4	0.4	0.4	0.4	0.4	0.4	0.4	1.7	1.7	7
Total 2016 and Prior	139.0	4.4	4.2	4.1	3.5	3.5	3.4	3.1	3.2	16.1	13.1	
Q12017	10.0	0.4	0.4	0.4	0.4	0.4	0.4	0.4	0.4	1.4	1.4	7
Q22017	12.0		0.4	0.4	0.4	0.4	0.4	0.4	0.4	1.3	1.7	7
Q32017	5.0			0.2	0.2	0.2	0.2	0.2	0.2	0.4	0.7	7
Q42017	12.0				0.4	0.4	0.4	0.4	0.4	0.4	1.7	7
Q12018	25.0					0.9	0.9	0.9	0.9	-	3.6	7
Q22018	62.0						2.2	2.2	2.2	-	6.6	7
Q32018	42.0							1.5	1.5	-	3.0	7
Q42018	12.0								0.4	-	0.4	7
Total Projected Acquisitions	180.0	0.4	0.8	1.0	1.4	2.3	4.5	6.0	6.4	3.5	19.2	
Total Depreciation	319.0	4.7	5.0	5.0	4.8	5.7	7.9	9.1	9.6	19.6	32.3	

already in service, including the timing of reduced depreciation when assets become fully depreciated. The depreciation for expected acquisitions is then estimated based on projected service date, cost, and useful life. Note the dramatic falloff in depreciation of prior assets and the subsequent increase when new assets are placed in service.

A version of this method for long-term projections is included in Chapter 14.

KEY PERFORMANCE INDICATORS FOR CAPITAL INTENSITY

Managers can utilize performance measures to provide visibility into drivers of capital intensity and the effectiveness of capital management. We will use the financial information introduced in Chapter 2 for Roberts Manufacturing Company (RMC).

Capital Asset Intensity (Fixed Asset Turnover)

Capital asset intensity or fixed asset turnover is computed as follows:

$$= \frac{\text{Sales}}{\text{Net Fixed Assets}}$$

For RMC in 2018,

$$= \frac{\$100{,}000}{\$20{,}000}$$

$$= 5 \text{ turns per year}$$

This measure reflects the level of investment in property, plant, and equipment relative to sales. Some businesses are very capital intensive (i.e. they require a substantial investment in capital), whereas others have modest requirements. For example, electric utility and transportation industries typically require high capital investments. On the other end of the spectrum, software development companies would usually require minimal levels of capital.

Capital Asset Intensity at Cost (Fixed Asset Turnover at Cost)

This is a variation of the previous formula that uses the original cost of the assets instead of the net book or depreciated value. It may be more useful in those situations where capital remains employed far beyond the original depreciation period, or to level set comparisons across companies with different depreciation policies.

$$= \frac{\text{Sales}}{\text{Fixed Assets}}$$

$$= \frac{\$100{,}000}{\$50{,}000}$$

$$= 2 \text{ turns per year}$$

Capital Reinvestment Rate

One way of measuring the rate of investment in capital is to compute the ratio of capital spending to depreciation.

$$= \frac{\text{Capital Expenditures}}{\text{Depreciation}}$$

For RMC in 2018,

$$\frac{5{,}000}{3{,}750} = 1.33$$

Changes in depreciation levels lag capital investment because assets are depreciated over several years. For businesses with little or modest top-line growth, a reinvestment index of 1 or lower may be appropriate. For high-growth businesses, capital expenditures will typically exceed depreciation, resulting in a high capital reinvestment rate.

Asset Write-Offs and Impairment History

Significant charges to write off or write down assets may indicate an ineffective decision or implementation process for capital investment. Companies that have frequent asset write-offs and impairment charges (and other nonrecurring charges) likely have an opportunity to improve capital investment, strategic, and related processes.

INTANGIBLE ASSETS

Unlike tangible fixed assets, intangible assets are not associated with a specific identifiable asset like property or equipment. Intangible assets typically arise from acquisitions, where the purchase price of an acquisition target exceeds the fair market value of tangible assets. The excess of the purchase price is recorded as goodwill or assigned to other intangible assets as shown in Table 18.3.

A company that has made one or several acquisitions is likely to have a substantial balance in goodwill and intangible assets. Companies that focus exclusively on internal growth will not have goodwill or related intangibles.

Figure 18.3 compares goodwill and intangibles as a percentage of total assets of several well-known companies with a range of acquisition activity ranging from minimal to extensive.

Companies that have done a poor job in evaluating, valuing, and integrating acquisitions will likely have been forced to write off or write down

TABLE 18.3 Acquisition Purchase Price Allocation

Purchase Price	$ 100,000
Assigned to Tangible Assets:	
Accounts Receivable	15,000
Inventories	12,000
Property, Plant, and Equipment	17,000
Other Assets	2,000
Accounts Payable	(4,000)
Accrued Liabilities	(6,000)
Net Tangible Assets	36,000
Excess of Purchase Price over Tangible Assets	64,000
Value of Identifiable Intangibles*	15,000
Remainder ("Goodwill")	49,000

*Includes Patents, Trademarks, Customer Lists, etc.

FIGURE 18.3 Goodwill and Intangible Assets as a Percentage of Total Assets

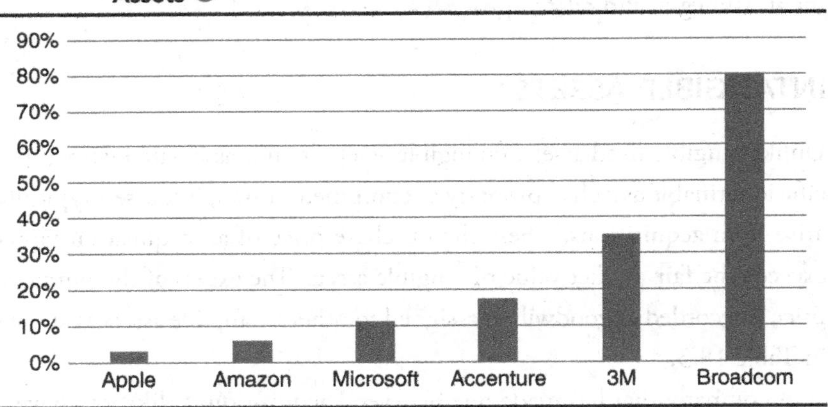

Source: Author analysis of company reports.

goodwill arising from failed acquisitions. Companies that are successful with mergers and acquisitions (M&A) will continue to carry the goodwill as an asset. Goodwill and certain acquisition intangibles must be evaluated each year to determine if the assets are "impaired." Stated simply, the performance of acquisitions is monitored to determine if the purchase price paid and resulting assets on the balance sheet are supported by current performance expectations.

The level of goodwill and related intangibles for firms that have completed acquisitions must be evaluated in the context of other value drivers, including sales growth and return on invested capital (ROIC). Refer to the analysis and economics of M&A in Chapter 23 for additional discussion of acquisitions.

KEY PERFORMANCE INDICATORS: GOODWILL AND INTANGIBLE ASSETS

Intangible Asset Turnover

Intangible asset turnover is a ratio helps explain the overall measure of asset turnover. A company that has made significant acquisitions will have a larger intangible balance and lower asset turnover than a company that has grown organically. The measure provides an indication of how significant acquisition activity has been relative to sales levels, and is computed as:

$$= \frac{\text{Annual Sales}}{\text{Intangible Assets}}$$

(Intangible Assets = Goodwill + Other Intangibles)

For RMC, the intangible asset turnover is:

$$\frac{100{,}000}{11{,}000} = 9.1 \text{ times}$$

Goodwill Impairment Charges

Goodwill impairment charges result from acquisitions failing to perform to expectations that supported the original purchase price. Significant charges to write off or write down assets may indicate an ineffective decision or implementation process for business acquisitions. Companies that have recorded impairment (and other nonrecurring) charges likely have an opportunity to improve acquisition and strategic processes.

Performance of Acquisitions: Synergies and Strategic Objectives

One way to determine if the intangibles related to a specific acquisition are safe or will be required to be written down in the future is to track key performance indicators on the value drivers that are critical to the success of the acquisition. Examples include key integration milestones such as sales force consolidation, the introduction of new products based on combined technologies, sales growth resulting from distribution synergies, and headcount reductions. Achieving these objectives, as set out in the acquisition plan and reflected in the acquisition pricing, should result in a favorable impairment test result.

EXCESS CASH BALANCES

In Chapter 17, we indicated that we would exclude financing accounts from our discussion of capital efficiency. However, we do need to address the impact of holding excessive levels of cash or short-term investments. What is excess cash? Most businesses need a minimum level of cash to operate the business. The minimum level of cash to operate will be a function of several factors, including business seasonality, cash generation and requirements, life cycle stage, international complexities, and management preference. This minimum level may be reduced if the company has ready access to a short-term credit facility. Many companies hold cash at a level significantly higher than levels necessary to support operations. Typically, this occurs in profitable firms with good returns where investments to support future growth have declined. Many firms retain excess cash as a cushion against unforeseen challenges or as a "war chest" to allow the company to pursue large investments, including acquisitions. In some cases, what appears as excess cash for US-based multinationals is often a result of a surcharge tax that would be due if the cash and earnings were repatriated to the United States. Some of these firms hold on to the excess cash year after year despite their stated intention to invest the cash. One of the most notable cash hoarders is Apple, having amassed a cash and investment balance exceeding $66 billion as of September 30, 2016. The combination of high growth and low cash requirements has created this "challenge" for one of the most successful companies over the past quarter century.

Maintaining this flexibility by holding excess cash dilutes shareholder returns. The interest earned (after tax) on cash and short-term investments is typically much lower than the firm's cost of capital. Table 18.4 illustrates the impact of retaining excess cash. Retainage Inc. has a $600 million cash balance, of which $100 million is required to support the business. The firm has net income of $150 million and total assets of $1,500 million. The cash earns 6% and is taxed at 30%. The firm's cost of capital is 15%.

The analysis estimates that retaining excess cash reduces economic profit by $54 million and reduces return on assets by 29.0%.

TABLE 18.4 Estimating the Economic Cost (Penalty) of Retaining Excess Cash

	Retainage Inc			
Estimate of "Excess Cash"		**$m**		
Year end cash balance		600.0		
Assume $100k required to support business		−100.0		
"Excess Cash"		500.0		
Estimate of Impact on Economic Profit				
Earnings (6% interest rate, 30% tax rate)				
After-tax interest rate of		4.2%		
Profit after Tax		21.0		
Cost of Capital:	15.0%			
WACC	500.0	−75.0		
Excess Cash				
Economic Profit (Loss) on Excess Cash		−54.0		
Estimated Impact on ROA	**Including Cash**	**Excess Cash**	**Excluding Cash**	**% Change**
Net Income	150.0	−21.0	129.0	−14.0%
Assets	1,500.0	−500.0	1,000.0	−33.3%
ROA	10.0%	4.2%	12.9%	29.0%

Managers and boards should carefully evaluate the trade-off involved in retaining excess cash. In some situations, some (or all) of the excess cash should be returned to shareholders in the form of dividends or share repurchases. This methodology can also be used to estimate the economic impact of retaining other underperforming assets, for example a unit with low profitability or returns.

LONG-TERM CAPITAL DASHBOARD

Based on the specific facts and circumstances, managers can combine several key performance measures into a dashboard to monitor key drivers of long-term capital assets (Figure 18.4).

FIGURE 18.4 Long-Term Capital Dashboard

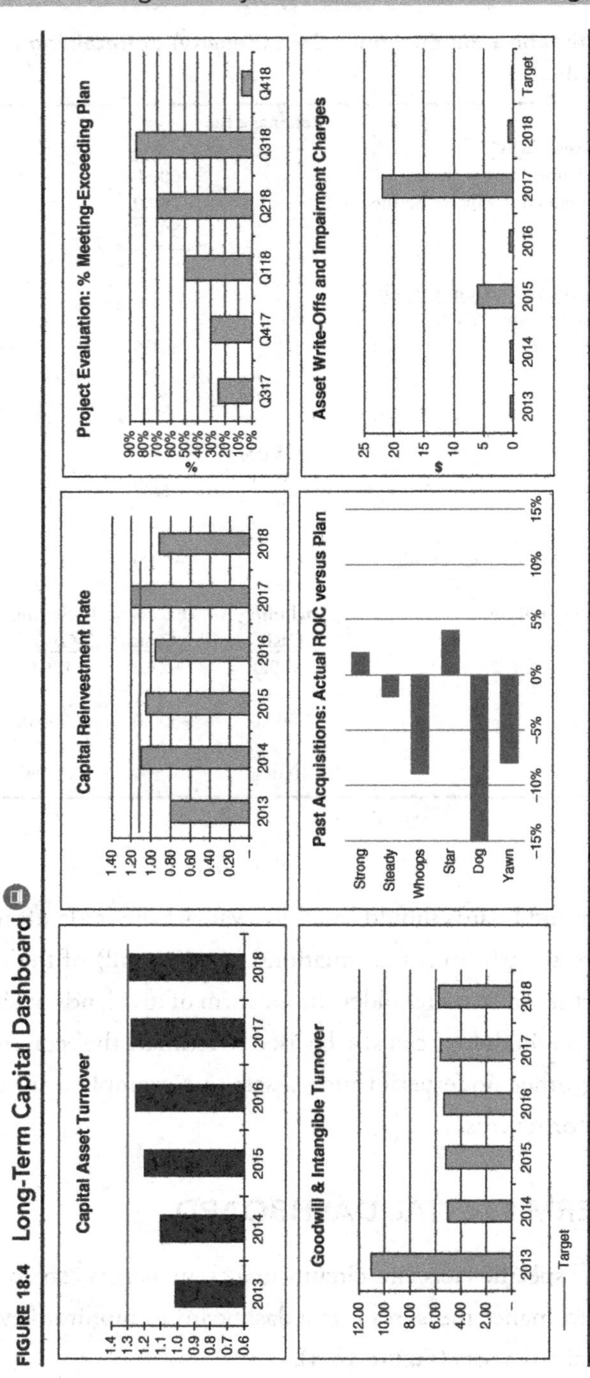

SUMMARY

The capital required to support a business and the effectiveness of management in managing capital assets are significant drivers of performance and value. Major components of capital include operating capital; property, plant, and equipment; and intangible assets. The level of assets required to support a business is driven by a number of factors, including the nature of the industry, the business model, and the level of efficiency in key businesses processes. Improvements to the capital investment process such as postimplementation and utilization reviews can lead to improved cash flow, profitability, asset turnover, and return on equity. Goodwill and intangibles are largely a function of acquisition activity and the effectiveness of the acquisition process, including the evaluation, valuation, and integration of acquisitions. Companies should estimate the economic impact of retaining excess levels of cash and other underperforming assets and consider this in their evaluation of these assets.

19

RISK, UNCERTAINTY, AND THE COST OF CAPITAL

CHAPTER INTRODUCTION

Risk and uncertainty impact all projections about future performance that support everything from forecasts and plans to investment decisions and valuations. We will deal with uncertainty in this chapter in the form of discounting future cash flows. Risk and uncertainty are addressed, in part, in two fundamental financial principles: the time value of money and the cost of capital. Additional mechanisms to understand and deal with risk and uncertainty are addressed in Chapters 20 and 21 covering capital investment decisions.

THE TIME VALUE OF MONEY

The time value of money (TVOM) is an important financial concept. Essentially, the TVOM recognizes that a dollar today is worth more than an expectation of receiving a dollar in the future. Several factors contribute to this:

- Inflation reduces the purchasing power in the future.
- Uncertainty reduces the value of future cash or income payments (you may never get paid in full).
- If you hold or invest a dollar, there is an "opportunity cost" (i.e. you are forgoing other opportunities to use that dollar). If you leave your savings in a passbook savings account with very modest interest rates, you have passed on an opportunity to invest in a stock or bond with potentially higher returns. If a company invests in a project, it is passing on the opportunity of investing the capital in another project or financial security (or returning it to shareholders).

We will review the key aspects of TVOM before proceeding to the cost of capital.

Compounding

Compounding is used to estimate the future value of a present sum. This enables us to estimate the future value of an investment, as in compound interest or compound growth rates.

Simple Compounding Illustration

Simple compounding is determining the future value (FV) of a present value (PV) or sum growing at an interest rate (i). The formula for determining the future value of a single cash flow for a single year is:

$$FV = PV + PV(i)$$

$$FV = \$100,000 + \$100,000(.04)$$

$$= \$104,000$$

For multiyear compounding, that is, to determine the future value (FV_n) of a sum growing at an interest rate (i) for multiple years (n), the formula is:

$$
\begin{aligned}
FV_n &= PV(1 + i)^n \\
&= \$100{,}000(1 + 0.04)^4 \\
&= \$116{,}986
\end{aligned}
$$

This growth in value or compounding is illustrated in Figure 19.1. Note an important feature of compounding: the interest earned in prior periods earns interest!

Applications of compounding include:

- Calculating how much a $5,000 savings balance will grow to in 10 years.
- Estimating sales with a compound annual growth rate (CAGR).

Future Value of an Annuity

An annuity is a stream of equal cash flows that occur at regular intervals over time. Examples of annuities include determining the future value of a regular savings plan, such as contributions to a 401(k) or IRA.

FIGURE 19.1 Compounding Illustration

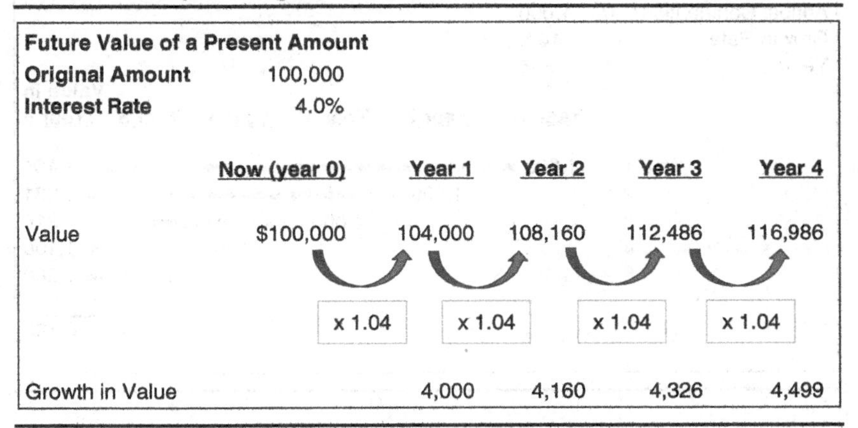

Future Value of a Present Amount
Original Amount 100,000
Interest Rate 4.0%
Now (year 0)
Year 1
Year 2
Year 3
Year 4
Value
$100,000
104,000
108,160
112,486
116,986
x 1.04
x 1.04
x 1.04
x 1.04
Growth in Value
4,000
4,160
4,326
4,499

To compute the future value of an annuity (FVA_n), with periodic payments (PMT) for (n) years, at a periodic interest rate (i), we use the following formula:

$$FVA_n = PMT \times \frac{[(1+i)^n] - 1}{i}$$

For example, what is the value in year 5 of annual contributions to an investment earning 10% per annum?

$$FVA_n = \frac{\$1{,}000 \times [(1+0.10)^5] - 1}{0.10}$$

$$FVA_n = \$6{,}105$$

Figure 19.2 details the growth of each contribution and provides important insight into the TVOM. The initial $1,000 contribution grows to $1,464 over five years, while subsequent contributions have shorter periods to compound.

Application:

How much will my annual IRA contribution be worth in 20 years?

FIGURE 19.2 Future Value of Annuity Illustration

Future Value of an Annuity (end of each year)						
Annual Contribution	1,000					
Growth Rate	10%					
Years	5					
	Year 1	**Year 2**	**Year 3**	**Year 4**	**Year 5**	**Value in Year 5**
Year 1	1,000 →					1,464
2		1,000 →				1,331
3			1,000 →			1,210
4				1,000 →		1,100
5					1,000 →	1,000
						6,105

Discounting

Discounting is the methodology we employ to estimate the present value of a future sum or payment. Discounting is a key tool used in business and investment valuation and evaluating capital investments.

Discounting a Future Payment

Let us assume that we will get a $100,000 payment (FV) in four years (*n*) from today. Based on the risk and opportunity costs, we have determined that a 4% interest rate (*i*) is appropriate. What is the value of this future payment today (PV_0), given this risk and opportunity cost? Figure 19.3 shows that the future payment must be discounted by 4% per year to arrive at the present value.

The formula for computing the present value (PV_0) of a future sum (FV_n) is:

$$
\begin{aligned}
PV_0 &= FV_n/(1+i)^n \\
&= \$100{,}000/(1+0.04)^4 \\
&= \$100{,}000/1.17 \\
&= \$85{,}480
\end{aligned}
$$

FIGURE 19.3 Discounting Illustration

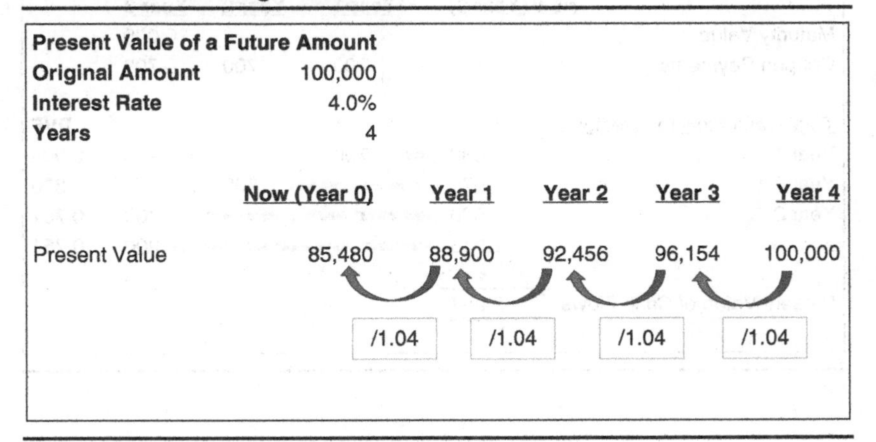

Present Value of a Future Amount
Original Amount 100,000
Interest Rate 4.0%
Years 4
Now (Year 0)
Year 1
Year 2
Year 3
Year 4
Present Value
85,480
88,900
92,456
96,154
100,000
/1.04
/1.04
/1.04
/1.04

Application:

How much money do I need to invest today for *n* years to pay for my kids' college educations?

Discounting Future Cash Flows

In many business decisions, the future cash flows will be realized in several future periods. The cash flow for each of the periods will have to be estimated and then discounted to its present value. We'll start with a simple example, determining the present value of a bond (see Figure 19.4).

Bond Pricing Illustration:

How much should you pay for a $10,000 bond, maturing in two years, with a coupon rate of 7%, paid annually, if the current rate on comparable bonds is 10%?

FIGURE 19.4 **Bond Valuation Illustration**

Value of a Bond					
Value at Maturity	10,000				
Interest Rate (Coupon)	7.0%				
Discount Rate	10%				
	Now (Year 0)	**Year 1**	**Year 2**	**Year 3**	
Maturity Value				10,000	
Coupon Payments		700	700	700	
Total Cash Flow to Investor					**PVF**
Year 1	636 ←	700			0.909
Year 2	579 ←	←	700		0.826
Year 3	526 ←	←	←	700	0.751
	7,513 ←	←	←	10,000	0.751
Present Value of Cash Flows	9,254				

The Value of an Annuity in Perpetuity

An annuity in perpetuity is a fixed payment every year, forever! In practice these rarely exist, but they provide a basis for valuing long-term payment streams such as the value of annual payments to lottery winners and the terminal (or post-horizon) value in business valuations (covered in Chapter 22).

Example:

What is the PV_t on a \$100,000 annuity (PMT) in perpetuity if the discount rate is 10% (i)? The present value of an annuity in perpetuity is computed as follows:

$$PV_t = \frac{PMT}{i}$$
$$= \frac{\$100{,}000}{0.10}$$
$$= \$1{,}000{,}000$$

Present Value of a Growing Annuity in Perpetuity

A growing annuity in perpetuity provides a periodic cash flow that is expected to grow at a constant rate (g) forever. Examples include terminal values in valuation and in valuing stocks using the dividend method.

$$PV_t = \frac{PMT_t + 1}{i - g}$$

where $PMT_t + 1$ = PMT next year.

Example:

What is the PV of a \$100,000 annuity growing at 5% per year in perpetuity if the discount rate is 10%?

$$PV_t = \frac{\$100{,}000(1.05)}{0.10 - 0.05}$$
$$= \$2{,}100{,}000$$

Note the significant difference from the value computed for the present value of an annuity in perpetuity ($1,000,000). This illustrates the importance of growth as a driver of value.

Present Value of Uneven Cash Flows

Frequently, the application of TVOM involves uneven cash flows over a number of years. This occurs in most real-world business problems such as valuing businesses and acquisitions and capital investment decisions.

Uneven Cash Flows Illustration:

What is the present value (PV) of a project that requires a $1 million investment now, will generate cash flows of 0 in year 1, $50,000 in years 2 and 3, and $100,000 in year 4, and has an estimated terminal value in year 5 of $1.4 million? Assume a discount rate of 10%. Will the investment in this project create value for the firm? See Table 19.1.

The construction of cash flow timeline by year is the critical first step. Next, we will compute the present value factor (PVF) for each year and multiply the cash flow for each year by the respective PVF. The sum of the PVs of cash flows for each year is known as the net present value (NPV).

As we will fully explore in Chapter 20, Capital Investment Decisions: Introduction and Key Concepts, this project has a positive NPV, indicating that the project will create value and should be approved and implemented.

Discounting uneven cash flows will be utilized throughout Part Five, Valuation and Capital Investment Decisions.

TABLE 19.1 Uneven Cash Flows Illustration

Year	0	1	2	3	4	5
Cash Flow	(1,000,000)	–	50,000	50,000	100,000	1,400,000
Present Value Factor (PVF)	1.000	0.909	0.826	0.751	0.683	0.621
Present Value (PV)	(1,000,000)	–	41,322	37,566	68,301	869,290
NPV (Sum of Present Value)	16,479					
Discount Rate	10%					

THE COST OF CAPITAL

Introduction

The cost of capital is a significant determinant of shareholder value. It is the rate used by investors to discount future cash flows, as shown in Figure 19.5. For investors that value companies using multiples of earnings or sales, it is one of the implicit assumptions made in selecting the multiple to use. Value is inversely related to the cost of capital. As the cost of capital declines, the value of the firm will increase, and vice versa.

Cost of capital can have a significant impact on the value of a firm. Figure 19.6 plots the relationship between cost of capital and enterprise value for Roberts Manufacturing Company based on the DCF model used in Chapter 22.

A fundamental aspect underlying the cost of capital is the relationship between risk and return. We all recognize that a riskier investment must have a higher potential return than a safer one, as otherwise we would simply invest in the safer investment. For example, few sensible people would

FIGURE 19.5 Discounted Cash Flow (DCF)

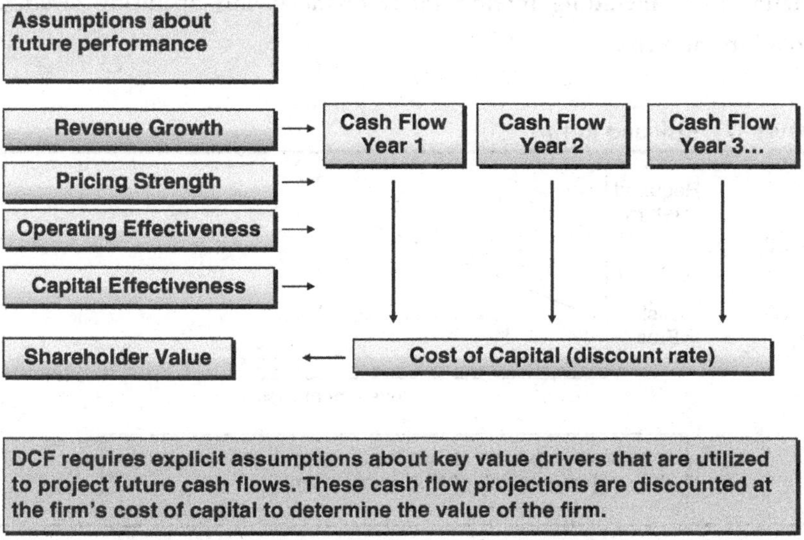

Assumptions about future performance

Revenue Growth →
Pricing Strength →
Operating Effectiveness →
Capital Effectiveness →

Cash Flow Year 1
Cash Flow Year 2
Cash Flow Year 3...

Shareholder Value ← Cost of Capital (discount rate)

DCF requires explicit assumptions about key value drivers that are utilized to project future cash flows. These cash flow projections are discounted at the firm's cost of capital to determine the value of the firm.

FIGURE 19.6 Sensitivity of Value to Cost of Capital

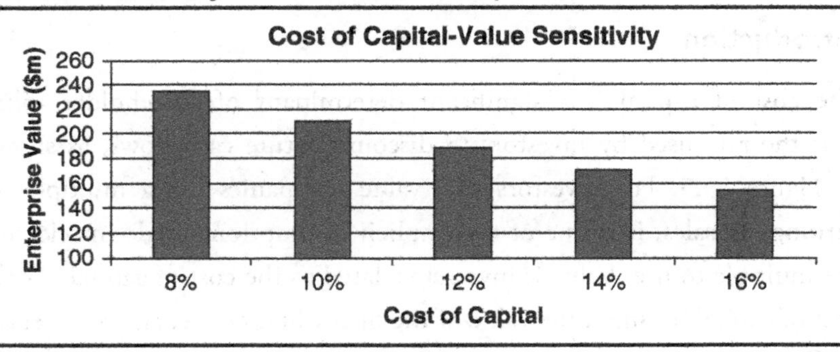

invest in a start-up company that, if successful, was expected to return a rate close to the risk-free rate on US Treasury bonds. Most would invest in the much safer investment providing the same return. We all would expect a risk premium for the higher-risk start-up investment. This risk-return trade-off is pictured in Figure 19.7.

Cost of Capital Drivers

The cost of capital for a firm is driven by several factors as illustrated in Figure 19.8, including interest rates, financial and operating leverage, volatility, and risk.

FIGURE 19.7 Risk and Return

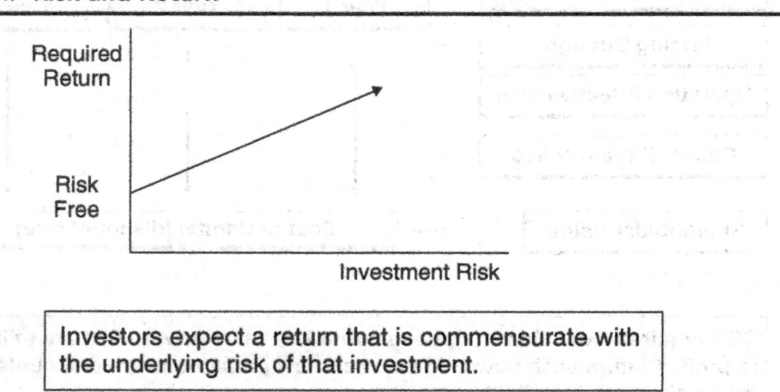

FIGURE 19.8 Cost of Capital Drivers

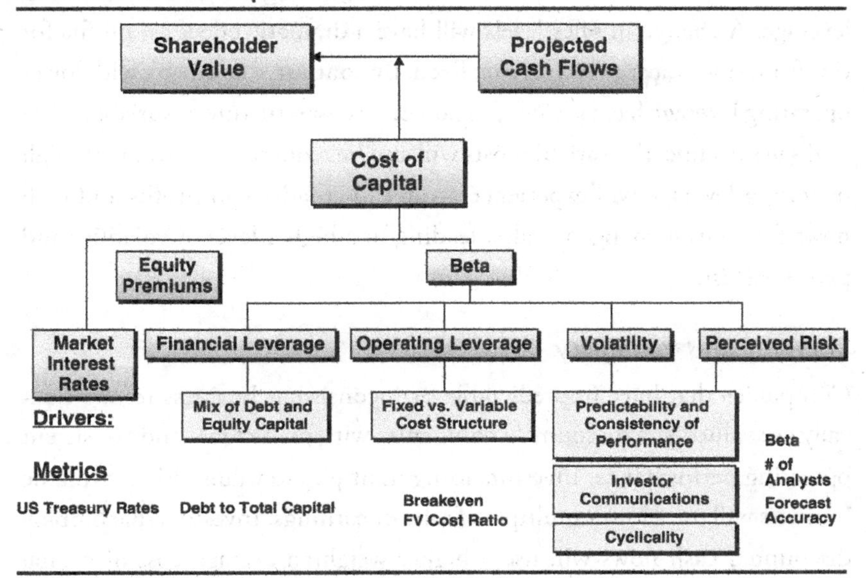

Market Interest Rates

The starting point in determining the cost of capital is typically the risk-free rate of return. Investors have the opportunity to invest in an essentially risk-free investment, US Treasury notes. This rate will form the baseline for setting required rates of return for alternative investments with progressively higher risks.

Financial Leverage

Another significant driver of the cost of capital for a firm is the mix of capital used to run the business. Typically, the cost of debt is lower than the cost of equity, as interest rates are generally well below expected rates of return on equity investments. In addition, the cost of debt is reduced by the related tax savings, since interest expense is a deduction in computing taxable income in most cases.

Operating Leverage

Operating leverage refers to the composition of costs and expenses for a company and was covered in detail in Chapter 3. A firm that has most of its costs fixed in the short term is said to have a high degree of operating leverage. A change in sales levels will have a dramatic effect on profits for this firm, since most of its costs are fixed. By contrast, a company with lower operating leverage has a greater portion of its cost structure as variable. That is, if sales decline, the variable costs will also be reduced. The firm with high operating leverage will experience greater fluctuations in profits and cash flows for a given change in sales, leading to a higher level of volatility and perceived risk.

Volatility and Variability

Companies that have unpredictable or inconsistent business results typically are valued at a discount to companies with predictable and consistent operating performance. Investors using multiples to value a highly volatile business will use a lower multiple of sales or earnings. Investors that employ discounted cash flows will use a higher weighted average cost of capital (WACC), used to discount future projected cash flows.

Perceived Risk

Investors will demand returns commensurate with the risk level they perceive in a business. Examples of additional factors leading to higher perceived risk:

- Geopolitical factors, for example developing countries or unstable regions
- Currency exposure
- Competitive pressure
- Technological obsolescence
- Management departures

Estimating the Cost of Capital

The most common method used to estimate the cost of capital is the weighted average cost of capital (WACC) method. The WACC methodology computes a blended or weighted cost of capital, considering that capital is often supplied to the firm in various forms. The most common are equity, provided by shareholders, and debt, provided by bondholders. In addition, there are many other forms that combine elements of both debt and equity. Examples of these hybrid securities include preferred stock and convertible bonds. It is important to emphasize that the cost of capital represents an estimate or approximation. Recognizing this, we should test the inputs to the WACC formula and use sensitivity analysis to understand the impact of these assumptions on the valuation of a company.

WACC Computation

Following are the steps to compute the WACC:

1. Estimate the cost of equity.
2. Estimate the cost of debt.
3. Weight the cost of equity and debt to compute the WACC.

The information in Table 19.2 will be used to illustrate the WACC computation.

Step 1: Estimate the Cost of Equity

The cost of equity represents the estimated return expected by shareholders and potential shareholders. Three components are considered: the risk-free

TABLE 19.2 WACC Illustration Inputs

Market Information	
Current Risk-Free Rate on US Treasury Notes	4.0%
Historical Market Premium for Stocks (vs. Risk-Free)	5.5%
Company Information:	
Market Value of Equity ($ millions)	90.0
Beta of Company Stock (Measure of Volatility)	1.09
Market Value of Debt ($ millions)	10.0
Interest Rate (Yield to Maturity*) YTM	6.0%
Tax Rate	40%

*Yield to maturity is used in WACC computation, not coupon rate.

rate, the premium expected for equity investments (market premium), and risk attributable to the specific company (beta). The cost of equity for this firm would be computed as follows:

$$\text{Cost of Equity} = \text{Risk-Free Rate} + (\text{Beta} * \text{Market Premium})$$
$$= 4.0\% + 1.09(5.5\%)$$
$$= 10.0\%$$

Step 2: Estimate the Cost of Debt

Since interest expense is generally tax deductible, the cost of debt is reduced by the tax savings and is computed as follows:

$$\text{Cost of Debt} = \text{Yield to Maturity} \times (1 - \text{Tax Rate})$$
$$= 6\%(1 - 40\%)$$
$$= 3.6\%$$

Step 3: Weight the Cost of Equity and Debt to Compute WACC

Table 19.3 shows the WACC computation.

Figure 19.9 provides a visual summary of how these elements come together in the WACC computation. Investors that invest in equity securities expect a premium over returns obtainable from risk-free securities (US Treasury notes). This market premium results in an expected return for the market (e.g. S&P 500), in the illustration, just above 10%. The cost of capital for a particular security is then computed by adding a premium for the risk of investing in an individual security. The cost of equity is then

TABLE 19.3 WACC Computation

	Cost	Market Value	Market Value %	Weighting
Debt	3.6%	10.0	10%	0.36%
Equity	10.0%	90.0	90%	9.00%
Total/WACC		100.0	100%	9.36%

FIGURE 19.9 WACC Visual Summary

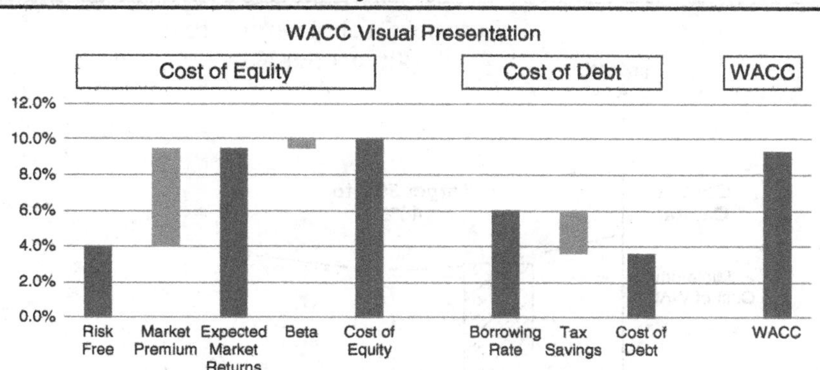

blended with the after-tax cost of debt to estimate the weighted average cost of capital.

Since the cost of debt is typically lower than the cost of equity, it is easy to conclude that some blend of debt and equity would result in the lowest cost of capital. The combination of debt and equity that results in the lowest cost of capital is called the optimal capital structure. This concept is illustrated in Figure 19.10. A firm with no debt will have a WACC equal to the cost of equity. As the firm adds debt to the mix, the WACC will be reduced to a point. However, at some point the increased risk associated with high borrowings will increase the required interest rates and will also increase the required cost of equity. The combined effects will increase the WACC above the minimum level projected at the optimum capital structure.

Most firms do not operate at or near the optimal capital structure. There are several reasons for this. First, some managers do not fully accept the concept of discounted cash flow/cost of capital or WACC. Others are very conservative and are opposed to the risk introduced by using or increasing debt. Even managers that accept the basic concept choose not to add leverage, or will add reasonable levels of debt that leave them far short of the

FIGURE 19.10 Optimal Cost of Capital and Capital Structure

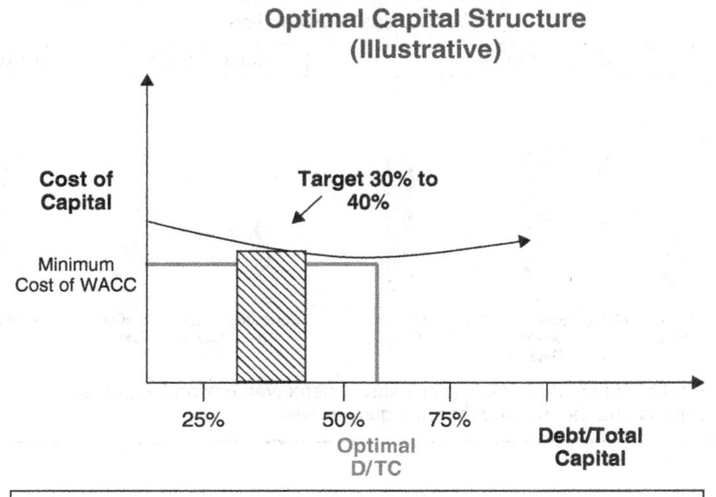

theoretical optimum capital structure. Typically, companies will set a target capital structure, expressed as a ratio of debt to total capital, for example 30% to 40%. Figure 19.11 captures some of the factors that influence decision makers in setting a target capital structure. Tolerance for risk, capital requirements, and growth rates are a few examples. Firms will then often deviate from this target capital structure. For example, they may choose to exceed the target range to finance a strategic opportunity such as an acquisition. Typically, the corporation would plan to return to the target range within a couple of years or reset the range to a higher level.

Key Ways Managers Can Reduce the Cost of Capital

Some of the factors that determine cost of capital are out of the firm's control. For example, market interest rates are the foundation for estimating cost of capital. Unless they have influence over the general

FIGURE 19.11 Capital Structure and Financial Policy

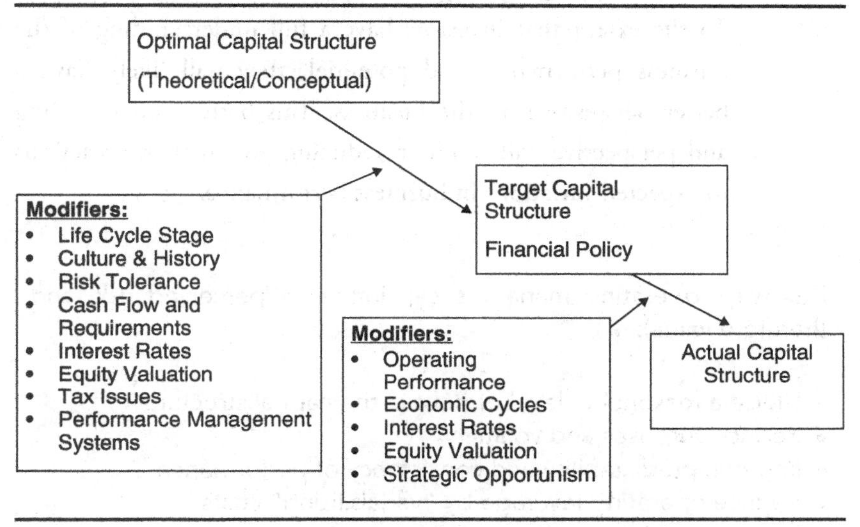

economy, inflation, or the chairman of the Federal Reserve Bank, there is little managers can do about interest rates. Here are some specific actions managers can take to reduce the cost of capital:

1. First, managers can reduce surprises and volatility, which will result in a lower beta and cost of capital and therefore higher valuation. Managers should strive to improve the predictability and consistency of business performance for several reasons. In addition to reducing surprises and volatility that affect the cost of capital, improvements in this area will result in lower working capital requirements and operating costs.
2. Second, managers can consider using a reasonable level of debt in the capital structure. Utilizing a sensible level of debt provides leverage to equity investors and reduces the cost of capital. The level of debt should be lower than theoretical borrowing capacity, to provide for a cushion to service this debt during a business downturn or unforeseen future challenges.

3. Third, managers can improve communications with investors. To the extent that investors have a full understanding of the business performance and potential, they will likely have a better perspective on the business. This better understanding and perspective will result in reducing potential overreactions to expected variations in business performance.

Key ways operating managers can influence perceived risk (and therefore value):

- Utilize a reasonable level of debt in the capital structure.
- Reduce surprises and volatility.
- Improve predictability and consistency of performance.
- Reduce operating leverage by "variabilizing" costs.
- Improve communications with investors.

PERFORMANCE MEASURES

A number of measures can be tracked to provide insight into the firm's WACC and identify potential opportunities to reduce the cost of capital.

Financial Leverage: Debt to Total Capital

In Chapter 2, we reviewed key financial ratios that measure financial leverage and capital structure. The mix of debt and equity in the capital structure is an important variable in the cost of capital and valuation. For evaluating financial leverage, the measure is usually computed using book values:

$$\text{Debt to Total Capital} = \frac{\text{Interest-Bearing Debt}}{\text{Total of Interest-Bearing Debt and Equity}}$$

Stock Volatility/Beta

For a public company, the volatility of the company's stock price is an important indicator of the level of risk perceived by investors. Investors attempt to estimate the risk inherent in future performance and cash flows by looking at historical measures of stock volatility or beta. Beta compares the change in the firm's stock price to the change in a broad market measure. Beta, which measures the correlation of an individual stock to the S&P 500, is available in many financial reporting services. Services use different time horizons to calculate beta and stock volatility, often going back several years. Since we want to track beta or stock volatility to use in estimating a cost of capital for future performance, we must ensure that the historical measure is indicative of future performance. Care should be exercised in circumstances where significant changes have recently occurred, or are anticipated, in the company's market, strategic direction, or competitive environment. In these cases, managers and investors may focus on recent history or expected future stock price volatility or beta as a better indicator of current investor confidence and perceived risk.

Operating Leverage

In Chapter 3 we concluded that the mix of variable and fixed cost components has a significant impact on the earnings and cash flow of a firm as sales levels vary. Where sales volatility is likely, for example in cyclical businesses, managers should closely monitor and evaluate the cost structure of the company. Fixed cost levels or breakeven sales levels should be measured and evaluated periodically.

Actual versus Projected Performance

Preparing business forecasts is an important activity for most companies. These forecasts will be the basis for making important decisions and in investor communications. For many firms, future estimates of revenue are typically the most important and difficult operating variables to forecast. In Part Three: Business projections and Plans, we presented a number of tools to monitor and evaluate the accuracy and effectiveness of forecasts. Forecast variances should also be reviewed in the context of the firm's cost of

FIGURE 19.12 Cost of Capital Dashboard

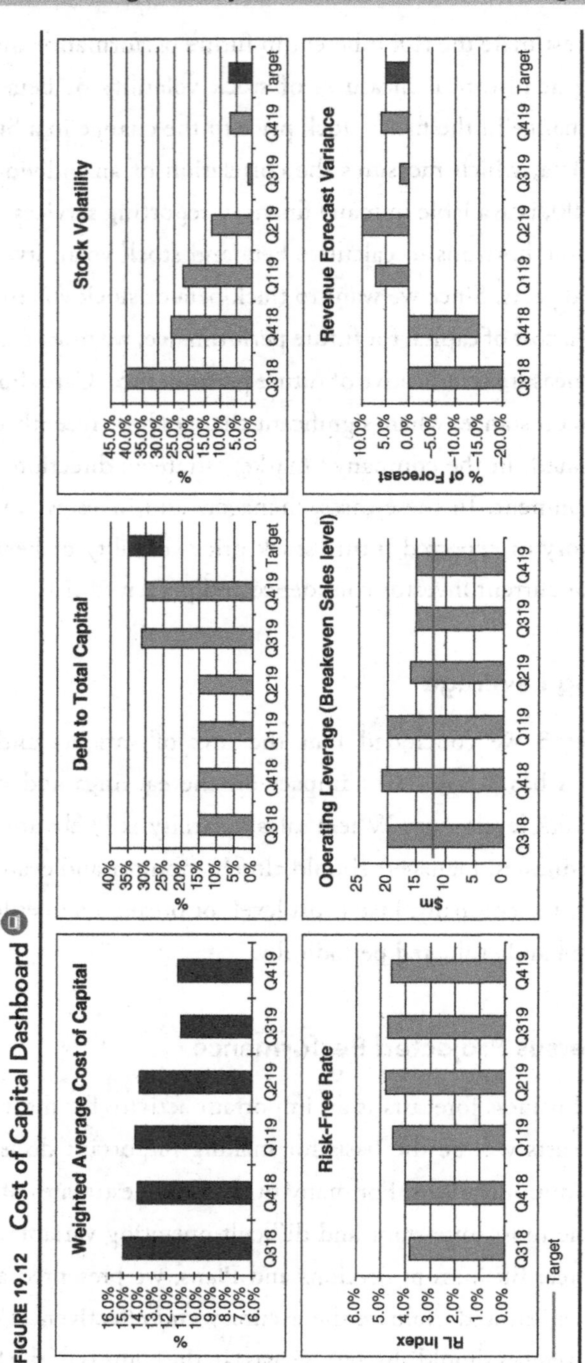

capital, since the predictability and consistency of operating performance will affect stock volatility.

Illustrative Dashboard: Cost of Capital

A dashboard for the cost of capital should be utilized, incorporating key performance indicators appropriate to the specific issues and priorities for each company. An illustrative cost of capital dashboard is presented in Figure 19.12.

SUMMARY

The time value of money is a core financial concept. Simply stated, a dollar promised in the future is worth less today. The value today must recognize risk and the opportunity cost of not having that dollar today to invest in other alternatives.

The cost of capital for a firm is a significant value driver. Cost of capital is inversely related to the firm's value. Managers should be aware of the sensitivity of the company's valuation to the cost of capital. Management can reduce the cost of capital, thereby increasing value, by reducing risk and volatility and by using an appropriate mix of debt and equity. Key factors impacting the firm's cost of capital should be identified and measured.

Part Five

Valuation and Capital Investment Decisions

20

CAPITAL INVESTMENT DECISIONS

Introduction and Key Concepts

CHAPTER INTRODUCTION

Capital investment decisions (CIDs) are some of the most important business decisions that managers make. Capital decisions are generally defined as relatively large investments that will have an economic life of several years. We will define capital investments broadly, including purchases of equipment, new product development projects, acquiring a product line or a company, and many others. The capital investment decision is a determination of whether the project is likely to create value for shareholders. In this chapter, we will introduce capital investments, evaluation, and key decision criteria, and outline the steps required to evaluate CIDs. In Chapter 21, we will cover advanced topics of CIDs, including dealing with risk and uncertainty, monitoring projects, and presenting capital investment decisions.

THE CAPITAL INVESTMENT PROCESS

A strong capital investment process is critical to ensure a thorough evaluation and decision. Figure 20.1 outlines key steps in an effective capital investment process.

Companies should identify potential capital projects as part of their strategic and annual operating planning activities. The capital budget should be an important element of each plan. For strategic plans, the managers should look out three to five years and anticipate significant capital expenditures to support growth, strategic initiatives, and other requirements. Integrating the capital plan into the financial projections will afford the opportunity to review cash flow projections and determine the adequacy of returns over the strategic planning horizon.

For significant expenditures, a capital investment proposal (CIP) should be prepared to document key aspects of the project, including business justification, economic case, alternatives, and implementation plan. The scope

FIGURE 20.1 Capital Investment Process Overview

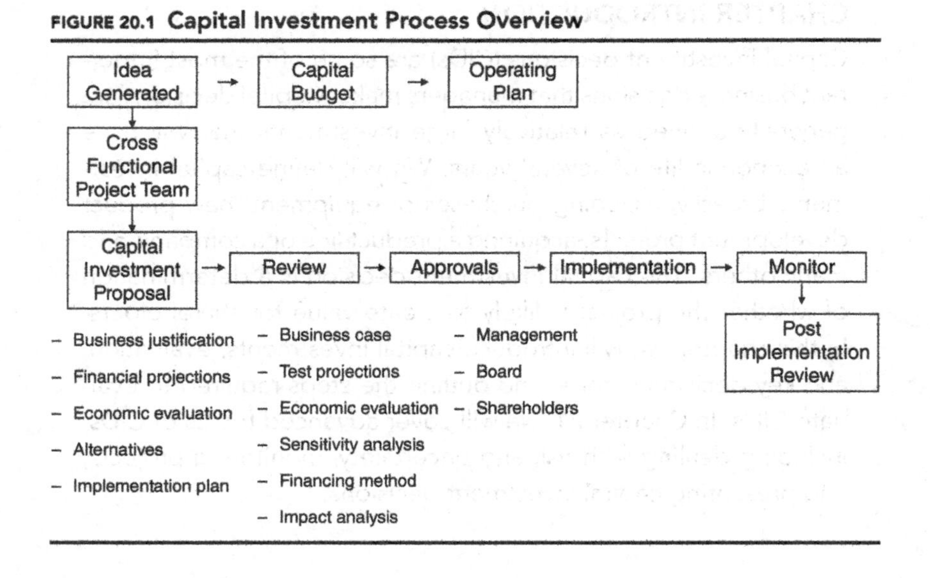

of the CIP and the management approval level should scale with the size and importance of the project.

Business Case. The business case should define the strategic and business objectives that will be achieved or supported with this use of capital. In addition to passing certain economic tests, the project must be clearly linked to a strategic or operational objective. Some projects may make economic sense but be outside or even inconsistent with the strategic direction of the company.

Economic Case. All capital investment projects should be supported by financial projections and an economic evaluation. The financial projections should be based on the business case and implementation plan and include the following:

- Estimated costs to purchase and start up the project.
- Incremental revenues, costs, and capital requirements that result from undertaking the project.
- Estimated salvage or terminal value at the end of the project life.

Alternatives. Most projects have several alternative courses of action. These should be explored as part of the capital investment decision and documented in the capital investment proposal. Reviewers should test the basis of selecting the recommended plan to ensure that this alternative provides the best balance of technical, business, and economic performance.

Implementation Plan. Execution and implementation are always critical success factors for any project. Capital projects should be supported with a detailed implementation plan. This plan will provide a road map to achieve the objectives of the capital investment. A good implementation plan is a strong indication that the project is well planned, including identification of resource requirements, risks, and alternatives. The implementation plan also provides a basis for monitoring and reviewing progress of the project. Identifying key assumptions, checkpoints, and go/no-go decision points will also allow managers to consider redirecting or terminating projects that may be at risk. The characteristics of a good implementation plan are detailed in the sidebar.

CHARACTERISTICS OF GOOD IMPLEMENTATION PLANS

Identify and address obstacles and barriers.
Identify critical success factors
Identify resource requirements and key assumptions.
Assign responsibility.
Include sufficient detail:

- Specific tasks: What should I be doing today?
- Interdependencies/critical path
- Monitoring and communication value
- Measurable objectives and targets

Make sure these link to and support financial targets.
Identify key performance indicators.

Executive Review of Capital Investment Projects

Most companies require management approval for investments over a certain limit. Approval requirements typically escalate to higher levels of management, the board of directors, or even shareholders based on the nature and size of the investment and source of financing. The sidebar ("Executive Review of Capital Projects") highlights key points that executives should consider in their evaluation of significant investments.

EXECUTIVE REVIEW OF CAPITAL PROJECTS

Key points:
Consistency with mission/strategy
Strategic and business case
Economic case:

- Projections, market size and share, adoption rate, business model, and investment requirements

Identify and test assumptions:
- What are the critical assumptions? Are they realistic? How will we monitor these over the course of the project?

Review scenario and sensitivity analysis:
- Can we live with downside scenarios?

Project management and ownership:
- Experience/knowledge
- Track record
- Passion for program

Implementation plan; human and financial resource requirements

Risk identification and mitigation plans

EVALUATING THE ECONOMIC MERITS OF CAPITAL INVESTMENTS

No matter how simple or complex the project, the same basic three steps should be employed to evaluate and select appropriate capital investments. The three steps are:

1. Estimate relevant cash flows associated with the project.
2. Measure the project's expected performance against investment decision rules.
3. Accept or reject based on decision rules.

These three steps focus on the financial or economic part of the evaluation. Of course, there also needs to be a review of other business issues and to ensure the project is consistent with the firm's strategic direction, as described earlier.

Step 1: Estimate Relevant Cash Flows Associated with the Project

Economic evaluations should be based on projected cash flows. The first step will be to estimate the *incremental* investments and profit and loss

(P&L) on the project, and then to estimate cash flows, reflecting the capital investment, depreciation, and working capital requirements.

Estimating both the acquisition or development cost and future cash flows of a project are by far the most important and most difficult part of CIDs. There are three categories of cash flow to consider for most projects: the initial cash outflow or investment, the stream of annual cash flows over the project's expected life, and a residual or terminal value at the end of the project (or projected cash flow).

The definition and application of incremental cash flows is a source of confusion in estimating relevant cash flows. Incremental revenues, investments, costs, and expenses should be limited to those that directly result from undertaking the project. The test is to identify those expenses and revenues that are not incurred if the project is not undertaken.

For significant and complex projects, we should utilize the techniques covered in developing long-term projections of future business in Chapter 14.

Initial Investment

We need to estimate the total investment or cash outflows associated with the project. This can be as simple as the purchase cost of a new piece of equipment. However, if the machinery is shipped to us and includes freight, installation, setup, and training, then these costs also must be reflected as the total cost of acquiring the asset.

The project investment can become very complex and extend over several years. For example, the total design, approval, and construction of a new refinery or nuclear plant can extend for a decade or longer. Similarly, the development of a new product such as a prescription pharmaceutical can extend over many phases with a high degree of uncertainty of effectivity and approval by regulatory agencies. The investment in these cases may be very difficult to estimate.

All cash outflows must be considered, regardless of the accounting treatment. These include operating expenses (after tax), purchases of property and equipment, development of facilities, and working capital required to support the project.

Cash Flows over Project Life

The second set of cash flows to consider are the estimated annual cash flows over the project's life. For simple projects, such as purchasing a more efficient piece of manufacturing equipment, the savings may be as simple to define as reduced labor or scrap costs. At the other end of the spectrum are complex projects such as new products or the acquisition of a company. In both these cases, a complete set of financial projections would be required, including a complete P&L, balance sheet, cash flow statement, and supporting schedules (see Chapter 14, Long-Term Projections).

Residual or Terminal Value

We need to estimate what, if any, value may exist at the end of the project's expected (or projected) useful life. For projects involving manufacturing or transportation equipment, the value at the end of life may be trade-in, salvage, or resale value. For more complex and longer-term programs such as the acquisition of a business or development of a product line, we must estimate the value of the business at the end of its useful life (or forecast horizon). This value may be a liquidation value if the business would be shut down and the remaining assets sold at liquidation value. If the business could be sold or continue to operate beyond the projected life or forecast horizon, then we need to estimate the terminal or post-horizon value.

Capital Investment Examples

Case Study 1: Automate Manufacturing Process

Vance Pharmaceutical is considering automating a key part of its manufacturing process. The equipment will cost $100,000 and is expected to reduce manufacturing cycle time, improve yield, and decrease test costs.

What incremental cash flows are likely to result from undertaking this project? This project will probably involve the following incremental cash flow items, among others:

- Cost of equipment
- Installation cost
- Reduced labor and test costs

- Reduced material costs due to yield improvement
- Increased depreciation expense
- Increased taxes on profit improvement

Case Study 2: Develop and Introduce New Treatment

Vance Pharmaceutical is considering the development of a breakthrough treatment for procrastination. The project will require several years of development and will result in a significant increase in sales. The treatment can be produced in the company's existing facilities.

What incremental cash flows are likely to result from undertaking this project? This project will probably involve the following incremental cash flow items, among others:

- R&D investment
- Cost of FDA approval
- Investment in manufacturing process
- Distribution channel and training
- Marketing and promotion
- Revenue and profits
- Working capital required to support program
- Increased depreciation expense
- Increased taxes on profit improvement

Step 2: Measure the Project's Expected Performance against Investment Decision Rules

A variety of measures or decision criteria are used to evaluate the economic characteristics of the investment. In addition to satisfying these economic tests, the project must also be justified on a business and strategic basis. The three most common measures are net present value (NPV), internal rate of return (IRR), and payback. In special situations, additional measures are utilized. Most of the decision rules are based on the economic principle of the time value of money (TVOM). Refer to Chapter 19 to review TVOM, discount rates (DRs), and cost of capital.

We illustrate the measurement criterion with the following simple example:

Project life: 5 years
Initial investment: $24,000
Projected after-tax savings for 5 years: $8,000
Project terminates at end of year 5 with no residual value.
Discount rate: 10%

Net Present Value (NPV)

Net present value (NPV) utilizes the discounted cash flow methodology described in Chapter 19 to account for the time value of money and project risk. The cash flow for each year is discounted back to the equivalent value today ("year 1") using a discount or hurdle appropriate for the risk level of the project. NPV is the sum of all discounted cash inflows and outflows. A positive NPV indicates that the project has a rate of return that exceeds the discount rate used, and therefore should be approved. A negative NPV indicates that the project has a return under the discount rate, and should not be undertaken.

In the example in Table 20.1, the NPV is +$5,751, indicating that the project has a return above the expected return (discount rate) and should be implemented. Note that we provided the present value factor (PVF) and present value (PV) for each annual cash flow. This provided insight into the TVOM and the dynamics of the project's NPV.

TABLE 20.1 NPV Illustration

	Discount Rate (10%)					
	Year 1	**Year 2**	**Year 3**	**Year 4**	**Year 5**	**Year 6**
Project Cash Flows:						
Cash Inflows	−24,000	8,000	8,000	8,000	8,000	8,000
Present Value Factor	0.91	0.83	0.75	0.68	0.62	0.56
Present Value	−21,818	6,612	6,011	5,464	4,967	4,516
Net Present Value (Sum of PV)	5,751					

Internal Rate of Return (IRR)

The internal rate of return (IRR) of a project is the actual rate of return implied in the project's cash flows. If the IRR exceeds the discount rate (DR), the project should be approved. If the IRR is less than the cost of capital, the project should be rejected. Prior to the widespread availability of spreadsheet and finance application software, the IRR would be computed by trial and error by guessing at the IRR and recomputing until NPV = 0.

The project in the example in Table 20.2 has an IRR of 19.9%, which is above the 10% discount rate used for the project. Note that IRR and NPV are consistent decision criteria, using estimated cash flows and the discount rate as key inputs. The use of IRR and NPV will result in consistent decisions as follows:

IRR	NPV	Result
IRR > DR	NPV > 0	Approve
IRR < DR	NPV < 0	Reject

Payback

The investment payback is a simple measure that estimates how long (in years and fractions of years) it will take to recover the investment in a project. Investments with shorter payback periods are typically viewed

TABLE 20.2 IRR Illustration

	Internal Rate of Return					
	Year 1	**Year 2**	**Year 3**	**Year 4**	**Year 5**	**Year 6**
Project Cash Flows:						
Cash Inflows	−24,000	8,000	8,000	8,000	8,000	8,000
Present Value Factor	0.83	0.70	0.58	0.48	0.40	0.34
Present Value	−20,024	5,569	4,646	3,876	3,234	2,698
Sum PV	0					
NPV	0					
IRR	19.9%					

as positive; investments with longer payback periods may be rejected or require additional review. This method does not consider the time value of money (that is, cash flow in future years does not have the same value as an equivalent cash amount now). Despite this criticism, it has high acceptance and usage because it is easily understood and measures an important characteristic: How long until we recover our initial investment? Many organizations have rules of thumb based on payback, requiring a certain class of investments to have a payback of three years or less.

In this example, the cumulative cash flow for the project becomes positive in year 3. We estimate the payback as shown in Table 20.3.

Typically, the payback will not end exactly at the end of a year and will require as estimation of partial-year payoffs, using interpolation.

All three methods should be utilized, since they each provide different views into the economic dynamics of the project (see Table 20.4).

While NPV indicates whether the project should be undertaken based on a given discount rate, IRR provides the precise rate of return on the project. By comparing the IRR to the DR, you can get a sense of the return "slack." Payback complements these measures by estimating the number of years until cash outlays are fully recovered. For example, a project may have a positive NPV and a high rate of return, but the bulk of the cash may be recovered late in the project life, or even in the terminal or salvage value. This long payback should be evaluated in the context of project risks.

TABLE 20.3 Payback Illustration

	Payback					
	Year 1	Year 2	Year 3	Year 4	Year 5	Year 6
Project Cash Flows:						
Cash Inflows		8,000	8,000	8,000	8,000	8,000
Cash Outflow	−24,000					
Cumulative	−24,000	−16,000	−8,000	–	8,000	16,000
Payback	3.0					

TABLE 20.4 Combined Illustration

	Discount Rate (10%)					
	Year 1	**Year 2**	**Year 3**	**Year 4**	**Year 5**	**Year 6**
Project Cash Flows:						
Cash Flows	−24,000	8,000	8,000	8,000	8,000	8,000
Cumulative	−24,000	−16,000	−8,000	–	8,000	16,000
Present Value Factor	0.91	0.83	0.75	0.68	0.62	0.56
Present Value Cash Flow	−21,818	6,612	6,011	5,464	4,967	4,516
Net Present Value	5,751					
IRR	19.9%					
Payback	3.0					

We used a discount rate of 10% in the example. The discount rate for each project should be based on the level of risk associated with the project. For practical reasons, companies often set a hurdle rate above the company's cost of capital (covered in Chapter 19) to ensure that projects will earn an acceptable return. If individual projects are perceived as having very low or high risk, the discount rate may be adjusted accordingly, as discussed in Chapter 21.

Other Measures

In addition to NPV, IRR, and payback, the following measures are occasionally used to evaluate capital projects. Their primary utility is to relate the level of NPV to the value of the investment or outflow. This can be useful in ranking projects based on their relative return.

Benefit-Cost Ratio (BCR). The BCR is computed as follows:

$$\frac{\text{PV of Cash Inflows}}{\text{PV of Cash Outflows}}$$

For our illustration,

$$\text{BCR} = \frac{\$27{,}569}{\$21{,}818}$$
$$= 1.26$$

Profitability Index (PI). The PI is also used in ranking projects in capital rationing applications. Essentially it scales the NPV of the investment to each dollar of investment. The PI is computed as follows:

$$= \frac{\text{NPV}}{\text{Initial Investment}}$$

$$= \frac{\$5{,}751}{\$24{,}000}$$

$$= 0.24$$

Step 3: Accept or Reject the Project

Financial theory provides that projects should be approved if the following requirements are met:

IRR exceeds the discount rate.
NPV is greater than 0.
Payback < limit (e.g. 3 years).

Of course, these decision criteria must be applied in a sensible manner. Projects that marginally satisfy these requirements should be subjected to further review, including evaluating the projections and sensitivity and scenario analyses.

What Is a "Strategic Investment"?

Organizations (and most commonly CEOs) often refer to strategic investments as including any investment that is of strategic importance to the enterprise. This may include new products, geographic expansion, or even the acquisition of a firm. Many cynical CFOs jokingly refer to a strategic investment as any investment the CEO is firmly committed to that does not meet the economic criteria described previously! As a result, it is ascribed some unquantifiable "strategic value."

In some cases, these projects may indeed have dubious value other than as a favorite initiative of the CEO. In other cases, this dichotomy arises because the analysis does not reflect all potential sources of value. The analyst should persevere to identify and estimate other scenarios and options that may not be reflected in the base case of the investment analysis. More on this in Chapter 21.

ILLUSTRATIONS

Two illustrations of capital investment decisions are presented next. The illustrations include the projected cash flows and the evaluation criteria for each investment. Table 20.5 is an example of an analysis of a project to automate manufacturing. Table 20.6 is an illustration of a new product development analysis. These examples were introduced earlier in the chapter to illustrate the identification of incremental cash flows for a project.

In both examples, the shaded part of the worksheet develops the incremental cash flows associated with the project. As discussed earlier in the chapter, each project will have unique characteristics and therefore unique cash flows. In addition to the incremental cash flow per year, we include the cumulative cash flow per year to highlight the timing of cash flows. Note that the cumulative cash flow for the new pharmaceutical remains negative through 2024 (six years) while the cumulative cash flow for the manufacturing project becomes positive in 2021 (three years).

The unshaded portion presents the economic evaluation of each project. In addition to presenting the project NPV, IRR, and payback, we include the present value factor and present value of cash flow for each year. This provides insight into the dynamics of the economic valuation, and the importance of accelerating cash flows in any project.

This project has a positive NPV, an IRR that exceeds the discount rate, and a relatively quick payback (3.0 years).

This project has a positive NPV and an IRR that exceeds the discount rate. As expected, the payback (six years) is longer than the manufacturing example, but certainly acceptable for a product development initiative. Note that the discount rate of 15% is higher than that of the

TABLE 20.5 Capital Expenditure: Manufacturing Project

Vance Pharma Co.		**Project Investment Analysis**				$000's (Unless otherwise noted)				
Automate Manufacturing Process										
Incremental Changes		**2018**	**2019**	**2020**	**2021**	**2022**	**2023**	**2024**	**2025**	**Terminal Value**
Revenues										
Cost of Revenues										
On Incremental Revenues	30%	–	–	–	–	–	–	–	–	
Project Savings		–	–25,000	–40,000	–75,000	–75,000	–75,000	–75,000	–75,000	
Incremental Cost of Revenues		–	–25,000	–40,000	–75,000	–75,000	–75,000	–75,000	–75,000	
Gross Margin Impact		–	25,000	40,000	75,000	75,000	75,000	75,000	75,000	
Operating Expenses:										
On Incremental Revenues	15%	–	–	–	–	–	–	–	–	
Project Savings										
Project Costs and Expenses		50,000								
Depreciation on Project Capital			30,000	30,000	30,000	30,000	30,000			
Incremental Operating Expenses		50,000	30,000	30,000	30,000	30,000	30,000	–	–	
Operating Profit		–50,000	–5,000	10,000	45,000	45,000	45,000	75,000	75,000	

TABLE 20.5 *(continued)*

Vance Pharma Co. Automate Manufacturing Process			**Project Investment Analysis**			$000's (Unless otherwise noted)			
Incremental Changes		**2018**	**2019**	**2020**	**2021**	**2022**	**2023**	**2024**	**2025**	**Terminal Value**
Tax	40%	20,000	2,000	−4,000	−18,000	−18,000	−18,000	−30,000	−30,000	
Operating Profit After Tax		−30,000	−3,000	6,000	27,000	27,000	27,000	45,000	45,000	
Operating Cash Flow:										
Depreciation			30,000	30,000	30,000	30,000	30,000			
(Inc) Dec in Accounts Receivable										
(Inc) Dec in Inventories			50,000	25,000						
Capital Expenditures		−150,000								
Incremental Cash Flows		−180,000	77,000	61,000	57,000	57,000	57,000	45,000	45,000	–
Cumulative Cash Flow		−180,000	−103,000	−42,000	15,000	72,000	129,000	174,000	219,000	
Present Value Factor		0.909	0.826	0.751	0.683	0.621	0.564	0.513	0.467	
Present Value of Cash Flows		−163,636	63,636	45,830	38,932	35,393	32,175	23,092	20,993	
NPV		$96,414								
IRR		28%			Discount Rate		10%			
Payback		3 years			PH Growth Rate		0%			

TABLE 20.6 Capital Expenditure: Pharmaceutical Product Development

Vance Pharma Co.		**Project Investment Analysis**				$000's (Unless otherwise noted)				
New Treatment for Procrastination										
Incremental Changes		**2018**	**2019**	**2020**	**2021**	**2022**	**2023**	**2024**	**2025**	**Terminal Value**
Revenues		–	–	–	25,000	75,000	125,000	200,000	225,000	
Cost of Revenues										
On Incremental Revenues	25%	–	–	–	6,250	18,750	31,250	50,000	56,250	
Project Savings		–								
Incremental Cost of Revenues		–	–	–	6,250	18,750	31,250	50,000	56,250	
Gross Margin Impact		–	–	–	18,750	56,250	93,750	150,000	168,750	
Operating Expenses:										
On Incremental Revenues	15%	–	–	–	3,750	11,250	18,750	30,000	33,750	
Project Savings										
Project Costs and Expenses		20,000								
Depreciation on Project Capital			10,000	10,000	10,000	10,000	10,000			
Incremental Operating Expenses		20,000	10,000	10,000	13,750	21,250	28,750	30,000	33,750	
Operating Profit		−20,000	−10,000	−10,000	5,000	35,000	65,000	120,000	135,000	

TABLE 20.6 *(continued)*

Vance Pharma Co.			Project Investment Analysis				$000's (Unless otherwise noted)			
New Treatment for Procrastination										
Incremental Changes		**2018**	**2019**	**2020**	**2021**	**2022**	**2023**	**2024**	**2025**	**Terminal Value**
Tax	40%	8,000	4,000	4,000	−2,000	−14,000	−26,000	−48,000	−54,000	
Operating Profit After Tax		−12,000	−6,000	−6,000	3,000	21,000	39,000	72,000	81,000	
Operating Cash Flow:										
Depreciation			10,000	10,000	10,000	10,000	10,000			
(Inc) Dec in Accounts Receivable			–	–	−938	−2,813	−4,688	−7,500	−8,438	
(Inc) Dec in Inventories			–	−1,875	−5,625	−9,375	−15,000	−16,875	−16,875	
Capital Expenditures		−50,000								
Incremental Cash Flows		−62,000	4,000	2,125	6,438	18,813	29,313	47,625	55,688	371,250
Cumulative Cash Flows		−62,000	−58,000	−55,875	−49,438	−30,625	−1,313	46,313	102,000	473,250
PV Factor		0.870	0.756	0.658	0.572	0.497	0.432	0.376	0.327	0.284
PV Cash Flow		−53,913	3,025	1,397	3,681	9,353	12,673	17,904	18,204	105,532
NPV		$117,856				Discount Rate		15%		
IRR		37%				PH Growth Rate		0%		
Payback		6 Years								

manufacturing project due to the higher level or risk (and therefore higher expected return) for developing a new product.

Monitoring Capital Investment Projects

After approving capital investment projects, organizations should have a process for tracking and evaluating the progress and revalidating the continued investment in resources. The critical assumptions and implementation progress can be compared to the original assumptions and project plan in the capital investment proposal (CIP).

This is especially important for mid- to long-term projects such as product development. In these times of rapid change, it is entirely possible that the underlying assumptions for a project have changed to an extent that continued investment is not justified. Have market or competitive factors changed significantly? Will the product meet targeted cost and performance attributes? Similarly, implementation may have incurred delays or unforeseen hurdles that need immediate attention or may threaten the success of the project, including economic justification. Are we on schedule to introduce the product as planned? Will the project meet the expectations for revenue, profits, and NPV that were established in the CIP? By monitoring critical projects, early detection is possible, providing the greatest window for consideration and action. If the ongoing project is determined to be dubious, investments can be terminated and resources redirected to other, more promising opportunities. Venture capital firms are masters of using this method. Their continued investment in a firm or project is dependent on progress or the attainment of specific objectives that foretell ultimate success.

Organizations should also evaluate the performance of completed projects and review utilization of assets on a periodic basis. These topics are covered in Chapter 18, Capital Management and Cash Flow: Long-Term Assets.

SUMMARY

Capital investment decisions are a critical aspect of managing an enterprise. Each CID requires a determination of whether that project will create value for the owners of the firm. Accordingly, firms must establish a rigorous process to allocate capital and evaluate individual uses of capital.

Capital investments include a wide spectrum of projects and purchases, from purchases of equipment to development of new products to acquiring a company. Common economic evaluation measures include payback, net present value, and internal rate of return.

Since CIDs require projections of future results, they incorporate a significant level of risk and uncertainty. Techniques for identifying and addressing risk and uncertainty are covered in Chapter 21.

21

CAPITAL INVESTMENT DECISIONS

Advanced Topics

CHAPTER INTRODUCTION

In Chapter 20, we introduced key elements of capital investment decisions. In this chapter, we will cover advanced topics, including dealing with risk and uncertainty, capital budgeting and rationing, and methods of evaluating the effectiveness of the capital investment decision process. Finally, we will review best practices in presenting capital investment decisions.

DEALING WITH RISK AND UNCERTAINTY IN CAPITAL INVESTMENT DECISIONS

Since we are dealing with expectations, predictions, and projections of *future* performance, capital investment decisions have an inherent level of risk and uncertainty. The risk and uncertainty can be extreme in projects that extend over a long period or involve rapidly changing environmental and competitive factors (almost all markets now!).

SOURCES OF RISK AND UNCERTAINTY

Project-specific risk
Competitive risk
Industry risk
Global and international risk
Geopolitical risk
Financial market risk
Estimation bias

There are two broad techniques for addressing risk and uncertainty in capital investment decisions:

1. Use of an appropriate discount rate for the project risk.
2. Analysis, evaluation, and flexing of financial projections.

Utilize an Appropriate Discount Rate

Many firms use a single discount rate for all capital projects. In many cases, the origin and basis of the discount rate is not known or well understood. The discount rate should be reviewed periodically, and the appropriateness of using it on a specific project should always be considered.

The starting point for selecting the discount rate should be the firm's overall cost of capital. This weighted average cost of capital (WACC) is a blend of all risk and return factors for the company. The rate for a specific project should be reviewed to determine if it is appropriate for the specific risk characteristics of that project.

Let's begin with the security market line, commonly known as the risk-return graph. While its origin lies in the capital asset pricing model (CAPM) for financial securities, the concept transfers to real investments as well. Investors and managers can choose to invest in a wide range of investment alternatives, each with its own level of a risk. As you move down the investment risk axis, the theory holds that investors should have a higher return expectation. (See Figure 21.1.)

FIGURE 21.1 Risk and Return

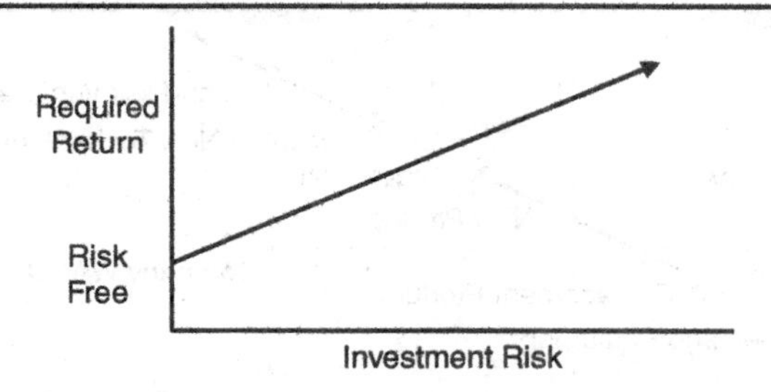

Investors expect a return that is commensurate with the underlying risk of that investment.

The firm's weighted average cost of capital is simply one point on this curve, representing the required return for all investors in the company's debt and equity. The spectrum of potential investments for a firm ranges from low-risk investments such as replacing equipment on the manufacturing line to investing in a high-risk venture. Figure 21.2 illustrates typical investments a firm may evaluate; the actual placement and ranking would be very situation and project specific. Replacing the equipment on the manufacturing line would generally have low risk since the firm already has experience in this activity and there is little risk of loss since it appears to be needed to support revenue. Replacing an existing product would also likely have lower risk than the firm-wide composite (WACC). However, investments to develop a new product, acquire a business, or develop a new technology would likely be higher than the firm's WACC.

If the firm uses the WACC to evaluate higher-risk programs, it runs the risk of approving projects that have higher risk than expected returns. Conversely, if the WACC is used to evaluate projects with lower risk, it may reject projects that should be approved. Refer to Chapter 19 for a more complete discussion on the cost of capital and WACC.

In theory, the firm could research similar investments and develop an expected return (discount rate) for each individual project. This can be time-consuming and difficult. Most firms would develop a practical

FIGURE 21.2 Risk and Expected Return

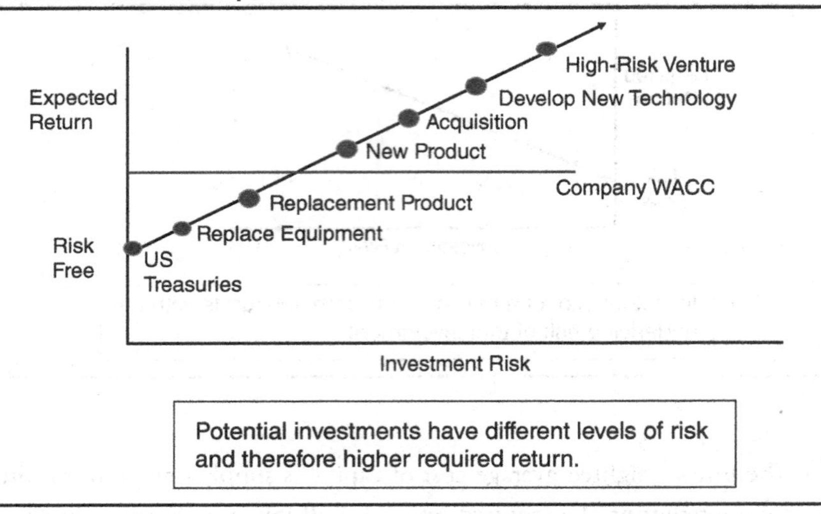

framework that allows for some recognition of differing risk levels, as illustrated in Figure 21.3.

In this example, the firm's WACC is estimated to be 12%. The firm could establish an overall hurdle rate of 14% by tacking on a premium or cushion of 2%. For project categories with lower risks, the hurdle rate would be reduced. For investment categories with higher risks, the hurdle rate would be increased to require a higher expected return to be approved. The firm can override the hurdle rate for any specific project if that is deemed appropriate. The firm's WACC and hurdle rates are typically reviewed and updated if appropriate, on an annual basis. Any significant events that change the risk profile would also warrant reconsideration.

Analysis, Evaluation, and Flexing of Financial Projections

I have always found that understanding and evaluating the financial projections in a capital decision are among the most important *and* difficult aspects of the review process. For significant projects, it may be appropriate to look at several projection scenarios and analyses. The best practices in

FIGURE 21.3 Setting Hurdle Rates Based on Risk

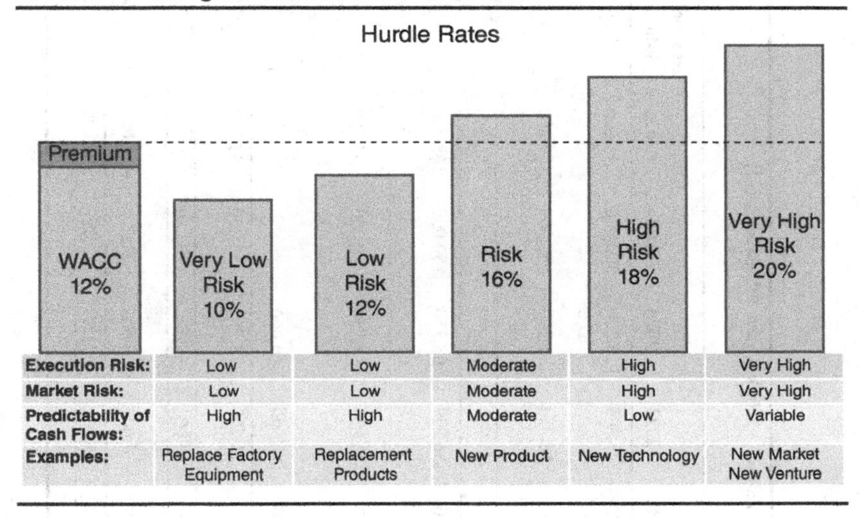

projecting and evaluating long-term projections discussed in Chapter 14 should be employed in significant projects.

For significant projects with extended time horizons, a thorough plan and financial projection should be developed to support the capital investment decision. The following capital investment decisions would warrant a complete business plan and detailed financial projections:

- New product
- New business unit
- Acquiring a business or company

There are several tools that have proven effective in dealing with risk and uncertainty in capital investment decisions. We will build on our illustration of the new pharmaceutical development to treat procrastination.

Base Case. The base case employs a discounted cash flow (DCF) analysis using the most likely estimates for all variables. This case represents a single outcome from a range of potential outcomes and includes many assumptions about future events and performance. The base case is the project investment analysis in Table 21.1.

TABLE 21.1 Project Investment Analysis: Procrastination Pharmaceutical

Vance Pharma Co.					**Project Investment Analysis**		**$000's (Unless otherwise noted)**			
New Treatment for Procrastination										
Incremental Changes		**2018**	**2019**	**2020**	**2021**	**2022**	**2023**	**2024**	**2025**	**Terminal Value**
Revenues		–	–	–	25,000	75,000	125,000	200,000	225,000	
Cost of Revenues										
On Incremental Revenues	25%	–	–	–	6,250	18,750	31,250	50,000	56,250	
Project Savings		–								
Incremental Cost of Revenues		–	–	–	6,250	18,750	31,250	50,000	56,250	
Gross Margin Impact		–	–	–	18,750	56,250	93,750	150,000	168,750	
Operating Expenses:										
On Incremental Revenues	15%	–	–	–	3,750	11,250	18,750	30,000	33,750	
Project Savings										
Project Costs and Expenses		20,000								
Depreciation on Project Capital			10,000	10,000	10,000	10,000	10,000			
Incremental Operating Expenses		20,000	10,000	10,000	13,750	21,250	28,750	30,000	33,750	
Operating Profit		−20,000	−10,000	−10,000	5,000	35,000	65,000	120,000	135,000	
Tax	40%	8,000	4,000	4,000	−2,000	−14,000	−26,000	−48,000	−54,000	
Operating Profit After Tax		−12,000	−6,000	−6,000	3,000	21,000	39,000	72,000	81,000	

TABLE 21.1 *(Continued)*

Vance Pharma Co. New Treatment for Procrastination			Project Investment Analysis		$000's (Unless otherwise noted)				
Incremental Changes	**2018**	**2019**	**2020**	**2021**	**2022**	**2023**	**2024**	**2025**	**Terminal Value**
<u>**Operating Cash Flow:**</u>									
Depreciation		10,000	10,000	10,000	10,000	10,000			
(Inc) Dec in Accounts Receivable		–	–	–938	–2,813	–4,688	–7,500	–8,438	
(Inc) Dec in Inventories		–	–1,875	–5,625	–9,375	–15,000	–16,875	–16,875	
Capital Expenditures	–50,000								
Incremental Cash Flows	–62,000	4,000	2,125	6,438	18,813	29,313	47,625	55,688	371,250
Cumulative Cash Flows	–62,000	–58,000	–55,875	–49,438	–30,625	–1,313	46,313	102,000	473,250
PV Factor	0.870	0.756	0.658	0.572	0.497	0.432	0.376	0.327	0.284
PV Cash Flow	–53,913	3,025	1,397	3,681	9,353	12,673	17,904	18,204	105,532
NPV	$117,856			Discount Rate			15%		
IRR	37%			PH Growth Rate			0%		
Payback	6 Years								

Sensitivity Analysis. This technique determines the sensitivity of the decision criteria (e.g. NPV) to changes in the assumptions used in the base case. Table 21.2 presents the traditional sensitivity analysis, showing the base case of $117.8 and the resultant NPV values at different assumptions of revenue and development costs.

Table 21.2 shows that this project could have a NPV as low as $77.0 million to a high of $154.0 million within the ranges of these assumptions. This provides great context to the decision makers, giving insight into the dynamics of the investment.

Breakeven Analysis. Table 21.3 presents a different form of sensitivity analysis that highlights the impact of a 10% change in each variable and determines how far the assumptions can change before resulting in a breakeven NPV value.

Scenario Analysis. This important tool determines projected NPV of the project under specified scenarios (e.g. recession, best case, competitive reaction, etc.). Projections for each specific scenario are developed, and the investment is evaluated under each scenario.

Steps to develop scenarios:

1. Select potential scenarios (e.g. general economic, price of oil, competitive reaction, adoption rates).
2. Develop projections under each scenario. This is a critical aspect of scenario planning. Unlike sensitivity analysis, where we

TABLE 21.2 Sensitivity Analysis

		Procrastination Pharmaceutical				
		Sensitivity Analysis			NPV	
				Revenues (M)		
		175.0	**200.0**	**225.0**	**250.0**	**275.0**
	$ **18.0**	88.0	105.0	122.0	137.0	154.0
Development	**19.0**	86.0	103.0	120.0	135.0	152.0
Costs (M)	**20.0**	83.0	101.0	117.8	133.0	150.0
	21.0	81.0	98.0	115.0	131.0	149.0
	22.0	77.0	94.0	111.0	129.0	146.0

TABLE 21.3 Sensitivity and Breakeven Analysis

	Procrastination Pharmaceutical Sensitivity and Breakeven Analysis				
	Key Assumptions				Breakeven Approx. Value
	Base	10% Change	NPV	% Change in NPV	NPV=0
Base			117.9		117.9
Sales (2025)	225.0	202.5	101.8	−13.6%	56.5
Cost & Expense Levels	40%	44.0%	87.9	−25.4%	56.0%
Tax Rate	40.0%	44.0%	103.3	−12.4%	NMF
Initial Outlay	70.0	77.0	114.2	−3.1%	250.0*
Terminal Value	371.3	334.1	107.3	−9.0%	0
Discount Rate	15.0%	16.5%	93.2	−20.9%	30.0%

*Dependent on assumptions capital vs. expense

simple flex selected variables, we will revise the base projections for expected changes under the scenario. For example, in a recession, a company may experience price pressure and lower demand. That company may also expect different interest rates, labor rates, and commodity pricing.

3. Measure scenario using NPV, IRR, payback, and so forth.
4. Use this insight in evaluating the project.

In our example of the development of a procrastination treatment, there are several potential scenarios to consider, including:

- Product development efforts fail, and the project is abandoned.
- Product development is successful but revenues do not meet projections because a competitor introduces a similar product.
- Revenues exceed the base projections.

Others:

- Prices are controlled by government.
- A recession occurs.

FIGURE 21.4 Scenario Recap

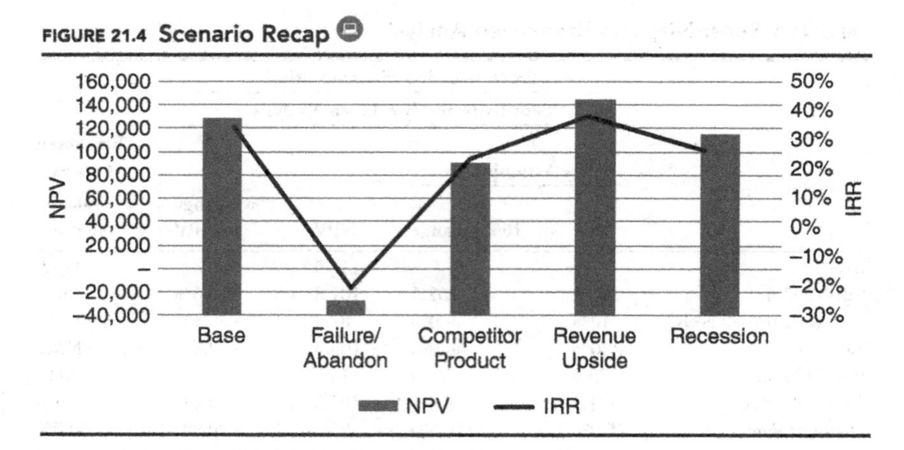

The results of each of each scenario can be evaluated and presented to decision makers. (See Figure 21.4.) In addition to providing insight into all potential outcomes, an important benefit is that it encourages the identification of important checkpoints and management options. For example, an executive should insist on identifying and monitoring the key drivers that will lead to abandonment of the project. Timely determination of ultimate failure will allow the project to be terminated at the earliest possible time, resulting in minimizing the loss on the project and allowing resources to be deployed to other, more promising projects.

Event, Decision, and Option Trees. Event, decision, and option trees can be very effective tools in evaluating and presenting capital investment decisions. An event tree generally refers to a presentation of alternative events or outcomes. Decision or option trees include future management decisions (options) as one or more events in the future. They build on the concept of scenario analysis described earlier. Decision and event trees are a useful way to visualize, communicate, and evaluate various scenarios, especially future projects or other decisions where the outcomes are uncertain. Projects may result in several different outcomes (success, failure, delay) and may also be subject to management decisions after the initial project approval (delay, cancel, etc.). For example, a firm may face a choice to

FIGURE 21.5 Decision Tree

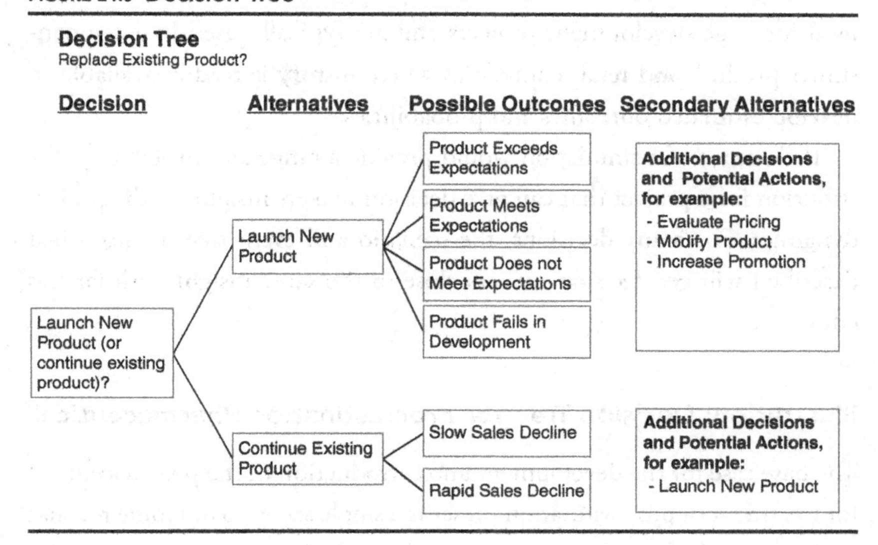

replace an existing product with a new product or continue to sell the existing one. This is unlikely to be a single decision point. How successful will the new product be? What will happen to the sales of the existing product if not replaced? What subsequent options will management have to optimize the result? A decision tree identifies and presents decisions and probable outcomes at each stage of a project.

The simple illustration in Figure 21.5 is a very effective way to lay out various management decisions and to describe potential outcomes resulting from each alternative scenario/decision. Each of the six potential outcomes will have a probability of occurrence and an estimated value (e.g. NPV, sales, earnings per share). Each of these six outcomes will also have a second level of management options or decisions.

Simulations. In simulations, decision criteria would be estimated across an entire probability distribution for key variables. For example, revenues, margins, investments, and other key variables would be analyzed to develop a spectrum of potential outcomes and associated probabilities. The biggest downside is the need to develop estimates and probabilities across the entire distribution of potential outcomes for each variable and then to determine value (e.g. NPV) under each combination of variables. Simulations can be used for large development projects and are typically used by large consumer product and retail companies where history is readily available to develop estimated outcomes and probabilities.

The output of a simulation would provide a range and probability distribution for a project that can give decision makers insight on the project dynamics. For many decisions, the scenario and event tree methods just described will get decision makers close to the same insight with far less effort.

Illustration: Decision Tree for Procrastination Pharmaceutical

The base case for the development and introduction of the pharmaceutical for treatment of procrastination presents a single scenario outcome for that project. It includes many assumptions about the timing and success of the development process and also assumes that management has no ability in the future to change the course of development and introduction if circumstances change. Figure 21.6 provides a simple illustration of multiple outcomes for this project. Note that this illustration is a gross oversimplification of the process for developing and obtaining approval for new pharmaceuticals!

This analysis provides several additional insights. First, the base case assumes approval and a solid revenue stream resulting in an NPV of $117,856. However, there is a 30% chance that the pharmaceutical will not be approved, resulting in a negative NPV of $12,000 ($20,000 research expense less 40% tax savings). Second, it highlights that there are also additional scenarios that revenues will fall short or exceed the base case, with the shortfall resulting in a negative NPV of $2,226.

Clearly the addition of this analysis adds significant insight to the decision. The results of this analysis can be summarized in Figure 21.7, but the decision tree also has outright value in understanding and communicating the dynamics of the investment decision.

FIGURE 21.6 Event/Option Tree

Event/Option Tree New Pharma

Development and Testing	Success? Proceed?	Invest in Manufacturing	Potential Outcomes	Result 2021	2022	2023	2024	2025	TV	NPV	Probability	Expected Value
			Upside Case 20%	7,413	24,738	39,438	66,675	77,963	519,750	181,900	14%	25,466
Invest in Development –20,000	70%	50,000	Base Case 60%	6,438	18,813	29,313	47,625	5,568	371,250	117,856	42%	49,500
			Downside Case 20%	4,609	7,703	10,328	11,906	13,922	92,813	–2,226	14%	–312
	30%	Stop								–12,000	30%	–3,600
										Total	100%	71,054

FIGURE 21.7 Option Event Summary for Procrastination Pharmaceutical

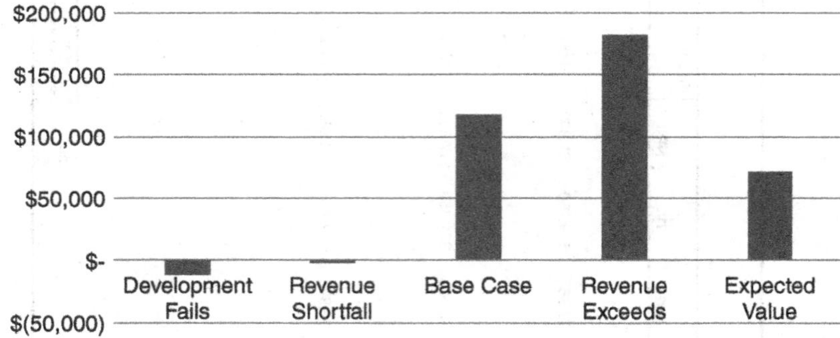

Real Options and Option Value

Real options build on the principles of option trees illustrated earlier. Essentially, the advocates of real options apply option pricing models for securities to "real" investments. While this is a fascinating area for math majors, I find it difficult to effectively utilize in most practice situations. In addition, presenting a value from a complex formula is difficult to explain and doesn't add value in terms of understanding the dynamics of an investment decision.

A related concept that is often used is the option value. An investment may have a positive (or negative) NPV based on the primary opportunity under evaluation. It may also provide a platform or ability to pursue another opportunity. For example, the procrastination treatment may also be the foundation for another treatment, for smart phone attention deficit (SPAD). Another plan and projection can be developed for this new treatment to commence after the procrastination treatment is completed. The potential NPV of this second project can be estimated and considered in the evaluation of the program (see Figure 21.8).

FIGURE 21.8 Option Value Illustration

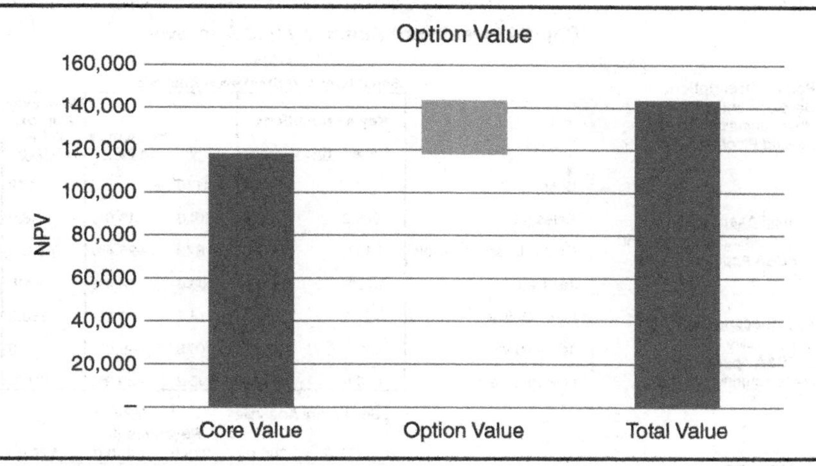

The option value is often used to justify a program that has negative or marginal NPV (prospect for value creation). Of course, this can be abused if not managed properly.

PRESENTING CAPITAL INVESTMENT DECISIONS

Capital investment decisions are a critical aspect of the management process, since it is the determination of what projects should be approved to create value for shareholders. In addition to effectively developing plans and investment evaluations for significant projects, it is important that FP&A teams also develop effective presentations to management in order to facilitate the overall evaluation and approval of projects.

Many projects, for example a large developmental project or acquisition, will be accompanied by a complete business plan that supports the economic valuation and analysis described in this chapter.

Figure 21.9 provides an illustration of a recap or approval summary for a capital investment decision. The advantage of this one-page summary

FIGURE 21.9 **Capital Investment Summary**

Capital Investment Summary and Approval

Project Description:
Development of New Pharmaceutical for treating Procrastination

Critical Assumptions:
o Successful Development
o FD&A Approval

Key Checkpoints:
o Feasibility
o FD&A Approval
Manufacturing

Alternatives:
o Forgo Opportunity
o
o

Sensitivity and Breakeven Analysis

	Key Assumptions Base	Key Assumptions 10% Change	NPV	% Change in NPV	Breakeven Approx. Value NPV=0
Base			117.9		117.9
Sales (2025)	225.0	202.5	101.8	–13.6%	56.5
Cost & Expense Levels	40%	44.0%	87.9	–25.4%	56.0%
Tax Rate	40.0%	44.0%	103.3	–12.4%	NMF
Initial Outlay	70.0	77.0	114.2	–3.1%	250.0
Terminal Value	371.3	334.1	107.3	–9.0%	0
Discount Rate	15.0%	16.5%	93.2	–20.9%	30.0%

Sensitivity Analysis NPV

Development Costs (M)	Revenues (M) 175.0	200.0	225.0	250.0	275.0
$ 18.0	88.0	105.0	122.0	137.0	154.0
19.0	86.0	103.0	120.0	135.0	152.0
20.0	83.0	101.0	117.8	133.0	150.0
21.0	81.0	98.0	115.0	131.0	149.0
22.0	77.0	94.0	111.0	129.0	146.0

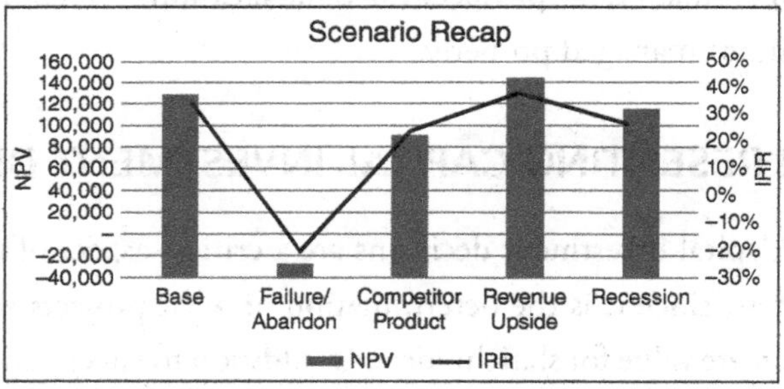

Base Case
Revenue
Operating Income
NPV
RR

Approvals

Preparer	
Operating Executive	
FP&A Analyst	
Controller	
CFO	
CEO	

Scenario Recap
NPV: 160,000; 140,000; 120,000; 100,000; 80,000; 60,000; 40,000; 20,000; –; –20,000; –40,000
IRR: 50%; 40%; 30%; 20%; 10%; 0%; –10%; –20%; –30%
Base
Failure/ Abandon
Competitor Product
Revenue Upside
Recession
NPV — IRR

is that all relevant information is presented on this single document. Of course, this recap will likely be supported by a detailed presentation and business case.

CAPITAL BUDGETING AND RATIONING

Although in theory we assume that capital is available for any investment opportunity with a positive NPV, as a practical matter firms must allocate capital and evaluate many potential projects for possible investment.

This process often occurs as part of the strategic and operational planning process and product development activities. Typically, operating and business unit executives identify more potential capital projects than the company is able or willing to fund, with reasons ranging from cash or profit constraints to management capacity. Firms employ several techniques to provide insight on which projects should be selected.

Raise the Hurdle or Discount Rate. If the hurdle or discount rate were raised for all projects, some investments would no longer have positive NPV and would be rejected. However, this has the effect of penalizing all projects.

Profitability Index (PI). The PI is a tool used to measure the value of a project compared to the initial investment.

The profitability index is computed as follows:

NPV/Initial Investment

For our drug development example, the PI is computed as follows:

$$PI = \frac{\text{NPV}}{\text{Initial Investment}} = \frac{\$117,856}{\$70,000}$$
$$= 1.68$$

The firm can then rank projects by the index and approve those projects with the highest PI as illustrated in Table 21.4. In this example, if the capital budget for the coming year must be held to $325,000, then the last five projects would not be pursued.

The problem with using only a financial measure to evaluate projects is that many projects have important nonfinancial attributes that must be considered, ranging from executive preferences to statutory requirements. In this case, the casualties of PI ranking would prohibit repairing the roof and addressing the wastewater issue, an apparent Environmental Protection Agency (EPA) requirement.

Holistic Approach. To reflect both the financial rankings and other important business issues, leading finance organizations develop a holistic view of all capital investments and rank them, taking into account a

TABLE 21.4 Capital Investment Allocation 

Vance Pharmaceutical
Capital Investment Allocation

Overall Rank	Project Description	Investment	NPV	IRR	Profitability Index	Cumulative Investment
6	Airplane for CEO	4,000	8,000	60.0%	2.000	4,000
3	Procrastination Drug	70,000	117,856	0.37	1.684	74,000
11	Replace Building 2 Equipment	3,200	2,900	50.0%	0.906	77,200
5	Laziness Treatment	32,000	22,000	17.0%	0.688	109,200
10	Info Technology-Enterprise System	12,000	6,100	15.0%	0.508	121,200
7	Automate Manufacturing	200,000	96,414	28.0%	0.482	321,200
5	Expand Distribution Center	4,875	2,265	18.5%	0.465	326,075
8	All Other < 1,000	16,000	4,200	0.17	0.263	342,075
12	New Corporate Headquarters	4,000	23	0.1%	0.006	346,075
2	New Roof	1,200	−120	−11.0%	−0.100	347,275
4	Info Technology-Security	7,000	−2,100	−7.0%	−0.300	354,275
1	Wastewater Treatment	15,000	−5,260	−15.0%	−0.351	369,275
	Total	369,275	252,278	25%	0.683	

multitude of factors, including PI, EPS impact, strategic importance, and statutory requirements. Table 21.5 incorporates all factors in a single summary. This presentation will generally facilitate the decision around capital priorities.

Note that the statutorily required projects top the list, since they are mandated by law. Of course, the airplane for the CEO still made the cut!

EVALUATING THE EFFECTIVENESS OF THE CAPITAL INVESTMENT DECISION PROCESS

Firms should evaluate the effectiveness of the CID process. The process should identify any estimation bias, execution failures, root causes, and possible corrective actions. This insight can then be used to revise the current process to improve future results. The process can also be used to identify problematic programs that require management attention and action on a real-time basis. Even in the simple illustration in Table 21.6, it is clear

TABLE 21.5 **Capital Plan Ranking**

		Vance Pharmaceutical Capital Investment Allocation									
Overall Rank	Project Description	Investment	NPV	IRR	Profitability Index	Cumulative Investment	EPS Accretive Year	EPS Accretive $0.00	Strategic Importance	Statutory Requirement	Notes
1	Wastewater Treatment	15,000	−5,260	−15.0%	−0.351	15,000			Low	Yes, EPA Requirement	
2	New Roof	1,200	−120	−11.0%	−0.100	16,200					Leaking roof jeopardizing FDA License
3	Procrastination Drug	70,000	117,856	0.37	1.684	86,200	2021	0.11	High	No	Most important PD effort
4	Info Technology-Security	7,000	−2,100	−7.0%	−0.300	93,200			High	No, but …	Cyber threats increasing
5	Laziness Treatment	32,000	22,000	17.0%	0.688	125,200	2024		Yes		
5	Expand Distribution Center	4,875	2,265	18.5%	0.465	130,075			No	Yes	Support sales growth, new products
6	Airplane for CEO	4,000	8,000	60.0%	2.000	134,075	2018		Yes		Expense/time savings
7	Automate Manufacturing	200,000	96,414	28.0%	0.482	334,075	2020	0.200	Moderate	No	
8	All Other < 1,000	16,000	4,200	0.17	0.263	350,075					
10	Info Technology-Enterprise System	12,000	6,100	15.0%	0.508	362,075				No	Replace existing/add functionality
11	Replace Building 2 Equipment	3,200	2,900	50.0%	0.906	365,275	2020				
12	New Corporate Headquarters	4,000	23	0.1%	0.006	369,275			Yes	No	Image/Locate in Financial Center
	Total	369,275	252,278	25%	0.683						

TABLE 21.6 Review of Capital Investments

		Review of Significant Capital Investments									
	% Complete	Cost/Investment			NY Revenue			Net Present Value			
Project	Status	Original	Act/Est	Variance	Original	Current	Variance	Original	Act/Est	Variance	Indicated Actions
Plant Expansion	Complete	1,400,000	1,480,000	–80,000		N/A		125,000	45,000	–80,000	None, 6% cost overrun
Network Update/ Expansion	70% Complete, Delay	2,600,000	2,725,000	–125,000		N/A		54,000	–71,000	–125,000	Cost Overrun, delayed. Review Needed
Wastewater Treatment Facility	Complete	800,000	875,000	–75,000		N/A			N/A		
Replace Manufacturing Cells 3–7	On Schedule	1,200,000	1,175,000	25,000		N/A		67,500	92,500	25,000	On schedule, no action required
New product 1	Complete	950,000	975,000	–25,000	1,200,000	1,135,000	–65,000	1,200,000	1,160,000	–40,000	6 month delay, outlook positive
New product 2	Delay	825,000	962,000	–137,000	750,000	125,000	–625,000	800,000	420,000	–380,000	Design delays, Review Needed
New product 3	20% Complete, Delay	1,400,000	1,425,000	–25,000	750,000	–	–750,000	1,450,000	265,000	–1,185,000	On Sched but competitor product introduced. Review Needed.

this company has a pattern of poor execution and underestimating costs. These issues should be addressed by improving the CID process.

In Chapter 18, we also discussed the asset utilization process for all prior significant investments in property, plant, and equipment.

SUMMARY

Capital investment decisions are of critical importance in creating value for shareholders. A CID, by definition, involves an extended planning horizon. The future is uncertain, and many factors and assumptions can impact the success of the project and the prospect of creating value for shareholders.

Techniques for dealing with uncertainty include:

- Identify, document, and monitor key assumptions.
- Adjust discount (hurdle) rates for risk.
- Utilize sensitivity and scenario analyses and other tools to understand the dynamics of the investment and projected results.

Owing to the importance and complexity of many CIDs, it is important to thoroughly evaluate and develop comprehensive presentations to decision makers.

22

BUSINESS VALUATION AND VALUE DRIVERS

CHAPTER INTRODUCTION

Nearly all valuation techniques are based on estimating the cash flows that an asset, for example real estate or a firm, can generate in the future. Two critical points are worth emphasizing. First, the value of any asset should be based on the expected *cash flows* the owner can realize by holding that asset or selling it to another party. Second, only the *future* expectations of cash flows are relevant in determining value. Historical performance and track records are important inputs in estimating future cash flows, but "the market prices forward" based on expectations of future performance.

It is important to recognize that valuation is both an art and a science. While we outline a number of quantitative, objective approaches to valuing a business, many other nonquantitative and perhaps even irrational factors do affect the value of the firm, especially in the short term. It is a marvel that each day millions of shares of stock are traded on the public exchanges, with buyers and sellers on both sides of the transaction, one deciding to sell at the same value at which the other has decided to purchase.

Commonly used valuation techniques fall into two major categories: (1) estimating the value by discounting future cash flows, and (2) estimating the value by comparing to the value of other similar businesses. This chapter is not intended to be an exhaustive work on business valuation; that has been the objective of some very well written books.[1] The goal in this chapter is to provide a foundation in key valuation concepts and to highlight key analytical tools and measures.

ESTIMATING THE VALUE OF A BUSINESS BY DISCOUNTING FUTURE CASH FLOWS

This discounted cash flow (DCF) valuation method is based on sound fundamental economic theory. Essentially, the value of a firm is equal to the present value of expected future cash flows. These future cash flows are "discounted" to arrive at the value today. Since DCF is based on projections of future cash flows, it requires that financial statement projections be prepared. In order to prepare financial statement projections, assumptions must be made about the firm's performance in the future. Will sales grow, and, if so, at what rate? Will margins improve or erode? Why? What capital will be required to support the future business levels? Financial projections are covered in more depth in Part Three: Business projections and Plans. The DCF technique also allows us to determine the magnitude of improvement in key operating variables necessary to increase the value of the firm by, say, 20%.

Figure 22.1 presents an overview of DCF methodology. Estimates of key financial and operating variables result in projected cash flows. These projected cash flows are then discounted to estimate the value of the firm. The discount rate considers a number of factors, including the time value of money and the level of risk of the projected cash flows. The discount rate, or cost of capital, was more fully explored in Chapter 19.

A sample worksheet for a DCF valuation is presented in Table 22.1. This example builds on the Roberts Manufacturing Company (RMC) example introduced in Chapter 2, utilizing the financial performance and other

FIGURE 22.1 **Discounted Cash Flow (DCF)**

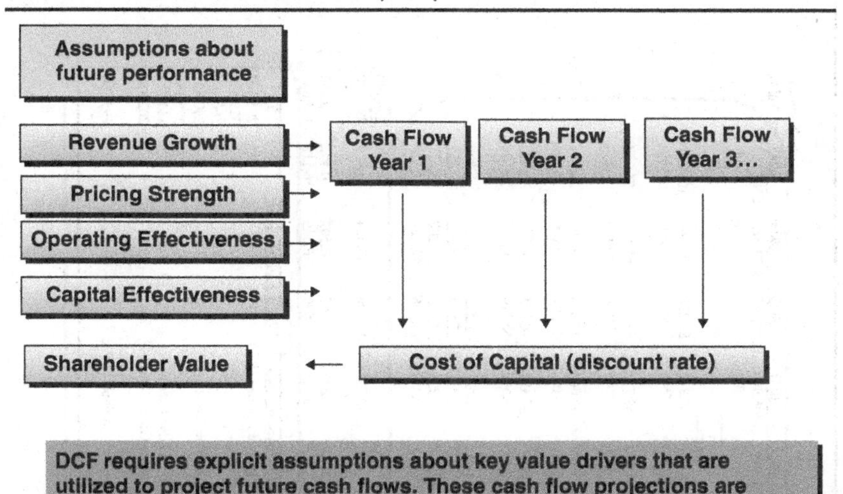

information presented in Table 2.5. This DCF valuation worksheet was developed for the primary purpose of understanding the overall dynamics of a firm's valuation, and may require modification to be used to as a valuation tool. For example, the model uses a single estimate of future sales growth and other key variables. Generally, a valuation would be based on estimates of key financial inputs for each period, supported by detailed projections and assumptions.

At first glance, the model presented in Table 22.1 can be overwhelming. We will review the model by breaking it into six key steps:

1. Review and present the firm's financial history.
2. Project future cash flows by estimating key elements of future operating performance.
3. Estimate the terminal or postplanning horizon value.
4. Discount the cash flows.
5. Estimate the value of the firm.
6. Explore the dynamics of the valuation.

TABLE 22.1 DCF Valuation Model

Roberts Manufacturing Company	($m) 2014	2015	2016	2017	Estimates	2018	2019	2020	2021	2022	2023	2024	2025	Terminal Value
Revenues	$79,383	$85,734	$92,593	$100,000		$108,000	$116,640	$125,971	$136,049	$146,933	$158,687	$171,382	$185,093	
Year over Year Growth		8%	8%	8%	8.0%	8%	8%	8%	8%	8%	8%	8%	8%	
Cost of Goods Sold	35,722	38,580	41,667	45,000										
Gross Margin	43,661	47,154	50,926	55,000	55.0%	59,400	64,152	69,284	74,827	80,813	87,278	94,260	101,801	
% Sales	55%	55%	55%	55%		55%	55%	55%	55%	55%	55%	55%	55%	
Operating Expenses	31,753	34,294	37,037	40,000	40.0%	43,200	46,656	50,388	54,420	58,773	63,475	68,553	74,037	
% Sales	40%	40%	40%	40%		40%	40%	40%	40%	40%	40%	40%	40%	
Operating Income (EBIT)	11,907	12,860	13,889	15,000		16,200	17,496	18,896	20,407	22,040	23,803	25,707	27,764	
% Sales	15.0%	15.0%	15.0%	15.0%		15.0%	15.0%	15.0%	15.0%	15.0%	15.0%	15.0%	15.0%	
– Taxes	–3,843	–4,166	–4,516	–4,894	–34.0%	–5,508	–5,949	–6,425	–6,938	–7,494	–8,093	–8,741	–9,440	
OPAT	8,065	8,694	9,373	10,106		10,692	11,548	12,471	13,469	14,546	15,710	16,967	18,324	
+ Depreciation/Amortization	2,800	2,930	3,197	3,750		5,000	5,400	5,832	6,299	6,802	7,347	7,934	8,569	
– Capital Expenditures	–3,000	–4,200	–4,800	–5,000	–5.0%	–5,400	–5,832	–6,299	–6,802	–7,347	–7,934	–8,569	–9,255	
(Increase) Decrease in OC		–2,228	–2,249	–2,130	30%	–2,400	–2,592	–2,799	–3,023	–3,265	–3,526	–3,808	–4,113	
Free Cash Flow	7,865	5,196	5,521	6,726		7,892	8,524	9,205	9,942	10,737	11,596	12,524	13,526	
						0								
+ Terminal Value														293,190
`						7,892	8,524	9,205	9,942	10,737	11,596	12,524	13,526	293,190
Present Value Factor						1.000	0.893	0.797	0.712	0.636	0.567	0.507	0.452	0.452
Present Value of Cash Flow (PVCF)						7,892	7,610	7,338	7,076	6,824	6,580	6,345	6,118	132,624

Sum PVCF	55,784
Present Value of Terminal Value	132,624
Estimated Value of Firm (Enterprise Value)	188,408
Add: Excess Cash and Nonoperating Assets	7,944
Subtract: Value of Debt	10,000
Estimated Value of Equity	186,352
Number of Shares Outstanding	17,000
Estimated Value per Share	$10.96
Cost of Capital	12.00%

Terminal Value (TV) Assumptions		Multiple/Rate	TV
	Multiples of Earnings (P/E)	16.0	293,190
		18.0	329,838
		20.0	366,487
	Multiples of Revenue	1.3	240,621
		2.0	370,186
	Perpetuity No Growth	0%	112,714
	Perpetuity Growth	5%	202,885
Use	Multiple of P/E	16.0	293,190

Note:
Key Assumptions:
Source: Company press release(w/o restructuring) and analyst reports

Step 1: Include and Review the Firm's Financial History

While the DCF valuation will be based on expected future cash flows, it is essential to review and consider recent history and trends in developing the projected financial results. The DCF model should present three or four years of history alongside the projections. In addition to providing a base from which the preparer estimates future cash flows, it provides a basis for others to evaluate the future projections in the context of recent performance. For example, if sales have grown at 3% to 5% over the past several years, why are we projecting 8% growth over the next several years?

Step 2: Project Future Cash Flows by Estimating Key Elements of Future Operating Performance

After reviewing the historical performance and identifying the key drivers of current and future performance, the analyst or manager can project the expected future financial performance. It is deceptively easy to plug in estimated sales, margins, expenses, and so forth, to arrive at financial projections and estimated cash flows. However, significant analysis, understanding, and thought are required to project key variables such as revenue or gross margins. For example, to predict revenue for a firm, multiple factors must be considered, including:

- Economic factors (growth, recession, etc.)
- Market size and growth
- Competitive factors
- Unit volume
- Pricing trends
- Product mix
- Customer success
- New product introduction
- Product obsolescence

It is extremely important to document the critical assumptions about revenue and all other key elements of financial performance. These assumptions can then be evaluated, changed, monitored, and "flexed" to understand the significance of each in the estimated value of the firm. Since no one has a crystal ball, we know that actual results will vary from our projections. Much of the value in business planning results from the *process* of planning, as opposed to the plan or financial projection itself. Additional information on developing long-term projections is contained in Chapter 14.

Another critical decision in DCF valuations is to determine the *forecast horizon*, the period for which we project future financial performance in detail. In theory, a company has an extended, if not infinite, life. However, it typically is not practical or necessary to attempt to forecast financial results for 20 or 30 years. The forecast horizon selected should vary according to the individual circumstances. Most discounted cash flow estimates for ongoing businesses will determine the value of the projected cash flows for the forecast horizon (5 to 10 years) and will then add to that an estimate of the value of the business at the end of that period, called the "terminal value" (TV) or "post-horizon value."

Two key factors should be considered in setting the forecast horizon. First, ensure that there is a balance between the value of the cash flows generated during the forecast horizon and the estimated terminal value. If substantially all of the estimated value is attributable to the terminal value, the forecast horizon should be extended. The second and related consideration is to extend the forecast horizon to a point where the financial performance reaches a sustainable or steady-state basis. For example, if a firm is in a period of rapid growth, the cash flows at the end of the horizon will still reflect significant investments in expenses, working capital, and equipment. The forecast horizon should extend beyond this rapid growth phase to a point beyond where it reaches a long-term sustainable growth rate. This will ensure that the key variables impacting cash flow reach a steady state, allowing this to be used as a base for estimating the terminal value.

Step 3: Estimate the Terminal or Post–Planning Horizon Value

The use of a terminal value or post-horizon value is an effective practical alternative to very long forecast horizons, subject to proper application. First, the factors in setting the forecast horizon as just described must be utilized. Second, care must be exercised in selecting the multiple or valuation technique utilized in calculating the terminal value. The terminal value is usually estimated by using one of two methods:

The first method involves taking the base performance in the past year (or average of the past several years) and estimating the value of the firm by applying a multiple to earnings or sales – for example, taking the final estimated earnings in year 2025 of $18,324 and applying a multiple of 16× to arrive at an expected terminal value of $293,190. Multiples could be applied in this manner to EBIT, EBITDA, and sales, as well as cash flow.

In the second method, the economic value of cash flows is determined beyond the forecast horizon by assuming that the cash flows will continue to be generated at the level of the last projected year, forever. More common is to assume that the future cash flows will continue to grow from the last projected year at some level, say 3% to 5%, in perpetuity.

Assuming no future growth beyond 2025, the estimated value of annual cash flows of $13,526 continuing in perpetuity is:

$$\text{TV} = \text{Cash Flow}_{\text{Final Year}}/\text{Discount Rate}$$

For Roberts Manufacturing Company:

$$\text{TV} = \$13{,}526/12\%$$

$$\text{TV} = \$112.7 \text{ million}$$

Assuming future growth after 2025 at g%:

$$\text{TV} = [\text{Cash Flow}_{\text{Final Year}}\,(1+g)]/(\text{Discount Rate} - g)$$

For Roberts Manufacturing Company:

$$TV = (\$13{,}526 \times 1.05)/(12\% - 5\%)$$

$$TV = \$202.8 \text{ million}$$

Since a case can be made supporting both methods, I recommend computing a range of estimated terminal values using both multiples and economic value. Understanding the underlying reasons for the different values is informative and should be explored. One of the estimates must ultimately be selected and used for the terminal value. Since the estimate of TV is usually significant to the overall valuation, a sensitivity analysis using multiple estimates of the terminal value should be created. This analysis should provide a more comprehensive understanding of the impact of key assumptions on the valuation of the company.

Common mistakes in estimating the terminal value include using inappropriate price-earnings (P/E) multiples or unrealistic post-horizon growth rates. The P/E multiple used in the TV estimate should be consistent with the performance estimated for the post-horizon growth period. This may be significantly different from current P/E ratios reflecting current performance. Post-horizon growth rates should be modest, since perpetuity means forever! Few companies achieve high levels of growth over extended periods, and many companies' growth rates slow to overall economic growth levels or even experience declines in sales over time.

Step 4: Discount the Cash Flows

Discounted cash flow (DCF) can be utilized to estimate the total value of the firm or the value of equity. Typically, we will estimate the total value of the firm by projecting total cash flows available to all investors, both equity and debt. We will then discount the cash flows at the weighted average cost of capital (WACC), which is an estimate of the returns expected by investors. Discount rates and the cost of capital are explored in greater detail in Chapter 19.

Step 5: Estimate the Value of the Firm and Equity

The resultant discounted cash flow is the *total* value of the firm, also referred to as the *enterprise value* (EV). To compute the value of equity, two adjustments must be considered. First, if the firm has a substantial cash reserve, this adjustment is added to the discounted value of projected cash flows. Second, in order to compute the value of equity, we deduct the value of the debt. The estimated value of an individual share can then be determined by dividing the market value of equity by the number of shares outstanding. Where there are significant stock options or other common stock derivatives outstanding, these should also be considered in the share count. In some cases, analysts may also make an adjustment to reflect the absence of ready liquidity for smaller privately owned enterprises.

Step 6: Explore the Dynamics of the Valuation

Arguably the most important part of valuing a business is to explore, evaluate, and communicate the dynamics of the valuation. This can be accomplished by performing sensitivity analysis, scenario analysis, and value decomposition using DCF. One of the criticisms of discounted cash flow analysis is that it requires assumptions about the future. In my view, this is a major strength of DCF analysis. We all recognize that it is not possible to predict the future, including specific projections of sales, costs, and numerous additional variables required for completing a thorough DCF analysis.

Sensitivity Analysis. By using sensitivity analysis, we can identify and quantify the sensitivity of shareholder value to key assumptions. The analysis allows us to identify the most critical factors impacting the value of a firm, such as revenue growth and profitability. Using the DCF worksheet, the analyst can change or flex key assumptions such as sales growth and profitability, and record the resultant value. The results can then be summarized as illustrated in Table 22.2.

Scenario Analysis. While sensitivity analysis is simply a math exercise to determine the effect of changing specific assumptions, scenario analysis

TABLE 22.2 DCF Sensitivity Analysis

DCF Value Sensitivity Analysis						
					Stock Price	
Roberts Manufacturing Co.		Sales Growth Rate				
		4%	6%	8%	10%	12%
	20.0%	$12.11	$13.49	$15.04	$16.80	$18.77
	17.5%	10.52	11.68	13.00	14.49	16.17
Operating Income %	15.0%	8.92	9.88	10.96	12.18	13.56
	12.5%	7.33	8.08	8.92	9.87	10.95
	10.0%	5.74	6.27	6.88	7.57	8.34

requires that a different "story" be told. The base or primary case undoubtedly contains critical assumptions about product introductions, competitor and customer actions and performance, the economy, and many others.

Under each scenario, multiple assumptions must be revisited. For example, a recession might affect sales volume and pricing, and may also reduce material and labor costs.

For Roberts Manufacturing Company, additional scenarios could be created. Each scenario would be supported by a financial projection that would be used to revalue the enterprise.

Value Decomposition. Using our DCF model, we can decompose or estimate the contribution to total value of any specific variable. For example, I find it useful to highlight the value of current performance for an enterprise versus the value associated with improvements to performance, including future growth and profitability improvements (see Figure 22.2). The value of current performance levels (i.e. assuming that the current cash flow remains constant in perpetuity) can be estimated using the formula for an annuity in perpetuity introduced in Chapter 19.

$$\text{Value} = \frac{\text{Cash Flow Year 2018}}{\text{Cost of Capital}}$$

$$\$65{,}768 = \frac{\$7{,}892}{0.12}$$

This value compares to our DCF valuation of $188,408, indicating that a disproportionate amount of the valuation is associated with assumptions about improved performance in the projections. In the

FIGURE 22.2 Value Decomposition

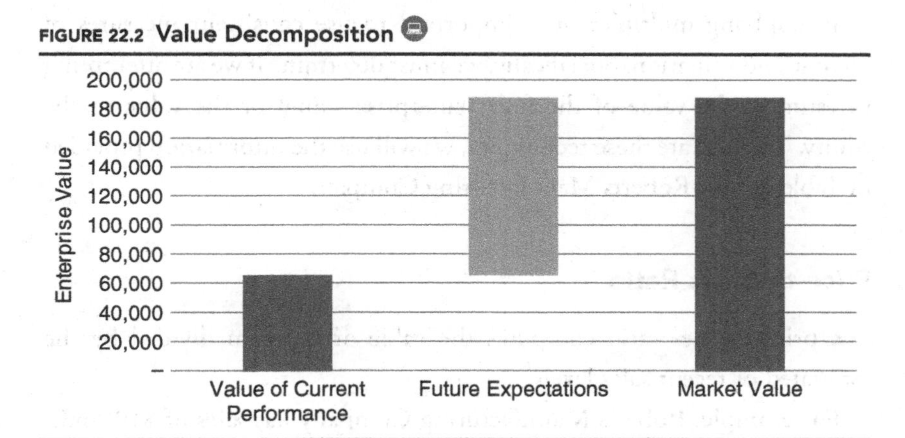

Roberts Manufacturing case, this improvement is due to the assumption of 8% growth per year (all other assumptions are held constant).

ESTIMATING THE VALUE OF FIRMS BY USING THE VALUATION OF SIMILAR FIRMS: MULTIPLES OF REVENUES, EARNINGS, AND RELATED MEASURES

The other commonly used valuation technique is based on using measures of revenues, earnings, or cash flow and capitalizing these amounts using a multiplier that is typical for similar companies. These methods are essentially shortcuts or rules of thumb based on economic theory. Users of these methods tend to establish ranges for certain industries. For example, retail companies may trade at a multiple of 0.5 to 1.0 times revenues, while technology companies may trade at 2 to 3 times revenues, or higher. The significant difference between the multiples for the two industries is explained by many factors that are independent of the current revenue level. For example, expected growth in revenues, profitability, risk, and capital requirements will have an impact on the revenue multiple. The use of multiples is common among operating executives and bankers as an easily understood basis for valuation. It also facilitates comparing relative valuations across companies.

In applying multiples, it is important to use consistent measures of income and valuation. Specifically, we must determine if we are attempting to estimate the value of the firm (enterprise value) or the value of the equity. To illustrate these techniques, we will use the information provided in Table 2.5 for Roberts Manufacturing Company.

Price-to-Sales Ratio

The price-to-sales ratio computes the value of the firm divided by the estimated or recent sales levels.

For example, Roberts Manufacturing Company has sales of $100 million and an estimated (enterprise) value of $190 million (debt of $10.0 million and equity of $180.0 million).

$$\frac{\text{Enterprise Value}}{\text{Sales}} = \frac{\$190\text{m}}{\$100\text{m}} = 1.9\times$$

Other companies in this industry have price-to-sales ratios of 1.3 to 2.0. This would indicate a comparable valuation range of $130 million to $200 million for Roberts Manufacturing Company. The value-to-sales ratio for Roberts Manufacturing Company is within the range of similar or comparable companies, although at the high end of that range.

Advantages: The price-to-sales ratio is a simple, high-level measure.

Disadvantages/Limitations: The measure requires many implicit assumptions about key elements of financial performance, including growth rates, margins, capital requirements, and capital structure.

Price-Earnings (P/E) Ratio

The price-earnings (P/E) ratio compares the price of the stock to the firm's earnings. Using per-share information, the P/E ratio is calculated as follows:

$$\text{P/E Ratio} = \frac{\text{Stock Price}}{\text{Earnings per Share}}$$

For Roberts Manufacturing Company:

$$\frac{\$10.59}{\$0.56} = 18.95$$

The valuations of companies comparable to Roberts Manufacturing Company indicate a P/E ratio range of 16 to 20 times earnings. Roberts Manufacturing Company's stock price of \$10.59 is within the range indicated by the market research (\$8.94 to \$11.18) using the comparable P/E range.

This measure can also be computed at the firm level:

$$\frac{\text{Market Value of Equity}}{\text{Net Income}} = \frac{\$180.0\text{m}}{\$9.5\text{m}} = 18.95\times$$

Advantages: This method is simple to employ and commonly used in practice.

Disadvantages and Limitations: Several problems exist with this technique. First, earnings are accounting measures and not directly related to economic performance or cash flows. This has become an increasing problem in recent years as accounting profit continues to diverge from the underlying economic performance. Second, this measure also requires many implicit assumptions about key elements of financial performance, including growth rates, capital requirements, and capital structure.

Enterprise Value/Earnings before Interest and Taxes (EBIT)

This method compares the total value of the firm to the earnings before interest and taxes. Recall that EBIT generally approximates operating income. Since it is a measure of income before deducting interest expense, it represents income available to all investors, both equity (shareholders) and debt (bondholders). Therefore, we will compare this measure to the total value of the firm (EV).

$$\text{EV} = \frac{\text{Market Value of Equity} + \text{Market Value of Debt}}{\text{EBIT}}$$

For Roberts Manufacturing Company:

$$\text{EV} = \frac{\$180.0\text{m} + \$10.0\text{m}}{\$15.0\text{m}}$$

Advantages: This method is also simple to use. It results in valuations based on earnings available to all investors.

Disadvantages and Limitations: This method does not directly take into account other key elements of performance, such as growth or capital requirements.

Enterprise Value/EBITDA

This measure is very close to EV/EBIT, but uses EBITDA as a better approximation of cash flow, since it adds back the noncash charges, including depreciation and amortization (D&A).

For Roberts Manufacturing Company:

$$\frac{\text{EV}}{\text{EBITDA}} = \frac{\$190.0}{\$15.0 + \$3.75} = 10.13$$

Other similar companies are valued at 8 to 10 times EBITDA. Based on ratios for comparable companies, Roberts Manufacturing Company is valued just outside the high end of this range.

Advantages: This method is simple to apply and is based on an approximation of cash flow.

Disadvantages and Limitations: The primary limitation with this method is that it does not explicitly account for growth or future capital requirements.

Price-Earnings Growth or "PEG" Ratio

The price-earnings growth (PEG) ratio is a derivative of the price-earnings ratio that attempts to factor in the impact of growth in price-earnings multiples. The logic here is that there is a strong correlation between growth rates and P/E multiples. Companies with higher projected growth rates of earnings, for example technology companies, should have higher P/E ratios than firms with lower expected growth rates.

The PEG ratio is computed as follows:

$$\frac{\text{P/E Ratio}}{\text{Estimated EPS Growth Rate}}$$

For Roberts Manufacturing Company:

$$\frac{P/E}{\text{Growth } (\%)} = \frac{18.95}{8.0} = \text{PEG of } 2.37$$

Roberts Manufacturing Company has a very high PEG ratio relative to the peer group. This may reflect a number of factors: perhaps strong cash flows, or consistent operating performance relative to the benchmark group.

Advantages: This method reflects a key driver of valuation: expected growth.

Disadvantages and Limitations: Again, this measure does not directly reflect other key elements of financial performance.

BUILDING SHAREHOLDER VALUE IN A MULTIPLES FRAMEWORK

Many investors, analysts, and managers use multiples of earnings in investment and valuation decisions. Using multiples, there are two ways to build value. First, the firm can improve the base performance measure, for example earnings. The second way is to command a higher multiple. For illustration, let's assume that Roberts Manufacturing Company's valuation is being driven by capitalizing earnings (P/E ratio). The stock is valued at $10.59 because the firm earned $0.56 per share in earnings and the market has capitalized those earnings at approximately 19 times. The price of Roberts Manufacturing Company stock will rise when the earnings increase and/or if the market applies a higher multiple, for example increasing to 22 times earnings. In the latter case, the stock would trade at $12.32 (22 × $0.56).

Factors That Affect Multiples

What factors would cause the multiples to expand or contract? A variety of factors can contribute, including some specific to the firm and others that relate to the industry or even the general economy. Examples include expected growth rates, the quality of earnings, cash generation, perceived risk, and interest rates. A firm's P/E multiple should expand if it demonstrates a higher expected growth rate, improved working capital management, and/or more consistent operating performance. It will likely contract if it consistently misses financial targets, utilizes capital less effectively, or increases the perceived risk by entering a new market. In addition, economic factors such as changes in interest rates or expected economic conditions will cause multiples to expand or contract.

Use of Multiples in Setting Acquisition Values

Most of the multiples used in the previous discussion are typically derived from the valuation of other similar companies, industry averages, or broad market indexes. This is commonly referred to as the "trading multiple" – that is, the value set by trades in the equity markets. If a company is being considered as a potential acquisition target, the multiples will typically be adjusted to reflect a likely control or acquisition premium. These *acquisition values* are referred to as *transaction values* versus trading values, and the multiples would be derived by looking at transactions involving similar companies. Control premiums are typical for two reasons. First, boards and management teams are unlikely to surrender control of a company unless there is an immediate reward to the selling shareholders. In addition, the acquirer should be able to pay more than a passive investor, since it will be able to control the company and should be able to realize a higher growth in earnings and cash flow due to synergies with the acquiring company. Valuation for acquisition purposes is covered in Chapter 23, Analysis of Mergers and Acquisitions.

Trailing and Forward Multiples

When applying multiples of earnings, sales, and other measures, the analyst must select a base period. The value of the multiple will vary depending on whether the multiple is applied to actual past results (e.g. "trailing

12 months earnings") or a future period's estimated performance (e.g. "forward 12 months earnings"). The multiple applied to trailing earnings will be higher than the multiple applied to future earnings for two reasons: risk and the time value of money. There is risk associated with future earnings projections; they may not be achieved. The time value of money suggests that a dollar to be received next year is not worth a dollar today. These two factors result in a discount of the multiples used for future periods.

Adjusting or Normalizing the Base

Using multiples requires us to use a measure for a single period, typically a year. Many of the measures, such as sales or earnings, for the selected period may have been or are anticipated to be significantly impacted by a number of anomalous, or one-time, factors. For example, the current year earnings may include income that is not expected to continue into the future. Or perhaps the income includes a so-called nonrecurring adjustment to record a legal settlement or the closing of a plant. In these situations, companies and analysts may adjust the base to normalize the earnings, often referred to as pro forma or non-GAAP earnings.

This practice became very prevalent in the 1990s and led to a number of abuses. Certain companies were accused of being selective in choosing items to exclude, leading to a perceived overstatement of the earnings on a pro forma basis. The Securities and Exchange Commission subsequently placed significant constraints on reporting adjusted earnings. Several reasons gave rise to the use of pro forma measures:

Deficiencies in Generally Accepted Accounting Principles (GAAP). There has been a continuing divergence between GAAP accounting measures and economic results. Specific issues relate to accounting for acquisitions, income taxes, stock options, and pension plans.

Significant Restructuring, Divestitures, and Acquisitions. One-time or nonrecurring charges are reflected in earnings in a specific period based on very precise rules established by the accounting rule makers. However, a significant restructuring may be viewed as an investment for economic and valuation purposes. Acquisitions and divestitures may result in a disconnect between historical performance trends and future projections.

Some advocate using other measures, such as cash flow or economic profit, which adjust the accounting earnings to a measure with greater relevance in evaluating the economic value and performance of the firm.

Problems with Using Multiples

The use of multiples has several inherent limitations, especially for our purposes in linking shareholder value to operating performance.

- **Circular reference.** The basic logic with multiples is that one company's value is determined by looking at the valuation of other companies. This is very useful in comparing relative valuations and in testing the fairness of a company's valuation. Management teams and boards rely heavily on the use of multiples to review the fairness of acquisition prices. However, if the industry or peer group is overvalued, then this method will result in overvaluing the subject enterprise. This was a contributing factor to the technology/Internet (and other) market bubbles. The logic was that since dot.com1 was valued at 50 times sales, so should dot.com2, notwithstanding the fact that neither valuation was supported by basic economic fundamentals.
- **Implicit performance assumptions.** Another problem with this methodology is that it is not directly related to key value drivers or elements of financial performance. It is very difficult to understand the assumptions underlying values computed using multiples. If a firm is valued at 18 times earnings, what are the

underlying assumptions for revenue growth, working capital requirements, and other similar factors?

The market often attempts to cope with this limitation by increasing or decreasing the multiple over benchmarks to reflect factors such as consistency of performance, quality of earnings, lower or higher risk, and so forth. Such stocks would be described as "trading at a premium to the market based on" certain identified factors.

- **Selecting appropriate comparables.** Using multiples requires the analyst to select a set of comparable companies or a peer group. This can be a significant challenge. Few companies are so-called pure plays that are serving a single industry or match up closely with other companies. Further, choosing an appropriate benchmark or peer group can lead to great debates, since the process is both subjective and often emotionally charged.

INTEGRATED VALUATION SUMMARY FOR ROBERTS MANUFACTURING COMPANY

The individual valuation techniques described in this chapter should be combined to form a summary analysis of estimated valuation for Roberts Manufacturing Company. Each measure contributed a view of valuation that contributes to an overall picture. The numerical summary shown in Table 22.3 can be converted into a more user-friendly visual summary in Figure 22.3.

Roberts Manufacturing Company's current value is at the high end of the 12-month trading range and near or exceeding the top of the range for comparable companies. In this case, it would be important to understand the underlying performance characteristics of the benchmark group compared to Roberts Manufacturing Company. Is Roberts Manufacturing Company's valuation supported by better performance or higher future expectations of growth? The current market value approximates our estimate of the DCF value. This indicates that the market is probably expecting future performance in line with our projections used in the DCF.

TABLE 22.3 Roberts Manufacturing Company Valuation Summary Table

Valuation Analysis: Multiples					
				Benchmark Range	
	Value Basis		Roberts	Low	High
Sales		2018 Result	$100,000		
		Multiple	1.9	1.3	2.0
	Enterprise	Value/Indicated Range	$190,030	$130,000	$200,000
	Equity	Value/Indicated Range	$180,030	$120,000	$190,000
Earnings		2018 Result	$9,501		
		Multiple	18.95	16	20
	Equity	Value/Indicated Range	$180,030	$152,011	$190,014
		Per Share	10.59	8.94	11.18
EBITDA		2018 Result	$18,750		
		Multiple	10.13	8.00	10.00
	Enterprise	Value/Indicated Range	$190,030	$150,000	$187,500
	Equity	Value/Indicated Range	$180,030	$140,000	$177,500
Price-Earnings Growth		P/E	18.95		
		Estimated Growth (%)	8		
		PEG	2.37	1.3	2.0
DCF		Equity	Value	$186,352	NA	NA

FIGURE 22.3 Roberts Manufacturing Company Valuation Summary Graph 

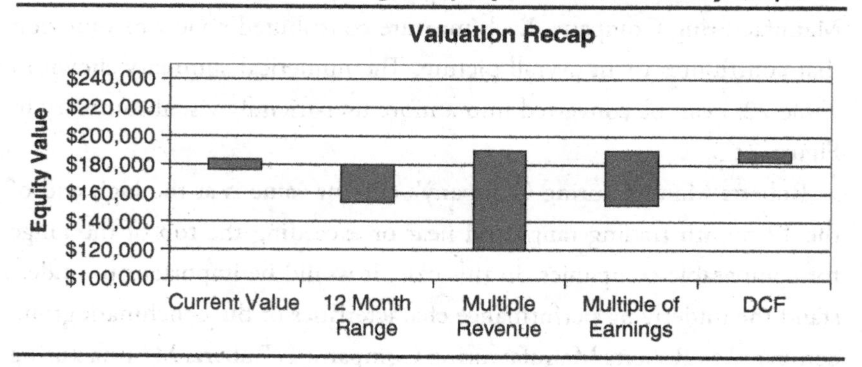

Comprehensive Valuation Summary

For fans of dashboards or one-page recaps, the comprehensive valuation summary (Figure 22.4) may be of interest. It combines a number of the

FIGURE 22.4 Valuation Summary

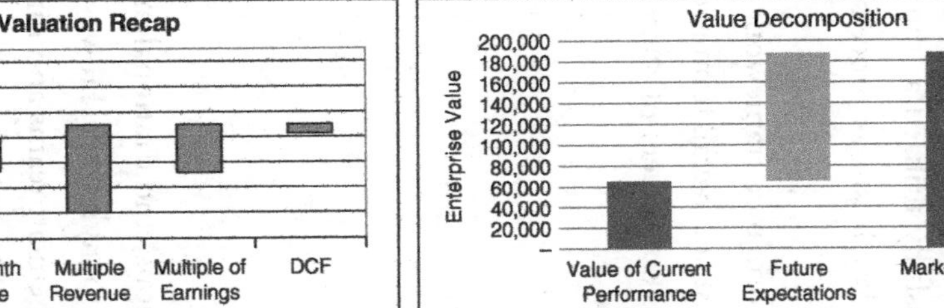

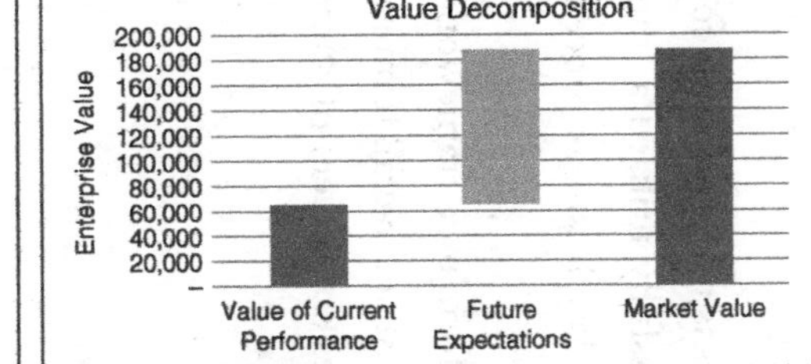

DCF Value Sensitivity Analysis

Roberts Manufacturing Co. — Stock Price

		Sales Growth Rate				
		4%	**6%**	**8%**	**10%**	**12%**
Operating Income %	**20.0%**	$12.11	$13.49	$15.04	$16.80	$18.77
	17.5%	$10.52	11.68	13.00	14.49	16.17
	15.0%	$8.92	9.88	10.96	12.18	13.56
	12.5%	$7.33	8.08	8.92	9.87	10.95
	10.0%	$5.74	6.27	6.88	7.57	8.34

Key DCF Assumptions:

- Sales Growth: 8% CAGR
- Profitability: Gross Margins and Expenses are assumed to remain constant from 2018 performance
- Historical Cap Ex and Operating Capital %'s

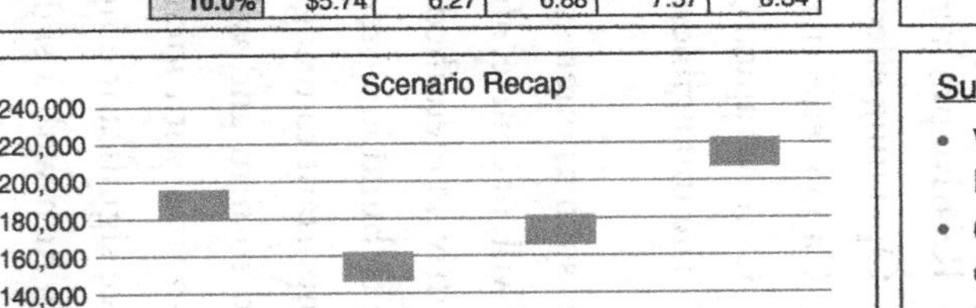

Summary

- Valuation is highly sensitive to Operating Income and Revenue Growth
- Current Performance accounts for only 35% of total value
- Sales Growth is critical to valuation!

tools we have reviewed in the chapter to present a very comprehensive view into the dynamics of the valuation of this company.

VALUE DRIVERS

The fundamental objective for most companies is to create value for shareholders. For these enterprises, we have successfully utilized a framework that links value creation and value drivers to key business processes and activities.

In Chapter 7, we introduced the value performance framework (VPF) (Figure 22.5) as one of several options to establish an overall framework for performance management. The VPF identifies six drivers of shareholder value:

1. Sales growth
2. Relative pricing strength
3. Operating effectiveness
4. Capital effectiveness
5. Cost of capital
6. The intangibles

Factors such as interest rates, market conditions, and irrational investor behavior will, of course, affect the price of a company's stock. However, the six value drivers identified are those that management teams and directors can drive to build long-term sustainable shareholder value.

It is important to recognize that the significance of each driver will vary from firm to firm and will also vary over time for a particular firm. For example, a firm with increased competition in a low-growth market will likely place significant emphasis on operating and capital effectiveness. In contrast, a firm with a significant opportunity for sales growth is likely to focus on that driver and place less emphasis on capital management or operating effectiveness. At some time in the future, however, this high-growth firm may have to deal with a slower growth rate and may have to shift emphasis to other drivers, such as operating efficiency and capital management.

FIGURE 22.5 The Value Performance Framework

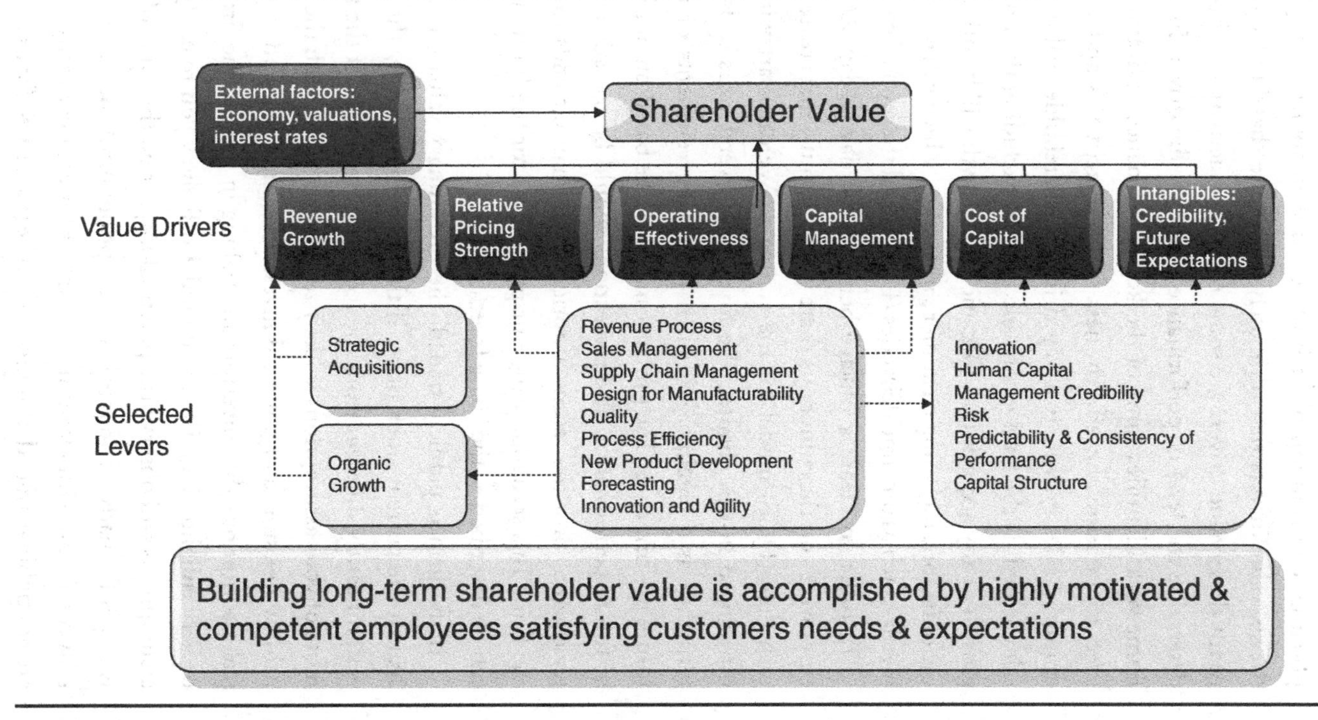

In order to attain its full potential value, a firm must understand the potential contribution of each driver to shareholder value. It starts with the six value drivers that ultimately determine shareholder value. Underneath these value drivers are some of the key activities and processes that determine the level of performance in each value driver. In addition, the framework identifies some of the key performance indicators that can be used to measure the effectiveness of these activities and processes. For example, sales growth is a key driver of shareholder value. A subset of sales growth is the level of organic growth, excluding the impact on sales growth of any acquisitions. Organic sales growth will be driven by a number of factors, including customer satisfaction, which can be tracked by key metrics such as on-time deliveries (OTDs) and the level of past-due orders.

In order to create a linkage between the day-to-day activities of the employees and the company's share value, we must first create a discounted cash flow (DCF) model for the company. We can start with the model introduced in this chapter. We first input several years of historical performance as a baseline, and then project key elements of the expected future performance. The projections should be based on our best estimate of future performance. The projections should be realistic and should be reviewed against the recent historical performance trends experienced by the firm. This scenario, using our projections for the future performance, can be described as the "base forecast."

If the firm is publicly traded, the preliminary valuation can be tested against the current stock price. If the value indicated by the DCF model is significantly different from the recent trading range of the stock, one or more of your assumptions is likely to be inconsistent with the assumptions held by investors and potential investors. Identifying and testing the critical assumptions that investors are making in valuing the firm's stock can be very enlightening. The DCF model will allow you to easily change key assumptions and observe the potential impact on the value of the stock. It is very informative to iterate key assumptions until you can achieve a valuation consistent with recent market values for your company. For firms that are not publicly traded, this process can be performed for a comparable firm or firms that are in the same industry. Growth rates, other key drivers, and valuation metrics can then be transferred to the private firm to understand value drivers and expectations for the industry.

After developing a perspective on valuation and value drivers, the second step is to identify the critical activities and processes that impact each value driver. While many of these critical processes and activities are common from business to business, their relative importance will vary significantly among companies. Further, every industry and firm has certain unique characteristics that must be identified and reflected in the framework. In Chapters 15 through 19, we examined each of the value drivers and linked those drivers to critical processes and activities.

This framework allows managers to evaluate potential improvement projects and identify high-leverage opportunities in the context of value creation. Too often, companies or functional managers embark on initiatives to improve certain aspects of the business without fully considering the impact on value creation. Will the initiatives be worth the investment of time and valuable resources? The VPF allows managers to rank various programs and address the following questions:

- How much value will be created if we accelerate sales growth from 5% to 10%?
- How much value will be created if we reduce manufacturing defects by 20%?
- How much value will be created if we reduce accounts receivable days sales outstanding (DSO) from 65 to 50 days? If we improve inventory turns from 4 to 6?
- Which of these programs will have the greatest impact on value?

Identifying High-Leverage Improvement Opportunities and Estimating Full Potential Value

Utilizing the tools of business process assessment, benchmarking, and discounted cash flow analysis, managers can estimate the potential

TABLE 22.4 Benchmarking Summary

Benchmarking Summary and Target Worksheet						
	Roberts Co.	Median	Top Quartile	Best in Class	Best Practice	Performance Target
Revenue Growth	8.0%	8.0%	12.0%	15.0%	25.0%	12.0%
Gross Margin %	55.0%	52.0%	56.0%	60.0%		56.0%
Operating Expenses	40.0%	40.0%	38.0%	35.0%		38.0%
Operating Margins	15.0%	12.0%	18.0%	20.0%	25.0%	18.0%
Tax rate	34.0%	30.0%	25.0%	15.0%	10.0%	25.0%
Operating Capital % Sales	30.0%	25.0%	15.0%	10.0%	15.0%	15.0%
WACC	11.99%	10.59%	10.13%	9.77%	9.07%	10%
Cost of Equity	12.4%	11.3%	11.0%	10.7%	9.8%	
Beta	1.24	1.05	1.00	0.95	0.80	
Debt to Total Capital						
Book	15.3%	30.0%	40.0%	50.0%	50.0%	
Market	5.3%	10.0%	13.3%	16.7%	16.7%	

improvements in the value drivers and quantify the effect on the value of the firm if the targeted performance is achieved. We start with the benchmarking summary developed in Chapter 11 (see Table 22.4).

In this case, Roberts Manufacturing Company has set preliminary performance targets to achieve top-quartile performance in each key measure in Table 22.4. Using the DCF model, the value created by each change can be estimated. The value of the firm could be increased from $196.4 million to $389 million if each of the performance improvements is realized. (See Table 22.5.) This may be a good place to start, but requires additional vetting. The targets should be refined by evaluating processes and operating effectiveness and testing the relative impact on value creation to develop a target business model. This exercise is not meaningful unless the team has a plan for *how* these improvements will be achieved.

A graphic presentation of this analysis is shown in Figure 22.6.

Projecting improved performance on spreadsheets is very easy. Achieving these improvements in actual results requires substantial planning, effort, and follow-through. Central to achieving these performance goals is the selection and development of effective performance measures.

TABLE 22.5 Summary of Full Potential Value

	From	To	Value	Enterprise Increment	How?
Current Value			196.4		Current Performance Expectations
Increase Sales Growth Rate	8%	12%	241	44.6	Improve Quality and On-Time Delivery
Improve Gross Margin %	55%	56%	259	18	Reduce Material Costs
Reduce Operating Expenses	40%	38%	294	53	Process Initiatives
Reduce Tax Rate	34%	25%	338	97	Tax Benefits from New Manufacturing Facility
Reduce Operating Capital %	30%	15%	352	111	Improve Supply Chain and Revenue Process
Reduce WACC	12%	10%	389	148	Improve Forecasting and Change Capital Structure

FIGURE 22.6 Estimating Full Potential Valuation

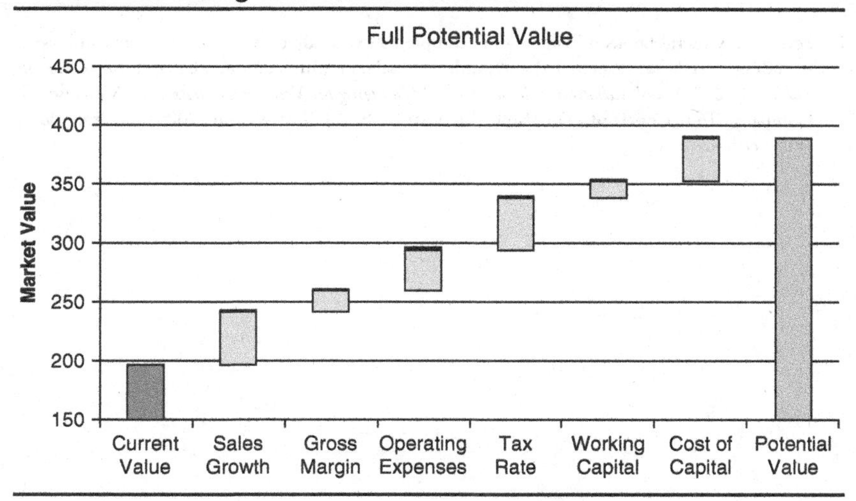

SUMMARY

While each of the valuation techniques has limitations, they do provide insight from a variety of perspectives. It is best to use a combination of measures and techniques in reviewing the valuation of a firm. When an analyst summarizes these measures for a firm and compares them to key benchmarks, significant insights can be gained. Conversely, inconsistencies across the valuation measures for a company are worth exploring and can usually be explained by identifying a specific element of financial performance that the measure doesn't reflect. For example, a company that consistently meets or exceeds operating plans and market expectations will typically be afforded a higher P/E multiple than its peers, and the company will trade at a premium to the industry norms.

Managers can use the DCF valuation model to estimate potential growth in value resulting from improving performance across key value drivers.

Given this foundation in valuation, we will turn our attention to unique issues in analyzing and valuing mergers and acquisitions in Chapter 23.

NOTE

1. Several very useful books provide a more comprehensive study on valuation concepts and tools, including *Investment Valuation* by Aswath Damodaran (3rd edition, 2012), *Damodaran on Valuation* (2006), and *Valuation: Measuring and Managing the Value of Companies* by McKinsey & Company, Tom Copeland, Tim Koller, and Jack Murrin (3rd edition, 2000), all from John Wiley & Sons.

23

ANALYSIS OF MERGERS AND ACQUISITIONS

CHAPTER INTRODUCTION

There probably is no other business decision that can create or destroy value more than mergers and acquisitions (M&A). Managers and boards pursue acquisitions for many reasons. Understanding the rationale for an acquisition is a key element of evaluating a potential deal, assessing the likelihood of success, and determining the reasonableness of the deal price. Successful acquirers have a clear acquisition strategy that flows out of a well-defined business strategy. In addition, they typically have competencies in evaluating and valuing potential acquisitions, discipline in pricing deals, and managers with experience in integrating acquisitions. We will focus on the analysis and economics of mergers and acquisitions in this chapter.

THE ACQUISITION CHALLENGE

Many managers, academics, and advisers believe that it is difficult to create value through acquisitions. Research studies over the years consistently report a low percentage of acquisitions that are ultimately successful in creating value for the shareholders of the acquiring firm. The cards are stacked against acquirers, since they typically have to pay a premium to close the transaction and assume risk of integration and execution. In addition, many common mistakes lead to problems in valuing, negotiating, and integrating acquisitions and are discussed later in this chapter. However, many companies do have successful acquisition programs that have resulted in building value for shareholders over a long period of time. The best practices that these companies employ are also discussed later in this chapter.

The stock market's reaction to proposed transactions can be informative. Following the announcement of a proposed transaction, the price of the acquirer's stock will typically fall. At the same time, the price of a target's stock will generally rise to a price at or just under the announced acquisition price.

Why does the market react this way? The market typically reacts negatively to the acquiring firm's announcement for several reasons. First, investors recognize that acquirers generally are forced to pay a significant premium and that most deals do not build value for the shareholders of the acquiring firm. Second, they may feel that this specific deal is overpriced. Finally, they recognize that all the risk of implementing the combined strategy and integrating the two organizations is transferred to the acquiring firm. It is interesting to note, though, that the market doesn't always react negatively to acquisition announcements. For companies with strong acquisition programs and track records, a clear strategic rationale, and a reputation for disciplined pricing, the market price of the acquirer's stock may hold steady or even increase on news of a deal.

The price of the acquired company's stock will rise to approximate the proposed value of the deal. Since there is a good chance that the selling shareholders would receive the deal value at the time of closing, the price trades up toward that level. If, however, the market perceives significant risk that the deal will not be completed, for example due to expected difficulty in obtaining regulatory approvals, then the stock will trade at a discount to the proposed deal price. As impediments to the deal are removed, the stock will trade closer to the deal price. If the market was speculating that another potential buyer might make an offer for the target, the stock price may even rise above the announced deal value in anticipation of an offer from another bidder.

KEY ELEMENTS IN VALUING AN ACQUISITION

In valuing acquisitions, it is useful to identify and value two components: the value of the company to be acquired (the target) as a stand-alone company and the value of any potential synergies arising from the acquisition.

Stand-Alone Value

The stand-alone value is the worth of a company presuming that it continues to operate on a stand-alone or independent basis. Most publicly traded companies are valued on this basis, unless there are rumors or expectations that the company is a potential acquisition candidate. The stand-alone value is computed using the methodologies described in Chapter 22, Business Valuation and Value Drivers. We will illustrate the mergers and acquisitions (M&A) valuation concepts in this chapter building on the Roberts Manufacturing Company example, presented previously in Table 22.1.

Synergies

Synergies are a critical element in valuing acquisitions. Few, if any, companies will be sold on the basis of the value of that company on a stand-alone basis. Synergies are generally understood to result where the combined results exceed the sum of the independent parts. For purposes of this discussion, we will use synergies to mean the additional economic benefits that will be achieved by combining two companies. The term *economic benefit* is used here to emphasize that any synergy must be realizable in future cash flows to be relevant in valuation.

Synergies can take many forms. Common types of synergies include higher sales growth, reduced costs and expenses, financial benefits, and improved management practices.

Sales Growth. Sales growth is always an important consideration in valuation. Drivers of sales growth resulting from M&A transactions include:

- *Leverage existing distribution channel(s).* The sales growth rate of the target may be accelerated if the acquirer can sell the target's products through existing distribution channels (or vice versa). For example, the acquirer may have a strong international distribution organization in a region where the target's presence is weak or nonexistent.
- *Address a new market or develop new products with combined competencies.* The combination of technical competencies from two organizations may result in a new product, channel, or technology that will accelerate sales growth.

Reduced Costs. Nearly all acquisitions contemplate some reduction in costs. Common examples include:

- *Eliminate redundant costs and expenses.* The acquirer may not need to maintain the target's procurement or administrative functions. For example, when two publicly traded companies are combined, many of the corporate functions at one of the companies can be eliminated, including the board of directors, investor relations, and financial reporting.
- *Leverage scale and purchasing power.* The combined purchasing power of the two organizations may result in reduced prices for materials or services.

Financial Synergies. Significant value can be created by leveraging the acquirer's lower cost of capital to the target. This is sometimes viewed as financial engineering by many operating managers. However, the cost of capital is a significant driver of value, and even a modest reduction can result in a significant increase to value. By providing a previously independent firm with the acquirer's access to capital, borrowing power, and lower interest rates, a substantial increase in earnings power and valuation may be realized.

Transferance of Best Practices. The acquiring company may have innovative business practices that can be transferred to the target (or vice versa). For example, a highly effective product development process may reduce the product development cycle and time to market, thereby reducing product development costs and increasing sales. One of the companies may have a highly effective strategic planning framework or experience in improving operations that will lead to tangible improvements in financial performance for its merger partner.

Beware of Vague Synergies

Over time, the word *synergies* has taken on negative connotations because of the loose use of this term in describing benefits from M&A transactions. Many deals have been justified over time by invoking the *synergy* word to describe vague or intangible benefits resulting from the transaction. Synergies must be specifically identified, supported by detailed implementation plans, and assigned to managers who will be held accountable for capturing the benefits that result in growth in value for shareholders.

Potential Acquisition Value

The potential economic value resulting from an acquisition is the sum of the stand-alone value and the value of expected synergies as shown in Figure 23.1.

METHODS AND METRICS FOR VALUING AN ACQUISITION

A variety of valuation methods and metrics are utilized in practice, including:

- Accounting and comparable methods
    - Earnings per share accretive-dilutive test

FIGURE 23.1 Stand-Alone and Synergies Value

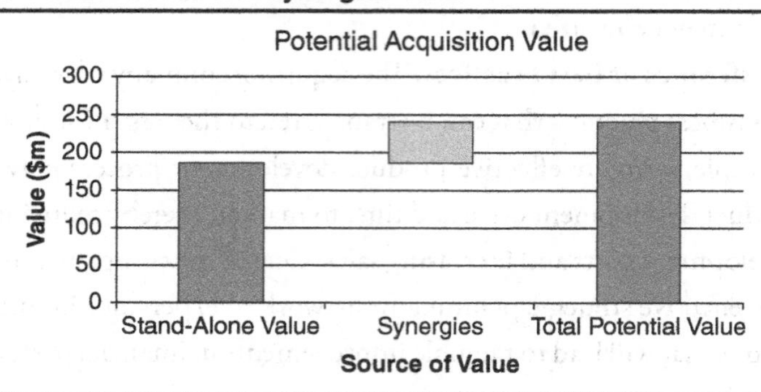

- Comparable or relative pricing methods: multiples of revenues, earnings, and cash flow
  - Control premium analysis
- Economic measures and tests
  - Discounted cash flow
  - Economic profit/ROIC test
  - Internal rate of return (IRR)/net present value (NPV)

Each of these methods has strengths and limitations. Each can play a role in developing a comprehensive view of a potential deal. We will illustrate these methods using a proposed acquisition of Roberts Manufacturing Company (RMC) by Sheridan Acquisition Company (SAC). SAC is offering to acquire all of the outstanding shares of Roberts Manufacturing Company for $233.8 million in cash and will assume the $10 million in debt outstanding, resulting in a total acquisition cost of 243.8. Key assumptions are detailed in Table 23.1.

Accounting and Comparable Methods

Earnings per Share (EPS) Accretive-Dilutive Test. Since EPS is a critical measure of performance for a company, especially those

TABLE 23.1 Sheridan Acquisition Company Acquires Roberts Manufacturing Company

$m		Assumptions	
SAC Forecast		**2020E**	
Sales		1,000	
PBT		100	
Tax		−34	
PAT		66	
Shares		64	
EPS		1.03	
Price-Earning Ratio		20.0	
Acquisition Financing:			
	Debt, at interest rate of:	6%	
Synergies			
Revenue	The merger would result in $20m of additional sales beginning in 2020. The sales are estimated to result in a 55% gross margin and 30% operating expenses. Working capital requirements are estimated at 30% of sales; no additional capital expenditures will be required.		
Cost savings	The merger would result in $6m of annual savings beginning in 2020 and would cost $2m in 2019 to implement.		
	Cost Savings:		
	G&A		2.0
	R&D		1.0
	Material cost savings		1.0
	Plant closings		2.0
			6.0

trading in public capital markets, it is very important to understand the impact of an acquisition on EPS. The basic test is to determine if the acquirer's EPS will increase (accrete) or decrease (dilute) as a result of pursuing a specific acquisition. A rule of thumb used by many managers, bankers, and investors is that a deal should be accretive within a short period of time, often 12 months. The method involves identifying all of the various ways an acquisition will affect EPS. Examples include:

Favorable to EPS	Unfavorable to EPS
Profits contributed by the acquired firm	Expenses related to the acquisition
Profits from sales synergies	Amortization of goodwill (in certain cases)
Reduced costs	Amortization of other intangibles
	Capital required to finance the acquisition:
	Additional shares issued to acquire company
	Interest expense on debt issued to finance deal
	Forgone interest on cash utilized

Goodwill arising from an acquisition is carried on the balance sheet and evaluated for recoverability on an annual basis. Historically, prior to 2001, goodwill was amortized and reported as an expense in the income statement. Under current rules, goodwill amortization expense is typically excluded from the income statement, thereby lowering the bar in the accretive-dilutive test. Since the EPS test does not fully reflect the true cost of capital for the acquisition, it will result in a positive impact on earnings long before earning an economic return. Table 23.2 illustrates the accretive-dilutive test for the Sheridan Acquisition Co.–Roberts Manufacturing Co. transaction.

This deal as presented would be accretive to earnings in the first full year after the acquisition, since the earnings contributed by the target and expected synergies exceed the financing costs. EPS will increase from $1.03 prior to the acquisition to $1.17 reflecting the acquisition. If the investors are focusing on EPS and using a P/E multiple to value the company (and if the P/E multiple remains constant), the price of the acquiring company's stock will rise from $20.63 to $23.49 per share.

TABLE 23.2 Accretive-Dilutive Test Illustration

Steady State- First Fiscal Year (2020)

	Sheridan	**Acquisition**					
$m	**Acq. Co.**	Roberts Co.	Synergies	Financing	Amortization	Total	**Combined**
Sales	1,000.0	116.6	20.0			136.6	1,136.6
PBT	100.0	17.5	11.0	−14.6		13.9	113.9
Tax	−34.0	−5.9	−3.7	5.0	0.0	−4.7	−38.7
PAT	66.0	11.5	7.3	−9.7	0.0	9.2	75.2
Shares	64.0	64.0	64.0	64.0	64.0	64.0	64.0
EPS	1.03	0.18	0.11	−0.15	0.00	0.14	1.17
Implied SAC Stock Price	$ 20.63						$ 23.49

What about the economics of the transaction? What is the hurdle rate implied in this EPS analysis? That is, what is the required rate of return on the capital used to purchase this company to break even on EPS? The hurdle rate implied in this EPS accretion test is 4.0%. If profit after tax (PAT) exceeds the after-tax financing costs of $9.7 million, the deal will be accretive to (i.e. add to) earnings. Since the total purchase price of the acquisition, including assumed debt, is $243.8 million, the hurdle rate is 4.0%, as follows:

$$\frac{\text{After-Tax Financing Expense}}{\text{Purchase Price}} = \frac{\$9.7\text{m}}{\$243.8\text{m}} = 4.0\%$$

Is 4.0% an appropriate return for shareholders on this transaction? Hardly. Historically, investors could typically earn a higher rate by investing in essentially risk-free US Treasury notes. In all investment decisions, the hurdle rate should be based on the specific risk associated with the investment. In acquisitions, the hurdle rate should be based on the target's risk profile adjusted for any perceived addition/reduction in risk due to the acquisition.

In spite of the reduced usefulness (under the rules eliminating goodwill amortization) of the accretive-dilutive metric, bankers, managers, and analysts continue to use it as a primary measure of the financial performance of an acquisition. If you listen to any conference call announcing an acquisition, EPS accretion-dilution will likely be prominently featured. It is certainly important to understand and communicate the EPS effect of a deal. However, it is not a comprehensive economic test.

Comparable or Relative Pricing Methods: Multiples of Revenues, Earnings, and Cash Flow

Nearly all acquisition decisions will include an analysis of the pricing of similar companies in recent acquisitions. This is an important tool to determine how pricing of a proposed transaction compares with the pricing of other recent deals. This process is no different than evaluating the pricing of residential real estate. Prior to negotiating on the purchase price of a home, real estate brokers provide a "comp listing," which summarizes transaction prices on recent home sales in the area. In a similar way, investment bankers and corporate development managers will identify recent transactions in the industry and compute key valuation metrics such as enterprise value/EBITDA and EV/revenue. These valuation metrics are then used to set or evaluate the pricing of the deal under review.

Generally, acquirers must pay a "full" or "strong" value (often euphemisms for overpaying) in order to convince the target's management and board that they should sell the company. Sometimes acquirers offer preemptive bids to discourage the target from considering other potential acquirers. Further, many companies are sold through auctions, where they are essentially marketed to a large number of potential buyers. The winner of this process is typically the highest bidder. All of these factors put upward pressure on the transaction prices. Therefore, managers who wish to build economic value through an acquisition program must recognize that the comparable transaction valuation methodology has a strong upward bias on transaction pricing.

Control Premium Analysis. A control or acquisition premium is the difference between the acquisition price and the market value of a public company prior to the acquisition announcement. Control premiums are often measured from the date preceding the announcement of a transaction. If the market is anticipating an acquisition, it is likely that a substantial part of an expected premium is already reflected in the stock price. Therefore, it is important to examine the stock trading history for the target over the past 12 to 18 months. It is possible that investors are expecting an acquisition and have partially or fully reflected an acquisition premium in the price of the stock. Table 23.3 shows the control premiums for the Sheridan Acquisition Co.–Roberts Manufacturing Co. transaction.

SAC's proposed purchase price of $13.75 per share represents a 30% premium over the price the day preceding the announcement of the deal. It represents a 30% premium over the 12-month high and a 49% premium over the 12-month low.

Economics-Based Measures

Despite their shortcomings, both the accretive-dilutive test and comparable methods are useful tools in the decision process. The danger in placing too much reliance on these methods results from two factors. First, neither method reflects the full economics of the deal, since they do not utilize an appropriate measure of return on the capital invested. Second, the measures do not require explicit assumptions about the total performance

TABLE 23.3 Control Premium Analysis

Roberts Manufacturing Co.			
Shares Outstanding (m)	17.0		
		%	$m
Acquisition price (per share)	13.75		233.8
Price (1 day prior to announcement)	10.59		180.0
Acquisition premium	3.16	30%	53.7
12 month trading range -High	10.59	30%	
-Low	9.22	49%	

of the combined businesses. Therefore, it is difficult to understand the performance expectations that are built into a comparables pricing analysis. How can operating managers understand what performance they are signing up for under these measures?

The use of the EPS accretive-dilutive test and multiples pricing methods should be complemented by economic tools, including discounted cash flow (DCF). The DCF analysis should include a "base case" valuation and sensitivity/scenario analyses to understand the impact of critical assumptions on valuation. Similarly, acquirers should estimate the expected economic return using return on invested capital (ROIC) or similar measures.

Discounted Cash Flow. Discounted cash flow (DCF) should be an integral element of any valuation and certainly in acquisition analysis. The advantage in using DCF is that it requires managers to make explicit assumptions about future performance. We would start with the discounted cash flow projection presented earlier in Table 22.1. This DCF for Roberts Manufacturing Company would be for a stand-alone or independent valuation, since we have not yet considered any changes that may result from an acquisition by another company. A simplified version of the stand-alone DCF for Roberts Manufacturing Company is presented in Table 23.4.

We must now determine the potential value of Roberts Manufacturing Company if acquired by Sheridan Acquisition Co. There are two ways to estimate the economic value of proposed synergies. One method is simply to change the financial projections in the DCF for higher sales growth or reduced costs arising from the acquisition in the DCF analysis and record the revised value (Table 23.5).

The second method is to compute the economic value of each synergy directly. The projected cash flow for each synergy is discounted to estimate the economic value today in Table 23.6. Note that the two methods result in the same value.

TABLE 23.4 DCF Stand-Alone

			Roberts Manufacturing Co.								
			2018	2019	2020	2021	2022	2023	2024	2025	2026
Sales		0	100,000.0	108,000.0	116,640.0	125,971.2	136,048.9	146,932.8	158,687.4	171,382.4	185,093.0
Gross Margin	55%			59,400.0	64,152.0	69,284.2	74,826.9	80,813.0	87,278.1	94,260.3	101,801.2
%				55%	55%	55%	55%	55%	55%	55%	55%
Cost Synergies											
SG&A				43,200.0	46,656.0	50,388.5	54,419.6	58,773.1	63,475.0	68,553.0	74,037.2
Total Operating Expenses				43,200.0	46,656.0	50,388.5	54,419.6	58,773.1	63,475.0	68,553.0	74,037.2
%				40%	40%	40%	40%	40%	40%	40%	40%
Operating Income				16,200.0	17,496.0	18,895.7	20,407.3	22,039.9	23,803.1	25,707.4	27,764.0
%				15%	15%	15%	15%	15%	15%	15%	15%
Tax	34%			5,508.0	5,948.6	6,424.5	6,938.5	7,493.6	8,093.1	8,740.5	9,439.7
EBIAT				10,692.0	11,547.4	12,471.1	13,468.8	14,546.3	15,710.1	16,966.9	18,324.2
Depreciation				5,000.0	5,400.0	5,832.0	6,298.6	6,802.4	7,346.6	7,934.4	8,569.1
Capital Expenditures				−5,400.0	−5,832.0	−6,298.6	−6,802.4	−7,346.6	−7,934.4	−8,569.1	−9,254.7
WC Increase	−30%			−2,400.0	−2,592.0	−2,799.4	−3,023.3	−3,265.2	−3,526.4	−3,808.5	−4,113.2
FCF				7,892.0	8,523.4	9,205.2	9,941.6	10,737.0	11,595.9	12,523.6	13,525.5
Acquisition Costs				0.0	0.0	0.0	0.0	0.0	0.0	0.0	0.0
TV											293,187.3
Cash Flow (CF)				7,892.0	8,523.4	9,205.2	9,941.6	10,737.0	11,595.9	12,523.6	306,712.8
Present Value CF (discount rate):		12%		7,892	7,610	7,338	7,076	6,824	6,580	6,345	138,741
Sum PVFCF			188,406								
Excess Cash			7,944								
Estimated Value of the Enterprise			196,350								
Value of Debt			10,000						TV P/E 16x	16.00	
Estimated Value of Equity			186,350								

TABLE 23.5 DCF Synergy and Stand-Alone

		2018	2019	2020	2021	2022	2023	2024	2025	2026
						DCF Synergy + Stand-Alone				
					SAC acquires Roberts Manufacturing Co.					
Sales		100,000	108,000	136,640	145,971	156,049	166,933	178,687	191,382	205,093
GM	55%		59,400	75,152	80,284	85,827	91,813	98,278	105,260	112,801
%			55%	55%	55%	55%	55%	55%	55%	55%
Cost Synergies			2,000.0	−6,000.0	−6,000.0	−6,000.0	−6,000.0	−6,000.0	−6,000.0	−6,000.0
SGA			43,200.0	52,656.0	56,388.5	60,419.6	64,773.1	69,475.0	74,553.0	80,037.2
Total Operating Expenses			45,200.0	46,656.0	50,388.5	54,419.6	58,773.1	63,475.0	68,553.0	74,037.2
%			42%	34%	35%	35%	35%	36%	36%	36%
Operating Income			14,200.0	28,496.0	29,895.7	31,407.3	33,039.9	34,803.1	36,707.4	38,764.0
%			13.1%	20.9%	20.5%	20.1%	19.8%	19.5%	19.2%	18.9%
Tax	34%		4,828.0	9,688.6	10,164.5	10,678.5	11,233.6	11,833.1	12,480.5	13,179.7
EBIAT			9,372.0	18,807.4	19,731.1	20,728.8	21,806.3	22,970.1	24,226.9	25,584.2
Depreciation			5,000.0	5,400.0	5,832.0	6,298.6	6,802.4	7,346.6	7,934.4	8,569.1
Capital Expenditures			−5,400.0	−5,832.0	−6,298.6	−6,802.4	−7,346.6	−7,934.4	−8,569.1	−9,254.7
WC Increase	−30%		−2,400.0	−8,592.0	−2,799.4	−3,023.3	−3,265.2	−3,526.4	−3,808.5	−4,113.2
FCF			6,572.0	9,783.4	16,465.2	17,201.6	17,997.0	18,855.9	19,783.6	20,785.5
Acquisition Costs			–	–	–	–	–	–	–	–
TV										353,687.3
Cash Flow			6,572.0	9,783.4	16,465.2	17,201.6	17,997.0	18,855.9	19,783.6	374,472.8
			6,572.0	9,783.4	16,465.2	17,201.6	17,997.0	18,855.9	19,783.6	374,472.8
Present Value (discount rate)	12%		6,572	8,735	13,126	12,244	11,437	10,699	10,023	169,392
Sum PVFCF		242,229								
Excess Cash		7,944								
Estimated Value of the Enterprise		250,173								
Value of Debt		10,000					TV Roberts Co.: P/E 16x			
Estimated Value of Equity		240,173					TV PHG Synergies: 0%			

The value of equity from Table 23.5 is $240.2 million. This is consistent with the sum of:

Roberts Manufacturing Co. Stand-Alone (Table 23.4)	$186.4m
Value of Synergies (Table 23.6)	53.8
Total	$240.2m

The advantage in using the detailed synergy method in Table 23.6 is that managers understand the specific contribution to value of each projected synergy as well as the stand-alone value of Roberts Manufacturing Company. This is useful in evaluating the probability and risks associated with each synergy. Not all synergies are created equal. For example, there may

TABLE 23.6 Synergy Valuation and Control Premium Test

Roberts Manufacturing Co.					
Cost of Capital	12%				
Tax Rate	34%				
Synergy Valuation:		EBIT	EBIAT/CF	PV	
Revenue	20.0	5.0	3.3	27.5	
Cost Savings					
G&A		2.0	1.3	11.0	
R&D		1.0	0.7	5.5	
Material cost savings		1.0	0.7	5.5	
lant closings		2.0	1.3	11.0	
Total		11.0	7.3	60.5	
PV of Synergies			60.5		
Less Working Capital on Revenue Growth	30%		−5.4(1)		
Implementation Costs (synergies)	2.0		−1.3(2)		
PV of Estimated Synergies			53.8		Excess/GAP
Control Premium ($m)			53.7		0.1

Notes
(1) $6m in year 2020, discounted for 1 period
(2) $2m pretax in 2019

be substantially more risk associated with sales growth expected in three to four years. However, the probability of achieving expected administrative savings should be relatively high.

In addition to estimating the value of each synergy, this analysis indicates that the total value of estimated synergies approximates the control premium in this deal. Presuming that the market is valuing the Roberts Manufacturing Company at a reasonable economic value (indicated by the stand-alone DCF analysis), the full value of potential synergies is being transferred to the shareholders of the selling firm. Comparing the value of potential synergies to the control premium is a useful test. The dynamics of this macro test are shown in Figure 23.2.

Combining the estimated stand-alone valuation with the estimates of each projected synergy results in the DCF valuation summary in Figure 23.3.

Economic Profit Test. Another sobering test in M&A analysis is to estimate the economic profit required to earn an acceptable return on the capital invested to acquire the business. Management must earn a return at least equal to the firm's cost of capital to create value for shareholders. Table 23.7 illustrates the economic profit/ROIC test for the Roberts Manufacturing Company acquisition. The total economic purchase price

FIGURE 23.2 Control Premium–Synergies Macro Test

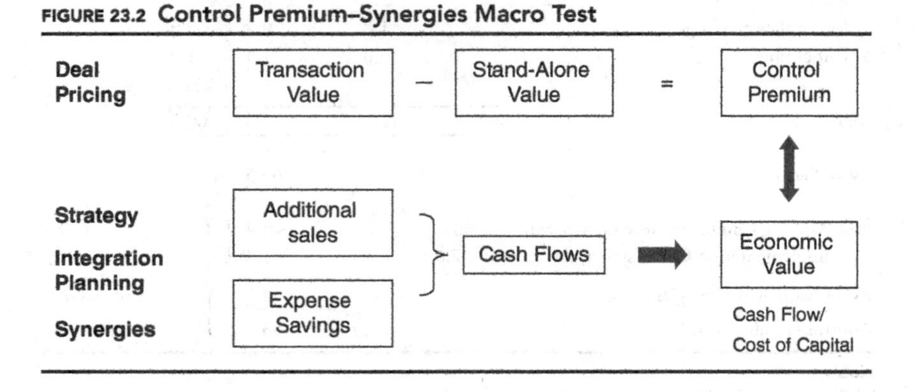

FIGURE 23.3 Sources of Acquisition Value

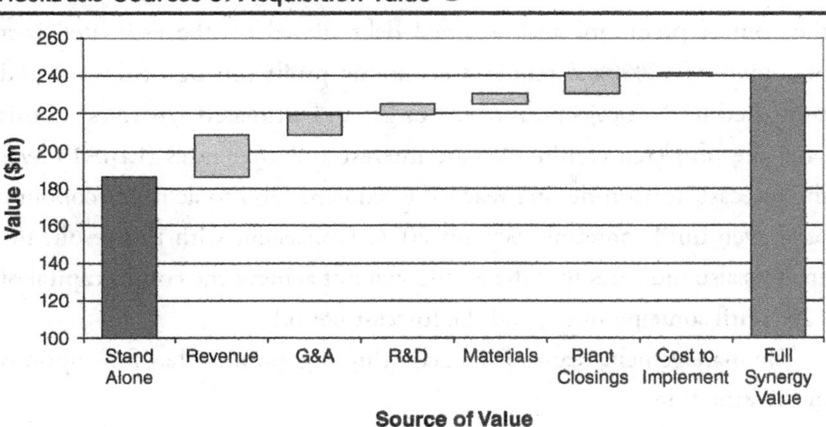

TABLE 23.7 Economic Profit/ROIC Test

$m	Economic Profit Test SAC acquires Roberts Manufacturing Co.								
Market Value of Company (prior to announcement)	$180.0								
Control Premium	53.7								
Assumed Debt	10.0								
Total Transaction Value (Invested Capital)	243.8								
Cost of Capital	12%								
Required Annual EBIAT for Economic Breakeven	29.3								
		2019	2020	2021	2022	2023	2024	2025	2026
Projected EBIAT (Table 23.5)		9.4	18.8	19.7	20.7	21.8	23.0	24.2	25.6
Required		29.3	29.3	29.3	29.3	29.3	29.3	29.3	29.3
Excess (deficit) EBIAT		−19.9	−10.4	−9.5	−8.5	−7.4	−6.3	−5.0	−3.7
ROIC (on transaction value)		3.8%	7.7%	8.1%	8.5%	8.9%	9.4%	9.9%	10.5%

of $243.8 million will include the market value of the target (stand-alone), the control premium, and assumed debt. Based on the estimated cost of capital of 12%, the required economic profit can be computed and compared to the projections of the target and estimated synergies. In this case, the projected earnings before interest and after taxes (EBIAT) over the forecast horizon doesn't reach the required level to achieve economic breakeven until sometime beyond 2026. Consistent with this result, the analysis also indicates that the ROIC will not achieve the cost of capital of 12% until some point beyond the forecast period.

The management team of the acquiring organization has four options in this situation:

1. Consider reducing the acquisition price.
2. Walk away.
3. Increase the projected performance to justify the price.
4. Proceed with the transaction (and overpay).

Unfortunately, too often managers select either option 3 or 4. Many proceed with the deal terms and argue that the economic analysis is not relevant or indicative of the value in the transaction. Often, they argue that the deal is strategic and that the financial analysis does not properly capture the strategic value. If the financials do not fully reflect the strategic case and expected synergies, then they should be revised. In other cases, the financial projections are increased to support the deal price. Presuming that the base projections were realistic estimates of future performance, this option may increase the risk of failing to achieve the financial results.

Internal Rate of Return and Net Present Value Analysis. An acquisition of a company is a specific and complex form of a capital investment. Therefore, it should be subject to the same tests as a new product proposal, plant expansion, or other capital expenditures described in Chapter 20.

		Source
Present Value of Cash Flows—Stand-Alone	$186.4	Table 23.4
Present Value of Cash Flows—Synergies	53.8	Table 23.6
Total Present Value of Cash Flows to Equity	240.2	
Purchase Price of Equity	(233.8)	
NPV	6.4	
IRR	12.5%	

The NPV is a small positive result and the IRR just exceeds of the cost of capital of 12%. This test indicates that the economics of the transaction satisfy the economic tests, although marginally. These results in NPV and IRR are consistent with the economic profit/ROIC test that indicated that breakeven returns would not be attained until sometime after 2026. While technically satisfying the economic tests, management of Sheridan Acquisition Co. should consider whether the value created and returns earned are commensurate with the effort and risk in proceeding with the transaction.

Comparative Summary of Valuation Methods

We have reviewed a number of different valuation methodologies and metrics. It is helpful to summarize the indicated values from these differing methods, as illustrated in Figure 23.4. It is quite common for the methods to result in a wide range of potential transaction values. A useful exercise is to compare and contrast the estimated value ranges and understand the underlying factors resulting in wide valuation ranges and sometimes even inconsistent results.

Day of Reckoning for Underperforming Acquisitions

The goodwill resulting from an acquisition (illustrated previously in Table 18.3) will be tested for recoverability at least annually under the accounting rules affecting most organizations. This test will require an annual review

FIGURE 23.4 Comparative Value Summary: Acquisition of Roberts Manufacturing Company

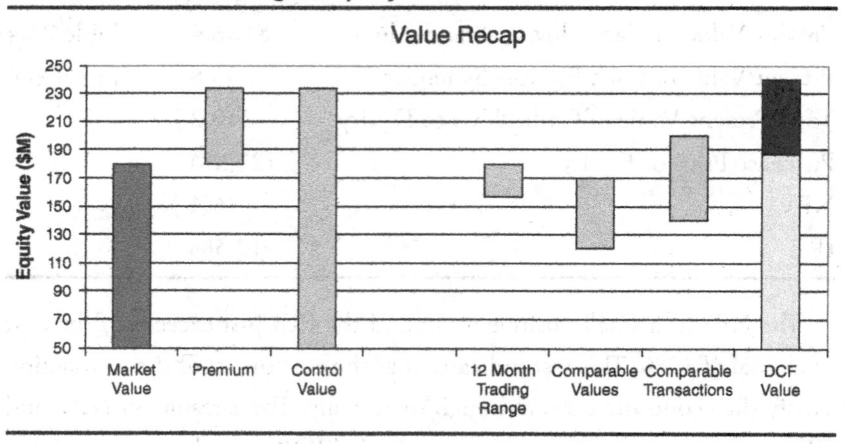

to determine if the acquisition is performing at levels sufficient to justify carrying the assets on the balance sheet. The test utilized is essentially a market-based valuation, often utilizing discounted cash flow analysis. This annual test has and will continue to result in a day of reckoning for many acquisitions. In fact, since the new standard was adopted, billions of dollars of goodwill have been written off, indicating that the acquisitions did not perform at a level that would earn an acceptable return on the original purchase price.

COMMON MISTAKES IN M&A

A number of common mistakes contribute to the difficulty in earning a return for shareholders of the acquiring firm. Many managers feel compelled to pursue acquisitions because their companies' organic growth rate has slowed or is about to slow. Sales growth is a key value driver, and the public capital markets place a huge premium on growth. Associates, executives, and directors want to serve growing organizations. In addition, mature organizations typically generate cash that exceeds operating requirements and are pressured to deploy this cash (or return it to shareholders). As the business matures and organic growth begins to slow, they may embark on an acquisition program. This is fine if the program is well thought out and if the team acquires or develops resources necessary to execute an effective acquisition program. Many do not.

Poor Strategic Rationale and Fit

Some acquisitions are based on soft strategic cases. On the surface, the acquirer believes and articulates a strategy for the combined companies and points to synergistic benefits. Observers who are knowledgeable of the markets and the companies involved may recognize that the strategic case is weak and that some, or all, of the expected synergies may be difficult to attain. In these cases, a year or two after the deal is closed the company will announce that the acquisition is not meeting expectations and will have difficulty in achieving the strategic and economic goals.

Poor Planning, Communication, Integration, and Execution

Well-planned and well-executed integration activities and strong communication plans are essential to achieve the objectives of an acquisition. Most successful acquirers also value speed in integrating acquisitions. Time is money, and getting the benefits of the acquisition earlier is better. More important, there is significant uncertainty and concern in the management and employee ranks about the potential impact of an acquisition. The sooner changes are made, the sooner employees will settle down to the tasks at hand. In the absence of well-planned, well-communicated, and timely changes, employees will lose significant productivity to speculation and fear. In addition, many will explore opportunities outside the firm.

Overpaying

Several factors cause managers to overpay for an acquisition. Paying too much for an acquisition may make it next to impossible to earn an acceptable rate of return on the investment, even if all other aspects are executed flawlessly. Many advisers and academics believe that it is difficult to purchase a public company at a price that will allow the acquiring shareholders to earn a return. Managers and boards have a fiduciary responsibility to maximize shareholder value. They have an obligation when selling the company to obtain the highest potential price for shareholders.

Managers often become emotionally charged when engaged in the acquisition process. After spending a great deal of time and emotional energy, it feels like losing to walk away from a deal. Winning is defined as "doing the deal," contrasted with doing the deal at a sensible valuation. Projections are often modified upward to support a higher offer. It is very easy to change expected savings or growth rates on a spreadsheet to yield a higher potential transaction value. Of course, achieving those lofty projections is another matter. The objective should be to buy a good company at a sensible price, not to buy a good company at any price. Ground the pricing discussions with DCF and other economic tests so that all parties understand the assumptions about future performance required to earn an economic return.

Managers should establish walk-away boundaries on price and other terms early in the process. The walk-away price should be supported by key assumptions. By putting a stake in the ground (or at least on paper), it will be easier for managers to recognize the inevitable upward pressure in transaction pricing. Only when significant changes in assumptions can be validated should they consider migrating to another pricing level.

Unrealistic or Unspecified Synergies

Acquirers should be cautious about unrealistic or unspecified synergies. Red flags include unsupported statements such as:

- Sales growth rates will increase from 3% to 10% as a result of the acquisition.
- Selling, general, and administrative (SG&A) levels will decrease 5% after the acquisition.

Test these statements with questions such as these:

- What new products will contribute to this growth? And how much?
- What territories and customers will contribute to the growth? Have they been identified?
- Has the sales organization signed up to these projections?
- How many jobs will be eliminated to achieve the lower SG&A levels? Have these positions been identified? When will they be eliminated? Have related costs been quantified?
- Do we have commitment from the managers who will be responsible for the financial performance of the acquisition?

Failure to Anticipate and Address Soft Issues

People make acquisitions work. Too often, key managers are excluded from early stages of the M&A process. Unless everyone is in the boat and rowing hard, it will be difficult to make forward progress and achieve the challenging objectives of most acquisitions. Clear, timely, and well-communicated decisions about organizational structure are essential.

Inadequate Due Diligence

Due diligence must go far beyond traditional areas such as accounting, legal, and environmental. Strong acquisition programs will test the key areas contributing to future value, including people, intellectual property, customer relationships, and other critical drivers of future performance.

BEST PRACTICES AND CRITICAL SUCCESS FACTORS

Companies that have track records of success with acquisitions avoid these common mistakes and potential pitfalls with a strong acquisition process. Successful programs tend to adopt best practices that improve the probability of creating value through acquisitions.

Sound Strategic Justification

Acquirers always present a strategic case for a transaction. The key for managers, directors, and investors is to understand and test the strength of the strategic case. Most deals make sense, at least at a high level. Some questions to consider:

- Is this a move that is consistent with stated strategy and prior actions? Or did it come out of the blue?
- Does the acquisition address a competitive disadvantage?
- Does it leverage a key advantage?
- Does the acquisition accelerate progress on a key strategic initiative?

Discipline in Valuation

The objective of an M&A program is to acquire a strategic asset at a price that will create value for shareholders. It should not be to complete a transaction at any price. It is very useful to establish a walk-away price at the beginning of an acquisition review. Managers and boards must not view walking away from a potential deal that is overpriced as a failure. After passing on or being outbid on a potential deal, managers do a lot of hand-wringing and questioning. What is wrong with our valuation methodology? Are we too conservative?

Different buyers will determine value very differently. Some buyers will perceive and are also capable of realizing higher synergies from a potential deal than others. It is also possible that another buyer may not have priced the deal on a rational basis. Remember that most acquisitions are not successful, and many are overpriced. After one particularly emotional postmortem session with a management team over a deal that got away, some members of the team predicted that the buyer would have substantial difficulty in earning an acceptable return at the final price. Within a short time, the management team of the buyer announced that the deal would not meet expectations, wrote off the goodwill, and announced that the company was exploring "strategic options" for the unit. That company was available again, for substantially less than the value that would have been required to win the deal from an irrational buyer the first time around.

Identify Specific Synergies

Synergies must be specific. They must be supported by detailed estimates and implementation plans. There must be buy-in by key managers, and accountability must be established. Incentive and compensation plans must incorporate key value drivers in the deal, including achieving projections.

Strong Acquisition Process

Companies with solid track records in M&A have a strong acquisition process. Candidates are identified in the context of the firm's strategic assessment and plan. These companies devote considerable attention and resources to identifying, evaluating, and valuing potential targets. Thorough due diligence is conducted, well beyond the legal and financial basics, to confirm key value drivers, including customer relationships and intellectual property. Synergies are confirmed and detailed execution plans are developed. Substantial effort is made to communicate the deal to key constituencies, including employees, customers, and investors. Integration is achieved as quickly as possible and monitored against the detailed implementation plans. Postacquisition reviews are conducted to ensure follow-through and to identify lessons learned to improve the process for future transactions.

Identify and Address Key Issues before Finalizing Deal

Successful acquirers identify and address key issues before announcing and proceeding with a deal. These issues often relate to posttransaction organization and people issues. How will the combined organizations be structured? Who will be the CEO and CFO of the combined organizations? What will happen to redundant organizations and positions? Will compensation and benefit plans be changed?

Communicate with, Retain, and Motivate Key Human Resources

It is extremely important to reduce uncertainty in the workforce as soon as possible. Details of integration plans and combined organizations should be communicated soon after the deal is announced. Key employees must be signed up and on board on day one to ensure a smooth transition and integration. Employees whose positions will be eliminated should be informed and provided with details of termination dates and benefits.

BEST PRACTICES SUMMARY

Sound strategic justification
Discipline in valuation:
- Success defined as acquiring a strategic asset at the right price

Identification of specific synergies
Action plan and timely execution
Solid acquisition programs:
- Objectives
- Acquisition criteria
- Process
- Predeal planning
- Due diligence teams and rigor
- Integration speed

Establish line manager ownership early in process,
Address key issues before finalizing deal.
Retain and incentivize critical human resources.

UNDERSTANDING SELLER BEST PRACTICES

I have learned as much about acquisitions by participating in the *sales* of companies as I have learned by participating in the acquisitions of many businesses. In addition to watching buyer behavior and practices, it has been enlightening to understand the advice of investment bankers and consultants retained to assist in selling businesses. Here is what I took away as seller best practices.

"Dress Up the Performance"

Most sellers of businesses attempt to improve the performance of the business to increase the potential sales price. Obviously, it makes sense to paint the house and clean the carpets before listing the property. It also makes sense to address any areas that may detract from the value of a business that will be sold. However, no buyer would be happy if a major flaw was hidden by some surface paint. Similarly, potential buyers need to be thorough in their evaluation of businesses. For example, a business may be sold because of an emerging competitive or market risk. Other sellers may reduce investment in R&D or marketing to increase profitability in the short term; this may have a negative impact on the competitiveness of the company and future sales and earnings.

Meet the Current Plan

Sellers are advised to meet or exceed their current operating plan. Falling short of the current plan provides a potential buyer with an opportunity to question future projections and the ability of the organization to execute to those plans. Beware of either modest plans or Herculean, unsustainable actions taken to meet the current plan.

Sell through an Auction Process or Sell to Best Potential Parent or Partner

Sellers and their advisers recognize that they are likely to realize a higher selling price if they create a competitive bidding process. Many establish processes that encourage as many as 20 to 30 companies to consider preliminary bids for a business. Obviously, the relative bargaining position tilts to the seller in these situations. In addition, sellers should identify the best potential parents or strategic partners, since those parties are likely to identify the highest level of potential synergies and therefore to offer a higher price.

Sell into a Strong Market

This is a variation of the investment advice to "buy low and sell high." Where possible, managers tend to offer businesses for sale at the top of valuation/market cycles. If the company is cyclical, the valuation will be substantially higher at the top of the cycle than at the bottom. There have been dramatic swings in the values of companies over the past 20 years, and only a small part of the variation can be explained by the underlying performance or prospects of the companies.

KEY PERFORMANCE INDICATORS FOR M&A

Managers can use performance measures to evaluate the effectiveness of the M&A process and to track the progress in achieving the objectives for a specific acquisition.

Effectiveness of M&A Process

Companies that are serial acquirers should look at the performance of each of their acquisitions to evaluate the overall effectiveness of the entire process. Are we achieving the sales, profits, and returns anticipated in the acquisition proposal? What is the level of intangible assets arising from acquisitions? Have these acquisitions resulted in subsequent write-down of goodwill? This evaluation may identify potential improvement opportunities in the acquisition process.

Actual versus Planned Sales and Profits. Compare the actual sales to the level planned for in the acquisition proposal for the current year. Are the acquisitions achieving the sales estimates in the plan? If not, then the team should identify the reasons for the shortfall and consider these in future acquisition proposals.

Actual versus Planned ROIC. Are the acquisitions achieving the return on invested capital (ROIC) projected in the acquisition proposal? ROIC is an important measure in M&A since it reflects the invested capital in the transaction. Again, what can we learn to improve our process for future acquisitions?

Goodwill and Intangibles Turnover. This measure provides a view into the relative significance of acquisitions to the firm. For highly acquisitive firms, this ratio will likely be low and will have a significant impact on return measures such as return on equity (ROE) and ROIC.

Asset Write-Offs and Impairment Charges. Goodwill impairment charges result from acquisitions failing to perform to expectations that supported the original purchase price. Significant charges to write off or write down assets may indicate an ineffective decision or implementation process for capital investment. Companies that have frequent asset write-offs and impairment charges (and other nonrecurring charges) likely have an opportunity to improve capital investment, acquisition, and strategic processes.

Specific Acquisitions

The following measures are intended to provide real-time feedback on the performance of a specific acquisition. The objective is to select measures that provide a leading indication of progress toward achieving the financial and strategic objectives of the transaction.

Progress on Key Acquisition Activities. During a sound acquisition process, a number of actions are identified that are vital to achieving the objectives of the acquisition. These may include retention of critical human resources, benefits integration, consolidation of the sales force, and manufacturing plants. Progress on these action plans is a leading indicator of being able to achieve the financial goals of the acquisition.

Acquired Sales and Synergies. Most acquisition plans anticipate growing the acquired sales base from the time of the acquisition and realizing revenue synergies from the combined companies. Both components of sales growth should be closely monitored on a frequent basis.

Annualized Cost Synergies Achieved. Cost savings from combining organizations are an important contributor to the economic success of the merger or acquisition. Progress toward achieving the annual synergies included in the acquisition proposal should be tracked frequently (e.g. monthly or quarterly).

Key Human Resources Retention. The success of most acquisitions is predicated on retaining and motivating key human resources. Key human resources may include some or all of the executive team, functional managers, and technical, manufacturing, and customer relationship personnel. During the acquisition planning process, these individuals should be identified and a program put in place to encourage continuation of employment. Success in retaining the key people should be closely monitored.

DASHBOARDS FOR M&A

Based on the specific facts and circumstances, several performance measures may be combined to measure the overall effectiveness of the M&A activity and the progress in achieving the objectives for a specific acquisition. These dashboards are illustrated in Figures 23.5 and 23.6, respectively, included at the end of this chapter.

SUMMARY

Do acquisitions create value for shareholders? The answer is that value is nearly always created for the selling shareholders, but not as consistently for the shareholders of acquiring firms. Firms that have strong acquisition programs have developed competencies to execute well on all steps in the acquisition process. A key element of a successful acquisition program is to be disciplined in setting pricing and other terms. Ensure that the acquisition pricing is supported by economic analysis based on realistic projections of future performance. *Synergies* is not a bad word if they are specifically identified and supported by a detailed implementation plan with clear accountability. The objective should be to do a good strategic deal at a reasonable price.

FIGURE 23.5 M&A Dashboard

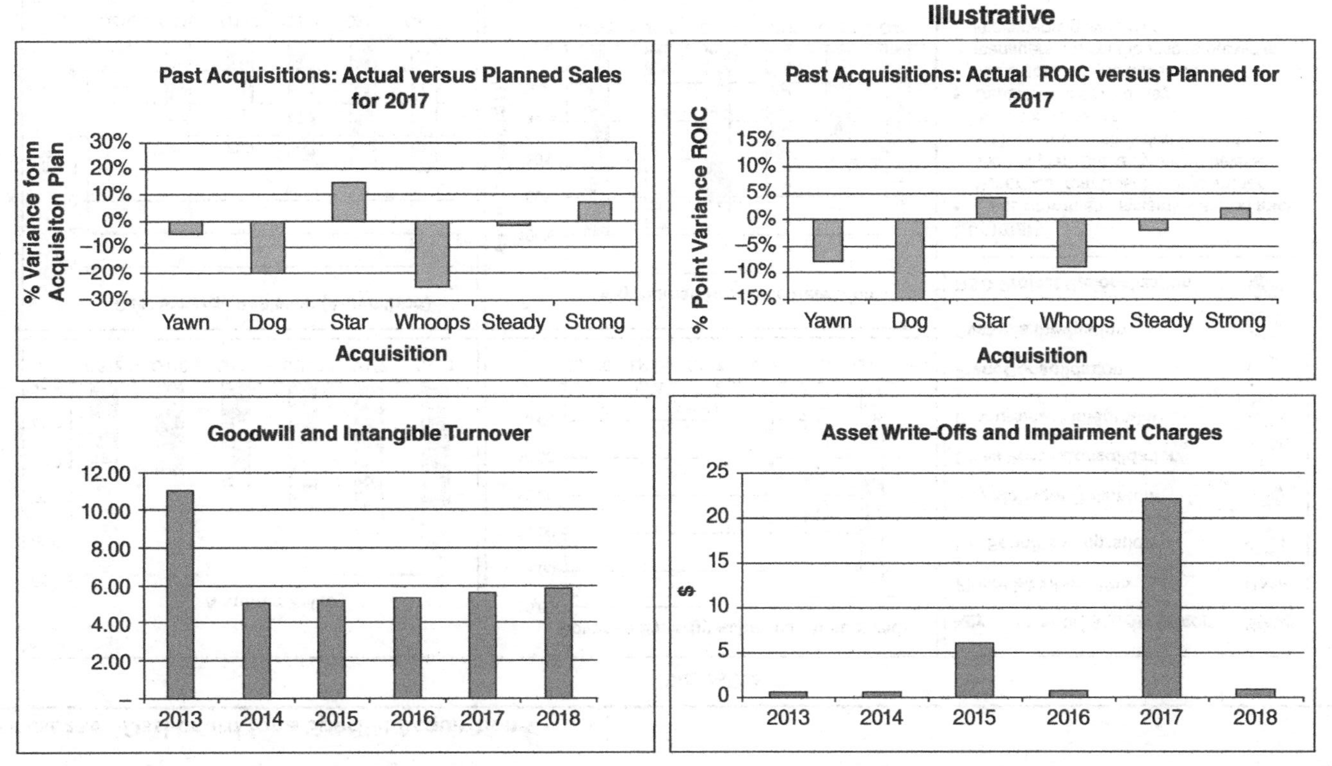

FIGURE 23.6 Dashboard for a Specific Acquisition

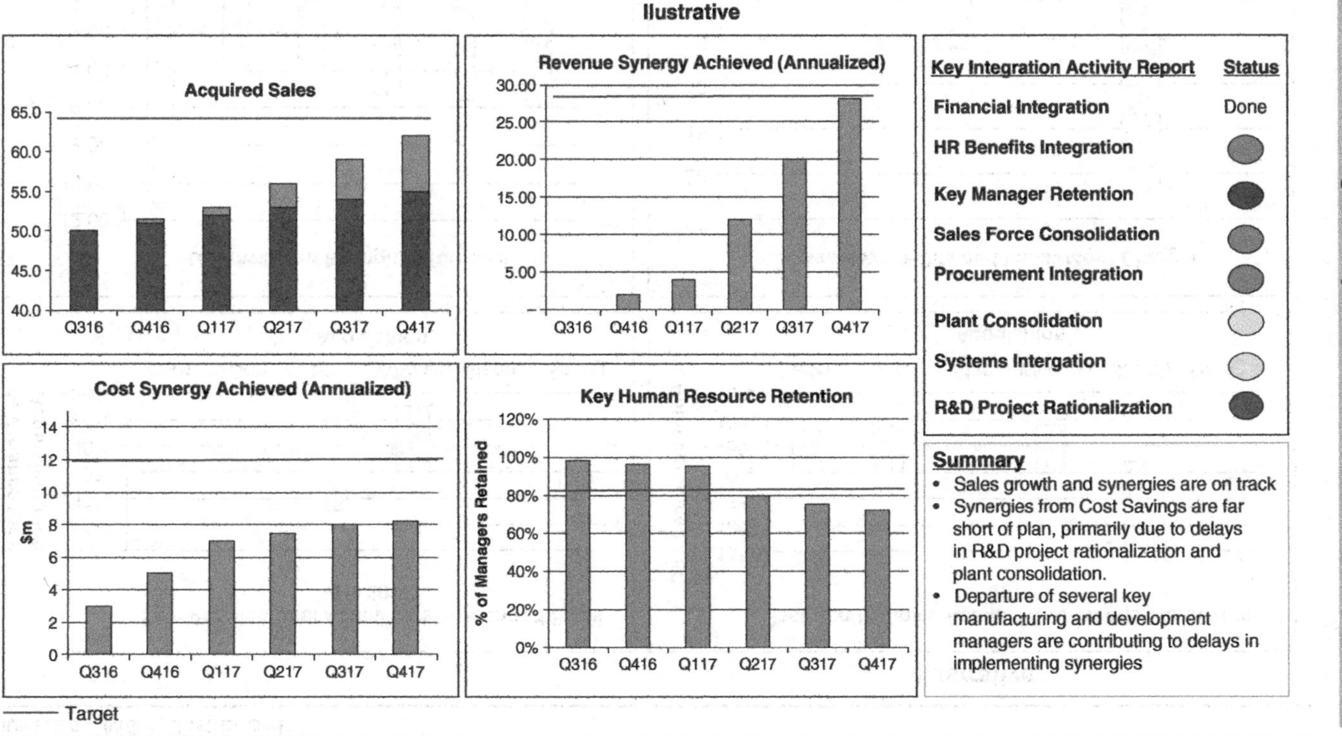

Part Six

Summary

24

SUMMARY AND WHERE TO FROM HERE?

CHAPTER INTRODUCTION

This chapter will recap key takeaways from this book and provide suggestions for accelerating improvements in Financial Planning & Analysis (FP&A).

KEY TAKEAWAYS

Whether you have read this book from cover to cover or focused on topics of current interest to you and your organization, I offer the following summary of key points on transforming Financial Planning & Analysis (FP&A) and Performance Management (PM).

The current business and economic climates, as well as the pace of change, have significantly increased the need for effective FP&A and performance management. Most **clients of these functions desire better analysis, advice, and service.** Finance teams must rise to the occasion and improve the effectiveness of FP&A.

FP&A and performance management generally represent the areas of greatest potential impact for the finance organization.

Organizations should **assess the current effectiveness of FP&A** and develop a plan to implement best practices and other improvements. In Chapter 5, we introduced several tools, including a best practices assessment and client survey to identify improvement opportunities. Finance teams must develop or acquire skills and competencies to meet high expectations and needs of our clients.

Analytical works are incomplete and ineffective until they are **presented and communicated** to our clients. Spreadsheets are seldom the best communication tool. The ability to develop and present the findings of our analysis is a critical skill for analysts. Improving our ability to deliver the message will improve the effectiveness of the analysis and the standing of the analyst. Chapter 6 detailed actions that can be taken to improve our ability to communicate and also provided specific examples of graphics, dashboards, and reports.

Performance management, including the use of key performance indicators (KPIs) and dashboards, must be integrated with FP&A efforts in order to maximize effectiveness. A key to successful performance management is to develop a context that allows us to focus on key business and value drivers, strategic issues and objectives, and other critical issues. The selection of KPIs and the development of dashboards are very important since they implicitly define priorities and key areas of emphasis. There is a tendency to measure areas and activities that are easy to track. Care should be exercised to include areas of great importance, including innovation, agility, human capital, and external forces. Finally, performance management must be fully integrated into other management processes, especially those dealing with acquiring, evaluating, and compensating team members. These topics on performance management were covered in Part Two, Business Performance Management.

The ability to develop reliable **financial projections** is a core competency for finance teams. Because the future is increasingly difficult to predict, new techniques and practices must be employed. Detailed financial budgets must be replaced with operating plans and business outlooks that focus on key drivers, operating processes and activities, upsides and downsides, and an ability to monitor key assumptions and indicators of future performance. Part Three, Business Projections and Plans, presented best practices in developing projections, including on-demand business outlooks and long-term projections.

FP&A teams must be able to plan, measure, review, and identify improvements in **critical business and value drivers**, including revenue growth, margins, and operating and capital effectiveness. Each of these drivers was reviewed in detail in Part Four, Planning and Analysis of Critical Business and Value Drivers. These business and value drivers typically are the core of most analytical efforts.

Capital investment decisions (CIDs) play a critical role in the overall success of any organization and have a direct impact on value creation. They are instrumental in purchases of equipment, product development projects, and acquisitions. Since CIDs require estimates of future performance, often over an extended time horizon, analysts must identify risks and upsides, a range of potential outcomes, and management options to optimize the project results under different scenarios. Capital investment decisions were covered in Chapters 20 and 21.

Valuation and shareholder value are important factors in assessing business decisions, setting goals, and purchasing businesses. Identifying value drivers and understanding the relationship between operating processes and activities, financial results, and value creation are essential. Valuation and value drivers were covered in Chapters 22 and 23.

Finally, it is important to direct our efforts in FP&A and performance management to **important business drivers and issues**. Specific suggestions to assist in this challenge were provided in Chapter 5, Building Analytical Capability, and in Chapter 11, The External View: Benchmarking Performance and Competitive Analysis.

WHERE TO FROM HERE?

Many finance teams struggle with the overwhelming number and magnitude of possible improvements to the current state of FP&A and performance management (PM). This problem is exacerbated by other demands on finance and the limited resources to deal with those demands. In addition, many teams encounter resistance to improved performance management, typically because of fear and misinformation that arise about how performance management will be utilized, in some cases to limit discretion or intuition or to more objectively evaluate employees' performance.

These initiatives to improve FP&A and PM represent changes for the finance team as well as the entire organization. Those in leadership roles must consider these soft issues and utilize change management principles. In addition to the suggestions in Chapters 5 and 11, the following suggestions may be useful in driving for significant improvements in FP&A and performance management.

Develop a Case. Document the current state of FP&A and PM. This can be accomplished in two areas. First, an assessment of FP&A effectiveness can be made. This can include a benchmark and identification of best practices, as well as client feedback. The second area of assessment is a view of the overall performance of the company or organization. This can include benchmark comparisons on everything from value creation to capital management and from revenue growth to costs and expense levels. These assessments will identify different needs for each organization and help to identify the specific areas warranting attention.

Build Consensus and an Execution Team. I cannot recall any successful endeavor of this magnitude that did not include building consensus and developing an execution team. The development of a case for change will provide a starting point for building consensus. Many executives are surprised at the amount of effort required to effectively communicate the case. In addition, catalysts for change also find that they must repeatedly drive home the message. The creation of a project plan with clear deliverables, milestones, and responsibilities is critical.

The execution team should include representatives from FP&A, information technology (IT), and key business processes and business units across the organization. This will help ensure that the changes and solutions are accepted, rather than viewed as a finance or IT project.

Provide Tools and Resources. Most efforts to significantly improve FP&A and PM will require investments in technology, training and development, and outside resources. In addition, a significant amount of FP&A human resources must be devoted to improving and then subsequently delivering high-quality FP&A service.

Build Momentum. An important aspect of leading change is to identify and execute on some early successes. The overall project should be planned to address some low-hanging fruit – in other words, relatively easy tasks that have high visibility. In organizations that resist adopting performance management, it is useful to direct initial efforts toward problem areas. For example, if the organization has difficulty in developing and meeting projections or in managing receivables, initial efforts can be directed to those areas. Skeptical managers can be won over after witnessing the useful role that performance management can play.

Monitor and Adjust. Progress on the plan should be reviewed frequently. In addition, the project results must be reviewed to ensure that intended objectives of the plan are achieved. For example, if one of the efforts is directed at improving the planning and forecasting process, has the project resulted in intended and measurable improvements?

Circumstances and priorities change frequently. Efforts to improve FP&A and PM must be continually reviewed to ensure that they are directed at important areas and drivers of performance.

It Is a Journey. Efforts to improve FP&A and PM will likely be an ongoing challenge. Changes in business conditions, technology, and competition will ensure that FP&A and PM will continue to evolve and rotate focus across various aspects of the enterprise.

FP&A and performance management generally represent the areas of greatest impact for the finance organization.

Good luck and enjoy the journey!

GLOSSARY

Accrual Accounting A basic principle of accounting that requires revenues to be recorded when earned and expenses recorded when incurred, regardless of the timing of cash payments.

Agility The ability to observe, recognize, and respond to changes in the environment.

Amortization A periodic charge to earnings to reduce the book value of intangible assets, including goodwill.

Analytics The discovery, collection, interpretation, and communication of meaningful patterns and trends in data.

Asset Any tangible or intangible item or claim owned by a firm.

Asset Turnover A measure of how efficiently assets are being used to generate revenue, computed by dividing sales by total assets.

Backlog The level of open (i.e. not shipped) customer orders at a point in time.

Balance Sheet One of the three primary financial statements, providing a schedule of assets, liabilities, and owner equity.

Benchmarking A process of comparing processes, performance, and valuation of one company to another company or group of companies.

Beta The risk associated with a specific investment or security estimated by the correlation of price movements in an individual stock to a broad market index.

Book Value The value of an asset on the balance sheet, reflecting original cost less any accumulated depreciation.

Breakeven The level of a particular assumption (e.g. sales) that results in a measure, such as NPV or income, equaling zero.

Business Model A financial representation of a firm's strategy and operating practices, usually expressed as a percentage of each income statement line item (e.g. SG&A) to sales.

Business Outlook A preferred term to describe a forecast, generally inferring a broader business perspective than simply a financial projection.

Capital Asset A tangible asset of a firm, such as real estate and machinery.

Capital Effectiveness A key driver of value, representing the firm's ability to manage and control capital levels in the business, computed as sales divided by net fixed assets.

Capital Intensity A measure of the level of capital requirements for a business, which varies significantly across industries.

Capital Structure The mix of capital sources for a company, including debt and equity.

Cash Flow Statement One of the three primary financial statements, providing a reconciliation of accounting income to cash flow.

Common Stock Equivalent An instrument such as stock options and convertible bonds that can be converted into common stock under certain conditions.

Comparables A method used to value a company that involves selecting similar public companies to compare valuation measures such as the price-earnings (P/E) ratio.

Compound Annual Growth Rate (CAGR) A multiyear measure of growth that reflects compounding.

Control Premium The premium over market value required to purchase a company.

Cost of Capital The weighted average return expected by all investors in a firm, based on the opportunity cost incurred in making an investment in that firm.

Cost of Equity The return expected by shareholders in a firm, based on the opportunity cost incurred in making an investment in that stock.

Cost of Goods Sold (COGS) The total cost of products sold, including material, labor overhead, and other manufacturing costs and variances.

Dashboard A one-page, visual summary or screen presenting graphs and charts of key performance measures.

Data Visualization The visual representation of data, using graphics and other visuals to identify and communicate patterns and trends that might not otherwise be evident.

Days Sales of Inventory (DSI) A measure of the level of inventories on hand relative to sales.

Days Sales Outstanding (DSO) A measure of the average time to collect accounts receivable from customers.

Debt A formal borrowing obligation of the firm, including bonds, notes, loans, and short-term financing.

Depreciation A periodic charge to earnings to reduce the book value of long-term assets, including equipment.

Depreciation and Amortization (D&A) Periodic charges to earnings to reduce the value of long-term and intangible assets. D&A is a noncash charge and is often an adjustment to income to estimate cash flows for valuation purposes.

Discounted Cash Flow (DCF) A valuation and decision tool that considers the cash flows of an asset or project and the time value of money.

Distribution Channel Refers to the method of selling and distributing the firm's products, including internal sales force, third-party distributors, and value-added resellers.

Earnings before Interest and after Taxes (EBIAT) Also called net operating profit after taxes (NOPAT), this measure estimates the after-tax operating earnings. It excludes financing costs but does reflect income tax expense. It is useful in comparing the operational performance of firms, excluding the impact of financing costs.

Earnings before Interest and Taxes (EBIT) Also called operating income, this measure reflects the income generated by operating activities before subtracting financing costs (interest) and income tax expense.

Earnings before Interest, Taxes, Depreciation, and Amortization (EBITDA) EBITDA adjusts EBIT (operating income) by adding back noncash charges, depreciation, and amortization. This measure is used in valuation and financing decisions, since it approximates cash generated by the operation. It does not include capital requirements such as working capital and expenditures for property and equipment.

Earnings per Share (EPS) The accounting net income per share of common stock and equivalents outstanding.

Earnings per Share (EPS) Accretive-Dilutive Test A decision test to determine if a project, an acquisition, or a financing alternative will increase or decrease earnings per share.

Economic Profit A financial measure of performance that subtracts a capital charge from earnings to arrive at an economic profit, consistent with other economic techniques such as NPV and DCF.

Engineering Change Notice/Engineering Change Order (ECN/ECO) A document used to initiate changes in a product's bill of materials or manufacturing process.

Enterprise Value The sum of a firm's market value of equity and debt.

Equity The book value of shareholders' equity or investment in the firm, including common stock and earnings retained in the business.

Financial Accounting Standards Board (FASB) The accounting standards setter in the United States.

Financial Leverage The use of debt and other liabilities to leverage the investment of equity investors; computed as assets divided by equity.

Fixed Assets A term used to describe property, plant, and equipment.

Fixed Cost A cost that cannot be eliminated in the short term (e.g. six months) and does not vary with changes in sales levels.

Forecast A financial projection, generally referring to a short-term horizon, less than 12 to 18 months.

Free Cash Flow to Equity (FCFE) The cash flow available to equity investors after providing for working capital requirements; investments in property, plant, and equipment; and payments to service debt (interest and principal).

Free Cash Flow/Free Cash Flow to the Firm (FCF/FCFF) The cash flow available to all investors after providing for working capital requirements and investments in property, plant, and equipment.

Generally Accepted Accounting Principles (GAAP) The cumulative body of accounting rules issued by the FASB, SEC, and other rule-making organizations.

Gross Margin The residual of sales minus cost of goods sold (COGS).

Income Statement One of the three primary financial statements, providing a summary of the firm's sales, costs, and expenses for a period.

Innovation The introduction of something new or the process of radically changing, transforming, or achieving breakthrough results.

Intangible Assets Assets of a firm that are not tangible, physical assets, such as reputation, brands, trademarks, patents, and goodwill.

Internal Rate of Return (IRR) The economic return of a project based on its cash inflows and outflows.

Invested Capital The total capital invested in a business, including equity and interest-bearing debt.

Key Performance Indicator/Key Performance Measure (KPI/KPM) A measure of a business process, activity, or result that is significant to the overall performance of the firm.

Lagging Performance Measure A measure that is computed after an event, transaction, or the close of an accounting period, such as DSO or ROE.

Liability An amount or service due another party.

Market Capitalization (Value) The market value of common stock outstanding, computed as the price per share times the number of common shares outstanding.

Multiple A ratio of value to one of several financial measures, including price-earnings and price-to-sales ratios. These ratios are used to compare values of similar companies.

Net Income Represents the bottom line of the income statement, the excess of sales over all costs and expenses for a period.

Net Present Value (NPV) The present value of cash inflows less the present value of cash outflows.

Operating Capital The level of net working capital required to support the business, reflecting the excess of current operating assets over current operating liabilities. The measure excludes financing components of working capital such as cash and debt.

Operating Effectiveness An important value driver that reflects the effectiveness and efficiency of the firm's business processes and activities.

Operating Income/Profit A pretax measure of operating performance, reflecting all operating income and expenses for a period.

Operating Leverage A measure of the proportion of fixed costs to total costs that causes wider variations in profits resulting from changes in sales levels.

Operating Profit after Tax (OPAT) A measure that estimates the after-tax operating earnings. It excludes financing costs but does reflect income tax expense. It is useful in comparing the operational performance of firms, excluding the impact of financing costs.

Payback The period of time it takes to recover the original investment in a project.

Performance Management Framework (PMF) A comprehensive system of management practices to measure, report, and improve business performance.

Perpetuity A measure of time meaning forever, typically used in valuing an asset or cash flow.

Predictive (Leading) Performance Measure A measure that covers key business processes and activities on a current basis, providing an early indication of future business and financial results.

Present Value The value today of a future payment or cash flow, reflecting a discount for the time value of money.

Price-Earnings (P/E) Ratio A key valuation measure representing the ratio of the firm's share price to earnings per share.

Pricing Strength The ability of a firm to command a premium price for its products and services based on a competitive advantage that will result in acceptable or above-average economic performance for the firm.

Proxy Statement A filing with the SEC required for publicly traded companies that presents matters to be voted on by shareholders. The proxy statement also contains disclosures on the company's stock performance (TRS) and management compensation levels and policies.

Return on Assets A measure of overall effectiveness, computed as net income divided by total assets.

Return on Equity A measure of overall effectiveness, computed as net income divided by total shareholders' equity.

Return on Invested Capital (ROIC) A measure of overall effectiveness, computed as after-tax operating profit divided by the total of shareholders' equity and interest-bearing debt. Since it considers all capital invested in a firm, this measure is independent of the mix of capital.

Revenue Linearity The pattern of revenue within a period (e.g. quarter). A linear pattern would result from a constant level of shipments over the entire period.

Revenue Process The entire process that supports delivering a product or service to a customer, commencing with presales activities and concluding with the collection of cash from customers.

Rolling Forecast A technique for extending the horizon of financial projections by adding on additional months or quarters into the future.

Scenario Analysis A projection or forecast version based on a specific set of conditions (e.g. a recession).

Securities and Exchange Commission (SEC) The US federal agency tasked with monitoring securities markets and financial reporting of publicly traded companies.

Selling, General, and Administrative (SG&A) Expenses An income statement line item that captures all costs and expenses associated with sales, marketing, and administrative activities of the firm.

Sensitivity Analysis A summary of the changes in a decision outcome (e.g. net present value) based on changes in one or more input variables.

Supply Chain Management A key business process incorporating all aspects of planning, procuring, manufacturing, and distributing a firm's product.

Synergies The incremental savings or income that results from an acquisition beyond the sum of the two independent companies.

Terminal Value The estimated value of a company at the end of the forecast period in discounted cash flow valuations.

Times Interest Earned A measure of the ability to service debt, computed by dividing profit before tax by interest expense.

Total Return to Shareholders (TRS) An overall measure of returns earned by shareholders that reflects both capital appreciation and dividends paid over a period of time.

Valuation The process of estimating the value of an asset or a company using one or more commonly accepted techniques such as multiples, comparables, and discounted cash flow analysis.

Value Driver A factor that has a significant impact on the value of the firm (e.g. sales growth).

Value Performance Framework (VPF) A comprehensive performance management framework that emphasizes building and sustaining long-term shareholder value.

Variable Cost A cost that varies with changes in sales levels.

Vertical Integration The extent to which a firm directly owns its supply chain and distribution channels.

Weighted Average Cost of Capital (WACC) The blend of returns expected by all suppliers of capital to the firm (weighted by market value).

Working Capital The excess of current assets (cash, accounts receivable, inventories, and prepaid expenses) over current liabilities (accounts payable, debt, and accrued expenses).

Yield to Maturity The current rate an investor will earn on a bond, adjusting the bond's stated (coupon) rate for current market conditions.

ACKNOWLEDGMENTS

I have been blessed in many ways in my career and in life. In my professional career, I have been blessed to have exposure to a number of businesses and industries, work with and for great people, and observe and participate in business from several different perspectives. The experience gained as a division finance and general manager, controller and CFO, educator, small business owner, and consultant have all contributed to the development of the tools and insights incorporated into this book.

I was first introduced to performance measures in the mid-1980s, primarily related to manufacturing and inventory management. Over time, the scope, depth, and use of performance measures have greatly expanded, as has the need to integrate these with financial results and value.

Prior to embarking on my teaching and consulting track, most of my professional career was with a terrific company, EG&G, Inc. The company had a large and diverse portfolio of businesses that provided ample opportunity for learning, as did the period of radical transformation during the 1990s. EG&G had very strong financial management and strategic planning practices that continue to influence me to this day. I had the pleasure of working with and learning from a number of terrific people at the division, group, and corporate levels, including Bob Nicol, Gary Hammond, Dave Botten, Luciano Rossi, Mike Gallucio, Paul D'Adamo, Jim Mellencamp, Sam Rubinovitz, Murray Gross, Fred Parks, Dan Heaney, Mark Allen, Peter Broadbent, Dan Valente, Ted Theodores, Debbie Lorenz, Jim Dobbins, Peter Walsh, Don Peters, Bill Ribaudo, Will Weddleton, and many more. Special thanks to John Kucharski, for both his leadership and as a model of managing with integrity.

Acknowledgments

The time spent teaching at Babson College was both rewarding and enlightening. I learned a great deal by teaching, especially how people learn and process information. I also learned a great deal from my time at Coopers & Lybrand in Philadelphia. The exposure to a wide range of client companies, process orientation, accounting and reporting, and great people provided a solid foundation for future growth.

I also benefited greatly by knowing and working with a number of external business partners over the years, including investment bankers, consultants, and public accountants. Working with many directors, analysts, and investors over the years also contributed to my understanding of business, finance, and value.

A number of friends and colleagues were very helpful in providing encouragement and feedback on this project, including Nate Osborne, Sally Curley, Paul McGowan, Sharleen Thornley, Warren Davis, Phil Franchois, Mike Vance, Dick Fickes, Ron McGurn, and Gary Olin. Finally, thanks to Bill Falloon and the team at Wiley for guidance and assistance on this project.

Thanks to my parents for everything, including passing on values of faith, integrity, hard work, and perseverance. And special thanks to my wife, Suzanne, for her unending support and love.

For from him and through him and to him are all things.

To him be the glory forever!

Romans 11:35

ABOUT THE AUTHOR

JACK ALEXANDER

Jack is an experienced CFO and operating executive turned consultant, author, lecturer, and entrepreneur. As the founder of Jack Alexander & Associates, LLC, he provides CFO Advisory Services to businesses across a wide range of financial and operating areas, including Financial Planning & Analysis (FP&A) and Business Performance Management (BPM), Strategy, Shareholder Value, CFO development and performance improvement. The firm also offers customized training and workshops on FP&A. He is a frequent speaker on FP&A and BPM.

Prior to founding the consulting practice, Jack served as CFO of EG&G, Inc. (renamed PerkinElmer), a global $2.5 billion technology and services company with more than 40 operating units, and also as CFO with Mercury Computer Systems. He was previously employed by General Refractories and Coopers & Lybrand.

Jack was a Senior Lecturer in Babson College's MBA program and School of Executive Education. He is a CPA and earned an MBA from Rider University and a BS from Indiana University of Pennsylvania.

In addition to the present book, *Financial Planning & Analysis and Performance Management*, he is the author of *Performance Dashboards and Analysis for Value Creation* (Wiley, 2006).

INDEX

Page references followed by *f* indicate a figure; and page references followed by *t* indicate a table.

B